ALSO BY JOHN BOLTON

Surrender Is Not an Option: Defending America at the United Nations

How Barack Obama Is Endangering Our National Sovereignty

THE ROOM WHERE IT HAPPENED

A White House Memoir

JOHN BOLTON

Former National Security Advisor
of the United States

Simon & Schuster

NEW YORK   LONDON   TORONTO   SYDNEY   NEW DELHI

Simon & Schuster
1230 Avenue of the Americas
New York, NY 10020

First Simon & Schuster hardcover edition June 2020

SIMON & SCHUSTER and colophon are registered trademarks
of Simon & Schuster, Inc.

For information about special discounts for bulk purchases, please contact Simon &
Schuster Special Sales at 1-866-506-1949 or business@simonandschuster.com.

The Simon & Schuster Speakers Bureau can bring authors to your
live event. For more information, or to book an event, contact
the Simon & Schuster Speakers Bureau at 1-866-248-3049
or visit our website at www.simonspeakers.com.

Interior design by Paul Dippolito

Manufactured in the United States of America

11   13   15   17   19   20   18   16   14   12

Library of Congress Cataloging-in-Publication data has been applied for.

ISBN 978-1-9821-4803-4 (hardcover)
ISBN 978-1-9821-4805-8 (ebook)

For Gretchen and Jennifer Sarah

Hard pounding, this, gentlemen. Let's see who will pound the longest.

—THE DUKE OF WELLINGTON,
RALLYING HIS TROOPS AT WATERLOO, 1815

CONTENTS

THE ROOM
WHERE IT
HAPPENED

THE LONG MARCH
TO A WEST WING
CORNER OFFICE

One attraction of being National Security Advisor is the sheer multiplicity and volume of challenges that confront you. If you don't like turmoil, uncertainty, and risk—all while being constantly overwhelmed with information, decisions to be made, and the sheer amount of work, and enlivened by international and domestic personality and ego conflicts beyond description—try something else. It is exhilarating, but it is nearly impossible to explain to outsiders how the pieces fit together, which they often don't in any coherent way.

I cannot offer a comprehensive theory of the Trump Administration's transformation because none is possible. Washington's conventional wisdom on Trump's trajectory, however, is wrong. This received truth, attractive to the intellectually lazy, is that Trump was always bizarre, but in his first fifteen months, uncertain in his new place, and held in check by an "axis of adults," he hesitated to act. As time passed, however, Trump became more certain of himself, the axis of adults departed, things fell apart, and Trump was surrounded only by "yes men."

Pieces of this hypothesis are true, but the overall picture is simplistic. The axis of adults in many respects caused enduring problems not because they successfully managed Trump, as the High-Minded (an apt description I picked up from the French for those who see themselves as our moral betters) have it, but because they did precisely the opposite. They didn't do nearly enough to establish order, and what they did do was so transparently self-serving and so publicly dismissive of many of Trump's very clear goals (whether worthy or unworthy) that they fed Trump's already-suspicious mind-set, making it harder for those who came later to have legitimate policy exchanges with the President. I had long felt that the role of the National Security Advisor was to ensure that a President understood what options were open to him for any given decision he needed to make, and then to ensure that this decision was carried out by the pertinent bureaucracies. The National Security Council process was certain to be different for different Presidents, but these were the critical objectives the process should achieve.

Because, however, the axis of adults had served Trump so poorly, he second-guessed people's motives, saw conspiracies behind rocks, and remained stunningly uninformed on how to run the White House, let alone the huge federal government. The axis of adults is not entirely responsible for this mind-set. Trump is Trump. I came to understand that he believed he could run the Executive Branch and establish national-security policies on instinct, relying on personal relationships with foreign leaders, and with made-for-television showmanship always top of mind. Now, instinct, personal relations, and showmanship are elements of any President's repertoire. But they are not all of it, by a long stretch. Analysis, planning, intellectual discipline and rigor, evaluation of results, course corrections, and the like are the blocking and tackling of presidential decision-making, the unglamorous side of the job. Appearance takes you only so far.

In institutional terms, therefore, it is undeniable that Trump's transition and opening year-plus were botched irretrievably. Processes that should have immediately become second nature, especially for the many Trump advisors with no prior service even in junior Executive Branch positions, never happened. Trump and most of his team never read the government's "operators' manual," perhaps not realizing doing so wouldn't automatically make them members of the "deep state." I entered the existing chaos, seeing problems that could have been resolved in the Administration's first hundred days, if not before.

Constant personnel turnover obviously didn't help, nor did the White House's Hobbesian bellum omnium contra omnes ("war of all against all"). It may be a bit much to say that Hobbes's description of human existence as "solitary, poor, nasty, brutish and short" accurately described life in the White House, but by the end of their tenures, many key advisors would have leaned toward it. As I explained in my book *Surrender Is Not an Option*,[1] my approach to accomplishing things in government has always been to absorb as much as possible about the bureaucracies where I served (State, Justice, the United States Agency for International Development) so I could more readily accomplish my objectives.

My goal was not to get a membership card but to get a driver's license. That thinking was not common at the Trump White House. In early visits to the West Wing, the differences between this presidency and previous ones I had served were stunning. What happened on one day on a particular issue often had little resemblance to what happened the next day, or the day after. Few seemed to realize it, care about it, or have any interest in fixing it. And it wasn't going to get much better, which depressing but inescapable conclusion I reached only after I had joined the Administration.

Former Nevada Senator Paul Laxalt, a mentor of mine, liked to say, "In politics, there are no immaculate conceptions." This insight powerfully explains appointments to very senior Executive Branch positions. Despite the frequency of press lines like "I was very surprised when President Smith called me . . . ," such expressions of innocence are invariably only casually related to the truth. And at no point is the competition for high-level jobs more intense than during the "presidential transition," a US invention that has become increasingly elaborate in recent decades. Transition teams provide good case studies for graduate business schools on how not to do business. They exist for a fixed, fleeting period (from the election to the inauguration) and then disappear forever. They are overwhelmed by hurricanes of incoming information (and disinformation); complex, often

competing, strategy and policy analyses; many consequential personnel decisions for the real government; and media and interest-group
scrutiny and pressure.

Undeniably, some transitions are better than others. How they unfold reveals much about the Administration to come. Richard Nixon's
1968–69 transition was the first example of contemporary transitions,
with careful analyses of each major Executive Branch agency; Ronald
Reagan's in 1980–81 was a landmark in hewing to the maxim "Personnel is policy," intently focused on picking people who would adhere
to Reagan's platform; and Donald Trump's 2016–17 transition was . . .
Donald Trump's.

I spent election night, November 8–9, in Fox News's Manhattan studios, waiting to comment on air about "the next President's"
foreign-policy priorities, which everyone expected would occur in
the ten p.m. hour, just after Hillary Clinton was declared the winner.
I finally went on the air around three o'clock the next morning. So
much for advance planning, not only at Fox, but also in the camp of
the President-Elect. Few observers believed Trump would win, and, as
with Robert Dole's failed 1996 campaign against Bill Clinton, Trump's
pre-election preparations were modest, reflecting the impending
doom. In comparison with Hillary's operation, which resembled a
large army on a certain march toward power, Trump's seemed staffed
by a few hardy souls with time on their hands. His unexpected victory,
therefore, caught his campaign unready, resulting in immediate turf
fights with the transition volunteers and the scrapping of almost all
its pre-election product. Starting over on November 9 was hardly auspicious, especially with the bulk of the transition staff in Washington,
and Trump and his closest aides at Trump Tower in Manhattan. Trump
didn't understand much of what the huge federal behemoth did before
he won, and he didn't acquire much, if any, greater awareness during
the transition, which did not bode well for his performance in office.

I played an insignificant part in Trump's campaign except for
one meeting with the candidate on Friday morning, September 23, at
Trump Tower, three days before his first debate with Clinton. Hillary
and Bill were a year ahead of me at Yale Law School, so, in addition

to discussing national security, I offered Trump my thoughts on how Hillary would perform: well prepared and scripted, following her game plan no matter what. She hadn't changed in over forty years. Trump did most of the talking, as in our first meeting in 2014, before his candidacy. As we concluded, he said, "You know, your views and mine are actually very close. Very close."

At that point, I was widely engaged: Senior Fellow at the American Enterprise Institute; Fox News contributor; a regular on the speaking circuit; of counsel at a major law firm; member of corporate boards; senior advisor to a global private-equity firm; and author of opinion articles at the rate of about one a week. In late 2013, I formed a PAC and a SuperPAC to aid House and Senate candidates who believed in a strong US national-security policy, distributing hundreds of thousands of dollars directly to candidates and spending millions in independent expenditures in the 2014 and 2016 campaigns, and preparing to do so again in 2018. I had plenty to do. But I had also served in the last three Republican Administrations,[2] and international relations had fascinated me since my days at Yale College. I was ready to go in again.

New threats and opportunities were coming at us rapidly, and eight years of Barack Obama meant there was much to repair. I had thought long and hard about America's national security in a tempestuous world: Russia and China at the strategic level; Iran, North Korea, and other rogue nuclear-weapons aspirants; the swirling threats of radical Islamicist terrorism in the tumultuous Middle East (Syria, Lebanon, Iraq, and Yemen), Afghanistan and beyond; and the threats in our own hemisphere, like Cuba, Venezuela, and Nicaragua. While foreign-policy labels are unhelpful except to the intellectually lazy, if pressed, I liked to say my policy was "pro-American." I followed Adam Smith on economics, Edmund Burke on society, *The Federalist Papers* on government, and a merger of Dean Acheson and John Foster Dulles on national security. My first political campaigning was in 1964 on behalf of Barry Goldwater.

I knew senior Trump campaign officials like Steve Bannon, Dave Bossie, and Kellyanne Conway from prior associations, and had spoken to them about joining a Trump Administration should one happen. Once the transition began, I thought it reasonable to offer my services as Secretary of State, as did others. When Chris Wallace came off the Fox set early on November 9, after the race was called, he shook my hand and said, smiling broadly, "Congratulations, Mr. Secretary." Of course, there was no dearth of contenders to lead the State Department, which generated endless media speculation about who the "front-runner" was, starting with Newt Gingrich, proceeding to Rudy Giuliani, then Mitt Romney, and then back to Rudy. I had worked with and respected each of them, and each was credible in his own way. I paid special attention because there was constant chatter (not to mention pressure) that I should settle for being Deputy Secretary, obviously not my preference. What came next demonstrated Trumpian decision-making and provided (or should have) a cautionary lesson.

While all the early "leading contenders" were broadly conservative philosophically, they brought different backgrounds, different perspectives, different styles, different pluses and minuses to the table. Among these possibilities (and others like Tennessee Senator Bob Corker and former Utah Governor Jon Huntsman), were there common, consistent attributes and accomplishments Trump sought? Obviously not, and observers should have asked: What is the real principle governing Trump's personnel-selection process? Why not have Giuliani as Attorney General, a job he was made for? Romney as White House Chief of Staff, bringing his undeniable strategic planning and management skills? And Gingrich, with decades of creative theorizing, as White House domestic policy czar?

Was Trump looking only for people from "central casting"? Much was made of his purported dislike of my moustache. For what it's worth, he told me it was never a factor, noting that his father also had one. Other than shrinks and those deeply interested in Sigmund Freud, which I assuredly am not, I don't really believe my looks played a role in Trump's thinking. And if they did, God help the country. Attractive women, however, fall into a different category when it comes to Trump. Loyalty was the key factor, which Giuliani had proved beyond peradventure in the days after the *Access Hollywood* tape became public in early October. Lyndon Johnson once reportedly said of an aide, "I want real loyalty. I want him to kiss my ass in Macy's window at high noon and tell me it smells like roses." Who knew Trump read so much history? Giuliani was later extremely gracious to me, saying after he withdrew from the Secretary of State melee, "John would probably be my choice. I think John is terrific."[3]

The President-Elect called me on November 17, and I congratulated him on his victory. He recounted his recent calls with Vladimir Putin and Xi Jinping, and looked ahead to meeting that afternoon with Japanese Prime Minister Shinzo Abe. "We'll have you up here in the next couple of days," Trump promised, "and we are looking at you for a number of situations." Some of the new President's first personnel announcements came the next day, with Jeff Sessions picked as Attorney General (eliminating that option for Giuliani); Mike Flynn as National Security Advisor (appropriately rewarding Flynn's relentless campaign service); and Mike Pompeo as CIA Director. (A few weeks after Flynn's announcement, Henry Kissinger told me, "He'll be gone within a year." Although he couldn't have known what was about to happen, Kissinger knew Flynn was in the wrong job.) As the days passed, more Cabinet and senior White House positions emerged publicly, including, on November 23, South Carolina Governor Nikki Haley as Ambassador to the UN, with Cabinet rank, a bizarre step to take with the Secretary of State still unchosen. Haley had no qualifications for the job, but it was ideal for someone with presidential ambitions to check the "foreign policy" box on her campaign résumé. Cabinet rank or no, the UN Ambassador was part of State, and coherent US foreign policy can have only one Secretary of State. Yet here was Trump, picking subordinate positions in State's universe with no Secretary in sight. By definition, there was trouble ahead, especially when I heard from a Haley staff person that Trump had considered her to be Secretary. Haley, her staffer said, declined the offer because of lack of experience, which she obviously hoped to acquire as UN Ambassador.[4]

Jared Kushner, whom Paul Manafort had introduced me to during the campaign, called me over Thanksgiving. He assured me I was "still very much in the mix" for Secretary of State, and "in a whole bunch of different contexts. Donald is a big fan of yours, as we all are." Meanwhile, the *New York Post* reported on decision-making at Mar-a-Lago at Thanksgiving, quoting one source, "Donald was walking around asking everybody he could about who should be his secretary of state. There was a lot of criticism of Romney, and a lot of people like Rudy. There are also many people advocating for John Bolton."[5] I knew I should have worked the Mar-a-Lago primary harder! Certainly, I was grateful for the considerable support I had among pro-Israel Americans (Jews and evangelicals alike), Second Amendment supporters, Cuban-Americans, Venezuelan-Americans, Taiwanese-Americans, and conservatives generally. Many people called Trump and his advisors on my behalf, part of the venerable transition lobbying process.

The transition's spreading disorder increasingly reflected not just organizational failures but Trump's essential decision-making style. Charles Krauthammer, a sharp critic of his, told me he had been wrong earlier to characterize Trump's behavior as that of an eleven-year-old boy. "I was off by ten years," Krauthammer remarked. "He's like a one-year-old. Everything is seen through the prism of whether it benefits Donald Trump." That was certainly the way the personnel-selection process appeared from the outside. As one Republican strategist told me, the best way to become Secretary of State was to "try to be the last man standing."

Vice President–Elect Pence called on November 29 to ask to meet in Washington the next day. I knew Pence from his service on the House Foreign Affairs Committee; he was a solid supporter of a strong national-security policy. We conversed easily about a range of foreign and defense policy issues, but I was struck when he said about State: "I would not characterize this decision as imminent." Given subsequent press reports that Giuliani withdrew his candidacy for Secretary at about that time, it could be the entire selection process for State was starting all over again, an almost certainly unprecedented development that far into the transition.

When I arrived at the transition offices the next day, Representative Jeb Hensarling was leaving after seeing Pence. Hensarling, it was reported, was so sure of getting Treasury that he told his staff to begin planning. His not being named matched Representative Cathy McMorris Rodgers's finding she was not to be Interior Secretary after being told she would, as well as former Senator Scott Brown's learning he would not become Secretary of Veterans Affairs. The pattern was clear. Pence and I had a friendly half-hour talk, during which I recounted, as I had several times with Trump, Acheson's famous remark when asked why he and President Truman had such an excellent working relationship: "I never forgot who was President, and who was Secretary of State. And neither did he."

Trump announced Jim Mattis as Defense Secretary on December 1, but the uncertainty about State continued. I arrived at Trump Tower the next day for my interview and waited in the Trump Organization lobby with a State Attorney General and a US Senator also waiting. Typically, the President-Elect was behind schedule, and who should emerge from his office but former Defense Secretary Bob Gates. I surmised later that Gates was there to lobby for Rex Tillerson as Secretary of Energy or State, but Gates gave no hint of his mission, just exchanging pleasantries as he left. I finally entered Trump's office, for a meeting lasting just over an hour, also attended by Reince Priebus (soon to become White House Chief of Staff) and Bannon (who would be the Administration's Chief Strategist). We talked about the world's hot spots, broader strategic threats like Russia and China, terrorism, and nuclear-weapons proliferation. I started with my Dean Acheson story, and, in contrast with my previous Trump meetings, I did most of the talking, responding to questions from the others. I thought Trump listened carefully; he didn't make or receive any phone calls, and we weren't interrupted until Ivanka Trump came in to discuss family business, or perhaps try to get Trump vaguely back on schedule.

I was describing why State needed a cultural revolution to be an effective instrument of policy when Trump asked, "Now, we're discussing Secretary of State here, but would you consider the Deputy job?" I said I would not, explaining that State could not be run successfully from that level. Moreover, I was uneasy about working for someone who knew I had competed for his job and who might wonder constantly if he needed a food taster. As the meeting ended,

Trump took my hand in both of his and said, "I am sure we will be working together."

Afterward, in a small conference room, Priebus, Bannon, and I caucused. Both of them said the meeting had gone "extremely well," and Bannon said Trump had "never heard anything like that before" in terms of the scope and detail of the discussion. Nonetheless, they pressed me to take Deputy Secretary, which told me they were not optimistic I would get the top job. I explained again why the Deputy idea was unworkable. The next day, I learned Trump would interview Tillerson for State, the first time I heard Tillerson's name raised, which likely explained why Priebus and Bannon asked me about being nominated for Deputy. Neither Trump nor the others raised the issue of Senate confirmation. Most Trump nominees could expect significant or even unanimous Democratic opposition. Rand Paul's well-known isolationist views meant he would be a problem for me, but several Republican Senators (including John McCain, Lindsey Graham, and Cory Gardner) told me his opposition would be overcome. Nonetheless, after this meeting, there was silence from Trump Tower, convincing me that I would remain a private citizen.

Tillerson's December 13 nomination, however, only unleashed another wave of speculation (for and against) about my becoming Deputy. One Trump advisor encouraged me, saying, "In fifteen months, you'll be Secretary. They know his limitations." One of those limitations was Tillerson's relationship from his years at ExxonMobil with Vladimir Putin and Russia, precisely at a time Trump was coming under early but steadily increasing criticism for "colluding" with Moscow to defeat Clinton. While Trump was ultimately vindicated on collusion, his defensive reaction willfully ignored or denied that Russia was meddling globally in US and many other elections, and public-policy debate more broadly. Other adversaries, like China, Iran, and North Korea, were also meddling. In comments at the time, I stressed the seriousness of foreign interference in our politics. McCain thanked me in early January, saying I was a "man of principle," which likely wouldn't have endeared me to Trump had he known.

At Defense, there was also turmoil over the Deputy Secretary job, as Mattis pushed for Obama-era official Michèle Flournoy. Flournoy, a Democrat, might have been Secretary of Defense herself had Clinton won, but why Mattis wanted her in a Republican Administration was hard to fathom.[6] Subsequently, Mattis also pressed for Anne Patterson, a career Foreign Service officer, to fill the critical job of Under Secretary of Defense for Policy. I had worked several times with Patterson and knew her to be philosophically compatible for a senior policy position in a liberal Democratic Administration, but hardly in a Republican one. Senator Ted Cruz questioned Mattis about Patterson, but Mattis was unable or unwilling to explain his reasons, and the nomination, under increasing opposition from Republican Senators and others, ultimately collapsed. All this turmoil led Graham and others to counsel that I stay out of the Administration in its early days and wait to join later, which I found persuasive.

For a time, there was consideration of my becoming Director of National Intelligence, to which former Senator Dan Coats was ultimately named in early January. I thought that the office itself, created by Congress after the 9/11 attacks to better coordinate the intelligence community, was a mistake. It became simply a bureaucratic overlay. Eliminating or substantially paring back the Director's Office was a project I would have enthusiastically undertaken, but I concluded quickly Trump himself was insufficiently interested in what would necessarily be a hard slog politically. Given the ensuing, prolonged, almost irrational war between Trump and the intelligence community, I was lucky the Director's job didn't come my way.

And so the Trump transition ended with no visible prospect of my joining the Administration. I rationalized the outcome by concluding that if Trump's post-inaugural decision-making process (using that word loosely) was as unconventional and erratic as his personnel selections, I was fine staying outside. If only one could say that for the country.

Then, less than a month into the Administration, Mike Flynn self-destructed. It started with Flynn's facing criticism for alleged remarks to Russian Ambassador Sergei Kislyak, someone I knew well; he had been my Moscow counterpart for a time when I was Under Secretary of State for Arms Control and International Security in the Bush 43 Administration. The criticism intensified dramatically when Flynn seemingly lied to Pence and others about the Kislyak conversation. Why Flynn would lie about an innocent conversation, I never understood. What senior Administration aides, and indeed Trump himself, told me a few days later made more sense, namely, that they had already lost confidence in Flynn for his inadequate performance (much as Kissinger had predicted), and the "Russian issue" was simply a politically convenient cover story. Flynn resigned late on February 13, after a day of White House Sturm und Drang, just hours after Kellyanne Conway unhappily received the unfair and unfortunate job of telling the ravenous press corps that Flynn had Trump's full confidence. This is the very definition of confusion and disorder.

Confusion and disorder unfortunately also marked the NSC staff in the Administration's first three weeks. Personnel choices were in disarray, as CIA Director Mike Pompeo personally took the stunning, nearly unprecedented step of denying "sensitive compartmented information" clearance to one of Flynn's choices to be a Senior Director, one of the top-rung NSC jobs.[7] Denying this critical clearance, as everyone knew, effectively barred that person from working at the NSC, a stinging blow to Flynn. He also faced innumerable battles with career officials detailed to the NSC during Obama's tenure but, as is customary, still there as the Trump presidency began. These battles provided frequently leaked accounts of bureaucratic blood on the floor at the White House and the Eisenhower Executive Office Building, the great gray granite Victorian pile across West Executive Avenue housing the bulk of the NSC staff.

Similarly, on one of Trump's signature campaign issues—stemming illegal immigration—the White House stumbled through one mistake after another in the early days, trying to craft Executive Orders and policy directives. Judicial challenges were inevitable, and likely to be hotly litigated in a judiciary filled with eight years of Obama appointees. But the White House entirely owned the initial immigration debacles, betraying a lack of transition preparation and internal co-ordination. A "dissent channel" cable at State, intended to be internal, found its way onto the Internet, signed by over a thousand employees, criticizing the immigration initiative. The press feasted on it, although the cable's arguments were weak, disjointed, and poorly presented. But somehow the cable, and similar arguments by media commentators and Hill opponents, went unanswered. Who was in charge? What was the plan?

Surprisingly, Tillerson called three days after the Senate Foreign Relations Committee approved his nomination on January 23 by an 11–10 party-line vote, pulling me from a corporate board meeting. We talked for thirty minutes, mostly about State organizational issues and how the interagency decision-making process worked. Tillerson was gracious and professional, and utterly uninterested in having me as his Deputy. Of course, had I been in his shoes, I would have felt the same way. Tillerson later told Elliott Abrams, whom he also considered, that he wanted someone who would work behind the scenes supporting him, not someone who had gained public attention, as I had at the UN and as a Fox commentator. Tillerson asked if I was interested in anything at State other than Deputy, and I said no, having already had the second-best job as UN Ambassador. Tillerson laughed, and we talked about the often-fraught relations between Secretaries and UN Ambassadors. It was clear he had not spoken with Haley about their relationship and that he had no idea how to handle this ticking time bomb.

I worried that Tillerson was susceptible to capture by the State Department bureaucracy. He had spent his entire forty-one-year ca-reer at Exxon, in an environment where there were clear metrics for performance, profit-and-loss statements being harsh taskmasters, and where the corporate culture was hardly subject to revolutionary change from within. After years of perching at the top of Exxon's hi-erarchy, believing that all his subordinates were on the same team, it would have been remarkable for Tillerson, sitting in the Secretary's seventh-floor suite, to assume anything else about the careerists on the floors below him or posted around the world. Precisely because of his background, Tillerson should have surrounded himself with people familiar with the Foreign and Civil Services' strengths and weaknesses, but he went a very different way. He neither sought a cultural revolution (as I would have done), nor embraced "the building" (as all who worked there referred to it), nor sought to control the bureaucracy without fundamentally changing it (as Jim Baker did). Instead, he isolated himself with a few trusted aides, and paid the inevitable price.

But with Flynn, fairly or unfairly, crashing and burning, the National Security Advisor job, which I hadn't previously considered because of Flynn's closeness to Trump, was now open. The press speculated that Flynn's successor would be another general, mentioning David Petraeus, Robert Harwood (formerly Navy, now at Lockheed, pushed vigorously by Mattis), or Keith Kellogg (a longtime Trump supporter and now NSC Executive Secretary). Tillerson seemed to be uninvolved, another sign of trouble, both because he was not in the loop and because he didn't seem to realize the potential problem for him if a Mattis ally got the job, potentially making Tillerson's relations with the White House more difficult. Indeed, news stories were noting Tillerson's low profile generally.[8]

Bannon texted me on Friday, February 17, asking me to come to Mar-a-Lago to meet Trump over President's Day weekend. That day, MSNBC's Joe Scarborough tweeted, "I strongly opposed @Amb JohnBolton for SecState. But the former UN ambassador is Thomas Jefferson in Paris compared to Michael Flynn." In Trumpworld, this could be helpful. During the Mar-a-Lago primary that weekend, a guest told me he had heard Trump say several times, "I'm starting to really like Bolton." Hadn't I concluded before that I needed to work that crowd harder? Trump interviewed three candidates: Lieutenant General H. R. McMaster, author of *Dereliction of Duty*, a superb study of civil-military relations in America; Lieutenant General Robert Caslen, Commandant of West Point; and me. I had met and spoken with McMaster years before and admired his willingness to espouse controversial positions. Meeting Caslen for the first time, I saw him as a personable and highly competent official. Both were in full-dress uniform, immediately demonstrating their marketing skills. Me, I still had my moustache.

Trump greeted me warmly, saying how much he respected me and that he was happy to consider me to be National Security Advisor. Trump also asked if I would consider a "title like Bannon's" (who was also present in the private bar on Mar-a-Lago's first floor, along with Priebus and Kushner), covering strategic issues. Thus, apparently, I could be one of many generic "Assistants to the President," of which there were already too many in Trump's White House, with only slap-dash efforts at defining their roles and responsibilities. This was a complete nonstarter for me, so I politely declined, saying I was only interested in the National Security Advisor job. As Henry Kissinger once reportedly said, "Never take a government job without an inbox."

The President assured me that Flynn's successor would have a free hand in organizational and personnel matters, which I believed essential in running an effective NSC staff and interagency process. We covered the full range of world issues, a tour d'horizon, as the State Department loves to call it, and Trump interjected at one point, "This is so great. John sounds just like he does on television. I could just keep listening. I love it." Kushner asked, "How do you handle the point that you're so controversial, that people either love you or hate you?" As I was opening my mouth to answer, Trump said, "Yeah, just like me! People either love me or hate me. John and I are exactly alike." I added only that one should be judged on performance, list-ing a few of what I considered to be my foreign-policy achievements. The meeting ended with a discussion about Russia, as Trump said, "I saw you talking the other day about the INF issue," referring to the Intermediate-Range Nuclear Forces Treaty with Russia. He then ex-plained why it was so inequitable that no nations other than Russia and America (such as China, Iran, or North Korea) were limited in de-veloping intermediate-range capabilities, and that the Russians were violating the treaty. This was almost exactly what I had said, so I had no doubt he was still watching and absorbing Fox News! I suggested we tell Putin to comply with Russia's INF obligations or we would withdraw, which Trump agreed with.

Bannon and I left together, Bannon saying, "That was great." Nonetheless, my clear impression was that Trump was going to pick a general. I returned to my hotel, and later in the day Bannon and Priebus asked me to breakfast with them at Mar-a-Lago the next morning. Priebus suggested alternatives to the National Security Advisor position, saying of Trump, "Remember who you're dealing with." They promised real influence, access to Trump, and the inevitability of Administration turnover, meaning I would eventually become Secretary of State or something. Based on my government experience, I explained that to run the bureaucracy, you needed to control the bureaucracy, not just watch it from the White House. The NSC was a mechanism to coordinate the national-security agencies, and the job required someone who had experience at lower levels on how it worked and didn't work. I didn't make an impression. I think Trump had said to them, in effect, "Get him into the Administration so he can defend us on television." That was exactly the last thing I intended to do, regarding policies I had little or nothing to do with formulating. At one point, Bannon said, "Help me out here, Ambassador," which was actually what I was trying to do, although he meant that I should tell him what else would induce me to join the Administration.

Flying back to Washington, I saw on the airplane Wi-Fi that Trump had picked McMaster. That was no surprise, but I was surprised to hear Trump then say: "I know John Bolton. We're going to be asking him to work with us in a somewhat different capacity. John is a terrific guy. We had some really good meetings with him. He knows a lot. He had a good number of ideas, that I must tell you, I agree with very much. So, we'll be talking to John Bolton in a different capacity."

I clearly hadn't made my point about the best role for me, certainly not to Kushner, who texted me shortly thereafter, "Great spending time together—we really want to get you on the team. Let's talk this week to find the right spot as u have a lot to offer and we have a unique chance to get some good done." Madeleine Westerhout, Trump's secretary in "the Outer Oval" (the room where Trump's personal assistants sat), called on Tuesday to connect me to Trump, but I had my cell phone on silent and didn't catch it. Predictably, Trump was tied up when I later called back, so I asked Westerhout if she knew what the subject was, fearing a true full-court press. She said, "Oh, he just wanted to tell you how wonderful you are," and said he wanted to thank me for coming to Mar-a-Lago. I told her that was very kind, but not wanting to burden his schedule, I said he didn't really need to call again, hoping to dodge the bullet. A few days later, Westerhout, always exuberant back then, left another message saying the President wanted to see me. I was convinced I would be pitched on some amorphous position, but fortunately I left the country for almost two weeks and dodged the bullet again.

You can run, but you cannot hide, and a meeting with Trump was finally scheduled for March 23, after lunch with McMaster at the White House mess. I texted Bannon in advance to be transparent: I was only interested in the Secretary of State or the National Security jobs, and neither was open as far as I could tell. By coincidence, I entered the West Wing for the first time in over ten years as the press scrum waited outside to interview Republican House members meeting with Trump on the failing effort to repeal Obamacare. Just what I needed, even though I didn't plan to answer any questions. In the Twitter era, however, even a nonstory is a story, as one reporter tweeted:

> **GLENN THRUSH** John Bolton just walked into the West Wing—I asked him what he was doing, he smiled and said 'health care!!!!'

I saw later that the *Washington Post*'s Bob Costa had tweeted while I was walking in:

> **ROBERT COSTA** Trump wants to bring John Bolton into the administration. That's why Bolton is at the WH today, per a Trump confidant. Ongoing convo.

I had a perfectly pleasant lunch with McMaster, discussing Iraq, Iran, and North Korea, and we then went to the Oval to see Trump, who was just finishing lunch with Treasury Secretary Steven Mnuchin and Nelson Peltz, a New York financier.

Trump was sitting behind the *Resolute* desk, which was completely bare, unlike the desk in his New York office, which seemed
always covered with newspapers, reports, and notes. He had a picture
taken of the two of us, and then McMaster and I sat down in front of
the desk for our discussion. We talked a bit about the Obamacare repeal effort and then turned to Iran and North Korea, repeating much
of the ground McMaster and I had covered at lunch. Trump said, "You
know, you and I agree on almost everything except Iraq," and I replied,
"Yes, but even there, we agree that Obama's withdrawal of American
forces in 2011 led us to the mess we have there now." Trump then said,
"Not now, but at the right time and for the right position, I'm going to
ask you to come into this Administration, and you're going to agree,
right?" I laughed, as did Trump and McMaster (although I felt somewhat uncomfortable on his behalf), and answered, "Sure," figuring I
had again dodged the bullet I had feared. No pressure, no rush, and no
amorphous White House job without an inbox.

The meeting lasted about twenty-plus minutes, and then Mc-
Master and I left, stopping by Bannon's office on the way out. Bannon
and I visited for a while with Priebus, running into Sean Spicer in the
hallway and then later the Vice President, who greeted me warmly.
The atmosphere reminded me of a college dorm, with people wan-
dering in and out of each other's rooms, chatting about one thing or
another. Weren't these people in the middle of a crisis trying to repeal Obamacare, one of Trump's signature 2016 issues? This was not
a White House I recognized from past Administrations, that was for
sure. The most ominous thing I heard was Mike Pence saying, "I'm really glad you're coming in," which was not what I thought I was doing!
I finally left at about two fifteen, but I had the feeling I could have hung
around all afternoon.

I could see this pattern of contact with the Trump White House
lasting for an indefinite period, and to an extent it did. But I ended
the Administration's first hundred days secure in my own mind about
what I was prepared to do and what I wasn't. After all, as Cato the
Younger says in one of George Washington's favorite lines from his

favorite play, "When vice prevails, and impious men bear sway, the post of honor is a private station."

Life under Trump, however, did not resemble life in Joseph Addison's eponymous *Cato*, where the hero strove to defend the failing Roman Republic against Julius Caesar. Instead, the new Administration resembled much more closely the Eagles song "Hotel California": "You can check out any time you like / But you can never leave."

It was not long before Bannon and Priebus were again calling and texting me to come into the White House in some capacity, as they sought to overcome the mismatches between Trump, McMaster, and Tillerson. The most palpable manifestation of the problems was Iran, specifically the 2015 nuclear deal, which Obama considered a crowning achievement (the other being Obamacare). The deal was badly conceived, abominably negotiated and drafted, and entirely advantageous to Iran: unenforceable, unverifiable, and inadequate in duration and scope. Although purportedly resolving the threat posed by Iran's nuclear-weapons program, the deal did no such thing. In fact, it exacerbated the threat by creating the semblance of a solution, diverting attention from the dangers, and lifting the economic sanctions that had imposed substantial pain on Iran's economy, while allowing Tehran to proceed essentially unimpeded. Moreover, the deal did not seriously address other threats Iran posed: its ballistic-missile program (a thinly disguised effort to develop delivery vehicles for nuclear weapons); its continuing role as the world's central banker for international terrorism; and its other malign activity in the region, through the intervention and growing strength of the Quds Force, the Islamic Revolutionary Guard Corps's external military arm, in Iraq, Syria, Lebanon, Yemen, and elsewhere. Freed from sanctions, benefiting from the transfer of $150 million in "cash on pallets" in cargo airplanes and the unfreezing of an estimated $150 billion in assets globally, Tehran's radical ayatollahs were back in business.

Trump and other 2016 GOP candidates campaigned against the

Joint Comprehensive Plan of Action, the lumbering formal title of the Iran deal, and it was widely believed to be ready for extreme unction following his inauguration. But a combination of Tillerson, Mattis, and McMaster frustrated Trump's efforts to break free from this wretched deal, earning them the plaudits of the adoring media as an "axis of adults" restraining Trump from indulging in wild fantasies. If only they knew. In fact, many of Trump's supporters saw their efforts as preventing him from doing what he had promised voters he would do. And McMaster wasn't doing himself any favors by opposing the phrase "radical Islamic terrorism" to describe things like . . . radical Islamic terrorism. Jim Baker used to tell me when I worked for him at Bush 41's State Department and pressed for something Baker knew Bush didn't want, "John, the guy who got elected doesn't want to do it." That was usually a signal I should stop pushing, but in the Trump Administration's infant national-security apparatus, what "the guy who got elected" wanted was only one of many data points.

In early May, after I had another White House discussion with Priebus and Bannon, they took me to what turned out to be a photo opportunity with Trump and Pence in the colonnade that connects the Residence to the West Wing. "John, so good to see you," said Trump as we walked along the colonnade, surrounded by photographers. We talked about the Philippines and the Chinese threat to bring nearly the entire South China Sea under its sovereignty. When we finished, Trump said loud enough for the trailing mob of reporters to hear, "Is Rex Tillerson around? He should talk to John." And with that, Trump was off to the Oval. Priebus said, "That was great. We want to get you back over here regularly."

Life at the White House developed its own rhythm, with Trump firing FBI Director James Comey later in May (at Kushner's suggestion, according to Bannon), then meeting with Russian Foreign Minister Sergei Lavrov (whom I had known for over twenty-five years at that point) and allegedly being less than cautious in discussing classified material, calling Comey a "nutjob," according to the unbiased *New York Times*.[9] I was in Israel in late May to give a speech and met with Prime Minister Bibi Netanyahu, whom I had first met in the Bush

41 years. Iran's threat was the centerpiece of our attention, as it should have been for any Israeli Prime Minister, but he was also dubious about assigning the task of bringing an end to the Israel-Palestinian conflict to Kushner, whose family Netanyahu had known for many years. He was enough of a politician not to oppose the idea publicly, but like much of the world, he wondered why Kushner thought he would succeed where the likes of Kissinger had failed.

I was back at the White House in June to see Trump, walking with Priebus to the Outer Oval. Trump saw us through his open door and said, "Hi, John, give me just a minute, I'm signing judges' commissions." I was happy to give him all the time he needed, because Trump's growing record on judicial nominations, in due course to be graced by the confirmation of Justices Neil Gorsuch and Brett Kavanaugh, was for conservatives the highest priority and greatest achievement of his tenure. When Priebus and I entered, I congratulated Trump on withdrawing from the Paris climate agreement, which the "axis of adults" had failed to stop him from doing and which I saw as an important victory against global governance. The Paris Agreement was a charade, for those truly concerned about climate change. As in many other cases, international agreements provided the semblance of addressing major issues, giving national politicians something to take credit for, but made no discernible real-world difference (in this case giving leeway to countries like China and India, which remained essentially unfettered). I gave Trump a copy of a 2000 article of mine called "Should We Take Global Governance Seriously?" from the *Chicago Journal of International Law*, not because I thought he would read it, but to remind him of the importance of preserving US sovereignty.

I warned Trump against wasting political capital in an elusive search to solve the Arab-Israeli dispute and strongly supported moving the US embassy in Israel to Jerusalem, thereby recognizing it as Israel's capital. On Iran, I urged that he press ahead to withdraw from the nuclear agreement and explained why the use of force against Iran's nuclear program might be the only lasting solution. "You tell Bibi that if he uses force, I will back him. I told him that, but you tell him again," Trump said, unprompted by me. As the conversation ranged on,

Trump asked, "Do you get along with Tillerson?" and I said we hadn't spoken since January. Bannon told me a few days later that Trump was pleased with the meeting. And indeed, a few weeks on, Tillerson called to ask me to be special envoy for Libyan reconciliations, which I saw as another exercise in box-checking; if asked, Tillerson could tell Trump he had offered me something but I turned it down. Tillerson almost simultaneously asked Kurt Volker, a close associate of McCain's, to become special envoy for Ukraine. Neither job required full-time government employment, but my view was you were either in the Administration or not, and halfway houses wouldn't work.

North Korea was also on the Administration's mind, with the release of Otto Warmbier, who suffered barbaric treatment at Pyongyang's hands and died upon returning to the United States. The North's brutality told us everything we needed to know about its regime. Moreover, Pyongyang was launching ballistic missiles, including on the Fourth of July (how thoughtful), followed by another on July 28, which ultimately led to further UN Security Council sanctions on August 5. A few days later, Trump was prompted to threaten "fire and fury like the world has never seen" against North Korea,[10] though Tillerson immediately said Americans should "sleep well at night" and have "no concern about this particular rhetoric of the past few days," hardly clarifying things.[11] I wondered if Tillerson was pooh-poohing North Korea or Trump, who upped the ante on August 11 by saying the US was "locked and loaded" on North Korea.[12] There was little visible evidence that any new military preparations were under way.

On August 30, Trump tweeted that we had talked to North Korea for twenty-five years without result, and there wasn't much point in talking further. Trump reiterated the point on October 7:

> Presidents and their administrations have been talking to North Korea for 25 years, agreements made and massive amounts of money paid . . . hasn't worked, agreements violated before the ink was dry, makings fools of U.S. negotiators. Sorry, but only one thing will work!

Mattis, in South Korea, almost immediately contradicted Trump, saying there was always room for diplomacy, although he quickly walked it back, claiming there was no daylight between him and the President.[13] The dissonance was getting louder. North Korea had chimed in with its sixth nuclear-weapons test on September 3, this one almost certainly thermonuclear, followed twelve days later by firing a missile over Japan, underlining Trump's point in his tweet. Almost immediately thereafter, Japanese Prime Minister Abe wrote a *New York Times* op-ed concluding that "more dialogue with North Korea would be a dead end" and saying, "I fully support the United States position that all options are on the table," which is as close as any Japanese politician can get to saying he could support offensive military operations.[14] By contrast, Tillerson was announcing we wanted "to bring North Korea to the table for constructive, productive dialogue."[15] He was obviously deep in the grip of "the building." When Trump announced new financial sanctions on North Korea, China responded by saying its central bank had directed all Chinese banks to cease doing business with Pyongyang, which was quite a step forward if actually carried out (and many were dubious).[16]

Iran remained the most visible flashpoint, however, and in July Trump faced his second decision whether to certify Iran was complying with the nuclear deal. The first decision to do so had been a mistake, and now Trump was on the verge of repeating it. I wrote an op-ed for *The Hill* that appeared on its website on July 16,[17] apparently setting off a daylong battle inside the White House. McMaster and Mnuchin held a conference call to brief reporters on the decision to certify Iranian compliance, and the White House e-mailed "talking points" to the media explaining the decision as their call was under way. But an outside analyst told me, "There's chaos at the NSC," the talking points were pulled back, and the decision to certify compliance was reversed.[18] The *New York Times*, citing a White House official, reported on a nearly hour-long confrontation between Trump, on one side, and Mattis, Tillerson, and McMaster, on the other, on the certification issue, confirming what I had heard earlier. Other sources said the same thing.[19] Trump ultimately succumbed, but not happily, and only after yet again asking for alternatives, of which his advisors said there were none. Bannon texted me, "POTUS loved it . . . Your op-ed drove him on Iran."

Trump called me a few days later to complain about how the Iran certification issue had been handled, and especially about "people in the State Department" who hadn't given him any options. Then he said, referring to my last conversation with Tillerson, "I hear what Rex talked to you about won't work. Don't take some half-assed position over there. If he offers you something that's really great, okay, whatever, but otherwise just wait. I'm going to call you," concluding the call by saying I should "come and see [him] next week" on Iran. Bannon texted me right afterward, "We talk about it/u everyday." I told Bannon I would write a plan about how the US could withdraw from the Iran deal. It would not be hard.

The next day, Sean Spicer resigned as White House spokesman to protest Anthony Scaramucci's being named Communications Director, with Sarah Sanders picked as Spicer's successor. One week later, Trump fired Priebus, naming John Kelly, then Homeland Security Secretary and a former four-star Marine general, as White House Chief of Staff. On Monday, July 31, Kelly fired Scaramucci. In mid-August, controversy erupted over Trump's comments about neo-Nazi demonstrators in Charlottesville, Virginia. He fired Bannon on August 18. Was this what business schools taught about running large organizations?

What was not happening was any White House sign of life on my Iran-deal exit strategy, which I had earlier transmitted to Bannon. When I sought a meeting with Trump, Westerhout suggested I first see Tillerson, which would have been a waste of time for both of us. I suspected that Kelly's efforts to bring discipline to White House operations and limit Oval Office anarchy in particular had resulted in my "walk-in" privileges' being suspended, along with those of many others. I thought it would be a shame to let my Iran plan wither, so I suggested to *National Review* editor Rich Lowry that he publish it, which he did at the end of August.[20] Iran's Foreign Minister, Javad Zarif, immediately denounced my plan as "a huge failure for Washington."[21]

I knew I was on the right track. Most of the Washington media, instead of focusing on the plan's substance, wrote instead on my loss of access to Trump, probably because they understood palace intrigue better than policy. Kushner texted me to say, "You are always welcome at the White House," and "Steve [Bannon] and I disagreed on many things, but we were in sync on Iran." In fact, Kushner invited me to meet on August 31 to go over his emerging Middle East peace plan, along with Iran. After a relatively long hiatus, I didn't think this meeting was accidental.

Nonetheless, still no word from Trump, although another Iran compliance certification, required every ninety days by statute, came due in October. The White House announced Trump would make a major Iran address on October 12, so I decided to stop being shy, phoning Westerhout to ask for a meeting. By then, Tillerson had reportedly called Trump "a fucking moron," which he refused to deny flatly. Rumors flew that Kelly wanted to resign as Chief of Staff and that Pompeo would replace him, although it was also regularly rumored that Pompeo would replace McMaster. I was still focused on Iran and wrote another op-ed for *The Hill*, hoping the magic might work again.[22] It appeared on October 9, the same day I had lunch with Kushner in his West Wing office. Although we talked about his Middle East plan and Iran, what really got his attention was the photo I brought of the gaudy entrance to Special Counsel Robert Mueller's office, located in the building where my SuperPAC was located.

The media reported Trump's advisors were urging he decline to certify Iran as complying with the nuclear agreement but that the US nonetheless stay in the deal. I saw this as self-humiliation, but so desperate were the deal's advocates that they were willing to concede a critical point on compliance just to save the deal. Trump called me in the late afternoon of October 12 (the speech having been moved to Friday the thirteenth) to talk. "You and I are together on that deal, you may be a little tougher than I am, but we see it the same," he said. I answered that I could see from the press coverage he was likely to decertify Iran but still remain in the deal, which I said was at least a step forward. I asked to discuss the issue further when there was more time.

"A hundred percent," said Trump. "Hundred percent. I know that's your view. I watch what you say very carefully." I asked if he would put a line in his speech that the agreement was under 24/7 review and that it was subject to being terminated at any time (thus eliminating the need to wait ninety days before having another shot at withdrawal and plainly making the fight over withdrawal rather than "compliance," as the deal's supporters preferred). We talked about the language Trump might actually use as he dictated to others in the room.

Trump then raised the topic of Iran's Islamic Revolutionary Guard Corps, asking if he should designate it as a Foreign Terrorist Organization, thereby subjecting it to additional penalties and constraints. I urged him to do so because of the organization's control of Iran's nuclear and ballistic-missile programs, and its extensive support for radical Islamic terrorism, Sunni and Shia. Trump said he was hearing Iran would be particularly upset by this specific designation, and there might be blowback against US forces in Iraq and Syria, which I learned later was Mattis's position. But his argument was misdirected; if Mattis was correct, the answer was to provide more protection for our troops or withdraw them to focus on the main threat, Iran. As it turned out, it would take nearly two years to get the Revolutionary Guard designated as a Foreign Terrorist Organization, showing the immense staying power of a dug-in bureaucracy.

Trump also said he was thinking of saying something on North Korea, which I urged him to do. On Friday, he said: "There are also many people who believe that Iran is dealing with North Korea. I am going to instruct our intelligence agencies to do a thorough analysis and report back their findings beyond what they have already reviewed."[23] I was delighted. I said I looked forward to talking with him again, and Trump said, "Absolutely." (Later, in November, on my birthday, purely coincidentally I am sure, Trump returned the North to the list of state sponsors of terrorism, from which the Bush 43 Administration had mistakenly removed it.)

I thought the Trump call had accomplished four things: (1) having the speech announce that the Iran deal was under continuous review and subject to US withdrawal at any time; (2) raising the connection between Iran and North Korea; (3) making it clear the Revolutionary Guard should be designated as a Foreign Terrorist Organization; and (4) getting a renewed commitment that I could see him without other approvals. Ironically, by having me on the speakerphone, all of those points were clear to whoever was in the Oval with him. I wondered, in fact, if I could do much more if I were actually in the Administration, rather than just calling in from the outside a few hours before a speech like this one.

Kushner had me back to the White House on November 16 to discuss his Middle East peace plan. I urged that we withdraw from the UN Human Rights Council, rather than follow Haley's plan to "reform" it. (See chapter 8.) The Council was a sham when I voted against it in 2006, having abolished its equally worthless predecessor.[24] We should never have rejoined, as Obama did. I also advocated defunding the UN Relief and Works Agency, ostensibly designed to aid Palestinian refugees but that over decades had become, effectively, an arm of the Palestine apparat rather than the UN. Kushner said twice how much better I would be handling State than present management. In early December, Trump, fulfilling a 2016 commitment, declared Jerusalem as Israel's capital and announced that he would move the US embassy there. He had called me a few days before, and I'd expressed support, although he had clearly already decided to act. It was long overdue and utterly failed to produce the crisis in "the Arab street" regional "experts" had endlessly predicted. Most Arab states had shifted their attention to the real threat, which was Iran, not Israel. In January, the US cut its funding for the UN Relief and Works Agency, contributing only $60 million of an expected tranche of $125 million, or roughly one-sixth of the estimated total fiscal year 2018 US contribution of $400 million.[25]

Trump again invited me to the White House on December 7. I was sitting in the West Wing lobby admiring the huge Christmas tree when Trump came in leading Chuck Schumer and Nancy Pelosi, just after a congressional leadership meeting. We all shook hands, and the various leaders began posing for pictures in front of the tree. As I was watching, John Kelly grabbed my elbow and said, "Let's get out of here and go back for our meeting." We went to the Oval and Trump came in almost immediately, along with Pence; we exchanged greetings; and then Pence departed and Kelly and I sat in front of Trump, who was behind the *Resolute* desk. I welcomed the embassy move to Jerusalem, and we quickly turned to Iran and North Korea. I explained some of the linkages between the two rogue states, including the North's sale of Scud missiles to Iran over twenty-five years ago; their joint missile testing in Iran after 1998 (following Japanese protests, Pyongyang had declared a moratorium on launch testing from the Peninsula after landing a projectile in the Pacific east of Japan); and their shared objective of developing delivery vehicles for nuclear weapons. On nuclear capabilities, Pakistani proliferator A. Q. Khan had sold both countries their basic uranium-enrichment technology (which he stole for Pakistan from Europe's Urenco Ltd.) and nuclear-weapons designs (initially provided to Pakistan by China). North Korea had been building the reactor in Syria destroyed by Israel in September 2007,[26] almost certainly financed by Iran, and I described how Iran could simply buy what it wanted from North Korea at the appropriate time (if it hadn't already).

The threat of North Korea's acquiring deliverable nuclear weapons manifests itself in several ways. First, strategy depends on analyzing intentions and capabilities. Intentions are often hard to read; capabilities are generally easier to assess (even granted that our intelligence is imperfect). But who wants to bet on what is really on the minds of the leaders in the world's only hereditary Communist dictatorship, in the face of hard evidence of accelerating nuclear and missile capabilities? Second, a nuclear-armed North Korea can conduct blackmail against nearby non-nuclear-weapons states like Japan and South Korea (where we have large deployed forces ourselves) and even against the United States, especially under a weak or feckless President. The dangers do not come simply from the risk of a first strike but from mere possession, not to mention the incentives for onward proliferation in East Asia and elsewhere created by a nuclear Pyongyang. Third, the North had repeatedly demonstrated it will sell anything to anybody with hard cash, so the risks of its becoming a nuclear Amazon are far from trivial.

I explained why and how a preemptive strike against North Korea's nuclear and ballistic-missile programs would work; how we could use massive conventional bombs against Pyongyang's artillery north of the DMZ, which threatened Seoul, thereby reducing casualties dramatically; and why the United States was rapidly approaching a binary choice, assuming China didn't act dramatically, of either leaving the North with nuclear weapons or using military force. The only other alternatives were seeking reunification of the Peninsula under South Korea or regime change in the North, both of which required cooperation with China, which we had not even begun to broach with them. Trump asked, "What do you think the chances of war are with North Korea? Fifty-fifty?" I said I thought it all depended on China, but probably fifty-fifty. Trump turned to Kelly and said, "He agrees with you."

In the course of this conversation (which lasted about thirty-five minutes), Trump raised his dissatisfaction with Tillerson, saying he didn't seem to have control of State. Trump asked why, and I said it was because Tillerson hadn't filled the subordinate ranks with appointees who would advance the Administration's policies and that he had, in effect, been captured by the careerists. I also explained why State needed a "cultural revolution" because of its desire to run foreign policy on its own, especially under Republican Presidents, during which both Trump and Kelly nodded affirmatively. Trump asked Kelly what he thought Tillerson was doing wrong, and Kelly said Tillerson was trying to centralize decision-making too much in his own hands. I agreed but said delegating authority had to go hand in hand with getting the right people in place to delegate it to. Kelly agreed, saying, "Delegation with supervision."

Trump then said to Kelly, "John knows that place [State] backwards and forwards." Kelly nodded agreement. I thought it was striking that Trump did not raise McMaster. As we ended the meeting, Trump said, "You're still ready to come in for the right position, am I right?" I laughed and said, "For the right position, yes." As Kelly and I walked back to the West Wing lobby, he said, "The guy loves you. After we've been here all day, he'll call me at home at nine thirty at night and say, 'Did you just see Bolton on television?'" I told Kelly to call me if I could be of help and left the building.

A week before Christmas, I met again with Kushner on the Middle East peace plan for about forty minutes and had a couple of other spare calls with him during the month. Other than that, things were quiet for the rest of the month. Happy New Year!

On January 6, 2018, during a maelstrom of press commentary on the new *Fire and Fury* book about Trump, he tweeted that he was a "very stable genius." With another statutorily required presidential decision approaching on whether to have the pre-Iran-deal sanctions come back into force, I decided to sit back. They knew how to get me if they wanted to, and no one made contact. Trump reprised what he had done in October, keeping the sanctions from coming back into effect but not certifying that Iran was complying with the deal. No progress.

And then North Korea returned to the spotlight as South Korea hosted the Winter Olympics. Pence and Ivanka Trump represented the US, amid speculation of talks with the North Korea delegation. I gave interviews applauding Pence for not letting the North gain a propaganda edge or drive wedges between us and South Korea. Pence tweeted in response, "Well said @AmbJohnBolton," a nice signal. Of course, South Korean President Moon Jae-in was going all out for domestic political purposes to highlight his "success" in having high-level North Koreans attend, particularly Kim Jong Un's younger sister, Kim Yo Jong (sanctioned by the US as a known violator of human rights). In fact, Kim Yo Jong did have a mission, inviting Moon to the North, which he accepted instantly. It trickled out later that Seoul had paid Pyongyang's costs of participating in the games, not from any Olympic spirit, but following a sad, well-established pattern.[27] South Korea's left worshipped this "Sunshine Policy," which basically held that being nice to North Korea would bring peace to the Peninsula. Instead, again and again, it merely subsidized the North's dictatorship.

On March 6, I had yet another meeting with Trump. Waiting in the West Wing lobby, I watched on television as reporters asked why he thought the North was now ready to negotiate, and Trump replied happily, "Me." I hoped he understood North Korea truly feared that he, unlike Obama, was prepared if necessary to use military force. I went to the Oval at about 4:40, once again sitting in front of the completely clean *Resolute* desk. Trump said to me, just as Kelly entered, "Did I ask for this meeting or did you?" I said I had, and he responded, "I thought I had, but I'm glad you came in because I wanted to see you." We started off talking about North Korea, and I explained I thought Kim Jong Un was trying to buy time to finish the relatively few (albeit critical) tasks still necessary to achieve a deliverable nuclear-weapons capability. That meant that Kim Jong Un now especially feared military force; he knew economic sanctions alone wouldn't prevent him from reaching that goal. I wasn't quite sure Trump got the point, but I also raised reports of North Korea's selling chemical-weapons equipment and precursor chemicals to Syria, likely financed by Iran.[28] If true, this linkage could be pivotal for both North Korea and Iran, showing just how dangerous Pyongyang was: now selling chemical weapons, soon enough selling nuclear weapons. I urged him to use this argument to justify both exiting the Iran nuclear deal and taking a harder line on North Korea. Kelly agreed and urged me to keep pounding away in public, which I assured him I would.

On the Iran nuclear deal, Trump said, "Don't worry, I'm getting out of that. I said they could try to fix it, but that won't happen." He turned to how much he wanted to fire Tillerson, saying, "You know what's wrong. I'd love to have you over there." But he said he thought confirmation, with just a 51–49 Republican majority, would be difficult. "That son of a bitch Rand Paul will vote against you, and McConnell is worried he may persuade other Republicans, who need his vote on judges and other things. What do you hear?" I said I wouldn't get Paul's vote, but I would be surprised if he dragged other Republicans along with him. (The real count in the Senate, however, increasingly looked to be 50–49, as John McCain's health continued to deteriorate, raising the prospect he might never return to Washington.) I also said, based on earlier conversations with Republican Senators, that we could roll up a handful of Democrats, especially in an election year.

I doubted I'd persuaded Trump, and he asked, "What else would you be interested in?" I answered, "National Security Advisor." Kelly broke his silence to underline that that job did not require Senate confirmation, and Trump asked happily, "So I don't have to worry about those clowns up there?" and both Kelly and I said, "Right."

I then launched into a description of what I thought the core duties of the National Security Advisor's job were, namely, ensuring that the full range of options was put before the President and that his decisions were then carried out, at which Kelly nodded vigorously. I said I thought my training as a litigator equipped me for that role, because I could present the options fairly but still have my own point of view (as one does with clients), and that I understood he made the final decisions, once again telling him the Dean Acheson/Harry Truman story. Trump and Kelly both laughed. Trump asked me what I thought McMaster had done right, and I said it was a real achievement to write a good national-security strategy in a President's first year in office, something that had not occurred, for example, in Bush 43's tenure, among others. Trump asked what I thought Mattis had done well, and I cited the major defense budget increase over the Obama years the Administration had recently won. Before I could finish, both Trump and Kelly said simultaneously the budget win was Trump's accomplishment, not Mattis's. I thought that was a real revelation about Trump's attitude toward Mattis.

The meeting ended after about thirty-five minutes, and Trump said, "Okay, stay patient, I'll be calling you." Kelly and I walked out of the Oval, and he asked, "Have you thought about the media reaction if you get named?" I had, saying I had been through it already when nominated to the UN ambassadorship. Kelly said, "Yes, that was outrageous. But think about it again, anyway, because he's serious." I had put up with so much from the media over the years that I really didn't care what their reaction was; by that point, my scar tissue had scars. As the Duke of Wellington once said (perhaps apocryphally), my attitude was, "Print and be damned."

I felt pretty good until that evening. While addressing a fundraiser in Northern Virginia for Republican Congresswoman Barbara

THE ROOM WHERE IT HAPPENED   33

Comstock, whom I first met at the Reagan Justice Department, I heard Kim Jong Un had invited Trump to meet, and he had accepted. I was beyond speechless, appalled at this foolish mistake. For a US President to grant Kim a summit with no sign whatever of a strategic decision to renounce nuclear weapons—in fact, giving it away for nothing—was a propaganda gift beyond measure. It was worse by orders of magnitude than Madeleine Albright clinking glasses with Kim Il Sung during the Clinton years. Fortunately, I had no Fox interviews that night because of the fund-raiser, so I had time to think about it. The next day, Sarah Sanders seemed to walk things back, saying our existing policy had not changed.

As I had left the White House earlier on Tuesday, the White House had announced Gary Cohn's resignation as Chairman of the National Economic Council. Larry Kudlow was named to replace him. In the meantime, in February, White House Staff Secretary Rob Porter resigned because of damaging personal information revealed in his FBI background investigation, followed shortly thereafter by Trump's longtime staffer Hope Hicks, then Communications Director. The bloodletting continued on March 13, with the announcement that Tillerson had been unceremoniously fired as Secretary of State; that Pompeo would be nominated to replace him; and that Pompeo's CIA Deputy, Gina Haspel, a career intelligence officer, would succeed him. Kushner called me the next day for another meeting on his Middle East peace plan, which I again found difficult to believe was entirely coincidental. Then, on March 16, Jeff Sessions resumed the bloodletting by firing FBI Deputy Director Andrew McCabe.

Life around the world, however, was still rolling along. A Russian hit squad, using chemical weapons from the Novichok family, attacked former Russian spy Sergei Skripal and his daughter in Salisbury, England. After Moscow disdainfully refused even to address the attack, Prime Minister May expelled twenty-three undeclared Russian intelligence agents.[29] In interviews, I took a very tough view of how America should respond to this attack, a view I still hold. So, it was unsettling to read that Trump had congratulated Putin on "winning" reelection as President of Russia, over McMaster's advice, which had been promptly and widely leaked to the media. Nonetheless, Trump later expelled over sixty Russian "diplomats" as part of a NATO-wide effort to show solidarity with London.[30] As several House members helping me with my National Security Advisor campaign confided, we were within days of Trump's deciding who would replace McMaster. I gritted my teeth, because the job was looking more arduous than before, but I decided not to pull back now.

On Wednesday, March 21, my cell phone rang as I was riding down a snowy George Washington Memorial Parkway to do an interview at Fox's DC studio (the federal government and most area schools and businesses being closed). "Good morning, Mr. President," I said, and Trump replied, "I've got a job for you that is probably the most powerful job in the White House." As I started to answer, Trump said, "No, really better than Chief of Staff," and we both laughed, which meant Kelly was probably in the room with him. "And you won't have to deal with the Democrats in the Senate, no need for that. You should come in and we'll talk about this, come in today or tomorrow. I want someone with gravitas, not some unknown. You have great support, great support, from all kinds of people, great support, like those Freedom Caucus guys" (a group of Republicans in the House). I thanked Trump and then called my wife and daughter, Gretchen and JS (Jennifer Sarah), to tell them, stressing that for Trump it was never over until something was publicly announced, and sometimes not then.

I met with Trump in the Oval the next day at four o'clock. We started into what seemed like another interview, talking about Iran and North Korea. Much of what Trump said harked back to his campaign days, before a series of speeches had positioned him in the broad Republican mainstream foreign-policy thinking. I wondered if he was having second thoughts about making me an offer, but at least he said unequivocally he was getting out of the Iran deal. He said almost nothing about the supposed upcoming summit with Kim Jong Un, an omission I found hard to read. The largest single block of time was spent discussing again how I thought the NSC should work. Although I didn't mention Brent Scowcroft by name, the system I explained, as Kelly well knew, was what Scowcroft had done in the Bush

41 Administration. First, it was the NSC's responsibility to provide the President with the available options and the pluses and minuses of each. Second, once a decision was made, the NSC was the President's enforcer to ensure that the bureaucracies carried out the decision. All this resonated with Trump, although he didn't directly offer me the job, asking instead, "So you think you want to do this?" I was beginning to wonder if this now hour-long meeting was just going to dribble off inconclusively when Westerhout came in to tell Trump he had another meeting. He stood up, and of course so did I. We shook hands over the *Resolute* desk. Although there had been no clear "offer" and "acceptance," both Kelly and I knew what had in fact happened, in the Trumpian way.

Given the experiences already recounted here, and more, why accept the job? Because America faced a very dangerous international environment, and I thought I knew what needed to be done. I had strong views on a wide range of issues, developed during prior government service and private-sector study. And Trump? No one could claim by this point not to know the risks in store, up close, but I also believed I could handle it. Others may have failed for one reason or another, but I thought I could succeed. Was I right? Read on.

Outside the Oval, I encountered White House Counsel Don Mc-Gahn going in with folders on potential judicial nominations. Kelly and I spoke for a few minutes, and I said it was clear to me that neither one of us could accomplish anything unless we worked together, which was my intention, and he readily agreed. I also asked what the timing of an announcement might be, and he thought the next day or the following week at the earliest. I later learned (as did Kelly) that within minutes of my leaving the Oval, Trump called McMaster to tell him he would be announcing the switch later that same afternoon. I went to the West Wing lobby to retrieve my coat, and the receptionist and a White House communications staffer said there was a mob of reporters and photographers waiting for me to exit the north door to the driveway. They asked if I would mind going out the "back way," through the White House's Southwest Gate onto Seventeenth Street, and walking "behind" the Eisenhower Executive Office Building to miss the press, which I happily did. I called Gretchen and JS again, and began to think about preparations for starting at the White House.

On my way to the Fox News studio for an interview on Martha MacCallum's show, Trump tweeted:

> I am pleased to announce that, effective 4/9/18, @AmbJohnBolton will be my new National Security Advisor. I am very thankful for the service of General H.R. McMaster who has done an outstanding job & will always remain my friend. There will be an official contact handover on 4/9.

At that point, my cell phone felt like a hand grenade going off, with incoming calls, e-mails, tweets, and news alerts.

I now had some two weeks to make the necessary transition away from private life to government service, and the pace was frenetic. The next day, Trump called me during his intelligence briefing, saying, "You're getting great press," that the announcement was "playing very big," getting "great reviews . . . the base loves it," and so on. He said at one point, "Some of them think you're the bad cop," and I replied, "When we play the good cop/bad cop routine, the President is always the good cop." Trump responded, "The trouble is, we've got two bad cops," and I could hear the others in the Oval for the intel briefing laughing, as was I.

Since Trump had announced I would start on April 9, the first priority was the White House Counsel's vetting process. This consisted of filling out extensive forms and undergoing questioning by the Counsel's Office lawyers on financial disclosure issues, possible conflicts of interest, requirements for divestiture of assets (not that I had all that much to divest), unwinding existing employment relationships, freezing my PAC and SuperPAC during my government service, and the like. Also required was what baby boomers called the "sex, drugs and rock and roll" interview, where typically the trap was not what foolish things you had done in your life but whether you admitted them in response to questions or volunteered them if they were exotic enough. Since my last government job as UN Ambassador, I had received plenty of media coverage, so I took care to mention even the outlandish things that lazy, biased, incompetent reporters had published at my expense, including that Maria Butina had tried to recruit me as a Russian agent. (I do not think the press is "an enemy of the people," but, as Dwight Eisenhower said in 1964, its ranks are filled with "sensation-seeking columnists and commentators" whose writings mark them as little more than intellectualoids.) Then there was the mandatory urine sample I provided for drug testing; let's not forget that.

I also tried to consult with former National Security Advisors, starting of course with Kissinger, who said, "I have great confidence in you, and I wish you every success. You know the subject. You know the bureaucracy. I know you are able to handle it." And most important, Kissinger, like every predecessor with whom I spoke, Republican and Democrat alike, offered their support. I spoke with Colin Powell (who had been my boss when he was Secretary of State in Bush 43's first term), Brent Scowcroft, James Jones, Condi Rice, Steve Hadley, Susan Rice, John Poindexter, and Bud McFarlane, as well as Bob Gates, who had been Scowcroft's Deputy and later Secretary of Defense. Scowcroft said succinctly, "The world is a mess, and we're the only ones who can straighten it out."

I spoke with former Secretaries of State for whom I had worked, including George Shultz and Jim Baker (Powell and Condi Rice, of course, fell into both categories), and also Don Rumsfeld and Dick Cheney. Finally, I spoke with President George W. Bush, who was very generous with his time, wishing me "all the best." I asked about calling his father, for whom I had also worked, and he said it would be "difficult" at that time, so I simply asked that he pass on my regards.

I had lunch with McMaster on March 27 in the Ward Room, part of the White House Navy mess facility. He was gracious and forthcoming in his assessments of issues, policies, and personnel. A few days later, I had breakfast with Jim Mattis at the Pentagon. Mattis showed his flair with the press, as he greeted me at the entrance, by saying he had heard I was "the devil incarnate." I thought of replying, "I do my best," but bit my tongue. We had a very productive discussion. Mattis suggested that he, Pompeo, and I have breakfast once a week at the White House to go over pending issues. Although we were all on the telephone with each other several times most days, the breakfasts proved to be a very important opportunity for the three of us alone to discuss key issues. When one might be traveling, the other two would get together, usually in the Ward Room, but often at State or the Pentagon.

When Mattis and I finished, he took me to meet Joe Dunford, Chairman of the Joint Chiefs of Staff, whose term as Chairman would last through September 2019. I recalled to Dunford his remarks on the North Korea nuclear issue at the summer 2018 Aspen Security Forum:

> Many people have talked about the military options with words such as unimaginable. I would probably shift that slightly and say it would be horrific and it would be a loss of life unlike any we've experienced in our lifetime, and I mean anyone who's been alive since World War II has never seen a loss of life that could occur if there is a conflict on the Korean Peninsula. But as I've told my counterparts, both friend and foe, it is not unimaginable to have military options to respond to North Korea's nuclear capability. What is unimaginable to me is allowing the capability to allow nuclear weapons to land in Denver, Colorado. My job will be to develop military options to make sure that doesn't happen.[31]

Dunford seemed surprised I knew of his comments, and we had a good discussion. Dunford had a reputation as an outstanding military officer, and I had no reason to doubt that, then or later.

I broached Mattis's three-way-breakfast idea with Mike Pompeo at the CIA a few days later. He readily agreed. He and I had already exchanged a number of e-mails, one from him saying, "I'm truly excited to get started as a co-founder of the war cabinet. I will send Sen. Paul your regards." I also had a chance to meet his Deputy and likely successor, Gina Haspel.

I had watched Trump closely during his nearly fifteen months in office, and I had no illusions that I could change him. Any number of National Security Council "models" might have been academically sound but would make no difference if they simply spun in a vacuum, disconnected, admiring themselves and lauded by the media but not actually engaging the sitting President. I was determined to have a disciplined, thorough process, but I would judge my performance on how it actually shaped policy, not how outsiders compared it to prior Administrations.

Several decisions flowed from this analysis. First, the NSC staff (roughly 430 people when I arrived, 350 when I left) was not a think tank. Its product was not discussion groups and staff papers but effective decision-making. The organization should be simple and direct. I planned to eliminate many duplicative, overlapping structures and staff. Since Trump had given me full hiring and firing authority, I acted quickly and decisively, among other things naming only one Deputy National Security Advisor, instead of several, to strengthen and simplify the National Security Council staff's effectiveness. This critical role I filled first with Mira Ricardel, a longtime defense expert with extensive government service and as a senior Boeing executive, and later with Dr. Charles Kupperman, a defense expert with similar credentials (including Boeing!). They had strong personalities; they would need them.

On the Saturday before Easter at six thirty p.m., I had a somewhat bizarre conversation with Trump. He did almost all the talking, starting with "Rex was terrible" and then explaining why, focusing on a decision to commit $200 million for Syrian reconstruction. Trump didn't like it: "I want to build up our country, not others." As a US Agency for International Development alumnus, I supported using US foreign assistance to advance national-security objectives, but I also knew such efforts had their weaknesses as well as strengths. I tried to get a word in edgewise, but Trump rolled right along, saying periodically, "I know you get this." He then said, "You've got a lot of leakers down there. You can get rid of anybody you want," which I was already preparing to do. Finally, the conversation ended, and we both said, "Happy Easter."

On Easter Monday, Trump called again. I asked, "How's the Easter

Egg Roll going, Mr. President?" "Great," he said as Sarah Sanders, her children, and others came in and out of the Oval, and then returned to his Saturday-night monologue, saying, "I want to get out of these horrible wars [in the Middle East]." "We're killing ISIS for countries that are our enemies," which I took to mean Russia, Iran, and Assad's Syria. He said his advisors were divided into two categories, those who wanted to stay "forever," and those who wanted to stay "for a while." By contrast, Trump said, "I don't want to stay at all. I don't like the Kurds. They ran from the Iraqis, they ran from the Turks, the only time they don't run is when we're bombing all around them with F-18s." He asked, "What should we do?" Figuring the Easter Egg Roll might not be the best time to discuss Middle East strategy, I said I was still waiting to get my temporary security clearance lined up. Pompeo, who had arrived in the Oval, said, "Give John and me a little bit of time—" before he was cut off by more children and parents traipsing through. It was pretty clear Trump wanted to withdraw from Syria, and indeed at an NSC meeting the next day (see chapter 2), he voiced precisely these sentiments. Still, much remained to be decided, giving me confidence we could protect US interests as the struggle to destroy the ISIS territorial caliphate neared a successful conclusion.

On Friday, April 6, heading into the weekend before my first official day, I met again with Kelly and several others to review West Wing procedures. I explained some of the NSC personnel changes I planned and the reorganizations I intended. I had Trump's authority to do these things, but I didn't mind informing Kelly in advance. He spent the rest of the meeting, which lasted an hour, explaining how Trump acted in meetings and on phone calls. The President used "very rough language," said Kelly, which was true, "and of course, he's entitled to do that," also true. Trump despised both Bush Presidents and their Administrations, leading me to wonder if he had missed my almost ten years of service in those presidencies. And Trump changed his mind constantly. I wondered listening to all this how close Kelly was to just walking away. Kelly concluded by saying graciously, "I'm glad you're here, John. The President hasn't had a National Security Advisor for the past year, and he needs one."

I spent the weekend reading classified materials and otherwise preparing for April 9. But as the next chapter will show, the Syria crisis came unannounced and unexpected, like much of the next seventeen months. Acheson had written about Roosevelt's replacement of Cordell Hull as Secretary of State with Edward Stettinius, which had led the press to speculate that Roosevelt "would continue to be . . . his own Secretary of State." Acheson had a firm view: "The President cannot be Secretary of State; it is inherently impossible in the nature of both positions. What he can do, and often has done with unhappy results, is to prevent anyone else from being Secretary of State."[32] Although not written about the National Security Advisor position, Acheson's insight was profound. Perhaps that is what Kelly was trying to say in his final comment to me before I started. And as Condi Rice said to me much later, "Secretary of State is the best job in the government, and National Security Advisor is the hardest." I am sure she is right.

CHAPTER 2

CRY "HAVOC!" AND LET SLIP THE DOGS OF WAR

O
n Saturday, April 7, 2018, Syrian armed forces, using chemical weapons, attacked the city of Douma in southwest Syria and other nearby locations. Initial reports had perhaps a dozen people killed and hundreds wounded, including children, some grievously sickened by the dangerous chemicals.[1] Chlorine was the likely base material for the weapons, but there were claims of sarin gas activity and perhaps other chemicals.[2] Bashar al-Assad's regime had similarly used chemical weapons, including sarin, one year earlier, on April 4, 2017, at Khan Shaykhun in northwest Syria. Only three days later, the United States responded forcefully, launching fifty-nine cruise missiles at the suspected site from which the Syrian attack emanated.[3]

Syria's dictatorship obviously had not learned its lesson. Deterrence had failed, and the issue now was how to respond appropriately. Unhappily, a year after Khan Shaykhun, Syria policy remained in disarray, lacking agreement on fundamental objectives and strategy.[4] Now it was again in crisis. Responding to this latest Syrian chemical-weapons attack was imperative, but we also urgently needed conceptual clarity on how to advance American interests long-term. An NSC meeting held the week before Douma, however, pointed in exactly the opposite direction: US withdrawal from Syria. Leaving would risk losing even the limited gains achieved under Barack Obama's misbegotten Syria-Iraq policies, thereby exacerbating the dangers his approach fostered. Responsibility for this policy disarray, one year after Khan

Shaykhun, rested at that iconic location where the buck stops: the *Resolute* desk in the Oval Office.

At about nine a.m. on April 8, in his own personal style and the style of our times, Donald J. Trump, President of the United States of America, tweeted:

> Many dead, including women and children, in mindless CHEMICAL attack in Syria. Area of atrocity is in lockdown and encircled by Syrian Army, making it completely inaccessible to outside world. President Putin, Russia and Iran are responsible for backing Animal Assad. Big price . . .

> . . . to pay. Open area immediately for medical help and verification. Another humanitarian disaster for no reason whatsoever. SICK!

Minutes later, he tweeted again:

> If President Obama had crossed his stated Red Line In The Sand, the Syrian disaster would have ended long ago! Animal Assad would have been history!

These were clear, forceful statements, but Trump tweeted before consulting his national security team. Lieutenant General H. R. McMaster, my predecessor as National Security Advisor, had left Friday afternoon, and I didn't start until Monday. When I tried to pull together a meeting on Sunday, White House lawyers blocked it, because I would not officially become a government employee until Monday. This gave the word "frustration" new meaning.

Trump called me Sunday afternoon, and we (mostly he) talked for twenty minutes. He mused that getting out of the Middle East the right way was tough, a theme he raised repeatedly during the call, interspersed with digressions on trade wars and tariffs. Trump said he had just seen Jack Keane (a four-star general and former Army Vice

Chief of Staff) on Fox News and liked his idea of destroying Syria's five main military airfields, thereby essentially knocking out Assad's entire air force. Trump said, "My honor is at stake," reminding me of Thucydides's famous observation that "fear, honor and interest" are the main drivers of international politics and ultimately war. French President Emmanuel Macron had already called to say France was strongly considering participating in a US-led military response.[5] Earlier in the day, presidential son-in-law Jared Kushner had told me that UK Foreign Secretary Boris Johnson had phoned him to relay essentially the same message from London. These prompt assurances of support were encouraging. Why a foreign minister was calling Kushner, however, was something to address in coming days.

Trump asked about an NSC staffer I planned on firing, a supporter of his since the earliest days of his presidential campaign. He wasn't surprised when I told him the individual was part of "the leak problem," and he continued, "Too many people know too many things." This highlighted my most pressing management problem: dealing with the Syria crisis while reorienting the NSC staff to aim in a common direction, a bit like changing hockey lines on the fly. This was no time for placid reflection, or events would overtake us. On Sunday, I could only "suggest" to the NSC staff that they do everything possible to ascertain all they could about the Assad regime's actions (and whether further attacks were likely), and develop US options in response. I called an NSC staff meeting for six forty-five a.m. Monday morning to see where we stood, and to assess what roles Russia and Iran might have played. We needed decisions that fit into a larger, post-ISIS Syria/Iraq picture, and to avoid simply responding "whack-a-mole" style.

I left home with my newly assigned Secret Service protective detail a little before six a.m., heading to the White House in two silver-colored SUVs. Once at the West Wing, I saw that Chief of Staff John Kelly was already in his first-floor, southwest-corner office, down the hall from mine on the northwest corner, so I stopped by to say hello. Over the next eight months, when we were in town, we both typically arrived around six a.m., an excellent time to sync up as the day began. The six forty-five NSC staff meeting confirmed my—and what seemed to be Trump's—belief that the Douma strike required a strong, near-term military response. The US opposed anyone's use of WMD ("weapons of mass destruction")—nuclear, chemical, and biological— as contrary to our national interest. Whether in the hands of strategic opponents, rogue states, or terrorists, WMD endangered the American people and our allies.

A crucial question in the ensuing debate was whether reestablishing deterrence against using weapons of mass destruction inevitably meant greater US involvement in Syria's civil war. It did not. Our vital interest against chemical-weapons attacks could be vindicated without ousting Assad, notwithstanding the fears of both those who wanted strong action against his regime and those who wanted none. Military force was justified to deter Assad and many others from using chemical (or nuclear or biological) weapons in the future. From our perspective, Syria was a strategic sideshow, and who ruled there should not distract us from Iran, the real threat.

I called Defense Secretary Jim Mattis at 8:05 a.m. He believed Russia was our real problem, harking back to Obama's ill-advised 2014 agreement with Putin to "eliminate" Syria's chemical weapons capability, which obviously hadn't happened.[6] And now here we were again. Unsurprisingly, Russia was already accusing Israel of being behind the Douma strike. Mattis and I discussed possible responses to Syria's attack, and he said he would be supplying "light, medium, and heavy" options for the President's consideration, which I thought was the right approach. I noted that, unlike in 2017, both France and Britain were considering joining a response, which we agreed was a plus. I sensed, over the phone, that Mattis was reading from a prepared text.

Afterward, UK national security advisor Sir Mark Sedwill called me to follow up Johnson's call to Kushner.[7] It was more than symbolic that Sedwill was my first foreign caller. Having our allies more closely aligned to our main foreign-policy and defense objectives strengthened our hand in critical ways and was one of my top policy goals. Sedwill said deterrence had obviously failed, and Assad had become "more adept at concealing his use" of chemical weapons. I understood from Sedwill that Britain's likely view was to ensure that our next use of force was both militarily and politically effective, dismantling Assad's chemical capabilities and re-creating deterrence. That sounded right. I also took a moment to raise the 2015 Iran nuclear deal, even in the midst of the Syria crisis, emphasizing the likelihood, based on my many conversations with Trump, that America now really would be withdrawing. I emphasized that Trump had made no final decision, but we needed to consider how to constrain Iran after a US withdrawal and how to preserve trans-Atlantic unity. Sedwill was undoubtedly surprised to hear this. Neither he nor other Europeans had heard it before from the Administration, since, before my arrival, Trump's advisors had almost uniformly resisted withdrawal. He took the point stoically and said we should talk further once the immediate crisis was resolved.

At ten a.m., I went down to the Situation Room complex for the scheduled Principals Committee meeting of the National Security Council, a Cabinet-level gathering. (Old hands call the area "the Sit Room," but millennials call it "Whizzer," for the initials "WHSR," "White House Situation Room.") It had been completely renovated and much improved since my last meeting there in 2006. (For security reasons as well as efficiency, I later launched a substantial further renovation that began in September 2019.) I normally would chair the Principals Committee, but the Vice President decided to do so, perhaps thinking to be helpful on my first day. In any case, I led the discussion, as was standard, and the issue never arose again. This initial, hour-long session allowed the various departments to present their thoughts on how to proceed. I stressed that our central objective was to make Assad pay dearly for using chemical weapons and to re-create structures of deterrence so it didn't happen again. We needed political and economic steps, as well as a military strike, to show we had a comprehensive approach and were potentially building a coalition with Britain and France. (UK, US, and French military planners were already talking.)[8] We had to consider not just the immediate response but what Syria, Russia, and Iran might do next. We discussed at length what we did and didn't know regarding Syria's attack and how to increase our understanding of what had happened, especially whether sarin nerve agent was involved or just chlorine-based agents. This is where Mattis repeated almost verbatim his earlier comments, including that the Pentagon would provide a medium-to-heavy range of options.

Further work on Syria, not to mention filling out more government forms, swirled along until one p.m., when I was called to the Oval. UN Ambassador Nikki Haley (who had participated in the Principals Committee via secure telecommunications from New York) was calling to ask what to say in the Security Council that afternoon. This was apparently the normal way she learned what to do in the Council, completely outside the regular NSC process, which I found amazing. As a former UN Ambassador myself, I had wondered at Haley's untethered performance in New York over the past year-plus; now I saw how it actually worked. I was sure Mike Pompeo and I would be discussing this issue after he was confirmed as Secretary of State. The call started off, however, with Trump asking why former Secretary of State Rex Tillerson, before he left office, had approved $500 million in economic assistance to Africa. I suspected this was the amount approved by Congress in the course of the appropriations process, but said I would check. Trump also asked me to look into a news report on India's purchasing Russian S-400 air defense systems because, said India, the S-400 was better than America's Patriot defense system. Then we came to Syria. Trump said Haley should basically say, "You have heard the President's words [via Twitter], and you should listen." I suggested that, after the Security Council meeting, Haley and the UK and French Ambassadors jointly address the press outside the Council chamber to present a united front. I had done that many times, but Haley declined, preferring to have pictures of her alone giving the US statement in the Council. That told me something.

In the afternoon, I met with NSC staff handling the Iran nuclear-weapons issue, asking them to prepare to exit the 2015 deal within a month. Trump needed to have the option ready for him when he decided to leave, and I wanted to be sure he had it. There was no way ongoing negotiations with the UK, France, and Germany would "fix" the deal; we needed to withdraw and create an effective follow-on strategy to block Iran's drive for deliverable nuclear weapons. What I said couldn't have been surprising, since I had said it all before publicly many times, but I could feel the air going out of the NSC staff, who until then had been working feverishly to save the deal.

I was back in the Oval at four forty-five p.m. for Trump to call Macron.[9] I typically joined in the President's calls with foreign leaders, which had long been standard practice. Macron reaffirmed, as he was doing publicly, France's intention to respond jointly to the chemical attacks (and which, after the fact, he actually took credit for!).[10] He noted UK Prime Minister Theresa May's desire to act soon. He also raised the attack earlier on Monday against Syria's Tiyas airbase, which housed an Iranian facility, and the risk of Iran's counterattacking even as we planned our own operations.[11] I spoke later with Philippe Étienne, my French counterpart and Macron's diplomatic advisor, to coordinate carrying out the Trump-Macron discussions.

As I listened, I realized that if military action began by the weekend, which seemed likely, Trump couldn't be out of the country.[12] When the call ended, I suggested he skip the Summit of the Americas conference in Peru scheduled for that time and that Pence attend instead. Trump agreed, and told me to work it out with Pence and Kelly. When I relayed this to Kelly, he groaned because of the preparations already made. I responded, "Don't hate me on my first day," and he agreed a switch was probably inevitable. I went to the VP's office, which was between my office and Kelly's, to explain the situation. While we were talking, Kelly came in to say the FBI had raided the offices of Michael Cohen, a Trump lawyer and chief "fixer" for nondisclosure agreements with the likes of Stormy Daniels, not exactly a matter of high state. Nonetheless, in the time I spent with Trump the rest of the week, which was considerable, the Cohen issue never came up. There was no trace of evidence to suggest Cohen was on Trump's mind, in my presence, other than when he responded to the incessant press questioning.

On Monday evening, Trump hosted a semiannual dinner with the Joint Chiefs of Staff and the military combatant commanders to discuss matters of interest. With all of them in town, it also provided an opportunity to hear their views on Syria. Had this not been my first day, with the Syria crisis overshadowing everything, I would have tried to meet them individually to discuss their respective responsibilities. That, however, would have to wait.

The next day, at eight thirty, I spoke again with Sedwill, calling to prepare for May's telephone conversation to Trump, scheduled shortly thereafter. Sedwill again pressed on the timing issue, and I wondered if domestic political pressures in Britain were weighing on May's thinking, given that parliament was coming back into session on April 16. Former Prime Minister David Cameron's failure to obtain House of Commons approval to attack Syria, after the Assad regime crossed Obama's "red line" on chemical weapons, worried me as a precedent. Obviously, if we acted before Parliament came back into session, I thought that risk would be eliminated.[13] Sedwill was also happy to hear that the Pentagon was thinking heavier rather than lighter for the military response, which was consistent with UK preferences, and in seeking a broader conceptual framework for Syria. When May and Trump spoke, she echoed Sedwill's comments on the need to act promptly.[14] Throughout the call, Trump seemed resolved, although it was clear he didn't like May, a feeling that struck me as reciprocal. I also spoke frequently through the week with my Israeli counterpart, Meir Ben-Shabbat, about reports regarding an air strike against Syria's Tiyas air base, and Iran's highly threatening presence in Syria.[15]

Through the week, more information on the attacks came in, and I spent considerable time reviewing this data, as well as reams of classified material on the rest of the world. My practice in prior government jobs had always been to consume as much intelligence as I could. I might have agreed or disagreed with analyses or conclusions, but I was always ready to absorb more information. Proof of the Assad regime's chemical-weapons usage was increasingly clear in public reporting, although left-wing commentators, and even some on Fox, were saying there was no evidence. They were wrong.

The second Syria Principals Committee meeting convened at one thirty and again consisted largely of the various agencies reporting on their developing planning and activity, all consistent with a strong response. I soon realized Mattis was our biggest problem. He hadn't produced any targeting options for the NSC or for White House Counsel Don McGahn, who needed to write an opinion on the legality of whatever Trump ultimately decided. From long, unhappy experience, I knew what was going on here. Mattis knew where he wanted Trump to come out militarily, and he also knew that the way to maximize the likelihood of his view's prevailing was to deny information to others who had a legitimate right to weigh in. It was simple truth that not presenting options until the last minute, making sure that those options were rigged in the "right" direction, and then table-pounding, delaying, and obfuscating as long as possible were the tactics by which a savvy bureaucrat like Mattis could get his way. The Principals Committee meeting ended inconclusively, although Mattis gave some ground to McGahn in the end after a little temper-flaring around the Sit Room table. I was determined that this obstructionism would not happen, but Mattis had clearly dug in. I didn't think he was over the line yet, but he was right on it, as I said to both Pence and Kelly after the meeting.

Starting at about three p.m., I spent about two hours in the Oval, in a "meeting" rolling from one issue to another. Trump was worried about the possibility of Russian casualties in Syria, given Russia's extensive military presence there, which had climbed dramatically during the Obama years. This was a legitimate concern, and one we addressed by having the Chairman of the Joint Chiefs of Staff, Joe Dunford, call his Russian counterpart, Valery Gerasimov, to assure him that whatever action we decided to take, it would not be targeted at Russian personnel or assets.[16] The Dunford-Gerasimov channel had been and remained a critical asset for both countries over time, in many instances far more suitable than conventional diplomatic communications to ensure Washington and Moscow both clearly understood their respective interests and intentions. Another Trump-Macron call went through at three forty-five, with Macron pushing for prompt action and threatening to act unilaterally if we delayed too long, an assertion he had earlier stated publicly.[17] This was preposterous and potentially dangerous; it was showboating, and Trump ultimately reined the French back in. Macron was right, however, in seeking prompt action, which weighed against Trump's mistaken inclination to move slowly. The quicker the retaliation, the clearer the message to Assad and others. We had still not seen options from the Pentagon, and the two leaders did not discuss specific targets. It seemed, nonetheless, that Macron wanted the medium option among the target packages, whatever that turned out to be. Low is too low, he said, and high is too aggressive. I had no idea what he meant, wondering whether he did either, or whether he was just posturing.

While briefing Trump for a later call with President Recep Tayyip Erdogan of Turkey, I stressed that we had the right formula: (1) a proposed three-way attack option with France and Britain, not just a unilateral US strike as in 2017; (2) a comprehensive approach, using political and economic as well as military means, combined with effective messaging to explain what we were doing and why; and (3) a sustained—not just a one-shot—effort. Trump seemed satisfied. He also urged me, "Do as much TV as you want," saying, "Go after Obama as much as you want," which he called "a good thing to do." I actually didn't want to do media that week, and there were enough other people clawing to get on television that no shortage of Administration voices would be heard.

The Erdogan call turned out to be an experience. Listening to him (his remarks were always interpreted), he sounded like Mussolini speaking from his Rome balcony, except that Erdogan was talking in that tone and volume over the phone. It was as if he were lecturing us while standing on the *Resolute* desk. Erdogan seemed to avoid any commitment to join US strike plans but said he would be speaking to Putin imminently.[18] Trump urged Erdogan to stress that we were seeking to avoid Russian casualties. The next day, Thursday, Ibrahim Kalin, my Turkish counterpart (and also Erdogan's press spokesman, an interesting combination), called to report on the Erdogan-Putin call. Putin had emphasized he did not want to see a broader confrontation with the United States over Syria, and that everyone should act with common sense.[19]

At eight a.m. Thursday, Dunford called to debrief his conversation with Gerasimov late the night before. After the obligatory Russian defense of the Assad regime, Gerasimov got down to business, taking Dunford seriously when he stressed our intention was not to target Russians. Dunford characterized Gerasimov as "very professional, very measured." Dunford and I agreed it was a positive result, which I conveyed to Trump later in the morning, along with the Erdogan-Putin phone call.

I met with Trump and Pence at one thirty in the small dining room down a short hall from the Oval. Trump spent a lot of time in this dining room, with a wide-screen television on the wall opposite his chair, usually turned to Fox News. It was here that his collection of official papers, newspapers, and other documents usually resided, rather than on the *Resolute* desk in the Oval. Trump wanted to withdraw most US troops from Syria and persuade Arab states to deploy more of their own forces there, as well as pay for the remaining US presence. He did not see this substitution of Arab for US forces as a strategic redirection, but as a way of deflecting US domestic political criticism for his increasingly blunt public comments about withdrawing from Syria. I said I would look into it. With a full NSC meeting (the proper term only when the President chairs the meeting) coming that afternoon, I also told Trump we were essentially being sandbagged by Mattis on the range of target options. Trump seemed troubled, but he offered no real direction.

The NSC meeting convened at three o'clock in the Sit Room, lasted about seventy-five minutes, and ended inconclusively. The Pentagon's proposed response to Syria's chemical-weapons attack was far weaker than it should have been, largely because Mattis had stacked the options presented to Trump in ways that left little real choice. Instead of three choices (light, medium, and heavy), Mattis and Dunford (who didn't seem to be doing anything Mattis didn't want, but who also didn't seem very happy about the whole thing) presented five options. I had only seen these options a few hours before the NSC meeting, which made a truly considered analysis by NSC staff impossible. Most unhelpfully, the five options didn't scale up or down in any particular order. Instead, two were characterized as "low risk," and three were deemed "high risk." Only one option was categorized as ready to go (one of the low-risk ones), with one partially ready (the other low-risk one). Moreover, even within the alternatives, the potential targets were combined in incomprehensible ways; picking and choosing among the various elements of the five options would have left things even more confused. We were not looking at options along an understandable scale but a collection of apples, oranges, bananas, grapes, and pears, "incommensurables," as nuclear targeteers said.

Given the imperative to strike soon to emphasize our seriousness, which Trump now accepted, this left little or no choice, especially since Britain and France, for their own reasons, had impressed on us their desire to strike sooner rather than later. Had Trump insisted on one of the "riskier options," several more days would have passed, and we were already close to one full week since Syria's attack. If we were following the 2017 timeline, the retaliation should have been happening today. Moreover, because Mattis was recommending to strike only chemical-weapons-related targets, even options Trump and others had asked about had not been included. Moreover, Mattis said without qualification that causing Russian casualties would mean we would be at war with Russia, notwithstanding our efforts to avoid such casualties and the Dunford-Gerasimov conversation. In the April 2017 attack with cruise missiles, the United States had struck targets at one end of a Syrian military airfield where no Russians were, even though we knew Russians were located near another runway at the same airfield.[20] No one seemed to care particularly about potential Iranian casualties, although both Russians and Iranians were increasingly located throughout Syrian territory held by Assad's forces. This increased foreign presence was an ever-larger part of the strategic problem in the Middle East, and acting like it wasn't simply allowed Assad to use them as human shields. Mattis was looking for excuses not to do much of anything, but he was wrong tactically and strategically.

Ultimately, although Trump had said all week he wanted a

significant response, he did not decide to make one. And his ultimate choice among the options missed the central strategic point, which Mattis had to know. The very reason we were in the Sit Room was that the 2017 US strike had failed to establish conditions of deterrence in Assad's mind sufficiently powerful that he never used chemical weapons again. We knew he had used chemical weapons not just at Douma a few days before but in several other cases since April 2017, and there were other possible cases where we were less sure.[21] The April 7, 2018, attack was simply the worst of the lot. The analysis in 2018 should have been: how big does it have to be to succeed in establishing deterrence this time, given that we failed the last time? Inevitably, in my view, that should have included attacks beyond facilities housing Syria's chemical-weapons program. We should have destroyed other Syrian military assets, including headquarters, planes, and helicopters (i.e., targets related to the decision to use chemical weapons and the delivery systems to drop the bombs containing the weapons themselves), and also threatened the regime itself, such as by attacking Assad's palaces. These were all points I made, unsuccessfully. That we measurably failed to scale up the level of our response virtually guaranteed that Assad, Russia, and Iran would all breathe a sigh of relief.

Mattis pushed relentlessly for his innocuous options. While Pence tried to help me out, Treasury Secretary Steven Mnuchin strongly backed Mattis, although he manifestly had no idea what he was talking about. Nikki Haley explained that her husband was in the National Guard, so we should try to avoid military casualties. When McGahn again sought more information on the targets, Mattis flatly refused to provide it, even though McGahn was still asking for it only for his legal analysis, not to act as a targeteer, which was outside his purview (as were Mnuchin's and Haley's comments). It was stunning. McGahn told me later he didn't challenge Mattis directly because he didn't want to disrupt the meeting further; he was later able to get what he needed for his legal opinion. The best we could say, as Dunford phrased it, was that Trump had decided to strike "the heart of the [Syrian chemical-weapons] enterprise." We would be firing over twice as many missiles as in 2017, and at more physical targets.[22] Whether

that would result in anything more than a few additional buildings'
being destroyed, however, was a very different question.

Even if the President had decided on the optimal strike, the
decision-making process was completely unacceptable. We'd experienced a classic bureaucratic ploy by a classic bureaucrat, structuring
the options and information to make only *his* options look acceptable
in order to get his way. Of course, Trump didn't help by not being
clear about what he wanted, jumping randomly from one question
to another, and generally frustrating efforts to have a coherent discussion about the consequences of making one choice rather than
another. The media portrayed the meeting, the details of which were
promptly leaked, as Mattis prevailing because of his "moderation." In
fact, the spirit of Stonewall Jackson lived in Mattis and his acolytes.
("There stands Jackson like a stone wall," as the Confederates said at
the First Battle of Bull Run.) Achieving a better outcome, however,
would require more bureaucratic infighting and a further NSC meeting, thereby losing more critical time. That was a nonstarter, and Mattis knew it. Indeed, Syria had already moved equipment and materials
away from several targets we hoped to destroy.[23] I was satisfied I had
acted as an honest broker, but Mattis had been playing with marked
cards. He knew how Trump responded in such situations far better
than I did. As McGahn often whispered to me during our overlapping
White House tenures, reflecting the contrast with our earlier experiences in government, "This is not the Bush Administration."

As the meeting ended, I sensed that Trump just wanted to decide
on something and get back to the Oval, where he felt more comfortable
and in control. I had been outmaneuvered by an expert bureaucratic
operator. I was determined it would not happen again. Far more important, the country and the President had not been well served. I was
determined that wouldn't happen again either. Over the next several
months, I tried many ways to pry open the Pentagon's military planning for similar contingencies, to get more information in advance to
help make the politico-military decision-making process more comprehensive and agile, sometimes successfully, sometimes not.

After we left the Sit Room, we indicated to the press that we hadn't made any *final* decisions and that the NSC would meet again on Friday at five p.m., thus leading everyone to think that any military action would come several days later. But we were clear among ourselves that we were aiming for a Trump speech to the nation at five p.m. on Friday (the middle of the night Syria time) in which he would announce the trilateral attack. I went immediately into a brief video conference call with Sedwill and Étienne, using another room in the Sit Room complex. I explained what our decisions were, so we would all be prepared for the coming calls between Trump, Macron, and May. I then ran up to the Oval, where Trump spoke first with May at about four forty-five; she was happy with the outcome of the NSC meeting, which the UK and French militaries had already discussed, another sign we had been completely gamed by Mattis.

While waiting in the Oval for the Macron call, Trump railed away about Tillerson and how much he disliked him, recalling a dinner with Tillerson and Haley. Haley, said Trump, had some disagreement with Tillerson, who responded, "Don't ever talk to me that way again." Before Haley could say anything, Tillerson said, "You're nothing but a cunt, and don't ever forget it." In most Administrations, that would have gotten Tillerson fired, so I wondered if he ever actually said it. And if he hadn't, why did Trump tell me he had? After that, the Macron call was unremarkable. Meanwhile, our preparations accelerated. When I was finally leaving late in the evening, Kushner came into my office to say Trump thought I had done "a great job." I didn't think so, but it meant I would probably make it through the end of my fourth day on the job.

On Friday, I made calls to various Arab states to check their interest in putting together the Arab expeditionary force Trump sought to substitute for US troops in Syria and Iraq. He had imagined that, in addition to manpower, the Arabs would pay the US "cost plus twenty-five percent," and then he went up to "cost plus fifty percent" for our remaining forces. I could only imagine the reactions. It was clear to me, however, that without something from the Arab nations, Trump would almost certainly withdraw the few remaining US forces in Syria, and sooner rather than later. I spoke with Qatari Foreign Minister

Mohammed bin Abdulrahman al-Thani; Sheikh Tahnoon bin Zayed al-Nahyan, my counterpart in the United Arab Emirates; and Abbas Kamel, the head of Egypt's national intelligence service. I made it clear the idea came directly from the President, and they all promised to take it very seriously. Later, explaining the background, I turned all this over to Pompeo when he became Secretary of State, saying we were going nowhere fast. He readily agreed, and there it ended.

At nine fifteen a.m., Kelly asked me to his office, saying Trump had just called, among other things wanting to revisit the strike package he had agreed to the day before. We got Mattis and Dunford on the phone and then connected to Trump, who was still in the Residence. "I don't love the targets," he said, "it could be criticized as nothing," thus making essentially the point I had raised in Thursday's NSC meeting. He was now also "a little concerned" about "chemical plumes" after the attack, although Mattis had emphasized the day before that the Defense Department didn't think there would be any. Trump said he was thinking of tweeting that he had planned to attack but had called it off because there were no good targets anymore, although he would keep his "finger on the trigger." I nearly imploded, and I could only imagine what Mattis and Dunford were doing. Kelly seemed nonchalant, having doubtless been through this drill countless times. "We're knocking out nothing," Trump repeated.

I said that we should have agreed on a heavier strike, but we were now past the point of changing our mind and doing nothing but tweeting; the others agreed. Trump was irritated at Germany and prepared to get out of NATO, and also determined to stop Nord Stream II (a natural-gas Baltic pipeline project directly connecting Russia to Germany). Nord Stream II was not directly relevant here, but once reminded of it, he asked Mnuchin to make sure he was working on it. "Don't waste this [Syria] crisis on Merkel," he said, referring to the pipeline project. Trump then launched into possible Russian actions in retaliation for a Syria strike, such as sinking a US Navy vessel, which Mattis assured him was very unlikely, despite the presence of several Russian warships in the Eastern Mediterranean. After more rambling, Trump seemed to settle on going ahead, and Kelly said quickly, "We'll take that as a go order for 2100," meaning the time now projected for Trump's Friday night speech announcing the attack. Trump said, "Yes." Trump's call to Kelly, and Kelly's intervention, reflected "how much of [my] job Kelly [was] doing," as McMaster had put it to me the week before. Nonetheless, I was glad this time that Kelly's experience in the Trump White House stopped the spreading chaos of this telephone discussion and allowed a fully considered (if inadequate, in my view) decision to go forward.

Fortunately, the day brought no more hiccups, and we began calling key House and Senate lawmakers. Macron called again to say that, after speaking with Putin, all seemed well in Moscow. Putin had given the standard line that Assad's forces had not conducted a chemical-weapons attack, but it was clear that we and Macron all knew Putin was lying. Putin had also commented how unfortunate it would be in public-relations terms if Assad's attacks had been falsely reported, from which I understood Macron to surmise that Russia was running influence campaigns in Britain and France about Syria, and possibly also in America. After the call, I stayed with Trump in the Oval for another half hour. Trump asked how things were going, observing, "This is what you've been practicing for." As he had done a few days before, he raised the possibility of a pardon for Scooter Libby, which I strongly supported. I had known Libby since the Bush 41 Administration and felt his treatment in the Valerie Plame affair demonstrated all the reasons why the "independent counsel" concept was so badly flawed and so unjust. Trump signed the pardon a few hours later. In the afternoon, Stephen Miller brought in the President's speechwriting team to talk about his evening address to the nation. The draft looked good, and at about 5:00 p.m., back in the Oval, Trump went over the speech word by word until he was satisfied. Pompeo called at about 3:40, and I congratulated him on his successful confirmation hearings on Thursday. He had asked Gina Haspel to tell Trump that he was prepared to take even stronger action against Syria, which was good to know in case things came unstuck again in the next few hours. Actual operations for the attack were well under way by the early evening. Because this was a "time-on-target" attack, some weapons were launched well before others so that they all arrived as close as possible to simultaneously on their targets.

At eight thirty, several of us walked to the Diplomatic Reception Room, where the speech would be broadcast. We did not walk through the colonnade, to avoid tipping anyone off that something was about to happen, but across the dark South Lawn, thereby getting a breathtaking close-up view of the White House illuminated at night. Trump was upstairs in the living quarters and took the elevator to the ground floor at about eight forty-five. We went quickly through the speech one more time. Trump delivered it well, shook hands with the aides around him, and returned to the living quarters. I went back to my office to pack up and head home, finding to my amazement that the West Wing was full of tourists at nine thirty at night!

The strike went nearly perfectly, with Syrian air defenses firing over forty surface-to-air missiles, none of which hit our incoming cruise missiles.[24] We believed Assad was surprised by the extent of the destruction, and there were no chemical plumes. On Saturday, Trump tweeted happily about the attack and spoke with May and Macron,[25] who were equally pleased with the retaliation and the Western unity it had demonstrated. UN Secretary General Antonio Guterres criticized the strike for not having Security Council authorization, and therefore its inconsistency with "international law," which some of us thought was ridiculous. I spent most of the day in the West Wing just in case follow-up activity might be needed.

Did we succeed in deterring Assad? Ultimately, we did not. After my resignation, the world learned that Assad had again used chemical weapons against civilian populations in May 2019,[26] and there had likely also been other uses. In short, whereas in 2017 the US strike produced perhaps twelve months of deterrence, the somewhat larger 2018 strike produced roughly only thirteen months. And on broader Syria policy, and the handling of Iran's growing regional hegemony, this Syria debate only underscored the confusion that would dog US policy during my tenure and beyond. To borrow Professor Edward Corwin's famous phrase, Syria policy remained "an invitation to struggle."

CHAPTER 3

AMERICA BREAKS FREE

On the Monday after the Syria attack, I flew with Trump to Florida, taking my first ride on Marine One from the South Lawn to Joint Base Andrews, and then Air Force One to Miami. Our destination was nearby Hialeah for a rally boosting Trump's efforts to create a positive business climate. The over-five-hundred-strong audience consisted largely of Cuban- and Venezuelan-Americans, and when Trump introduced me, in the context of the Syria strike, I got a standing ovation. Trump, obviously surprised, asked, "Are you giving him all the credit? You know that means the end of his job." What fun. Senator Marco Rubio, however, had foreshadowed the ovation earlier when he raised my appointment as National Security Advisor: "It's a bad day for Maduro and Castro, and a great day for the cause of freedom." I had long worked on these issues, and the crowd knew it even if Trump didn't. Air Force One flew afterward to Palm Beach, and we then motorcaded to Mar-a-Lago. I continued preparing for Trump's summit with Japanese Prime Minister Abe, with a heavy focus on North Korea's nuclear-weapons program, the main purpose of Abe's trip.

Even the simple task of preparing Trump for Abe's visit turned out to be arduous, and a sign of things to come. We arranged two briefings, one largely on North Korea and security issues, and one on trade and economic issues, corresponding to the schedule of meetings between Abe and Trump. Although the first Abe-Trump meeting was on political matters, our briefing room was filled with trade-policy types who, having heard there was a briefing, wandered in. Trump was late, so I said we would have a brief discussion on trade and then get to North Korea. It was a mistake. Trump, set off by a comment that we had no better ally than Japan, jarringly complained about Japan's attack on Pearl Harbor. Things went downhill from there. Before long, Abe arrived, and the session ended. I pulled Kelly aside to discuss the fruitless "briefing," and he said, "You're going to be very frustrated in this job." I answered, "No, I'm not, if there are minimal rules of order. This is not a Trump problem; this is a White House staff problem." "I don't need a lecture from you," Kelly shot back, and I replied, "I'm not lecturing you, I'm telling you the facts, and you know it's true." Kelly paused and said, "It was a mistake to let them [the trade people] in," and we agreed to fix the problem next time. But in truth, Kelly was right and I was wrong. It was a Trump problem, and it never got fixed.

Abe and Trump first had a one-on-one meeting, and then they and their delegations convened in Mar-a-Lago's White and Gold Ballroom, which was indeed very white and very gold, at three p.m. Abe greeted me by saying, "Welcome back," because we had known each other for over fifteen years. As is typical at such meetings, the press mob then stampeded in, cameras rolling. Abe explained that, during the one-on-one, he and Trump had "forged a mutual understanding" that all options were on the table regarding North Korea, where we needed "maximum pressure" and the threat of overwhelming military power.[1] Certainly, that was my view, although at that very moment Pompeo was busy negotiating where Trump's summit with Kim Jong Un would occur. The Abe visit was perfectly timed to stiffen Trump's resolve not to give away the store. After the media shuffled reluctantly out, Abe and Trump had a lengthy discussion on North Korea and then turned to trade issues.

While this meeting continued, the press was exploding on something else. In the hectic hours before the Syria strike, Trump had initially agreed to impose more sanctions on Russia. Moscow's presence in Syria was crucial to propping up Assad's regime, and perhaps facilitating (or at least allowing) chemical-weapons attacks and other atrocities. Afterward, however, Trump changed his mind. "We made our point," Trump told me early Saturday morning, and we could "hit them much harder if need be later." Moreover, the US had just imposed substantial sanctions on Russia on April 6, as required by the "Countering America's Adversaries Through Sanctions Act,"[2] which Trump detested because Russia was its target. Trump believed that acknowledging Russia's meddling in US politics, or in that of many other countries in Europe and elsewhere, would implicitly acknowledge that he had colluded with Russia in his 2016 campaign. This view is wrong as a matter of both logic and politics; Trump could have had a stronger hand dealing with Russia if he had attacked its efforts at electoral subversion, rather than ignored them, especially since the concrete actions, such as economic sanctions, taken by his Administration were actually quite robust. As for his assessment of Putin himself, he never offered an opinion, at least in front of me. I never asked what Trump's view was, perhaps afraid of what I might hear. His personal take on the Russian leader remained a mystery.

I tried to persuade him to proceed with the new sanctions, but he wasn't buying. I said Mnuchin and I would make sure Treasury didn't make any announcement. Fortunately, since many senior officials were all too familiar with the roller-coaster ride of Administration decisions, there was a built-in pause before Trump's initial approval of new sanctions would actually be carried out. A final go/no go decision was to be made on Saturday, so I told Ricky Waddell, McMaster's Deputy and still on board, to get the word out to stop any forward motion. NSC staff informed Treasury first, then all the others, and Treasury agreed it would also alert everyone the sanctions were off.

On the Sunday-morning talk shows, however, Haley said Treasury would be announcing Russia sanctions on Monday. Immediately, there were red flags and alarm bells. Jon Lerner, Haley's political advisor, told Waddell that the US Mission to the UN in New York knew the orders on the Russia sanctions, and said, "She [Haley] just slipped," a breathtaking understatement. Magnetic attraction to television cameras, a common political ailment, had created the problem, but it was also a process foul: the sanctions were for Treasury to announce. The Ambassador to the UN had no role to play, except, in this case, mistakenly stealing the limelight. Trump called me at six thirty p.m. to ask how the Sunday shows had gone, and I told him about the Russia mistake and what we were doing to fix it. "Yeah, what's up with that?" Trump asked. "This is too much." I explained what Haley had done, and Trump said, "She's not a student, you know. Call the Russians and tell them." That I did, ringing Moscow's US Ambassador, Anatoly Antonov, whom I knew from the Bush 43 Administration, shortly thereafter. I wasn't about to tell him what had actually happened, so I just said Haley had made an honest mistake. Antonov was a lonely man, since people in Washington were now afraid to be seen talking to Russians, so I invited him to the White House to meet. This pleased Trump when I later debriefed him, because now we could start talking about the meeting he wanted with Putin. I also filled in Pompeo on Haley and the day's Russia events, and I sensed over the phone he was shaking his head in dismay.

Notwithstanding that Moscow was calm, the US press on Monday was raging away on the Russia sanctions story. Trump gave Sanders press guidance that we had hit Russia hard with sanctions and were considering more, hoping that would stop the bleeding caused by Haley's comments. I spoke to State's Acting Secretary, John Sullivan, who agreed State bore some generic responsibility, since in the Tillerson-Haley days, there had been essentially no communication between State and our UN mission in New York. Haley was a free electron, which she had obviously gotten used to, communicating directly with Trump. I told Sullivan of the screaming matches between Al Haig and Jeane Kirkpatrick in the early days of the Reagan Administration, and Sullivan laughed, "At least they were talking."

By Tuesday, the press was still baying away. Haley called me at nine forty-five, worried about being left out on a limb: "I'm not going to take it. I don't want to have to answer for it." She denied she or the US mission had been informed of the Saturday rollback. I said I would check further, even though her own staff had admitted on Sunday that she had made a misstep. I had Waddell check again with Treasury, which was getting tired of being blamed. They emphasized they had made clear to everyone on Friday, including the UN Ambassador's representative, that, whatever Trump's decision, no announcement would be made until Monday morning, just before US markets opened. I thought that was a telling point. Treasury also confirmed they had called around on Saturday, as the NSC staff had done, to follow up. And anyway, why should our UN Ambassador make the announcement? Waddell spoke again with Haley aide Jon Lerner, who said, "She shouldn't have done it . . . it was a slip of the tongue." Meanwhile, Trump groused about how the press was spinning what was, without doubt, a reversal of policy, because he worried it made him look weak on Russia.

The wildfire, however, was about to break out on another front, as Larry Kudlow briefed the press on the Trump-Abe discussions. Sanders wanted me to join Kudlow, but I chose not to, for the same reason I declined to go on the Sunday talk shows: I didn't see any point in being a TV star in my first week on the job. In live coverage of Kudlow's briefing, asked the inevitable question about the Russia sanctions, Kudlow said there had been some momentary confusion and then made the points Trump had dictated to Sanders on Air Force One. Haley immediately fired off a message to Fox's Dana Perino: "With all due respect, I don't get confused," and, boom, the war was on again, at least for a while. Haley got a good book title out of the incident. But, with all due respect, Haley wasn't confused. She was wrong.

After Trump and Abe golfed on Wednesday morning, there was a working lunch, largely on trade matters, which did not begin until three p.m. The two leaders held a joint press conference, and a dinner between the two delegations started at seven fifteen, a lot of food in a short period. I flew back to Washington on the First Lady's plane, considering this summit a real success on substantive issues like North Korea.

My focus now, however, was Iran, and the opportunity presented by the next sanctions waiver decision, on May 12, to force the issue of withdrawal. Pompeo had called me in Florida on Tuesday evening, spun up about what to do on the Iran nuclear deal. I couldn't tell if he was still wired after his difficult confirmation process, which was entirely understandable, or if he was being played by people at State who were getting increasingly agitated that we might finally withdraw. After a difficult, sometimes testy, back-and-forth about the inevitable criticism from the High-Minded a withdrawal decision would cause, Pompeo said he would have State think more thoroughly about what would follow from our exit, something they had adamantly resisted doing thus far. I worried that Pompeo's evident nervousness about blowing away the Iran nuclear deal could lead to even more delay. Knowing that State's bureaucracy would seize on indecisiveness to obstruct the demise of yet another hallowed international agreement, hesitation at the Administration's political level could be fatal.

Trump stayed in Florida the rest of the week, but back in Washington, I focused on Iran. I had long believed that Iran's nuclear threat, while not as advanced operationally as North Korea's, was as dangerous, potentially more so because of the revolutionary theological obsessions motivating its leaders. Tehran's nuclear program (as well as its chemical and biological weapons work) and its ballistic-missile capabilities made it both a regional and global threat. In the already tense Middle East, Iran's progress in the nuclear field inspired others— Turkey, Egypt, Saudi Arabia—to take steps ultimately consistent with having their own nuclear-weapons capabilities, evidence of the proliferation phenomenon at work. Iran also had the dubious distinction of being the world's central banker of international terrorism, with an active record particularly in the Middle East of supporting terrorist groups with weapons and finance, and by deploying its own conventional military capabilities in foreign countries in aid of its strategic objectives. And after forty years, the fervor of Iran's Islamic Revolution showed no signs of abating in its political and military leaders.

I met with the UK's Mark Sedwill, then with my German counterpart, Jan Hecker, and spoke at length by phone with France's Philippe Étienne. While I said repeatedly no final decision had been made, I also tried every way possible to explain there was no avenue for "fixing" the agreement, as the State Department had pleaded for well over a year. For all three of my counterparts, and their governments, this was hard news. That was why I kept repeating it, knowing, or at least hoping, that Trump would withdraw from the deal in a matter of weeks. The news would be a thunderclap, and I wanted to be certain I did everything possible so that our closest allies were not surprised.

With imminent visits to the White House by Macron and Merkel, there were ample opportunities for full discussion of these issues, but they needed to know in advance that this time Trump meant to get out. Probably.

I expected, despite his wobble when I was at Mar-a-Lago, that Pompeo would instill some discipline at State, but he had run into a confirmation problem with Rand Paul. Paul eventually declared support for Pompeo, in exchange for Pompeo's saying (1) that the 2003 Iraq war had been a mistake, and (2) at least according to a Paul tweet, that regime change was a bad idea and that we should withdraw from Afghanistan as soon as possible. I felt sorry for Pompeo, because I was sure those were not his real views. I was never faced with having to recant my views in order to get a vote, or even to get the NSC job from Trump, so I never had to make the decision Pompeo faced. State's John Sullivan told me later that day about his courtesy call with Paul during his confirmation process. Paul had said he would vote for Sullivan for one reason only: "Your name is not John Bolton." Kelly had also told me that, in the course of the Pompeo negotiations, Paul said I was "the worst fucking decision" Trump had made. Kelly replied, "He seems like a nice guy to me," which set Paul off on another tirade. It all made me proud.

During these hectic first two weeks, I also participated in several trade-related meetings and calls. I was a free trader, but I agreed with Trump that many international agreements reflected not true "free trade" but managed trade and were far from advantageous to the US. I particularly agreed that China had gamed the system. It pursued mercantilist policies in the supposedly free-trade World Trade Organization (WTO), all the while stealing US intellectual property and engaging in forced technology transfers that robbed us of incalculable capital and commerce over decades. Trump understood that a strong domestic US economy was critical to the effective projection of US political and military power (not, as I began to understand, that he wanted to do much projecting), which precept applied to China and everyone else. And I had no truck whatever with WTO decision-making and adjudication processes that were intended to subsume national decision-making. I completely agreed on this point with US Trade Representative Bob Lighthizer, a former colleague from Covington & Burling, where we had been associates together in the mid-1970s.

Decision-making on trade issues under Trump, however, was painful. There could have been an orderly path, using the NSC's interagency structure, cochaired with Kudlow's National Economic Council, to develop trade-policy options, but there was only one person who thought that was a good idea: me. Instead, the issues were discussed in weekly meetings, chaired by Trump, in the Roosevelt Room or the Oval, that more closely resembled college food fights than careful decision-making, with no lower-level interagency effort to sort the issues and the options. After these sessions, had I believed in yoga, I probably could have used some. I attended my first trade meeting in late April, in preparation for a Mnuchin-Lighthizer trip to Beijing. Trump allowed as how "tariffs are a man's best friend," which was chilling, but at least he said to Mnuchin, "You're going to China to kick their ass." That I liked. Looking at me, Trump said China was strictly enforcing sanctions against North Korea because they feared a trade war with us, which was only partially correct: In my view, China was *not* strictly enforcing sanctions.[3] Mnuchin and Kudlow predicted a global depression if a real trade war erupted, but Trump brushed them aside: "The Chinese don't give a shit about us; they are cold-blooded killers [on trade]." I could see that trade issues would be a wild ride.

Macron arrived on April 24 for the Trump Administration's first State visit, replete with a ceremony that must have impressed even the French. Sadly for the press, nothing went wrong. The French and US delegations lined up on the South Lawn, with the President and First Lady in the Diplomatic Reception Room, waiting for the Macrons to arrive, and the military bands playing away. I asked Dunford at one point the name of one of the songs, and he asked the Washington Military District's commander, but neither of them knew. "Another disappointment," said Dunford, and we both laughed. The military pageantry was impressive, especially when the Old Guard Fife and Drum Corps, dressed in Revolutionary War uniforms, marched in review, playing "Yankee Doodle." It made up for a lot of bureaucratic agony.

Before the Macron-Trump one-on-one in the Oval, the press mob shambled in for the customary pictures and questions. Trump characterized the Iran deal as "insane," "ridiculous," and the like.[4] I wondered if this time people would take it seriously. With the press cleared from the Oval, Trump and Macron spoke alone for much longer than expected, the bulk of which consisted, as Trump told me later, of his explaining to Macron that we were exiting the Iran deal.[5] Macron tried to persuade Trump not to withdraw but failed. Instead, Macron worked to ensnare Trump in a larger negotiating framework of "four pillars" that was discussed in the expanded meeting in the Cabinet Room after the one-on-one (the four pillars being: handling Iran's nuclear program now; handling it tomorrow; Iran's ballistic-missile program; and regional peace and security).[6] Macron was a clever politician, trying to spin a clear defeat into something that sounded at least somewhat positive from his perspective. Speaking almost entirely in English during the meeting, he said unambiguously about the agreement: "No one thinks it's a sufficient deal,"[7] arguing we should work for "a new comprehensive agreement" based on the four pillars. During the meeting, Trump asked for my opinion of the Iran deal. I said it wouldn't stop Iran from getting nuclear weapons and that there was no way to "fix" the deal's basic flaws. Knowing of Trump's penchant to deal on anything, I mentioned Eisenhower's famous observation "If you can't solve a problem, enlarge it," and said I thought that was what Macron seemed to be doing. It was something we could explore after withdrawing and reimposing US sanctions, which Mnuchin affirmed we were "completely ready" to do.

Said Trump the builder, "You can't build on a bad foundation. Kerry made a bad deal. I'm not saying what I'm going to do, but if I end the deal, I'm open to making a new deal. I'd rather try to solve everything than leave it like it is." We should, he said, "get a new deal rather than fixing a bad deal."[8] (Macron told Trump in a subsequent call that he was eager to rush to find a new deal, which didn't produce any resonance from Trump.) The meeting then turned to trade and other issues, and broke around 12:25 to prepare for the joint press conference. At that event, neither leader said much that was new or different on Iran, although, at one point, Trump observed, "nobody knows what I'm going to do . . . , although, Mr. President, you have a pretty good idea."[9] Later, the black-tie state dinner was very nice, if you like eating until 10:30 at night. Even at that, Gretchen and I skipped the subsequent entertainment, as did John Kelly and his wife, Karen, whom we ran into as we all picked up briefcases and work clothes from our offices on the way home.

Preparations to leave the deal took a giant step forward when Mattis agreed on April 25, "If you decide to withdraw, I can live with it." Hardly an enthusiastic endorsement, but it at least signaled that Mattis wouldn't die in a ditch over it. Even so, Mattis extensively restated his opposition to withdrawal every chance he got, to which Trump said resolutely a few days later, "I can't stay in." That was the definitive statement that we were leaving. Later in the morning of April 25, Trump again emphasized to me that he wanted Mnuchin fully ready with "the heaviest possible sanctions" when we exited. I also met that morning with Étienne, and my clear impression was that Macron had not briefed the French side fully on the one-on-one with Trump. This was excellent news, since it meant Macron fully understood that Trump had told him we were about to withdraw.

The Trump-Merkel April 27 summit was a "working visit" rather than a "state visit," so not as grand as Macron's. Trump's one-on-one with Merkel lasted only fifteen minutes before the larger Cabinet Room meeting, which he opened by complaining about Germany's "feeding the beast" (meaning Russia) through the Nord Stream II pipeline, moving on to the European Union (EU), which he thought treated the US horribly. It was clear to me that Trump thought Germany was Russia's captive. Trump also used a line I later heard countless times, that "the EU is worse than China except smaller,"[10] adding that the EU was set up to take advantage of the US, which Merkel disputed (in English, as the whole meeting was). She also asked for three to four months' delay in imposing global steel and aluminum tariffs Trump was considering, so the EU could negotiate with the US. Trump answered that he didn't want to negotiate with the EU. Too bad he didn't feel that way about North Korea, I thought to myself.[11] Trump had already turned to Germany's failure to meet its NATO commitment to increase defense expenditures to 2 percent of GDP, describing Merkel as one of the great tap dancers on NATO, which she was now doing on trade.[12] Merkel kept pressing for an extension, even two months, on the tariffs, but Trump said it would be a waste of time, just like NATO. He asked when Germany would reach 2 percent, and Merkel answered 2030, innocently, which caused even Germans to smile and Trump to say that she had been saying the same thing for sixteen months. On tariffs, Merkel finally said he could do whatever he wanted because he was a free man.

Mention of Iran was desultory. Merkel asked us to stay in the deal, and Trump reacted with indifference. At the press event, Trump said of Iran, "They will not be doing nuclear weapons," and that was pretty much it. Possibly more eventful was yet another putative Israeli attack on Iranian positions in Syria the day after,[13] which Mattis and others at the Pentagon worried could prompt Iranian retaliation (probably through surrogate Shia militia groups in Iraq) on US forces. None happened, and in any event Trump seemed unconcerned. Briefing Netanyahu on his Iran thinking, Trump said that the whole deal was based on lies, Iran had played the United States for fools, and that Israel should feel free to flay the deal publicly, which of course Netanyahu was already busily doing.

As the days went by, I quietly confirmed with Mnuchin, Haley, Coats, Haspel and others that everything pointed to an early May withdrawal from the Iran deal, and that we all needed to think of the decision's appropriate rollout and follow-up steps in our respective areas. Mnuchin insisted he needed six months to get the sanctions back in place, which I couldn't understand. Why not make the reimposed sanctions effective immediately, with some short grace period, say three months, to allow businesses to adjust existing contracts and the like? This was a perennial problem with Treasury under Mnuchin. He seemed as concerned with mitigating the impact of sanctions as with imposing them to begin with. No wonder Iran, North Korea, and others were so good at evading sanctions: they had plenty of time to get ready under Mnuchin's approach (which was, in essence, the same as Obama's). Pompeo agreed with me that the sanctions should take immediate effect. We did score a small victory when Mnuchin reduced the "wind-down" period on most goods and services from 180 days to 90 days, except for oil and insurance, which he kept at 180 days. Of course, oil was the overwhelmingly most important economic issue at stake, so Mnuchin's retreat was hardly significant. And we were not talking just about "winding down" existing contracts, but a grace period within which new contracts could be entered and performed with no prohibition at all. It was unnecessarily self-defeating.

Pompeo, Mattis, and I had our first weekly breakfast at the Pentagon on May 2 at six a.m., and Mattis continued to make his case against withdrawing. It was clear that Trump had made up his mind. Throughout the rest of the day and the week, and over the weekend, preparations intensified for the withdrawal announcement, particularly drafting the official presidential decision document, to make sure there were no loopholes that supporters could crawl back through. Stephen Miller and his speechwriters were also working away on Trump's speech, which was progressing well. Trump had plenty to add, so the drafting went right until the text had to be prepared for the teleprompters. Although I had aimed for Trump's announcement to be on May 7, Sanders told me that the First Lady had an event scheduled that day, so we moved the withdrawal to May 8. Thus are weighty matters of state disposed. And, in fact, even there Trump wavered, wondering about one date or another, literally until almost the last minute.

There was a final, perfunctory Trump-May phone call on Iran and other issues on Saturday, May 5,[14] and Foreign Secretary Boris Johnson arrived in Washington Sunday night for further discussions. That night as well, Mattis sent me a classified document at home again opposing the withdrawal, but still not requesting a high-level meeting to discuss it. I felt like saying that his position was well preserved and well papered for history, but I refrained. The Pentagon still wasn't telling us what it would have to do operationally if the US withdrew, having moved from overt opposition into guerilla warfare. It didn't slow us down.

I saw Johnson in my office at nine a.m. Monday, having first met him in London in 2017, discussing Iran and North Korea at length. We reviewed Trump's recent meetings with Macron and Merkel, and Macron's "four pillars" idea; Johnson said they had been thinking along the same lines. I said I would be happy to call the idea "Johnson's four pillars," and we all laughingly agreed. He, like Macron, stressed that Britain fully understood the existing deal's weaknesses, which would have surprised many supporters who still worshipped at its altar.[15] I explained why the announcement would be coming soon, although, knowing Trump, I did not say it would be the next day. We would not then simply lapse into inaction but would bring back into force all the nuclear-related US sanctions the deal had put on ice. As we parted, I reminded Johnson that I had said to him the previous summer that I wanted to help out on Brexit, and still did, although we had had little chance to talk about it. I spoke later with Sedwill about this conversation and was later on the phone with Étienne when he exclaimed that Trump had just tweeted:

> I will be announcing my decision on the Iran Deal tomorrow from the White House at 2:00pm.

No suspense left there. Étienne had been watching Trump's tweets more carefully than I! There was little doubt what was coming, which I confirmed to Israeli Ambassador Ron Dermer and a few others, not that anyone needed much explanation.

On D-day itself, Trump called China's Xi Jinping at eight thirty a.m. on several issues, including North Korea. Trump said he would be making a statement on Iran shortly and asked, in an almost childlike way, if Xi wanted to know what he would say. Xi said it sounded like Trump wanted to tell him, a completely on-target insight. Trump, in a "why not?" moment, said that, feeling trust in confiding in Xi, he was terminating the nuclear deal, which was bad, and that we would see what happened. Xi said he would keep the news confidential, adding simply that the US knew China's position, meaning Xi did not plan to make it a major bilateral issue. Macron called and asked what Trump planned to say on Iran, but Trump wanted to be sure Macron would be circumspect. He admonished Macron not to make it public, asking for Macron's word. Macron replied affirmatively, believing that Iran should not leave the deal, nor would France as they worked to achieve a comprehensive new deal, as the two leaders had discussed previously. Trump didn't think Iran would exit, because they were making too much money. Trump mused that at some point he should meet with Iranian President Rouhani, flattering Macron as the best of the Europeans, and that he should tell Rouhani Trump was right.

Trump delivered the speech at about two fifteen p.m., which went according to script, with Pence, Mnuchin, Ivanka, Sanders, and myself in attendance. Afterward, we all walked back to the Oval Office feeling things had gone off as planned and that the speech would be well received. A few minutes after two thirty, I conducted a close encounter with reporters in the White House briefing room, which was on the record but not on camera so that the media pictures would be, appropriately, of the President giving his speech. With that, we were done.

It had taken one month to shred the Iran nuclear deal, showing how easy it was to do once somebody took events in hand. I did my best to prepare our allies Britain, Germany, and France for what happened, because they had seemed completely unready for a possible US withdrawal. A lot remained to be done to bring Iran to its knees, or to overthrow the regime, Trump's stated policy to the contrary notwithstanding, but we were off to a great start.

For several months after the withdrawal, work proceeded to follow up on Trump's decision to reimpose economic sanctions, and to take other steps to increase pressure on Tehran consistent with his decision to withdraw from the nuclear deal. Basically, the initial plan was to bring back into effect all the previous sanctions suspended by Obama's nuclear deal and then make adjustments to close loopholes, increase enforcement activity, and turn the campaign into "maximum pressure" on Iran.[16] By July 26, it was time to hold a restricted Principals Committee meeting to see how we were doing, which we did at two p.m. in the Sit Room. The most interesting part of the meeting was Mattis's efforts to downplay the overall importance of Iran in the international threat matrix facing the US. He said Russia, China, and North Korea were bigger threats, although his reasons were vague, and I was pleased to see Pompeo and Mnuchin both push back, given that Iran was one of the top four threats identified in the National Security Strategy Trump had approved before my arrival. But the ghost of Mattis's protestations about taking Iran seriously would dog us right until the end of 2018, when he departed, and beyond. So momentous was this meeting that it leaked to the press and was reported the next day.[17] In the meantime, Iran's currency was dropping through the floor.

In mid-August 2018, and then again in January 2019, I traveled to Israel to meet with Netanyahu and other key Israeli officials on a range of issues, but especially Iran. This was existential for Israel, and Netanyahu had become the leading strategist on rolling back Iran's nuclear-weapons and ballistic-missile programs. He also clearly understood that regime change was far and away the most likely way to permanently alter Iranian behavior. Even if that was not the Trump Administration's declared policy, it certainly could happen as the effects of sanctions took hold. Moreover, given the views of the Middle East's Arab oil-producing states, there was, and had been tacitly for years, agreement on the common threat Iran posed to them and Israel among themselves, albeit for different reasons. This Iran consensus was also contemporaneously making possible a new push to resolve the Israel-Palestine dispute, which strategically could very much benefit America. Whether we could make the most of these new alignments operationally, of course, was very different.

By early September, attacks on the US embassy in Baghdad and the US consulate in Basra, undoubtedly, in my view, by Shia militia groups acting at Iran's behest, revealed new tensions within the Administration, as many in State and Defense resisted forceful responses.[18] The unwillingness to retaliate, thereby raising the costs to the attackers and hopefully deterring them in the future, reflected the hangover of Obama-era policies. Even twenty months into the Trump presidency, new appointees and new policies were not yet in place. If it were still early 2017, the problem might have been understandable, but it was sheer malpractice that bureaucratic inertia persisted in such critical policy areas. The debate over responding to these sorts of attacks lasted right through my tenure, because of obstructionism and Trump's impulsive desires to reduce America's troop presence in the region, leading uniformly in a more passive direction. For all that Trump hated about the Obama Administration, it was no small irony that his own idiosyncratic views simply reinforced the bureaucracy's existing tendencies, all to the detriment of US interests in the Middle East more broadly.

I was also troubled by Treasury's unwillingness to bear down on Iran's participation in the global financial messaging system known as SWIFT. There was considerable interest among congressional Republicans in stopping Iran's continued connection to the system, but Mnuchin and Treasury objected. They had understandable concerns, but invariably they pushed for no change in existing policy, the characteristic attribute of bureaucratic inertia. The real answer was to squeeze Iran ever harder and work to find more ways to comprehensively monitor Iran, not to give it a pass simply to continue with monitoring mechanisms that could be replaced and perhaps even improved with a little effort.[19] The NSC staff and I kept pushing on this, largely behind the scenes, and succeeded later in the year, but even more difficult obstacles to our Iran policy emerged in the coming year.

CHAPTER 4

THE SINGAPORE SLING

Even as we neared withdrawing from the wretched Iran nuclear deal, Trump's focus on North Korea's nuclear-weapons program resumed. The more I learned, the more discouraged and pessimistic I became about a Trump-Kim summit. I was deeply skeptical of efforts to negotiate the North out of its nuclear-weapons program,[1] which Pyongyang had already sold many times to the US and others in exchange for economic benefits. Despite breaching its commitments repeatedly, North Korea always cajoled a gullible America back to the negotiating table to make more concessions, ceding time to a proliferator, which invariably benefits from delay. Here we were, at it again, having learned nothing. Worse, we were legitimizing Kim Jong Un, commandant of the North Korean prison camp, by giving him a free meeting with Trump. It called to mind Winston Churchill's dark 1935 observation about Britain's failed policies toward Germany:

> When the situation was manageable, it was neglected, and now that it is thoroughly out of hand, we apply too late the remedies which then might have effected a cure. There is nothing new in the story. It is as old as the Sibylline books. It falls into that long, dismal catalogue of the fruitlessness of experience, and the confirmed unteachability of mankind. Want of foresight, unwillingness to act when action would be simple and effective, lack of clear thinking, confusion of counsel until emergency comes, until self-preservation strikes its jarring gong—these are the features which constitute the endless repetition of history.[2]

Having endured eight years of Obama mistakes, which I constantly feared would include dangerous concessions to North Korea, as his Iran policy had, not to mention the Bush 43 Administration's failed Six-Party Talks and Clinton's failed Agreed Framework, I was sick at heart over Trump's zeal to meet with Kim Jong Un. Pompeo told me that Trump's fascination with meeting Kim dated to the Administration's outset; clearly the options were very limited.

On April 12, in the midst of the Syria whirlwind, I met with my South Korean counterpart, Chung Eui-yong, Director of their National Security Office. In March, in the Oval, Chung had extended Kim's invitation to meet to Trump, who accepted on the spur of the moment. Ironically, Chung later all but admitted that it was he who had suggested to Kim that he make the invitation in the first place![3] This whole diplomatic fandango was South Korea's creation, relating more to its "unification" agenda than serious strategy on Kim's part or ours. The South's understanding of our terms to denuclearize North Korea bore no relationship to fundamental US national interests, from my perspective. It was risky theatrics, in my view, not substance. I urged Chung to avoid discussing denuclearization at the upcoming April 27 North-South summit, to prevent Pyongyang from driving a wedge between South Korea, Japan, and the US, one of its favorite diplomatic strategies. I told Trump that we needed the closest possible coordination with Moon Jae-in to avoid North Korea's engineering a split between Washington and Seoul. I wanted to preserve US–South Korean alignment, and avoid the headline "Trump rejects South Korea compromise," but he seemed unconcerned.

Later in the morning, I met with my Japanese counterpart, Shotaro Yachi, who wanted me to hear their perspective as soon as possible. Tokyo's view of the looming Trump-Kim meeting was 180 degrees from South Korea's—in short, pretty much like my own. Yachi said they believed the North's determination to get nuclear weapons was fixed, and that we were nearing the last chance for a peaceful solution. Japan wanted none of the "action for action" formula that characterized Bush 43's failed Six-Party Talks.[4] "Action for action" sounded reasonable, but it inevitably worked to benefit North Korea (or any proliferator) by front-loading economic benefits to the North but dragging out dismantling the nuclear program into the indefinite future. The marginal benefits to Pyongyang of even modest economic aid (or release from pain, like easing sanctions) was much greater than the marginal benefits to us of the step-by-step elimination of the nuclear program. Kim Jong Un knew this just as well as we did. At that point, Japan wanted dismantlement to begin immediately upon a Trump-Kim agreement and to take no longer than two years. I urged, however, based on the experience in Libya, that dismantlement should take only six to nine months. Yachi only smiled in response, but when Abe met Trump at Mar-a-Lago the following week (see chapter 3), Abe asked for dismantlement to take six to nine months![5] Yachi also stressed North Korea's abduction of Japanese citizens over many years, a powerfully emotional issue in Japan's public opinion and a key element in Abe's successful political career. At Mar-a-Lago and later, Trump committed to pursuing this issue and followed through faithfully in every subsequent encounter with Kim Jong Un.

Pompeo, the Administration's initial contact for North Korea as CIA Director, was already negotiating the summit's venue and date, and the prospect of releasing three American hostages. Kim wanted the meeting in Pyongyang or Panmunjom, both of which Pompeo and I agreed were nonstarters. Pompeo saw Geneva and Singapore as the two most acceptable choices, but Kim didn't like to fly. North Korea's rickety airplanes couldn't reach either city anyway, and he didn't want to be too far from Pyongyang. My hope: maybe the whole thing would collapse!

At Mar-a-Lago, Abe spoke at length about North Korea's nuclear program, stressing as had Yachi in our earlier meeting in Washington, that we needed a truly effective agreement, unlike the Iran nuclear deal which Trump had so frequently criticized, and which the Obama Administration itself had emphasized was not even signed.[6] Of course, Pyongyang was just as capable of lying about a signed as an unsigned document, but it might just trip them up. Abe also urged Japan's long-standing positions that, in discussing ballistic missiles, we include short- and medium-range missiles (which could hit significant parts of Japan's home islands) as well as ICBMs (which the North needed to hit the continental United States). Similarly, Japan also wanted to eliminate the North's biological and chemical weapons, which I agreed should be part of any agreement with Pyongyang.[7] Trump asked Abe what he thought of Kim's recent visit to see Xi Jinping in China, and Abe said it reflected the impact of America's implicit threat to use military force, and the cutoff, under international sanctions, of much of the oil flow from China. Abe emphasized that the US strike against Syria a few days before had sent a strong signal to North Korea and Russia. Kim Jong Un's father, Kim Jong Il, had been frightened when Bush 43 included the North in the "Axis of Evil," and military pressure was the best leverage on Pyongyang. I thought Abe's convincing presentation would sway Trump, but the impact turned out to be limited. The Japanese had the same sense that Trump needed continual reminders, which explained why Abe conferred so frequently with Trump on North Korea throughout the Administration.

On April 21, the North announced with great fanfare that it was forgoing further nuclear and ballistic-missile testing because it was already a nuclear power. The credulous media took this as a major step forward, and Trump called it "big progress."[8] I saw just another propaganda ploy. If the necessary testing were now concluded, Pyongyang could simply complete the work necessary for weapons and delivery-system production capability. Chung returned on April 24 before Moon's inter-Korean summit with Kim at the DMZ. I was relieved Chung contemplated that the leaders' "Panmunjom Declaration" would only be two pages, which meant whatever it said about denuclearization could not be very specific. I sensed that South Korea believed Kim Jong Un was desperate for a deal because of the pressure imposed by sanctions, and that economic development was the North's top priority, now that it was a "nuclear-weapons state." I did not find this reasoning comforting. Meanwhile, Pompeo was narrowing the options on timing and location for the Trump-Kim meeting, probably June 12 or 13, in either Geneva or Singapore.

The April 27 Moon-Kim festival at the DMZ had everything but doves with olive branches flying around but was actually almost substance-free. On Friday morning Washington time, I gave Trump a copy of a *New York Times* op-ed by Nick Eberstadt,[9] one of America's most astute Korea watchers, which rightly called the summit "P. T. Barnum–style, a-sucker-is-born-every-minute diplomacy." I didn't think Trump would read it, but I wanted to emphasize my view that South Korea's agenda was not always ours, and that we needed to safeguard our own interests. Fortunately, the Panmunjom Declaration was remarkably anodyne, especially on the nuclear issues. Moon called Trump on Saturday to report on his talks. He was still ecstatic. Kim had committed to "complete denuclearization," offering to close their Punggye-ri nuclear test site. This was just another sham "concession," like blowing up the Yongbyon reactor's cooling tower under Kim Jong Il. Moon pushed hard for the Trump-Kim meeting to be at Panmunjom, followed immediately by a trilateral with both Koreas and the US. This was largely a Moon effort to insert himself into the ensuing photo op (as we would see again in June 2019). Trump seemed swept up in the rapture, even suggesting advancing the Kim meeting to mid-May, which was logistically impossible. Fortunately, Moon conceded that Kim preferred Singapore, which helped nail down the venue. Trump said finally that Pompeo and I would work with Moon on the dates, which was reassuring.

Moon had asked Kim to denuclearize in one year, and he had agreed, agreeably close to a timeframe I had suggested.[10] Ironically, in the months that followed, it was harder to get State to agree to a one-year schedule than to persuade Kim. The two leaders strategized about how to proceed, and Trump asked Moon to specify what we should request from North Korea, which was quite helpful. This was clever diplomacy, because whatever Moon wrote, he could hardly object if we asked for it, and if we were tougher than Moon, he had at least had his say. Moon complimented Trump's leadership. In turn, Trump pressed him to tell South Korea's media how much Trump was responsible for all this. He then spoke with Abe, to strategize further about the Trump-Kim Summit in light of Moon's report on his meeting with Kim. Abe repeated all the key points he had made at Mar-a-Lago, in contrast with Moon's over-optimistic perspective.

Not trusting Kim, Japan wanted concrete, unambiguous commitments, on both the nuclear and the abductee issues. Abe stressed to Trump that he was tougher than Obama, showing clearly that Abe thought it necessary to remind Trump of that point.

I spoke later with Pompeo, then traveling in the Middle East, who listened to the Abe and Moon calls from there. The Moon call especially had been "a near-death experience," I said, and Pompeo responded, "Having cardiac arrest in Saudi Arabia." After a few more gyrations, we settled on Singapore for the summit meeting on June 12 and 13. On Monday morning, Trump called me about my appearances on two of the Sunday talk shows, where much of the discussion concerned North Korea. I had been "very good on television," he said, but I needed to praise him more because "there's never been anything like this before." After all, Moon said he would recommend Trump for the Nobel Peace Prize. Trump said, however, that he didn't like my reference to the "Libya model" for denuclearizing North Korea because of Muammar Qaddafi's overthrow seven years later during the completely unrelated Middle East Arab Spring. I tried explaining that the "model" for nonproliferation analysts was completely removing Libya's nuclear program, not Qaddafi's subsequent unpredictable demise.

History showed that I didn't get through. Trump failed to understand that the unforeseen Arab Spring, which swept dramatically through the region beginning in 2011, was the reason for Qaddafi's subsequent downfall, not his 2003 renunciation of nuclear weapons. This was not Trump's error alone. Many engaged in the classic logical fallacy of "post hoc, ergo propter hoc" ("after this, therefore because of this"), exemplified in this sentence from a 2019 New York Times story: "Libya's dictator, Muammar el-Qaddafi, was killed in 2011 after relinquishing his country's nascent nuclear program."[11] Nonetheless, Trump ended the conversation by saying, "Great job." Ironically, Trump himself said at a later press conference that when he referred to "the Libya model" he meant the "total decimation" of Libya: "Now, that model would take place [with North Korea] if we don't make a deal, most likely."[12] A few minutes after Trump made those remarks, the Vice President gave me a high five and said, "He's got your back!" Trump himself said, "You're clear, I fixed it!"

There were also significant developments on the hostage front, where we were getting increasing indications that North Korea would release three US prisoners if Pompeo personally flew to the North to receive them and return them to America. He and I didn't like the idea of his going to Pyongyang, but freeing the hostages was sufficiently important that we decided to swallow it. (Trump cared nothing about who picked up the hostages, not seeing it as an issue.) Chung came to see me a third time on May 4, providing more details on the Panmunjom meeting. He stressed that he had pushed Kim hard to agree to "complete, verifiable, and irreversible denuclearization," which had long been our formulation going back to the Bush 43 Administration,[13] and would be an important rhetorical step for North Korea. According to Moon, Kim had seemed amenable, in the pre-Singapore context, but Kim never made the commitment publicly. Moon urged Kim to reach "a big deal" with Trump, after which specifics could be discussed at working levels, stressing that whatever benefits the North might receive would come *after* accomplishing denuclearization. Kim, said Chung, said that he understood all this. Moon wanted to confer with Trump in Washington in mid to late May before the Trump-Kim summit, which we ultimately agreed to. Later that day, Japan's Yachi also came to my office to discuss the Moon-Kim summit, showing just how closely Japan followed the entire process. Yachi wanted to counter the euphoria emanating from Seoul, not that I was overcome by it, stressing we should not fall for the North's traditional "action for action" approach.

Pompeo left for Pyongyang on Tuesday, May 8, picked up the three American hostages, and returned with them to Washington, arriving at Andrews after two a.m. on Thursday morning. Trump greeted the returning men in an incredible, hastily arranged, middle-of-the-night, broadcast-live arrival ceremony. The three released Americans were understandably exuberant, raising their arms in celebration when they exited the plane into the bright spotlights. They loved speaking to the press and were the hit of the night, enjoying, thankfully, a return from

North Korea far different from that of the fatally tortured and brutal-
ized Otto Warmbier. The Marine One flight back to the White House,
passing very near the illuminated Washington Monument, was almost
surreal. Trump was on cloud nine, even at three thirty a.m., when we
landed on the South Lawn, because this was a success even the hostile
media could not diminish.

Maneuverings for the Trump-Kim meeting continued apace.
In particular, we worried about what China was doing to influence
the North Koreans, and closely followed what key Chinese players
like Yang Jiechi, China's former Ambassador to Washington during
Bush 43, former Foreign Minister, and now State Councilor (a position superior to Foreign Minister in China's system), were saying
to their counterparts and in public. I had concerns that Beijing was
setting the stage to blame the United States if the talks broke down,
warning that North Korean "hardliners" were undercutting Kim Jong
Un for releasing the American hostages without any "reciprocity"
from the US. Under this scenario, there was no consensus within the
system in the North, and that strong resistance from Pyongyang's military meant that the talks were in jeopardy before they even began.
The answer? More preemptive concessions by the United States. This
was one of the oldest games in the Communist playbook: frighten-
ing gullible Westerners with tales of splits between "moderates" and
"hardliners" so that we accepted otherwise unpalatable outcomes to
bolster the "moderates." Chung did worry about the North's recent
announcement that only journalists would attend the "closure" of
the Punggye-ri test site, not nuclear experts, as they had previously
committed to. Pyongyang might just as well invite the Bobbsey Twins.
While this ploy was "destroying" something rather than "building" it,
Grigory Potemkin's ghost was nonetheless undoubtedly celebrating
his continued relevance.

Chung and I were on the phone constantly over the following
week preparing for Moon Jae-in's visit to Washington and the Trump-
Kim Singapore meeting. We spoke repeatedly about the Punggye-ri
"closure," which was pure fluff, starting with the lack of any US or
international site inspections, particularly examining the tunnels and

underground facilities before any preparations for or detonations closing the adits (the tunnel entrances). By precluding such inspections, North Korea was concealing key information. Nuclear forensics experts, as was common practice, could have extrapolated significant conclusions about the size and scope of the nuclear-weapons program, other locations in the North's nuclear gulag that we wanted disclosed and inspected, and more.[14] We knew from the IAEA's experience in Iraq in 1991 and thereafter, which I had lived through personally during the Bush 41 Administration, that there were enormous amounts of information that could be very effectively concealed without adequate, persistent on-site inspections before, during, and after any denuclearization. Subsequent international monitoring, such as the International Atomic Energy Agency's taking soil samples outside the adits, was no substitute for inspections inside Punggye-ri mountain, as the North fully understood. This propaganda charade was evidence not of Pyongyang's good faith but of its unmistakable bad faith. Even CNN later characterized North Korea's approach as "like trampling on a crime scene."[15] Chung thought the issue could be raised at an inter-Korean meeting at Panmunjom later in the week, but the North canceled the meeting at the last minute, another typical Pyongyang gambit. They then expressly threatened to cancel the Trump-Kim meeting, complaining about an annual US–South Korean military exercise called "Max Thunder." This was another propaganda ploy, but it and later complaints about these military exercises, absolutely vital to our joint military preparedness, turned out to influence Trump beyond the North's wildest expectations.

I told Trump about this North Korean eruption at about six thirty p.m., and he said our press line should be, "Whatever the situation is, is fine with me. If they would prefer to meet, I am ready. If they would prefer not to meet, that is okay with me too. I will fully understand." I called again at about seven o'clock and listened at length to Trump criticize the South Korean–US military exercise: he had been against it for a year, couldn't understand why it cost so much and was so provocative, didn't like flying B-52s from Guam to participate, and on and on and on. I couldn't believe that the reason for these exercises—to be fully ready for a North Korean attack—hadn't been explained be-fore. If it had, it clearly hadn't registered. Competent militaries exer-cise frequently. Especially in an alliance, joint training is critical so that the allied countries don't cause problems for themselves in a time of crisis. "Fight tonight" was the slogan of US Forces Korea, reflect-ing its mission to deter and defeat aggression. A decrease in readiness could mean "fight next month," which didn't cut it. As I came to re-alize, however, Trump just didn't want to hear about it. The exercises offended Kim Jong Un and were unnecessarily expensive. Case closed.

In the meantime, we were working on logistics for Singapore; on one critical point, Pompeo suggested that he, Kelly, and I be with Trump whenever he was around Kim, to which Kelly and I readily agreed. I also worried how cohesive we could be given the daily ex-plosions everyone became inured to in the Trump White House. One such bizarre episode in mid-May involved disparaging remarks by Kelly Sadler, a White House communications staffer, about John Mc-Cain. Her comments, dismissing McCain and how he might vote on Gina Haspel's nomination as CIA Director because "he's dying any-way," leaked to the press, immediately creating a storm. Trump wanted to promote Sadler, while others wanted to fire her, or at least make her apologize publicly for her insensitivity. Sadler refused and got away with it because Trump, who despised McCain, allowed her to. Sadler turned her own insensitivity into a weapon by accusing others of leak-ing, a frequent offensive tactic in the Trump White House. In an Oval Office meeting, Trump rewarded her with a hug and kiss. Although this debacle was hardly my issue, I went to see Kelly at one point, fig-uring that surely rational people could get an apology out of this in-subordinate staffer. After a brief discussion, with just the two of us in his office, Kelly said, "You can't imagine how desperate I am to get out of here. This is a bad place to work, as you will find out." He was the first to see Trump in the morning and the last to see him at night, and I could only conjecture how many mistakes he had prevented during his tenure. Kelly attacked the press, fully justifiably in my view, and said, "They're coming for you, too," which I didn't doubt.

North Korea continued to threaten canceling the Trump-Kim

meeting and attacked me by name. This was nothing new, dating to 2002 under Bush 43, when North Korea honored me by calling me "human scum." They attacked my citing the Libya model of denuclearization (I wondered if they had a source inside the White House who knew Trump's reaction), saying, "We shed light on the quality of Bolton already in the past, and we do not hide our feelings of repugnance toward him."[16] Of course, it was clear to everyone on our side of the negotiations that they were really denouncing the very concept of "complete, verifiable, and irreversible denuclearization." South Korea remained concerned about the North's efforts to scale back the joint military exercises. Even the dovish Moon Administration understood full well the exercises were critical to their security and worried this was yet another Pyongyang effort to drive a wedge between Seoul and Washington. Chung said the North was clearly trying to split Trump away from me, relating that at the April 27 Moon-Kim meeting, several North Korean officials asked about my role in the Trump-Kim meeting. I felt honored once again. But more important, North Korea continued denouncing the joint military exercises, now attacking Moon: "The present South Korean authorities have been clearly proven to be an ignorant and incompetent group . . ."[17] Such attacks were the North's not-so-subtle way of intimidating Moon into doing the North's work for it by pressuring us, a ploy we were determined wouldn't succeed.

More seriously, Kim's chief of staff did not arrive in Singapore as scheduled on May 17. Preparations for the North's paranoid leader were formidable, even if dwarfed by what it took for a US President to make such a journey. Delay in laying the groundwork could ultimately postpone or even cancel the meeting itself. By Monday, May 21, no North Korean advance team had arrived, hence there were no meetings with our team in Singapore. Trump began to wonder what was up, telling me, "I want to get out [of Singapore] before they do," which sounded promising. He recounted how with the women he had dated, he never liked to have them break up with him; he always wanted to be the one doing the breaking up. ("Very revealing," said Kelly when I told him later.)[18] One question was whether to cancel Singapore just as Moon Jae-in came to town or wait until he departed. I urged Trump to act now, because doing so after Moon left would seem like an explicit rebuff of Moon, which was unnecessary. Trump agreed, saying, "I may tweet tonight." At Trump's request, I spoke with Pence and Kelly, who both agreed he should tweet away. I reported this back to Trump, and Trump started dictating what his tweet might say. After several drafts (suitably retyped by Westerhout), it (or they) emerged as:

> Based on the fact that dialogue has changed pertaining to North Korea and its denuclearization, I have respectfully asked my representatives to inform North Korea to terminate the June 12th meeting in Singapore. While I very much look forward to meeting and negotiating with Kim Jong Un, perhaps we will get another chance in the future. In the meantime, I greatly appreciate the release of the 3 Americans who are now at home with their families.

A follow-up tweet would say:

> I am disappointed that China has been unable to do what is necessary, primarily at the border [meaning sanctions enforcement], to help us obtain peace.

The Oval was then filling with staffers to prepare Trump for a dinner with state governors. As he left, Trump said he would probably tweet after dinner at "eight or nine o'clock." I returned to my office to brief Pompeo, and he said, "I get it, let's go with the strategy." I walked to Pence's office to tell him about the tweets; both of us were very confident Trump would cancel Singapore that evening. But when we awoke the next morning, no tweets had emerged. Trump explained to Kelly later that his cell phone had not been working the night before, but he told me he wanted to let Moon have his say before canceling. So, it was with a distinct lack of enthusiasm that I met Chung and his colleagues for breakfast in the Ward Room, to discuss the Moon-Trump meeting later in the day. The South still wanted Moon in Singapore for a trilateral after the Trump-Kim meeting.

Another important topic in our discussion was a declaration "ending the Korean War." I originally thought the "end-of-war declaration" was the North's idea, but I later started to suspect that it was Moon's, emanating from and supporting his reunification agenda, another good reason not to buy it. Substantively, the "end of war" idea had no rationale except that it sounded good. With the possibility nothing much else would emerge in Singapore, we risked legitimizing Kim Jong Un not only by having him meet with a US President, but also by holding a gauzy "peace summit" undermining economic sanctions by suggesting the North was no longer dangerous, and not just at the nuclear level. I was determined to stop anything legally binding, and also to minimize the damage of whatever objectionable document Trump might agree to. I worried about Moon's pitching Trump on these bad ideas, but, after all, I couldn't stop it.

I walked to Blair House to meet Pompeo ahead of our ten a.m. meeting with Moon, Foreign Minister Kang Kyung-wha, and Chung. Moon was characteristically optimistic about Singapore, and after an hour, I returned to the White House (Pompeo headed to State) to tell Trump what we had discussed. I joined one of the intelligence briefings Trump had every week from Director of National Intelligence Coats, CIA Director Haspel, and briefers who accompanied them. I didn't think these briefings were terribly useful, and neither did the intelligence community, since much of the time was spent listening to Trump, rather than Trump listening to the briefers. I made several tries to improve the transmission of intelligence to Trump but failed repeatedly. It was what it was. When I arrived from Blair House, Trump was telling the briefers he had written tweets about canceling Singapore the night before but concluded he could wait a little bit longer "because there was still some chance it might come off," and he didn't want to cancel "before the absolute last minute." It made me feel worse to see just how close we had come.

Moon arrived, and the two leaders soon thereafter greeted the press hordes in the Oval. The extended questioning, mostly on China

issues, substantially shortened Moon's one-on-one with Trump. After
the two leaders entered the Cabinet Room, Trump opened by saying
there was about a 25 percent chance the Singapore meeting would
happen, which I suspect he also told Moon privately. In response,
Moon stressed his support for complete, verifiable, and irreversible
denuclearization, and his optimistic view there was "a zero percent
chance" Singapore wouldn't happen. Trump was worried about appearing "too anxious," but Moon hastened to assure him it was really
North Korea that was anxious, since nothing like this had ever happened before. Trump said he wanted a structured meeting in Singapore, which shocked me (and which didn't happen in any event). He
asked why no experts were being allowed to visit Punggye-ri, and we
explained that many believed, myself included, that Kim had made a
verbal commitment to close the test site without really understanding
what he was saying.

As if things were not already messy, Nick Ayers, the VP's Chief
of Staff, phoned in the late evening to say North Korea's Vice Foreign
Minister Choe Son Hui had issued a stinging attack on Pence, calling him a "political dummy" and basically threatening nuclear war
because of Pence's remarks in a recent interview with Fox's Martha
MacCallum.[19] Pence came on the line to suggest I tell Trump, which
I set out to do immediately. After quickly obtaining and reviewing
Pyongyang's full screed, I reached Trump at ten p.m. I explained the
situation and suggested we demand an apology, at least implying Singapore would be canceled without one. Trump wanted to sleep on it,
which I relayed back to Pence (and which Trump also did himself).
I called Pompeo at 10:25 to brief him, suggesting he join us early the
next morning. As Vice President, Pence maintained the strong views
on national security that he'd had during his years in the House of
Representatives, and I regarded him as a consistent ally. At the same
time, he followed the prudent example of other Vice Presidents who
were circumspect in their advocacy of policies without knowing first
where Trump was headed. I respected the inherent difficulties of his
job, believing he did much of his best work in private conversations
with Trump.

I went in even earlier than usual the next day, surveying the extensive Asian press coverage of the North Korean blast but noting little US coverage, probably because of the hour the statement was released. I told Kelly what had happened and said we had an eight a.m. call with Trump in the Residence. Ayers entered to say both he and Pence thought Singapore should be canceled; Kelly agreed, as did Pompeo, who had come over. We were all around the speakerphone to call Trump, and I gave a full description of the North's attack on Pence, and the international and US press coverage. Trump asked me to read the full text of Vice Foreign Minister Choe Son Hui's remarks, which I did. "Jesus," said Trump, "that's strong." We all agreed that so vitriolic a statement could have come only with Kim Jong Un's express approval; this was not just some rogue official sounding off. Our critics would likely accuse us of overreacting, because, after all, North Korea frequently spoke in vitriolic terms. That was true, but it was also true prior US Administrations had simply accepted North Korea's rhetoric without imposing consequences. That had to stop, and this was the time to do it.

Trump didn't hesitate to cancel the Singapore meeting. He dictated a letter, which we took through several iterations but which emerged as truly Trump's. The final version, edited for small corrections, went public about nine forty-five a.m., followed by two presidential tweets. We also drafted a statement he could read at an already-scheduled bill-signing ceremony that morning, emphasizing that "maximum pressure" on North Korea would continue. I called Singaporean Foreign Minister Vivian Balakrishnan to tell him what was happening, catching him in Dubai while changing planes. He took the news very graciously, as he had a few weeks earlier taken the initial news that Singapore had "won" the prize of hosting the Trump-Kim summit. The South Koreans weren't so gracious. Chung called me in the late morning to say our cancellation was a big political embarrassment to Moon, coming right after his return from Washington, a trip that had raised big expectations in South Korea. I told Chung to read carefully what Choe Son Hui had said about America's Vice President, but he was not mollified, nor was Moon, who issued a watered-down version of Chung's remarks to me.[20] Japan's Yachi, by contrast, said they were greatly relieved Singapore had been canceled.[21] While this drama was unfolding, the North presented a little theater of its own, "closing" Punggye-ri in exactly the Potemkin-village-in-reverse style we had expected.

That very evening, less than twelve hours after announcing Singapore's cancellation, the roof fell in. Trump seized on a slightly less belligerent statement by a different North Korean foreign ministry official to order us to get the June 12 meeting back on schedule. This was a clear mistake in my view, an open admission Trump was desperate to have the meeting at any price, which produced media reports of "head-snapping diplomacy" that unnerved our friends worldwide. Of course, the media had no clue we had also almost canceled Singapore on Monday before Trump backed away. In resurrecting the meeting, Pompeo talked to Kim Yong Chol, his counterpart in the US–North Korea negotiations when he was CIA Director, and decided this Kim would come to New York for further preparations. Pompeo, Kelly, and I agreed we should insist on a public statement by Kim Jong Un himself, rather than relying on statements by foreign ministry officials, and that we should postpone Singapore for a month as insurance. We called Trump at about 8:50 a.m. to make these recommendations, but he wasn't having any. Instead, he rhapsodized about what an "extremely warm letter" (meaning North Korea's statement) we had received. He didn't want to "risk the momentum" we now had. I was tempted to respond, "What momentum?" but I stifled it. On he went: "This is a big win here. If we make a deal, it will be one of the greatest deals in history. I want to make him [Kim] and North Korea very successful." It was depressing. We had come so close to escaping the trap.

On Saturday, we learned to our collective surprise that Moon and Kim had met for two hours earlier that day at the DMZ.[22] Foreign Minister Kang told Pompeo that Kim had requested the meeting, and Moon, predictably, had immediately agreed. Chung also debriefed me, saying he had not been at the DMZ but all had gone well, with the two leaders reaffirming agreement on complete, verifiable, and irreversible denuclearization and other matters. Kim told Moon he expected to reach a "comprehensive deal" at Singapore, for which the

North was making extensive preparations. Kim had been a bit surprised by Trump's decision to "suspend" the meeting and was very relieved the US had changed its position. Moon stressed that the US wouldn't accept "action for action," although he then turned around and essentially implied there could be US political compensation if the North made substantial progress on our concept of denuclearization, thus demonstrating, in my view, why we needed to get Moon out of the business of negotiating the issue. At the same time, my concern grew that some State working-level types would revert predictably and quickly into the failed Six-Party Talks approach without even noticing the change from our present approach. Meanwhile, Trump was busy tweeting there was no division on his team:

> Unlike what the Failing and Corrupt New York Times would like people to believe, there is ZERO disagreement within the Trump Administration as to how to deal with North Korea . . . and if there was, it wouldn't matter. The @nytimes has called me wrong right from the beginning!

The next day at the DMZ, North Korea, led by the ever-pleasant Choe Son Hui, refused in bilateral talks with the US even to use the word "denuclearization" on the agenda for the Trump-Kim meeting. This was unhappily familiar territory and why I worried it was only a matter of time before State began to buckle, not to mention Trump, who was so eager for "success" in Singapore. We were in near-constant contact with our South Korean counterparts, and the pace of our preparations rose dramatically. Abe and the Japanese were also pouring it on, hoping they could hold Trump in line with his previous commitments. Abe told Trump on Memorial Day that the way he handled the summit was completely different from the way other US presidents had handled them, and that Kim never expected he would dare to cancel the meeting. Trump, said Abe, was now in a position of strength, obviously hoping Trump wouldn't make his predecessors' errors. Abe pressed Trump to advocate not just our concept of denuclearization but, reflecting Japan's long-standing positions, also dismantling Pyongyang's biological and chemical-weapons programs, as well as all their ballistic missiles, whatever the ranges.

I discussed the state of play with Trump the day after Memorial Day, and, unpredictably, Trump said, "We can't have a bunch of doves take over the delegation. Tell Pompeo. I'll have to take this deal over. We've got to discuss denuclearization [in the Singapore communiqué], got to have it." Then he said, "Get the leader of the delegation on the phone," which we did quickly, speaking to a very surprised American Foreign Service officer in Seoul. After initial pleasantries, Trump said, "I'm the one to sell the deal . . . you shouldn't negotiate denucleariza-tion, and you should tell them that. You have to say 'denuclearization,' with no wiggle room." Trump allowed as how he didn't want a "big, formal agenda" and wanted "no great formality." That was that. A few minutes later, Pompeo called, upset Trump had spoken directly with the delegation. I explained what had happened, including my concern about weak language in the draft communiqué. "I'm right with you on that," said Pompeo, meaning we had to discuss "denuclearization," but it was not clear he realized State's negotiators were not "right with" us on holding the line in the negotiations. Pompeo then told me Trump wanted to bring Kim Yong Chol to meet in the Oval Office, which Trump thought was "genius." We both thought it was a mistake, as did Kelly when I briefed him, although Pompeo seemed resigned to it. About then, I wondered if I should just recede from the North Korea issue and let Trump own it, instead of constantly fighting rearguard actions and wild Trump policy swings. On the other hand, we were dealing with nuclear weapons in the hands of a bizarre regime, as I saw it, so I was reluctant to turn my back on it or resign.

Trump personally still seemed undecided about whether he wanted Singapore to happen. As we discussed strategy before Pompeo left for New York to meet Kim Yong Chol, he went back and forth before concluding, "I would rather have it [Singapore] than not have it. But if we don't get denuclearization, we can't do anything else." He said, "[If the meeting fails] I would impose massive tariffs [either he meant sanctions, or he was referring to China, not North Korea]. I have decided to delay them for now, but they are waiting." Then came the bottom line: "I want to go. It will be great theater." There was no discussion of Kim Yong Chol's coming to the White House, and Pompeo and I agreed as we walked out of the Oval that we might yet escape. That, unfortunately, overlooked the lesser Kim, who, as Pompeo said to Kelly and me shortly after nine p.m. that evening, was "hell-bent on getting in front of Trump" to hand him a letter from Kim Jong Un. Kim Yong Chol was also obdurate on all the substantive issues. The only good news was that he had no use for Moon and no interest in a trilateral summit. This was between us, with no need for the South Koreans. We got Trump on the line, Pompeo reported on the dinner, and we came finally to Kim Yong Chol's desire to hand him Kim Jong Un's letter. "Very elegant," Trump exclaimed, "let's do it." Kelly and I explained why we opposed it, but to no avail. Neither arguments about the potential political impact nor about Kim Yong Chol himself (a brutal killer, and the man very likely personally responsible for the effectively fatal torture of Otto Warmbier) made a dent. We tried later, with the Vice President's agreement, at least to move the meeting out of the Oval Office, but that didn't work either. I dug out a picture of Bill Clinton sitting in the Oval with two North Korean generals, to show Pyongyang had played this game before, and even that didn't work.

State's Diplomatic Security people drove the lesser Kim from New York for the one p.m. Oval meeting with Trump. We met to brief Trump, and Pence tried again to persuade him to hold it somewhere else, such as the Diplomatic Reception Room. Trump wasn't listening. In fact, he began musing about taking Kim Yong Chol to the Lincoln Bedroom, which we also tried to talk him out of. I collected the US interpreter and walked over to the Residence's South Entrance, where Kelly was already waiting to meet the North Koreans and escort them to the Oval. While we were there, a Secret Service agent told me the President wanted me back in the Oval. I was puzzled, but downright amazed when I walked into the Oval and ran into Pence, who said neither he nor I would be in the meeting with Kim. I could tell from both Pence and Ayers that they were somewhat in shock, and Ayers said Trump wanted "to keep the meeting small"; it would just be

Trump, Pompeo, and the interpreter on the US side, and Kim and his interpreter on theirs. There would be the absolute minimum number of people present to hear what Trump said. By this time, Trump was in a near frenzy, piling up standard-issue White House gifts (such as cuff links) to give away. One box was slightly creased, and Trump told Madeleine Westerhout harshly, "You've ruined this one, get another one." He then berated the White House official photographer, whom he wanted to stay only briefly while Kim Yong Chol was there. I had never seen Trump so wrought up. Pence said to me, "Why don't you hang out in my office?" which was generous; neither of us thought that handing over Kim Jong Un's letter would take more than a few minutes. I was still stunned at being excluded, but not more stunned than Pence, who was stoical throughout.

Kim Yong Chol arrived at one fifteen, and Kelly escorted him to the Oval along the colonnade. Kelly told us later that Kim seemed very nervous, and just as they entered the West Wing, he remembered he had left Kim Jong Un's letter in the car. The North Korean interpreter was sent racing back to retrieve it. One can only imagine Kim Yong Chol thinking about how to explain to "the Great Successor" that he had forgotten his letter. In the VP's office, we watched the television as the press on the South Lawn desperately tried to see what was happening inside. Time dragged, to say the least. We had one light moment when Don McGahn came to tell us that Trump's gifts were almost certainly sanctions violations, which he would have to retroactively waive. As McGahn said frequently, this was not the Bush White House. The meeting finally ended at two forty-five. Trump and Pompeo emerged from the Oval with Kim Yong Chol and walked him to the driveway where his cars were waiting, and then Trump spoke to the press on his way back to the Oval.

Once we saw that Kim had left the Oval, Pence and I went in, and Kelly gave me the original and a rough translation of Kim Jong Un's letter to Trump, saying, "This is the only copy." The letter was pure puffery, written probably by some clerk in North Korea's agitprop bureau, but Trump loved it. This was the beginning of the Trump-Kim bromance. The First Family was going to Camp David for the weekend, and they had all assembled to walk to Marine One, which had landed in the interim. Trump smiled and gave me a thumbs-up as he left the Oval again.

The rest of us repaired to Pence's office, where Kelly and Pompeo debriefed us. Kim Yong Chol had said nothing new or different about the North's position. Clearly, what they wanted were political assurances before agreeing to any denuclearization, and Trump had seemed inclined to give them just that. Strikingly, as in earlier discussions with the North, economic sanctions seemed to be secondary. This probably meant that North Korea feared US military power more than it feared economic pressure, and also quite likely indicated that sanctions weren't as effective as we thought. Kelly said the North could have come away with any impression they wanted regarding what Trump might do. Trump had said he was willing to reduce the US–South Korean military exercises and had gone off on a riff about how expensive and provocative they were. This may have been the worst point, because North Korea had now just heard from America's Commander in Chief that our military capabilities on the Peninsula were up for negotiation, despite our earlier denials. This was a concession that could upset even Moon Jae-in and his "Sunshine Policy" advocates, whose calculations rested on a strong US presence. To many people, it was the US presence that allowed the South Korean political left to engage in the fantasy of the "Sunshine Policy" to begin with. If we ever left Korea, they would be effectively on their own and would feel the consequences of their foolishness, which I believed they themselves feared. As bad as it sounded, I felt we could walk Trump back off the ledge, so perhaps no real damage had been done. How could this meeting have lasted for an hour and fifteen minutes? Consecutive translation was one answer, but in truth any meeting with Trump could last that long or longer. "I'm a talker," I heard him say several times during my tenure. "I like to talk."

What to do next? Kelly said he thought Trump was ready for the possibility nothing would happen in Singapore. I thought that was optimistic. We talked about establishing a timeline to show we didn't have forever to play this out, all while North Korea was still developing and/or manufacturing nuclear components and ballistic missiles. We broke up around 3:45, and I returned to my office. To my surprise, at around 4:10, my phone rang and a voice said, "This is the Camp David switchboard," the first time I had ever heard that greeting. The operator said the President wanted to speak to me. "The letter was very friendly, don't you think?" he asked, and I agreed, although I also said it was "nonsubstantive." "It's a process," said Trump. "I understand that now. We'll just have a meeting to get to know each other, and then we'll see what happens. It will take longer than I first thought." I stressed my view that neither sanctions relief nor an "end of the Korea War" declaration should come until complete, verifiable, and irreversible denuclearization was concluded, which was what the Administration's policy always had been. He seemed to be amenable to this analysis and advice. I said that having the discussions play out over time was acceptable, with one major qualification. Time was almost always on the side of the proliferator, and simply running the clock had long been a central part of North Korea's strategy. Our time was not indefinite, which he seemed to accept. "It was pretty good," he concluded, and the call ended. In fact, Trump got precisely what he wanted from the press; the headlines were, effectively, "June 12 meeting in Singapore back on."

Over the weekend, I briefed Chung about the Kim Yong Chol meeting, and he said Moon was just delighted by the outcome. Unknowingly echoing Trump, Chung also said that we were facing "a process," not just one meeting in Singapore. That was exactly what I had feared their reaction would be. Meanwhile, at the bilateral US–North Korea talks in the DMZ, the North rejected our draft approach to Singapore. The State Department, faced with rejection, wanted to offer a compromise, in effect saying, "You don't like that one? How about this one?" And if the North didn't like "this one," the State negotiators would probably offer them "another one," all the while, in reality, negotiating with themselves to see if they could produce a smile from the North Koreans. I had seen it many times before. Fortunately, Pompeo agreed with my view that we should produce no new drafts but wait for Pyongyang to respond to ours. The North finally commented verbally on our draft and said they would provide written comments the next day. Amazing how that works. I also pushed to get the negotiations moved to Singapore, to get the North Koreans out of their DMZ comfort zone. After a struggle with the US delegation more than with the North, we did so. Even Chung agreed it was time this moveable feast arrived in Singapore.

I then decided to confront the growing press speculation I was being cut out of North Korea matters and would not go to Singapore. I told Kelly, "I've been around this track a few times before," and I didn't think my exclusion from the Kim Yong Chol meeting was accidental. Kelly said he was "surprised" I wasn't in the room when he walked into the Oval with Kim in tow. I explained what Pence had said and why we had gone to the VP's office without my asking Trump directly why we wouldn't be included. Kelly said he hadn't expected to be in the meeting either, but Trump had asked him to stay. I recounted the speculation I would not be going to Singapore, which, if true, meant I couldn't do my job and would accordingly resign. Kelly said, "I wouldn't have expected you to say anything else," and said he would talk to Trump, which I accepted as a first step. Later that morning, Kelly reported that Trump had "meant nothing" by not having me in the Kim Yong Chol meeting and that I would be in all the Singapore meetings. That satisfied me for the moment.

Immediately after his lunch with Trump that day, June 4, Mattis came in to discuss the Trump-Kim summit, stressing he was worried about the squishiness of our position on the North's nuclear program, and asked, given the press speculation, if I was going to Singapore. When I said "Yes," Mattis said, "Good," emphatically, explaining he was sure, in his assessment, that Japan and several other key states in the region all supported my position not to lift sanctions before complete denuclearization, which showed the extent of backing for our approach. I wondered at this conversation, because, for the first time, I sensed Mattis was uncertain and nervous. I didn't understand why until Ayers told me a few days later that Trump had spent much of the lunch with Mattis, according to what he had heard, beating up on him—for, among other things, being a Democrat—in "ways no one had ever seen before." Mattis had to know what that meant. This was something to watch.

On Tuesday, June 5, Pompeo and I had lunch with Trump, one important topic of which was Moon's continuing desire to be present in Singapore, which was a topic that had already broken out into the Asian press because of leaks in South Korea.[23] Both Pompeo and I explained to our counterparts in Seoul what our thinking was. The bad news at lunch was Trump's fascination with the prospect he could say he had ended the Korean War. I didn't mind selling that concession to the North at some point, but I thought we certainly shouldn't give it away for free, which Trump was ready to do. It simply didn't matter to him. He thought it was just a gesture, a huge media score, and didn't see any international consequences. After lunch Pompeo and I walked to my office. We decided we had to develop something to offer as an alternative, but no good ideas popped up. I knew that Japan would be particularly disturbed that we might make this concession, so I couldn't wait to hear what Yachi would say to me during yet another Washington visit that afternoon.

I also took the opportunity to ask Pompeo if he had some issue with me, as media stories were alleging. He said flatly that he did not, recalling how, just in the past few days, I had helped him stop an errant US Ambassador from making an appointment with Trump directly without seeking permission from him. Pompeo, at the time, had said, "Bless you, John," at which we both laughed. Whether even at this early stage there was more to it than that, I can't say, but there didn't appear to be. When Pompeo and I had breakfast in the Ward Room the next morning (Mattis being out of the country yet again), we discussed what to extract from North Korea in return for an "end of war" communiqué, including perhaps a baseline declaration of their nuclear-weapons and ballistic-missile programs. I doubted the North would agree, or agree on any of our other ideas, but it might at least prevent a gratuitous US concession "ending" the Korean War.

Later that day, Prime Minister Abe stopped briefly in Washington on his way to the annual G7 summit, held that year in Charlevoix, Canada, to press Trump one more time not to give away the store. Abe stressed that the North Koreans "are survivors," saying, "They have staked their lives on their system. They are very tough, very shrewd politicians . . . if they think this is business as usual, they will go back to their old ways." Although the two leaders had a good conversation on Pyongyang, trade issues were not so sunny, with long riffs by Trump on the unfair trade deficits, especially since the US had agreed to defend Japan: "We defend you, by treaty. We defend you, but not the other way around. We had bad negotiators, right, John?" he asked, looking at me. "We'll defend you without a treaty," Trump continued, but said, "It's not fair."

With that, our attention turned from meeting Kim Jong Un to attending the G7. It turned out the road to Singapore was paved with the ruins of Charlevoix. The G7 meetings and similar international gatherings had a rhyme and reason at one point in history, and at times do good work, but in many respects, they have simply become self-licking ice-cream cones. They're there because they're there.

On June 8, Trump was over an hour late leaving the White House on Marine One for Andrews. Air Force One landed at the Bagotville Canadian Air Force base, from which we helicoptered to the summit location, the Fairmont Le Manoir Richelieu in La Malbaie, Quebec, still about an hour late. It seemed like a nice location, pretty much in the middle of nowhere. Not that it mattered; as usual, we only saw the inside of the spacious hotel where all seven heads of government and their delegations stayed. Trump arrived fixated on inviting Russia to rejoin the G7, from which it was expelled in 2014 after invading and annexing Crimea. He found an ally in Italy's new Prime Minister, Giuseppe Conte, on the job less than a week before arriving at Charlevoix.[24] Conte was in office because of an unusual left-right populist coalition that made Italian politics some of the most unstable in Europe. The G7 opening plenary sessions were contentious, with Trump under siege for his trade policies, until he fired back: the G7 should abolish all tariffs, all non-tariff trade barriers, and all subsidies. That subdued the Europeans in particular, who had no intention of doing any such thing. The discussion really showed the rampant hypocrisy of international trade talks, where free trade was invariably good for everyone else but not for favored domestic sectors, particularly farmers in places like France and Japan, not to mention the US and Canada.

Trump had bilateral meetings with Canada's Trudeau and France's Macron, where the conversations on bilateral trade were far from amicable. Trump didn't really like either Trudeau or Macron, but he tolerated them, mockingly crossing swords with them in meetings, kidding on the straight. I assume they understood what he was doing, and they responded in kind, playing along because it suited their larger interests not to be in a permanent tiff with the US President. Trump rightly complained to both that China did not play by the applicable rules in international trade and had gotten away with it far too long. With Canada, Trump wanted the new North American Free Trade Agreement (NAFTA) ratified, which would largely satisfy his trade objectives with Mexico and Canada. With France, Trump's real target was the EU. As usual, he trotted out that old stand-by, "The EU is worse than China, only smaller." Trump also complained about China and many other WTO members that called themselves "developing" in order to take advantage of more favorable trade treatment. This was only one of many areas where the WTO could stand thorough reform, which the other G7 states professed to support but never quite got around to. Trump ended the Macron meeting by saying, "You know, John's been preparing all his life for this job. He was a genius on Fox TV, you know, and now he's got to make hard decisions, which he didn't have to do on TV, but he's doing a great job." The French got a kick out of that. So did I for that matter.

In true G7 fashion, there was then an elaborate dinner for the leaders, followed by a Cirque du Soleil performance. I skipped all the fun to continue preparations for Singapore. Unfortunately, also in true G7 fashion, the "sherpas," the senior officials responsible for the substance of the summit, were gridlocked on the traditional final communiqué. The Europeans loved playing games with these communiqués, forcing the US into the unpleasant choice of either compromising on core policy principles or appearing "isolated" from the others. For most professional diplomats, being isolated is worse than death, so compromising principles looked good by comparison. Another fate the Europeans couldn't contemplate was not having a final communiqué at all, because if there was no final statement, maybe the meeting never took place, and how terrible that would be for mankind. Therefore, instead of enjoying Cirque du Soleil, the other leaders began harassing Trump, complaining that the US sherpa was being "hard-line." The dinner had also been contentious, with the other leaders opposing Trump's ill-conceived idea of bringing Russia back into the G7, and the mood had grown somewhat churlish. Since the G7 was originally conceived in the 1970s as a forum to discuss economic issues, most of the work fell to National Economic Council Chairman Larry Kudlow. The US sherpa and his international economics staff reported jointly to Kudlow and me.

Trump should have said, "Leave it to the sherpas, and let them work all night." He concluded, however, since he was a "closer," he and the other leaders would gather in one of the lounges and negotiate themselves. By this point, Kudlow had joined the group, with the aim of being friends with the European leaders on international economic issues. Kelly, sensing trouble, sent for me at about ten thirty p.m. As I was walking in, Kelly was walking out, saying, "This is a disaster," which, after a few minutes of observation, was clear. The leaders were on plush couches and chairs, with several dozen aides hovering around. No good could come of this. Trump himself seemed very tired; in fairness, so were many others, but not Macron and Trudeau, and certainly not their aides, who were pushing policy agendas contrary to ours. This was déjà vu for me; I had engaged in scores of these slow-moving debacles over the years. I tried to judge whether Trump really wanted a G7 communiqué and would therefore make more concessions, or whether he was indifferent. I couldn't tell, but Trump (who had not troubled to prepare himself) didn't really have much of an idea what was at stake. By the time I arrived, Trump and Kudlow had already given away a number of hard-fought positions. I intervened on one point against a German idea on the WTO, but no one really seemed to understand what was at issue, reflecting that it was not Trump alone who didn't grasp the specifics of what the sherpas were debating. Finally, at about eleven o'clock, the leaders agreed the sherpas should continue on their own, which they dutifully did until five thirty a.m. Saturday. I would have said, "Why bother? Let's just not have a communiqué," which might have brought Europe and Canada up short. But as Jim Baker would have reminded me, I was not "the guy who got elected."

I found Kudlow and our sherpa at about 7:20 a.m., and they confirmed not much had happened overnight. Because Trump woke late, however, we did not have a briefing session before G7 events resumed. I still didn't mind leaving Charlevoix with no communiqué, but I wanted to be sure Trump understood the implications. We never had that conversation. Instead, I suggested we advance the time of our departure from Canada to ten thirty a.m. in order to force a decision. We were already leaving well before the G7's scheduled end so we could arrive Sunday evening in Singapore at a reasonable hour, and I was just suggesting leaving a bit earlier. My theory was that once out of the summit's hothouse atmosphere, Trump could decide more calmly how to handle the communiqué. Kelly and Kudlow agreed. Trump was already bored, tired, and late for a breakfast on gender equality. Upon hearing of his accelerated departure, the Europeans, who had other ideas, descended before we could spirit him from the room. The now-famous picture (taken by Germany) shows we didn't get him out in time:

It felt like Custer's Last Stand. The whole thing was a waste of time, but on and on the discussions went, with Kudlow and me doing most of the negotiating. We picked up nickels and dimes (eliminating a European provision that Iran was in compliance with the nuclear deal, which it was not). But basically all we did was produce carbon emissions that simply contributed to global warming, which the Europeans professed to be concerned about. Trump was still bored, but we agreed on a final document, and off we went for a press conference before boarding Marine One and heading back to Bagotville air force base, leaving Kudlow behind to hold the fort. We joined up with Pompeo, and Air Force One left for Singapore, twelve hours ahead in time zones, via NATO's Souda Bay base on Crete for a refueling stop. We were done with the G7, I thought.

Trump was delighted to be on his way to meet Kim Jong Un. Once we were airborne, I explained to Pompeo what happened at Charlevoix. I tried to nap to adjust to Singapore time and awoke on Sunday Greek time, shortly before landing at Souda Bay. Except for POTUS, Air Force One is not designed for luxury travel, with no lie-flat seats, and many people simply stretched out on the floor. While I was asleep, Trump had fired off two tweets withdrawing support for the G7 communiqué, which was unprecedented. He had had Pompeo awakened some hours earlier to come to his office, where he was throwing a fit about Trudeau's using his closing press conference to score points against him. Trump had been gracious to Trudeau in his press event, and he was infuriated Trudeau had not reciprocated. The communiqué was collateral damage. No one rousted me, and when I did wake, I obviously couldn't recall the tweets, which predictably dominated the news until we landed in Singapore. I called Kudlow to find out what had happened, and he said things had ended in good order but for Trudeau's press conference. The immediate issue was what Kudlow should say on the Sunday talk shows, and Trump's direction was clear: "Just go after Trudeau. Don't knock the others. Trudeau's a 'behind your back' guy." Trump also wanted to invoke the coming Kim Jong Un meeting, saying that rejecting the G7 communiqué showed "we don't take any shit," a point definitely worth making. There was no doubt Trump wanted Kudlow and Peter Navarro (another Assistant to the President, whom I briefed) unleashed, as well as Lindsey Graham (whom I also briefed). Navarro said "there [was] a special place in hell" for Trudeau because of the way he had treated Trump; Navarro was criticized, but it was just what Trump wanted.

Looking more tired than before, as if he had not slept much on the flight, Trump was now obsessed with watching press coverage of Kim Jong Un's arrival in Singapore and what coverage of his own arrival early Sunday evening would be. After landing, Trump decided he didn't want to wait until Tuesday to meet Kim but wanted to meet on Monday. I agreed. Although we had scheduled downtime for Trump to prepare and recover from jet lag before coming face-to-face with Kim, the less time we spent in Singapore, the less time there was to make concessions. If we could escape Singapore without complete disaster, we might be able to get things back on track. On Monday, Trump met with Singaporean Prime Minister Lee Hsien Loong at the Istana [Palace], former residence of British Governors General and now the Prime Minister's residence and main office. Pompeo and I rode with Trump in "the Beast" (the presidential limo's informal name) and found him in a bad mood. He thought the Kim meeting would fail, and he attributed that to Chinese pressure. Trump and Lee had a one-on-one, and then Lee hosted a working lunch. Singaporean Foreign Minister Balakrishnan had just visited Pyongyang to prepare for the summit and said North Korea was not hurting economically and believed they were a nuclear-weapons state. Trump replied that he had taken a long flight for a short meeting. Balakrishnan said the US had already given away three things: first, having the meeting to begin with, a "give" that everyone except Trump saw; second, the difficulty in returning to our "maximum pressure" campaign, also obvious to everyone but Trump; and third, to China, because we were focusing on North Korea when China was the real strategic game. Balakrishnan was very convincing, and Trump couldn't have been happy to hear any of it.

After lunch, back at our hotel, Pompeo briefed us on the state of negotiations with North Korea, where we were at an impasse. "This is an exercise in publicity," said Trump, which is how he saw the entire summit. Kelly said to me while Trump did a meet-and-greet with the Singapore US embassy staff, "The psychology here is that Trump wants to walk out in order to preempt Kim Jong Un." I agreed, and became somewhat hopeful we could avoid major concessions. After the meet-and-greet, Trump told Sanders, Kelly, and me he was prepared to sign a substance-free communiqué, have his press conference to declare victory, and then get out of town. Trump complained that Kim Jong Un had been meeting with China and Russia to put us at a disadvantage, but he said Singapore would "be a success no matter what," saying, "We just need to put on more sanctions, including on China for opening up the border.[25] Kim is full of shit, we have three hundred more sanctions we can impose on Friday." This all threw logistics back into disarray (not that they had been in much array since we left Canada), but Kelly and I said we'd get back to him with options later that day. Trump spoke to Moon Jae-in, who still wanted to come to Singapore, but it should have been apparent to Moon by then that there wasn't going to be a trilateral meeting: he wasn't even in the right country. We also showed Trump the brief "recruitment" video the NSC staff and others had produced to lure Kim with the promise of economic success for Pyongyang if he gave up nuclear weapons. Trump agreed to show it to Kim on Tuesday (and he later played it at his closing press conference).

Negotiations with the North continued through the day, purportedly reaching near-agreement. I reviewed what was marked as the "six p.m. text" shortly thereafter with a group of State, Defense, and NSC officials. I told them flatly I would not recommend Trump sign it. Pompeo and other State people then arrived, and we met in the White House staff area to discuss the text. I explained again why I wouldn't sign it, even if all the language still in dispute were resolved favorably to the US, which was unlikely. North Korea was refusing to agree to complete, verifiable, and irreversible denuclearization, even though they had repeatedly done so before. They weren't rejecting just "magic words" but the entire concept, which rendered the whole summit meaningless to me. I said we shouldn't agree to any language about the end of the war without getting something concrete in return. Pompeo grew increasingly agitated, as he had over the phone to me in Mar-a-Lago in April discussing withdrawal from the Iran deal. I made the point that congressional Democrats would rip us to pieces on this text because that's what they did, and congressional Republicans would rip us because they knew it was inconsistent with everything they and we believed. Pompeo didn't defend the language I criticized, and he understood we were better off not signing any document rather than signing a bad one. All Pompeo knew was that Trump wanted to sign something. He couldn't bring himself to admit, at least in front of the State staffers, what we both knew: that they had led us into a cul-de-sac, where we conceded one point after another and got nothing in return. Now here we were at the very last moment, with few options, none of them good.

There was a second or two of silence, and then, as if by unspoken consent, everyone else exited, leaving just Pompeo and me in the room. After going back and forth for a while, we agreed we would insist on including references to our notion of denuclearization and Security Council Resolution 1718 (requiring North Korea not to conduct nuclear tests or ballistic-missile launches), adding new paragraphs on the Japanese-abductee issue, and pledging the return of US Korean War remains. If this didn't work, we would revert to a very brief statement, the principal virtue of which was that it would be short. Pompeo and I explained this to the State, Defense, and NSC officials, all knowing they were likely to go long into the night negotiating. Trump had already crashed earlier, for his own good, frankly, and would sleep until Tuesday morning.

NSC Asia Senior Director Matt Pottinger woke me at one a.m. to say the negotiations had stalled, no surprise, and that Pompeo and Kim Yong Chol would meet at seven a.m. at the Capella hotel, the venue for the later Trump-Kim meeting, to see what could be done. Trump finally emerged at eight a.m., and we left for the Capella. Trump declared himself satisfied with the "short statement" that we had come up with, which surprised me because it came nowhere near declaring an end to the Korean War. In fact, it didn't say much of anything. We had dodged another bullet. During all this, Trump was preparing a tweet on a 5–4 Supreme Court victory in an Ohio voting case, and also wishing a speedy recovery to Kudlow, who had had a heart incident, fortunately minor, possibly brought on by the G7.

Then we were off to the Trump-Kim arrival ceremony and meeting, then their one-on-one, followed by Kim Jong Un and four aides' entering the room where the main meeting was to take place. He shook hands with the US side, including yours truly, and we sat down and let the press take pictures for what seemed like an eternity. When the mob finally departed, Kim speculated (all through interpreters) what kinds of stories they would try to cook up, and Trump objected to the tremendous dishonesty in the press. Trump said he thought the one-on-one meeting had been very positive, and anticipated that the two leaders would have direct contact over the telephone thereafter. Laughing, Kim distinguished Trump from his three predecessors, saying they would not have shown the leadership to hold the summit. Trump preened, saying that Obama had been ready to make significant mistakes on North Korea, without even talking first, alluding to their initial meeting (presumably during the transition). Trump said he knew he and Kim were going to get along almost immediately. In response, Kim asked how Trump assessed him, and Trump answered that he loved that question. He saw Kim as really smart, quite secretive, a very good person, totally sincere, with a great personality. Kim said that in politics, people are like actors.

Trump was correct on one point. Kim Jong Un knew just what he was doing when he asked what Trump thought of him; it was a question designed to elicit a positive response, or risk ending the meeting right there. By asking a seemingly naïve or edgy question, Kim actually threw the burden and risk of answering on the other person. It showed he had Trump hooked.

Kim claimed strenuously that he was committed to the denuclearization of the Korean Peninsula. Even though he knew there were people who doubted his sincerity, those people were mistakenly judging him by the actions of his predecessors. He was different. Trump agreed that Kim had changed things totally. Following the decades-old, standard North Korean line, however, Kim blamed the troubled US–North Korea history on the hostile policies of past US Administrations. He said that as he and Trump met frequently, they could work to dispel mistrust and accelerate the pace of denuclearization. I had heard all this before, but Trump had not, and he agreed with Kim's assessment, noting that there were some very militant people on the US side, especially with regard to Kim's criticism of past US Administrations. Interestingly, Trump said he would seek Senate approval of any nuclear agreement with North Korea, contrasting his approach positively with Obama's unwillingness to seek ratification of the Iran nuclear deal. At this point, Pompeo passed me his note pad, on which he had written, "he is so full of shit." I agreed. Kim promised there would be no further nuclear tests, and that their nuclear program would be dismantled in an irreversible manner.

Then came the catch, perfected by Joseph Stalin in his wartime summits with Franklin Roosevelt, when "hardliners" were first discovered in the Soviet Politburo. Kim "confessed" that he had domestic political hurdles he could not easily overcome, because there were hardliners in North Korea as well as America. Kim needed a way to build public support in North Korea, he said, actually maintaining a straight face, and he bored in on the South Korean–US joint exercises, which, he said, got on people's nerves. Kim wanted us to reduce the scope or eliminate the exercises altogether. He said he had raised the military exercises with Moon in their first Summit (which produced the Panmunjom Declaration), and Moon had said that only the US could make the decision. Trump answered exactly as I feared, reiterating to Kim his constant refrain that the exercises were provocative and a waste of time and money. He said he would override his generals, who could never make a deal, and decide that there would be no exercises as long as the two sides were negotiating in good faith. He said brightly that Kim had saved the United States a lot of money. Kim was smiling broadly, laughing from time to time, joined by Kim Yong Chol. You bet. We certainly were having fun. In later US press coverage, there were leaks, obviously from DoD, that Mattis was displeased he was not consulted before Trump made this concession. Of course, neither were Kelly, Pompeo, nor I, and we were sitting right there. Trump said he had known from his first day in office that, for him, deal-making or negotiating such as this summit would be easy. Trump asked Kelly and Pompeo if they agreed. Both said yes. Luckily, he didn't ask me. Kim said the hardliners in North Korea would be impressed by Trump's decision on the exercises, and that further steps could be taken in the next phase of the negotiations. He joked that there would be no more comparisons of the sizes of their respective nuclear buttons, because the US was no longer under threat from North Korea, agreeing to dismantle a rocket-engine test facility.

As the meeting continued, Kim congratulated himself and Trump for all that they had accomplished in just one hour, and Trump agreed that others couldn't have done it. They both laughed. Trump then pointed to Kim, and said he was the only one that mattered. Kim agreed he was doing things his way, and that he and Trump would get along. Trump returned to the military exercises, again criticizing his generals, whom he was overruling to give the point to Kim at this meeting. Kim laughed again. Trump mused that six months earlier, he was calling Kim "little rocket man," and asked if Kim knew who Elton John was. He thought "rocket man" was a compliment. Kim kept laughing. At this point, Trump asked that we play the Korean-language version of the "recruitment" film, which the North Korean side watched very intently on the iPads we gave them. When it ended, Trump and Kim wanted to sign the joint statement as soon as possible, but it turned out that translation inconsistencies were holding it up, so the conversation continued. Kim repeated that they had had a good discussion, saying he was glad that he and Trump had agreed to follow the "action for action" approach. Somehow, I had missed Trump making that concession, but those were indeed magic words, exactly the ones I wanted to avoid, but which Kim thought he was walking away with. Kim asked if UN sanctions would be the next step, and Trump said he was open to it and wanted to think about it, noting that we had literally hundreds of new sanctions poised to announce. Pompeo and I had no idea what he meant. Trump handed out mints to the North Koreans. Kim was optimistic about moving forward quickly, and wondered why their predecessors had been unable to do so. Trump answered quickly that they had been stupid. Kim agreed that it took the likes of him and Trump to accomplish all this.

Then, a delicate moment. Kim looked across the table and asked what the others on our side of the table thought. Trump asked Pompeo to start, and Pompeo said that only the two leaders could agree on the day's historic document. Trump said happily that the US couldn't have made the deal with Tillerson, who was like a block of granite.

Fortunately, Kim changed the subject to returning American war remains, and I didn't have to speak. A second bullet dodged. Official photographers from both sides then entered, and the meeting ended at about 11:10. After stopping briefly in a holding room for Trump to check out the massive, ongoing television coverage, we started a working lunch at 11:30. Another press mob stumbled in and then out, and Kim said, "It's like a day in fantasy land." Finally, something I completely agreed with. The opening conversation was light, with Kim's describing his visit the night before to Sheldon Adelson's Sands casino and hotel complex, one of the standouts of Singapore's nightlife. Kim and Trump talked about golf, Dennis Rodman, and the US women's soccer team's defeating North Korea in the 2016 Olympics.

The conversation drifted around, and then Trump turned to me and said, "John was once a hawk, but now he's a dove. Anything to say after that introduction?" Fortunately, everyone laughed. Trying to keep a straight face, I said, "The President was elected in large part because he was different from other politicians. He's a disrupter. I look forward to visiting Pyongyang, it will certainly be interesting."

Kim thought that was funny for some reason and said, "You will be warmly welcomed. You may find this hard to answer, but do you think you can trust me?"

This was tricky, one of those questions he was good at asking. I couldn't either tell the truth or lie, so I said, "The President has a finely tuned sense of people from his days in business. If he can trust you, we will move forward from there."

Trump added that I was on Fox News all the time, calling for war with Russia, China, and North Korea, but it was a lot different on the inside. This really had all the North Koreans in stitches. Kim said, "I heard a lot about Ambassador Bolton saying not good things about us. At the end, we must have a picture so I can show the hard-liners that you are not such a bad guy."

"Can I go to Yongbyon?" I asked. More laughter.

Trump said, "John is a big believer in this, I can tell you," showing just how far the truth could be stretched.

I added, "Mr. Chairman, I'm delighted you watch Fox News," and everyone laughed. (Trump told me on the flight back to Washington, "I rehabilitated you with them." Just what I needed.)

The lunch ended shortly thereafter, at twelve thirty, but we were still stuck because the joint statements weren't ready. Trump and Kim decided to walk in the hotel garden, which produced endlessly rebroadcast television footage but nothing else. Finally, we held the signing ceremony. The North Korean delegation was very impressive. They all clapped in perfect unison, loud and hard, for example whenever Kim said or did something noteworthy, which was quite a contrast with the raggedy performance of the US delegation. Trump did several one-on-one press interviews before the huge media event began shortly after four p.m., when he unexpectedly played our "recruitment" video. The coverage was extraordinary, and then we were off to Washington, my fondest wish, before anything else went wrong. Shortly after Air Force One was airborne, Trump called Moon and then Abe to brief them. (Pompeo stayed in Singapore, traveling on to Seoul, Beijing, and Tokyo to provide more-detailed readouts of what had happened.) Trump told Moon that things could not have gone better, and they both spoke glowingly of what was accomplished. Trump asked Moon, a little belatedly, about how to implement the agreement. repeating what he said in the press conference, that he had been up for twenty-seven straight hours, something Kelly and I knew for sure was not true. Moon stressed, as Seoul's representatives did subsequently in public statements, that Kim had made a clear commitment to denuclearization. Abe expressed gratitude that Trump had brought up the abductee issue in his one-on-one with Kim, not wanting to rain on the parade. Trump said he believed Kim wanted to make a deal; it was time to close on one.

I also made briefing calls, speaking particularly to Pence to discuss the "war games" point, which congressional Republicans were already criticizing. Pompeo, stuck in Singapore because his plane had engine problems, said Mattis had called him, quite worried about the concession. Pompeo and I agreed the two of us, Mattis, and Dunford should talk once we all returned to Washington, to think through what to do to avoid dangerous impairments to US readiness on the Peninsula. Our approach should be, "Don't just do something; sit there," until we assessed what was necessary. This point was proven when I was in Trump's Air Force One office with him watching Fox News. A reporter, citing an unnamed Pentagon spokesman, said planning for exercises was continuing as before, sending Trump through the roof. Trump wanted me to call Mattis and have him stop everything, but I instead asked Mira Ricardel, also on Air Force One, to call others at the Pentagon to tell them to avoid public statements until told otherwise.

We landed at Andrews a little after five thirty a.m. on Wednesday, June 13, and Trump motorcaded back to the White House. My Secret Service detail drove around the Washington Beltway to my home, and I noticed on the way that Trump tweeted out:

> Just landed—a long trip, but everybody can now feel much safer than the day I took office. There is no longer a Nuclear Threat from North Korea. Meeting with Kim Jong Un was an interesting and very positive experience. North Korea has great potential for the future!

There was no stopping it. I spoke with Yachi the next day, and the Japanese, in my judgment, were clearly concerned about what we had given away and how little we had gotten in return. I tried to keep things calm, but the Singapore outcome was ambiguous enough that we needed to reel things back in or risk rapidly losing control of events. Both Japan and South Korea were particularly confused about the approach Trump seemed to take in his conversations with Moon and Abe, saying Moon in particular would be the "closer" on the nuclear deal. What exactly did the President have in mind? they wanted to know. Neither Pompeo nor I had the slightest idea, but we were also both certain neither did Trump. In fact, I was revising my earlier view, wondering if greater South Korean involvement in denuclearization might not complicate things so much that we could prevent a total collapse of both our nuclear nonproliferation policy and our conventional deterrence strategy on the Peninsula and in East Asia more broadly.

I also spoke with Mattis regarding the "war games" and explained how I thought we should proceed. Mattis said his Japanese and South Korean counterparts were already calling him, understandably very concerned. He also said, which I had not heard before, that six months earlier, Trump had also almost canceled the exercises because Russia and China complained about them, which was disturbing, to say the least. Dunford was compiling a list of exercises that might be affected, and we agreed to meet back in Washington. But Mattis wouldn't leave well enough alone, saying later that day he wanted to issue a press statement. Whatever it said, in my view, risked another presidential edict, the substance of which Mattis would doubtless dislike. Why roll the dice? Probably because it was a Defense Department bureaucratic ploy: if the Pentagon could produce enough blowback in Congress, it could avoid responsibility for any degradation in readiness in Korea. But it was a risky strategy, given the danger Trump might make his exercises prohibition even more sweeping and stringent. Mattis, finally, agreed his department would remain silent, but it was an effort.

Pompeo, Mattis, and I met for breakfast in the Ward Room on Monday, June 18, by which time Dunford's list of exercises was complete. Mattis argued that readiness started to deteriorate when any exercises were canceled, and the decline would accelerate the more time passed. We were all concerned about the objective, both near- and long-term, of not degrading readiness on the Peninsula. As regularly scheduled officer rotations began to ripple through the ranks and new people replaced more experienced people, the lack of exercises could take its toll. This discussion made September 1 a potentially important date.

Mattis was worried about canceling too few exercises and incurring Trump's wrath, but I thought it was ridiculous to cancel too many, provoking unnecessary confrontations with Hill Republicans and only making things worse. We finally agreed the Pentagon would issue a statement that the two biggest annual exercises would be "suspended," a key word we thought (i.e., not "canceled"). Overall, however, and remembering that the Chinese had suggested to Pompeo in Beijing that we press very hard in the next two months to make progress with Pyongyang, we set September 1 as a date by which to assess whether the negotiations were in fact productive.

During the rest of the week after returning from Singapore, Trump was euphoric. On Friday, during an intel briefing, he exclaimed, "I never could have gotten this done with McMaster and Tillerson. Pompeo's doing a great job. This guy's doing great too," he said, pointing at me. Trump was happy there would be no more war games and said he was glad he had been "overruled" in his previous efforts to cancel them because otherwise, he "wouldn't have had something to give away!" Trump also said Kim Jong Un "has a vicious streak in him," and that he could be "mercurial," remembering an irritated look Kim Jong Un shot at one of his officials during the talks. Trump had signed notes and pictures and newspaper articles for Kim Jong Un to remember the glow of Singapore, which couldn't fade rapidly enough for me.

One important point Trump made at the end of June underscored the potential of a division growing between the US and Moon Jae-in, which increasingly concerned us. Having watched Moon in action, Trump came to understand that Moon had a different agenda from ours, as any government prioritizes its national interest. For Moon, this likely meant emphasizing inter-Korean relations over denuclearization. Moreover, Trump wanted good news on North Korea before the 2018 congressional election. To that end, he wanted the South to ease up on pushing for reunification with North Korea, because denuclearization was the US priority. That had always been an accurate statement of US interests. Having it fixed in Trump's mind gave us at least one guardrail to keep us from completely losing our perspective. I worried that Trump only wanted to hear good news before the election, which was, of course, impossible to guarantee. I also worried that Pompeo particularly didn't want to be the bearer of bad news, a role too easily avoided by making concessions to North Korea.

In what passed for speed in diplomacy with North Korea, Pompeo scheduled a return to Pyongyang on July 6. I worried that State's bureaucracy was so delighted negotiations were resuming that, as in the Six-Party Talks, each new meeting was an opportunity to give things away. Indeed, State was already drafting charts with "fallback positions" for the US delegation before they even sat down with real, live North Koreans post-Singapore. I stressed vigorously to Pompeo that no serious negotiations should begin until we had Pyongyang's commitment to provide a full, baseline declaration on their nuclear and ballistic-missile programs. For arms controllers, this was a basic step, if hardly one that guaranteed success. It was elemental tradecraft that negotiators would compare what was being declared to what was already known about an adversary's weapons capabilities, and that such comparisons amounted to a test of good faith in the negotiations, and in the case of North Korea, the sincerity of their "commitment" to denuclearization. If a country grossly misstated its nuclear assets, that would show us exactly how serious these negotiations would be. I often said that "unlike a lot of other people, I have faith in North Korea. They never let me down." I also pressed Pompeo on what NSC and IC nonproliferation experts agreed: if the North Koreans were serious on renouncing weapons of mass destruction, they would cooperate on the critical disarming work (another test of their seriousness), which could then be done in one year or less. State staffers wanted a much longer period for disarmament, which was a prescription for trouble. Pompeo was not enthusiastic about a rapid denuclearization schedule, perhaps because he worried that the North would resist, thus meaning bad news for Trump, who wanted none before the election, thus causing potential headaches for Pompeo.

Pompeo left for Pyongyang after the Fourth of July fireworks on the Mall, which he viewed from the State Department, hosting the traditional reception for foreign Ambassadors. He called back to Washington on Friday evening at six thirty p.m. (Saturday morning Korea time) to speak with Trump, Kelly, and me. Pompeo said he had spent five hours in two separate meetings with Kim Yong Chol, which had been "incredibly frustrating," producing "almost no progress." Pompeo had meetings again on Saturday, and he called back to

Washington at five fifteen p.m. to report he had seen Kim Yong Chol
again, but not Kim Jong Un, which said a lot about who the North
wanted to talk to. (South Korea's Chung told me a few days later even
they were surprised and disappointed there had been no Kim Jong
Un meeting.) After Pompeo left Pyongyang, the North described the
talks as "regrettable," presenting a "unilateral and gangster-like demand for denuclearization."[26] So much for all the good news. Pompeo
said North Korea wanted "security guarantees" before denuclearization, and there would be "verification" only after denuclearization, not
before, meaning no baseline declaration, and thus no way to have a
meaningful "before and after" comparison. This was a total nonstarter,
in my view.

Trump agreed, saying, "This 'trust building' is horseshit," the smart-
est thing on Pyongyang he had said in months. Pompeo added, "It's all
an effort to weaken the sanctions, a standard delaying tactic," which
was correct. Trying to deliver some good news, Pompeo referred to
an item in North Korea's press statement, saying something like Kim
Jong Un "still has trust in President Trump." In both the Friday and
Saturday phone calls, Trump asked what impact China was having on
North Korea. Pompeo downplayed China's influence, whereas Trump
thought it was much more important. I thought Pompeo's assessment
the more accurate, though China's role was well worth watching. Then
Trump was off riffing that he didn't understand why we had fought the
Korean War and why we still had so many troops on the Peninsula,
not to mention those war games. "We're going to end being chumps,"
said Trump. Turning to North Korea, he said, "This is a waste of time.
They're basically saying they don't want to denuke," which was clearly
right. Until the end of the call, Trump didn't seem to realize Pompeo
hadn't actually seen Kim Jong Un, asking if Pompeo had handed over
the Trump-autographed copy of Elton John's "Rocket Man" CD, which
Pompeo had not. Getting this CD to Kim remained a high priority for
several months. Pompeo called me back separately after the Trump
phone call to discuss how to handle the press in Japan, where he had
stopped for refueling. The only thing that surprised me about North

Korea's behavior was how quickly they became difficult after Singapore. They weren't wasting any time.

Trump obviously wanted to suppress bad news so it didn't become public in the middle of the congressional campaign, especially the lack of any evidence whatever that North Korea was serious about denuclearization. So instead, he stressed the North was not testing missiles or nuclear weapons. I tried to explain that delay worked in North Korea's favor, as it usually did for proliferators. In all probability, the North was moving its weapons, missiles, and production facilities into new, more secure locations, as it had for decades, and continuing production of weapons and delivery systems, having concluded that for now, at least, their testing programs had accomplished their missions.[27] This was certainly Japan's view, shared repeatedly, as in a phone call I had with Yachi on July 20. Perhaps some items were even stored in other countries. That didn't bother Trump, who said, "They've been doing that for years." Of course they had; that was the very essence of the problem! But he again saw the contrast between the South's reunification agenda and our goal of denuclearization, and he therefore decided against signing the KORUS trade deal until Seoul demonstrated it was still tightly enforcing sanctions against Pyongyang. Perhaps he thought he could use KORUS for bargaining leverage, but, while the deal's signing was slightly delayed. it was ultimately signed on September 24, 2018.[28] But you could ignore the risks from North Korea only so long, especially since Trump believed China was behind the North's recalcitrance. He may have thought he would resolve the trade issues with China and then everything else would fall into place. If so, he was dreaming.

On Friday, July 27, I convened a Principals Committee to discuss what had happened since Singapore, and there was no dissent that the conclusion was "nothing much." Pompeo was emphatic that North Korea had made no significant steps toward denuclearization and that there was "zero probability of success." My take exactly. There was general agreement on tightening sanctions in a variety of ways, diplomatically, economically, and militarily. Neither Mattis, Pompeo, nor I raised our September 1 target date, but it was certainly on my mind, with just five weeks to go.

North Korea's approach was different. Kim sent Trump one of his famous "love letters" at the beginning of August, criticizing the lack of progress since Singapore and suggesting the two of them get together again soon.[29] Pompeo and I agreed such a meeting needed to be avoided at any cost, and certainly not before the November election. Under such political pressure, who knew what Trump might give away? We also agreed the best response to the letter was to say Pompeo was ready to return to Pyongyang at any time. When I showed Trump Kim Jong Un's letter and explained our recommendation, however, Trump said immediately, "I should meet with Kim Jong Un. We should invite him to the White House." This was a potential disaster of enormous magnitude. I suggested instead meeting in New York at September's UN General Assembly opening, but Trump wasn't having it: "No, there are too many things going on then." By this time, others had come into the Oval, including Kelly, to whom I whispered on the way out, "There is no way he should meet again with Kim." Kelly completely agreed. Pompeo, traveling in Asia, called in the late afternoon, and I explained what had happened. He said, "I want to see the picture of the look on your face when POTUS said he wanted a White House visit!" That would have been hard, I said, because they would first have had to peel me off the rug on the Oval Office floor. Trump tweeted to Kim that afternoon, "Thank you for your nice letter—I look forward to seeing you soon!" Although it was dicey, we drafted a letter Trump signed the next day, offering up Pompeo in Pyongyang. Trump said he didn't like the idea, which he thought was insulting to Kim: "I disagree with you and Pompeo. It's not fair to Kim Jong Un, and I hope it doesn't ruin things," he said as he wrote in his own hand at the bottom of the letter, "I look forward to seeing you soon."[30] At least he signed it.

Despite plans for another Pompeo trip to North Korea, at the end of August, just before he was due to depart for Pyongyang, the North Koreans warned that Pompeo would not see Kim Jong Un on this trip, and shouldn't even bother coming unless he was bringing completely new proposals, including the end-of-war declaration. They basically warned denuclearization was not on the agenda, but Pompeo wanted to ignore the threat, and tweet that he was looking forward to meeting Kim Jong Un. Unexpectedly, Trump said Pompeo shouldn't go at all. Pence and Pompeo argued back, pushing for the trip, but Trump was still deciding how to send the message. He ultimately reverted to the comfortable Twitter mode, and, as he did so often, he began dictating a tweet. "What do you think of that, John?" he asked, and I immediately said, "I agree. No way Mike should go to Pyongyang in the face of [all] that." Pence agreed we should show strength rather than weakness, and in short order, the tweets went out:

> I have asked Secretary of State Mike Pompeo not to go to North Korea, at this time, because I feel we are not making sufficient progress with respect to the denuclearization of the Korean Peninsula . . .

> . . . Additionally, because of our much tougher Trading stance with China, I do not believe they are helping with the process of denuclearization as they once were (despite the UN Sanctions which are in place) . . .

> . . . Secretary Pompeo looks forward to going to North Korea in the near future, most likely after our Trading relationship with China is resolved. In the meantime I would like to send my warmest regards and respect to Chairman Kim. I look forward to seeing him soon!

I was delighted. Another bullet dodged. Shortly afterward, I spoke to Pompeo, who was reconciled to Trump's decision. Trump himself said a few days later, "The sanctions should be as strong as you can make them. Don't give them any breathing room. Put more sanctions on."

Trump still wondered what Xi Jinping was telling Kim Jong Un, and I told him for sure it wasn't helpful. I gave Trump a one-pager I had drafted entirely on my own speculating on what Xi might be saying, based on my years of involvement in these issues. I hoped it might wake him up or get him thinking; I had tried everything else, so I figured I had nothing to lose. Trump read the "script" but didn't react to it. At least he had heard what I believed was the real situation. The "transcript" of my version of Xi's "comments" to Kim is as follows:

"Look, Jong Un, you can't trust Trump no matter how many nice letters he writes. He's trying to sucker you, like all capitalist salesmen. Don't fall for it. What Trump really wants is to turn North Korea into South Korea. Trump, Pompeo and Bolton are all the same. They only appear different so they can mess with your head. Americans have short-term minds. They are erratic and inconsistent, and they can't be trusted. What's more, Moon Jae-in thinks like they do, except he's even worse. He's a pacifist. We can run all over Moon, but the Americans understand power.

"That's why you have to stick with me. It's the only way for you to keep your nuclear-weapons program, get real financial aid, and hold on to power. If you proceed down this road of negotiations with the Americans, you're going to be hanging from a tree in Pyongyang before too long, I guarantee it. Stick with me.

"All you have to do is keep hiding your nuclear weapons, missiles, and production facilities. Our friends in Iran will continue testing your missiles as they have for two decades. In return, you can build them nuclear warheads in your hidden underground plants. I will buy more Iranian oil and increase our capital investment there, offsetting US sanctions. Iran will do what I say after that.

"To deceive the US, keep giving back their soldiers' bones. They get very emotional about such things. Same with Japan. Send back the bodies of the people your father kidnapped. Abe will weep in public, and start giving you suitcases full of dollar bills.

"Right now, I'm in a trade war with Trump. He's inflicting some damage on China's economy, and if this trade war continues, it could hurt us badly. Fortunately, Trump is surrounded by Wall Street advisors who are just as short-term as most Americans and just as weak as Moon Jae-in. I'll agree to buy more of their precious soybeans and some of their technology (which I will then steal and sell back to their consumers at lower prices), and that will get them to back off.

"When we get together next month, I'll explain in more detail. I'll also lay out aid packages that even Japan can't match. I won't violate any UN sanctions because I won't have to. I'll provide supplies and assistance the sanctions don't cover, and I'll hold the Border Police up from watching too closely at what's going on. You'll be fine. Not only do you not have to give up your nukes, pretty soon, you'll be able to have South Korea fall into your lap like ripe fruit.

"Think long-term, Jong Un. You want to be on the winning side of history, and that's China. The Americans are no friends of ours."

On August 29, for some reason, Mattis and Dunford held a disastrous press conference, during which Mattis was asked about US Forces Korea's readiness in light of the war games' being suspended. He gave a long, confused answer, the substance of which, however, taken fairly, indicated a split from Trump on the issue. That set Trump off, not surprisingly, riffing about what was wrong with Mattis, the generals, war games, and so on. I said Mattis was working to clear up the confusion, but Trump wanted to tweet, which he did later:

STATEMENT FROM THE WHITE HOUSE President Donald J. Trump feels strongly that North Korea is under tremendous pressure from China because of our major trade disputes with the Chinese Government. At the same time, we also know that China is providing North Korea with . . .

. . . considerable aid, including money, fuel, fertilizer and various other commodities. This is not helpful! Nonetheless, the President believes that his relationship with Kim Jong Un is a very good and warm one, and there is no reason at this time to be spending large amounts . . .

. . . of money on joint US-South Korea war games. Besides, the President can instantly start the joint exercises again with South Korea, and Japan, if he so chooses. If he does, they will be far bigger than ever before. As for the US-China trade disputes, and other . . .

. . . differences, they will be resolved in time by President Trump and China's great President Xi Jinping. Their relationship and bond remain very strong.

I thought this was all mostly laughable, but it didn't undercut our basic positions. In Trump White House terms, this was a victory, a good day at the office. The next day, China criticized the tweets—more progress in my view. Mattis told Pompeo and me at our weekly breakfast in the Ward Room on August 30 that he regretted even having the press conference that precipitated this, and I doubted he would hold another for a long time.

Moon and Trump spoke on September 4. Trump complained that he had had a phenomenal meeting in Singapore, and that a good friendship with Kim had been built, and now suddenly there's no deal. He wondered what had happened. Of course, Singapore had not been "phenomenal" unless you were a North Korean; KJU didn't make friends with his enemies; and there wasn't a real deal. Other than that . . . Moon was still singing the Sunshine Policy song, saying Kim was entirely committed to improving relations with the United States and denuclearizing, but Kim Yong Chol and others around him had rude manners, an interesting surmise. Moon suggested that Trump meet again with Kim Jong Un. Just what we needed. Moon was still pressing for his own summit with Kim in mid-September, something he likely wanted for domestic political reasons.

Pompeo, Kelly, and I gave Trump another Kim Jong Un letter on September 10,[31] which he read in the Oval, commenting as he went, "This is a wonderful letter," "This is a really nice letter," and "Listen to what he says about me," followed by his reading one oleaginous passage after another. As Kelly and I said later, it was as if the letter had been written by Pavlovians who knew exactly how to touch the nerves enhancing Trump's self-esteem. Trump wanted to meet Kim, and he didn't want to hear anything contrary, which is probably why he didn't want to hear me explaining that another meeting soon was a bad idea: "John, you have a lot of hostility," he said, to which I replied, "The letter is written by the dictator of a rat-shit little country. He doesn't deserve another meeting with you until he has met with Pompeo, as he agreed to just a couple of weeks ago." "You have such hostility," said Trump, "of course, I have the most hostility, but you have a lot of hostility." On we went, until, out of nowhere, Trump said, "I want the meeting the first week after the election, and Mike should call today and ask for it. You should say the [Kim] letter is extremely nice. The President has great affection for Chairman Kim. He wants to release the letter because it's so good for the public to see the strength of the relationship, and he wants to have a meeting after the election. Where would he like to meet?"

Outside the Oval, Kelly said to me, "I'm sorry that meeting was so rough on you," and Pompeo seemed discouraged. I said I was ecstatic at the outcome. After all, we had just gained a five-week delay in any possible Trump-Kim meeting, during which time anything could happen in Trumpworld. We should take it and run.

A continuing, very significant problem was Trump's relentless desire to withdraw US military assets from the Korean Peninsula, part of his general reduction of US forces worldwide. September 1 came and went, and Mattis reaffirmed in early October his concern for our military readiness on the Peninsula. He and Dunford would have to testify in Congress after January 1 during the budget process, and it seemed hard to imagine the problem wouldn't surface then. Pompeo finally obtained another meeting with Kim Jong Un in mid-October, where Kim complained at length about our economic sanctions but offered little in new ideas from his side. The main outcome of the meeting was to restart working-level discussions, which I considered inevitable but bad news nonetheless. Here is where the US concession train would really start steaming along. But we had at least survived past the November congressional elections without any major disasters and could now face the next round of Trump enthusiasm to meet with Kim Jong Un.

CHAPTER 5

A TALE OF THREE CITIES—SUMMITS IN BRUSSELS, LONDON, AND HELSINKI

Coming a month after June's Singapore encounter with Kim Jong Un were three back-to-back July summits: a long-scheduled NATO meeting in Brussels with our partners in America's most important alliance; Trump and Theresa May in London, a "special relationship" bilateral; and Trump and Putin in Helsinki, neutral ground to meet with our once and current adversary Russia. Before leaving Washington, Trump said: "So I have NATO, I have the UK—which is somewhat in turmoil . . . And I have Putin. Frankly, Putin may be the easiest of them all. Who would think? Who would think?" Good question. As I realized during this busy July, if I hadn't seen it earlier, Trump was not following any international grand strategy, or even a consistent trajectory. His thinking was like an archipelago of dots (like individual real estate deals), leaving the rest of us to discern—or create—policy. That had its pros and cons.

After Singapore, I traveled to various European capitals to prepare for the summits. One of my planned trips was to Moscow. That stop had its complications. When I told Trump about going there to lay the groundwork for his trip, he asked, "Do you have to go to Russia? Can't you do this in a telephone call?" Ultimately, he didn't object when I explained why reviewing the issues in advance would help in our preparations. Shortly thereafter, I asked Kelly why Trump was complaining, and Kelly said, "That's easy. He's worried you're going to upstage him." This would sound preposterous for any President other than Trump, and while it was flattering, if true, it was also dangerous. What exactly was I supposed to do now to overcome the problem? I obviously did not come up with a good answer.

Trump really wanted Putin to visit Washington, which the Russians had no intention of doing, and we had been skirmishing over Helsinki and Vienna as possible meeting venues. Russia pushed Vienna, and we pushed Helsinki, but it turned out Trump didn't favor Helsinki. "Isn't Finland kind of a satellite of Russia?" he asked. (Later that same morning, Trump asked Kelly if Finland was part of Russia.) I tried to explain the history but didn't get very far before Trump said he too wanted Vienna. "Whatever they [the Russians] want. Tell them we'll do whatever they want." After considerable further jockeying, however, we agreed on Helsinki.

I landed at Moscow's Vnukovo airport on Tuesday, June 26, and went the next morning to Spaso House, the longtime US Ambassador's residence in Moscow. Jon Huntsman had arranged a breakfast with Russian think-tankers and influencers, including former Foreign Minister Igor Ivanov, whom I had known and worked with during the Bush 43 Administration, and NSC and embassy officials. The Russians were near-unanimous in their pessimism about the prospects for improving US-Russia relations, notwithstanding what they read about Trump. They believed that fundamental American views, both in Congress and among the general public, on Russia had not changed, which was true. I pushed hard on the election-interference issue, knowing most of those present would promptly report to their contacts in the Kremlin and more broadly. I wanted the word out.

Huntsman and our delegation then rode to the Russian Federation Security Council's offices on Staraya Ploshad, hard by the Kremlin, to meet our counterparts. My opposite number, Nikolai Patrushev, Secretary of the council, was out of the country, but we had full teams on both sides to cover all the issues, from Iran to arms control, that Putin and Trump might later discuss. Putin himself had once very briefly been Secretary of the Russian Security Council, and Patrushev, like Putin a veteran of the KGB (and the FSB, its successor handling domestic intelligence and security matters), had succeeded Putin in 1999 as FSB Director. Patrushev was reputedly still very close to Putin, not surprising given their common background. We had lunch with Russian Foreign Minister Sergei Lavrov at the Osobnyak guesthouse, an estate owned in pre-revolutionary times by a wealthy industrialist who sympathized with the Bolsheviks, and where I had been a frequent guest. I continued to press on the election-interference issue, which Lavrov dodged by saying that, while they couldn't rule out hackers, the Russian government hadn't had anything to do with it.

From Osobnyak, we rode to the Kremlin to meet with Putin at two thirty. We arrived early, and while we were waiting, Defense Minister Sergei Shoygu, there with a military delegation of some sort, came in to introduce himself (and later joined the Putin meeting). We were escorted into the room where the main event would occur, almost certainly the same room where I had first met Putin in October 2001, accompanying Defense Secretary Donald Rumsfeld immediately after the 9/11 attacks.[1] The room was huge, painted in white and blue, with gold trim, and an impressive oval, white-and-blue conference table. The press mob was already present, ready to take pictures of Putin as he entered through a door at the far end of the room (and it was the *far* end). As instructed by Russian protocol officers, I waited in the center of the room for Putin to greet me, and we shook hands for the cameras. He seemed relaxed and very self-assured, more so than I remembered from that first meeting in 2001. I also greeted Lavrov, Shoygu, and Yuri Ushakov (Putin's diplomatic advisor and former Ambassador to the US), and we sat down at the elegant conference table. The Russian press later reported (incorrectly) that Putin was on time for the meeting, contrary to his practice of keeping visitors waiting, including the Pope and the Queen of England. I didn't see any need to correct them.

With the media present, Putin started by noting the decline in Russian-American relations, blaming US domestic politics. I didn't take the bait. I wasn't going to compete publicly with Putin when he had the home-court advantage. Since Moscow was then hosting the

2018 FIFA World Cup, and the US (with Mexico and Canada) had just won the games for 2026, I replied that I looked forward to hearing from him how to stage a successful World Cup. The press then cleared out in a disciplined way, and we got down to business.

Putin's style, at least at the start, was to read from index cards, pausing for the interpreter, but frequently he would put the cards down to say something like, "You tell President Trump this." Ushakov, Shoygu, and Lavrov said nothing at the meeting except to answer Putin's questions, nor did those on our side (Ambassador Huntsman, NSC Europe/Russia Senior Director Fiona Hill, NSC Russia Director Joe Wang, and our interpreter). Putin spoke for almost forty-five minutes, including consecutive translation, mostly on the Russian arms-control agenda (US national missile-defense capabilities, the INF Treaty, the New START agreement, and proliferation of weapons of mass destruction). When my turn came, I said we could follow one of two conceptual approaches to arms control: negotiations between adversaries to constrain each other, or negotiations between competitors to deconflict activities that could lead to problems. I used America's 2001 withdrawal from the 1972 Anti-Ballistic Missile Treaty as an example of the latter, which set Putin off on a soliloquy about why he felt Bob Gates and Condi Rice had later shafted Russia on that issue. I responded that Putin had left out much of the history from 2001 to 2003, where we tried to induce Moscow also to withdraw from the ABM Treaty and cooperate mutually on national missile-defense capabilities, which Putin had declined to do—quite likely, I had surmised—because they then had an effective missile-defense technology and we did not! Arms control was not an issue much discussed thus far in the Trump Administration. It clearly warranted much longer conversations before Trump would be ready to engage.

On Syria, Putin asked, regarding our desire to see Iranian forces withdraw, who would accomplish that? This was one of those moments where Putin pointed at me and said I should tell Trump directly that the Russians didn't need Iranians in Syria, and that there was no advantage for Russia in having them there. Iran was pursuing its own agenda, given their goals in Lebanon and with the Shia, that had nothing to do with Russian goals, and was creating problems for them and Assad. Russia's goal, said Putin, was to consolidate the Syrian state to prevent chaos like in Afghanistan, whereas Iran had broader goals. While Russia wanted Iran out of Syria, Putin didn't think he could ensure that complete withdrawal would happen, and he didn't want Russia to make promises it couldn't deliver on. And if the Iranians were withdrawn, what would protect Syrian forces against large-scale aggression, presumably meaning from the Syrian opposition and its Western supporters. Putin had no intention of substituting Russian for Iranian forces in the internal Syrian conflict while Iran sat back and said, "You fight it out in Syria." He wanted a clear understanding with the US on Syria, then running through various aspects of the US and Russian military dispositions there, focusing especially on the At Tanf exclusion zone (near the tri-border area where Syria, Jordan, and Iraq come together). Putin said confidently, following a long-standing Russian propaganda line, that up to 5,000 "locals" near At Tanf were, in fact, ISIS fighters, who would ostensibly follow American direction, but then betray us when it suited them. (Putin said the ISIS fighters would kiss a certain part of our anatomy, although his interpreter didn't translate it that way!) I thought this exchange on the situation in Syria was the most interesting of the entire meeting. Referring to the Syrian Opposition, Putin pressed strongly that they were not reliable allies for us, and could not be trusted from one day to the next. Instead, he urged that we advance the Syrian peace process. I said our priorities were to destroy ISIS and remove all Iranian forces. We were not fighting Syria's civil war; our priority was Iran.

Putin took a very hard line on Ukraine, discussing in detail the conflict's political and military aspects. Moving to a more confrontational tone, he said US military sales to Ukraine were illegal, and that such sales were not the best way to resolve the issue. He refused even to discuss Crimea, dismissing it as now simply part of the historical record. Then, in the meeting's second most-interesting moment, he said that Obama had told him clearly in 2014 that if Russia went no further than annexing Crimea, the Ukraine confrontation could be settled. For whatever reason, however, Obama had changed his mind, and we arrived at the current impasse. By the time I responded, near the ninety-minute mark, sensing the meeting coming to its end, I said only that we were so far apart on Ukraine there was no time to address things in detail, so we should simply agree to disagree across the board.

Putin also raised the subject of North Korea, where Russia supported the "action for action" approach the North wanted, but he basically seemed less than fully interested in the issue. On Iran, he scoffed at our withdrawal from the nuclear deal, wondering, now that the United States had withdrawn, what would happen if Iran withdrew? Israel, he said, could not conduct military action against Iran alone because it didn't have the resources or capabilities, especially if the Arabs united behind Iran, which was preposterous. I replied that Iran was not in compliance with the deal, noted the connection between Iran and North Korea on the reactor in Syria the Israelis had destroyed in 2007, and said we were carefully watching for evidence the two proliferators were cooperating even now. In any event, reimposing sanctions on Iran had already taken a heavy toll, both domestically and in terms of their international troublemaking. Because Trump was still euphoric about North Korea, I merely explained Xi Jinping's advice to proceed speedily in our negotiations.

Putin hadn't raised election meddling, but I certainly did, stressing there was even more interest than before because of the approaching 2018 congressional elections. Every member of Congress running for reelection, and all their challengers, had a direct personal interest in the issue, which they had not fully appreciated in 2016, with the attention on allegations of meddling at the presidential level. I said it was politically toxic for Trump to meet with Putin, but he was doing so to safeguard US national interests regardless of the political consequences, and to see if he could advance the relationship. After a few closing pleasantries, the roughly ninety-minute meeting ended. Putin struck me as totally in control, calm, self-confident, whatever Russia's domestic economic and political challenges might have been. He was totally knowledgeable on Moscow's national-security priorities. I was not looking forward to leaving him alone in a room with Trump.

Brussels

In years gone by, NATO summits were important events in the life of the alliance. Over the past two decades, however, the gatherings became almost annual, and therefore less than exciting. Until the 2017 NATO summit in Brussels, that is. Trump livened things up by not referring to the North Atlantic Treaty's iconic article 5, which stated that "an armed attack against one or more of them in Europe or North America shall be considered an attack against them all." This provision is actually less binding than its reputation, since each alliance member will merely take "such action as it deems necessary." It had been invoked only once, after the 9/11 attacks on New York and Washington. Nonetheless, NATO had been a successful deterrence structure, for decades blocking the Red Army from knifing through Germany's Fulda Gap and deep into the heart of Western Europe. Of course, the United States was always the overwhelmingly greatest force contributor. It was our alliance, and it was primarily for our benefit, not because we were renting ourselves out to defend Europe, but because defending "the West" was in America's strategic interest. As a Cold War bulwark against Soviet expansionism, NATO represented history's most successful politico-military coalition.

Did NATO have problems? Of course. Not for nothing was Henry Kissinger's famous 1965 work entitled *The Troubled Partnership: A Reappraisal of the Atlantic Alliance.* The list of NATO deficiencies was long, including, after the Soviet Union's 1991 collapse, the feckless abandonment by several European members of their responsibility to provide for their own self-defense. Under President Clinton, America suffered its own military declines, as he and others saw the collapse of Communism as "the end of history," slashing defense budgets to spend on politically beneficial domestic welfare programs. This "peace dividend" illusion never ended in much of Europe, but it ended in America with the September 11 mass murders in New York and Washington by Islamicist terrorists. NATO's future has been intensely debated among national-security experts for decades, with many urging a broader post–Cold War agenda. Barack Obama criticized NATO members for being "free riders," not spending adequately on their own defense budgets, but, typically, had simply graced the world with his views, doing nothing to see them carried out.[2]

Trump, at his first NATO summit in 2017, complained that too many allies were not meeting their 2014 commitment, collectively made at Cardiff, Wales, to spend 2 percent of GDP for defense by 2024, which for most Europeans meant defense in the European theater. Germany was one of the worst offenders, spending about 1.2 percent of GDP on defense, and always under pressure from Social Democrats and other leftists to spend less. Trump, despite, or perhaps because of, his father's German ancestry, was relentlessly critical. During consultations on the strike against Syria in April, Trump asked Macron why Germany would not join in the military retaliation against the Assad regime. It was a good question, without an answer other than domestic German politics, but Trump rolled on, criticizing Germany as a terrible NATO partner and again attacking the Nord Stream II pipeline, which would see Germany paying Russia, NATO's adversary, substantial revenues. Trump called NATO "obsolete" during the 2016 campaign but argued in April 2017 that the problem had been "fixed" in his presidency. His noteworthy failure in 2017 to mention article 5 allegedly surprised even his top advisors because he personally deleted any reference to it from a draft speech.[3] True or not, the 2017 summit set the stage for the potential crisis we faced in 2018.

This storm had been brewing well before I arrived in the West Wing, but it was now directly ahead. Trump was correct on the burden-sharing point, as Obama had been, a convergence of views that might have shaken Trump's confidence in his own had he paid attention to it. The problem, from the perspective of US credibility, steadfastness, and alliance management, was the vitriol with which Trump so often expressed his displeasure with allies' not achieving the objective, or in some cases not even seeming to be interested in trying. In fact, earlier Presidents had not succeeded in keeping the alliance up to the mark in burden-sharing in the post–Cold War era. I certainly believed that, under Clinton and Obama in particular, the US had not spent enough on its own behalf for defense, regardless of what any of the allies were doing or not doing. If this were merely a critique of Trump's style, which it seemed to be for many critics, it would be a triviality. Personally, I've never shied away from being direct, even with our closest friends internationally, and I can tell you they are never shy about telling us what they think, especially about America's deficiencies. In fact, it was not Trump's directness but the veiled hostility to the alliance itself that unnerved other NATO members and his own advisors.

Trump asked to call NATO Secretary General Jens Stoltenberg at nine a.m. on Friday, June 29, just a couple of weeks before the upcoming summit. As we met in the Oval beforehand, Trump said he would tell Stoltenberg the US was going to lower its "contribution" to NATO to Germany's level and ask him to inform the other members before the July 11–12 summit. (Here, we face a persistent problem with nomenclature. The Cardiff commitment is not about "contributions" to NATO, but about aggregate defense spending. Whether Trump ever understood this, and simply misused the word "contribution," I could never tell. But saying he would reduce the US "contribution" to Germany's level implied the US would drop its defense expenditures from over 4 percent of GDP by some 75 percent, which I don't think he meant. Adding to the confusion, NATO has a Common Fund to pay for its headquarters' operating expenses and the like, roughly $2.5 billion annually. Members *do* make "contributions" to the fund, but the fund's spending is not what Trump was referring to. Pursuant to my later suggestion, I did persuade Germany to increase its Common Fund contribution, and the US to reduce its correspondingly, although this didn't become final until December 2019.[4])

With Stoltenberg on the line, Trump said he had inherited a mess economically and that NATO was egregious, complaining that Spain (he had just met the King) spent only 0.9% of its GDP on defense. Rounding on Germany, Trump was pleased when Stoltenberg said he agreed that the Germans had to pay more, which, in fairness, Stoltenberg said consistently, urging NATO members to make plans to meet their Cardiff commitments by 2024 if not before. Trump rolled on, saying that the United States paid 80–90% of the cost of NATO, a number the source of which none of us ever knew. Aggregate US defense expenses (worldwide) amounted to slightly more than 70 percent of all military spending by all NATO members, but of course, much US spending was for global programs or other specific regions. Trump would later come to say he thought that, in truth, the US paid 100 percent of the cost of NATO. The source of that figure is also unknown. He told Stoltenberg that from then on, because this disparity in NATO payments was so unfair, America would pay only what Germany paid. Trump conceded that Stoltenberg regularly gave him credit for his efforts to increase NATO spending by the European allies, but argued that the only reason expenditures had increased was because the allies thought Trump would otherwise withdraw the United States from NATO. Trump stressed again that we simply would not continue to bear a disproportionate cost burden. Stoltenberg said he totally agreed with Trump that the situation was unfair, but he protested that after many years of declining NATO expenditure, we were now seeing an increase. Trump responded by urging Stoltenberg to tell that to the media, and asked him to speak with me to discuss the means by which the US would no longer "contribute" in the current, unjustified way to pay NATO's costs, which was not justified, and which didn't help the United States. Heretofore, said Trump, the US had been run by idiots, but no more. The Europeans didn't appreciate us, screwed us on trade, and we would no longer pay for the privilege, but pay only what Germany paid. On and on it went in that vein. Trump said at the end he was officially protesting.

Stoltenberg called me at about ten a.m., and I asked all NSC staff and Sit Room personnel to get off the call so I could be as straight as possible with Stoltenberg. I gave him my assessment that the now largely departed "axis of adults," worshipped by the US media, had so frustrated Trump he was now determined to do what he wanted to do on several key issues no matter what his current advisors told him. I said we had clear notice of what might happen at the NATO summit. There should be no thinking that small, palliative measures might head it off. This was clearly something Trump had thought about doing and wanted to do his way, which he had now done. Stoltenberg seemed to have trouble accepting how bad it was, but after thirty minutes of near-nonstop verbal assault by Trump, and my explanation, he got the point. Our Ambassador to NATO, Kay Bailey Hutchison, called me about noon, and I gave her a brief description of the Trump-Stoltenberg call. I said we would all be doing ourselves a disservice if we pretended the call hadn't happened and resumed business as usual.

Later that day, I briefed Pompeo. Rather than taking the issue of NATO on directly, he suggested we persuade Trump that, with so many other battles under way (notably the campaign to confirm Kavanaugh to the Supreme Court), we couldn't overload Republicans with other contentious issues. There were only fifty-one Republican Senators, and we didn't want to lose any of them because of threats to NATO. Pompeo and I agreed the two of us alone should present this case to Trump, with no generals present, so Trump didn't think the "axis of adults" was ganging up on him again. Kelly immediately agreed to our strategy, as did Mattis, who also agreed Dunford need not participate. I filled in McGahn, whose focus on confirming Kavanaugh made him more than willing to be "Plan B" if Pompeo and I failed.

We met with Trump on Monday, July 2, and it turned out to be easier and shorter than I expected. We explained the logic of not taking on more battles than we could handle, given the importance of Kavanaugh's nomination, and urged that we simply continue pushing for other NATO members to get their defense spending to the 2-percent-of-GDP level. Trump agreed without really debating. However, over the next several days, he asked me again why we just didn't withdraw from NATO entirely, precisely what we had tried to prevent. Clearly, our work was still cut out for us. One step I took to reduce the likelihood of a confrontation with our allies in Brussels, and thus reduce the possibility that Trump might deliver on the prospect of withdrawing from NATO, was to accelerate negotiations to reach agreement on the inevitable final communiqué. Yet another communiqué that no one would read, even a week after it was agreed as a possible flash point! I stressed to Hutchison that we should finalize the communiqué before leaders even arrived in Brussels to minimize the chances of another G7 debacle. This was new to NATO, and I saw that it caused extensive grumbling from those, like France, who—*quelle surprise!*—profited from strong-arming others near the end of international meetings with that most-dreaded diplomatic threat: agree with us or there will be no final communiqué! I would always welcome that outcome, but it required a considerable attitude adjustment for NATO to wrap up the final document in advance. We succeeded, but only after ceaseless aggravation.

In the meantime, on Monday, July 9, Trump began tweeting:

> The United States is spending far more on NATO than any other Country. This is not fair, nor is it acceptable. While these countries have been increasing their contributions since I took office, they must do much more. Germany is at 1%, the US is at 4%, and NATO benefits . . .

> . . . Europe far more than it does the U.S. By some accounts, the U.S. is paying for 90% of NATO, with many countries nowhere close to their 2% commitment. On top of this the European Union has a Trade Surplus of $151 Million with the U.S., with big Trade Barriers on U.S. goods. NO!

These tweets repeated what Trump had said to Stoltenberg and others, but it was the first time many saw them stated so publicly. More were coming.

We departed on Marine One for Andrews early Tuesday morning, with Trump exuberant about the Kavanaugh nomination the day before. The family was right from "central casting," said Trump. Just before boarding the helicopter, Trump spoke with the assembled press, as he regularly did in such circumstances, noting that with all the turmoil in NATO and the United Kingdom, his meeting with Putin "may be the easiest of them all. Who would think?"[5] In many conversations with Trump during the flight, however, I could see he was unhappy for some reason. We landed, and he rode with the three US Ambassadors in Brussels (one to Belgium, one to the EU, and one to NATO) in the Beast to the residence of our bilateral Ambassador to Belgium, where he was staying. In the car, he blasted Hutchison for her Sunday talk show interviews on NATO, saying she sounded like an Ambassador from the Obama Administration. He then rolled on to inadequate spending by US NATO allies and unfair trade deficits with the EU. I wasn't in the Beast, but I could recite the script from memory. It was not an auspicious start.

On Wednesday morning, I went to pre-brief Trump before breakfast with Stoltenberg and his advisors. Trump entered a small dining room on the residence's second floor, where Mattis, Pompeo, Kelly, Hutchison, and I waited, and said, "I know I don't have much support in this room." He then proceeded to rip NATO. It wasn't much of a briefing. Stoltenberg arrived, the press entered the breakfast room, and Trump riffed away: "Many [NATO allies] owe us a tremendous amount of money. This has gone on for decades." Stoltenberg explained the nearly $40 billion of annual increases in NATO member-country defense spending since Trump had taken office. Trump rolled on: "It's very sad when Germany makes a massive oil-and-gas deal with Russia. We're protecting all of these countries, and they make a pipeline deal. We're supposed to protect you, and yet you're paying all this money to Russia . . . Germany is totally controlled by Russia. Germany pays a little over one percent, we pay over four percent. This has been going on for decades . . . We're going to have to do something, because we're not going to put up with it. Germany is captured by Russia."[6]

Stoltenberg tried to start over after the press left by saying he was glad Trump was in Brussels. Trump was unappeased, saying that even the increases in NATO member defense spending that had been achieved were a joke. He was very unhappy about NATO and very unhappy with the European Union. He complained, yet again, about the new NATO headquarters building, the funds for which could have been spent on tanks—a fair point, like many points Trump made, important but often overwhelmed by the tsunami of words. He later asked why NATO hadn't built a $500 million bunker rather than the headquarters, which he called a target rather than a headquarters, which one tank could destroy. NATO, he marched on, was very important to Europe, but its value to the US was less apparent. He was one hundred percent for NATO, but America paid more than was fair. Stoltenberg tried occasionally to break in to answer, but he never got far. Nor was the EU spared, as Trump criticized Jean Claude Juncker [President of the European Commission] as a vicious man who hated the United States desperately. Juncker, said Trump, sets the NATO budget, although he did not describe how that was accomplished. Trump stressed again that he wanted to decrease rather than increase US payments to the same level as Germany's, as they had previously discussed in their recent telephone call. Trump reaffirmed his personal friendship with Stoltenberg but complained again that everyone knew we were being taken advantage of, paying more in every way, which wasn't going to continue. At this point, Mattis tried to say a few words defending NATO, but Trump swatted him away.

On Trump rolled, asking why we should enter World War III on behalf of some country not paying its dues, like Macedonia, which he then acknowledged didn't bother him as much as Germany, a wealthy country not paying enough. He complained about his own advisors, saying we didn't understand the problem, even though he told us the truth. Trump clearly believed that the only way the allies would spend more is if they thought the United States was leaving, which didn't bother him, because he didn't think NATO was good for America. Stoltenberg tried again, but Trump continued to say that too many NATO members were not paying, and repeated his fear of the United States entering World War III on behalf of one of them. Continuing on the theme, he asked why the United States should protect such countries, like Germany, and thereby bear a disproportionate share of NATO expenditures. He repeatedly asked why the United States should pay, complaining that the allies laughed behind our backs when the United States was absent, mocking how stupid we were. Then we were on to Ukraine and the Crimea, with Trump asking if Russia hadn't spent a lot of money in Crimea, which he wouldn't have allowed them to do, although Obama had. Why should the US risk war Trump wondered, and Stoltenberg answered that Ukraine was different, since it was not a NATO country. Trump responded that Ukraine was very corrupt, and the breakfast finally came to a close. He reassured Stoltenberg that he was with him one hundred percent, noting that he had supported extending Stoltenberg's term as NATO Secretary General. Still, the other allies had to pay up now, not over a thirty-year period, and in any case our spending was going down to Germany's level. By this point, Mattis had turned to me and said quietly, "this is getting pretty silly," shortly after which Trump said he was telling General Mattis not to spend more on NATO. Stoltenberg said in conclusion that we agreed on the fundamental message.

Quite the breakfast. Could the day get worse? Yes. We motorcaded to NATO headquarters, my first visit. It certainly was architecturally flamboyant, probably reflected in its cost. The summit's opening ceremony came first, and, due to the vagaries of seating assignments, I was next to Jeremy Hunt, in his second day on the job as UK Foreign Secretary. Watching the leaders mix and mingle for the de rigueur "family photo," he said, "Some leaders have small talk, and some don't; you can tell in a minute who they are," an interesting insight. After the ceremony, the first session of the North Atlantic Council began with Stoltenberg declaring the draft communiqué and other summit documents adopted, a small point here, unlike the G7, due to prior planning. Thank you. Trump was the first speaker. His opening statement, carefully crafted by his speechwriters, with assistance from yours truly and others, was pretty plain vanilla, intentionally so.

Trump's first bilateral was with Merkel, who said lightly, "We are not yet completely controlled by Russia."[7] She asked about Putin, but Trump ducked, saying he had no agenda. Instead, he wanted to talk yet again about the higher tariffs he was considering applying to US imports of cars and trucks, which would hit Germany hard, complaining, as he did frequently, that Germany's existing tariffs on US cars were four times higher than our tariffs on theirs. Then it was Macron, whom Trump accused of always leaking their conversations, which Macron denied, smiling broadly. Trump smiled too, looking at Mattis as if to imply he knew whence came the leaks on the US side. Macron wanted to know Trump's endgame in the trade wars with China and the EU, but Trump said it didn't matter. For the EU, he thought it would come down to the car and truck tariffs, likely to be 25 percent, and then went off on Jean-Claude Juncker, who, he believed, hated America. Macron still wanted a "broad deal" with Iran, as the two of them had discussed in April, but Trump seemed uninterested. With that, we motorcaded back to downtown Brussels. I gave my seat at the leaders' dinner to Hutchison that night, as a gesture for what she had been through. Besides, I had had enough, and things seemed to be settling down.

Wrong. I left the hotel at seven forty-five Thursday morning to meet with Trump, but he called me in the car first to ask, "Are you ready to play in the big leagues today? This is what I want to say," and he proceeded to dictate the following: "We have great respect for NATO, but we're being treated unfairly. By January one, all nations must commit to two percent, and we will forgive arrears, or we will walk out, and not defend those who have not. So long as we are not getting along with Russia, we will not go into a NATO where NATO countries are paying billions to Russia. We're out if they make the pipeline deal." This was not finely polished, but the direction was clear. As I wondered whether I would be resigning by the end of the day, the call cut off. I thought to myself I had ten minutes until I saw Trump to figure out what to do. I called Kelly, explained the situation, and told him that, contrary to his plans, he had to come out to NATO headquarters. All hands on deck. When I arrived at the embassy residence, I located the President's military aide (who carries the famous "football," which contains the nuclear launch codes) and asked him to find Mattis, whom I had been unable to raise (good thing we weren't at war) immediately. Mattis, it turned out, was meeting with Trudeau at NATO headquarters. Already engaging in gallows humor, I wondered if Mattis was defecting. Pompeo was waiting at the residence, and I explained Trump's mood: "He's going to threaten to withdraw today." Fortunately, Trump was typically late, so we considered what to do, concluding that the Kavanaugh play was still our best argument. We also thought about reducing the US contribution to NATO's operating budget, the Common Fund, to equal Germany's, reducing the current US share from 22 percent to 15 percent.

Trump entered at eight thirty a.m.; asked, "Do you want to do something historic?"; and then repeated what he had said earlier: "We're out. We're not going to fight someone they're paying." Then he mentioned that he hadn't wanted Hutchison at dinner with him. "You should have been at the dinner last night," he said to me. "I want to say we're leaving because we're very unhappy," Trump continued, and turned to Pompeo, saying, "I want you to get it."

Then out of nowhere, Trump said, "Keith Kellogg [Pence's National Security Advisor] knows all about NATO. You know I wanted him as National Security Advisor after McMaster. He never offers his opinions unless I ask. And he's not famous because he was never on TV. But I like John, so I picked him." (As Pompeo and I reflected later, this statement told us exactly who my likely replacement would be if I resigned soon. I said, "Of course, if you resign, maybe Keith would be Secretary of State." We laughed. Pompeo paused for a moment and said, "Or if we both resign, Keith could become Henry Kissinger and have both jobs." We roared. It was the high point of the day.)

With Trump, we made our Kavanaugh pitch as forcefully as possible and then departed for our respective vehicles in the motorcade. I reached Mattis on the way to NATO headquarters, extricating him from the plenary meeting ostensibly on Ukraine and Georgia that had already begun in Trump's absence, and briefed him.

When we arrived, Trump went to his seat between Stoltenberg and Theresa May (leaders were seated around the huge North Atlantic Council table in alphabetical order by country). Trump motioned me up and asked, "Are we going to do it?" I urged him not to, saying he should slam delinquent members for not spending adequately on defense but not threaten withdrawal or cutting US funding. "So, go up to the line, but don't cross it," was how I finished. Trump nodded but didn't say anything. I returned to my seat not knowing what he was going to do. It felt like the whole room was looking at us. Trump spoke at about 9:25 for fifteen minutes, saying nothing whatever about Ukraine and Georgia, but starting off by commenting he wanted to register something of a complaint. He observed that it was difficult, because many people in the United States felt European countries were not paying their fair share, which should be 4 percent (as opposed to the existing 2014 Cardiff agreement of 2 percent). For years, Trump said, US Presidents would come and complain, but then leave and nothing would happen, even though we paid 90 percent. We were being slow-walked, and nothing much was really being done. The US considered NATO important, said Trump, but it was more important for Europe, which was far away. He had great respect for Chancellor Merkel, noting that his father was German, and his mother Scottish. Germany, he complained, was paying only 1.2 percent of GDP, and rising only to 1.5 percent by 2025. Only five of twenty-nine NATO members currently paid 2 percent. If countries were not rich, Trump acknowledged that he could understand it, but these are rich countries. The US wanted to continue to protect Europe, he said, but he then veered into an extended riff on trade and the EU, which he thought should be tied together with NATO for analysis purposes. The EU wouldn't accept US products, and this was something the US couldn't allow to continue, but only Albania had addressed this point at dinner the evening before. This all left us in the same position we'd been in for four years. Trump disagreed with the Europeans on some things, like immigration and the EU's lack of control over its borders. Europe was letting people into its countries who could be enemy combatants, especially since most were young men coming in.

On it went. Trump said again that he had great respect for NATO and for Secretary General Stoltenberg. He complained that NATO members wanted to sanction Russia, but Germany would pay Russia billions of dollars for Nord Stream II, thereby feeding the beast, which was a big story in the United States. Russia was playing us all for fools, he believed, as we paid billions because of the new pipeline, which we shouldn't let happen.[8] The US wanted to be good partners with Europe, but the allies had to pay their share; Germany, for example, could meet the 2 percent target right now, not waiting until 2030, he said, calling Merkel by name across the huge chamber. The US was thousands of miles away, he said, noting for example that Germany was not helping with Ukraine. In any case, Ukraine didn't help the United States, it helped Europe, serving as Europe's border with Russia. Returning to the burden-sharing point, Trump said he wanted all the allies to meet the 2 percent target now, which only five of the twenty-nine were doing, even among the wealthiest countries, even friends like France. Trump said he didn't want to see press reports coming from this NATO summit that said everyone was happy. He wasn't happy, because the United States was being played. Then there was more, and then more.

Then, coming to a close, Trump said he was with NATO one hundred percent, a thousand million percent. But allies had to pay the 2 percent by January 1, or the United States was just going to do its own thing. Then he was back on why he didn't like the headquarters building where we were all sitting, repeating that a single tank shell could destroy it. Trump ended by saying he was very committed to NATO, but he was not committed to the current situation. He wanted members to pay what they could, and not in four or six years, because the current situation was not acceptable to the United States. He wanted that registered.

Trump had done what I hoped, although his toe was over that line several times. Still, despite the stunned reaction in the vast NAC chamber, Trump *had* said he supported NATO, making it hard to construe his remarks as an outright threat to leave. Perhaps the fever had broken. When people ask why I stayed in the job as long as I did, this was one of the reasons.

A few minutes later, Merkel came over to speak with Trump at his seat, suggesting that Stoltenberg convene an informal "roundtable" where everyone would have a chance to react to what Trump had said. At the meeting, various governments described their domestic political woes, as if we should feel sorry for them or didn't have any domestic political woes ourselves. Dutch Prime Minister Mark Rutte made the most telling point, stressing that he had consistently said that Trump was right, and that he had instilled a sense of urgency since he took office. By contrast, as the Europeans now understood, said Rutte, with Obama the 2 percent target it had been entirely pro forma. Times had changed. He had clearly gotten the message. The most inane comment came from the Czech Prime Minister, who said he was making every effort to get to 2 percent by 2024, but their GDP was rising so fast, he was unsure defense spending could keep up. In effect, this was saying they were getting rich too fast to defend themselves adequately. Trump jumped on it, saying he had a similar, actually much bigger, problem because of US economic growth. He said the situation was unfair and unsustainable, and needed to be brought to a conclusion, where the allies stepped up to their responsibilities, or there would be problems. Trump explained that the Nord Stream story was the biggest story in Washington. People were saying Germany had surrendered to Russia (and certainly that's what he had, in effect, said). How could we defend ourselves from the Russians, Trump wondered, if the allies wouldn't pay for it? Trump said he liked Hungary and Italy, but it wasn't fair to the United States that they weren't paying their allocated share. The US was protecting countries it wasn't allowed to trade with. He had no more to say, but he underlined again that there had to be a satisfactory conclusion, after which the US would be a great partner. Trump said he didn't want to hurt his country by saying how stupid we had been, such as by spending to protect Nord Stream.

Trump was bargaining in real time with the other leaders, trapped in a room without their prepared scripts. It was something to see. Some leaders said they couldn't accept what Trump asked for on defense expenditures because it contradicted the earlier-adopted communiqué, which I communicated to Stoltenberg would be a real mistake. He agreed and helped head off that problem, but it was clear things were in dire straits. Canada's Trudeau asked, "Well, John, is this one going to blow up too?" I answered, "Plenty of time left, what could go wrong?" and we both laughed. I gave Trump a note about reducing US Common Fund spending, which he passed to Stoltenberg, who blanched when he saw it. But at least that was now also on the table. With a few more comments from the crowd, the meeting ended, and we went off to prepare for Trump's closing press conference, which was restful compared to Singapore. Trump gave a positive spin to the day's events. The outcome was unmistakable: the United States expected its NATO allies to live up to the commitments they had made on defense spending. How unremarkable that should have been, but how much effort it had taken to get to something so banal. Indeed, this was definitely not the Obama presidency. Trump stopped off at the resumed leaders' conference on Afghanistan to give some prepared remarks, noting as well the great spirit he thought was developing at NATO. However, we then had to press him to head for the airport more or less as scheduled, to prevent Brussels's traffic from being even more gridlocked than it had already become. As we left, Merkel was speaking. Trump went up to her to say goodbye, and she rose to shake hands. Instead, he kissed her on both cheeks, saying, "I love Angela." The room broke into applause, and we left to a standing ovation. That night, Trump tweeted:

> Great success today at NATO! Billions of additional dollars paid by members since my election. Great spirit!

It was a wild ride, but NATO had sent Trump off to meet Putin in Helsinki with a publicly united alliance behind him, rather than exacerbating our already incredibly difficult position involving the very future of NATO itself.

London

Air Force One flew to London's Stansted Airport, where we took Marine One to Winfield House, our Ambassador's residence. We then motorcaded to our hotel to change into formal wear, raced back to Winfield House, and helicoptered to Blenheim Palace, where Prime Minister May was hosting dinner. Built to reward John Churchill, Duke of Marlborough, for his 1704 victory over Louis XIV's armies in the War of the Spanish Succession, marking Britain unarguably as one of the great world powers of the day, Blenheim was spectacular. We were told it was the only British building styled a "palace" not owned by the royal family. Winston Churchill was born there, a direct descendant of the first Duke. The arrival ceremony with red-coated troops and military band at sundown was most impressive, as was the interior of the huge palace. Sedwill and I sat at the head table with the leaders and their spouses, the current Duke of Marlborough, and the UK and US Ambassadors and their spouses. I could have hung around for a while, but bad weather was closing in. We either choppered back to London at ten thirty p.m., or there was no telling when we would get back. Time to go! Ta-ta!

The next day, Friday the thirteenth, opened with press stories about an interview Trump gave in Brussels to the *Sun* newspaper, basically trashing May's Brexit strategy. I thought the strategy was in free fall anyway, but it was, as they say in London, a spot of bother for this to happen as the leaders met, supposedly to demonstrate the special relationship at work. Brexit was an existential issue for the UK, but it was also critically important to the US. Brexit's fundamental impetus was the accelerating loss of citizen control over the Brussels-based mechanisms of the European Union. Bureaucracies were making rules that national parliaments had to accept as binding, and the loss of democratic sovereignty was increasingly palpable. For the Brits, ironically, Brussels was the new George III: a remote (politically if not physically), unaccountable, oppressive machine that a majority of British voters rejected in 2016, reversing forty-three years of EU membership. Yet implementing the vote had been disastrously mishandled, thereby threatening political stability in Britain itself. We should have been doing far more to help the Brexiteers, and I certainly tried. Unfortunately, apart from Trump and myself, almost no one in the Administration seemed to care. What a potential tragedy.

The US delegation helicoptered to Sandhurst, Britain's military academy, where the Ministry of Defence held a joint exercise for US and UK special forces to take down a terrorist camp. Trump apologized as he greeted May, and she brushed the press incident away. The exercise was loud and impressive, clearly getting Trump's attention. I kicked myself over the fact that someone in the last eighteen months hadn't taken Trump to a US exercise. Had he seen such things before, perhaps we could have saved the war games on the Korean Peninsula. From Sandhurst, we helicoptered to Chequers, the British Prime Minister's weekend retreat, for the main business meetings of the visit.

Jeremy Hunt and others joined May and Sedwill, and we began

the meeting in front of a fireplace in the two-story central living room. After starting with Yemen, a British obsession, May turned to Syria, particularly how to deal with Russia's presence there, stressing that Putin only valued strength, obviously hoping Trump would pay attention. I explained what Putin had told me a few weeks before (see above) on working to get Iran out of Syria, about which the Brits were rightly skeptical. I said, "I'm not vouching for Putin's credibility," to which May replied, "Well, we especially didn't expect it from you, John!" to general laughter.

That led to Russia's hit job on the Skripals (a defecting former Russian intelligence officer and his daughter),[9] described by Sedwill as a chemical-weapons attack on a nuclear power. Trump asked, oh, are you a nuclear power?, which I knew was not intended as a joke.

I asked May why the Russians did it, and Trump said he had asked the same question the night before at Blenheim, thinking it might be intended as a message. May thought the attack was intended to prove Russia could act with impunity against dissidents and defectors, to intimidate them and like-minded others. She stressed to Trump that, in Helsinki, he should go into the meeting from a position of strength, and Trump agreed, claiming that Putin asked for the meeting (the opposite of the truth), and assured her he would not give anything away. (I had learned earlier that the Justice Department was making public Mueller's indictments against twelve Russian GRU officers for election interference,[10] which I thought better announced before the summit, for Putin to contemplate.)

Over the working lunch that followed, we discussed the travails of Brexit, Trump's view of the North Korea negotiations, and then China and Trump's November 2017 visit. He said he was greeted by a hundred thousand soldiers and said, "There's never been anything like it before in the history of the world." In the concluding press conference, Trump went out of his way to tamp down the firestorm caused by his *Sun* interview, leading the UK press to label it "a complete reversal," which it certainly seemed to be. Trump called the US-UK relationship "the highest level of special," a new category.[11] After taking Marine One back to Winfield House, we helicoptered out to Windsor Castle for the Trumps to meet Queen Elizabeth, which brought another display of pageantry, and lots more red coats and military bands. Trump and the Queen reviewed the honor guard, and they (and FLOTUS) met for almost an hour. The rest of us had tea and finger sandwiches with members of the royal household, which was very elegant but hard on some of us ill-schooled colonials. Then it was back on Marine One, heading to Stansted and boarding Air Force One for Scotland, to stay at the Trump Turnberry golf resort.

The resort, on the Firth of Clyde, was huge, and many of us gathered outside to enjoy the view, until someone flying an ultralight vehicle, more like a bicycle with wings attached to it (a Greenpeace demonstrator, as we learned later), came peddling by flying a banner calling Trump "below par." The Secret Service hustled Trump inside, along with everyone else except Kelly and me, who for some reason stayed outside to watch as this ungainly contraption flew ever closer. The Service finally decided Kelly and I should go inside as well. It was quite a breach of security, but fortunately only entertainment.

We stayed at Turnberry until Sunday, Trump played golf, and we had several calls with Israeli Prime Minister Netanyahu. The key subject was Netanyahu's recent meeting with Putin, and particularly what they had discussed about Syria. As he had implied in his earlier meeting with me, Putin told Netanyahu that Iran had to leave Syria, saying that he shared our goal, but that Assad had problems that precluded Putin from getting him to press the Iranians; Assad was, of course, relying on Iranian forces to make progress in Idlib against the Syrian Opposition and numerous terrorist groups. Dealing with Idlib was one thing, but there was no excuse for Assad to import weapons systems that could only be used to threaten Israel. Putin said he understood, but couldn't make any promises. Israel rightly believed the United States was also concerned about Iran's continuing presence in Syria, which Putin also said he understood even if disagreed with it. Netanyahu pressed Putin for a "permanent border" on the Golan Heights, a long-standing Israeli objective, with Syria on one side and Israel on the other, meaning, to me, the elimination of the UN disengagement force and areas of separation, and returning to a "normal" border situation. Israel had long since annexed the Golan Heights and wanted that reality regularized, so normalizing the border situation would be a significant step. I was doubtful that Trump would raise this particular issue with Putin, involving as it did an issue at a level of specificity Trump had not previously encountered.

Air Force One left Prestwick Airport midafternoon on Sunday, July 15, for Helsinki. Trump was watching a World Cup soccer match in Moscow as I tried to brief him on the arms-control issues we might discuss with Putin. I explained why Obama's New START agreement, which Trump had criticized during the 2016 campaign, was a disaster and definitely not something we should extend for another five years, which Moscow wanted to do. I explained that Senate Republicans had voted against the treaty in 2010 by a 26–13 margin, which I hoped would be convincing to Trump. We also talked about the INF Treaty (and why I wanted to leave it) and our national missile-defense program (which I said we should not negotiate with the Russians), but I didn't get far. As we talked, while Trump watched the World Cup, he said of Mattis, "He's a liberal Democrat, you know that, don't you?" Trump asked if I knew Mark Milley, then Army Chief of Staff, which was interesting because Milley was a "candidate" to be Chairman of the Joint Chiefs when Dunford's term expired in September 2019. It was widely believed in the Pentagon that Mattis was determined to block Milley. I told Trump he should get at least three names from the Defense Department for all important military command and staff positions. The practice when I arrived was for Mattis to send over one name for each position, which I thought reflected a significant decline in civilian control over the military, an issue I pursued throughout my tenure as National Security Advisor with only mixed success.

Trump and I also discussed how to handle the issue of election meddling with Putin, especially now that Mueller's indictments of the GRU agents were public. Since we had no extradition treaty with Russia, and Russia's "constitution" prohibited extraditions anyway, the odds these defendants would be handed over were infinitesimal. Accordingly, I advised against demanding that the Russians do so, as many Democrats and Republicans were suggesting. Asking for something we knew we couldn't get made us look impotent. Instead, I suggested Trump say, "I'd love to have them come to the United States to prove their innocence," which he seemed to like. "You should get credit for this," said Trump. He wanted to say that if Russian hacking in 2016 was so serious, Obama should have done more about it, which was entirely true.

I gave Trump a paper I had asked the White House Counsel's office to draft, laying out our objections to Russian election meddling. Trump made several changes to it, reflecting his general unease with the subject. It was precisely to deal with that unease that I asked for the paper. Trump could make the point of our intense opposition to election interference by handing Putin the paper, obviating the need for a long conversation. Ultimately, Trump decided not to use the document. He wanted me to raise election interference, which I said I would do in the scheduled working lunch, but obviously I wouldn't be in the one-on-one with Putin he wanted so much.

Helsinki

We landed in Helsinki and drove to the Kalastajatorppa Hotel (go ahead, try pronouncing it). On Monday morning, I walked through the tunnel to the hotel's guesthouse to brief Trump for his breakfast with Finnish President Sauli Niinisto. I had first walked through this tunnel in September 1990 with Jim Baker, to help prepare George H. W. Bush for his meetings with Mikhail Gorbachev, after Saddam Hussein's August invasion of Kuwait. During the day, Finnish television ran endless footage of the Bush-Gorbachev summit, probably the last time US and Soviet/Russian leaders met in Helsinki. I was one of the few people in Trump's entourage who even remembered that summit, let alone had attended it. In our brief preparatory meeting, Trump mostly complained about Jeff Sessions for his latest transgression, saying he had "lost his mind." The substantive discussion we did have centered on Russian election meddling. Trump remained, as he had been from the beginning, unwilling or unable to admit any Russian meddling because he believed doing so would undercut the legitimacy of his election and the narrative of the witch hunt against him.

Off we went at nine thirty a.m. to the nearby Mantyniemi compound, home of Finland's President, for breakfast. Although we covered a number of topics, Niinisto wanted to make three points on Russia, the first being how to deal with Putin. Niinisto reminded Trump that Putin was a fighter, and Trump should therefore hit back if attacked. Second, Niinisto stressed the importance of respecting Putin, and that if trust were established, he might be more discrete. Finally, again as if preparing for a boxing match, Niinisto warned Trump never to provide an opening or give even one inch. He ended his pep talk with a Finnish saying, "The Cossacks take everything that's loose." Niinisto said Finland had an army of 280,000, if everyone was called up,[12] to make it clear the price would be high if they were invaded. Trump asked if Finland wanted to join NATO, and Niinisto gave the complicated Finnish answer, not saying yes or no, but leaving the door open. Niinisto went back to his pep talk, saying Putin was not stupid and wouldn't attack NATO countries. While Putin had made a mistake in engendering conflict in Ukraine's Donbas, he didn't believe Putin would give back Crimea. Trump blamed Obama, and promised not to accept such behavior, to my immense relief, underscoring that Putin would not have so acted had he been President at the time.

Back at the Kalastajatorppa, we had word that Putin's plane was late departing Moscow, following his pattern of making his guests wait. I hoped Trump would be irritated enough by this that he would be tougher on Putin than otherwise. We did consider canceling the meeting entirely if Putin were late enough, and we decided that in any event, we would make Putin wait for a while in Finland's presidential palace (where the summit was to be held, as in 1990) once he did arrive.

We sweated out a stunningly long, just-under-two-hour one-on-one meeting. Trump emerged at about four fifteen and briefed Kelly, Pompeo, Huntsman, and me. Most of the conversation was on Syria, with particular emphasis on humanitarian assistance and reconstruction (which Russia wanted us and the West generally to fund), and getting Iran out. Trump said Putin spent a lot of time talking, and he listened, which was a switch. In fact, the US interpreter told Fiona Hill and Joe Wang later that Putin had talked for 90 percent of the time (excluding translation); she also said Trump had told her not to take any notes, so she could only debrief us from her unaided memory. It was clear, said Trump, that Putin "wants out" of Syria, and that he liked Netanyahu. Trump also said Putin didn't seem to care much one way or the other about our leaving the Iran nuclear deal, although he did say Russia would stay in. On China trade issues, Putin commented on the tough US stance, and Trump had replied that he had no choice. Putin wanted the US to do more business in Russia, noting that the EU did twenty times more than America. The key point was there were no agreements on anything, no concessions, no real change in substantive foreign policy. I was delighted. And relieved. No successes, but that didn't trouble me at all, since I had long seen this entire summit as one massive exercise in damage control.

Then we came to election meddling, which Trump said he raised first. Unfortunately, Putin had a curveball ready, offering to try in Russia the just-indicted GRU agents (how thoughtful), under an unspecified treaty, saying further he would let Mueller's investigators come in to do their work, so long as there was reciprocity with respect to Bill Browder, a businessman whose lawyer in Russia, Sergei Magnitsky, had been arrested and killed by the Putin regime. Browder's grandfather Earl Browder had been General Secretary of the US Communist Party for many years in the 1930s and '40s, marrying a Soviet citizen. The capitalist grandson, now a British citizen, had done well financially in Russia, but Magnitsky's murder and the actions taken against his investments moved him to launch an international campaign against Moscow. He persuaded Congress to pass a law that enabled the US to sanction Russian human-rights violators; several other countries followed suit. The way Putin saw it, Browder had given Hillary Clinton's campaign, foundation, and other parts of the Clinton galactic empire some $400 million that he had basically stolen from Russia, which got Trump's attention. It was all hot air, but Trump was very excited about it. I tried to deflate his enthusiasm, at least until I could find out more about the treaty Putin had raised. This seemed like a trap if there ever was one. We then headed to the working lunch, now more like an early dinner.

Trump asked Putin to describe the one-on-one, and Putin said Trump had first raised the election-interference issue, and then said he hoped we could provide a common explanation of the matter (whatever that meant). Putin said we should all promise no more cyberattacks. Sure, that'll work. He followed with what they had said on Ukraine, Syria, Iran, and North Korea, with a few comments by Trump, and it all seemed uneventful, much like Trump had described it earlier. They also touched on arms control, but only superficially. I decided to let that last issue lie, worried it was simply risking problems to reopen it. Trump asked if anyone had any questions, so I asked Putin to expand on the 1974 Syria-Israel border question, to see if we could learn more on what he had said to Netanyahu. Putin made clear he was talking only about stiffening enforcement of the disengagement lines, not real "borders." I also asked about Syrian humanitarian aid and reconstruction, because I was sure the more Putin said about how much aid was necessary, the less interested Trump would be. What both of them really wanted to discuss was increasing US trade and investment in Russia, a conversation that lasted a surprisingly long time given there was so little to say, with so few US businesses really eager to dive into the Russian political and economic morass.

After the lunch broke, we walked to the Trump-Putin press conference, which started about six p.m.[13] As Kelly observed to me at some point, there were now two military aides in the room, each carrying his country's nuclear football. Putin read a prepared statement, written well before the meeting, but he did say publicly that Trump had raised the election-meddling issue first, answering "the Russian state has never interfered and is not going to interfere into internal American affairs, including the election process," as he had in my earlier meeting with him. Fiona Hill, a Russian speaker, noted this choice of words, because obviously if the meddling had been done by a "nongovernmental organization" or a "corporation" (not that there were many truly independent versions of either in Russia), one could say with a modestly straight face that it was not "the Russian state" that had acted. We should have done more to highlight that point, but, once again, that would have required explicitly agreeing there was meddling in the first place. Trump read his anodyne statement, and the press questions started. Putin at one point mentioned that Trump had stood by the well-known US position that the annexation of Crimea was illegal, but that got lost in the shuffle.

I thought we might actually be okay, for a while. A US reporter asked Putin why Americans should believe his denials of interference in our 2016 election, and Putin answered, "Where do you get this idea that President Trump trusts me or I trust him? He defends the interests of the United States of America, and I do defend the interests of the Russian Federation . . . Can you name a single fact that would definitively prove the collusion? This is utter nonsense." Then, after showing more knowledge about Mueller's recent indictments than might have been prudent, Putin raised the 1999 Mutual Legal Assistance Treaty. Putin misnamed it (or it was mistranslated) during the press conference, although we had concluded by then this must have been what he had raised in his one-on-one with Trump. Putin said Mueller could take advantage of the treaty, and Russia should also be able to take advantage of it to pursue Bill Browder for his alleged crimes, as he had related to Trump during their encounter. Putin's description of what might be possible under the treaty was a long way from what it actually provided, but by the time we explained it to the press, Putin had scored his propaganda point.

Worryingly, however, Putin also said he wanted Trump to win the 2016 election "because he talked about bringing the US-Russian relationship back to normal," a significant deviation from the standard public line that countries don't interfere in others' internal politics and would work with whomever was elected. That in turn paled before the Trump response near the end of the press conference, when Trump said, "My people came to me—Dan Coats came to me and some others—they said they think it's Russia. I have President Putin; he just said it's not Russia. I will say this: I don't see any reason why it would be, but I really do want to see the server. But I have—I have confidence in both parties . . . So I have great confidence in my intelligence people, but I will tell you that President Putin was extremely strong and powerful in his denial today." Kelly and I, sitting next to each other in the audience, were almost frozen to our seats by Trump's answer. It was obvious that major corrective action would be needed because of this self-inflicted wound, but what exactly that would be was far from evident. The immediate media coverage was catastrophic.

After Trump's individual interviews finished, we raced to the airport to board Air Force One, which took off at eight p.m. local time. Dan Coats had been trying to reach me, and I called him immediately after we were airborne. He was, to say the least, upset. "Shock waves are rolling across Washington," he said, and the intelligence community wanted a statement from him to prevent the community from being totally undermined. Coats had prepared something that in his view was necessary to defend the community, and I asked him to hold off issuing it for just a few minutes until I could talk to Kelly. I did not detect any hint that he was thinking of resigning, but his sense of urgency was palpable. I hung up and found Kelly, who thought a statement might be helpful if Coats talked about Trump Administration anti-meddling efforts, which were far greater than what Obama had done. Coats didn't want to make any changes to the statement, which he read to me over the phone. I didn't think, ceteris paribus, it was that bad, or unexpected. I still didn't see any indication Coats might resign, so I told him to go ahead and release the statement.

Coats's comments, issued moments later, added fuel to the fire but were minor compared to what the press was already doing. We were hard at work researching the MLAT, confirming the initial view that Putin had totally distorted the treaty, both how it applied to Bill Browder and what Mueller's team might be able to obtain. It was pure propaganda, Soviet-style. Nick Ayers called to say Pence wanted to point out that Trump had twice before said he had faith in the US intelligence community, which I said was a good idea. I told Trump what Pence was about to do, which he supported, and in fact he put out his own tweet to the same effect. Nonetheless, the press maelstrom continued unabated. After a little more thought, I wrote down the four points I thought Trump had to make: "(1) I have always supported the IC; (2) there was never any 'Russia collusion'; (3) Russian (or any other foreign) meddling is unacceptable; and (4) it will not happen in 2018." I typed this up and handed it to Kelly, Sanders, Sarah Tinsley (NSC Communications Senior Director), Miller, Bill Shine (former Fox News senior executive), Dan Scavino (Trump's social media guru), and others, and then (around midnight Finnish time) took a nap. We landed at Andrews at nine fifteen p.m. Washington time, and I headed home.

The next day, the entire senior White House communications team conferred with Trump in the Oval. Still surprised at the negative reaction, he had reviewed the press-conference transcript and decided he had misspoken. In the line where he said "I don't see any reason why it would be," meaning, "I don't see any reason why it would be Russia," he had meant to say "would not be [Russia]," thereby reversing the sentence's meaning. Trump was renowned for never backing away from something he said, in fact usually digging in when challenged, so this was a surprising turnaround. Of course, that change alone did not eliminate the problem of his other statements accepting moral equivalence between Putin's view and our own intelligence community's view. But for the press office people, Trump's making any kind of corrective statement was progress. Stephen Miller drafted prepared remarks, which Trump delivered in the early afternoon.

This was hardly the way to do relations with Russia, and Putin had to be laughing uproariously at what he had gotten away with in Helsinki. Condi Rice called to tell me she was not going to make any public comment on Helsinki, but she said, "You know, John, that Putin only knows two ways to deal with people, to humiliate them or dominate them, and you can't let him get away with it." I agreed. Lots of people were calling on various senior officials to resign, including Kelly, Pompeo, Coats, and myself. I had been in the job only a little over three months. Things sure moved fast in the Trump Administration!

CHAPTER 6

THWARTING RUSSIA

Defenestrating the INF Treaty

Since my days in George W. Bush's Administration, I had wanted to extricate the United States from the INF (Intermediate-Range Nuclear Forces) Treaty. This may seem like a tall order, but I had been there before. I knew what to do, having helped Bush 43 get America out of the dangerous, outmoded 1972 ABM Treaty, which precluded the US from mounting an effective national missile defense. There was no learning curve. And since one of Helsinki's few tangible outcomes was to be increased cooperation between the US and Russian national security councils, the tools were at hand. I proposed to Nikolai Patrushev we meet in Geneva, and he accepted for August 23.

Russia had been violating the INF Treaty for years, while America stayed in compliance and watched it happen. Barring missiles and launchers with ranges between 500 and 5,500 kilometers (310 to 3,420 miles), the Reagan-Gorbachev agreement between the US and the USSR was intended to prevent a nuclear war being fought in Europe. Over time, however, the INF's fundamental purpose was vitiated by persistent Russian breaches, changed global strategic realities, and technological progress. Even before Trump took office, Russia had begun actual deployment of missiles violating the INF's prohibitions in the Kaliningrad exclave on the Baltic Sea, laying the basis for a substantial threat to NATO's European members. Moreover, and of even greater long-term consequence, the treaty bound no other countries (apart from, in theory, other USSR successor states), including many of the biggest threats facing the US and its allies. China, for example, had the greatest proportion of its large, growing, already-deployed

missile capabilities in the INF-forbidden range, endangering US allies like Japan and South Korea, as well as India and Russia itself, a
fine irony. Iran's intermediate-range ballistic-missile force threatened
Europe and was poised to expand, as were North Korea's, Pakistan's,
India's, and those of other would-be nuclear powers. Finally, the
INF Treaty was outdated technologically. While it forbade ground-
launched missiles within its prohibited ranges, it did not forbid sea-
and air-launched missiles from nearby waters or airspace that could
hit the same targets as ground-launched missiles.

The real bottom line was that the INF Treaty bound only two
countries, and one of them was cheating. Only one country in the
world was effectively precluded from developing intermediate-range
missiles: the United States. It made no sense today, even if it did when
adopted in the mid-1980s. Times change, as liberals like to say.

Patrushev and I met at the US Mission to the UN in Geneva. Beforehand, NSC staff had consulted widely within the US government
on the agenda, and Pompeo and I had discussed arms-control issues
several times; he agreed with my approach to Patrushev. In typical
Cold War style, Patrushev and I started with arms control and nonproliferation, particularly Iran and North Korea. The Russians followed
Putin's approach in our Moscow meeting, focusing on "strategic stability," their foundational phrase for attacking our withdrawal from the
ABM Treaty. They asserted, which they had not done in 2001 when we
withdrew, that missile defense was inherently destabilizing strategically, and they clearly wanted more-detailed negotiations between the
two security councils on this proposition. I quickly disabused them
of that notion and then explained again that we had withdrawn from
the ABM Treaty to deal, at least initially, with threats to the homeland
from emerging nuclear-weapons states and accidental launches from
Russia and China. Patrushev said our respective levels of trust would
define how successful we will be, pointing to the INF Treaty, where
he claimed there were "conflicting" claims of "compliance." That was
pure propaganda. Russia had been violating the INF Treaty for well
over a decade, a point made repeatedly during the Obama Administration, to no avail whatever. As with all US treaties, the Defense and

State Departments were overgrown with lawyers; we couldn't violate a treaty if we wanted to.

As usual, the Russians had a long list of alleged US violations to discuss in excruciating detail; we had an even longer list of actual Russian violations I emphatically did not want to waste time on. We considered the theoretical possibility of "universalizing" the INF by bringing in China, Iran, and others, but it was a fantasy that they would voluntarily destroy large quantities of their existing missile arsenals, which would be necessary to comply with the treaty's terms. Instead, I wanted to make clear that US withdrawal from the INF was a real possibility, even though there was no official US position, something that must have astounded them.

I also said it was unlikely we could agree to a five-year extension of Obama's New START,[1] which Moscow and most US liberals were praying for. There were many reasons not to succumb to a knee-jerk extension, including the need to involve China in strategic-weapons negotiations for the first time, a view that I could see took the Russians by surprise. We also needed to cover tactical nuclear weapons (which New START did not) and new technologies being pursued aggressively by Russia and China (such as hypersonic glide vehicles) that were only in the early stages of design when New START was adopted in 2010, as I explained at some length. Finally, we needed to consider returning to the conceptually far simpler model of the 2002 Treaty of Moscow (negotiated by yours truly). There was much more to cover, but this was a good start. After Geneva, I went to Kiev to participate in Ukraine's Independence Day ceremonies and to confer with President Petro Poroshenko, his Prime Minister, and other officials. I briefed them on the INF discussions, which directly affected their defense planning. Who knew that just over a year later, Ukraine would figure so centrally in US politics?

On returning to Washington, I spent the next months preparing for the dramatic step of INF withdrawal. To prevent leaks that would agitate the press and foreign-policy establishment, I thought we should pursue a quiet, low-profile, but expedited approach, rather than endless meetings among staffers who had lived with the INF Treaty their entire government careers and couldn't bear to see it die. Trump, I believed, was on board, although I was never certain he understood the INF Treaty did not regulate nuclear weapons as such, but only their delivery vehicles. I wanted to launch US withdrawal from the treaty (which would be an important signal to China, among others), or possibly even mutual withdrawal, before my next meeting with Patrushev, in Moscow, in late October. Experience taught me that without action-forcing deadlines, bureaucracies could resist change with incredible tenacity and success.

We also needed to prepare our NATO allies for the INF's demise. Too many European political leaders believed they lived beyond "the end of history" and that nothing external should be allowed to roil their contented continent. It was a nice thought: tell it to Russia and China, not to mention all Europe's good friends in Iran. An example of the conversations we needed to have took place on October 3 with German Foreign Minister Heiko Maas. Maas, a Social Democrat, was part of Merkel's coalition, and doubtless an INF supporter. I didn't say how far along our thinking was, but I emphasized that Europe was already under growing threat as Russia proceeded unchallenged. I also explained why we wouldn't be discussing "strategic stability" with Moscow, meaning what Russia didn't like about America's national missile-defense program, which we had no intention of negotiating, let alone modifying or abandoning.

The best news came when Mattis and I had breakfast in the Ward Room a couple of days later (Pompeo being away), following a just-concluded NATO Defense Ministers' meeting. He had explained at length to his counterparts that Russia was in material breach of the INF, and he believed they fully understood. Mattis recommended that Pompeo repeat these arguments the first week in December at the NATO Foreign Ministers' meeting, giving Russia, say, ninety days to return to compliance with the treaty, or the US would withdraw. I thought we should skip the ninety-day pause, since there was no way Russia was coming back into compliance. Besides, the treaty itself provided, following notice of withdrawal, a six-month waiting period before withdrawal became effective. This was a standard provision in international agreements, basically the same as the ABM Treaty clause we invoked in 2001. With that built-in waiting period, there was no reason to give Moscow more time to sow further confusion and uncertainty among the Europeans; I urged we give notice and start the 180-day withdrawal clock running.

At one of our weekly breakfasts, on October 11, Mattis, Pompeo, and I confirmed we still all favored withdrawal. Mattis, however, was averse to mutual withdrawal, fearing it implied "moral equivalence." None of us believed there was moral equivalence, and notwithstanding Mattis's point, mutual withdrawal would give Trump something he could announce as a "success" with Russia, perhaps thereby reducing the pressure to make real concessions in other areas. I called NATO Secretary General Stoltenberg that afternoon and explained where we were headed. He stressed we shouldn't give Russia the pleasure of dividing us, especially from Germany. I agreed but explained to Stoltenberg and all who would listen that US withdrawal from the INF didn't threaten Europe. What *was* threatening were Russian violations of the treaty, and the capability they now possessed to strike most of Europe with INF-noncompliant missiles. Stoltenberg asked what we understood "material breach" to mean and whether we had totally given up on Russia coming back into compliance. As to "material breach," I thought Mattis's presentation at the Defense Ministers' meeting had proved "materiality" by anyone's definition. As for Russia, did anyone seriously believe they would junk existing assets that violated the treaty, especially since China's growing missile threat along its Asian borders was likely driving Moscow as much or more than what it was seeking to achieve in Europe? Stoltenberg was optimistic that we could play our cards right on this issue.

On October 17, before my meeting with Patrushev in Moscow the following week, I briefed Trump on where things stood, including all the interagency work we had done, our preliminary diplomacy with NATO allies and others, and our likely schedule for withdrawal, kicked off on December 4 by Pompeo's giving Russia notice to resume compliance or else. Trump responded, "Why do we have to wait so long? Why can't we just get out?" I said I was certainly ready. I explained that once we announced our intention to withdraw, the Russians would likely do the same, accusing us of violating the treaty, which was untrue but which could involve us in a series of recriminatory statements between Moscow and Washington. Instead, I suggested, why didn't I ask Patrushev that the two countries withdraw mutually; this approach could spare us a lot of grief and allow us to announce an agreement with Russia on something of importance. Trump, however, said, "I don't want to do that. I just want to get out." I had thought mutually withdrawing would be a more appealing route to Trump, but if not, so be it. For myself, I couldn't have cared less what Moscow did.

I left Joint Base Andrews on Saturday, flying uneventfully for all of twenty minutes until we saw that, responding to a reporter's question at an Elko, Nevada, campaign rally, Trump had said we were leaving the INF Treaty. My first thought was, "Well, that settles that." It wasn't the timing that Mattis, Pompeo, and I had agreed on, but apparently Trump had decided that "now" was better (subject, of course, to the treaty's 180-day waiting period). I immediately called Sanders in Washington, who hadn't heard Trump's remark, and suggested we quickly draft a statement to embody his comment, with which she agreed. I then called Pompeo, who said it was "horrific" Trump could make an announcement as significant as withdrawing from the INF just in response to a reporter's question, a rare occasion of Pompeo's being explicitly critical of something Trump did. I didn't agree, since all he had really done was accelerate our timetable, which was fine with me. As long as the decision was public, we might as well give formal notice of withdrawal to start the six-month clock ticking. I said we should also announce the immediate suspension of our treaty obligations, thus allowing us to begin the race to catch up to Russia, China, and other INF-capable countries. I had the NSC staff on the plane with me start calling their colleagues at State and Defense to get busy on drafting and clearing a statement. Unfortunately, the statement never got issued, for reasons I do not even now understand, but almost certainly because Mattis and possibly Pompeo didn't want to act on what Trump had already publicly said.

After refueling at Shannon, Ireland, we headed off to Moscow, and

I called Stoltenberg Sunday morning Europe time. He had, by then, heard about Trump's statement. I explained what had happened and that now we would simply accelerate our consultations with allies and others, because we obviously couldn't walk back what Trump had said openly. Stoltenberg was worried that, as of now, a NATO resolution on withdrawal would not be unanimous, and he wanted time to make it so. That was fine, since none of us had contemplated a NATO resolution this early anyway. Stoltenberg wasn't as panicky as some Europeans, but he was obviously nervous. I said I would report back after my meetings with the Russians.

When I landed in Moscow, Ambassador Jon Huntsman met me and said the Russians were agitating, playing on Europeans' fears we were abandoning them, leaving them defenseless. This line had also swept Europe during the ABM Treaty withdrawal. It hadn't been true then and wasn't true now. Someone should have said, "Steady in the ranks, Europeans." In any case, I still didn't know why Trump had made his Nevada comments or why the statement elaborating on them hadn't been issued. Inexplicably, Ricardel received word of a four p.m. Sunday meeting with Trump at the Residence, requested by Mattis. I called Pompeo, who didn't understand why the meeting was urgent, even after speaking with Mattis on Saturday. Pompeo believed Mattis would ask to return to our original timetable for announcing the withdrawal, not for reopening the underlying decision. Since Trump had already effectively made the announcement, I didn't see how to roll it back, and Pompeo agreed. There was no dispute we needed more discussions with our allies, but we were now in a fundamentally different position than before Trump's comments. Why not, therefore, file notice of withdrawal, suspend our treaty obligations, and get moving? Pompeo said that was what Mattis wanted to avoid, which led me to wonder if Mattis really only wanted to slow the pace of withdrawal, or if he had changed his mind on withdrawing and was now trying to play for time. I could imagine that Washington's High-Minded were already on the phone to Mattis, and I was intrigued he hadn't bothered to call me, rushing instead to schedule a weekend meeting when I was out of town. I asked Pompeo what he thought about the timing issue. He said he was agnostic and could live with it either way.

My meeting with Patrushev the next day was at 1A Olsufyevskiy Pereulok, which he happily described as the former headquarters of the FSB's "Alfa Group" of the Spetsnaz, or special forces, formed by the KGB in 1974. Alfa Group was a "counterterrorism task force," helping remind us, I thought, of Patrushev's prior role as head of the FSB. We again started off with arms control, as the Russians solemnly advised us that official Russian doctrine had no plans to use military power for offensive goals, and that defensive power was the key to strategic stability. Patrushev explained why they didn't want us to exit the INF, noting the critiques of our decision by certain of our helpful European allies. In response, I laid out the reasons we felt Russia was in violation and why the capabilities of China, Iran, and others made it impossible to universalize the treaty, as we had once thought possible. Former Foreign Minister Igor Ivanov best summed up the Russian reaction: "If you want to leave, go ahead, but Russia will stay in." That was fine by me.

We were then treated to a lecture on our alleged violations of New START. For the second time I explained to Patrushev and his delegation why it was unlikely we would simply extend New START, given the ratification debates, where many Republicans objected that key issues, such as tactical nuclear weapons, were not addressed at all. I pressed again for a 2002 Treaty of Moscow format, which was simpler, clearer, and had worked well. Patrushev did not dismiss the idea. Instead, he stressed that the 2002 treaty was more complicated than it seemed because it relied on START II verification provisions, which was not quite true, but I didn't take time to revisit the issue. What struck me was that, even with the INF disappearing, they seemed willing to consider the 2002 model. There might yet be hope.

Late in the afternoon, with the day's meetings concluded except for a dinner hosted by Foreign Minister Lavrov at Osobnyak, I called Ricardel to see what had happened at the Sunday meeting with Trump. She said Mattis had started with a filibuster on the eighteen-month plan he had to withdraw from the INF, which was now in shreds. He wanted to return to where we were before Trump spoke in Nevada and put out a press statement to that effect. I still couldn't comprehend how we could roll the clock back, pretending we were consulting about *whether* to leave the treaty, or that Russia *might* take some action to return to compliance (as to which there was not the slightest hint). What was the purpose of this charade? Trump said he didn't see any reason not to proceed with withdrawing as he had said, but he didn't object to making a formal announcement on December 4, which was contradictory and ignored the new reality his own statement had created. After the Trump meeting, Mattis, Pompeo, and Ricardel argued over Mattis's draft statement, which at best muddied the waters, but which in fact was aimed at rolling back what Trump had said. I told Ricardel to do everything she could to kill it.

The whole thing baffled me, but Trump made it even more moot (if that was possible) later in the day Monday, in another of his customary press encounters as he left the South Entrance to board Marine One. He said, "I'm terminating the agreement. Russia violated it. I'm terminating it . . ." Asked if that was a threat to Putin, Trump answered, "It's a threat to whoever you want. It includes China, and it includes Russia, and whoever wants to play that game. You can't play that game on me."[2] What else was there to say? I didn't realize it at the time, but I wondered later, with Mattis's resignation just two months away, whether this was his attempt at legacy creation, to show he had fought to the end to preserve the INF. The whole affair was a waste of time and energy, not to mention confusing to foreign friend and foe alike. I spoke with Pompeo later in the afternoon, and he insisted that Mattis was not really seeking any change in policy. I felt far away and frustrated, but I determined I would continue working to minimize the available time for opponents of our withdrawal to undo what Trump had already now said twice publicly. At about four p.m. Moscow time, I called Trump, and he confirmed that he couldn't see what all the fuss was about or why Mattis thought it was so important. I told Trump I was telling the Russians he had clearly stated we were getting out, and Trump said, "I like our way of doing it." That was all I needed.

The next day, I met with Russian Defense Minister Sergei Shoygu.

With respect to the INF, he appeared less concerned than Mattis. He said (through an interpreter) that Trump's message was unambiguous, and that the Russians had heard it clearly. He went further, saying that under current circumstances, a reasonable man could see the situation under the INF Treaty was unrealistic because of China and changes in technology since the 1987 INF. Shoygu favored trying to rewrite the treaty to get others to join it, because he thought our unilateral withdrawal was favorable only to our common enemies, which he repeated later. I thought the implicit reference to China was unmistakable. Shoygu added that it had been a while since it was signed, and the challenge was that the technologies were in the possession of countries that shouldn't have them. I remember him concluding by agreeing that the effectiveness of the Treaty had expired. This was the most sensible thing anyone in Russia said on the issue. Interestingly, Shoygu and Mattis had never met, and, indeed, as of then, Pompeo and Lavrov had not yet met, and here I was talking to these Russians all the time.

That afternoon, Huntsman and I placed a wreath on a bridge near the Kremlin, less than a hundred yards from St. Basil's Cathedral, where Boris Nemtsov had been murdered, many believed by Kremlin operatives. We then placed a wreath at Russia's Tomb of the Unknown Soldier, along the Kremlin wall, a ceremony I had first attended with Donald Rumsfeld almost exactly eighteen years earlier. My meeting with Putin followed right afterward, beginning precisely the same as the prior meeting, same ornately decorated room, same arrangements, same conference table. Putin was obviously determined to make the point while the media was present that he was unhappy the US had withdrawn from the INF Treaty. He noted that the eagle in the Great Seal of the United States is clutching olive branches in one talon (although he failed to note the eagle is clutching arrows in the other) and asked if the eagle had eaten all the olives. I said I hadn't brought any new olives with me. So much for Soviet-style banter.

Once the press exited, Putin said he had received reports on my earlier meetings and that their side valued our contacts a lot, and that it was always a pleasure to meet with me. We discussed our respective positions on the INF at length, but what really interested Putin was "What comes next?," meaning what were we contemplating regarding deployment in Europe? Having made the point earlier that Russia and America were effectively the only two countries bound by the INF, I replied that I thought Putin had said at our last meeting that Russia understood the strategic implications of that fact, meaning China's large and growing ballistic and hypersonic glide missile capabilities. Putin agreed that he had acknowledged the China issue but said he had not mentioned wishing to pull out of the INF, agreeing with my point that Russia and the United States were the only two countries bound by the treaty. As for now, he continued, withdrawal was not the most important point, but rather what Washington's future plans would be. As I would reiterate in my subsequent press conference, I told him that the US had not yet made any final decisions regarding future deployments.[3] Obviously, Putin was most worried about what we might deploy in Europe, and later that week he saw a way to intimidate the Europeans by implying we were returning to the mid-1980s confrontation over deploying US Pershing II missiles. Putin made that very point publicly, threatening to target any country that accepted US missiles noncompliant with INF terms.[4] Of course, *Russia was already doing just that through its deployments in Kaliningrad, among other things*, which was a major reason we were exiting the treaty.

Putin recalled that both of us were lawyers, saying, "We could go on talking like this until dawn," and we then exchanged jokes about lawyers. On New START, we reviewed our respective positions, and I again pressed the benefits of reverting to a Treaty of Moscow–type agreement. Why go through the agony of renegotiating New START, adding, for example, reductions or limitations on tactical nuclear weapons, which were of major importance to the US given the large number of such weapons Russia had?[5] In response to Putin's questions, I said we had no intention of withdrawing from New START, but we were also essentially certain not to allow it simply to be extended for five years as Russia was asking (along with almost all Senate Democrats). Fortunately, we avoided long discussions of who was, and who was not, violating the INF or New START, but I urged that such detours showed how disruptive such treaties could be, rather than advancing the much-touted objective of easing tensions.

On Syria, Putin emphasized that Russians had no need of an Iranian presence, and that the right thing for both of us to do was to incentivize them to leave. He mentioned that he had discussed the topic with Netanyahu. I pointed out that having withdrawn from the Iran nuclear deal, the US was reimposing sanctions on Iran, which we expected to bite sharply, and they were not tradable just to get Iran out of Syria. Putin said that he understood our logic, and acknowledged our view that the people of Iran were tired of the regime. He cautioned, however, that if we declared war against them economically, it would consolidate support for the regime. I explained why we didn't see it that way, and why strong sanctions would reduce support for the regime, which was already under enormous stress. Putin also acknowledged that we each had our theories about how to deal with Iran, and we would see which one worked out. Putin joked at our expense over Saudi Arabia and the Khashoggi murder, saying Russia would sell the Saudis arms if we didn't, which was undoubtedly correct, and underscored why Trump didn't want to renounce our pending arms sales. We ended at about 7:05, after an hour and three-quarters. (Putin subsequently told Trump at the November 11 Armistice Day centenary in Paris that he and I had a nice conversation in Moscow, and that I was very professional and specific, not that that had any impact on Trump.) As we were shaking hands good-bye, Putin smiled and said he saw that I was going to the Caucasus.

I returned home feeling that Russia, always happy to pin the blame on us, especially with perennially nervous Europeans, would run a pro forma opposition campaign against our INF withdrawal, irritating but not threatening. I did not foresee a major propaganda effort or anything that could frustrate our ultimate withdrawal. In the meantime, briefings to NATO allies in Brussels and in capitals were going well. Flying back from Tbilisi, my last stop, I spoke to Stoltenberg, who said more and more allies now understood the logic of our position. He also said, however, that several countries still resisted admitting that Russia was violating the INF because they were afraid that if they agreed the

Russians were in violation it might mean that one day down the road they therefore might have to accept nuclear weapons on their territory. This was crazy, in my view: NATO allies were prepared to deny reality because they feared the consequences of admitting it. Did they really believe if they didn't admit it, it wouldn't be true? Many pressed for more delay before withdrawal, a thinly veiled way to buy time to prevent it altogether, which is why Mattis's palpable obstructionism worried me. In Paris for the Armistice Day centenary in November, I met with Sedwill, Étienne, and Jan Hecker (our German counterpart) to discuss Germany's desire for another sixty-day delay in our withdrawal. I didn't agree to it, especially given Trump's evident desire to exit sooner rather than later, but the issue remained unresolved.

At a mid-November Association of Southeast Asian Nations Summit in Singapore, where I accompanied Vice President Pence, we had an impromptu "pull aside" bilateral with Putin in a corner of the large conference room. We were surrounded by Secret Service and other security personnel, so we drew a lot of attention as others were departing. Pence wanted to raise the issue of Russian election meddling, but the discussion quickly turned elsewhere. Putin asked where things stood on meeting with Trump at the upcoming G20 meeting in Argentina, to discuss strategic stability and New START, which would certainly be interesting. Putin seemed to have lost interest in the INF, saying to me (through an interpreter) that he understood our arguments and logic on the decision to withdraw from the INF, which I took to be an acknowledgment of our shared view on China. I said we would get back to them on scheduling for the G20.

Germany, however, continued to press for delay, so I explained to Trump on November 26 that we should announce withdrawal at the December 4 NATO Foreign Ministers' meeting, rather than give Germany another sixty days. Russia was still trying to intimidate the Europeans, and the risk of further delays was simply not worth it. Trump agreed, also now worried that further delays would make us look weak in Russia's eyes. Trump was in the right place. The next day, we were at it again, in a meeting with Trump on other subjects, when Mattis advocated the German position of an additional sixty days' delay. Was he working some unspoken agenda? I urged Trump yet again to pull the trigger on December 4, and he said, "I agree. This is going to be a win for John. We'll announce withdrawal on December 4." I then pressed him to announce simultaneously the suspension of our treaty obligations because of Russia's material breach, a concept separate from withdrawal, which would allow us to begin "violating" the treaty even as the 180-day clock was ticking, and Trump agreed. Kelly, also present, asked, "So, the full Monty, sir?" and Trump said, "Yes."

But, of course, it wasn't really over, and at the Buenos Aires G20 on December 1, Merkel took one more shot in her bilateral with Trump. She said she completely agreed that Russia was in violation, but complained that there had been no political talks between Russia and the US, which was nonsense, since we had held just such talks not only under Trump but even under Obama. Trump asked what I thought, and I urged him again to proceed as planned, giving notice of withdrawal on December 4. Trump said he didn't want to look weak to Russia, and Merkel promised she would back us if we gave her sixty days. After several more minutes of back-and-forth, Trump said he agreed with me but nonetheless would give Merkel the two months she wanted, so long as we could definitely leave the INF then. Pompeo and I stressed that it was just two months, and Merkel agreed. I then urged that, at that point in time, the Germans would say they "support" our decision to withdraw, and not use some other word (like "understand," which Hecker had previously tried with me), and Merkel agreed. I figured that was all I could get, but it was precious little compared to the potential agony we might endure by pulling the Band-Aid off slowly. We discussed explaining this to NATO allies, and Trump proposed saying, "At the request of Germany and others, we will terminate the INF Treaty sixty days from now." It struck me he still didn't appreciate the 180-day clock that had to run before withdrawal actually took effect, but it was too late by then to reopen the discussion.

The December 4 announcement went well, and we filed notice of withdrawal on February 1, 2019. The Russians announced immediate suspension of any new arms-control negotiations, an unexpected side benefit. The high priest of US arms controllers called me a "nuclear arms agreement hitman," which I took as a compliment. There was some fussing as the months wore on, but at 12:01 a.m. on Friday, August 2, the US broke free of the INF Treaty. A great day!

Other bilateral and multilateral treaties involving Russia and the United States should also come under the ax, not to mention numerous multilateral agreements the US has unwisely made. Trump, for example, readily agreed to unsign the Obama-era Arms Trade Treaty, which had never been ratified by the Senate, but which anti-gun-control groups in the US had long opposed, dating back to my days as an Under Secretary of State in the Bush 43 Administration.[6] Speaking to the annual NRA convention on April 26, 2019, in Indianapolis, Trump received a standing ovation while he actually unsigned the agreement right in front of the audience.

Trump also unsigned the Paris Agreement on climate change, a move I supported. That deal had all of the real-world impact on climate change of telling your prayer beads and lighting candles in church (which someone will try to forbid soon because of the carbon footprint of all those burning candles). The agreement simply requires signatories to set national goals but doesn't say what those goals should be, nor does it contain enforcement mechanisms. This is theology masquerading as policy, an increasingly common phenomenon in international affairs.

The list of other agreements to discard is long, including the Law of the Sea Convention and two others from which the US should be immediately unshackled. The 1992 Treaty on Open Skies (which only entered into force in 2002) in theory allows unarmed military surveillance flights over the territories of its thirty-plus signatories but has been contentious since its inception.[7] It has proven a boon to Russia[8] but is outdated and essentially valueless to the United States because we no longer need to overfly their territory. Withdrawing the US would clearly be in our national interest, denying Russia, for example, the ability to conduct low-altitude flights over Washington, DC, and other highly sensitive locations. When I resigned, consideration was under way regarding leaving Open Skies, and press reports indicated these efforts, which I still fully support, were continuing.[9]

Similarly, unsigning the Comprehensive Nuclear-Test-Ban Treaty should be a priority, so the United States can once again conduct underground nuclear testing. We have not tested nuclear weapons since 1992, and while we have extensive programs to verify the safety and reliability of our stockpile, there is no absolute certainty without testing. We never ratified the Comprehensive Nuclear-Test-Ban Treaty, but we are caught in "international law" limbo. Article 18 of the Vienna Convention on the Law of Treaties, arguably based on "customary international law," provides that a country that has signed but not ratified a treaty is prohibited from taking actions that would defeat "the object and purpose" of the treaty. Unsigning the Comprehensive Nuclear-Test-Ban Treaty would make it clear the US will make future judgments on underground nuclear testing based on its own national interests. Ironically, the US has signed but never ratified the Vienna Convention, and the applicability of "customary international law" is subject to heated debate.[10] Other nuclear powers like China and India have either not ratified or not signed the treaty, which is why it has still not entered into force. The US has unsigned other treaties, most notably under Bush 43 when we unsigned the Rome Statute establishing the International Criminal Court.[11]

Protecting US Elections from Acts of War

During the 2016 campaign, I called Russian efforts to interfere in the elections an "act of war" against our constitutional structures,[12] and I watched with dismay reports of Putin's meeting with Trump at the 2017 G20 meeting in Hamburg, Germany, where Putin flatly denied any Russian interference.[13]

We needed not just a law-enforcement response to international cyber threats, but substantial military and clandestine capabilities as well. Accordingly, one of the first things I addressed was our ability to undertake offensive cyber operations against our adversaries, including terrorist groups and other "nonstate actors." There was a long-simmering struggle under way between those who favored the Obama

Administration's approach, believing that only defensive cyber efforts, with the rarest of exceptions, were sufficient, versus the more robust view that offensive capabilities were crucial. Obama's strategy rested on the fallacy that cyberspace was relatively benign, even unspoiled, and that the best approach was to smooth over the problems and not risk making things worse. I didn't understand why cyberspace should be materially different from the rest of human experience: initially a state of anarchy from which strength and resolve, backed by substantial offensive weaponry, could create structures of deterrence against potential adversaries that would eventually bring peace. If, as we knew with increasing certainty, Russia, China, North Korea, Iran, and others were contesting us in cyberspace,[14] it was time to fight back. Such a strategy was not designed to increase conflict in this new domain but restrain it. In reality, a defense-only strategy guaranteed more provocations, more conflict, and more damage, to both businesses and other private entities as well as to the US government.

This forward-leaning approach was hardly revolutionary. Before I arrived in the West Wing, there were extensive interagency discussions to change the Obama-era rules governing cyber decision-making. These rules so centralized authority for cyber offense, and were so bureaucratically burdensome, that actual offensive cyber actions under Obama were rare. By stressing process rather than policy, Obama inhibited US operations in cyberspace without ever having to say so explicitly, thereby evading the legitimate public debate we should have been having over this new war-fighting domain. Unfortunately, bureaucratic inertia, turf fights, and some genuine unresolved issues paralyzed the Trump Administration, month after month. That had to change. One of the first things I did was clarify lines of authority within the NSC staff dealing with national and homeland security issues, since they were at bottom exactly the same thing. I also swept away duplicative, competitive billets and fiefdoms, and made it possible for the NSC staff to speak with one voice. With the deadwood cleared away, we were off, although incredibly frustrating bureaucratic battles and obstructionism still lay ahead.

We needed to do two things: first, we needed a Trump Administration cyber strategy, and second, we needed to scrap the Obama-era rules and replace them with a more agile, expeditious decision-making structure. Considerable work had already been done by the time I arrived, but it still took an enormous effort to make the last few bureaucratic first downs to achieve finality. I often thought that if our bureaucrats struggled as hard against our foreign adversaries as they did against each other when "turf issues" were at stake, we could all rest a lot easier. Despite considerable hard slogging, it still took five months, until September 20, before we could make the new cyber strategy public.[15] Although our determination to enable offensive cyber operations got the headlines, the overall strategy was comprehensive, thoughtful, and a good beginning.[16] Even an Obama Administration cyber expert said, "This document shows what a national strategy can look like on an issue that truly is nonpartisan. It strikes a good balance between defensive actions and seeking to impose consequences on malicious actors. Further, it's clear that this strategy is a reflection of a strong policy development process across administrations."[17]

Revamping the strategy was hard enough, but shredding the old rules was actually even harder. The interagency process was frozen solid. The Department of Homeland Security and others wanted to keep a stranglehold on the Defense Department, as did the intelligence community. The Pentagon didn't want oversight from anyone, including the White House, and took an "all or nothing" approach in negotiations that only infuriated everyone else involved. As a result, policy positions had become ever more hardened in the eighteen months since the Administration began. I felt like Ulysses S. Grant before Richmond, saying, "I propose to fight it out on this line, if it takes all summer," which looked optimistic. Mattis repeatedly claimed we wouldn't be able to undertake any offensive cyber operations before the November elections (which he knew was my top priority) if his view didn't prevail, which was standard operating procedure for him: stress that the timing was urgent, which is what Mattis said when it suited him, and predict doom and gloom if he didn't get his way.

We needed to move. On August 7, we had a Principals Committee meeting that I opened by saying that for nineteen months, after scores of unproductive lower-level meetings, the Trump Administration had failed to replace Obama's rules. We now had a draft presidential memorandum that gave policymakers more flexibility and discretion, but without excluding from decision-making those with legitimate stakes in the outcome. I said that if there were still dissents, I would put them before the President to get a decision. That got everyone's attention. As in many of these Cabinet-level meetings, however, several of the "principals" could only speak from prepared talking points, relying on their staff to help them. I felt there should be a rule that if it wasn't important enough for Cabinet Secretaries personally to understand the issues, they should not be in the meeting at all. Mattis still wanted major changes, but Gina Haspel, Sue Gordon (Dan Coats's Deputy), and Jeff Sessions (and the FBI) all liked the draft as it was. Pompeo and Mnuchin had little to say but did not disagree. Unfortunately, Mattis either couldn't or wouldn't explain the reasons for the changes he wanted. In the Administration's first year-plus, I had been told, the common pattern was that Mattis would hold forth, Tillerson would agree, everyone else would fold without significant comment, thereby ending the meeting. That may have worked earlier, but I wasn't having it. I ended the meeting saying we had broad consensus on the way ahead (even if Mattis didn't agree), and I hoped we could move rapidly to finalize the draft decision memorandum.

Mattis left quickly, but Defense lawyers and others hung around and agreed we were very close to something the department could live with, Mattis notwithstanding. Over the next few days of detailed negotiations, Mattis remained obdurate and there was some backsliding by elements of the intelligence community, which was jealous of the National Security Agency's authority. This reflected a long-standing, almost existential, CIA-Pentagon tension. Nonetheless, I told Trump we were making progress. After internal White House bureaucratic delays too tedious and inexplicable to recount, on August 15, Trump signed our directive and we were launched. We focused initially on election-related matters to get a fast start on creating deterrence against interference not only in 2018 but also in future US elections. Other steps would follow to lay the foundation for a comprehensive cyber capability.

We also drafted a new Executive Order, under existing presidential authorities, making it easier to carry out sanctions against foreign efforts to interfere with elections.[18] This avoided obtaining new legislation, which almost certainly would have been gridlocked in partisan wrangling. Even some Republicans, fearful of Trump's weak responses to Russian provocations, wanted to pursue legislation, but we patiently explained why our Executive Order would actually be more effective, without the partisan sniping any legislation would inevitably produce. Most important, there was no guarantee Congress could even get its act together before the 2018 election, and the imperative had to be moving quickly. On September 12, sitting in his small dining room with a number of people discussing the Mexico border-wall issue, I explained to Trump the thinking behind the Executive Order: it was a way to show our diligence and rebut criticisms about the Administration's not being aggressive in defending election integrity, as well as to hold off ill-advised action by Congress. He asked, "Whose idea is this?" and I said it was mine, whereupon he said, "Oh," and signed the order. As Shahira Knight, then the White House Director of Legislative Affairs, said to me later, happy to have the prospect of elections legislation effectively foreclosed, "Congratulations, that was amazing."

By the end of September, we had a substantial election-security policy framework in place, and we could accelerate our efforts to safeguard the November 2018 elections, not that we hadn't already been hard at work on defenses well beyond cybersecurity alone. Just a month after I arrived, on May 3, 2018, Sessions, FBI Director Wray, Department of Homeland Security Secretary Kirstjen Nielsen, Director of National Intelligence Coats, and others briefed Trump on what was already under way to increase security for November. Trump wanted the operating agencies to be more visible in generating news about the extensive work being done, which the media was underreporting. And indeed, the departments and agencies themselves felt they were doing a good job, they knew what the threat was, and no one was holding them back from trying to defend against it. We held a second NSC meeting on July 27 to take another look at our efforts, with all the operating agencies reporting they were substantially better prepared than they had been at this stage of the 2016 campaign and much more aware of the kinds of threats they would face in their respective areas.

We followed up this NSC meeting with a briefing in the White House press room on August 2, featuring Coats; Nielsen; Wray; General Paul Nakasone, Director of the National Security Agency, which was also the home of US Cyber Command; and myself. Each official told the story of what their agency was doing, which we should have done earlier, and the briefing was well received, if grudgingly, by the press. One story called the briefing an Administration "show of force" to prove we were actually doing something on election meddling. Unable to criticize the adequacy of the overall effort, the media therefore turned to saying Trump was following one policy and we were following another.[19] Unfortunately, there was something to that, as Trump repeatedly objected to criticizing Russia and pressed us not to be so critical of Russia publicly.

All this preparatory work was essential, especially because it might be necessary to brief Congress on particular threats. Within the limited group of agencies that had offensive cyber interests at stake, there were clear divisions of opinion on what to share with Congress and how quickly it would get into the press. These were often complex issues, since one of our adversaries' objectives was not just to affect particular elections, but to sow fear and mistrust throughout the body politic, thus undermining citizen confidence in the integrity of the system as a whole. With uncertain, incomplete information, from which hard conclusions did not immediately emerge, it could cause more damage to disclose it prematurely and too broadly, thus risking its becoming ammunition in partisan political battles. I did not believe we should be doing the attackers' work for them, spreading misinformation, whether to Congress or campaigns potentially under attack. Fortunately, foreign interference was sufficiently reduced in 2018 that the few incidents we had were ultimately resolved satisfactorily. But it was clear that the "posterior covering" instincts of some officials and bureaucracies were potentially serious problems if the stakes ever increased.

The Trump Administration had imposed substantial new economic sanctions on Russian citizens and entities in 2017, related to the Crimea annexation, adding to what Obama had done, as well as extending other sanctions; closed the Russian consulates in San Francisco and Seattle; expelled more than sixty Russian intelligence agents (operating in the US as "diplomats") after Moscow's attack on the Skripals;[20] imposed sanctions for violating the Chemical and Biological Weapons Control and Warfare Elimination Act, also required by the attack on the Skripals; sanctioned Russia's Internet Research Agency, an arm of Russia's cyber-offense machinery; and penalized over three dozen Russian officials for violations of US Syria-related sanctions.[21] As new violations were uncovered, further sanctions were imposed on each person and corporate entity involved.

Trump touted these as major achievements, but almost all of them occasioned opposition, or at least extended grumbling and complaining, from Trump himself. One example involved the sanctions related to the chemical-weapons attack on the Skripals. This statute had only recently been used for the first time, after Kim Jong Un ordered his half brother murdered in Malaysia via chemical weapons, and after the Assad regime's chemical-weapons attacks in Syria. There was criticism that the sanctions imposed were not sweeping enough, but Trump objected to having any sanctions at all. Trump finally approved sanctions before the Helsinki summit but postponed announcing them until the summit ended. We explained to Trump that these sanctions were only the first in what was likely a series, since the applicable statute provided for ever-more-stringent sanctions if the accused nation did not provide convincing evidence it had given up chemical and/or biological weapons, including allowing international inspectors to verify compliance. No one believed Russia would do so. When Helsinki concluded, State announced the sanctions, since no new decision was required. Trump, upon hearing the news, wanted to rescind them. I wondered if this entire crisis was caused by Rand Paul's recent visit to Moscow, which generated significant press coverage for him and where the Russians doubtless stressed that they were very unhappy about the sanctions. This was ironic, with libertarian politicians like Paul so worried about the Kremlin's tender sensibilities. Hearing of the controversy, Mnuchin called Pompeo and me to blame us for not telling him about the new sanctions, which was inaccurate because the sanctions had previously gone through a National Security Council review process without objection from anyone. Within hours, Trump concluded he was relaxed about this particular decision, but he still thought we were being too tough on Putin. Trump told Pompeo to call Lavrov and say "some bureaucrat" had published the sanctions—a call that may or may not have ever taken place.

In addition to objecting to sanctions, Trump stopped an anodyne statement criticizing Russia on the tenth anniversary of its invasion of Georgia, a completely unforced error. Russia would have ignored it, but the Europeans noticed its absence and became even more concerned about American resolve. This was typical of Trump, who in June 2019 also blocked a draft statement on the thirtieth anniversary of the Tiananmen Square massacres and criticized the State Department for a press release issued before he knew about it. Trump seemed to think that criticizing the policies and actions of foreign governments made it harder for him to have good personal relations with their leaders. This was a reflection of his difficulty in separating personal from official relations. I'm not aware of any case where Russia or China refrained from criticizing the United States for fear of irritating our sensitive leaders.

Trump's inconsistent views and decisions on Russia made all our work complicated, and cyber and noncyber issues often bled into each other. Moreover, establishing cyber deterrence was easier said than done, since almost all the cyber-offensive operations we wanted to undertake necessarily remained classified. So, those directly affected would know they had been hit, but not necessarily by whom unless we told them. Accordingly, there had to be some public discussion of our capabilities, to put our adversaries on notice that our years of passivity were over and to reassure our friends that America was on the march in cyberspace. In late October, I made public remarks in Washington intended to convey in broad terms what we had done to eviscerate the Obama-era rules.[22] Other Administration officials, such as General Nakasone, did the same.[23] This was a complicated field of decision, with difficult tradeoffs between what to make public and what to keep classified. The more we could tell, the greater the deterrence we could establish in the minds of publics and decision-makers around the world. But, unfortunately, the more we said publicly, the more we would reveal about capabilities that others could use to improve their own cyber programs, offensive and defensive. This is obviously an area of debate for future Administrations. But whatever Trump's own personal attitude, we had done substantial work to protect US elections, from Russia and everyone else.

CHAPTER 7

TRUMP HEADS FOR THE DOOR IN SYRIA AND AFGHANISTAN, AND CAN'T FIND IT

War by radical Islamist terrorists against the United States began long before 9/11 and will continue long after. You can like it or not, but it is reality. Donald Trump didn't like it, and acted like it wasn't true. He opposed "endless wars" in the Middle East but had no coherent plan for what followed withdrawing US forces and effectively abandoning key regional allies as the withdrawal unfolded. Trump liked to say, wrongly, it was all "thousands of miles away." By contrast, during my time at the White House I tried to operate in reality, with mixed success.

Syria: Lawrence of Arabia, Call Your Office

After our April retaliation for Assad's chemical-weapons attack on Douma, Syria reemerged indirectly, through Turkey's incarceration of Pastor Andrew Brunson. An apolitical evangelical preacher, he and his family had lived and worked in Turkey for two decades before his arrest in 2016 after a failed military coup against President Recep Tayyip Erdogan. Brunson was a bargaining chip, cynically charged as conspiring with followers of Fethullah Gulen, an Islamic teacher

living in America, once an Erdogan ally but now an enemy obses-
sively denounced as a terrorist. Just after Trump's return from Helsinki, Erdogan called to follow up on their brief encounter at NATO
(and later phone call) about Brunson and his "relationship" to Gulen.
Erdogan also raised another favorite subject, frequently discussed
with Trump: the conviction of Mehmet Atilla, a senior official of the
state-run Turkish bank Halkbank, for financial fraud stemming from
massive violations of our Iran sanctions.[1] This ongoing criminal investigation threatened Erdogan himself because of allegations he and his
family used Halkbank for personal purposes, facilitated further when
his son-in-law became Turkey's Finance Minister.[2] To Erdogan, Gulen
and his "movement" were responsible for the Halkbank charges, so it
was all part of a conspiracy against him, not to mention against his
family's growing wealth. He wanted the Halkbank case dropped, unlikely now that US prosecutors had their hooks sunk deep into the
bank's fraudulent operations. Finally, Erdogan fretted about pending
legislation in Congress that would halt the sale of F-35s to Turkey
because Ankara was purchasing Russia's S-400 air defense system. If
consummated, that purchase would also trigger mandatory sanctions
against Turkey under a 2017 anti-Russia sanctions statute. Erdogan
had a lot to worry about.

What Trump wanted, however, was very limited: when would
Brunson be released to return to America, which he thought Erdogan had pledged? Erdogan said only that the Turkish judicial process
was continuing, and Brunson was no longer imprisoned, but under
house arrest in Izmir, Turkey. Trump replied that he thought that
was very unhelpful, because he had expected to hear Erdogan tell
him that Brunson, who was just a local minister, was coming home.
Trump stressed his friendship with Erdogan, but implied it would be
impossible even for him to fix the hard issues facing the US-Turkey
relationship unless Brunson returned to the US. Trump was genu-
inely agitated. After a riff on Tillerson, and puzzled expressions about
Gulen (which Trump claimed was the first time he had heard about
it), he said incredulously (and inaccurately), that Erdogan was telling him that Brunson wouldn't be coming home. That was why no

one would do business with Erdogan, Trump complained, especially because America's entire Christian community was upset about this one pastor; they were going crazy. Erdogan answered that the Moslem community in Turkey was going crazy, but Trump interrupted to say they were going crazy all over the world, which they were free to do. If possible, the conversation went downhill thereafter.

Trump had finally found someone he relished sanctioning, saying "large sanctions" would ensue if Brunson wasn't returned to the US. On August 2, Treasury sanctioned Turkey's Justice and Interior Ministers,[3] and two days later, Turkey sanctioned their counterparts, Sessions and Nielsen, in response.[4] Although we had discussed these measures with Trump, he told me later that day he thought it was insulting to Turkey to sanction Cabinet officials. Instead, he wanted to double the existing steel tariffs on Turkey to 50 percent, which appalled the economic team. Trump had imposed worldwide steel and aluminum tariffs on national-security grounds in March 2018, under the authority of section 232 of the 1962 Trade Expansion Act, a little-known statute that found great favor in Trump trade policy. The "national security" grounds were gauzy at best; the 232 tariffs were classically protectionist. To use them now for political leverage to obtain Brunson's release violated any known statutory rationale, however worthy the cause. Trump, of course, sensed no one was going to challenge him in these circumstances. Away we went.

The Turks, worried about escalating problems with America, wanted a way out, or so we thought, trying to wrap an exchange for Brunson into the Halkbank criminal investigation. This was at best unseemly, but Trump wanted Brunson out, so Pompeo and Mnuchin negotiated with their counterparts (Mnuchin because Treasury's Office of Foreign Assets Control was also looking into Halkbank).[5] In three-way conversations, Mnuchin, Pompeo, and I agreed nothing would be done without full agreement from the Justice Department prosecutors in the Southern District of New York, where the case, involving over $20 billion in Iran sanctions violations, was pending. (In my days at the Justice Department, we called the Southern District the "Sovereign District of New York," because it so often resisted control by "Main Justice," let alone by the White House.) Several times, Mnuchin was exuberant he had reached a deal with Turkey's Finance Minister. This was typical: Whether Mnuchin was negotiating with Turkish fraudsters or Chinese trade mandarins, a deal was always in sight. In each case, the deal fell apart when Justice tanked it, which was why trying this route to get Brunson's release was never going to work. Pompeo said, "The Turks just can't get out of their own way," but it was in fact Justice prosecutors who rightly rejected deals worth next to nothing from the US government's perspective. In the meantime, Turkey's currency continued to depreciate rapidly, and its stock market wasn't doing much better.

We had a problem with multiple negotiators on both sides. Haley was conducting conversations with Turkey's UN Ambassador, which the Turks said they didn't understand. Neither did we. Pompeo said grimly he would resolve this problem by telling Haley to stop making unauthorized contacts with the Turks, confusing further what was already confused enough. Fortunately, this time it worked. Diplomatic efforts, however, produced nothing on Brunson. Trump allowed the negotiations to continue, but his instinct on Erdogan proved correct: only economic and political pressure would get Brunson released, and here at least Trump had no problem applying it despite Mnuchin's happy talk. Erdogan went almost instantly from being one of Trump's best international buddies to being a target of vehement hostility. It kept my hopes alive that Vladimir Putin, Xi Jinping, Kim Jong Un, or others would, in due course, inevitably show Trump their true colors, and we could at that moment reconnect our errant policies to reality. Also possible, of course, was Trump's returning again to "best buddy" mode, which did in fact happen here just a few months later. Ironically, although the media painted Trump as viscerally anti-Muslim, he never grasped—despite repeated efforts by key allied leaders in Europe and the Middle East and his own advisors to explain it—that Erdogan was himself a radical Islamicist. He was busy transforming Turkey from Kemal Ataturk's secular state into an Islamicist state. He supported the Muslim Brotherhood and other radicals across the Middle East, financing both Hamas and Hezbollah, not to mention being intensely hostile toward Israel, and he helped Iran to evade US sanctions. It never seemed to get through.

In the meantime, Trump tired of Turkish delays and obfuscation, and on August 10, dubious legal authority notwithstanding, he ordered Turkey's steel tariffs doubled to 50 percent and the aluminum tariffs doubled to 20 percent, probably the first time in history tariffs were raised by tweet:

> I have just authorized a doubling of Tariffs on Steel and Aluminum with respect to Turkey as their currency, the Turkish Lira, slides rapidly downward against our very strong Dollar! Aluminum will now be 20% and Steel 50%. Our relations with Turkey are not good at this time!

Turkey retaliated with its own tariffs, and Trump responded by requesting more sanctions. Mnuchin tried to slow-roll Trump on sanctions, which I thought would only frustrate him further. Then the Vice President suggested Jared Kushner call Turkey's Finance Minister, since they were both sons-in-law of their respective countries' leaders. Really, what could go wrong? I briefed Pompeo and Mnuchin on this new "son-in-law channel," and they both exploded, Mnuchin because the Turkish son-in-law was Finance Minister, his counterpart, and Pompeo because this was one more example of Kushner's doing international negotiations he shouldn't have been doing (along with the never-quite-ready Middle East peace plan). I always enjoyed bringing good news. Trump and Kushner were flying to a political fund-raiser in the Hamptons where Mnuchin had already arrived, and Kushner called me later to say Mnuchin had "calmed down." Kushner also said he had told the Turkish son-in-law he was calling in his "personal" capacity as a matter of "friendship" and in no way was signaling "weakness" to the Turks. I doubted the Turks believed any of that.

On August 20, Trump called me in Israel about a shooting that morning near the US embassy in Ankara. I had already checked the incident out, finding it to be a local criminal matter, unrelated to the US. Nonetheless, Trump wondered if we should close the embassy,

thereby increasing the heat regarding Brunson, and perhaps do something else, like canceling Turkey's F-35 contract. I called Pompeo and
others to fill them in and asked the NSC staff traveling with me to
consider what options might be available. Pompeo thought we should
declare Turkey's Ambassador persona non grata and directed State's
lawyers to contact the White House Counsel to confer further. These
steps were unorthodox, but we had spent considerable effort on Brunson and still not secured his release. In a few days, however, Trump
reversed course, deciding against doing anything on our embassy or
Turkey's Ambassador, instead returning to the idea of more sanctions.
"You have it on Turkey," he said to me, meaning, basically, figure out
what to do. He reaffirmed this view a few days later, saying, "Hit 'em,
finish 'em. You got it," and he told Merkel in a phone call that Erdogan was being very obtuse on the Brunson issue, saying we would be
imposing substantial sanctions in the next few days. The Qataris, who
were extending Turkey a massive financial lifeline,[6] also volunteered to
help on Brunson, but it was hard to see their effort having any success.

In fact, there was very little progress diplomatically, even as the
effects of sanctions and the obvious split with the United States over
Brunson and other issues (such as buying Russia's S-400 air defense system) continued to wreak havoc across Turkey's economy. Turkey, urgently needing more foreign direct investment, was rapidly moving in
the opposite direction, which eventually affected its decision-making.
Its judicial system ground its way to yet another hearing on Friday,
October 12, in Izmir, where Brunson had been under house arrest
since July. With strong indications the court was working toward
releasing him, the Defense Department prepared to stage a plane in
Germany in case it was needed to retrieve Brunson and his family.
Bizarrely, the court *convicted* Brunson of espionage and related crimes
(which was ridiculous), sentenced him to five years in jail, and then
decided because of time served and other mitigating factors, he was
free to go. This outcome showed that the political fix was in: Erdogan's
claim Brunson was a spy had been "vindicated" for his domestic political purposes, but Brunson went free.[7]

At 9:35 a.m., I called Trump, who was as usual still in the Residence, and said we were 95 percent certain Brunson was out. Trump was ecstatic, immediately tweeting away, mixed in with a tweet about why Ivanka would be a great UN Ambassador. He wanted Brunson brought immediately to the White House, not stopping at the US medical facility at Landstuhl, Germany, for medical observation and care if necessary. Delays in getting the Pentagon plane to Izmir meant Brunson had to overnight in Germany anyway. In turn, that meant his visit to the White House would be Saturday afternoon, when North Carolina members of Congress, his home state, and additional family and friends would attend. After seeing the White House physician just to ensure they were ready for the wild scene about to unfold, Brunson and his wife walked to the West Wing. I spoke to them briefly, surprised to hear that Brunson had followed me for a long time and almost always agreed with me. The Brunsons went to the Residence to meet Trump and then walked with him along the colonnade to the Oval Office, where those assembled greeted them with cheers. The press mob entered as the pastor and the President talked. At the end, Brunson knelt next to Trump's chair, put his arm on Trump's shoulder, and prayed for him, which, needless to say, was the photo du jour. So the Brunson matter ended, but bilateral relations with Turkey were at their lowest ebb ever.

Before his release, however, conditions in Syria were already deteriorating. We worried in September that Assad was planning to savage Idlib Governorate,[8] long an opposition stronghold in northwestern Syria. It was now home to hundreds of thousands of internally displaced Syrians, mixed with radical terrorists, as well as a Turkish military presence intended to deter any Assad attack. Russia and Iran would almost certainly assist Assad, producing bloodshed and chaos, and launching massive refugee flows from Syria into Turkey. Along with legitimate refugees, thousands of terrorists would escape, many of whom would head to Europe, their preferred destination. I was particularly worried Assad might again use chemical weapons, and I pushed urgently for the Defense Department to think about a possible military response (hopefully again with Britain and France) in case it happened. I didn't want to be unprepared, as in

April. If required, retaliation should not again just aim at degrading Syria's chemical-weapons capability but at permanently altering Assad's proclivity to use it. This time, Mattis freed the Joint Chiefs to do what they should do; there was extensive advance planning, based on alternative assumptions, limitations (e.g., rigorously avoiding the risk of civilian casualties), and objectives. Unlike in April, I felt that if worse came to worst, we were ready to present real options for Trump to choose from.

In the meantime, Israel wasn't waiting around, repeatedly striking Iranian shipments of weapons and supplies that could be threatening.[9] Jerusalem had its own communications with Moscow, because Netanyahu was not after Russian targets or personnel, only Iranians and terrorists. Russia's real problem was its Syrian allies, who shot down a Russian surveillance plane in mid-September,[10] which also prompted Moscow to turn over elements of its S-300 air defense system to the Syrians, troubling Israel greatly.[11]

In Iraq, on Saturday, September 8, Shia militia groups, undoubtedly supplied by Iran, attacked Embassy Baghdad and our Basra consulate, and Iran launched missiles against targets near Irbil in Kurdish Iraq.[12] Coming days before the anniversary of 9/11, and with the 2012 assault on our Benghazi diplomatic compound on our minds, we needed to think strategically about our response. We did not. Kelly told me that, after a campaign event, Trump "unleashed" to him yet again on wanting out of the Middle East entirely. Dead Americans in Iraq, tragic in themselves, might accelerate withdrawal, to our long-term detriment, and that of Israel and our Arab allies, if we didn't think this through carefully. By Monday, however, our "response" was down to a possible statement condemning Iran's role in the attacks. Mattis opposed even that, still arguing we weren't absolutely sure the Shia militia groups were tied to Iran, which defied credulity. Our indecision continued until Tuesday, when Mattis precipitated an Oval Office meeting on this one-paragraph statement, with Trump, Pence, Mattis, Pompeo, Kelly, and me. It was now so late few would notice it, whatever it said. This was Mattis obstructionism at work: no kinetic response, and perhaps not even a press release responding to attacks on US diplomatic personnel and facilities. What lesson did Iran and the militias draw from our complete passivity?

Predictably, there were renewed threats by Shia militia groups within weeks, and two more rocket attacks on the Basra consulate. Pompeo decided almost immediately to close the consulate (which employed over a thousand people, including government employees and contractors) to avoid a Benghazi-like catastrophe. This time, even Mattis could not deny the Iran connection. Betraying no sense of irony, however, and still opposing any kinetic action in response, he worried that shuttering the consulate would signal we were retreating from Iraq. Nonetheless, on September 28, Pompeo announced the consulate's closure.[13] When we come to the events of summer 2019, and the shooting down of US drones and other belligerent Iranian acts in the region, remember well these Administration failures to respond to the provocations one year earlier.

Shortly thereafter, Trump flipped again on Erdogan and Turkey. With the Brunson matter now six weeks behind us, the two leaders met bilaterally on December 1 at the Buenos Aires G20 summit, largely discussing Halkbank. Erdogan provided a memo by the law firm representing Halkbank, which Trump did nothing more than flip through before declaring he believed Halkbank was totally innocent of violating US Iran sanctions. Trump asked whether we could reach Acting US Attorney General Matt Whitaker, which I sidestepped. Trump then told Erdogan he would take care of things, explaining that the Southern District prosecutors were not his people, but were Obama people, a problem that would be fixed when they were replaced by his people.

Of course, this was all nonsense, since the prosecutors were career Justice Department employees, who would have proceeded the same way if the Halkbank investigation started in the eighth year of Trump's presidency rather than the eighth year of Obama's. It was as though Trump was trying to show he had as much arbitrary authority as Erdogan, who had said twenty years earlier as mayor of Istanbul, "Democracy is like a streetcar. You ride it to the stop you want, and then you get off."[14] Trump rolled on, claiming he didn't want anything bad to happen to Erdogan or Turkey, and that he would work very hard on the issue. Erdogan also complained about Kurdish forces in Syria (which Trump didn't address) and then raised Fethullah Gulen, asking yet again that he be extradited to Turkey. Trump hypothesized that Gulen would last for only one day if he were returned to Turkey. The Turks laughed but said Gulen needn't worry, since Turkey had no death penalty. Fortunately, the bilateral ended shortly thereafter. Nothing good was going to come of this renewed bromance with yet another authoritarian foreign leader.

In fact, the Europeans had already shifted attention from the risks of an Assad assault into Idlib Governorate to concern about a Turkish attack in northeastern Syria, the triangular region east of the Euphrates River, south of Turkey, and west of Iraq. Largely under Syrian Opposition control, and dominated by Kurdish fighters, several thousand US and allied troops were deployed there to assist the continuing offensive against ISIS's territorial caliphate. Begun under Obama, whose misguided policies in Iraq contributed heavily to the emergence of ISIS and its caliphate to begin with, the offensive was finally nearing success. It was close to eliminating ISIS's territorial holdings in western Iraq and eastern Syria, although not eliminating ISIS itself, which still held the allegiance of thousands of fighters and terrorists living in and roaming through Iraq and Syria but not controlling any defined territory.

Erdogan was purportedly interested in destroying the caliphate, but his real enemy was the Kurds, who, he believed with some justification, were allied to the Kurdistan Workers' Party, or PKK, in Turkey, which the US had long considered a terrorist group. Why we were affiliated with one terrorist group in order to destroy another stemmed from Obama's failure to see that Iran was a much more serious threat, now and in the future. Many parties to this conflict opposed ISIS, including Iran, its terrorist proxy Hezbollah, and its near-satellite Syria. Tehran, however, unlike Obama, was also focusing on the next war, the one after ISIS was defeated. As the ISIS caliphate shrank, Iran was expanding its span of control in the region, leaving the US with its awkward squad of allies. That said, America had long supported Kurdish efforts for greater autonomy or even independence from Iraq, and a Kurdish state would require border adjustments for existing states in the neighborhood. It was complicated, but what was not complicated was the strong US sense of loyalty to Kurds who had fought with us against ISIS, and fear that abandoning them was not only disloyal but would have severely adverse consequences world-wide for any future effort to recruit allies who might later be seen as expendable.

In the meantime, there was turmoil at the Pentagon. On Friday, December 7, at our weekly breakfast, Mattis said somberly to Pompeo and me, "You gentlemen have more political capital than I do now," which sounded ominous. Mark Milley's nomination to succeed Dunford as Chairman of the Joint Chiefs would be announced the next day, before the Army-Navy game, but we knew it was coming. Milley, then Army Chief of Staff, had impressed Trump and won the job on his own. Mattis had tried to force his preferred candidate on Trump, but many Trump supporters believed that the last thing he needed was a Mattis clone as Chairman. By pushing prematurely, perhaps because Mattis knew he would be leaving well before Dunford's term expired on September 30, 2019, Mattis had hurt his own cause. At our next Ward Room breakfast, Thursday, December 13, the mood was decidedly unhappy for several reasons, but largely because we all felt, silently to be sure, Mattis was coming to the end of his ride. It didn't bother me that Mattis's obstructionism would be leaving with him, but his departure was part of a problematic, almost inevitable pattern. None of the three prior Republican Administrations in which I served had seen anything approaching this extent and manner of senior-level turnover.

On December 14, Trump and Erdogan spoke by phone. I briefed Trump beforehand on the situation in Syria, and he said, "We should get the hell out of there," which I feared he would also say directly to Erdogan. Trump started by saying we were getting very close to a resolution on Halkbank. He had just spoken to Mnuchin and Pompeo, and said we would be dealing with Erdogan's great son-in-law (Turkey's Finance Minister) to get it off his shoulders. Erdogan was very grateful, speaking in English no less. Then he switched to Syria. He said Trump knew Turkey's expectations regarding the YPG (a Syrian Kurdish militia, part of the Opposition Syrian Defense Forces) and the FETO (Gulenist) terrorist network, which Erdogan characterized as threats to Turkish national security which were poisoning bilateral relations between Washington and Ankara. Nonetheless, whined Erdogan, contrary to fact, America was continuing to train YPG forces, including up to 30–40,000 new recruits. He complained of the discrepancy between Trump's political will and US military activities on the ground, which were causing questions in his mind. Turkey, said Erdogan, wanted to get rid of ISIS and the PKK, although, in my view, by "PKK" he was really referring to Kurdish fighters generally.

Trump said he was ready to leave Syria if Turkey wanted to handle the rest of ISIS; Turkey could do the rest and we would just get out. Erdogan promised his word on that point, but said his forces needed logistical support. Then came the painful part. Trump said he would ask me (I was listening in to the call, as was customary) to immediately work on a plan for US withdrawal, with Turkey taking over the fight against ISIS. He said I should work it out quietly but that we were leaving because ISIS is finished. Trump asked if I could speak, which I did, saying I had heard his instructions. As the call came to an end after further discussion on Halkbank, Trump said Erdogan should work with me on the military (telling me to do a good job) and Mnuchin on Halkbank. Erdogan thanked Trump and called him a very practical leader. Shortly thereafter, Trump said we should craft a statement that we had won the fight against ISIS, we had completed our mission in Syria, and we were now getting out.[15] There was little doubt in my mind that Trump had seized on withdrawing from Syria as another campaign promise, like Afghanistan, he was determined to say he had kept. I called Mattis shortly thereafter to brief him; needless to say, he was not thrilled.

This was a personal crisis for me. I felt that withdrawing from Syria was a huge mistake, because of both the continuing global threat of ISIS and the fact that Iran's substantial influence would undoubtedly grow. I had argued to Pompeo and Mattis as far back as June that we should end our piecemeal policy in Syria, looking at one province or area at a time (e.g., Manbij, Idlib, the southwest exclusion zone, etc.), and focus on the big picture. With most of the ISIS territorial caliphate gone (although the ISIS threat itself was far from eliminated), the big picture was stopping Iran. Now, however, if the US abandoned the Kurds, they would either have to ally with Assad against Turkey, which the Kurds rightly considered the greater threat (thereby enhancing Assad, Iran's proxy), or fight on alone, facing almost certain defeat, caught in the vise between Assad and Erdogan. What to do?

First, on December 18, Mattis, Dunford, Coats, Haspel, Pompeo, and I (and a few others) convened in "the Tank" in the Pentagon, rather than the Sit Room, to attract less attention. Based on the Trump-Erdogan call, the Turks were doubtless telling anyone who would listen that we were turning northeastern Syria over to their tender mercies. The potential dangers on the ground were daunting, starting with the thousands of ISIS prisoners held by the Kurds, pending some decision on their disposition. Estimates of the actual numbers of prisoners varied, in part due to differing definitions: Were they "foreign terrorist fighters," meaning from outside the Middle East? From outside Syria and Iraq? Or local? Whatever the number, we did not want them moving en masse to the United States or Europe. In mid-December, Trump suggested bringing the ISIS prisoners in northeastern Syria to Gitmo, but Mattis objected. Trump then insisted that other countries take back their own nationals from the Kurdish camps, which was hardly unreasonable, but which foreign governments strongly resisted, not wanting the terrorists coming home. No one did, but this resistance hardly contributed to a solution. As events developed, we did not resolve the issue before I left the White House.

Finally, exactly how long would it take for the US and other coalition forces to leave in a safe and orderly fashion? Dunford's planners estimated about 120 days; it certainly wasn't a matter of 48 hours. I asked about holding on to the At Tanf exclusion zone, located inside Syria at the tri-border junction of Syria, Jordan, and Iraq, not in northeastern Syria, but which US forces held. Control of At Tanf neutralized a key border crossing point on the road between Baghdad and Damascus, which forced Iran and others to cross from Iraq into Syria at a more distant border crossing to the north. Surprisingly, Mattis was skeptical of At Tanf's worth, probably because he was focused on ISIS rather than Iran. Iran was my main concern, and I stayed firm on At Tanf throughout my time as National Security Advisor. Besides, why give territory away for nothing?

As we had agreed, Mattis, Dunford, Pompeo, and I began to call our allies to prepare them for what was about to happen, receiving no sign of support. France's Étienne told me Macron would certainly want to talk to Trump about the decision, which didn't surprise me. Other reactions were equally predictable. I was in the Oval that afternoon when Macron's call came through, and he was not happy. Trump brushed him aside, saying we were finished with ISIS, and that Turkey and Syria would take care of any remnants. Macron replied that Turkey was focused on attacking the Kurds, and would compromise with ISIS. He pleaded with Trump not to withdraw, saying that we would win in a very short time, and should finish the job. Trump agreed to consult again with his advisors, telling me I should talk to Macron's people (which I had already done), and Mattis and Dunford that they should talk to their counterparts. Almost immediately, Mattis called to say that French Defense Minister Florence Parly was not at all happy with Trump's decision. Israel's Ambassador Ron Dermer told me that this was the worst day he had experienced thus far in the Trump Administration.

The next day, Wednesday, December 19, Mattis, Pompeo, and I had our weekly breakfast in the Ward Room, dominated by Syria, notwithstanding our extensive Pentagon discussion the day before. Numerous press stories had appeared, filled with inaccuracies,[16] which I thought came largely from the Pentagon, via allies in Congress. Later in the day, Trump tweeted a video with his own explanation, and press and congressional calls were overwhelming the White House, which, other than the NSC, was yet again focused on the Mexico border wall and related immigration topics. Republicans in Congress almost uniformly opposed Trump's Syria decision but largely said they would avoid the media, an inhibition Democrats did not share. Republican acquiescence in mistaken national-security policies, however, didn't help the country or ultimately the party. I reported on the negative Hill reaction that morning, but Trump didn't believe it, probably relying again on Rand Paul's assurances that he represented the party's real base. As if this weren't enough, Turkey detained a Texas National Guardsman on duty at Incirlik air base, near Adana (which problem, unlike Brunson's, was resolved quickly).

By Thursday, Trump understood he was getting mauled by media coverage of the Syria withdrawal, which was a small fraction of what would happen if he proceeded to leave Afghanistan completely. We concluded it was not wise to set a deadline for withdrawal but stressed it should be "orderly." The Turkish military provided a potential lifeline in that regard. They knew full well there had to be military-to-military talks on an orderly transfer of power in an otherwise essentially ungoverned region before the handover Trump proposed could succeed. Those talks would take time, and indeed the US delegation was making plans to travel to Ankara only on Monday, Christmas Eve, the next week.

That afternoon, I learned that Mattis was in the Oval alone with Trump, and a previously scheduled bill-signing ceremony was running very late. As we were talking, Mattis came out, with Trump right behind him. I could tell instantly something was up. Mattis seemed stunned to see me waiting, but he shook hands without much of an expression. Trump said, "John, come on in," which I did, with just the two of us in the Oval. "He's leaving," said Trump. "I never really liked him."

After the bill-signing ceremony, Trump and I talked for roughly twenty minutes on how to handle the Mattis departure. Trump wanted to put out a tweet before Mattis's public relations machine got rolling. Mattis had given Trump a long resignation letter explaining why he was leaving, unquestionably written for widespread public distribution, which Trump had not actually read. Instead, he had simply left it on the *Resolute* desk, from which it had been removed for the bill-signing ceremony. When we retrieved the letter, I read with surprise that Mattis wanted to serve until the end of February, spending his remaining time as Secretary of Defense testifying before Congress and speaking

at the February NATO Defense Ministers' meeting. Even more surprising to Trump, given the tenor of his conversation with Mattis, was
the letter's substance, rejecting Trump's policies. I explained to Trump
that the scheduling was completely untenable, though I was not sure
it sank in. He was, however, more and more expressive about how
much he didn't like Mattis. "I created a monster when I named him
'Mad Dog,'" said Trump, which was at least partially correct. (Mattis's
real moniker was "Chaos.") I returned to my office to call Pompeo at
5:20 p.m., and by then, Trump's tweet was out and the Mattis press
blitz under way. Pompeo said Mattis had stopped by State on the way
to the White House, giving him a copy of the resignation letter. Mattis
said, "The President doesn't pay attention to me anymore. It's his way
of saying he doesn't want me. It's time to leave." I thought all these
things were true, and Pompeo agreed.

All this turmoil over Mattis, of course, affected the Syrian and parallel Afghan dramas, especially because Mattis made Trump's order
for US forces to exit Syria the determining factor in his resignation.
Nonetheless, the succession question remained. By Saturday, two
days after the Mattis meeting in the Oval, Trump told me at about
six fifteen p.m. that he wasn't waiting around for February for Mattis's departure and had decided to name Deputy Defense Secretary Pat
Shanahan as Acting Secretary of Defense. (At this point, Trump was
torn between nominating Shanahan for the job full-time and naming
retired General Jack Keane.) In addition, Trump now wanted Mattis out immediately, not even coming to the Pentagon on Monday. I
pointed out it was almost Christmas, and Trump said, "Christmas isn't
until Tuesday. We should fire him today."

On Sunday, December 23, I spoke with Trump just before a ten
a.m. call with Erdogan. Trump had just finished "a good talk" with
Shanahan, whom he had found "very impressive." Trump wondered
why he had not been so impressed in their previous encounters. He
supplied his own answer, with which I agreed, that Shanahan "had
been held down over there [at the Pentagon] by Mattis," adding, "He
loves you and Pompeo." A January 1 start date, however, would still
leave Mattis in place until December 31, and Trump was rumbling

again that he wanted him out immediately. I said I would see what could be done and then immediately called Shanahan, who was in Seattle with his family. I suggested that, Christmas or no Christmas, he should think about returning to Washington immediately. I also called Dunford, reaching him as he landed at Bagram Air Base in Afghanistan. I told him what had happened with Erdogan on Syria, and with Mattis, which he appreciated because no one else had conveyed the Pentagon news. I assured Dunford that Trump wanted him to stay as Chairman of the Joint Chiefs, which I sort of made up, but which I expected was true, and appropriate to ease any concerns with the turmoil Mattis had caused. At least for now, we seemed to be steady again.

But Syria was still in flux. Over the weekend, Trump decided he wanted another call with Erdogan to make two points: first, don't attack any US troops in Syria, and second, be sure to attack ISIS and not Kurds, both points being correct, but it was a little late to fill them in after his earlier call with Erdogan and the subsequent publicity.[17] So after greetings and opening remarks, Trump said that, first, he wanted Erdogan to get rid of ISIS, and that we would provide assistance if Turkey need it. Second, he pressed Erdogan not to go after the Kurds and kill them, noting that a lot of people liked them for fighting with us for years against ISIS. Turkey and the Kurds should go after the remaining ISIS forces together. Trump acknowledged that such a strategy might be a change for Erdogan, but he stressed again how much support there was for the Kurds in the United States. Trump then came with what he thought was the clincher: the prospect of substantially greater US trade with Turkey. Erdogan took pains to say he loved the Kurds and vice versa, but added that the YPG-PYD-PKK (three Kurdish groups in Turkey and Syria, the nine initials of which Erdogan rattled off as if spelling his own name) were manipulating the Kurds, and did not represent them. He pointed out that his government had Kurdish MP's and ministers, that the Kurds had a special love and sympathy for him, and that he was the only leader who could conduct big rallies in the Kurdish areas. He had no intention of killing anyone but terrorists. We had heard all this before, and it was standard Erdogan regime propaganda.

Rallies! What an appeal to Trump! At this point, perhaps recognizing he was being drawn into a trap on the Kurds—those Erdogan planned to decimate versus those who loved coming to hear
him, a distinction we had no business trying to help Erdogan with—
Trump asked me to say what I thought of Erdogan's comments. On
the spur of the moment, I said we should leave it to the upcoming
military-to-military discussions to distinguish the terrorists from the
non-terrorists. My feeling was that parsing this question would go absolutely nowhere, thereby postponing our departure from Syria.

Christmas Eve and Christmas Day were quiet. At nine forty-five
p.m. Christmas night, my Secret Service detail and I left for Andrews,
where, under extraordinary security precautions, Trump, the First
Lady, and a small traveling party boarded Air Force One to head for
Iraq (eight hours ahead of Washington time). I got some sleep, and
woke up in time to see that word of the trip still hadn't broken and that
security was good enough that we could continue to our destination
at al-Asad Air Base, where we expected, among other things, to meet
with Iraqi Prime Minister Adil Abdul Mahdi and several top officials.
Trump also arose "early," although it was already afternoon Iraq time,
and we spent a fair amount of time in his office chatting away because
so few others were up yet. We ranged from what he would say to the
Army and Marine troops at al-Asad and in the State of the Union address in January, to sending a New Year's greeting to Xi Jinping and
whether Trump should get the Nobel Peace Prize. Trump also raised
the widespread political rumor he would dump Pence from the ticket
in 2020 and run instead with Haley, asking what I thought. White
House gossip was common that Ivanka and Kushner favored this approach, which tied in with Haley's leaving her position as UN Ambassador in December 2018, thus allowing her to do some politicking
around the country before being named to the ticket in 2020. The political argument in Haley's favor was that she could win back women
voters alienated from Trump. By contrast, it was said, the evangelicals
supporting Pence had nowhere else to go in 2020, so their votes were
not at risk if Haley took his place. I explained it was a bad idea to
jettison someone loyal, and that doing so risked alienating people he

needed (who could stay home, even if they didn't vote for Trump's opponent) without necessarily generating new support because of the replacement. That seemed to be Trump's thinking as well.

We landed at al-Asad about seven fifteen p.m. local time, in near-total darkness and under the tightest security possible. We careened away from Air Force One in heavily armored Humvees, heading for the tent where the US commanders would meet us. As we drove along, it became clear we were not really certain whether Abdul Mahdi was actually coming or not. For security reasons, he had received minimal notice, but we heard a plane was on the way from Baghdad, the only uncertainty being whether Abdul Mahdi was on it! Greeting the President and the First Lady in the tent, arranged with tables, chairs, and flags, were Army Lieutenant General Paul LaCamera, the commander of Operation Inherent Resolve (in Iraq and Syria); Air Force Brigadier General Dan Caine (nicknamed "Raisin'"); the Deputy Commander; and several others. I wanted a little more "inherent resolve" in the Administration, so I took LaCamera aside and urged him to stress the threat from Iran in Syria, in addition to whatever else he planned to say.

If I had to pick one clear point in time that saved the US military presence in Syria (at least through the end of my White House tenure), this was it: sitting in this tent, at the makeshift conference table, with the President and First Lady at the head, and the rest of us on the sides, after the obligatory performance before the traveling press pool. The press left about eight p.m., and LaCamera and his colleagues began what I'm sure they thought would be a standard briefing, where they talked and the President listened. Were they in for a surprise! LaCamera got only as far as "It's crystal clear that we are to get out of Syria," when Trump interrupted with questions and comments. LaCamera said at one point, "I can protect our interests in Syria while withdrawing, and I can do it from here." Trump said he had told Erdogan not to attack US forces in Syria, and LaCamera and Caine were explaining what they were currently doing against ISIS when Trump asked, "Can you knock the shit out of them on the way out?" They both responded, "Yes, sir," and Trump said, "That is my order; take it out from here."

LaCamera proceeded to explain that the US had been seeking to build "partnership capacity" over the years, but Trump interrupted to say he had given repeated extensions of the time needed to defeat ISIS and was tired of doing so. He then asked, "What can we do to protect the Kurds?" and I jumped in to tell the commanders that the President had expressly told Erdogan that he didn't want harm done to the Kurds who had helped us in Syria. LaCamera and Caine explained they could finish off the ISIS territorial caliphate in the next two to four weeks. "Do it," said Trump, "you have the okay on that," asking why Mattis and others couldn't have finished the job in the last year and a half. Trump came to believe he was hearing a lot of this information for the first time, which may or may not have been true but was his view nonetheless.

As the discussion moved on, LaCamera said that the al-Asad base was also critical to keep pressure on Iran. Trump asked quizzically, "Staying in Iraq puts more pressure on Iran?" US Ambassador to Iraq Douglas Silliman answered, "Yes," emphatically, and LaCamera and others agreed. Trump began to bring the meeting to a close by saying he wanted "a vicious withdrawal" from Syria and that he saw a continuing US presence in Iraq as being "a lynchpin" for a number of reasons. I decided to press my luck, asking LaCamera and Caine about the value of the At Tanf exclusion zone. LaCamera was saying, "I haven't briefed my bosses yet—" when I interrupted, pointed to POTUS, and said, "You are now." LaCamera, to his credit, recovered quickly and said we should hold on to at Tanf. Trump responded, "Okay, and we'll decide the schedule on that later." Trump and the First Lady shortly thereafter moved off to a mess tent nearby to meet service members, and Stephen Miller, Sarah Sanders, and I stayed back with LaCamera, Caine, and the other commanders to draft a statement we could release publicly. We wrote that the President and the commanders "discussed a strong, deliberate and orderly withdrawal of US and coalition forces from Syria, and the continuing importance of the US presence in Iraq to prevent a resurgence of the ISIS territorial threat and to protect other US interests," which all agreed was a fair summary of the meeting.[18]

I thought the outcome was fantastic, not because we had a final decision on US military activity in Syria, but because Trump had come away with a very different appreciation for what we were doing and why it was important. How long it would last was a separate question, but I planned to move while the impression was strong. And why had Trump's advisors not gotten him to Iraq or Afghanistan earlier? We had all collectively failed on that score.

By the time we finished drafting the statement, it was clear Prime Minister Abdul Mahdi was not coming, a big mistake on his part. His advisors convinced him it was unseemly for Iraq's Prime Minister to meet the President on an American base, notwithstanding that our facility was completely surrounded by an Iraqi base (which had once been ours as well). They had a good phone call instead, and Trump invited Abdul Mahdi to the White House, a positive sign. We rode to a hangar, where Trump addressed the troops, receiving an enthusiastic reception. Even Americans callous about our country and indifferent to its greatness would be moved by the enthusiasm, optimism, and strength of spirit of our service members, even in the middle of the Iraqi desert. This really was America's "inherent resolve" in the flesh. The rally ended at about 10:25 p.m., and we motorcaded in the dark back to Air Force One to fly to Ramstein Air Base in Germany to refuel.

I called Pompeo to report on the Iraq visit and then talked to Shanahan and Dunford (who was in Poland, having just left al-Asad the night before). We landed at Ramstein at one forty-five a.m. German time, met with the US commanders there, and then rode to a hangar with a large crowd of service members waiting to greet the Commander in Chief (at two in the morning!). Trump shook hands and took selfies with many service members along the rope line the base had fashioned. Then, back to Air Force One, headed for Andrews, where we landed at five fifteen a.m. on December 27, all of twenty minutes behind the original schedule.

Trump called me later in the afternoon to urge moving forward quickly with "the two-week plan" to finish off the ISIS territorial caliphate in Syria. I said I had heard "two to four weeks" from LaCamera and Caine, which he didn't contest, but he said anyway, "Call it 'the two-week plan.'" I briefed Dunford in more detail, having found al-most immediately after Mattis left that Dunford could handle the con-fused, often conflicting array of Trump's Syria priorities (withdraw, crush ISIS, protect the Kurds, decide how to handle At Tanf, don't release the prisoners, keep the pressure on Iran). These were presiden-tial outbursts, off-the-cuff comments, knee-jerk reactions, not a co-herent, straight-line strategy, but bits and pieces we needed to thread our way through to get to a satisfactory outcome. What Dunford and I feared, along with many others, was ISIS's making a comeback in regions it had formerly controlled, thereby once again threatening to become a base from which to launch terrorist attacks against America and Europe.

I also wanted to minimize any potential gains for Iran, something Mattis never seemed to prioritize but which Dunford understood bet-ter. He and I discussed developing a plan to accommodate all these priorities, which was difficult but far superior to the Mattis style, which veered from insisting we had to remain in Syria indefinitely to saying, in effect, he would spite the President by doing exactly what he said: withdraw immediately. Since Erdogan appeared to believe that "the only good Kurd is a dead Kurd," big rallies notwithstand-ing, Dunford thought Turkey's immediate military objective in Syria would be to expel Kurds from the area along the Turkey-Syria border and then move hundreds of thousands of Syrian refugees from Turkey back across the border into the now-largely-depopulated border zone. He suggested creating a NATO-based monitoring force, supported by American intelligence, surveillance, and reconnaissance; air cover; and a "dial 911" capability to intervene if elements of the monitoring force ran into trouble, with minimal US forces on the ground.[19] I was also happy when Dunford quickly agreed on keeping US forces in At Tanf, which Mattis had not. Perhaps there was a way ahead.

Dunford suggested he join the early January trip I was planning to Turkey and then stay afterward to talk to their military, which I agreed to. This way, the Turks would hear a unified US government message, thereby lessening their ability to exploit differences among the various American players, always a favorite foreign-government strategy. I briefed Pompeo on these discussions, saying we had prevented a very bad outcome in Syria and were verging now on constructing something adequate and doable. Pompeo wanted to be sure the State Department envoy handling Syria was present for the Turkey meetings, which I agreed to reluctantly. That's because Pompeo himself had told me two days before Christmas that Jim Jeffrey, a former US Ambassador to Turkey, "had no love lost for the Kurds, and still saw Turkey as a reliable NATO partner." Those were clear warning signs of an advanced case of "clientitis," a chronic State Department affliction where the foreign perspective becomes more important than that of the US.[20] Pompeo, Shanahan, Dunford, and I agreed to draft a one-page "statement of principles" on Syria to avoid misunderstandings, which Defense thought was particularly important.

Senate Majority Leader Mitch McConnell called on January 4 as I was leaving for Israel, my first stop before Turkey, to say, "I had you on my mind," about Syria and Afghanistan, noting there was "a high level of alarm" around the Senate over recent developments. I said the key objective of my trip was to get straight exactly what we were going to do in Syria. Indeed, in an on-the-record meeting with the press traveling with me on Sunday, January 6, at Jerusalem's King David Hotel, I said, "We expect that those who have fought with us in Syria, in the Opposition, particularly the Kurds, but everybody who's fought with us, is not put in jeopardy by the coalition withdrawal. It's a point the President has made very clear in his conversations with President Erdogan of Turkey."[21] That is in fact what Trump had said, and it was correct when I said it in Israel. Later in the day, Washington time, asked by a reporter about my remarks as he was boarding Marine One for Camp David, Trump said, "John Bolton is, right now, over there, as you know. And I have two great stars. And John Bolton is doing a great job, and Mike Pompeo is doing a great job. They're very strong and they work hard . . . We're coming up with some very good results."[22] It is also true, of course, that Trump changed his mind again when the Turks pushed back after reading this and other comments I made in Jerusalem, meeting with Prime Minister Netanyahu. But's that's where we were at the trip's start.

Trump called me at about eleven forty-five p.m. on January 6, say-ing, "You're awake, right?" which I assuredly was not. Someone had told him the Turks were unhappy with various of my remarks reported in the press. Of course, I hadn't said anything Trump hadn't said to Erdogan. Nonetheless, Trump said several times during this brief call, "My base wants to get out [of Syria]," which meant visiting Turkey would certainly be fun. Indeed, the next day, as we flew from Jerusa-lem, the embassy in Ankara was hearing Erdogan was so irritated that he might cancel the meeting scheduled with me. In diplomatic circles, this was seen as a slight, but I saw it as proof our Syria policy was right on the mark, from the US perspective, if not Turkey's.

After I arrived in Ankara at 4:35 p.m. local time, Pompeo called to report Trump was unhappy with a *New York Times* story, filled with even more than the usual quota of mistakes, recounting contradictions in our Syria policy, citing statements from Administration officials.[23] Of course, many of the contradictions came from Trump himself, and Pompeo agreed he had made a few statements tracking mine (such as saying we would not allow Turkey to "slaughter the Kurds," which had not received widespread media attention but which certainly irritated the Turks).[24] We agreed our embassy should not plead for a meeting with Erdogan and that we had perhaps reached the moment we knew was inevitable, where Trump's desire to exit Syria came crashing into his statement about protecting the Kurds. That was something Erdo-gan would not tolerate. Trump called me about an hour later. He didn't like the reporting on internal Administration disagreements, but he was mostly worried whether the Defense Department was still work-ing hard on "the two-week plan" to defeat the ISIS caliphate. I urged him to call Shanahan to reassure himself and said I was seeing Dun-ford shortly in Ankara, and would also follow up with him.

Ironically, the next day, the *Washington Post* reported unhap-pily that Trump and I were actually on the same page on Syria[25]—unhappily because the *Post* was contradicting its own story from the day before.[26] All this confused press coverage reveals both the in-consistencies within Trump's own thinking, and reporting based on second- and third-hand sources, exacerbated under a President who spent a disproportionate share of his time watching his Administration being covered in the press. It is difficult beyond description to pursue a complex policy in a contentious part of the world when the policy is subject to instant modification based on the boss's perception of how inaccurate and often-already-outdated information is reported by writers who don't have the Administration's best interests at heart in the first place. It was like making and executing policy inside a pinball machine, not the West Wing of the White House.

In the meantime, contrary to the statement of principles, Jim Jeffrey circulated a color-coded map showing which parts of northeastern Syria he proposed to allow Turkey to take over and which the Kurds could retain. Dunford didn't like what the map showed at all. I asked if our objective should not be to keep the Turks entirely on their side of the border with Syria east of the Euphrates River, and Dunford said that was certainly his position. I said I wanted to see northeastern Syria look much as it did now, but without US troops being present; I knew that might be "mission impossible" but thought it should at least be the objective we sought even if we couldn't reach it. Dunford agreed. At this point, Jeffrey finally wandered in, and we went through the draft statement of principles we could give to the Turks. I added a new sentence to make clear we didn't want to see the Kurds mistreated and took pains to show we didn't accept a Turkish presence, military or otherwise, in northeastern Syria. Dunford and Jeffrey agreed to the draft, which, along with the map, in light of developments after I left the White House, is now purely a matter of historical interest.

Not surprisingly, Erdogan let us know he was canceling his meeting with me because he had to deliver a speech in Parliament. As we learned later, Erdogan's speech was a preplanned attack on what I presented as the US position. Erdogan had not moved an inch from his insistence that Turkey have a free hand in northeastern Syria, which we could not allow if we wanted to prevent retribution against the Kurds. Erdogan essentially gave a campaign speech (just prior to nationwide local and provincial elections, in which Erdogan's supporters would soon fare badly) saying "no concessions," and that it was "not possible . . . to make compromises" on the point.[27] On the way back,

I spoke with Pompeo to brief him on the Turkey meetings. We agreed our views on the Kurds were "irreconcilable" with Turkey's and they needed to be "really careful." Pompeo said Turkish Foreign Minister Mevlut Cavusoglu was trying to reach him and that he planned to say: "You have a choice. You can either have us on your border, or the Russians and the Iranians [who would almost certainly move into northeastern Syria when we withdrew]. Your choice." I said that sounded right to me.

Next, I called Trump to report in. He thought the Turks had been ready months before to cross into Syria, which is why he wanted to get out to begin with, before Turkey attacked the Kurds with our people still in place. He continued, "Erdogan doesn't care about ISIS," which was true, and said the US would remain capable of hitting ISIS after we left Syria, also true. Trump was focused on his speech that evening on the Mexico border wall, the first of his Administration from the Oval Office, and he added, "Just don't show any weakness or anything," as if he didn't realize I was describing things that had already happened. "We don't want to be involved in a civil war. They're natural enemies. The Turks and the Kurds have been fighting for many years. We're not getting involved in a civil war, but we are finishing off ISIS."

Meanwhile, I learned that Dunford thought Turkish military commanders were a lot less interested in going into Syria than Erdogan and were looking for reasons they could use to avoid conducting military operations south of their border, while simultaneously saying they were protecting Turkey from terrorist attacks. To them, said Dunford, "this is our Mexico border on steroids." Dunford had proceeded consistently with the statement of principles, proposing a twenty-to-thirty-kilometer buffer zone, from which Kurdish heavy weapons would be removed, and which would be patrolled by an international force consisting largely of NATO allies and the like, who would ensure there were no Kurdish incursions into Turkey, and vice versa, as we had discussed earlier in Washington. The US would continue to provide air cover and search-and-rescue capabilities for the international force, which Dunford and I believed would also allow us to keep control of the airspace over northeastern Syria. Although

Dunford didn't stress it, because we were staying at al-Asad in Iraq, under Trump's direction, we would also be able, if the need arose, to return to northeastern Syria quickly and in force to suppress any serious reappearance of an ISIS terrorist threat. Since Erdogan's real priority was domestic politics, in my view, this arrangement might be enough. We now had to convince the Europeans to agree, but that was a problem for another day. While we played this string out, or developed a better idea, which might take months, we had a good argument for maintaining US forces east of the Euphrates.

As for the Kurds, Jeffrey would present the idea to their commander, General Mazloum Abdi, to see how he reacted. Dunford was fatalistic, believing that Mazloum's options were quite limited, and that he might as well consider some insurance now. I then spoke with Pompeo, who thought this the proper line to pursue and that others in the region would support it. The Arab states had no love for Turkey, and they had financial resources that could make it easier for NATO allies and others to justify participating in a multinational monitoring force. Getting more equitable burden-sharing from our allies, NATO in particular, was a constant Trump theme, and a correct one. In the 1990–91 Persian Gulf conflict, George H. W. Bush had financed our war efforts by soliciting contributions from the beneficiaries in the region, like Kuwait and Saudi Arabia, and also other, more distant beneficiaries, like Japan. It was done with a tinge of embarrassment, referred to lightly as "the tin cup exercise," but it had worked, and no one suggested it was dishonorable. There was no reason it might not work again.

I continued to explain this approach in Syria to Trump. In the Oval for another issue on January 9, Dunford made a more detailed presentation on why an international force in a buffer zone south of Turkey's border was doable, allowing us to extricate ourselves without profoundly endangering the Kurds and our other anti-ISIS allies, not to mention our international reputation. Dunford now vigorously defended staying in At Tanf, which Jordan's King Abdullah had also pressed on Pompeo during his visit, noting that the longer we stayed in At Tanf, the more secure Jordan was against the risk of the conflict in

Syria's spilling across the border into his country. Trump was pleased the "two-to-four-week plan" was under way, although he still expected results in two weeks, which wasn't happening. He seemed satisfied, but it didn't stop a long digression on Mattis's failure to win in Afghanistan and Syria. Then he was off wondering why, after having fought the Korean War in the 1950s, we were still there, as well as critiquing the freeloading and ingratitude of sundry allies around the world. Just for the record, I did discuss with Trump several times the history of the "temporary" 1945 division of the Korean Peninsula, the rise of Kim Il Sung, the Korean War and its Cold War significance—you know, that old stuff—but I obviously made no impact. We endured this cycle repeatedly, always with the same outcome. Every few days, someone would inadvertently press a button somewhere, and Trump would be repeating his lines from the same movie soundtrack.

Dunford did a good job defending himself, and with minimal interference-running by me, because I thought it was better to let Trump hear it from someone else for a change. Others in the room (Pence, Shanahan, Coats, Haspel, Mnuchin, Sullivan, and more) largely remained silent. This was the longest conversation between Dunford and Trump I had seen, the first one without Mattis present. Dunford handled himself well, and I wondered how different things might have been if Mattis hadn't acted like a "five-star general," commanding all the four-star generals, but a real Secretary of Defense, running the entire, vast Pentagon machinery. Watching Dunford perform, it occurred to me there was a hidden wisdom in the statutory prohibition against former general officers becoming Secretary of Defense. It was not fear of a military takeover, but, ironically, that neither the civilian nor the military side of the Pentagon's leadership performed so well when both were military. The Secretary's broader, inevitably political role ill suited someone with a military background, leaving Mattis just to supervise Dunford and the other Joint Chiefs, who really didn't need more military supervision. It also underscored how unpersuasive Mattis was in meetings in either the Sit Room or the Oval. He may have established a reputation as a warrior-scholar for carrying with him on the battlefield a copy of Marcus Aurelius's *Meditations*, but he was no debater.

All these negotiations about our role in Syria were complicated by Trump's constant desire to call Assad on US hostages, which Pompeo and I thought undesirable. Fortunately, Syria saved Trump from himself, refusing even to talk to Pompeo about them. When we reported this, Trump responded angrily: "You tell [them] he will get hit hard if they don't give us our hostages back, so fucking hard. You tell him that. We want them back within one week of today, or they will never forget how hard we'll hit them." That at least took the Trump-Assad call off the table. We didn't act on the talk about striking Syria.

Efforts to create the international monitoring force, however, did not make progress. One month later, on February 20, Shanahan and Dunford said it would be an absolute precondition for other potential troop contributors that there be at least some US forces on the ground in the "buffer zone" south of Turkey's border, with logistical support coming from al-Asad in Iraq. I certainly had no problem with the idea, but raising it with Trump was undoubtedly dicey. In an Oval Office pre-brief for another Erdogan call the next day, I said the Pentagon believed unless we kept "a couple of hundred" (a deliberately vague phrase) US troops on the ground, we simply could not put a multilateral force together. Trump thought for a second and then agreed to it. Erdogan said he really wanted Turkey to have exclusive control of what he called the "safe zone" inside northeastern Syria, which I thought unacceptable. With the speakerphone on the *Resolute* desk on mute, I suggested to Trump he simply tell Erdogan Dunford was handling those negotiations, the Turkish military would be in Washington the next day, and we should just let the military-to-military talks continue. Trump followed through.

Afterward, I raced to my office to tell Shanahan the good news. A few hours later, I called Dunford to be sure he had heard, and he said, "Ambassador, I don't have much time to talk because we're going outside right now for the ceremony to rename the Pentagon 'the Bolton

Building.'" He was as pleased as we all were and agreed that "a couple of hundred" was a good figure of speech (which could mean up to four hundred without too much poetic license). He would make clear to the Turks he didn't want any of their troops south of the border. I called Lindsey Graham, urging him to keep it quiet so others didn't have a chance to reverse it, which he said he would do, also volunteering to call Erdogan, with whom he had good relations, to urge full support for Trump's decision. Unfortunately, Sanders issued a press statement, without clearing it with anyone who knew the facts, which caused significant confusion.[28] We had to explain that "a couple of hundred" only applied to northeastern Syria, not At Tanf, where there would be another two hundred or so US forces, for a total north of four hundred. I deliberately never tried to pin it down more precisely, despite the media confusion. Dunford also assured me he had calmed down US Central Command, which was worried about contradictory news reports, saying, "Don't worry, the building is still named after you."

With occasional bumps in the road, this was the situation in northeastern Syria until I resigned. ISIS's territorial caliphate was eliminated, but its terrorist threat remained unabated. Prospects for a multilateral observer force deteriorated, but the US presence remained, fluctuating around fifteen hundred country-wide. How long this "status quo" could last was unknowable, but Dunford preserved it through the September 30 end of his term as Chairman of the Joint Chiefs. Erdogan's belligerence remained unchecked, perhaps because of Turkey's deteriorating economy and his own domestic political troubles. Trump refused to impose any sanctions for Erdogan's S-400 purchase, ignoring widespread congressional dismay.

When Trump finally erupted on October 6, 2019, and again ordered a US withdrawal, I had left the White House nearly a month earlier. The result of Trump's decision was a complete debacle for US policy and for our credibility worldwide. Whether I could have averted this result, as happened nine months before, I do not know, but the strongly negative bipartisan political reaction Trump received was entirely predictable and entirely justified. To have stopped it a second time would have required someone to stand in front of the bus again and find an alternative that Trump could accept. That, it seems, did not happen. There was some good news, however: after years of effort, on October 26, the Pentagon and the CIA eliminated ISIS leader Abu Bakr al-Baghdadi in a daring raid.[29]

Afghanistan: A Forward Defense

By late 2018, Afghanistan was undoubtedly a sore spot for Trump, one of his principal grievances against the "axis of adults" so beloved by the media. Trump believed, not without justification, he had given Mattis all the leeway he requested to finish the Taliban, as with finishing the ISIS territorial caliphate. In Iraq and Syria, the stated goal had been accomplished (whether it should have been the only goal is a different story). In Afghanistan, by contrast, the stated goal was not in sight, and things were undeniably going the wrong way. That grated on Trump. He believed he had been right in 2016, he believed he had been right after the military failures in 2017 and 2018, and he wanted to do what he wanted to do. A reckoning was coming.

Trump opposed a continuing US military presence in Afghanistan for two related reasons: first, he had campaigned to "end the endless wars" in faraway places; and second, the sustained mishandling of economic and security assistance, inflaming his instinct against so much frivolous spending in federal programs. Besides, Trump believed he had been right in Iraq, and everyone now agreed with him. Well, not everyone.

The argument I pressed again and again, regarding all the "endless wars," was that we hadn't started the wars and couldn't end them just by our own say-so. Across the Islamic world, the radical philosophies that had caused so much death and destruction were ideological, political as well as religious. Just as religious fervor had driven human conflicts for millennia, so it was driving this one, against America and the West more broadly. It wasn't going away because we were tired of it, or because we found it inconvenient to balancing our budget. Most important of all, this wasn't a war about making Afghanistan,

Iraq, Syria, or any other country nicer, safer places to live. I am not a nation builder. I do not believe what is, after all, an essentially Marxist analysis that a better economic way of life will divert people from terrorism. This was about keeping America safe from another 9/11, or even worse, a 9/11 where the terrorists had nuclear, chemical, or biological weapons. As long as the threat existed, no place was too far away to worry about. The terrorists weren't coming to America on wooden sailing ships.

By the time I arrived, this debate had been through many iterations, so I did not face a clean slate. My first involvement was May 10, 2018 (later in the day after the post-midnight return of the hostages from Korea), when Zalmay Khalilzad, a friend I had known since the Bush 41 Administration, who had succeeded me as Ambassador to the UN in 2007, came to visit. "Zal," as everyone called him, an Afghan-American and also former US Ambassador to Afghanistan, said he had been approached by people purporting to speak on behalf of various Taliban factions who wanted to talk peace. He had spoken to others in the US government who could evaluate the bona fides of these approaches, but he wanted to give me an early heads-up in case they proved real, which by late July Khalilzad told me they had. I saw no reason further contacts shouldn't proceed, not that I expected much, and he initially became a back-channel negotiator with the Taliban. Within a month, the role had expanded to Khalilzad's being one of the growing number of State Department "special envoys," a convenient role that avoided having them confirmed in more traditional State positions.

Given Trump's periodic eruptions on our continuing military presence in Afghanistan, there was a growing sense we should have a full NSC meeting, or at least a military briefing, before the end of the year. I wanted any briefing to be as far after the elections as possible, but for reasons I never understood, Mattis wanted it sooner. It was finally scheduled for November 7, the day after the congressional midterms. I was sure Trump would be unhappy about the Republicans' losing control of the House, no matter what happened in the Senate. Did Mattis in particular want a flat-out Trump decision to withdraw, so Mattis could then resign on a matter of principle? Or was this an institutional Pentagon effort to have Trump be squarely responsible, not US failings during the course of the war, and especially not the collapse of the beloved counterinsurgency strategy that had failed in both Afghanistan and Iraq? Pompeo agreed with me that the briefing should have been held later in November, but we couldn't stop it.

At one p.m. on Election Day, I met with Khalilzad, who thought he had more time to negotiate with the Taliban than I believed likely, given my expectation Trump would pull the plug, perhaps the next day. Pence told me Mattis still argued we were making military progress in Afghanistan and should not change course. Pence knew as well as I that Trump didn't believe that, and there was substantial evidence Mattis was wrong. Here, once again, it wasn't so much that I disagreed with Mattis substantively as it was frustrating that he was determined to run into the wall on Afghanistan (as on Syria), and that he had no alternative line of argument to avoid getting the "wrong" answer. Kellogg sat in on the Pence-Mattis meeting and told me later Mattis simply repeated what he had said for two years. No wonder Trump was frustrated with what he called "his" generals. To my litigator's instincts, this was the sure way to lose. In truth, I didn't have a better answer, which is why I wanted more space after the elections before having this briefing.

At two p.m. on November 8, we convened in the Oval, with Pence, Mattis, Dunford, Kelly, Pompeo, Coats, Haspel, myself, and others present. Pompeo led off, but Trump quickly interjected, "We're being beaten, and they know they're beating us." Then he was off, raging against the statutorily mandated Afghanistan Inspector General, whose reports repeatedly documented wasted tax dollars but also provided amazingly accurate information about the war that any other government would have kept private. "I think he's right," said Trump, "but I think it's a disgrace he can make such things public." Mentioning Khalilzad, Trump said, "I hear he's a con man, although you need a con man for this." Pompeo tried again, but Trump rolled on: "My strategy [meaning what 'his' generals had talked him into in 2017] was wrong, and not at all where I wanted to be. We've lost everything. It was a total failure. It's a waste. It's a shame. All the casualties. I hate talking about it." Then Trump raised the first combat use of the MOAB ("Massive Ordnance Air Blast"), "without your knowledge," said Trump to Mattis,[30] complaining for the umpteenth time that the MOAB had not had its intended effect. As was often the case, Trump had truth mixed with misunderstanding and malice. Mattis had delegated to the US commander in Afghanistan authority to use the MOAB, so further authorization was unnecessary. As for the MOAB's effects, that remained a matter of dispute within the Pentagon. One thing was sure: Mattis was not going to win this argument with Trump, who knew what he wanted to know, period. I knew I didn't want this briefing.

Predictably, Mattis ran right into his favorite wall, lauding the efforts of other NATO members.

"We pay for NATO," said Trump.

"ISIS is still in Afghanistan," said Mattis.

Trump said, "Let Russia take care of them. We're seven thousand miles away but we're still the target, they'll come to our shores, that's what they all say," said Trump, scoffing. "It's a horror show. At some point, we've got to get out." Coats offered that Afghanistan was a border-security issue for America, but Trump wasn't listening. "We'll never get out. This was done by a stupid person named George Bush," he said, to me. "Millions of people killed, trillions of dollars, and we just can't do it. Another six months, that's what they said before, and we're still getting our asses kicked." Then he launched into a favorite story, about how we helicoptered schoolteachers every day to their school because it was too dangerous for them to go on their own: "Costs a fortune. The IG was right," he said, veering off into a report about the construction of "a billion-dollar Holiday Inn" and saying, "This is incompetence on our part. They hate us and they shoot us in the back, blew the back of the guy's head off, arms and legs and things [referring to a recent "green-on-blue" attack where a Utah National Guardsman was killed].[31] India builds a library and advertises it all over."

On it went. "We've got to get out. My campaign was to get out. People are angry. The base wants out. My people are very smart, it's why [Dean] Heller lost [his Nevada Senate reelection bid]. He supported

Hillary." Mattis tried again, but Trump was on to Syria: "I don't understand why we're killing ISIS in Syria. Why aren't Russia and Iran doing it? I've played this game for so long. Why are we killing ISIS for Russia and Iran, Iraq, which is controlled by Iran?"

Pompeo gave in, saying, "If that's the guidance, we'll execute it, but the story is that we won't get victory."

Trump answered, "That's Vietnam. And why are we guarding South Korea from North Korea?" Pompeo said, "Just give us ninety days," but Trump responded, "The longer we take, the more it's my war. I don't like losing wars. We don't want this to be our war. Even if we did win, we get nothing."

I could see it coming; sure enough, Mattis said, "It's your war the day you took office."

Trump was ready: "The first day I took office, I should have ended it." And on and on it went. And on.

Trump finally asked: "How long do you need?" and Pompeo said, "Until February or March. We'll prepare the options to exit." Trump was furious, furious he was hearing what he had heard so many times before: "They've got it down so fucking pat." Then he was back to criticizing Khalilzad, and whether anything the Taliban signed would be worth anything. "How do we get out without our guys getting killed? How much equipment will we leave?"

Dunford spoke for the first time, saying, "Not much."

"How do we get out?" asked Trump.

"We'll build a plan," said Dunford.

I had been silent throughout because the whole meeting was a mistake. Inevitably, Trump asked, "John, what do you think?" I said, "It sounds like my option is in the rearview mirror," explaining again why we should counter terrorists in their home base and why Pakistan's nuclear-weapons program made it imperative to preclude a Taliban haven in Afghanistan that might accelerate Pakistan's falling to terrorists. Dunford said if we withdrew, he feared a terrorist attack on the US in the near future. Trump was off again—"Fifty billion dollars a year"—until he ran down and said to no one in particular, "You have until Valentine's Day."

Most participants filed out of the Oval dispirited, although Pompeo and I remained behind as Sanders and Bill Shine rushed in to say Jeff Sessions had resigned as Attorney General, the first of many year-end departures. One month later, Trump named Bill Barr to succeed Sessions. Also one month later, after another report we were losing ground to the Taliban, Trump exploded again: "I should have followed my instincts, not my generals," he said, reverting to the MOAB's not having its intended effect. He now didn't want to wait for Khalilzad but wanted to announce the withdrawal of US forces prior to the end of his second full year in office, or even before. If he waited until his third year, he would own the war, whereas if we exited in the second year, he could still blame his predecessors. I said he simply had to address how to prevent terrorist attacks against America once we withdrew. He answered, "We'll say we're going to flatten the country if they allow attacks from Afghanistan." I pointed out we had already done that once, and we needed a better answer. I said I might have been the only one worried about Pakistan if the Taliban regained control next door, but Trump interrupted to say he worried as well; the speech had to address that issue. Basically, as we talked, the outline of the speech emerged: "We've done a great job and killed a lot of bad people. Now we're leaving, although we will leave a counterterrorism platform behind." Fortunately, the concept of a counterterrorism platform was already well advanced in Pentagon thinking, but it was hardly the first choice.[32]

At my regular breakfast with Mattis and Pompeo, this one on Pearl Harbor Remembrance Day, I suggested we seek to answer three questions: Would the Afghan government collapse after we left, and, if so, how fast? How fast and in what ways would ISIS, al-Qaeda, and other terrorist groups react to withdrawal? And how fast could the various terrorist groups mount attacks on the United States?

We scheduled another Oval Office meeting for Monday, and Mattis had barely begun before Trump was all over him. I felt sorry for Mattis, not to mention the country as a whole. After a somewhat shortened version of what he'd said in the prior gathering, Trump concluded, "I want out before January 20. Do it fast." He then turned to his visits to Walter Reed, where the wounded soldiers had not had the impact on Trump they have on most people, impressing them with their bravery and commitment to their mission. Trump had simply been horrified by the seriousness of their wounds (oblivious also that advances in military medicine saved many men who would simply have died in earlier wars). Then we were back to the MOAB not having its intended effect and other refrains, including "that stupid speech" in August 2017 where Trump had announced his new Afghanistan strategy of moving onto the offense. "I said you could do whatever you wanted," he said, and glared, looking straight at Mattis. "I gave you complete discretion, except for nuclear weapons, and look what happened." Trump was bitter whenever his 2017 speech came up, but one wonders how he would have felt if the strategy had prevailed. Pompeo told me later that, from his CIA perch at the time, he felt Mattis had unfortunately wasted several months in 2017 doing nothing, afraid Trump would reverse himself and start talking again about withdrawing. We certainly could have used those months now.

"What's a win in Afghanistan?" Trump asked.

Mattis correctly responded, "The United States doesn't get attacked." Finally switching his tack, Mattis offered, "Let's say we're ending the war, not that we're withdrawing."

"Okay, you ready?" Trump asked no one in particular, but using this favorite phrase indicating something big was coming. "Say we have been there for eighteen years. We did a great job. If anybody comes here, they will be met like never before. That's what we say," he said, although Trump then expanded the withdrawal to include Iraq, Syria, and Yemen. Then Trump came back at Mattis: "I gave you what you asked for. Unlimited authority, no holds barred. You're losing. You're getting your ass kicked. You failed." This painful repetition demonstrates that Trump, who endlessly stresses he is the only one who makes decisions, had trouble taking responsibility for them.

"Can we delay it [the withdrawal] so we don't lose more men and diplomats?" Mattis asked.

Trump roared back, "We can't afford it. We've failed. If it were turning out differently, I wouldn't do it."

We wandered disconsolately down to Kelly's office, where we

reconnoitered what to do next. Dunford, who had been largely silent, said there was no way to withdraw everyone safely in the time frame Trump wanted, and he would insist on another meeting to explain why. Kelly, totally fed up by this point, said Trump cared only about himself (he was thinking at least in part about Trump's unwillingness, up until that point, to visit Iraq or Afghanistan). Mattis then told Dunford to withdraw everyone from the Afghan boonies back to four or five key bases, from which they would depart the country, and to secure the landing and takeoff flight paths of the planes that would lift the men and equipment, as if another four-star Marine general couldn't figure that out on his own. I honestly do not know how Kelly and Dunford restrained themselves from telling Mattis what he could do with his withdrawal plan, but this was the "five-star general" phenomenon at work. Mattis should have worried about persuading Trump, not nitty-gritty plans on the ground in Afghanistan.

Afterward, I walked Pompeo to his car outside the West Wing, agreeing that Trump's assessment of Republican views on Afghanistan was completely wrong. "He's going to get crushed politically," said Pompeo, "and deservedly so." I concluded the generals really were in a cliché, fighting the last war, not dealing effectively with Trump's attitude, which they were partly responsible for. As a latecomer, I saw that what seemed like successes to Mattis and his colleagues, such as the August 2017 Afghanistan speech, were, in retrospect, mistakes. Trump had been pushed far beyond where he wanted to go, and now he was overreacting in the other direction. The media's hallowed "axis of adults" was not alone in this mistake, but before we could recover, we had to admit the misperception of Trump it rested upon. Khalilzad could pick up the pace of his negotiations, but his efforts were disconnected from what was happening on the ground in his country. It looked like there were a grim couple of months ahead.

On December 20, as Pompeo later told me, just hours before his resignation, Mattis gave Pompeo not only his resignation letter but also other documents, one particularly important here. This was a draft public statement on the operational plans for the Afghan withdrawal, which basically preempted whatever Trump might say about it in his January State of the Union speech. Stunned, Pompeo told Mattis he simply could not release such a document and that there was no way to edit it to make it acceptable. Mattis asked if he would at least send it along to me, and Pompeo said he knew I would agree with him. Neither Pompeo nor I knew at the time that the Defense Department had drafted an "execute order" elaborating what the draft statement said, and distributed it to US commanders and embassies worldwide, all part of Mattis's resignation scenario. We obviously understood this only hazily in all the confusion, but it produced an explosion of press stories. It reflected a common Mattis tactic, one of spite, to say, in effect, "You want withdrawal? You've got withdrawal." They didn't call him "Chaos" for nothing.

Even after Mattis's departure, Shanahan, Pompeo, and I continued the weekly breakfasts. On January 24, reflecting our divergent views on key points, Shanahan and I worried that Khalilzad was giving away too much, not because he was a poor negotiator, but because those were Pompeo's instructions. The Taliban was insisting that the draft US-Taliban statement (itself a troubling concept) under negotiation say that all foreign forces (meaning us) would withdraw from Afghanistan.[33] That certainly wouldn't leave room for the counterterrorism capabilities, even though Trump said he wanted them. I worried that State was so wrapped up in getting a deal, it was losing the bigger picture—a congenital department problem. Pompeo vigorously disagreed, although he readily conceded the negotiations could go into a ditch at any point, hardly a vote of confidence in the Taliban as a "negotiating partner," a term they like at State. The central problem with the diplomatic strategy was that if the Taliban really thought we were leaving, they had no incentive to talk seriously; they could simply wait, as they had often done before, and as Afghans had done for millennia. As the Taliban saying went, "You have the watches, we have the time." The breakfast ended inconclusively, but Shanahan called later saying he remained very nervous about both the pace of the negotiations, which seemed to have picked up considerably, and their substance. Pompeo just wanted to negotiate a deal and declare success, without much more. This dichotomy characterized the internal debate for months to come.

The State of the Union was delayed for weeks due to the acrimonious budget fight and partial government shutdown. It was finally scheduled for February 5, and the key passage on Afghanistan was mercifully brief: "In Afghanistan, my Administration is holding constructive talks with a number of Afghan groups, including the Taliban. As we make progress in these negotiations, we will be able to reduce our troop presence and focus on counter-terrorism."[34] This comment received little attention, but it embodied struggles that persisted until my final days in the White House. At least at this point there was still hope.

CHAPTER 8

CHAOS AS A WAY OF LIFE

If you can keep your head when all about you
Are losing theirs and blaming it on you . . .

RUDYARD KIPLING, "IF—"

It took me about a month after my arrival at the Trump White House to have any chance to assess systematically how things worked inside. Dysfunctionality arose in many ways, often unfolding through specific policy issues, some of which I have described throughout this work.

There were many more. During the last months of 2018 and early 2019, as Trump's second year in office came to an end—roughly eight to nine months after my arrival—several seemingly disparate issues and individuals converged to push the Administration even deeper into uncharted territory.

In early June 2018, for example, Kelly tried a new tactic on Trump's schedule, beginning each day in the Oval, at eleven a.m., with "Chief of Staff" time, hoping to minimize the rambling lectures he delivered during his twice-weekly intelligence briefings. Of course, what most people found striking was that Trump's "official" day didn't start until almost lunchtime. Trump was not loafing during the morning. Instead, he spent considerable time working the phones in the Residence. He talked to all manner of people, sometimes US government officials (I spoke with him by phone before he arrived in the Oval nearly every day due to the press of events he needed to know about or I needed direction on), but he also spoke at length to people outside the government. It was an anomaly among contemporary Presidents by any definition.

By contrast, a regular day for President George H. W. Bush, described by his first Chief of Staff, former Governor John Sununu, started like this:

> The president began his formal day in the Oval Office with an 8:00 a.m. intelligence briefing that would include the president, the vice president, National Security Advisor Brent Scowcroft and me. That meeting, the President's Daily Briefing (PDB), was presented by the CIA and would take ten to fifteen minutes. Following that, always on the calendar for 8:15, was a separate half hour for Scowcroft to bring the president and us up to date on all foreign policy issues arising from the events that occurred overnight or were expected during the course of the upcoming day. That briefing segued into a similar one at 8:45 that I would lead, addressing all other issues beyond foreign policy. Scowcroft usually stayed for that as well. My meeting was scheduled to end at 9:15.[1]

I would have thought I had died and gone to heaven to have had such an orderly approach to preparing for an upcoming day. As it was, Trump generally had only two intelligence briefings per week, and in most of those, he spoke at greater length than the briefers, often on matters completely unrelated to the subjects at hand.

Trump's schedule was the easiest anomaly to deal with. One of the hardest was his vindictiveness, as demonstrated by the constant eruptions against John McCain, even after McCain died and could do Trump no more harm. Another example of his vindictiveness was Trump's August 15 decision to revoke former CIA Director John Brennan's security clearance. Now, Brennan was no prize, and during his tenure the CIA became more politicized than at any other time in its history. He denied any improper behavior, but Trump was convinced Brennan was deeply implicated in abusing the FISA surveillance process to spy on his 2016 campaign, all of which was exacerbated by his constant presence in the media criticizing Trump after he took office.

The press fastened on the revocation immediately after Sanders announced it during her daily noon briefing. Kelly said to me, "This Brennan thing is exploding," having spent much of the afternoon on it. "This is big." In an hour-long conversation just between the two of us, we went over what had happened. Kelly said that by mid to late July he thought he had gotten Trump off the idea of taking away people's clearances, but Trump returned to it because his favorite media sources kept pounding away on it. Earlier in the day, Trump had wanted to revoke clearances from a longer list of names but had settled for Sanders reading the names out at the briefing, implicitly threatening to revoke the clearances at some point in the future. I pointed out that the whole idea had started with Rand Paul. It was largely symbolic, because having a security clearance didn't mean Brennan or anyone else could just walk into the CIA and read whatever interested him. He had to have a "need to know," and, for anything really important, would have to be read into the appropriate "compartments."

Kelly said he had had an argument with Trump about it, not the first such confrontation, but one that had obviously been harsher than previous ones. Kelly told Trump it was "not presidential," which was true, and he told me it was "Nixonian," also true. "Has there ever been a presidency like this?" Kelly asked me, and I assured him there had not. I thought there was a case against Brennan for politicizing the CIA, but Trump had obscured it by the blatantly political approach *he* took. It would only get worse if more clearances were lifted. Kelly agreed.

In what by this point was already an emotional discussion for both of us, Kelly showed me a picture of his son, killed in Afghanistan in 2010. Trump had referred to him earlier that day, saying to Kelly, "You suffered the worst." Since Trump was disparaging the wars in Afghanistan and Iraq at the time, he had seemingly implied that Kelly's son had died needlessly. "Trump doesn't care what happens to these guys," Kelly said. "He says it would be 'cool' to invade Venezuela." I said relatively little during the conversation, which was mostly Kelly venting his frustrations, very few of which I disagreed with. I couldn't see how it was possible he would stay through the 2020 elections, though Trump had announced a few weeks before that he would. When I left Kelly's office, I said nothing to anyone else.

Perhaps uniquely in presidential history, Trump engendered controversy over attendance at funerals, starting with Barbara Bush's in April 2018, which Trump did not attend (although four former Presidents and the First Lady did), and then at John McCain's in late August. Kelly opened the weekly White House staff meeting on August 27 by saying, "I'm in a bad place today," because of ongoing disagreements with Trump over whether to fly US government flags at half-mast and who would attend which services. McCain's family didn't want Trump at the services either, so the feeling was mutual. The final decision was that Pence would lead the Administration's representation at both the Capitol Rotunda ceremony and the funeral service at Washington National Cathedral. The service was extremely well attended, with all the socializing that routinely accompanies even moments of passing. Among others I greeted were Bush 43 and Mrs. Bush, with Bush asking cheerily, "Still got a job, Bolton?" "For now," I answered, and we all laughed. When George H. W. Bush later died during the Buenos Aires G20, Trump declared a national day of mourning, issued a fitting presidential statement, and spoke cordially with both George W. and Jeb Bush during the morning. He and the First Lady attended the National Cathedral service on December 5 without incident. It wasn't so hard to do after all.

During the controversy over McCain's funeral, Trump tweeted that White House Counsel Don McGahn was leaving at the end of the Brett Kavanaugh confirmation battle. Although McGahn had often joked to me, "We're all only one tweet away," this was a classic example of Trump's announcing something already decided, without giving McGahn a chance to announce it first. I should have paid closer heed. As Kelly confirmed to me later, tensions between Trump and McGahn had become unsustainable because of McGahn's (truthful) testimony to, and cooperation with, Mueller's investigation. Even though Trump's outside attorneys had approved McGahn's role, they were all reportedly surprised by just how candid he was. In any event, the search for a replacement was immediately on.

Illegal immigration, a key Trump initiative, was a shambles. White House lawyer John Eisenberg approached me in mid-May 2018 to see if I had any interest in trying to repair the collapsed White House policy process on immigration generally and at the Mexican border in particular. I had no interest entering that arena without the White House Counsel's office and Justice fully on board. Don McGahn, who for the best of reasons focused every waking moment on judicial nominations, saw immigration policy for the swamp it was and decided to stay out of it. Justice had its own problems. Now alerted, however, I kept my eye on the issue but followed McGahn's example.

I saw the problem firsthand at a Cabinet meeting on immigration, held on May 9, the day after we escaped the Iran nuclear deal. Homeland Security Secretary Kirstjen Nielsen and Jeff Sessions were to report on what their respective departments were doing to close the Mexican border, followed by other Cabinet members discussing their areas. But this was not to be a "briefing" where Trump listened appreciatively to his team's efforts, asked a few questions, and then patted them on their backs. Things went downhill after Sessions concluded, just as Nielsen was starting. Trump asked her why we couldn't close the border, and Nielsen answered by listing all the difficulties she and her department faced. Trump interrupted, saying in front of the entire Cabinet and a coterie of White House aides, his voice rising, "You're wrong. There's no way we can't close the border. Tell them the country is closed. We don't have the people [such as immigration judges] to do all these things. That's it. It's like a movie theater when it gets filled."

This was already bad, but it got worse. Kelly tried to support Nielsen, who was effectively his protégé, but that was a mistake. Everyone knew Nielsen had the Homeland Security job largely because of Kelly, and his intervention made it look like she couldn't defend herself, which was unfortunately proving to be true before a packed

Cabinet Room. Kelly and Nielsen tried to turn things back toward Sessions, who appeared to say something new and different about the Department of Homeland Security's authority at the border. He was uncomfortable discussing the issue and seemingly reversed himself, basically saying the department did *not* have the authority he had just explained it did. Kelly fired back, "We're going to do what the Attorney General says is illegal and send them [the immigrants] back," and Sessions twisted a little more. But Trump was still after Nielsen, and she didn't have the wit to either remain silent or say, "We'll get back to you in a few days with a better answer." Finally, as if anyone could have missed the point, Trump said, "I got elected on this issue, and now I'm going to get unelected," which might not have been far from the political truth. I thought as the meeting drew to a close it was only a matter of time before both Nielsen and Kelly resigned. And, according to numerous press reports, Nielsen came very close in Kelly's office right afterward. This issue was a total mess, and unnecessary, because there was much that could be done to tighten up on fraudulent, unjustifiable, and made-up claims for asylum in the United States.

Things worsened further on June 20. In a "zero tolerance" policy, Trump had been prepared to separate children from their parents (or people claiming to be their parents, but who were frequently human traffickers) at the border, as prior Administrations, including Obama's, had done. But under political pressure, Trump reversed himself, in effect hanging Nielsen and Sessions out to dry. After the Executive Order revoking "zero tolerance" was signed, Kelly just went home. He confirmed to me the next day his view that Trump had "sold out Sessions and Nielsen," but no one had a real plan what to do next. Immigration was also jumbled in with the negotiation and ratification efforts to modify the NAFTA agreement with Canada and Mexico; foreign aid programs in Central America; and enormous turf fights among the Departments of Justice, Homeland Security, Health and Human Services, State, and others over who had what responsibility. These problems were due largely to the chaos in domestic policy making, a problem that showed no signs of abating.

Despite my efforts to stay out of the immigration stew, it kept chasing me. On October 4, Kushner, now involved in immigration because of the spillover from the NAFTA revision effort, came to see me. He said Nielsen and her department were negotiating with Mexico's government with no State Department clearance, an obvious process foul if true. A few days later, on a Saturday, Kushner called to say Trump had suggested that he take over the immigration portfolio; he had declined because he felt Kelly was protecting Nielsen from the consequences of her own incompetence, which made the problem unfixable. "What about Bolton?" Trump asked, "Could he take it over?" Kushner said he doubted I would be interested, but Trump replied, "John's great. He gets things done. He brings me all these decisions and stuff. Really great. Can you ask him if he'd do it?" Kushner said whomever Trump selected would be in a fight with Kelly, and Trump replied, "John's not afraid of fights. He'll take him [Kelly] on." Wonderful, I thought. Great Saturday.

On Monday morning, Columbus Day, I met with Stephen Miller, the White House policy lead on immigration. As we were talking, Kushner walked in and asked, "Can I join the conspiracy?" I had already e-mailed Pompeo, who had agreed Mexico-related immigration issues had to be brought more effectively into the NSC process, which had been frustrated for months if not years primarily by the Department of Homeland Security's lack of cooperation. The department just didn't want to be coordinated. My personal view was that America would benefit from far more legal, controlled immigration, whereas illegal immigration was undermining the foundational sovereignty principle that the US decided who was allowed in, not the would-be immigrants. I was clear on one thing: Nielsen's effort to bring in the UN High Commissioner for Refugees to help us decide who to admit to the US was badly flawed. We could hardly cede such basic sovereign decisions to an international body.

Later in the week, after an unrelated meeting in the Oval, attended by Nielsen, Pompeo, and others, Trump was pounding away again: "We're doing the worst job on the border of any Administration. I ran and won on the border. We have a national emergency," he said, and he then riffed on finding money in the Pentagon budget to build the border wall he had long promised. Trump's agitation was based in part on sensational media reporting about "caravans of illegal immigrants" heading through Central America toward our border, which he saw as visible proof he was not meeting his 2016 campaign pledge. Pointing to Nielsen, Trump said, "You're in charge of border security," and then, pointing to Pompeo, he said, "You're not involved." This was directly contrary to what Trump had told Kushner on Saturday and convinced me I was happy to be as little involved in this exercise as possible. On and on it went between Trump and Nielsen. At one point, Pompeo whispered to me, "Why are we still here?" Good question. We needed to find a way out of this train wreck before Trump blamed us for the collapse of his border policy!

According to Kushner, however, this latest encounter with Nielsen convinced Trump I should have control of the issue. "Kirstjen is not mentally able to do it," said Kushner. Two days later, Trump told me, "You take over the southern border. She loses every case. She's so weak." Trump wanted to declare a national emergency and had already talked to John Eisenberg about it. "You have my full authorization," said Trump, "the number one thing is the southern border. You and me. You are the fucking boss." A few hours later, with just Kelly and me in the Oval, Trump said, "I told John to take control of the border." This was getting serious. I decided to lay out for Trump the process required to get control of illegal immigration issues. If he agreed to it, I would step in, but if not, I had plenty of other work to do.

I drafted a one-page "plan" that included giving lead international negotiation authority to the State Department, rewriting all the relevant Homeland Security and Justice regulations, proposing sweeping new legislation on the issue, vesting policy development authority in the NSC, replacing Nielsen and Sessions, and more. I was writing for a one-person audience, but I showed drafts to Pompeo, Miller, Kushner, Eisenberg, and a few others, who generally concurred. In the meantime, the caravan issue was growing steadily more neuralgic. Trump, tweeting prodigiously, asked that Executive Orders closing the borders be drafted, and the White House atmosphere grew increasingly febrile. On the morning of October 18, Pompeo and I were in my office talking about the Khashoggi affair when Kelly asked both of us to come to his office. There, a mass meeting (perhaps fifteen people) was in progress on the Mexico border, which Kelly summarized when Pompeo and I entered. He then asked Nielsen to describe her plan, which had the United Nations High Commissioner for Refugees staffing processing facilities on the Guatemala-Mexico border. The High Commissioner's office would separate out legitimate refugees, who could then enter the United States (or another country), from those not qualifying, who would return to their countries of origin.

Kelly asked Pompeo what he thought, and he responded slowly, likely knowing little about what Nielsen was saying. I jumped in (and Pompeo happily receded) to point out that the High Commissioner had no real role in this kind of immigration processing work; that its budget and personnel were already overstrained by, among other things, the Venezuelan refugee crisis; and that in any case, the US shouldn't subcontract decisions on admission to the US to the United Nations. Nielsen couldn't answer these points, so I continued to probe on what the refugee agency's role would be as she stumbled through her responses. Kelly asked, "Well then, what's your plan, John?" Of course, my plan was something I had no intention of discussing in a stadium-sized crowd before I had even shown it to Trump. I simply said, "Yes, I have a plan, which he [Trump] asked for, and which I will discuss with him." That caused Nielsen to do a flounce and turn her back on me, saying "Huh!" or something like that. I said, "That's exactly why I want to see the President alone." The conversation meandered around for a few minutes more, nearing ten a.m., when I said to Kelly, "John, we should get down to the Oval to talk Saudi Arabia," just to remind everyone that the rest of the world was still out there. Off Pompeo, Kelly, and I went. Suffice it to say, this was not the "profanity-laced shouting match" the credulous media later reported.

In the Oval, we were addressing the Khashoggi issue with Trump when Madeleine Westerhout came in, saying Kushner wanted to report by phone on his conversation with Mexico's Foreign Minister. Kelly asked loudly, "Why is Jared calling the Mexicans?"

"Because I asked him to," said Trump in an equally loud voice. "How else are we going to stop the caravans?"

"Kirstjen Nielsen is working on this," said Kelly, still loudly, and Trump shot back, "None of you other geniuses have been able to stop the caravans," at which point Kelly stomped out of the Oval, Trump waving his hand dismissively at Kelly's back as he left. This conversation could qualify as "shouting," but there was no profanity here either. Kushner, now on the speakerphone, described his call with Luis Videgaray, while Pompeo steamed quietly, since Kushner was once again doing his job. There was some further desultory conversation, and then Pompeo and I headed back to Kelly's office. (In a December conversation with Trump as he decided on Kelly's successor, Trump acknowledged that this exchange with Kelly was the "shouting match" about which the press had spilled so many electrons.)

Several people were milling around in Kelly's outer office. He called Pompeo and me in; said, "I'm out of here"; and walked out. Somewhat dazed, I suppose, Pompeo and I spoke further on Saudi Arabia, but it then hit us that Kelly meant something more than just "you can use my office" when he walked out. I opened the door to ask where Kelly was, but no one knew. I went into the hallway; saw him speaking to someone; pulled him into the Roosevelt Room, which was empty; and shut the door. This was our second emotional conversation, even more intense than the first. "I've commanded men in combat," he said, "and I've never had to put up with shit like that," referring to what had just happened in the Oval.

I could see his resignation coming, so I asked, "But what is the alternative if you resign?"

Kelly said, "What if we have a real crisis like 9/11 with the way he makes decisions?"

I asked, "Do you think it will be better if you leave? At least wait until after the election. If you resign now, the whole election could go bad."

"Maybe it would be better that way," he answered bitterly, so I said, "Whatever you do will be honorable, but there's nothing positive about the likes of Elizabeth Warren and Bernie Sanders having more authority."

He answered, "I'm going out to Arlington," presumably to visit his son's grave, which he did at serious times. We knew this because it happened so often.

I left the Roosevelt Room for Kelly's office, where Pompeo was still waiting before going out to speak to the press about Khashoggi. After his press gaggle, we spoke in my office about what to do, Kelly having left. It was grim. "Mattis is always overseas," Pompeo said, "the VP is in Mississippi talking about religious freedom, and the only thing Mnuchin thinks about is covering his ass. This will just leave you and me," worrying that Kelly could go at any time. "If he [Trump] wants to know who the real warriors are, just look around [meaning us]. And Kelly is part of that." I agreed. Realizing how bad it all sounded, Pompeo said, "This whole thing could end up being the Donald, Ivanka, and Jared show!"

In the midst of all this, in the early afternoon, I showed Trump my one-page immigration plan. He read through it and said he agreed with it, but added, "You know, most of this I can't do until after the election," which I said I understood. He asked if he could keep the one-pager, folded it, and put it in his suit coat pocket. The ball was in his court. And from my perspective, that's where it stayed. The immigration issue rolled on, but largely without me. I had made my suggestions, which may or may not have worked had they been fully carried out, and ultimately Trump did pick bits and pieces of them. But he did it his own way in his own time, which was his prerogative. Immigration issues stumbled along, rather than forming a coherent policy.

During the immigration controversy came the bombshell of the disappearance and then the assassination of Saudi Arabian journalist Jamal Khashoggi at the Saudi consulate in Istanbul. Trump's handling of Khashoggi's murder was in stark contrast to his usual decision-making.

On October 8, Kushner asked how we should respond to the

growing storm. My advice to the Saudis was to get the facts out immediately, whatever they were, and get it over with. Kushner agreed, and the next day we spoke with Crown Prince Mohammed bin Salman, emphasizing how seriously this issue was already viewed. I urged the Crown Prince to find out exactly what had happened to Khashoggi and then publish the report before people's imaginations exploded. Pompeo later made the same point to him. I also proposed we send the Saudi Ambassador in Washington back to Riyadh to get the facts and then come back and brief us. This was unorthodox, but the Ambassador was the Crown Prince's younger brother and could reinforce firsthand what the temperature was in Washington.

Unlike with so many other issues, however, Trump had essentially already decided on his response, saying in a pretaped interview for *60 Minutes* for the coming weekend that he wasn't going to cut off arms sales to the Kingdom. On Saturday, when we welcomed Pastor Brunson to the White House after his release from Turkey, I suggested Pompeo go to Saudi Arabia, rather than sending a lower-ranking official, which he and Trump liked. No one could say we weren't taking this seriously. Trump raised the idea with King Salman on October 15, and the King said he would welcome Pompeo's visit. Trump was feeling pressure from the US media, but the pressure was unexpectedly moving him toward stronger public support for the Kingdom, not less. Pompeo's whirlwind trip bought some time, during which the Saudis would have more opportunity to get the facts out, but Trump was not waiting. The Saudis subsequently published their version of the events and fired several senior officials. The Saudi report didn't satisfy most analysts, but it reflected a narrative that obviously wasn't going to change. During this period, through tweets and statements, Trump supported the emerging Saudi version and never wavered from both the US-Saudi alliance generally or the massive arms sales already negotiated with the Kingdom.

With the media in a foaming-at-the-mouth frenzy, Trump decided to issue an unequivocal statement of support for Mohammed bin Salman, which he essentially dictated to Pompeo. The text was utterly unqualified and thus risked harming Trump himself if the facts changed. It was not all that difficult to make a few editorial changes to build in protection, but Pompeo would not accept any changes or even hold the draft a day for further review. Pompeo said, "He asked for it, and I'm sending it in," a characteristic "Yes, sir, roger that" answer. The next day, November 20, my birthday, Trump wanted to call bin Salman to tell him the statement was coming out, saying, "We're doing him a hell of a favor," namely stating that "whether he did it or not, we're standing with Saudi Arabia."

We debated whether Trump himself would read the statement from the White House podium or whether we would just release the text. "This will divert from Ivanka," Trump said. "If I read the statement in person, this will take over the Ivanka thing." (The "Ivanka thing" was a flood of stories about Ivanka's extensive use of her personal e-mail for government business, which the White House was trying to explain was actually quite different from Hillary Clinton's extensive use of her personal e-mail for government business.) "Goddamn it, why didn't she change her phone?" Trump complained. "What a mess we have because of that phone." Then he turned to Pompeo, settling on his calling the Crown Prince, and said, "Tell him it's unbelievable, what a great thing I'm doing. Then get his opinion, and we'll decide what to do." We decided to issue a statement and have Pompeo answer questions, but there was considerable debate over whether the text should be released before or after the annual ceremony pardoning the Thanksgiving turkey (pun not intended). Sorry, Crown Prince, but we have our priorities. (I met with Turkey's Foreign Minister that same day, another coincidence.) Pompeo and Trump both ultimately took questions, which Trump had wanted to do anyway. It was an all-Trump show, obvious to everyone except Rand Paul, who tweeted that he thought I had written the statement!

In hard-nosed geopolitical terms, Trump's was the only sensible approach. No one excused Khashoggi's murder, and few doubted it was a serious mistake. Whether or not you liked Saudi Arabia, the monarchy, Mohammed bin Salman, or Khashoggi, we had significant US national interests at stake. Withdrawing support would immediately trigger countervailing efforts by our adversaries in the region to exploit the situation to our detriment. Putin had earlier put it to me most bluntly in Moscow (see Chapter 6) on October 23, saying Russia could sell arms to the Saudis if we didn't. Trump wasn't necessarily deciding on the basis of geostrategic reality, but on the US jobs generated by the arms sales, and he ended up in more or less the right place. This approach was exactly Jeane Kirkpatrick's conclusion in her iconic 1979 essay, "Dictatorships and Double Standards"[2]: "Liberal idealism need not be identical with masochism, and need not be incompatible with the defense of freedom and the national interest."

Personnel management issues, also critical to policy development, portended a series of dramatic changes following the November 2018 congressional elections. Jim Mattis and his staff, for example, had a masterful command of press relations, carefully cultivating his reputation as a "warrior scholar." One story I was sure the media hadn't heard from Mattis was one told by Trump on May 25, as Marine One flew back to the White House from Annapolis after Trump's graduation speech to the Naval Academy. He said Mattis had told him, regarding Trump's appearing in a scheduled presidential debate with Clinton just days after the *Access Hollywood* story broke in the press, that "it was the bravest thing he had ever seen anyone do." Coming from a career military man, that was indeed something. Of course, Trump could have been making it up, but, if not, it showed Mattis knew how to flatter with the best of them.

There was no doubt Mattis was in troubled waters by the summer of 2018, and he grew steadily weaker as the year unfolded. At about nine forty-five p.m. on Sunday, September 16, Trump called me to ask if I had seen a prominently displayed *New York Times* article about Mattis[3] and "read it carefully," which I said I had. "I don't like it," said Trump. "Mattis is always doing this kind of thing." I said I thought the article was very unfair to Deputy National Security Advisor Mira Ricardel, brought on by the enmity she had earned from Mattis in her early days at the White House, where she resisted Mattis's efforts to hire Democrats with views incompatible with Trump's. "She stopped

Rex from bringing in some of his people too, right?" Trump asked, which was also true. "What do you think of Mattis?" Trump asked, in line with his management style, which almost no one believed was conducive to building trust and confidence among his subordinates. But he did it all the time. And only a fool would not assume that if he asked me questions about Mattis, he was surely asking others about me. I gave a partial answer, which was both true and important: I said Mattis was "good at not doing what he didn't want to do" and that he had "a high opinion of his own opinion." With that, Trump was off, explaining that he didn't trust Mattis and how tired he was of constant press stories about Mattis's outwitting Trump. I didn't say it to Trump, but this was the biggest self-inflicted wound by the "axis of adults." They thought themselves so smart they could tell the world how smart they were, and Trump wouldn't figure it out. They were not as smart as they thought.

Kelly came to my office late the next morning to talk about the article, saying, "Mattis is just in survival mode now," and that he was pointing the finger for the leaks at Ricardel, which showed amazing chutzpah. I explained Judge Larry Silberman's theory about assessing leaks, namely asking, "Cui bono?" which means "Who stands to gain?" and which, in this case, pointed squarely to Mattis and his associates' being the leakers. Kelly had served under Mattis in the Marines, as had Joe Dunford, a remarkable alignment the press never seemed to notice and that a spy novelist could not have convinced a publisher was plausible. Trump, Kelly, and I discussed the article again later in the day, and Trump asked, "Mattis didn't like canceling the Iran deal, did he?" which was an understatement. Shortly thereafter, the speculation on Mattis's replacement picked up again in earnest. I wondered if the leaks started in the Oval Office.

One week later, however, when I was in New York for the annual opening festivities of the UN General Assembly, Kelly called me to say the First Lady wanted Ricardel fired because her staff complained she had been uncooperative in preparing for FLOTUS's upcoming trip to Africa. I found this stunning, and Kelly said it was "not clear how it got to this level." He then characterized the First Lady's staff as a bunch of catty, gossipy sorority types. No one said anything further to me, and I thought it had died away. Kelly was still in Washington because of "this Rosenstein thing," meaning the stories about whether Deputy Attorney General Rod Rosenstein had ever proposed invoking the Twenty-Fifth Amendment against Trump, or that he wear a wire into the Oval to gather evidence to that end. This was also a first in presidential management history.

Being in New York reminded me why UN Ambassadors should not have Cabinet rank (the traditional Republican approach). Or, if they were going to have that rank, they needed to be told by the President that there was nonetheless only one Secretary of State. Haley had never gotten that reminder, and from everything I heard, including directly from Trump, she and Tillerson cordially detested one another (well, maybe not cordially). Early evidence of the Haley problem occurred in her mishandling of the Russia sanctions question in the immediate aftermath of the April US attack on Syria. It emerged again in June regarding US withdrawal from the UN's misbegotten Human Rights Council. Trump agreed to leave it, which all of his advisors recommended, confirming it in an Oval Office meeting with Pompeo, Haley, and me. Trump then asked Haley, "How's it going?" and she responded by talking about the trade negotiations with China, which formed no part of her responsibilities. After a lengthy trade riff by Trump, with all his favorite lines ("The EU is just like China, only smaller"), Haley asked him about a trip she wanted to take to India to visit the Dalai Lama. The purpose of this trip was unclear, other than getting a photo op with the Dalai Lama, always good for an aspiring pol. But the minefield she strayed into by raising the China trade issue showed a political tin ear: once Trump wondered how China would view Haley's seeing the Dalai Lama, the trip was essentially dead. This episode confirmed to Pompeo how far out of line Trump had allowed Haley to drift, and why it had to stop. In any case, on June 19, we withdrew from the Human Rights Council.

Replacing departing senior Administration officials could also be arduous, especially as the halfway mark in Trump's term neared. Choosing Haley's successor was one such marathon. After conferring alone with Trump, Ivanka, and Kushner on a "purely personal" matter, Haley told Kelly (but not Pompeo or me) on October 9 that she was resigning, although that resignation came with a long recessional extending until its effective date on December 31. Few doubted the 2024 race for the Republican presidential nomination had now begun. In a jaw-dropping statement, sitting next to the President in the Oval, Haley ruled out a 2020 run, just so she could remind everyone she was available: "No, I'm not running for 2020 . . . I can promise you what I'll be doing is campaigning for this one."[4] Many thought she was instead running to replace Pence as Trump's 2020 running mate, supported by Kushner and Ivanka, which was not idle speculation.[5]

One Trump prerequisite for Haley's successor was that it be a female. Early favorite Dina Powell had been at the NSC, and, preferred by the family, initially appeared to be a shoo-in. Enormous opposition developed, however, and the search was quickly on for other candidates. Pompeo and I agreed from the outset that the UN Ambassador should not have Cabinet rank, but we first had to persuade Trump. He said of Powell that Cabinet status "will help her out," which left me speechless. If someone needed that kind of help, they should have been looking for other work. In addition to the status issue, Pompeo and I discussed, over several weeks, possible alternatives, conferring with several of them to see if they were interested. When the sorting was done, we both concluded that Ambassador to Canada Kelly Craft was the most logical choice. In addition to being qualified, Craft was already in the Administration, had been fully vetted and granted appropriate security clearances, and was therefore ready quickly to assume new duties.

In the meantime, the White House lapsed into full conspiracy mode, as everyone had an opinion about who should succeed Haley. I never went through a time where more people told me not to trust other people on an issue. Perhaps they were all right. The internal politics were byzantine, much of it played out in the media. Candidates rose and fell, entered and withdrew, and then entered again, came close, or were actually picked, only to find some disqualifying factor took them out of the running and us back to the beginning. Even when Pompeo and I thought we had Trump decided on one candidate, we were often wrong. As Pompeo said at the November G20 meeting, "You can't leave him alone for a minute." It was like being in a hall of mirrors. As the weeks passed, I wondered if we would have a nominee in time to get her confirmed before Haley's three-month-long curtain call ended on New Year's Eve.

Indeed, we didn't. Not until February 22, in the Oval Office, when Trump called me down in midafternoon, did Trump and Kelly Craft shake hands on the nomination. I was delighted, as was Pompeo, but dismayed that nearly five months had disappeared on something that could have been resolved in just days after Haley's announcement. Trump said to Craft, "It's the best job in government next to mine," which I thought wasn't far from wrong. We were done, at least with the Executive Branch deliberations. Almost five months in the making.

As Mattis's troubles continued to rise, speculation turned to whether Kelly might also have finally had enough. Pompeo said, "If Mattis goes, Kelly goes too," which had a logic to it. This was now beyond personnel dysfunction but meant a major change in White House direction. Nielsen's unending problems with Trump also seemed to indicate her early departure, another incentive for Kelly to leave, but she hung on. Indeed, Nielsen lasted until April 2019, probably long after she should have left voluntarily for her own well-being. Kelly and Kushner also had not gotten along well since the controversy over Kushner's security clearance.

Kelly also had his troubles, not unlike those I experienced, with Treasury Secretary Mnuchin, a Trump confidant. In July 2018, for example, Mnuchin fussed endlessly about a press release he wanted to issue on new sanctions against a Russian bank that had facilitated North Korea's international financial transactions. Trump agreed the sanctions should proceed, but he didn't want a press release, to avoid potential negative reactions from Moscow and Pyongyang. Mnuchin feared Congress would grill him for covering up for Russia if he didn't issue something. I thought he was overwrought, and a few days later, Trump agreed to a release. Exasperated, Kelly told me Mnuchin cared more than anything not to be exposed to any risk, notwithstanding his inordinate desire to attend Oval Office meetings and travel the world. A few days before, Kelly and I had spoken about Mnuchin's efforts to get into meetings where he had no role, including calling Trump to get himself invited. Kelly said he was sure Mnuchin spent far less than half his time at his desk at Treasury, so eager was he to go to White House meetings or on presidential trips. "They hardly recognize him in his building," said Kelly disdainfully.

In the meantime, Mattis's long-standing efforts to fire Ricardel, combined with the clandestine efforts of the First Lady's staff, finally had their effect. I was in Paris for meetings in advance of Trump's arrival to attend the November 11 World War I Armistice Day centenary. On the evening of November 9, as I was walking to dinner with my British, French, and German counterparts, Kelly called me from Air Force One, which was nearing arrival in Paris. We were on non-secure phones, so we didn't talk fully until closer to midnight, when Kelly said the First Lady's office was still trying to get Ricardel fired. "I have nothing to do with this," said Kelly.

On Saturday, I went to the US Ambassador's residence, where Trump was staying, to brief him before his bilateral with Macron. The weather was bad, and Kelly and I spoke about whether to travel as planned to the Château-Thierry Belleau Wood monuments and nearby American Cemeteries, where many US World War I dead were buried. Marine One's crew was saying that bad visibility could make it imprudent to chopper to the cemetery. The ceiling was not too low for Marines to fly in combat, but flying POTUS was obviously something very different. If a motorcade were necessary, it could take between ninety and a hundred and twenty minutes each way, along roads that were not exactly freeways, posing an unacceptable risk that we could not get the President out of France quickly enough in case of an emergency. It was a straightforward decision to cancel the visit but very hard for a Marine like Kelly to recommend, having originally been the one to suggest Belleau Wood (an iconic battle in Marine Corps history). Trump agreed, and it was decided that others would drive to the cemetery instead. As the meeting broke up and we prepared to leave for the Élysée Palace to see Macron, Trump pulled Kelly and me aside and said, "Find another spot for Mira. Melania's people are on the warpath." Kelly and I assumed we were to find an equivalent position elsewhere in government in a calmer setting in Washington.

The press turned canceling the cemetery visit into a story that Trump was afraid of the rain and took glee in pointing out that other world leaders traveled around during the day. Of course, none of them were the President of the United States, but the press didn't understand that rules for US Presidents are different from the rules for 190 other leaders who don't command the world's greatest military forces. Trump blamed Kelly, unfairly, marking a possibly decisive moment in ending his White House tenure. Trump was displeased throughout the trip ("He's in a royal funk," as Sanders put it) because of the disappointing election results, and nothing made things better. The rest of the Paris visit was similar. Macron opened their bilateral meeting by talking about a "European army," as he had been doing publicly earlier,[6] which a large number of other Americans were fully prepared to let the ungrateful Europeans have, without us. Macron all but insulted Trump in his November 11 speech at the Arc de Triomphe, saying, "Patriotism is the exact opposite of nationalism. Nationalism is a betrayal of patriotism by saying: 'Our interest first. Who cares about the others?'" Trump said he didn't hear Macron's rebuff because his earpiece cut off at the critical point.

After Paris, I flew on to the United Arab Emirates and then Singapore to help support the Vice President's trip to the annual Association of Southeast Asian Nations Summit. At 2:20 a.m. on November 14, Ricardel called to say there was a *Wall Street Journal* story, obviously leaked from an unfriendly source, that she was about to be fired. The story was also full of speculation on Kelly and Nielsen's being fired, so I immediately called to reach Trump (Singapore being thirteen hours ahead of Washington) and others to find out what was happening. In the interim, an incredible tweet went out from "the office of the First

Lady" that Ricardel no longer deserved to work at the White House. Talk about unprecedented. I was still digesting this when Trump called me back at about 5:30 a.m. He asked, "What is this thing from the First Lady?" and called to Westerhout to bring him the tweet, which he read for the first time. "Holy fuck," he shouted, "how could they put that out without showing it to me?" Good question, I thought. "Let me work on this," Trump concluded. Trump later called Ricardel and the FLOTUS staffers into the Oval, where they presented their versions of the FLOTUS Africa trip Ricardel had tried to keep from going off the rails due to the ignorance and insensitivity of the First Lady's staffers. Ricardel had never actually met the First Lady; all the criticism was from her staff. Trump was justifiably irritated by the tweet from the "office of the First Lady," which the staffers denied they were responsible for. "That statement is crap," said Trump, correctly.

I spoke to Pence about Ricardel when the two of us had a private lunch. "She's great," he said, and promised to be totally supportive. Kelly called later in the day to say Trump had instructed him, after the Oval meeting, "Find a place for her to land . . . we should keep her in the government," and that he'd said, "She's not a bad person," despite what the FLOTUS staffers had alleged.

Kelly went on to say, "Paris was a complete disaster," and that Trump had complained incessantly on Air Force One flying back to Washington, and even thereafter. He kept rehashing what had gone wrong, along with demanding that Mattis and Nielsen be fired, largely due to the Mexican border issue. Kelly said he had gotten Trump "off a number of ledges" but was not at all sure what would come next. I asked him to keep me posted, and he said simply, "Okay, pal," which told me he didn't have a lot of friends left at the White House. Trump issued a statement the next day that Ricardel would be transitioning to a new job in the Administration, although we didn't have it nailed down yet. Unfortunately, the atmosphere had been so poisoned by the FLOTUS staff that Ricardel decided on her own simply to leave government entirely and rejoin the private sector. The whole thing was appalling to me, and grossly unfair to Ricardel.

I did my own evaluation of the NSC after almost nine months.

Substantively, we had met a "do no harm" standard, entering no new bad deals and exiting several inherited from days gone by (*e.g.*, the Iran nuclear deal, the INF Treaty). But I could sense turmoil was coming on other fronts.

As the November election approached, the rumor mills were going full speed. Especially given the disappointing results, and after Armistice Day, rumors circulated constantly about who might succeed Kelly. One persistent theory was that Trump would select Nick Ayers, Pence's Chief of Staff. It was unusual, to say the least, to move from working for the VP to working for the President, but Jim Baker had gone from being George H. W. Bush's campaign manager in 1980 to being Reagan's White House Chief of Staff. Ayers's political skills made him a logical choice, if Kelly decided to leave, for a President looking toward a reelection campaign, but the real question was whether Ayers wanted it. He sought in advance to define the terms of the role, and Trump seemed amenable to doing so but repeatedly reneged on key points or dismissed the entire idea of a job description as unworkable. Although Ayers was tempted by the job, the experiences of the past two years had convinced him that, without a piece of paper to fall back on in times of crisis, the risk was not worth taking. Of course, it was an open question whether the piece of paper would have ever been worth anything, but that question would never be answered.

While this personnel pot simmered, the Mattis pot came to a boil. Nonetheless, I still fully expected Ayers would be named to succeed Kelly, likely on Monday, December 10, 2018. Kelly told me that morning at six thirty a.m., one of our last early conversations, that, after two days working directly for Trump as an experiment, Ayers had decided it would simply not work. Kelly was also convinced Trump planned to swap Haley for Pence as the 2020 VP nominee, which would have put Ayers in an impossible position. In any case, we were back at square one, and the whole world knew it. The only good news was that on December 10, Pat Cipollone started as White House Counsel, not a minute too soon. Mattis's departure soon became highly public.

Many candidates, inside and outside, vied for the Chief of Staff role, but Trump tweeted on December 14 that Mick Mulvaney, Director of the Office of Management and Budget, would be Acting Chief of Staff once Kelly left. Kushner came by that afternoon to say he was delighted at the decision and that the "acting" part of the title was just a charade. As I pieced things together later, there were no real negotiations between Trump and Mulvaney over the terms of the job, so the decision struck me as somewhat impulsive. Pompeo thought Mulvaney would do essentially whatever Ivanka and Kushner wanted him to do, which worried both of us philosophically. The handover from Kelly to Mulvaney was effective January 2.

In an October 2019 interview, in the midst of the Ukraine impeachment crisis, Kelly said he had told Trump, "Whatever you do—and we were still in the process of trying to find someone to take my place— I said whatever you do, don't hire a 'yes man,' someone who won't tell you the truth—don't do that. Because if you do, I believe you will be impeached."[7] Trump flatly denied Kelly had made such a statement: "John Kelly never said that, he never said anything like that. If he would have said that I would have thrown him out of the office. He just wants to come back into the action like everybody else does."[8] And Stephanie Grisham, previously one of the First Lady's Furies, now White House press secretary, pronounced *ex cathedra* , "I worked with John Kelly, and he was totally unequipped to handle the genius of our great President."[9] These quotes speak volumes about the people who uttered them.

With Kelly's departure and Mulvaney's appointment, all effective efforts at managing the Executive Office of the President ceased. Both domestic policy strategy and political strategy, never strong suits, all but disappeared; personnel decisions deteriorated further, and the general chaos spread. The crisis over Ukraine followed. There was a lot of evidence that Kelly's hypothesis was entirely correct.

CHAPTER 9

VENEZUELA LIBRE

Venezuela's illegitimate regime, one of the Western Hemisphere's most oppressive, presented the Trump Administration an opportunity. But it required steady determination on our part and consistent, all-out, unrelenting pressure. We failed to meet this standard. The President vacillated and wobbled, exacerbating internal Administration disagreements rather than resolving them, and repeatedly impeding our efforts to carry out a policy. We were never overconfident of success supporting the Venezuelan opposition's efforts to replace Nicolas Maduro, Hugo Chavez's heir. It was almost the opposite. Maduro's opponents acted in January 2019 because they felt strongly this could be their last opportunity for freedom, after years of trying and failing. America responded because it was in our national interest to do so. It still is, and the struggle continues.

After the unsuccessful efforts to oust Maduro, the Trump Administration did not hesitate to discuss publicly, in detail, how close the Opposition had come to ousting Maduro, and what had gone wrong. Numerous press stories repeated details of what we had continuously heard from the Opposition during 2019, and which are discussed in the text. This was hardly a normal situation of diplomatic conversations and interchanges, and we heard as well from many members of Congress, and private US citizens, especially members of the Cuban-American and Venezuelan-American communities in Florida. Someday, when Venezuela is free again, the many individuals supporting the Opposition will be free to tell their stories publicly. Until then, we have only the memories of people like myself fortunate enough to be able to tell their stories for them.[1]

There is a two-decade-long history of missed opportunities in Venezuela, given the widespread, strongly held opposition to the Chavez-Maduro regime. Shortly after I became National Security Advisor, while Maduro was speaking at a military awards ceremony on August 4, he was attacked by two drones. While the attack failed, it showed vigorous dissent within the military. And the hilarious pictures of service members fleeing energetically at the sound of explosions, despite regime propaganda, showed just how "loyal" the military was to Maduro.

Maduro's autocratic regime was a threat due to its Cuba connection and the openings it afforded Russia, China, and Iran. Moscow's menace was undeniable, both military and financial, having expended substantial resources to buttress Maduro, dominate Venezuela's oil-and-gas industry, and impose costs on the US. Beijing was not far behind. Trump saw this, telling me after a New Year's Day 2019 call with Egypt's President Abdel Fattah al-Sisi that he worried about Russia and China: "I don't want to be sitting around watching." Venezuela hadn't topped my priorities when I started, but competent national-security management requires flexibility when new threats or opportunities arise. Venezuela was just such a contingency. America had opposed external threats in the Western Hemisphere since the Monroe Doctrine, and it was time to resurrect it after the Obama-Kerry efforts to bury it.

Venezuela was a threat on its own account, as demonstrated in a December 22 incident at sea, along the Guyana-Venezuela border. Venezuelan naval units tried to board ExxonMobil exploration ships, under licenses from Guyana in its territorial waters. Chavez and Maduro had run Venezuela's oil-and-gas industry into a ditch, and extensive hydrocarbon resources in Guyana would pose an immediate competitive threat right next door. The incident evaporated as the exploration ships, after refusing Venezuelan requests to land a chopper on board one of them, headed rapidly back into undeniably Guyanese waters.

Shortly after the drone attack, during an unrelated meeting on August 15, Venezuela came up, and Trump said to me emphatically, "Get it done," meaning get rid of the Maduro regime. "This is the fifth time I've asked for it," he continued. I described the thinking we were doing, in a meeting now slimmed down to just Kelly and me, but Trump insisted he wanted military options for Venezuela and then keep it because "it's really part of the United States." This presidential interest in discussing military options initially surprised me, but it shouldn't have; as I learned, Trump had previously advocated it, responding to a press question, almost exactly one year earlier, on August 11, 2017, at Bedminster, N.J.:

> "We have many options for Venezuela, and by the way, I'm not going to rule out a military option. We have many options for Venezuela. This is our neighbor . . . this is—we're all over the world, and we have troops all over the world in places that are very, very far away. Venezuela is not very far away, and the people are suffering, and they're dying. We have many options for Venezuela, including a possible military option, if necessary."[2]

I explained why military force was not the answer, especially given the inevitable congressional opposition, but that we could accomplish the same objective by working with Maduro's opponents. I subsequently decided to turn a spotlight on Venezuela, giving a widely covered speech in Miami on November 1, 2018, in which I condemned the Western Hemisphere's "troika of tyranny": Venezuela, Cuba, and Nicaragua. I announced that the Administration, in its ongoing reversal of Obama's Cuba policy, would impose new sanctions against Havana, and also carry out a new Executive Order sanctioning Venezuela's gold sector, which the regime used to keep itself afloat by selling gold from Venezuela's Central Bank. The "troika of tyranny" speech underlined the affiliations between all three authoritarian governments, laying the basis for a more forward-leaning policy. Trump liked the phrase "troika of tyranny," telling me, "You give such great speeches"; this one, as I pointed out, had been written by one of his own speechwriters.

Of course, Trump also periodically said that he wanted to meet with Maduro to resolve all our problems with Venezuela, which neither Pompeo nor I thought was a good idea. At one point in December,

I ran into Rudy Giuliani in the West Wing. He asked to come see me after a meeting of Trump's lawyers, which was why he was there. He had a message for Trump from Representative Pete Sessions, who had long advocated Trump meet with Maduro, as had Senator Bob Corker, for reasons best known to themselves. Discussing this later, Pompeo suggested we first send someone to Venezuela to see Maduro, although, as Trump's interest in talking with Maduro waned thereafter, nothing happened.

The big bang in Venezuela came on Friday, January 11. The new, young President of the National Assembly, Juan Guaidó, announced at a huge rally in Caracas that the Assembly believed Maduro's manifestly fraudulent 2018 reelection was illegitimate, and therefore invalid. Accordingly, the Assembly, Venezuela's only legitimate, popularly elected institution, had declared the Venezuelan presidency vacant. Under the vacancy clause of Hugo Chavez's own Constitution, Guaidó said he would become Interim President on January 23, which was the anniversary of the 1958 military coup that overthrew the Marcos Perez Jimenez dictatorship, and oust Maduro to prepare new elections.[3] The US had only late word the National Assembly would move in this direction. We played no role encouraging or assisting the Opposition. They saw this moment as possibly their last chance. It was now all on the line in Venezuela, and we had to decide how to respond. Sit and watch? Or act? I had no doubt what we should do. The revolution was on. I told Mauricio Claver-Carone, whom I had recently chosen as NSC Senior Director for the Western Hemisphere, to issue a statement of support.[4]

I briefed Trump on what had happened, interrupting a meeting with an outsider that had already run past its scheduled end. Trump, though, was irritated at being informed only of a *possible* change in Venezuela, saying I should put the statement out in my name, not his. I could have reminded him he had said not ten days before, "I don't want to be sitting around watching," and probably should have, but I just issued the statement as my own. Maduro reacted harshly, threatening National Assembly members and their families. Guaidó himself was arrested by one of the regime's secret police forces but then quickly released.[5] There was speculation it was actually Cubans who seized Guaidó, but his release indicated real confusion in the regime, a good sign.[6]

I also tweeted the first of many Venezuela tweets to come condemning the Maduro dictatorship's arrest of Guaidó. I was heartened that Maduro's government promptly accused me of leading a coup "against Venezuela's democracy,"[7] an approach followed by other adversaries who attacked Trump's advisors. More important, we began devising steps to take immediately against Maduro's regime, and also Cuba, its protector and likely controller, and Nicaragua. Why not go after all three at once? Oil sanctions were a natural choice, but why not declare Venezuela a "state sponsor of terrorism," something I first suggested on October 1, 2018, and also return Cuba to the list after Obama had removed it?

Under Chavez and now Maduro, Venezuela's revenues from petroleum-related exports had dropped dramatically, as production itself fell, from approximately 3.3 million barrels of oil pumped per day when Chavez took power in 1999 to approximately 1.1 million barrels per day in January 2019. This precipitous decline, dropping Venezuela to production levels not seen since the 1940s, had already substantially impoverished the country. Driving the state-owned oil monopoly's production as low as possible, which the Opposition fully supported,[8] might well have been enough to crash Maduro's regime. There were many other sanctions necessary to eliminate the regime's illicit income streams—especially drug trafficking with narco-terrorists operating primarily in Colombia, with safe havens in Venezuela—but striking the oil company was key.[9]

On January 14, I convened a Principals Committee in the Sit Room to consider our options for sanctioning the Maduro regime, especially the petroleum sector. I thought it was time to turn the screws and asked, "Why don't we go for a win here?" It rapidly became clear that everyone wanted to take decisive action except Treasury Secretary Mnuchin. He wanted to do little or nothing, arguing that if we acted, it risked Maduro's nationalizing what little remained of US oil-sector investments in Venezuela and raising international oil prices. Mnuchin essentially wanted a guarantee we would succeed, with Maduro overthrown, if we imposed sanctions. That, of course, was impossible. If I have one memory of Mnuchin from the Administration—and there were many carbon copies of this one, Mnuchin opposing tough measures, especially against China—this is it. Why were our sanctions often not as sweeping and effective as they might have been? Read no further. As Commerce Secretary Wilbur Ross (a renowned financier, much more politically conservative than Mnuchin, who was basically a Democrat) said to me in April, "Stephen's more worried about secondary effects on US companies than about the mission," which was completely accurate. Mnuchin's argument for passivity was entirely economic, so it was important that Larry Kudlow weighed in quickly to say, "John's view is my view too." Keith Kellogg added that Pence believed we should be "going all out" against Venezuela's state-owned oil company. That had enormous effect since Pence rarely offered his views in such settings, to avoid boxing in the President. Pompeo was traveling, but Deputy Secretary of State John Sullivan argued for sanctions, although not with great specificity. Energy Secretary Rick Perry was strongly in favor of tough sanctions, sweeping aside Mnuchin's concerns about the limited US oil-and-gas assets in Venezuela.

Mnuchin was a minority of one, so I said we would send Trump a split-decision memo; everyone should get their arguments in quickly because we were moving fast. Pence had earlier offered to call Guaidó to express our support, which, after hearing Mnuchin, I thought was a good idea. The call went well, increasing the urgency that America react with something more than just rhetoric praising Venezuela's National Assembly. Nonetheless, Mnuchin kept up his campaign for doing nothing; Pompeo told me he had had a thirty-minute call with Mnuchin on Thursday and had counterproposed doing the sanctions in slices. I responded that we had a shot to overthrow Maduro now, and it might be a long, long time before we had another one as good. Half measures weren't going to cut it. Pompeo agreed we didn't want to replicate Obama in 2009, watching pro-democracy protests in Iran suppressed while the US did nothing. That sounded like Pompeo was moving in the right direction. Even the Organization of American States, long one of the most moribund international organizations (and that's saying something), was roused to help Guaidó, as a growing number of Latin American countries stood up to declare support for Venezuela's defiant National Assembly.

The mere fact Guaidó remained free showed we had a chance. We needed Trump's decision on sanctions and whether to recognize Guaidó as the legitimate Interim President when he crossed the Rubicon on January 23. On the twenty-first, I explained to Trump the possible political and economic steps to take against Maduro and said a lot depended on what happened two days later. Trump doubted Maduro would fall, saying he's "too smart and too tough," which was yet another surprise, given earlier comments on the regime's stability. (He had said just a short time before, on September 25, 2018, in New York, that "it's a regime that, frankly, could be toppled very quickly by the military, if the military decides to do that."[10] Trump added that he also wanted the fullest range of options against the regime,[11] which request I conveyed to Dunford later in the day. Dunford and I also discussed what might be required if things went badly in Caracas, potentially endangering the lives of official US personnel and even private US citizens there, thereby perhaps necessitating a "non-permissive" evacuation of those in danger.

The more I thought about it, the more I realized the decision on political recognition was more important now than the oil sanctions. First, US recognition would have major implications for the Federal Reserve Board, and therefore banks worldwide. The Fed would automatically turn control over Venezuelan government assets it possessed to the Guaidó-led Administration. Unfortunately, as we were to find, Maduro's regime had been so proficient at stealing or squandering those assets, there weren't many left. But the international financial consequences of recognition were nonetheless significant, since other central banks and private bankers weren't looking for reasons to be on the Fed's bad side. Second, the logic of sanctioning the country's oil monopoly, and other measures Mnuchin and Treasury were resisting, would become unanswerable once we endorsed Guaidó's legitimacy.

To that end, I scheduled an eight a.m. meeting on January 22 with Pompeo, Mnuchin, Wilbur Ross, and Kudlow.

Inside Venezuela, tensions were rising. In the hours before we met, there had been all-night demonstrations, including *cacerolazos*, the traditional gatherings to bang pots and pans, in the poorest areas of Caracas, the original base of "Chavista" support. Shortages of basic goods were increasing, and demonstrators had briefly seized control of the roads to the Caracas airport. Only *colectivos*, the armed gangs of motorcycle thugs used by Chavez and Maduro to sow terror and intimidate the Opposition, and which the Opposition believed were equipped and directed by the Cubans,[12] appeared to reopen the roads. No military. Defense Minister Vladimir Padrino (one of many Latins with Russian first names, from Cold War days) and Foreign Minister Jorge Arreaza had both already approached the Opposition, tentatively exploring what the National Assembly's amnesty for defecting military officers would mean if the Opposition prevailed. Nonetheless, after years of hostility between the two sides, there was real mistrust within Venezuelan society.

With this backdrop, I asked if we should recognize Guaidó when the National Assembly declared him Interim President. Ross spoke first, saying it was clear we should support Guaidó, immediately seconded by Kudlow and Pompeo. Happily, Mnuchin concurred, saying we had already asserted that Maduro was illegitimate, so recognizing Guaidó was simply the next logical step. We didn't discuss what the economic consequences would be; either Mnuchin didn't see the connection, or he didn't want to fight the issue. I was fine either way. With recognition resolved, we discussed other steps: working with the informal "Lima Group" of Latin American nations for them to recognize Guaidó (which took little or no convincing), adjusting the level of our travel-advisory warnings, considering how to oust the Cubans, and handling the Russian paramilitaries reportedly arriving to protect Maduro.[13] I considered the meeting a total victory.

Later in the morning, I spoke with Trump, who now wanted assurances regarding post-Maduro access to Venezuela's oil resources, trying to ensure that China and Russia would not continue to benefit from their deals with the illicit Chavez-Maduro regime. Trump, as usual, was having trouble distinguishing responsible measures to protect legitimate American interests from what amounted to vast overreaching of the sort no other government, especially a democratic one, would even consider. I suggested Pence raise the issue with Guaidó in the call being scheduled for later in the day, and Trump agreed. I also called several members of Florida's congressional delegation, who were coming to see Trump on Venezuela that afternoon, so they were prepared if the oil-field issue arose. Senators Marco Rubio and Rick Scott, and Congressmen Lincoln Diaz-Balart and Ron DeSantis, gave very forceful support for toppling Maduro, with Rubio saying, "This may be the last chance," and that success would be "a big foreign-policy win." During the meeting, they explained that the National Assembly believed many Russian and Chinese business deals had been procured through bribes and corruption, making them easy to invalidate once a new government was installed.[14] The discussion was very helpful, and Trump agreed unequivocally to recognize Guaidó, which Pence, who was attending the meeting, was fully prepared to do. Trump later added unhelpfully, "I want him to say he will be extremely loyal to the United States and no one else."

Trump still wanted a military option, raising the question with the Florida Republicans, who were plainly stunned, except for Rubio, who had heard it before and knew how to deflect it politely. Later, I called Shanahan and Dunford to ask how their thinking was proceeding. None of us thought that a military option was advisable at this point. To me, this exercise was solely to keep Trump interested in the objective of overthrowing Maduro, without actually wasting a lot of time on a nonstarter. The Pentagon would have to begin at square one, because under the Obama Administration, Secretary of State John Kerry had announced the end of the Monroe Doctrine,[15] a mistake that had reverberated through all of the national security departments and agencies with predictable effects. But it is proof of what some people thought was a joke, when Trump later commented that I had to hold him back. He was correct on Venezuela. Dunford said politely at the end of our call that he appreciated my trying to help him understand how our military's involvement might arise. Of course, I had the easy job, closing by saying, "All I had to do was make the call." Now Dunford had the problem. He laughed and said, "Tag. I'm it!" At least he still had a sense of humor.

Pence asked me to join him in his office for the Guaidó call, which went through about six fifteen. Guaidó was very appreciative of a supportive video Pence had distributed earlier over the Internet, and the two had an excellent talk. Pence again expressed our support, and Guaidó answered positively, if very generally, about how the Opposition would perform if it prevailed. He said that Venezuela was very happy with the support the United States was providing, and would work hand in hand with us, given the risks we were taking. I felt this should satisfy Trump. After the call, I leaned over Pence's desk to shake hands, saying, "This is a historic moment." He suggested we go to the Oval to brief Trump, who was quite happy with the outcome, looking forward to the statement he would make the next day.

He called me about 9:25 a.m. on the twenty-third to say the draft statement to be issued when the National Assembly formally invoked the Venezuelan constitution to move against Maduro was "beautiful," adding, "I almost never say that."[16] I thanked him and said we would keep him posted. Guaidó appeared before a huge crowd in Caracas (according to our embassy, the largest in the twenty-year history of the Chavez-Maduro regime), and took the oath of office as Interim President. The die was cast. Pence came in to shake hands, and we issued Trump's statement immediately. We feared the imminent deployment of troops, but none came (although reports indicated that, overnight, *colectivos* killed four people).[17] Embassy Caracas presented its credentials to the new Guaidó government, along with the Lima Group Ambassadors, as a show of support. I briefed Trump on the day's events at about six thirty p.m., and he seemed to be holding firm.

The next day, Defense Minister Padrino and an array of generals held a press conference to declare loyalty to Maduro, which was not what we wanted, but which to this point was not reflected in actual military activity. The Opposition believed that 80 percent or more of the rank and file, as well as most junior officers, whose families were enduring the same hardships as Venezuela's civilian population generally, supported the new government. While the percentage figure cannot be confirmed given the authoritarian nature of the Maduro regime, Guaidó frequently contended he had the support of 90 percent of Venezuela's population overall.[18] Top military officers, like those at the press conference, however, were likely still too corrupted by years of Chavista rule to break ranks. On the other hand, they had not ordered the military out of their barracks to crush the rebellion, likely fearing such an order would be disobeyed, which would be the end of the regime. UK Foreign Minister Jeremy Hunt, in Washington for meetings, was delighted to cooperate on steps they could take, for example freezing Venezuelan gold deposits in the Bank of England, so the regime could not sell the gold to keep itself going.[19] These were the sorts of steps we were already applying to pressure Maduro financially. I urged Pompeo to have State more fully support the effort against the state-owned oil company, where I still worried Mnuchin was holding out, which he agreed to do. Pompeo was also disturbed by signs Maduro might be encouraging the *colectivos* to threaten US embassy personnel and said Trump was as well.[20]

The first troubling sign from Trump came that evening after eight thirty p.m. when he called to say, "I don't like where we are," referring to Venezuela. He worried about Padrino's press conference, saying, "The entire army is behind him." Then, he added, "I've always said Maduro was tough. This kid [Guaidó]—nobody's ever heard of him." And, "The Russians have put out brutal statements." I walked Trump back off the ledge, explaining that the military was still in its barracks, which was very significant, and that senior military figures had been talking to the Opposition for two days about what would be in it for them if they came over to the Opposition or retired. Things were still very much in play, and the more time passed, the more likely it was that the military would fragment, which was what we really needed. I don't think I satisfied Trump, but I at least talked him back into silence. God only knew who he was talking to or whether he had just gotten a case of the vapors because things were still uncertain. I was sure of one thing: any display of American indecision now would doom the entire effort. I suspected Trump knew that too, but I was amazed our policy was so close to shifting just thirty-plus hours after being launched. You couldn't make this up.

The next morning, I called Pompeo to tell him how Trump had all but jumped ship on Venezuela and to make sure Pompeo wasn't about to follow. Fortunately, I heard exactly the opposite reaction, Pompeo saying "we should go to the wall" to get Maduro out. Encouraged, I later asked Claver-Carone to follow up Guaidó's people to ensure that they were getting out letters, the sooner the better, to the International Monetary Fund, the Bank for International Settlements, and similar institutions announcing that they were the legitimate government.[21] Pompeo thought there was a way forward on the safety of US personnel in Caracas, thus allowing us to retain a slimmed-down mission, which he wanted to do. I explained how State often became so hung up on safety issues that it made concessions on policy issues, arguing it was required to protect official staff. I certainly wasn't arguing for ignoring risks to our people, but I did believe it was better to withdraw them rather than make substantive concessions to governments like Maduro's.

Just after nine a.m., I called Trump, finding him in somewhat better shape than the night before. He still thought the Opposition was "beaten down," referring again to the picture of Padrino and "all those good-looking generals" declaring support for Maduro. I told him the real pressure was about to begin, as we imposed the petroleum sanctions, taking away a significant share of the regime's revenues. "Do it," said Trump, which was the clear signal I needed to roll over Treasury if it was still obstructionist. On our Caracas diplomatic personnel, however, Trump wanted them all out, fearing the blowback if anything went wrong. Mostly, however, he seemed uninterested, which was explained later in the day when he announced a partial deal ending the government shutdown, interpreted across the political spectrum as a complete surrender on his Mexico border-wall project. No wonder he was in a grumpy mood.

I decided to call Mnuchin, who for some reason was in California again, and he agreed we had to apply oil sanctions "now that we've

After greeting me at the Pentagon's ceremonial entrance, Mattis and I enter the building for our first meeting, on March 29, 2018, ten days before my official start as National Security Advisor.

Happy times just before Pompeo's swearing-in ceremony as Secretary of State, at the Department, in Washington, on May 2, 2018.

At the G7 meeting in Canada on June 10, 2018, I was there as the Europeans pushed Trump into a corner, literally. It turned out not to be a good moment for the Western alliance.

I met with King Abdullah at the residence of Jordan's Ambassador to Washington on June 22, 2018, just before the King's meeting with Trump to discuss the continuing crisis in Syria, and Iran's support for the Assad regime.

Getting together with Russian Foreign Minister Sergei Lavrov for lunch at Osobnyak House in Moscow on June 27, 2018, to prepare for the Trump-Putin meeting in Helsinki. Unfortunately, the summit ended in disarray when Trump appeared to cast doubt on US intelligence about Russian interference in our elections. E. PESOV

Laying a wreath at the Yad Vashem Holocaust memorial in Jerusalem, Israel, on August 21, 2018, a traditional stop for high-level visitors.

I met Nicolas Patrushev, my Russian counterpart, for the first time, at the US mission in Geneva on August 23, 2018, and made a point of addressing Russian election interference.

Russian President Vladimir Putin welcomes me to our second 2018 meeting in Moscow's Kremlin, on October 23, where, among other things, Putin joked that Russia would sell weapons to Saudi Arabia if the US did not. Fiona Hill, NSC Senior Director for Europe and Russia, looks on.
AP PHOTO/ALEXANDER ZEMLIANICHENKO

Pompeo and I speak while waiting for Trump, typically late, to join the G20 meetings in Buenos Aires, Argentina, on November 30, 2018, as relations with Russia chilled after the seizure of Ukrainian ships in the Kerch Strait.

One of the turning points in Trump's decision making on Syria: being briefed by American military commanders at the Al-Asad air base in Iraq, December 26, 2018. AP PHOTO/ANDREW HARNIK

Trump speaks by phone with Iraqi Prime Minister Adil Abdul-Mahdi from Al-Asad air base in Iraq on December 26, 2018, after Abdul-Mahdi decided not to meet with Trump at the base.

The final meeting of the Hanoi Summit between the United States and North Korea, February 28, 2019, from which Trump walked away without a deal. AP PHOTO/ EVAN VUCCI

Always an experience: reporters accompanying me on one of several Middle East trips on board our military aircraft, March 23, 2019. SARAH TINSLEY

Trump's meeting with South Korean President Moon Jae-in, April 11, 2019, considered what to do next about North Korea's nuclear weapons and ballistic missile programs after two failed summits with Kim Jong-un.

Johnny Lopez de la Cruz, President of the Bay of Pigs Veterans Association Brigade 2506, gave me an enthusiastic introdution at the brigade's annual commemoration of their tragically unsuccessful 1961 effort to overthrow Castro's regime, in Coral Gables Florida, April 17, 2019. AP PHOTO/ WILFREDO LEE

After a sad day for the people of Venezuela, I explained to the press outside the West Wing on May 1, 2019, how close the opposition to the Maduro regime had had come to ousting him.

Trump meets with US service members, veterans, and their families at the UK celebration of the 75th anniversary of launching D-Day, on June 5, 2019, at Portsmouth, England, from which much of the Allied invasion armada sailed.

Helicoptering to the Jordan Valley with Israeli Prime Minister Bibi Netanyahu on June 23, 2019, Victoria Coates, NSC Senior Director for the Middle East is at left. AP PHOTO/ ABIR SULTAN/EPA POOL VIA AP

Bibi took me on a tour of the strategic geography of the Jordan Valley, June 23, 2019; here we overlook the valley from a secure Israeli position on the heights of the West Bank. CHRISTINE SAMUELIAN

Outside the West Wing on September 10, 2019, explaining to my daughter on my personal cell (normally kept in a secure box during the work day) that I am about to resign. TOM BRENNER/BLOOMBERG VIA GETTY IMAGES

acknowledged the new regime." I called Pompeo to tell him the good news, and he said Venezuela's Foreign Minister was coming to New York for the Saturday UN Security Council debate we and others had asked for. We both thought this might be an opportunity for Pompeo to see him alone and get a clear assessment of his state of mind without flunkies nearby to listen in, similar to what we were doing with other Venezuelans in diplomatic missions around the world. Because of the near certainty of Russian and probably Chinese vetoes, we didn't expect anything substantive from the Security Council, but it was a good forum to generate support for the Opposition cause. Guaidó helped out later in the day by calling on Cuba to take its people out of Venezuela and send them home.[22]

On Saturday, January 26, the Security Council met at nine a.m., and Pompeo laced into the Maduro regime. The European members said Maduro had eight days to call elections or they would all recognize Guaidó, a considerable improvement over what we thought the EU position was. Russia blasted the meeting as an attempted coup and denounced me personally for calling for a "Bolshevik-style" expropriation in Venezuela (an honor!), thereby showing we were on the right track going after the oil monopoly.[23] Potentially significant was news that Venezuela's military attaché in Washington had declared his allegiance to Guaidó. These and other defections brought the Opposition new advocates, which as a standard procedure the Opposition now asked to persuade officers and civilian officials still in Venezuela to bring as many of them around as he could.

Unfortunately, the State Department was in a tizzy over the assurances it wanted from Maduro about the safety of our diplomatic personnel. This was not about the substance of ensuring Venezuela's government provided adequate protection, but about how to exchange "diplomatic notes," completely oblivious to the broader political context. State had also held up notifying the Federal Reserve we had recognized a new government in Caracas, which was stunning. By Monday, State's Western Hemisphere Affairs bureau was in open revolt against petroleum sanctions, arguing, as I had feared, that so doing would endanger embassy personnel. Western Hemisphere

Affairs Assistant Secretary Kim Breier wanted a thirty-day delay in the sanctions, which was palpable nonsense. At first, I didn't take it seriously. But Breier's argument seemed to be expanding by the day, with essentially anything we did to put pressure on the Maduro regime leaving our embassy staff (most of whom by then were security personnel, not "diplomats") in danger. If I were just a tad more cynical, I might have concluded Breier and her bureau were actually trying to subvert our basic policy.

Pompeo called me Saturday afternoon, uncertain about what to do about the bureaucracy's resistance. I persuaded him that the Western Hemisphere bureau was simply playing for time; whatever delay he agreed to would only form the basis for the next request for delay. He agreed, finally, that he was "okay if we [went] tomorrow" on the sanctions, which we did. Nonetheless, the bureau's rebellion was not a good sign. Who knew what the bureaucracy was telling other governments, the strong left-wing Latin America think tank/lobby presence in Washington, and the media? Mnuchin and I spoke several times on Monday. He had talked to oil-company executives all weekend, and the sanctions would actually be more aggressive than he had first anticipated, which was good news. Predictions we could not act against the state-owned oil company because of negative impacts on Gulf Coast refiners turned out to be overstated; having appreciated the possibility of petroleum sanctions for years, these refineries were "well positioned," in Mnuchin's words, to find other sources of oil; imports from Venezuela were already less than 10 percent of their total work.

In the afternoon, we were to unveil the sanctions in the White House briefing room, but I got diverted to the Oval first. Trump was very happy with how "the Venezuela thing" was playing in the press. He asked if we should send five thousand troops to Colombia in case they might be needed, which I duly noted on my yellow legal pad, saying I would check with the Pentagon. "Go have fun with the press," Trump said, which we did, when my note, picked up by cameras, produced endless speculation. (A few weeks later, Colombian Foreign Minister Carlos Trujillo brought me a pack of legal pads like the one I had in the briefing room, so I didn't run out.) Substantively, we believed that the oil sanctions were a major blow to Maduro's regime, and many asserted that it was now just a matter of time before he fell. Their optimism was high, fueled in substantial part because they believed Maduro loyalists like Diosdado Cabello[24] and others were sending both their financial assets and their families abroad for safety, hardly a vote of confidence in the regime.

On January 30, my office filled with people, including Sarah Sanders, Bill Shine, and Mercedes Schlapp, to listen to Trump's call to Guaidó at about nine a.m. Trump wished him good luck on the large anti-Maduro demonstrations planned for later in the day, which Trump said were historic. Trump then assured Guaidó he'd pull off Maduro's overthrow, and offered as an aside that he was sure Guaidó would remember in the future what had happened, which was Trump's way of referring to his interest in Venezuela's oil fields. It was a big moment in the history of the world, said Trump. Guaidó thanked Trump for his calls for democracy and his firm leadership, which made me smile. Firm? If only he knew. Trump said Guaidó should feel free to tell the rallies later in the day he had called, and that he looked forward to meeting Guaidó personally. Guaidó responded that it would be very, very moving for the people to hear that he had spoken to Trump when they fight against the dictatorship. Trump said it was an honor to talk to him, and the call ended.[25] It was undoubtedly a boost to Guaidó to announce he had spoken with Trump, which of course is what we intended. Guaidó tweeted about the call even before Trump did, and the press coverage was uniformly favorable.

At one thirty p.m., I met with American executives of the Citgo Petroleum Corporation, which is majority-owned by Venezuela's state-owned oil company, to tell them we supported their efforts, and those of the Venezuelan Opposition, to keep control of Citgo's refineries and service stations in the United States, thereby shielding them from Maduro's efforts to assert control. (As I explained to them and others, we were also providing advice to Guaidó at his request in his efforts to nominate people to the oil company's various boards of directors which, through subsidiaries, ultimately held Citgo's ownership.) I referred the executives to Wilbur Ross, whom they met the next day, for

advice on avoiding the effects of a Russian government lien on Venezuela's oil company stock that might lead to a loss of control over the
US assets, which was right down his alley. (From Moscow, we learned
that Putin was allegedly very concerned about the roughly $18 billion
Venezuela owed to Moscow; the estimates of the actual amounts owed
varied widely, but they were all substantial.) The US executives told
me that, earlier in the day, Venezuelans loyal to Maduro, having tried
unsuccessfully to divert corporate assets before they left, had fled the
US with one of Citgo's corporate jets, headed for Caracas. I was sure
we could expect more of this in the days ahead.

Even Lukoil, the big Russian firm, announced it was suspending
operations with Venezuela's oil monopoly, which reflected at least
some desire by Russia to hedge its bets.[26] A few days later, PetroChina,
a major Chinese operation, announced it was dropping the oil monopoly as a partner for a Chinese refinery project, thus showing significant unease.[27] Subsequently, Gazprombank, Russia's third-biggest
lender, closely tied to Putin and the Kremlin, froze its accounts to
avoid running afoul of our sanctions.[28] We believed Guaidó and the
Opposition would take the opportunity to speak with Russian and
Chinese diplomats and business types, stressing it was in their interest
not to take sides in the intra-Venezuelan dispute. Within the US government, we were also planning for "the day after" in Venezuela and
considering what could be done to get the country's economy, in terrible disarray after two decades of economic mismanagement (which
even Putin disparaged), back on its feet. We gave significant thought
to how we could help a new government face both immediate needs
for the people and also the longer-term need to repair the systemic
destruction of what should have been one of Latin America's strongest
economies.

A drumbeat of diplomatic recognitions of Guaidó was picking
up and we hoped it would demonstrate even to Maduro loyalists that
his days were numbered, and also provide insurance against arrest for
Guaidó and other Opposition leaders. This was not hypothetical. Maduro's secret police broke into Guaidó's home and threatened his wife
and young daughter. They were not harmed, but the signal was clear.[29]

It looked very much like a Cuban-directed operation, underscoring again that the foreign presence in Venezuela, Cuban and Russian alike, was critical to keeping Maduro in power. Protests continued throughout the country, undeterred by the prospect of Maduro's cracking down. Continuous contacts were being made with top military officers about the terms under which they could come to Guaidó's side, and with former Chavista Cabinet members, labor union leaders, and other sectors of Venezuelan society to build alliances. We thought the momentum remained with the Opposition, but they needed to pick up the pace.

In Venezuela, a plan was being developed, which we thought promising, to bring humanitarian supplies across the borders from Colombia and Brazil to distribute around Venezuela. Until now, Maduro had effectively closed the borders, feasible because difficult terrain and thick forests and jungles made crossings all but impossible except at well-known and established border checkpoints. The humanitarian aid project would demonstrate Guaidó's concerns for Venezuela's people and also show that the international borders were open, reflecting Maduro's increasing lack of control.[30] There were also hopes that key military officials would not follow orders to close the borders, but that, even if they did, Maduro would be placed in the impossible position of denying humanitarian supplies to his impoverished citizens. Maduro was so troubled by this strategy that he again took to criticizing me by name, saying, "I have proof that the assassination attempt was ordered by John Bolton in the White House."[31] He was joined by Foreign Minister Arreaza, who complained, "What he's trying to do here is give us orders!"[32] Cuba was also now attacking me by name, so my spirits were high.

Colombian President Ivan Duque visited Trump in the White House on February 13, and the discussion centered on Venezuela. Trump asked the Colombians if he should have talked to Maduro six months earlier, and Duque said unequivocally it would have been a big victory for Maduro, implying it would be an even bigger mistake to talk to him now. Trump said he agreed, which relieved me greatly. He then inquired how the effort was going overall and whether the momentum was with Maduro or Guaidó. Here, Colombian Ambassador Francisco Santos was particularly effective, saying that even two months ago, he would have said Maduro had the edge, but he no longer believed it was true, explaining why. This clearly registered with Trump.

Nonetheless, I worried our own government was not displaying a proper sense of urgency. There was, across the government, an obstructionist, "not invented here" mentality, undoubtedly in large part because under eight years of Obama, the Venezuelan, Cuban, and Nicaraguan regimes were not seen as US adversaries. Little or no attention was given to what the US should do if, inconveniently, the people of these countries decided they wanted to run their own governments. Even more important, in my view, the growing Russian, Chinese, Iranian, and Cuban influence across the hemisphere had not been a priority. In effect, therefore, the Trump Administration faced an avalanche of due bills in Latin America with no preparation for how to handle them.

The Opposition refined its thinking on how to "force" humanitarian aid into Venezuela from Colombia and Brazil, and set Saturday, February 23, as the target date. The Saturday prior, some six hundred thousand people had signed up in Caracas to help. After much coordinating between the United States Agency for International Development and the Pentagon, C-17 cargo planes were now landing at Cúcuta, one of the principal Colombian border crossing points, offloading humanitarian assistance to go across the bridges connecting the two countries. Inside Venezuela, movement toward the Opposition continued. The Catholic bishop of San Cristóbal, who was also Vice President of the country's Catholic bishops' conference, spoke publicly, specifically referring to a transition in power away from Maduro. We had hoped the church would take a more active public role, and that now seemed to be happening. As February 23 approached, rumors intensified of a high-level military leader, likely Venezuelan Army Commander Jesús Suárez Chourio, publicly announcing that he no longer backed Maduro. There had been similar rumors before, but the humanitarian cross-border plan was the key factor why this time it might be true. Contemporaneously, Senator Marco Rubio specifically named Suarez Chourio, along with Defense Minister Padrino and four others, as key military figures who could receive amnesty if they defected to the Opposition.[33] There was also some feeling that defections of this magnitude would bring a significant number of troops with them, with the military units seemingly moving toward the borders, but then doubling back to Caracas to encircle the Miraflores Palace, Venezuela's White House. These optimistic forecasts, however, did not come to pass.

We were doing our bit, with a Trump speech at Miami's Florida International University on February 18, which could have been a campaign rally, so enthusiastic was the crowd. Plans for the twenty-third fell into place, as Colombia's President Duque announced he would be joined at Cúcuta by the Presidents of Panama, Chile, and Paraguay, and the Organization of American States Secretary General Luis Almagro. This would prove convincingly that Venezuela's revolution was hardly "made in Washington." Humanitarian supplies increased on the borders, and there was evidence that Maduro's security forces intensified their harassment of nongovernmental organizations inside the country. Guaidó left Caracas under cover on Wednesday, heading for the Colombian border, where, it was originally planned, he would wait on the Venezuelan side while the humanitarian aid came across the Tienditas International Bridge from Colombia. We heard, however, that Guaidó was thinking of actually crossing into Colombia to attend a Richard Branson-sponsored concert in Cúcuta on Friday night to support the assistance to Venezuela, and then leading the aid back across the border the next day, facing a confrontation with Maduro's forces, if one came, directly.

This was not a good idea, for several reasons. It was very dramatic but dangerous, not just physically, but more important, politically. Once across the border and outside Venezuela, it would likely be difficult for Guaidó to get back in. What would happen to his ability to direct and control Opposition policy if he were isolated outside the country, subject to Maduro propaganda saying he had fled in fear? We had no way of predicting the outcome on Saturday. It could swing from one extreme to another: things could go well, with the border effectively opened, which would be a direct challenge to Maduro's authority, or there could be violence and bloodshed at the crossing points, potentially with Guaidó arrested or worse. I thought trying to bring the humanitarian aid across the border was well conceived and entirely doable. More grandiose plans, however, were not well thought out and could easily lead to trouble.

In the midst of all this, with the Trump/Kim Jong Un Hanoi Summit looming, I cut short my planned itinerary in Asia, canceling meetings in Korea so I could stay in Washington until Sunday to see what happened in Venezuela. Although media attention focused on the Colombia-Venezuela border, especially at Cúcuta, there were also significant developments on the Brazil side. The Pemones, indigenous people inside Venezuela who detested Maduro, were fighting the government's National Guard forces. Both sides sustained casualties, and the Pemones reportedly captured twenty-seven guardsmen, including one General, and burned an airport checkpoint. By Friday, the Pemones also took control of several roads leading into Venezuela.[34]

Later on Friday, Guaidó crossed into Colombia reportedly via helicopter, assisted by sympathetic members of Venezuela's military.[35] These troops were also expected to help get the humanitarian aid through the border checkpoints on Saturday. I was disappointed, but at least we heard that night that Richard Branson's concert was much better attended than a competing Maduro concert inside Venezuela, which I guess was a victory of sorts. Maduro's Vice President Delcy Rodriguez announced that all border crossing points would be closed on Saturday, but we had conflicting information on what exactly was closed and what might still be open.

Saturday morning, large crowds massed on the Colombian side of the border, with riot police in Táchira on the Venezuelan side. Low-level violence continued on the Brazilian border as crowds gathered there as well. Aid supplies had been building for weeks at several checkpoints on both borders, and additional convoys were prepared to arrive at the checkpoints throughout the day, escorted across by volunteers from Colombia or Brazil, to be met on the other side by Venezuelan volunteers. At least that was the plan. Incidents of rock throwing, confrontations with the Venezuelan National Guard, and barricades being moved and replaced increased throughout the day as the times for the attempted crossings drew near. Several midlevel army and navy officers defected, and there were reports that National Guardsmen along the border were defecting as well.[36]

Guaidó arrived at the Tienditas International Bridge about nine a.m., prepared to cross. There were reports all day that he was about to cross, but it didn't happen, without real explanations. In fact, the operation simply fizzled out, with exceptions at some places where volunteers tried to bring aid across; they succeeded on the Brazil border, but not so on the Colombia border. The Pemones were still the most aggressive, seizing the biggest airport in the Brazilian border region and capturing more National Guard troops.[37] But between the *colectivos* and some National Guard units, the level of violence against attempted border crossings rose, and the level of aid getting through did not. There were large demonstrations in Venezuela's cities, planned to coincide with the humanitarian aid coming in, including outside La Carlota military base in Caracas, with the crowds trying to convince servicemen to defect, unfortunately without success.

By the end of Saturday, I thought the Opposition had done little to advance its cause. I was disappointed the military had not responded with more defections, especially at senior levels. And I was amazed Guaidó and Colombia did not execute alternative plans when the *colectivos* and others stopped aid shipments from coming in, burning trucks on the bridges. Things seemed haphazard and disconnected, whether through lack of advance planning or failure of nerve I couldn't immediately tell. But if things didn't pick up in the next few days and Guaidó didn't get back to Caracas, I was going to start getting worried.

We were hearing that among Venezuelans, the feeling was that Saturday had been a victory for Guaidó, which struck me as very optimistic. We learned much later that there was speculation that the Colombians had gotten cold feet, fearing a military clash along the border would draw them in, and that after years of fighting counterinsurgency and counternarcotics wars inside Colombia, their troops simply weren't ready for conventional conflict with Maduro's armed forces. Nobody figured this out until Saturday? Guaidó was in Bogotá by midafternoon, preparing for Monday's Lima Group meeting. I still didn't like the idea of Guaidó's crossing the border in the first place, let alone hanging out in Colombia for several days, which Maduro used to propagandize that Guaidó was seeking aid from Venezuela's traditional adversary.

I spoke to Pence, who was heading to Bogotá to represent the US to the Lima Group, and stressed the need to persuade Guaidó to return to Caracas. A key element of the opposition's success so far was its cohesion, whereas in the past it had always fragmented. Every day Guaidó was out of the country increased the risk Maduro would find a way to split them again. Pence agreed and said he would be meeting Guaidó in a trilateral with Duque. I also urged Pence to press for more sanctions against the Maduro regime, to show it had to pay a price for blocking the humanitarian aid. Trump had said at the Miami rally that the Venezuelan generals had to make a choice, and Pence could say he was elaborating on Trump's point.

I briefed Trump Sunday afternoon, but he seemed unconcerned, which surprised me. He was impressed by the number of defections from the military, which within a few days would be close to five hundred.[38] I suspected his mind was on North Korea and the upcoming Hanoi Summit. As the call ended, he said, "Okay, man," which was his usual signal he was pleased with what he had heard. As I flew to Hanoi, I spoke again with Pence, on his way back to Washington after a firm speech in Bogotá to the Lima Group, who said there was "tremendous spirit in the room," which was encouraging. Guaidó had impressed him: "Very genuine, very smart, and he gave an extremely strong speech in front of the Lima Group." I urged Pence to pass his judgment to Trump.

Venezuela fell off the radar screen while we were in Hanoi, but when I returned from Vietnam on March 1, it was again front and center. Guaidó, now touring Latin America, was at last seriously considering how to reenter Venezuela, whether overland or flying to Caracas directly. I kept Trump posted, and he said to me on Sunday, March 3, "He [Guaidó] doesn't have what it takes . . . Stay away from it a little; don't get too much involved," which was like saying "Don't get too pregnant." In any case, Guaidó seized the initiative the next day, despite the risks, flying into Venezuela that morning. This showed the courage he had demonstrated earlier and relieved me greatly. Live shots over the Internet throughout the day showed Guaidó's dramatic return to Caracas, which proved to be a triumph. One immigration inspector said to him, "Welcome home, Mr. President!" Riding from the airport through his home state, Guaidó was greeted by cheering crowds the whole way, and no sign of military or police efforts to arrest him.

Buoyed by Guaidó's successful return, I was prepared to do the most we could to increase pressure on Maduro, starting with imposing sanctions on the entire government and taking more steps against the banking sector, all of which we should have done in January, but which we ultimately put in place. At a Principals Committee to discuss our plans, Mnuchin was resistant, but he was overwhelmed by others, with Perry politely explaining to him how oil and gas markets actually worked internationally, Kudlow and Ross disputing his economic analysis, and even Kirstjen Nielsen chiming in for stricter sanctions. Pompeo was largely silent. I said, again, we had only two choices in Venezuela: win and lose. Using an analogy from the 1956 Suez Canal Crisis, I said we had Maduro by the windpipe and needed to constrict it, which made Mnuchin start visibly. He was worried that steps in the banking sector would hurt Visa and Mastercard, which he wanted to keep alive for "the day after."[39] I said, as did Perry and Kudlow, there wouldn't be any "day after" unless we increased pressure dramatically, the sooner the better. This wasn't some academic exercise. As for Mnuchin's concern for the harm we would cause the Venezuelan people, I pointed out that Maduro had already killed over forty during this round of Opposition activity, and hundreds of thousands risked their lives every time they went into the streets to protest.[40] They weren't thinking about Visa and Mastercard! The poorest people didn't have Visa or Mastercard, and they were already crushed by Venezuela's collapsed economy. Really, there was a revolution going on, and Mnuchin worried about credit cards!

At the end of March 7, we had word of massive power outages

across Venezuela, exacerbated by the decrepit state of the country's power grid. My first thought was that Guaidó or someone had decided to take matters into their own hands. But whatever the cause or the extent or duration of the outage, it had to hurt Maduro, emblematic as it was of the overall disaster the regime represented for the people. Reporting on the effects of the outage came slowly because almost all Venezuelan domestic telecommunications had been knocked out. What we learned as each day passed confirmed the devastation. Almost the entire country was blacked out, the Caracas airport was closed, the security services seemed to have disappeared, there were reports of looting, and the *cacerolazos* started again, showing sustained popular dissatisfaction with the regime. How bad was the damage? Some months later, we learned, a visiting foreign delegation concluded the country's electricity-generating infrastructure was "beyond repair." The regime tried to blame America, but people generally understood that, like the disintegration of Venezuela's petroleum industry, the national power grid had also deteriorated over two decades of Chavista rule, because the government had failed to undertake necessary maintenance and new capital investment. And where had the money gone that was required for the state-owned oil company and the national power grid? Into the hands of the thoroughly corrupt regime. If this wasn't the stuff of popular uprisings, it was hard to know what would qualify. We continued to increase the pressure, with Justice announcing the indictment of two Venezuelan drug-trafficking kingpins (both former regime officials),[41] and by the broadly supported ousting of Maduro's representatives by a majority of the members of the Inter-American Development Bank.[42]

Regime efforts to bring up the power grid faltered as power substations exploded under the renewed electrical loads, reflecting widespread, long-term lack of maintenance and antiquated equipment. The loss of telecoms also impaired the coordination of activities nationally, including in key cities like Maracaibo. Guaidó continued his rallies, still drawing sizable crowds, assuring people the Opposition was pressing ahead. The National Assembly declared a "state of alarm" over the outages, not that they had authority to do anything, but at least demonstrating to the people they were thinking about it, compared to Maduro's near invisibility, an indication of continuing regime disarray. Contacts with regime officials continued, as Guaidó sought leadership fissures to undermine Maduro's authority.

Unfortunately, there was also disarray within the US government, particularly at the State Department. Coupled with Treasury foot-dragging, each new step in our pressure campaign against Maduro's regime took far more time and bureaucratic effort than anyone could justify. Treasury treated every new sanction decision as if we were prosecuting criminal cases in court, having to prove guilt beyond a reasonable doubt. That's not how sanctions should work; they're about using America's massive economic power to advance our national interests. They are most effective when applied massively, swiftly, and decisively, and enforced with all the power available. This did not describe how we approached Venezuela sanctions (or most others in the Trump Administration). Instead, even relatively minor enforcement decisions could require Stakhanovite efforts by NSC staff and supporters in other agencies, all the while providing Maduro a margin of safety. The regime obviously wasn't sitting idly by. It was constantly taking measures to evade sanctions and mitigate the consequences of those it couldn't escape. Our slowness and lack of agility were godsends to Maduro and his regime, and its Cuban and Russian supporters. Unscrupulous global traders and financiers took advantage of every gap in our pressure campaign.[43] It was painful to watch.

Perhaps the most wrenching decision came March 11, when Pompeo decided to close Embassy Caracas and withdraw all US personnel. There were clearly risks to the remaining staff, and the thuggishness of the *colectivos* was undeniable. Pompeo had built a substantial part of his political reputation by justifiably criticizing the Obama Administration's errors during the Benghazi crisis in September 2012. As in the earlier reduction of staff levels at Embassy Baghdad and closing the Basra consulate, Pompeo was determined to avoid "another Benghazi" on his watch. Trump was even more sensitive. At Pompeo's mere indication of risk, Trump decided immediately to withdraw our personnel, which Pompeo did with alacrity.

Hindsight is always 20/20, but closing Embassy Caracas proved harmful to our anti-Maduro efforts. Most European and Latin American embassies stayed open without incident, but our in-country presence was obviously decreased. And because of Obama's relaxed attitude about authoritarian regimes and Chinese and Russian threats in the hemisphere, our eyes and ears were already substantially reduced. Even worse, the State Department utterly mishandled the aftermath, not sending Jimmy Story, our Venezuela Chargé d'Affaires, and at least some of his team immediately back to Colombia, where they could work closely with Embassy Bogotá to continue their work across the border. Instead, the Western Hemisphere bureau kept the team in Washington to hold them more closely under its control. It did nothing to help our efforts to oust Maduro.

More positively, Opposition negotiations with key regime figures indicated their view that the fissures we sought were beginning to emerge. Overcoming years of mistrust was not easy, but we tried to show potential defectors that both the Opposition and Washington were serious about amnesty and avoiding criminal prosecutions for earlier transgressions. This was realpolitik. Many top regime figures were corrupt, profiting from drug trafficking, for example, and their human-rights records were hardly exemplary. But I felt strongly it was better to swallow a few scruples to crash the regime and free Venezuela's people than to stand on "principles" that kept them oppressed, and Cuba and Russia dominant inside. That was why, playing head games with the regime, I tweeted to wish Maduro a long, quiet retirement on a nice beach somewhere (like Cuba). I didn't like it, but it was far preferable to his remaining in power. In the judgment of the Opposition, we also faced the problem of heavy surveillance, likely Cuban, of leading regime officials, obviously intimidating, and making trustworthy communications among potential coup plotters all the more difficult.

One ploy we considered to send signals to key figures in the regime was delisting from the sanctions people like wives and family members, a common practice in US policy to send signals to influence the behavior of selected individuals or entities. Such actions would likely get little public attention but would be powerful messages to regime officials that we were prepared to ease their paths either out of Venezuela entirely or into the arms of the Opposition as co-conspirators rather than prisoners. In turn, if they then cooperated in facilitating Maduro's ouster, they could be delisted themselves. In mid-March, the issue came to a head when Treasury flatly refused to delist certain individuals, despite the unanimous support of the other affected players. Pompeo called Mnuchin, once again reaching him in Los Angeles, and told him to fulfill Treasury's administrative role and stop second-guessing his department. Nonetheless, Treasury persisted, asking questions about Opposition negotiations with Maduro regime figures, second-guessing the State Department on whether delisting would produce the results desired. This was intolerable. It suggested that we should move the entire sanctions operation out of Treasury and put it elsewhere. Finally, Mnuchin said he would accept the State Department's guidance if I would send him a note saying it was acceptable to me. This was nothing but "cover your ass" behavior, but I was happy to send a brief memo to Pompeo, Mnuchin, and Barr laying out my view that Treasury was not entitled to its own foreign policy. I was gladdened later that Elliott Abrams, an old friend who had joined State as another "special envoy," sent me an e-mail saying, "Your letter is a classic. It should be studied in schools of government!" Sadly, the time and effort wasted here could have been spent advancing US interests.

We were simultaneously squeezing Havana. State reversed Obama's absurd conclusion that Cuban baseball was somehow independent of its government, thus in turn allowing Treasury to revoke the license allowing Major League Baseball to traffic in Cuban players. This action didn't endear us to the owners, but they were sadly mistaken if they didn't grasp that their participation in professional baseball's scheme meant they were sleeping with the enemy. Even better, the perennial presidential waivers of key provisions of the Helms-Burton Act were coming to an end. Helms-Burton allowed property owners with assets expropriated by Castro's government and sold to others, to sue in US courts, either to retrieve the property or to receive compensation from the new owners, but those provisions had never been deployed. Now they would be. Consistent with his public threats of a "full and complete embargo" on Cuba because of the oil shipments between Venezuela and Cuba, Trump also repeatedly asked the Defense Department for concrete options on how to stop such shipments, including interdiction.[44] Although military force inside Venezuela was a nonstarter, using force to slice Cuba's oil lifeline could have been dramatic. The Pentagon did nothing.

How bad was Cuba's influence in Venezuela? Even the *New York Times* understood the problem, running a major story on March 17 recounting how Cuban "medical assistance" had been used to shore up Maduro's support among Venezuela's poor and held back from those unwilling to carry out Maduro's orders.[45] The article demonstrated the extent of Cuba's penetration of Maduro's regime and how bad conditions in Venezuela were. In addition, a top Venezuelan General who defected to Colombia described publicly later in the week the extent of the corruption inside the country's medical program, adding further evidence of the rot within the regime.[46] The *Wall Street Journal* carried an article shortly thereafter detailing Maduro's loss of support among Venezuela's poor, something we'd believed since the outset of the rebellion in January.[47] I urged that we consider more measures to drive wedges between the Venezuelan military and the Cubans and their gangs of *colectivos*. The professional military despised the *colectivos*, and anything we could do to increase tensions between them, further delegitimizing the Cuban presence, would be positive.

Trump seemed to be holding up fine, saying at a March 19 White House press conference with new Brazilian President Jair Bolsonaro, "We haven't done the really tough sanctions yet on Venezuela." Of course, that comment begged the question "Why not?" What exactly were we waiting for? Story, Claver-Carone, and others continued to hear from Venezuela that the pace and extent of conversations between the Opposition and potential allies inside the regime continued to increase. It all seemed incredibly slow but was still moving in the right direction. In fact, evidence of division within the regime may have prompted the arrest of two top Guaidó aides, particularly his chief of staff, Roberto Marrero. Pence weighed in heavily on this, persuading Trump to overcome Treasury's objections to sanctioning a major Venezuelan government financial institution and four of its subsidiaries. Pence told me later Trump said to Mnuchin in giving him these instructions, "Maybe it's time to put Maduro out of business." Indeed. Treasury also now acquiesced in designating Venezuela's entire financial sector for sanctions, something it had long resisted strenuously. I was glad to get the right result, but the time lost in internal debate was equivalent to throwing Maduro a lifeline. In the meantime, in late March, Russia sent in new troops and equipment, labelling one shipment as humanitarian, and trying to obfuscate what its presence amounted to.[48] There were strong indications more were coming over the next several months. At that same time, however, Brazil's Defense Minister, Fernando Azevedo, was telling me that the end was in sight for Maduro. I also met in my office with Honduran President Juan Hernandez, who was similarly optimistic, in contrast to the situation in Nicaragua, on his border.

On March 27, Guaidó's wife, Fabiana Rosales, arrived at the White House for a meeting with Pence in the Roosevelt Room, for which we hoped Trump would drop by. She was accompanied by Marrero's wife and sister, and after photos and statements to the press by Rosales and Pence, we were instead ushered into the Oval Office. Trump greeted Rosales and the others warmly, and the press mob then lumbered in, for what turned out to be a twenty-minute, live-broadcast event. Rosales thanked Trump, Pence, and me for our support (saying, "Mr. Bolton, it is an honor to count on you as we do"). Trump did a good job with the press, saying, when asked about Russian involvement in Venezuela, "Russia has to get out," which made a strong impression and was exactly what I hoped he would say.[49]

Even more interesting was the discussion after the press left, as we listened to Rosales describe how bad things were in Venezuela, and Marrero's wife tell the story of the secret police breaking into her house and dragging her husband off to the Helicoide, its now-infamous Caracas headquarters building, which also served as a prison. As the discussion continued, Trump told me twice, regarding the Russians, "Get them out," and, with respect to the Cuban regime, "Shut them down [in Cuba]," both of which instructions I welcomed. At one point, Trump stressed that he wanted the "strongest possible sanctions" against Venezuela, and I turned to look at Mnuchin, who had come in for another meeting. Everyone, Venezuelan and American, laughed, because they knew Mnuchin was the main obstacle to doing what Trump said he wanted. Pence asked Rosales what was happening with the Venezuelan military, but Trump interrupted to say, "It's very slow. I thought they'd have come over already." Rosales answered with a description of the extreme violence she was seeing, and the close connections of Venezuela's military to Cuba.[50] After the Rosales meeting ended, Trump said to Mnuchin and me, "You can't hold back now," and I said, "Steve and I are both looking forward to it as soon as he [Mnuchin] gets back from China." I was sure Mnuchin was enjoying this as much as I was.

The most unexpected outcome of the meeting was Trump's perception that Rosales had not worn a wedding ring and how young she looked. The second point was true, although she seemed as resolute as they come, but the first I hadn't noticed. Later, when Guaidó's name came up, Trump would comment on the wedding ring "issue." I never did understand what it signified, but it was not good, in Trump's mind. He thought Guaidó was "weak," as opposed to Maduro, who was "strong." By spring, Trump was calling Guaidó the "Beto O'Rourke of Venezuela," hardly the sort of compliment an ally of the United States should expect. It was far from helpful but typical of how Trump carelessly defamed those around him, as when he began blaming me for the opposition's failure to overthrow Maduro. Perhaps Trump forgot he made the actual decision on policy, except when he said he was the *only* one who made decisions. Still, at the moment with Fabiana Rosales, Trump's performance in the Oval was the most emphatic he had given to date on Venezuela. Too bad the relevant Treasury and State Department subordinates hadn't also been there to see it.

One gambit was a string of tweets from me to Defense Minister Padrino, trying to inflame his Venezuelan patriotism against the Russians and Cubans, urging him to "do the right thing" by his country's Constitution. It appeared we got through. In response to a reporter's question, Padrino answered, "Mr. Bolton, I tell you that we are doing the right thing. Doing the right thing is doing what's written in the constitution . . . Doing the right thing is respecting the will of the people."[51] That was all we needed to start a new line of tweets that "the will of the people" was to get rid of Maduro, which was certainly true. At least we could now say we were inside Padrino's head, and perhaps others'. In fact, Rosales said to Abrams after the Trump meeting, "The regime wonders if the US military threat is credible, but they are most afraid when John Bolton starts tweeting." Now, that was encouraging!

In Venezuela, the Opposition and key regime figures were developing a play with the Supreme Tribunal of Justice, the equivalent of our Supreme Court, to declare the National Constituent Assembly, Maduro's fraudulently elected "legislature," illegitimate.[52] If Venezuela's top court, packed by Maduro cronies and hacks, and led by one of his nominally strongest supporters, delegitimized Maduro's sham legislature, it would dramatically undercut Maduro across the board in Venezuela. At the same time, Venezuelan civilians had now broken through barricades put up by Maduro's National Guard on the Simon Bolivar International Bridge near Cúcuta, the crossing point into Colombia, thus reopening contact with the outside world. The National Guard had simply scattered, and there were unconfirmed reports that provincial governors in several border provinces seemed to be taking matters into their own hands, but only temporarily. Final totals from the February 23 effort were that as many as fourteen hundred Venezuelan Army, National Guard, and police had defected,[53] and we still had no doubt the vast bulk of the remaining military firmly supported Guaidó.

If we wanted to win, we had to step up our game considerably. At an "informal" meeting of the principals I organized on April 8, Mnuchin was now more flexible, and we agreed on torqueing up pressure on Russia both within the Western Hemisphere and outside it, in Ukraine or the Baltics, for example, or on the Nord Stream II pipeline. He offered to press Russia's Finance Minister over the weekend at the annual International Monetary Fund/World Bank meetings, which was progress. With estimates of total Venezuelan debt owed to

Russia and China (primarily Russia) as high as $60 billion, or even higher, they obviously had a lot at stake, more so if the Opposition took power.[54] I just hoped Trump wouldn't object to our upping the ante with Moscow.

Claver-Carone and Story were hearing that April 20, the day before Easter, might be the target date for the negotiations to shatter the regime. Even the head of the secret police Manuel Cristopher Figuera, we heard, believed that Maduro was finished.[55] Talks with several senior Venezuelan military leaders, including Defense Minister Padrino, were becoming increasingly operational: not about whether Maduro would be ousted but about how it would happen.[56] These military leaders were also in consultation with top civil authorities, particularly Moreno,[57] which boded well for proceeding against Maduro and those who still showed loyalty to the regime. This was important, because real change required more than just throwing Maduro out of office. My impression was that much of the negotiation centered on what a "transition" period would look like, which was very dangerous, since Chavista movement supporters would still control key government institutions even after Maduro's ouster. I understood the tentative sequence was that the supreme court would declare the Constituent Assembly illegal; Maduro would then resign; the military would recognize Guaidó as Interim President; the National Assembly would be recognized as Venezuela's only legitimate legislature; and the supreme court would remain in place. This was not perfect, and there were certainly risks in my judgment that eliminating Maduro but having regime remain in power could be the hidden objective of some regime figures involved.

On April 17, at the Biltmore Hotel in Coral Gables, Florida, I spoke to the Bay of Pigs Veterans Association commemoration of the anniversary of their invasion of Cuba fifty-eight years before, in a failed effort to overthrow the Castro regime. The Brigade 2506 vets were a potent force in Cuban-American politics in Florida and around the country, and this yearly gathering was a big attention getter, something aspiring politicians never missed if at all possible. I was able to bring them news, at long last, of the end of the waivers of Helms-Burton title 2, thus allowing suits against the owners of property expropriated by the Castro regime, and the full enforcement of title 4, which could deny them visas to the US, a major problem for foreign corporations that now owned much of that property. There were a number of other noteworthy measures we were announcing against both Cuba and Venezuela, especially those targeting Venezuela's Central Bank. The overall impact was to show how resolved the Administration was against the "troika of tyranny," even though I was the only one in the packed Biltmore ballroom who knew how little resolve there was behind the *Resolute* desk.

After slippages for various reasons, the new target date for the Opposition to act became April 30. I felt time was rapidly moving against us, given Trump's evident worries about Guaidó and the wedding ring "issue." Earlier mistakes, like Guaidó's leaving the country, the February failure by the Opposition and Colombia to force their way across the border with humanitarian assistance, and the closure of Embassy Caracas were all on my mind. In any event, with April 30 fixed, and coming the day before Guaidó's previously announced mass country-wide demonstrations on May 1, perhaps the decisive hour was about to arrive.

Indeed, it was. Pompeo called me at 5:25 a.m. on April 30 to say, "There's a lot of movement down in Venezuela," and said that, among other things, Opposition leader Leopoldo Lopez had been released from his long-standing house arrest by the relatively new head of the SEBIN, a key secret police agency, General Manuel Cristopher Figuera. Pompeo said Padrino had gone to meet Guaidó, and he was planning to tell Maduro shortly that it was time for him to go. Padrino was said to be accompanied by three hundred military personnel, which indicated he had broken free of the Cubans, although we learned later that this information (both the purported meeting and the military personnel) was incorrect. The supreme court part of the plan (declaring the Constituent Assembly illegitimate) had still not happened, but other pieces seemed to be falling into place. I was already prepared to leave for the White House and departed slightly earlier than normal, expecting a full day of turmoil. By the time I reached the West

Wing, Guaidó and Lopez were at La Carlota air base in central Caracas, which had reportedly defected to the Opposition. Guaidó tweeted out a video message announcing the start of "Operation Liberty," calling on the military to defect and civilians to come into the streets to protest. But soon thereafter, we heard that the information about La Carlota air base was inaccurate, and that Guaidó and Lopez were never actually inside the base. Moreover, reports that military units supporting Guaidó had captured at least some radio and television stations, if they ever were true, were shown to be untrue within a few hours.

Confusing and contradictory reports continued through the morning, a "fog of war" phenomenon in these kinds of events, but it became increasingly clear that the endlessly discussed plan between the Opposition and key regime figures had come apart. The first wire service reports did not arrive until about 6:16 a.m. We were hearing that the supreme court members had been summoned by Moreno to play their assigned role, which would in turn trigger Padrino's moving into action. But it turned out, however, that the judges did not follow through. By the afternoon, my assessment was that senior regime civilian and military leaders with whom the Opposition had been negotiating, such as Moreno, were all recoiling from the effort because they thought it had been launched too soon. General Cristopher Figuera said that he personally alerted Padrino to the timetable's acceleration, but he could tell Padrino was nervous about the change of plans.[58] The timetable had moved up, but only because on Monday night the Cubans had likely gotten wind of the conspiracy, thus motivating those involved on the Opposition side to move forward outside the understood sequence. All the evidence, in my assessment, showed who was really in charge in Venezuela, namely, the Cubans, who had informed Maduro. As word spread within the regime's top levels that the security of the plan had been breached, supreme court President Moreno became increasingly nervous, resulting in his failure to have his court delegitimize Maduro's Constituent Assembly as planned, thus spooking the senior military leaders. Lacking "constitutional" cover, they hesitated, and the release of Lopez on Tuesday morning only further increased the senior military conspirators' unease. I thought that these generals may never have intended to defect, or had at least hedged their bets enough that they could jump either way on Tuesday, depending on what course events took.

Nothing ever goes as planned in revolutionary situations, and improvisation can sometimes make the difference between success and failure. But in Venezuela that day, things unraveled. We were certainly frustrated, largely because we were in Washington, distant from what was going on and mostly unable to know of events in fast-moving real time. As we learned later from Opposition leaders, after Cristopher Figuera released Lopez from house arrest, Lopez and Guaidó decided to move forward, hoping key regime officials would come along. History will record they were wrong, but they were not unreasonable in believing that once it was launched, they should play out the game. Cristopher Figuera later took refuge in a Caracas embassy, fearing for his life from the Maduro regime, later escaping to Colombia; his wife, and the wives of many other senior Maduro officials, had previously left Venezuela for the United States and other safer locations.

I had wrestled with the issue of when to wake Trump and decided to do so after arriving at the White House and quickly reviewing all the available information. I called him at 6:07 a.m., waking him for the first time in my tenure as National Security Advisor. I don't know if Flynn or McMaster ever did so. Trump was very sleepy, but when I told him what we knew, he said only, "Wow." I stressed that the outcome was far from certain. The day could end with Maduro in jail, with Guaidó in jail, or anything in between. I called Pence at 6:22 and gave him the same message, and then called around to other NSC members and key leaders on the Hill, where support on both sides of the aisle for our hard line in Venezuela was almost uniform. Throughout the day, Pompeo and I were on the phone constantly with foreign governments, telling them what we knew and soliciting their support for a struggle the duration of which we still couldn't predict.

No one gave Maduro the word it was time to go, as had been in the Opposition plan, but there was no doubt, despite all of his regime's surveillance, the rebellion took him by surprise. Maduro was hustled off to Fuerte Tiuna, a military headquarters near Caracas, where he was held under the tightest security for several days.[59] Whether that was to protect Maduro or to freeze him in place before he fled Venezuela, or some combination of both motives, was disputed then and remains unclear even now. (The Cubans had good reason to be worried about Maduro; Pompeo later said publicly that we believed that he had been on the verge of fleeing Venezuela that day.)[60] Padrino was also reportedly at Tiuna most of the day, the Opposition believed. But whatever the reasons, the Cubans and top regime figures were unquestionably very worried about what they were witnessing, which speaks tellingly about their own misperceptions of support for Maduro and the regime inside Venezuela.[61]

My concern now was that the failed uprising would prompt mass arrests of the Opposition and the possible bloodbath we had feared since January. But these worst-case outcomes did not take place that day and night, nor did they for weeks and months that followed. The most likely reason is that Maduro and his cronies knew full well that a crackdown could finally provoke the military, and even its highest officers, to move against the regime. Neither Maduro nor his Cuban handlers were willing to risk it, and that remains true even as of today.

On May 1, I scheduled a Principals Committee Meeting to discuss what to do. Everyone had suggestions, many of which we adopted, again begging the question of why we hadn't done them all and more in January. Now was when the effects of bureaucratic foot-dragging became all too evident, and the lack of constancy and resolve in the Oval Office all too apparent. Although the sides emerged essentially where they had been before the turmoil of April 30, there was no way to pretend this was anything other than an Opposition defeat. They had run a play and gained no yardage, and in a dictatorship, that was never good news. But the fact that one play had been unsuccessful did not mean the game was lost, despite the palpable disappointment on our side. The task now was for the Opposition to pick itself up, dust itself off, and get moving again.

One immediate effect was that Guaidó's previously planned May 1 mass demonstrations, while far larger than the regime's counterdemonstrations, were not nearly as big as they might have been. Many citizens, obviously uncertain how the regime would react, were nervous about being on the streets, although television pictures from Caracas showed young men and women in the Opposition spoiling for a fight, attacking the police armored vehicles that were trying to restrain the demonstrators. Guaidó was out in public speaking all day, calling for continuous protests and strikes from public-sector unions, which he had worked with some success to break away from their long-standing support for the Chavista movement behind Maduro. The wretched state of the economy meant even government employees knew there had to be a major change before things got better. Maduro, by contrast, remained invisible, not coming out in public, probably holed up in Fort Tiuna, reportedly laying the foundation for large-scale arrests, which the Opposition and the general public feared, but which fortunately never materialized.

An unnecessary negative development was Trump's decision to call Putin on May 23, primarily on other subjects, but including Venezuela at the end. It was a brilliant display of Soviet-style propaganda from Putin, which I thought largely persuaded Trump. Putin said our support for Guaidó had consolidated support for Maduro, which was completely divorced from reality, like his equally fictitious assertion that Maduro's May 1 rallies had been larger than the Opposition's. In a way guaranteed to appeal to Trump, Putin characterized Guaidó as someone who proclaimed himself, but without real support, sort of like Hillary Clinton deciding to declare herself President. This Orwellian line continued, as Putin denied that Russia had any real role in the events in Venezuela. Russia had, Putin admitted, sold arms to Venezuela under Chavez ten years earlier, and maintained responsibility for repair and maintenance under the contract signed at that time, but nothing more than that. He said that Cristopher Figuera (although he did not use his name, but his title) was probably our agent, could fill us in. What a comic! Putin could easily have come away from this call thinking he had a free hand in Venezuela. Shortly afterward, so Treasury informed us, Trump spoke with Mnuchin, who happily concluded that Trump wanted to go easy on more Venezuela sanctions.

Over the next several months, Venezuela's economy deteriorated, continuing the twenty-year-long decline under Chavez and Maduro. The President of the International Committee of the Red Cross, after visiting Venezuela, told me that he hadn't seen hospitals in such condition since his last trip to North Korea. Negotiations between the Opposition and key regime figures resumed. Progress varied, and there were long periods when negotiations seemed stalled. The Opposition struggled to find a new strategy after the April 30 failure, with mixed success. One potentially attractive route would be to foment competition within the regime to overthrow Maduro. If setting these scorpions in a bottle against each other produced Maduro's removal, even if "the regime" remained in place, it could increase instability and sharpen infighting, affording the Opposition more opportunities to act. Florida's Venezuelan-American community, depressed by the outcome, rebounded quickly because of the continuing imperative to relieve the oppression of their friends and families. And US politicians, from Trump down, realized that Venezuelan-American voters, not to mention Cuban-Americans and Nicaraguan-Americans, critical in Florida and elsewhere, would be judging candidates based on their support for the Opposition.

But the fundamental gridlock in Venezuela continued. Neither side could take down the other. It would still be a mistake to say, as many commentators have, that the military remained loyal to Maduro. The military stayed in its barracks, which, without question, on net, benefits the regime. Nonetheless, that doesn't mean, in my judgment, that the more junior officers and enlisted personnel feel any sense of loyalty to a regime that has devastated the country, where economic conditions continue to deteriorate day by day. Instead, in my view, senior military officers are almost certainly still more concerned about the cohesiveness of the armed forces as an institution. An order to suppress the Opposition could lead to civil war, with most regular military units likely supporting the Opposition, against the several forms of secret police, militias, and Cuban-directed *colectivos*. Such a conflict is one of the rare developments that could actually make things worse than they already are in Venezuela. But that is precisely why, in the right circumstances, the military is still perfectly capable of ousting the regime, not just Maduro, and allowing a return to democracy.

What now stands primarily in the way of freeing Venezuela is the Cuban presence, critically supported by Russian financial resources. If Cuba's military and intelligence networks left the country, the Maduro regime would be in serious, probably terminal, trouble. Everyone understands this reality, especially Maduro, who many believe owes his position as President to Cuban intervention in the struggle for control after Chavez's death.[62] Looking back, it's clear to me that Havana saw Maduro as the more malleable of the leading contenders, and time has proven this thesis accurate.

At the end of that last day in April 2019, two decades of mutual mistrust; cowardice on the part of several regime leaders who had committed to act but who lost their nerve at the critical moment; some tactical mistakes by the inexperienced Opposition; the absence of any US advisors on the ground who might, and I underline "might," have helped make a difference; and the cold, cynical pressure of the Cubans and the Russians, brought the attempted uprising to a halt the day it started. I laid all this out at the time, hoping both to continue the Opposition's efforts, and to make the historical record clear.[63] Recriminations after failure are inevitable, and there were plenty to go around, including from Trump directly.

But make no mistake: this rebellion came very close to succeeding. To believe otherwise ignores the reality that, as further information comes to light in the years ahead, will only become clearer. In the aftermath of the April 30 failure, the Opposition continued to oppose, and American policy should continue supporting them. As Mitch McConnell said to me in early May, "Don't back down." All credit to those who risked their lives in Venezuela to free their countrymen, and shame on those who second-guessed them. Venezuela will be free.

CHAPTER 10

THUNDER OUT OF CHINA

merica's economic and geopolitical relations with China will determine the shape of international affairs in the twenty-first century. Deng Xiaoping's decision to shift Chinese economic policy away from orthodox Marxism, starting in 1978, and the US decision to recognize the People's Republic of China (and derecognize the Republic of China on Taiwan) in 1979 were critical turning points. The history of these decisions and their consequences is complex, but US strategy and the West's more broadly, as well as "informed" public opinion for the next several decades, rested on two basic propositions. First, those who supported these developments believed China would be changed irreversibly by the rising prosperity caused by market-oriented policies, greater foreign investment, ever-deeper interconnections with global markets, and broader acceptance of international economic norms. As the phrase went, China would enjoy "a peaceful rise" and be a "responsible stakeholder" or "constructive partner" in international affairs.[1] Bringing China into the World Trade Organization in 2001 was the apotheosis of this assessment.

Second, proponents of the benign view of China's rise argued that, almost inevitably, as China's national wealth increased, so too would democracy. Nascent patterns of free elections, which observers saw in isolated local village elections in rural China, would spread to other locales, and then rise to the provincial level, and then finally to the national level. There was a strong correlation, they said, between the growth of economic freedom and the emergence of true middle classes, on the one hand, and political freedom and democracy on the other. Then, as China became more democratic, the consequences of the "democratic peace" theory would kick in: China would avoid competition for regional or global hegemony, the world would thereby avoid the "Thucydides trap," and the risk of international conflict, hot or cold, would recede.

But both these views were fundamentally incorrect. In economics, after joining the World Trade Organization, China did exactly the opposite of what was predicted. Instead of adhering to existing norms, China gamed the organization, successfully pursuing a mercantilist policy in a supposedly free-trade body. Internationally, China stole intellectual property; forced technology transfers from, and discriminated against, foreign investors and businesses; engaged in corrupt practices and "debt diplomacy" through instruments such as the "Belt and Road Initiative"; and continued managing its domestic economy in statist, authoritarian ways. America was the primary target of these "structural" aspects of China's policy, but so were Europe, Japan, and virtually all industrial democracies, plus others that are neither but were still victims. Moreover, China sought politico-military benefits from its economic activity that free-market societies simply do not contemplate. It did so through purportedly privately owned companies that are in fact tools of China's military and intelligence services,[2] by fusing its civil and military power centers,[3] and by engaging in aggressive cyber warfare that targeted foreign private interests as much or more than government secrets.

Politically, China began moving away from becoming a democracy, not toward it. In Xi Jinping, China now has its most powerful leader, and the most centralized governmental control, since Mao Tse-tung. Every dictator has to run his chances, so internal disagreement within an all-powerful Communist Party structure is hardly evidence of democratic "green shoots." If further proof is necessary, the citizens of Hong Kong have provided it, seeing the "one country, two systems" promise in existential jeopardy. Ethnic (Uighurs and Tibetans) and religious (Catholic and Falun Gong) persecution on a massive scale continues. Finally, China-wide, Beijing's use of "social credit" measures to rank its citizenry[4] provides a chilling vision of a future that hardly seems free to American eyes.

All the while, as I said repeatedly in speeches and articles before

I joined the Trump Administration, China's military capabilities have expanded: creating one of the world's top offensive cyber warfare programs; building a blue-water navy for the first time in five hundred years; increasing its arsenal of nuclear weapons and ballistic missiles, including a serious program for submarine-launched, nuclear-capable missiles; developing anti-satellite weapons to blind US space-based sensors; designing anti-access and area-denial weapons to push our Navy back from Asia's coast; reforming and modernizing the People's Liberation Army's conventional warfare capabilities; and more. Watching China's transformation over the years, I saw all this as deeply threatening to US strategic interests, and to our friends and allies globally.[5] The Obama Administration basically sat back and watched it happen.

America has been slow to awaken to basic mistakes made decades ago. We have suffered extensive economic and political harm, but fortunately, the game is far from over. As the knowledge spreads that China has not played by "our" rules, and quite likely never intends to, we are still capable of responding effectively. To do so, it is essential that enough Americans see the nature of China's challenge and act in time. If that happens, we need not worry. As Japanese Admiral Isoroku Yamamoto reputedly said after Pearl Harbor, "I fear all we have done is to awaken a sleeping giant and fill him with a terrible resolve."

Trump in some respects embodies the growing US concern about China. He appreciates the key truth that politico-military power rests on a strong economy. The stronger the economy, the greater the capacity to sustain large military and intelligence budgets to protect America's worldwide interests and compete with multiple would-be regional hegemons. Trump frequently says explicitly that stopping China's unfair economic growth at US expense is the best way to defeat China militarily, which is fundamentally correct. These views, in an otherwise bitterly divided Washington, have contributed to significant changes in the terms of America's own debate about these issues. But having grasped some notion of China's threat, the real question is what Trump does. On this score, his advisors are badly fractured intellectually. The Administration has panda huggers like Mnuchin; confirmed free-traders, like Kevin Hassett, Chairman of the Council of Economic Advisors, and Kudlow; and China hawks, like Ross, Lighthizer, and Navarro.

I had the most futile role of all: I wanted to fit China trade policy into a broader China strategic framework. We had a slogan, a good one, calling for a "free and open Indo-Pacific" region (unfortunately acronymed as "FOIP").[6] Conceptually, broadening the strategic environment to include South and Southeast Asia is important, showing that not everything revolves around China. But a bumper sticker is not a strategy, and we struggled to elaborate it and avoid being sucked into the black hole of China trade issues, which happened all too often. And that, at least in summary fashion, is where we turn next.

By the time I joined the White House, trade discussions of all sorts with China had been under way for some time. Trump approached trade and trade deficits as if reading a corporate balance sheet: trade deficits meant we were losing, and trade surpluses meant we were winning. Tariffs would reduce imports and increase government revenues, which was better than the opposite. In fact, free-traders, and I consider myself one before, during, and after my time with Trump, scoffed at such arguments. Still, trade deficits often indicated other problems, such as the enormous benefits China reaped from intellectual property theft, which in turn allowed it to compete more successfully against the very firms it had stolen the intellectual property from. Compounding the problem, Beijing subsidized its businesses to lower their prices internationally. Major decreases in US manufacturing jobs resulted from lower labor costs of production in China and other developing countries. It was therefore trade deficits as symptoms of other problems, not as problems in themselves, that warranted more attention, whether Trump fully understood or not.

In the midst of US trade delegations going to Beijing and Chinese delegations coming to Washington, Ross called me in mid-April, my second week on the job, to talk about ZTE, a Chinese telecom company. ZTE had committed massive violations of both our Iran and our North Korea sanctions, had been successfully prosecuted by Justice, and was operating under a criminal-consent decree[7] monitoring and regulating its behavior. A court-appointed master overseeing the decree had just reported extensive violations, which could result in significant additional fines, as well as cutting ZTE off from the US market, which Ross was prepared to do. I didn't consider this a trade issue but a law-enforcement matter. If ZTE had been a US company, we would have toasted them, and I saw no reason to hold back because ZTE was Chinese. Nonetheless, the State Department worried about offending China, so Ross wanted to know how to proceed the next day with a planned Commerce Department announcement. I told him to go ahead, which he did.[8]

Within a few weeks, however, Trump was unhappy with Ross's decision and wanted to modify the hefty penalties he had proposed, with Mnuchin quickly agreeing. I was appalled, because by rescinding what Ross had already told China, Trump was undercutting him (which, as I learned shortly, was standard operating procedure for Trump) and forgiving ZTE's unacceptable criminal behavior. Even so, Trump decided to call Xi Jinping, just hours before announcing that the US was withdrawing from the Iran nuclear deal. Trump began by complaining about China's trade practices, which he believed were so unfair, and said China needed to buy more US agricultural products. Xi actually raised ZTE first, and Trump called our actions very strong, even harsh. He said he had told Ross to work something out for China. Xi replied that if that were done, he would owe Trump a favor and Trump immediately responded he was doing this because of Xi. I was stunned by the unreciprocated nature of the concession, and because, as Ross told me later, ZTE had almost been destroyed by the penalties imposed. Reversing the decision would be inexplicable. This was policy by personal whim and impulse.

Whim and impulse continued on Sunday, May 13, when Trump tweeted:

> President Xi of China, and I, are working together to give massive Chinese phone company, ZTE, a way to get back into business, fast. Too many jobs in China lost. Commerce Department has been instructed to get it done!

When had we started to worry about jobs in China?

On Monday, I heard Navarro was trying to get a miscellaneous group of people into the Oval to tell Trump what a bad idea backtracking on ZTE was. Substantively, I obviously agreed, but this was a completely chaotic way to make policy. Unfortunately, this is exactly how trade matters were handled within the Administration from day one. I tried to restore order by organizing a Principals Committee. Unfortunately, the various economic departments and agencies were riled at being put into the process run by the National Security Council, indicating it had happened only rarely before. They would all rather take their chances with the existing policy-making roulette rather than follow process discipline. The only conclusion to emerge clearly from this moment was that international economic policy remained utterly unstructured, and this was unlikely to change without superhuman effort, not to mention a President who agreed such change would be beneficial.

In fact, Trump's favorite way to proceed was to get small armies of people together, either in the Oval or the Roosevelt Room, to argue out all these complex, controversial issues. Over and over again, the same issues. Without resolution, or even worse, one outcome one day and a contrary outcome a few days later. The whole thing made my head hurt. Even where there were occasional areas of agreement, it did not afford a basis from which to develop broader policy. For example, Hassett's economists had done some careful modeling of the impact of China tariffs if an open trade conflict broke out. His data showed that tariffs on approximately $50 billion of Chinese exports to the US that Lighthizer had been crafting would actually advantage the US.[9] Trump heard that and said, "This is why they will negotiate." Whether China was a currency manipulator was also a favorite subject of discussion, with Navarro insisting that Beijing was, and Mnuchin insisting it was not. I also tried to create process discipline in this area, together with the National Economic Council, but that too failed. As time went on, Trump didn't hide his view (strongly shared by Chuck Schumer, just for context) that China was manipulating its currency for trade advantage, telling Mnuchin in mid-November, "I was with you two months ago. I was okay with your analysis, but I'm not with you now." On and on it went. And then it went on some more.

Part of the contentiousness arose because in the Administration's earlier days, Mnuchin had embedded himself into trade negotiations, although Treasury's role in prior presidencies was always far smaller than the role of the United States Trade Representative or the Commerce Secretary. Not only was his outsized role institutionally unusual, Mnuchin's pro-China, zeal-for-the-deal approach was substantively dangerous. From time to time, even Trump saw this. At one Roosevelt Room session, on May 22, Trump all but yelled at Mnuchin, "Don't be a trade negotiator. Go after Bitcoin [for fraud]." Mnuchin, also all but yelling, said, "If you don't want me on trade, fine, your economic team will execute whatever you want." That didn't necessarily mean the United States Trade Representative would resume its traditional role as primary negotiator, because Trump also lashed out at Lighthizer: "You haven't made one deal yet!"

What did process matter anyway when Trump tweeted on his own, as he did on May 14:

> ZTE, the large Chinese phone company, buys a big percentage of individual parts from U.S. companies. This is also reflective of the larger trade deal we are negotiating with China and my personal relationship with President Xi.

What was that all about? Worse was the explicit linkage of a law-enforcement matter to a trade deal, not to mention with Trump's "personal relationship" with Xi. For Xi, personal relationships of any sort did not get in the way of his advancing Chinese interests, just as Putin's personal relationships didn't hamper his advancing Russian interests. I don't think Trump ever got this point. Here, it was all about Trump and Xi. In countless other episodes, he had trouble divorcing the personal from the official.

On May 16, Trump struck again: "The Washington Post and CNN have typically written false stories about our trade negotiations with China. Nothing has happened with ZTE except as it pertains to the larger trade deal. Our country has been losing hundreds of billions of dollars a year with China . . ." This continued linkage of ZTE to overall trade issues was quite disturbing not only to Commerce but also to Justice, which was still monitoring ZTE's performance under the consent decree. Of course, by then Trump was barely talking to Attorney General Sessions, let alone considering his advice. Instead, Trump was writing Xi personal handwritten notes, which had the White House Counsel's office climbing the walls. What Trump wanted from ZTE now was a billion-dollar fine. That sounds like a lot, but it was chump change compared to ZTE's shutting down altogether, which is what Commerce's actions were doing to it. It was also slightly *smaller* than the fine ZTE had paid *initially* when the consent decree was first imposed.[10] The settlement Ross negotiated under Oval Office duress was finally announced in June. ZTE would theoretically have an independent board of directors and a continuing outside monitor.[11] Most business observers thought Trump had given ZTE not just a reprieve but a new lease on life. And what did we receive in exchange? Good question.

On the other hand, Trump came increasingly to view China as trying to influence the 2018 congressional elections against Republicans, and more important (to him), as working for his defeat in 2020. There was plenty of logic supporting both propositions, with good reason if you looked at the significant increase in US military spending under Trump, and the trade war. In our public statements on foreign-government efforts to meddle in US elections, we correctly referred to both China and Russia. China was also trying to leverage Trump's primal urge to make deals to its economic advantage, hoping to push us into "trade agreements" that didn't resolve the structural issues that were the real cause of the economic and political disputes between us. Beijing had to know how deeply divided Trump's China advisors were, because they could read about it routinely in the media.

We looked at China's election-related efforts as part of one of the broadest influence operations ever undertaken, far broader than what Democrats and the media obsessed over in 2016. Viewed without partisan blinders, China could bring considerably greater resources to bear on this effort than Russia. This was serious, and required a serious response. One answer was a judicious declassification review, done with care and prudence, especially not to jeopardize intelligence sources and methods, but enabling us to lay before the American people what we were up against. Trump referred publicly to China's efforts when he addressed the UN Security Council in September 2018, but it received little press attention.[12]

Pence took the opportunity of a speech at the Hudson Institute to describe the nature of China's influence operation, using both the newly declassified information and a wide range of other data already in the public domain.[13] The drafting involved difficult choices, because it was obvious Trump did not want the Vice President saying anything that could damage his prized personal relationship with Xi. Otherwise, he was prepared to take Beijing on, because he saw its efforts aimed at him personally. In private, Trump said both China and Russia were threats, which I wish the press could have heard. So interested was he in the final draft that the day before its delivery, Pence, Ayers, and I sat with Trump in his small dining room, going over it line by line. In short, Trump knew and personally approved everything that Pence said. The next day, we were all delighted with the press coverage. Pence said to Ayers and me that it was "the boldest China speech ever," which I think is true. As we discussed press coverage with Trump, he said, revealingly, "Other Presidents just didn't think it was appropriate to talk about money. That's all I know how to talk about."

With November's elections looming, there was little progress on the trade front, and attention inevitably turned to the Buenos Aires G20 meeting at the end of the month, when Xi and Trump could meet personally. Trump saw this as the meeting of his dreams, with the two big guys getting together, leaving the Europeans aside, cutting the big deal. What could go wrong? Plenty, in Lighthizer's view. He was very worried about how much Trump would give away once untethered. The day after the election, I met with Chinese State Councilor Yang Jiechi in Washington for a series of meetings ahead of the G20. We gathered in the Ward Room, which was crowded with participants, including Kushner, who had told me on Election Day, "The President has asked me to get more involved in the China trade issue," I am sure thereby delighting the dozens of other senior people jostling to be heard on China trade.

As was customary with senior Chinese officials in these kinds of meetings, Yang read carefully from a prepared text, saying the G20 meeting was the top priority in the relationship. We discussed how to structure the meeting, and my contribution to world peace was suggesting that Xi and Trump, each accompanied by seven aides, have dinner on December 1, which is what ultimately happened, after a lot of to-ing and fro-ing. Trade was the top priority. Yang assured me that China wanted strategic trust, and had no intention to challenge or displace the United States. They did not want conflict or confrontation, but win/win solutions. This went on and on, but the only problem we solved was the dinner arrangement. That was hard enough, given how many others on the US side wanted to weigh in on that mega-question.

Saturday, December 1, in Buenos Aires came quickly, and dinner with Xi was the last event before Trump flew home. In the late afternoon, we met Trump for a final briefing. Mnuchin had been beavering away all day with Liu He, China's economic-policy czar and top trade negotiator, widely viewed as number three in Xi's regime. Liu laid out what he expected Xi would say at dinner, including how Xi thought a trade deal should be structured. Mnuchin said all but explicitly that Trump should just accept it. Tough bargainer, Steve. It was unclear how much Lighthizer had been involved, but Navarro hadn't been involved at all, and the fireworks began. (Russia and North Korea were also on the dinner agenda; we never got to Russia and spent less than two minutes on Korea. In many ways, I was relieved.)

Lighthizer said he thought a "free-trade agreement" with China would be almost suicidal, but Mnuchin was fired up by his success in getting China to agree to purchase more soybeans, other agricultural products, and minerals, just as if we were a Third World commodity supplier to the Middle Kingdom.

I said I didn't think any of the numbers being bandied about were the real issues. This wasn't a trade dispute but a conflict of systems. The "structural issues" we raised with China weren't trade tactics but a fundamentally different approach to organizing economic life. Negotiations should begin on these issues, so we could see whether there was any real chance China was serious about changing its ways (and I certainly didn't believe it was). Kudlow agreed, taking a position more distant from Mnuchin than ever before, and Mnuchin didn't react well. During the ensuing debate, I suggested we bar all Chinese goods and services from America if they were based in whole or in part on stolen intellectual property. "I like that idea," said Trump, but of course Mnuchin didn't. I said we would need additional legislative authority, but it was a battle worth fighting. Trump said again (several times in fact) that he liked the idea, so I thought at least some progress had been made. The briefing ended minutes later, at four forty-five.

Dinner started at five forty-five, after the mandatory session with the press mob for pictures, and lasted until eight o'clock. Xi began by telling Trump how wonderful he was, laying it on thick. Xi read steadily through note cards, doubtless all of it hashed out arduously in advance planning for this summit. For us, the President ad-libbed, with no one on the US side knowing what he would say from one minute to the next. One highlight came when Xi said he wanted to work with Trump for six more years, and Trump replied that people were saying that the two-term constitutional limit on Presidents should be repealed for him. I was aware of no such chatter. Knowing Xi was effectively "President for life" in China, Trump was trying to compete with him. Later in the dinner, Xi said the US had too many elections, because he didn't want to switch away from Trump, who nodded approvingly. (Indeed, in a subsequent telephone conversation on December 29, Xi said expressly that China hoped Trump would have another term by amending the Constitution so he could stay longer.) Xi denied the idea of the

"100-year marathon"[14] to gain world dominance, or replace the United States, saying that was not China's natural strategy. They respected our sovereignty and our interests in Asia, and merely wanted the 1.4 billion Chinese to enjoy a better life. How nice.

Xi finally shifted to substance, saying that since their November 1 phone call, their staffs had worked hard and reached consensus on the key economic issues. He then described China's positions, essentially what Mnuchin had earlier urged we agree to: the US would roll back Trump's existing tariffs; there would be no competitive currency manipulation; and we would agree not to engage in cyber thievery (how thoughtful). There were no winners in a trade war, said Xi, so we should eliminate the current tariffs, or at least agree there would be no new tariffs. "People expect this," said Xi, and I feared at that moment that Trump would simply say yes to everything Xi had laid out. He came close, unilaterally offering that US tariffs would remain at 10 percent rather than rise to 25 percent as he had threatened. In exchange, Trump asked merely for some increases in farm-product purchases (to help with the crucial farm-state vote). If that could be agreed, all the tariffs would be reduced. Intellectual property was left to be worked out at some unspecified point. There would be a ninety-day period of negotiations to get everything done. It was breathtaking. Then he asked Lighthizer if he had left anything out, and Lighthizer did what he could to get the conversation back onto the plane of reality, focusing on the structural issues and ripping apart the Chinese proposal so beloved by Mnuchin.

Trump also asked Xi to reduce China's exports of fentanyl, a deadly opioid causing havoc across America and a politically explosive issue, which Xi agreed to do (but then later did essentially nothing). Trump also asked for the release of Victor and Cynthia Liu, whom China was holding hostage because of allegations against their father, Liu Changming, who was in the US. Xi said, as if this were the answer, that the Lius were dual US-Chinese citizens. Trump shrugged his shoulders disdainfully and dropped the issue. So much for protecting US citizens. The Chinese probably hoped the dinner would go on all night.

Trump closed by saying Lighthizer would be in charge of the

deal-making, and Kushner would also be involved, at which point all the Chinese perked up and smiled. You bet. Trump pointed out Lighthizer and Navarro (whose very presence must have irritated the Chinese) as the hawks, Mnuchin and Kudlow as the doves, and said about Pompeo and me, "They don't care about the money." Hard to say what the Chinese made of all that, but Xi certainly didn't offer up a reciprocal scorecard for his side of the table. The diminution of Mnuchin's role was the day's best news. At the end, after discussing press statements, we all headed for our respective airports. In the telling later, the dinner got longer and longer, three hours, three and a half, and finally "over four hours," as Trump regaled listeners with the triumphs he had enjoyed.

Back in Washington, on Monday, December 3, we gathered in the Oval to assess the results. Trump was delighted, happy with the reaction of global stock markets, and he still liked my idea to bar Chinese exports based on stolen US intellectual property. Mnuchin, however, was fighting his new role, asking, "Who's in charge?" about the coming negotiations. Trump stuck with Lighthizer as the lead, saying, "I don't see what's wrong with that. Treasury is a whole different world." He wanted Lighthizer: "Mnuchin puts out a different kind of signal. I don't know why you [Mnuchin] want to be involved. Do you know how to help him [Lighthizer]? Get the dollar fixed." And then away Trump went, attacking Fed Chairman Powell, his favorite punching bag, for keeping interest rates too high. Then, turning to Lighthizer, Trump said, "On this, I want your attitude, not Steve's. Double or triple the purchases of ag products . . . If we don't get a great deal, forget it. We'll be back here where we were [increasing tariffs]. Schumer likes this. Tariffs will be much better received in ninety days." And the new rounds of negotiations began for what Trump called more than once "the biggest deal in history. Not just the biggest trade deal, but the biggest deal ever."

The negotiations came complete with theatricals in the Oval Office starring Trump and Liu He, broadcast live on cable news. As time passed, the March 1 deadline became clearly unattainable, so Trump blew past it, saying "substantial progress" had been made.[15] I thought it signaled weakness, showing what he really wanted was a deal. In fact, of course, the ninety-day period was always illusory; it was impossible to believe China would concede on the "structural issues" in three months, having developed its practices over decades. But the decisive play came in May, when the Chinese reneged on several key elements of the emerging agreement, including on all the key "structural issues" that were really the heart of the matter. At the time, I was consumed with Iran's growing threat in the Persian Gulf region, but Lighthizer's call snapped me to attention. This was a serious setback for the deal advocates, which Lighthizer said he and Mnuchin believed was attributable to Liu He and his allies' having lost control of the politics back in Beijing.

Lighthizer came by my office the next morning, May 6, at eight a.m. to discuss the situation. He said that in Beijing the week before, the Chinese had retreated widely on specific commitments they had made, such as amending existing regulations, repealing statutes and passing new ones (for example, to protect intellectual property), and similar concrete steps that would show they were serious on the structural issues. Without these specific commitments, only vague assertions of intent were left, which, going back years with China, had always failed to produce results. Liu He said he was proposing merely an optical "rebalancing" of the draft deal's text, which enumerated many steps China would take but very few by the United States (with good reason!). The overall impact was to water down what Beijing would actually have to do, and the Chinese were also now pressing many other unhelpful revisions. Lighthizer said both he and Mnuchin concluded that Liu had lost control of the negotiations, and which they believed Liu had in effect admitted to them in Beijing. Liu was still planning to be in Washington at the end of the week, in the pattern of home-and-away meetings the negotiators had followed, but it was unclear whether he would have anything new or different to say.

There was now no prospect of reaching agreement in what Mnuchin had billed as "the last round" of talks, especially since many other serious issues remained unresolved. Trump had been tweeting threats of new tariffs, so it was also entirely possible Liu would not come at all. Later in the day, Lighthizer announced he was teeing up the next round of tariff increases to go into effect on Friday, which

Trump was clearly prepared to impose. Liu came to Washington with nothing new, and the discussions at his offices ended early. There was no Liu He meeting with Trump. The trade war was still on.

Trump spoke with Xi Jinping by phone on June 18, ahead of 2019's Osaka G20 summit, when they would next meet. Trump began by telling Xi he missed him, and then said that the most popular thing he had ever been involved with was making a trade deal with China, which would be a big plus politically. They agreed their economic teams could continue meeting. The G20 bilateral arrived, and during the usual media mayhem at the start, Trump said, "We've become friends. My trip to Beijing with my family was one of the most incredible of my life."[16]

With the press gone, Xi said this is the most important bilateral relationship in the world. He said that some (unnamed) political figures in the United States were making erroneous judgments by calling for a new cold war, this time between China and the United States. Whether Xi meant to finger the Democrats, or some of us sitting on the US side of the table, I don't know, but Trump immediately assumed Xi meant the Democrats. Trump said approvingly that there was great hostility among the Democrats. He then, stunningly, turned the conversation to the coming US presidential election, alluding to China's economic capability to affect the ongoing campaigns, pleading with Xi to ensure he'd win. He stressed the importance of farmers, and increased Chinese purchases of soybeans and wheat in the electoral outcome. I would print Trump's exact words, but the government's prepublication review process has decided otherwise.

Trump then raised the negotiations' collapse in May, urging China to return to the positions it had retracted. Breezing by China's failure to do anything on fentanyl and its seizure of Canadian hostages (not to mention the American hostages), both discussed in Buenos Aires, Trump urged that the two sides start from where they had left off in May and pursue the negotiations to conclude the most exciting, largest deal ever made. Out of nowhere, Xi answered by comparing the impact of an unequal deal with us to the "humiliation" of the Treaty of Versailles, which had taken Shandong province from Germany but given it to Japan. Xi said with a straight face that if China suffered the same humiliation in our trade negotiations, there would be an upsurge of patriotic feeling in China, implicitly indicating that that feeling would be directed against the United States. Trump manifestly had no idea what Xi was referring to, but said that a treaty of non-equals was not in Xi's blood. History being a very easy subject for Trump once it was broached, he implied China owed the US a favor for knocking Japan out of World War II. Xi then lectured us on how China fought for nineteen years, and relied mainly on themselves to defeat the Japanese aggressors. Of course, this was just as nonsensical; the Chinese Communists had spent most of the war ducking Japan and trying to undercut the Chinese Nationalists. The war ended when it did because we used atomic bombs, but Xi was reciting history from the Communist catechism, not that Trump understood that either.

Toward the end of the trade issue, Trump proposed that for the remaining $350 billion of trade imbalances (by Trump's arithmetic), the US would not impose tariffs, but he again returned to importuning Xi and China to buy as many American farm products as they could. Then, they would see if a deal were possible. Trump asked Liu He if we could make a deal from where we were before China backtracked in May. Liu looked like a deer in the headlights, speechless, clearly not wanting to answer. After a pregnant silence, Trump highlighted Liu's awkwardness by saying he had never seen him so quiet. Turning to Xi, Trump asked him what the answer was, since he was the only one with the courage to answer it. Xi agreed that we should restart the trade talks, welcoming Trump's concession that there would be no new tariffs, and agreeing that the two negotiating teams should resume discussions on farm products on a priority basis. "You're the greatest Chinese leader in three hundred years!" exulted Trump, amending it a few minutes later to be "the greatest leader in Chinese history." After a drive-by discussion of North Korea, since Trump was on his way to Seoul that evening, that was that on trade.

Xi returned to the Liu children, recalling that they had been discussed in Buenos Aires on December 1, calling them Chinese citizens (they were actually dual US-Chinese citizens). Stunningly, he said quite casually were barred from leaving China to get them to cooperate in a money-laundering investigation of their father, arguing that by failing to cooperate, the Lius were endangering Chinese national security. Xi then said pointedly that December 1 was the same night that Meng Wanzhou, Huawei CFO, had been arrested. He concluded vaguely that the two sides could stay in touch. Of course, Xi was then perfectly comfortable complaining that not enough visas were being issued for Chinese students who wanted to come to the United States!

Trade talks with China resumed after Osaka, but progress was negligible. Trump seemed inclined to hedge, tweeting on July 30, against the advice of Mnuchin and Lighthizer:

> China is doing very badly, worst year in 27 – was supposed to start buying our agricultural product now – no signs that they are doing so. That is the problem with China, they just don't come through. Our Economy has become MUCH larger than the Chinese Economy is last 3 years . . .

> . . . My team is negotiating with them now, but they always change the deal in the end to their benefit. They should probably wait out our Election to see if we get one of the Democrat stiffs like Sleepy Joe. Then they could make a GREAT deal, like in past 30 years, and continue . . .

> . . . to rip off the USA, even bigger and better than ever before. The problem with them waiting, however, is that if & when I win, the deal that they get will be much tougher than what we are negotiating now . . . or no deal at all. We have all the cards, our past leaders never got it!

As the negotiations continued, there was simply no indication of real movement from China. After yet another Lighthizer-Mnuchin visit to Beijing, they reported to Trump in the Oval on August 1. Trump had nothing good to say, opening with, "You shouldn't have gone there. It

makes us look weak." He had actually been musing about more tariffs the day before, saying to me with a wink and a smile, "I'm much
more like you than you know." Trump was now even more convinced
China was waiting to see who won in 2020, believing "they want the
President to lose." Trump finally said, "I want to put tariffs on. They're
tapping you along," and we turned to whether to impose tariffs on another $350 billion of Chinese exports to the United States. Trump said
to Mnuchin, "You talk too much. Don't be scared, Steve." Lighthizer for
some reason worried that our trade war with China was hurting Europe, which only added fuel to the fire, provoking the familiar Trump
refrain, "The EU is worse than China, only smaller," as he decided to
impose the next round of tariffs on Beijing, via Twitter, of course:

> Our representatives have just returned from China where
> they had constructive talks having to do with a future Trade
> Deal. We thought we had a deal with China three months
> ago, but sadly, China decided to re-negotiate the deal prior
> to signing. More recently, China agreed to . . .

> . . . buy agricultural product from the U.S. in large quantities,
> but did not do so. Additionally, my friend President Xi
> said that he would stop the sale of Fentanyl to the United
> States—this never happened, and many Americans
> continue to die! Trade talks are continuing, and . . .

> . . . during the talks the U.S. will start, on September 1st,
> putting a small additional Tariff of 10% on the remaining
> 300 Billion Dollars of goods and products coming from
> China into our Country. This does not include the 250
> Billion Dollars already Tariffed at 25% . . .

> . . . We look forward to continuing our positive dialogue with
> China on a comprehensive Trade Deal, and feel that the
> future between our two countries will be a very bright one!

This was a huge decision, causing great angst in Trump's economic team, which was pretty much where things stood when I resigned on September 10. Subsequent negotiations did lead to a "deal" announced in December, which was, in substance, less than met the eye.

On December 1, 2018, the same day as the lengthy Xi-Trump dinner in Buenos Aires and as they discussed at the meeting in Osaka, Canadian authorities in Vancouver arrested Meng Wanzhou, the CFO of Huawei, another Chinese mega-telecom firm. (We had heard on Friday the arrest might occur on Saturday, when Meng, daughter of Huawei's founder, landed in Canada.) Because this arrest was based on our case of financial fraud against Huawei for, among other things, concealing massive violations of our Iran sanctions, it struck me as straightforward. Things were busy in Buenos Aires, to say the least, and I had learned enough watching Trump with Erdogan to understand I needed to have all the facts in hand before I briefed Trump.

As the implications of the arrest spread through the media, however, China's US friends grew upset. At the December 7 White House Christmas dinner, Trump raised Meng's arrest, riffing about how much pressure this put on China. He said to me across the table that we had just arrested "the Ivanka Trump of China." I came within an inch of saying, "I never knew Ivanka was a spy and a fraudster," but my automatic tongue-biting mechanism kicked in just in time. What Wall Street financier had given Trump that line? Or was it Kushner, who had been engaged in a mutual courtship on China matters with Henry Kissinger since the transition? Trump complained that Huawei was China's largest telecom company. I said Huawei wasn't a company but an arm of China's intelligence services,[17] which slowed him down. Combined with what Trump later said about the Uighurs during this same dinner, I could tell we were in a different cycle of Trump's thinking on how to handle China. I wondered what it would take to get him off appeasement and back onto his more aggressive approach, as when he gave Lighthizer the lead in trade negotiations.

Trump made matters worse on several occasions by implying

that Huawei also could be simply another US bargaining chip in the trade negotiations, ignoring both the significance of the criminal case and also the far larger threat Huawei posed to the security of fifth-generation (or 5G) telecom systems worldwide. This is what the black-hole-of-trade phenomenon did in twisting all other issues around Trump's fascination with a big trade deal. Huawei posed enormous national-security issues, many of which we could only allude to in public statements. The idea that this was merely trade bait both discouraged and confused our friends. Mnuchin fretted constantly about how this or that prosecution for hacking or other cybercrimes would have a negative effect on the trade negotiations, which Trump sometimes bought and sometimes didn't. At one point, he said to Mnuchin, "Steve, the Chinese see fear in your eyes. That's why I don't want you negotiating with them." Those were the good days. There were more that weren't.

As the trade negotiations proceeded, we began producing draft Executive Orders to secure US telecom systems and information technology assets generally. Each step of the way, we had to fight the alleged impact on the China trade negotiations. At times, some Administration economic-policy officials didn't think Huawei was a threat, just another competitor, whom we national-security types were trying to disadvantage as a protectionist measure to help US firms.[18] Trench by trench, we overcame this resistance. I urged in several Oval Office meetings that we follow Zhou Enlai's World War II admonition, in conducting negotiations with Chiang Kai-shek even as Communist and Kuomintang forces were locked in armed combat, that their policy should be "fighting while talking." How could Xi Jinping object to our following Zhou's advice? It didn't get a rise out of Mnuchin. Trump said, nonetheless, "I don't disagree with John," but he followed through only fitfully and grudgingly. We continued putting important defenses in place, but far more slowly than was prudent. And, of course, Trump himself continued to be part of the problem, asking Lighthizer, at one point in April, whether we should say something in the trade deal about cyberwarfare. This idea bordered on the irrational, or worse, and it quickly disappeared from official US circles, but where else might it be toddling along, leading to incalculable mischief if it reemerges in the next Xi-Trump meeting?

We ran into similar obstacles internationally as we sought to alert our allies to Huawei's threat and that of other state-controlled Chinese firms. We also spread awareness of how treacherous China's Belt and Road Initiative was, based on "debt diplomacy," luring countries with seemingly advantageous credit terms, then getting them hooked financially, from which Third World nations especially couldn't extract themselves. In December 2018, at the Heritage Foundation, I laid out the Administration's Africa strategy, stressing our concern for the unfair advantage China had taken of many African nations. In Europe, many countries had done so much business with Huawei, they found it hard to disentangle themselves. With the UK, for example, the discussions were very difficult, although attitudes changed significantly once Johnson became Prime Minister and installed a new Cabinet. But even then, it was hard slogging because of the high level of dependence on Huawei that Britain had built up over an extended period. These legitimate worries should have led us to focus on rapidly getting new entrants into 5G markets, not how we would mitigate the consequences of continuing to patronize Huawei.[19]

Japan took a tough view.[20] During Trump's May state visit, Abe had said China is the largest strategic challenge in the mid- to long-term. They completely disregard established rules and order. Their attempts to change the status quo unilaterally in the East and South China Seas are unacceptable. Abe encouraged Trump to maintain US-Japan unity against China, and much more. This was how to conduct a strategic dialogue with a close ally. Australia's Prime Minister Scott Morrison was also clear-eyed, seeing Huawei pretty much the way I did, and New Zealand also took a surprisingly but gratifyingly hard line.[21]

We had to admit we were all late to realize the full extent of Huawei's strategy, but that was not an excuse to compound our earlier mistakes. Even as we discussed these issues, China was showing its teeth, unlawfully detaining Canadian citizens in China, just to show they could.[22] Canada was under great domestic pressure, which Trudeau was having difficulty resisting. Former Prime Minister Jean Chretien, never a friend of the US, was arguing that Canada should simply not abide by our extradition treaty.[23] Pence, Pompeo, and I all urged Canada to stand firm, stressing we would support them every way we could, including directly raising with China the mistreatment of Canadian citizens. As we pointed out, this was the way China behaved even as some people continued to praise its "peaceful rise" as a "responsible stakeholder." How would China act as it became dominant, if we let it? This is a national-security debate that will go on well into the future. Tying it to trade degrades our position both in trade and in national security.

By early May, Ross was prepared to put Huawei on the Commerce Department's "entity list," as had been done to ZTE, precluding US firms from selling to Huawei without specific licenses, which could deal Huawei a body blow. I strongly supported the measure, for the same reasons we barred US government purchases of Huawei goods and services. This was not a commercial company as we know that concept, and it should not have been treated as one. At yet another Oval Office roll-around on May 15, Mnuchin said listing Huawei would effectively shut it down, which wasn't true, but it was fine with me if it did. To be fair, Mnuchin may have been a little unhinged by the collapse just a week before of five months of intensive trade negotiations with China, which now appeared to be broken beyond repair. Mnuchin said Ross's draft press statement on Huawei was extreme, so Ross asked if he could read it aloud and let others decide, which he did. Said Trump, "It's a fucking great statement. It's beautiful. Add 'with the approval of the President' next to one of the references to Commerce adding Huawei to the entity list." Mnuchin wouldn't give up but was finally overwhelmed, saying snippily to Trump, "I gave you my advice, and you followed the wrong person."

In the June 18 Xi-Trump phone call (see above), Xi pressed hard on Huawei. Trump repeated his point that Huawei could be part of the trade deal, along with all of the other factors being discussed. Xi warned that, if not handled properly, Huawei would harm the overall bilateral relationship. In an amazing display of chutzpah, Xi described Huawei as an outstanding private Chinese company, having important relations with Qualcomm and Intel. Xi wanted the ban on Huawei lifted, and said he wanted to work jointly with Trump personally on the issue, and Trump seemed amenable. He tweeted his delight at the call shortly after the two leaders hung up. Sensing weakness, Xi kept pushing at the G-20, saying we should resolve Huawei as part of the trade talks. Trump forthwith reversed his earlier position, saying he would now allow US companies to sell to Huawei immediately, thereby effectively reversing Ross, as Trump had reversed him on ZTE earlier. Fortunately, after this meeting, we re-reversed all this, and Trump's loose comment had little real-world impact. But what impact did it have in the minds of the Chinese to see this behavior on Trump's part? We were just lucky China didn't move more quickly to pin Trump's concession down before we prevented any damage.

I briefed Mnuchin on the call a few hours later. More than a little concerned, Mnuchin said, "We've got to try to protect the President on the Huawei stuff. People thought he was trading national security for trade on ZTE, and if we allow him to do it again on Huawei, we'll get the same kind of backlash, or worse." That was true then and remains true today.[24]

Former Vice President Dan Quayle told me as far back as October 2018, after a trip to Hong Kong, that China had become increasingly aggressive, kidnapping from Hong Kong businessmen who had somehow crossed Beijing, many of whom were simply never heard from again. The business community was too scared to say much or get it reported in the international press. Quayle believed one reason China was prepared to behave so cavalierly was that Hong Kong's economy now amounted to only 2 percent of China's total, whereas at the time of the handover from Great Britain in 1997, it amounted to 20 percent. Those were stunning numbers.

Dissatisfaction in Hong Kong had been growing, although without receiving media attention. The pervasive feeling was that Beijing was steadily eroding the "one country, two systems" concept, and that time was running out before Hong Kong simply became just another

Chinese city. An extradition bill proposed by Hong Kong's govern-ment provided the spark, and by early June 2019, massive protests were under way. I first heard Trump react on June 12, upon hearing the number of people at the demonstrations the Sunday before, some 1.5 million: "That's a big deal," he said, but immediately added, "I don't want to get involved," and "We have human-rights problems too." That pretty much ended my Twitter campaign pressing China to honor its deal with Great Britain, highlighting how little respect China paid to international agreements, for all those so excited at the prospect of a trade deal.

I hoped Trump would see these Hong Kong developments as giving him leverage over China, although not necessarily because he supported the demonstrators' efforts to preserve Hong Kong's unique status. I should have known better. During the UK state visit, on June 4, the thirtieth anniversary of the Tiananmen Square massacre, Trump refused to issue a White House statement. Mnuchin told Trump he worried about the effects of the draft statement on the trade negotia-tions and wanted to water it down. That was bad enough, but Trump said he didn't want any statement at all. "That was fifteen years ago," he said, inaccurately. "Who cares about it? I'm trying to make a deal. I don't want anything." And that was that.

The demonstrators, however, won a major victory when Beijing's handpicked Hong Kong Chief Executive Carrie Lam backed off the extradition bill, effectively killing it. Protests continued, next putting two million "HongKongpeople," pronounced as one word, into the streets the following weekend, now demanding Lam's resignation.

In the June 18 phone call, along with trade and Huawei, Trump said that he saw what was happening in Hong Kong, that it was a do-mestic Chinese issue, and he had told his advisors not to discuss Hong Kong publicly in any way, shape, or form. Xi was appreciative, saying that what happened in Hong Kong was indeed a purely Chinese do-mestic affair. He said that the extradition issue, which had touched off the demonstrations, was to close existing loopholes in Hong Kong law, and was for serious criminal matters. He also stressed that sta-bility and prosperity in Hong Kong was a plus for both China and the United States, and others should refrain from interfering in Hong Kong affairs. Trump acquiesced. With that, Hong Kong's fate might have all but disappeared from our agenda.

However, as Pompeo pointed out when we spoke later that day, several statutory reporting requirements would obligate the State Department, at some point, to opine on the Hong Kong situation, with no way to duck. "What are you going to say on the Sunday talk shows?" he asked rhetorically. "Or me, or any of us?" By mid-August, there were increasing media reports about the possibility of a Chinese crackdown in Hong Kong. I briefed Trump on what we knew, and he said he might tweet about it. I urged him, if he did so, to rely only on public sources, but as was so often the case, he ignored this warning, tweeting instead:

> Our Intelligence has informed us that the Chinese Government is moving troops to the Border with Hong Kong. Everyone should be calm and safe! Many are blaming me, and the United States, for the problems going on in Hong Kong. I can't imagine why?

So much for stopping all those leaks from the "deep state."

On August 13, after our discussion on F-16 sales to Taiwan (see below), Trump tweeted again:

> I know President Xi of China very well. He is a great leader who very much has the respect of his people. He is also a good man in a 'tough business.' I have ZERO doubt that if President Xi wants to quickly and humanely solve the Hong Kong problem, he can do it. Personal meeting?

Of course, with so much at stake in Hong Kong, there was little doubt Xi personally was calling the shots. As October 1, the seventieth anniversary of the founding of the People's Republic of China, approached, tensions grew accordingly. No one believed Beijing would accept extensive demonstrations in Hong Kong, especially if they turned violent, raining on Xi's parade. China's news agency Xinhua warned the demonstrators, "The end is coming," about as explicit a threat as you could make.[25]

In November, however, pro-democracy advocates turned local council elections into a referendum on the city's future. Stunningly, HongKongpeople voted in unprecedented numbers, overwhelming pro-Beijing candidates, and completely reversed the political coloration of the local councils. This fight was on.

China was also busily repressing ethnic minorities—in Tibet, for example—as it had been doing for decades. Beijing's repression of the Uighurs also proceeded apace. Trump asked me at the 2018 White House Christmas dinner why we were considering sanctioning China because of its treatment of the Uighurs, a non–Han Chinese, largely Muslim people, who lived primarily in China's northwest Xinjiang Province. Ross had warned me that morning Trump didn't want sanctions because of the China trade negotiations. The issue of the Uighurs had been wending its way through the NSC process, but it was not yet ready for decision. It only got worse. At the opening dinner of the Osaka G20 meeting, with only interpreters present, Xi explained to Trump why he was basically building concentration camps in Xinjiang. According to our interpreter, Trump said that Xi should go ahead with building the camps, which he thought was exactly the right thing to do. Pottinger told me Trump said something very similar during the 2017 trip to China, which meant we could cross repression of the Uighurs off our list of possible reasons to sanction China, at least as long as trade negotiations continued.[26]

Religious repression in China was also not on Trump's agenda; whether it was the Catholic Church or Falun Gong, it didn't register. That was not where Pence, Pompeo, and I were, but it was Trump's call. US Ambassador-at-Large for International Religious Freedom Sam Brownback, pressing for Trump to do a religious freedom event at the upcoming September 2019 opening of the UN General Assembly, thought China was "horrible across the board," which was just about right.

Trump was particularly dyspeptic about Taiwan, having listened to Wall Street financiers who had gotten rich off mainland China investments. Although it came in several variations, one of Trump's favorite comparisons was to point to the tip of one of his Sharpies and say, "This is Taiwan," then point to the *Resolute* desk and say, "This is China." So much for American commitments and obligations to another democratic ally. Taiwan very much wanted a free-trade agreement with the US, which generated absolutely no interest that I could discern. China pounded away during my tenure, sensing weakness at the top, doubtless having heard from those Wall Street financial types. Yang Jiechi, in our November 8 meeting, gave me the customary lecture about Taiwan's being the most important and sensitive issue in US-China relations. Remarkably, he said that we had a mutual stake in preventing Taiwanese independence as if we were co-conspirators, which I certainly didn't believe. He talked endlessly about the "one China" policy, which he mischaracterized in Beijing's favor. At the Buenos Aires dinner, Xi urged us to be prudent on Taiwan, which Trump agreed he would be alert to, meaning we escaped with our lives. I was delighted the discussion was so brief.

Xi returned to Taiwan at Osaka, saying it involved Chinese sovereignty and national integrity, and warning that our entire bilateral relationship could become unhinged. He asked for Trump's personal attention to the issue, probably figuring he had identified his mark and wasn't going to let him get away. Always infuriating to me, Xi urged that we not allow Taiwanese President Tsai Ing-wen to travel to the United States, or to sell arms to Taiwan, both of which Xi deemed critical for stability across the Taiwan Strait. Much of Xi's position directly contradicted the Taiwan Relations Act of 1979, US legislation that authorizes US arms sales to Taiwan for purposes of self-defense, including an important sale of F-16s to significantly upgrade Taiwan's defense capabilities. In fact, Taiwan was far from behaving belligerently. Quite the contrary. Dan Quayle told me in October that Taiwan had shrunk its military dramatically, by more than half in recent years, which struck me as a huge mistake.

Pompeo was holding back a congressional notification on the F-16 sale, worried that, in addition to generally grousing, as Trump did on all Taiwan sales, this time he might actually refuse to proceed with it. Given our delicate circumstances on military sales to Ukraine, this was not fanciful. We strategized on persuading Trump and got Mick Mulvaney on board, as a former congressman from South Carolina, a state with major Boeing manufacturing facilities. On August 13, in an afternoon conference call with Trump at Bedminster, we explained the enormous political blowback if the sale didn't proceed. There was no US subsidy or foreign aid involved, and Taiwan was paying full costs for the F-16s, for a total sales price of $8 billion and lots of jobs in South Carolina. We also said it was better to go forward now, before something dramatic happened in Hong Kong. Trump asked, "Did you ever give any thought to not making the sale?" to which, of course, the answer was no. Trump finally said, "Okay, but do it quietly. John, you're not going to give a speech about it, are you?" which I actually hadn't thought about. But I probably should have.

After I left the White House, when Trump abandoned the Kurds in Syria, there was speculation about who he might abandon next.[27] Taiwan was right near the top of the list, and would probably stay there as long as Trump remained President, not a happy prospect.

More thunder out of China, in the form of the coronavirus pandemic, came in early 2020. Although epidemiologists (not to mention biological weapons experts) will be studying this catastrophe long into the future; the mark of China's authoritarian government and social-control systems is all over it. There is little doubt that China delayed, withheld, fabricated, and distorted information about the origin, timing, spread, and extent of the disease;[28] suppressed dissent from physicians and others;[29] hindered outside efforts by the World Health Organization and others to get accurate information; and engaged in active disinformation campaigns, actually trying to argue that the virus (SARS-CoV-2) and the disease itself (COVID-19) did not originate in China.[30] Ironically, some of the worst effects of China's cover-up were visited on its closest allies. Iran, for example, looked to be one of the worst-hit countries, with satellite photos showing the excavation of burial pits for the expected victims of COVID-19.[31]

With 2020 being a presidential election year, it was inevitable that Trump's performance in this global health emergency would become a campaign issue, which it did almost immediately. And there was plenty to criticize, starting with the Administration's early, relentless assertion that the disease was "contained" and would have little or no economic effect. Larry Kudlow, Chairman of the National Economic Council, said, on February 25, "We have contained this. I won't say [it's] airtight, but it's pretty close to airtight."[32] Market reactions to these kinds of assertions were decidedly negative, which may finally have woken the White House up to the seriousness of the problem. And obviously, in addition to the humanitarian implications, the economic and business consequences would certainly continue to reverberate through the November elections and beyond. Trump's reflex effort to talk his way out of anything, however, even a public-health crisis, only undercut his and the nation's credibility, with his statements looking more like political damage control than responsible public-health advice. One particularly egregious example was a news report that the Administration tried to classify certain public-health information regarding the United States on the spurious excuse that China was involved.[33] Of course China was involved, which is a reason to disseminate the information broadly, not restrict it. This, Trump was reluctant to do throughout the crisis, for fear of adversely affecting the elusive definitive trade deal with China, or offending the ever-so-sensitive Xi Jinping.

Other criticisms of the Administration, however, were frivolous. One such complaint targeted an aspect of the general streamlining of NSC staffing that I conducted in my first months at the White House. To reduce duplication and overlap, and enhance coordination and efficiency, it made good management sense to shift the responsibilities of the directorate dealing with global health and biodefense into the existing directorate dealing with weapons of mass destruction (biological, chemical and nuclear). The characteristics of bioweapons' attacks and pandemics can have much in common, and the medical and public-health expertise required to deal with both threats went hand in hand. Combining the two directorates therefore maximized the opportunities for working more effectively together, as well as raising the priority of biosecurity, by structurally recognizing that the threat could come from either of two directions, natural or man-made. Most of the personnel working in the prior global health directorate simply moved to the combined directorate, and continued doing exactly what they were doing before. One person moved to the international organizations directorate and continued to work there on health issues in the UN system and other bodies. Like all NSC directorates, most staffers come from other Departments and agencies, and rotate after one- or two-year assignments at the NSC back to their home bases. That process continued. Tim Morrison, the senior director I brought in to handle these matters, and his successor, Anthony Ruggiero, have successfully kept global health a focus.[34]

I personally made it clear that global health remained a top priority, and that the NSC's role remained unchanged. That criticisms of the reorganization came from Obama Administration alumni who had initially created the separate global health office signaled their underlying political basis. Obama's staffing reflected the view that the White House had to be involved in often-minute operational details, which was contrary to Scowcroft's model of a non-operational NSC, as well as the management philosophy that properly delegated authority was a far more effective way to administer programs and policies than constant second-guessing from on high.[35]

The reorganized directorates performed perfectly well, as I had fully expected. In real-world terms, the renewed Ebola outbreaks in the eastern Congo and nearby areas in 2018–19 were handled with great skill across the interagency process.[36] Apart from continual monitoring, my personal interventions were limited to helping ensure adequate security and protection for Centers for Disease Control experts to access the affected Congo regions. Trump himself told Kupperman, when OMB raised budgetary objections to sending the teams, to have OMB make available whatever funds would be needed "to keep Ebola out of the US." In addition, the Directorate oversaw the creation of a fully revised national biodefense strategy in 2018,[37] and also produced two important presidential decisions, one (following on the new strategy) on support for biodefense in September, 2018,[38] and one on modernizing influenza vaccines in September, 2019.[39] These and other less publicly visible achievements are the hallmark of an effectively functioning interagency process.

The idea that a minor bureaucratic restructuring could have made any difference in the time of Trump reflected how immune bureaucratic pettifoggery is to reality. At most, the internal NSC structure was no more than the quiver of a butterfly's wings in the tsunami of Trump's chaos. Even so, and despite the indifference at the top of the White House, the cognizant NSC staffers did their duty in the coronavirus pandemic. As the *New York Times* reported in a historical review in mid-April:

> The National Security Council office responsible for tracking pandemics received intelligence reports in early January predicting the spread of the virus to the United States, and within weeks was raising options like keeping Americans home from work and shutting down cities the size of Chicago. Mr. Trump would avoid such steps until March.[40]

Thus, responding to the coronavirus, the NSC biosecurity team functioned exactly as it was supposed to. It was the chair behind the *Resolute* desk that was empty.

And fundamentally, after all the human and economic costs of the coronavirus are reckoned, there are two chilling conclusions. First, we must do everything possible to ensure that China, and its contemporaneous disinformation campaign about the origin of the virus, will not succeed in proving that the Big Lie technique is alive and well in the twenty-first century. We must tell the truth about China's behavior, which Trump was consistently loath to do, or we will suffer the consequences and the risk well into the future.

Second, after decades in which biological (and chemical) warfare have been belittled as "the poor man's nuclear weapon"—given what the likes of North Korea, Iran, and others have just seen happen worldwide—we must treat these other two weapons of mass destruction with at least the vigilance we now afford to nuclear weapons. And, in fact, by combing the biosecurity directorate with the Directorate responsible for weapons of mass destruction, I intended to do just that.[41] The reorganization was not a downgrading of biosecurity, but an effort to increase the salience of biological threats to US national security.

CHAPTER 11

CHECKING INTO THE HANOI HILTON, THEN CHECKING OUT, AND THE PANMUNJOM PLAYTIME

When the 2018 congressional elections concluded, another Trump-Kim summit looked depressingly inescapable. Trump's fascination with obtaining "a deal" with the North waxed and waned, but with over six months having passed since the Singapore summit and nothing much happening, waxing was becoming ascendant. Pompeo was to meet North Korea's Kim Yong Chol in New York on Thursday, November 8, and Kim wanted another White House meeting that day or the next. Fortunately, I would be in Paris preparing for Trump's upcoming visit, so there would be no repeat of the spring 2018 scene. It still turned my stomach to imagine Kim Yong Chol back in the Oval. Then, mercifully, Kim Jong Un canceled the trip. Prospects for a Moon-Kim summit were also going nowhere, at best being kicked into 2019.

After New Year's, though, the pace increased, not that it took much to fire up Trump. Kim Jong Un flew unexpectedly to Beijing on his birthday, January 8, very likely to prepare for another Trump meeting. Sure enough, next up was a Kim Yong Chol visit to Washington on January 17 and 18, with a Trump meeting on Friday the eighteenth. I couldn't wait. I explained to Pompeo I had a minor surgery long scheduled for that day; he asked if I was sure I didn't need some help.

Kim Yong Chol brought along another Kim Jong Un letter, and the Oval Office meeting lasted ninety minutes, obviously making surgery preferable.[1] Charlie Kupperman (who had recently replaced Ricardel) attended the session, reporting that the discussion rambled, typically, and loose language was undoubtedly used. Nonetheless, he saw no *real* Trump commitments, and at the end, Trump said he couldn't lift sanctions until North Korea denuclearized, or he would look like a fool, which was true, and it was good Trump still remembered it. That may not normally be the basis for grand strategy, but it's what we had to work with. Staff-level negotiations were scheduled over the weekend in Sweden, and it was there I feared things would start slipping out of control. Indeed, according to press reports,[2] that seemed ever more likely, especially since North Korea had finally named a counterpart to the State Department's special envoy Steve Biegun, one Kim Hyok Chol, a veteran of the Bush 43–era Six-Party Talks. This was not a good sign.

With the summit venue and dates fixed for Hanoi on February 27 and 28, I thought hard about how to prevent a debacle. Remarks by Biegun at Stanford strongly implying that the Administration was prepared to follow the "action for action" formula demanded by North Korea only increased my concern,[3] compounded by the State Department's reversion to type: uncooperative and uncommunicative on what they were telling the North Koreans. The State Department had done exactly the same thing to the NSC during the Six-Party Talks. It was possible that Pompeo was not fully aware that Biegun's personal agenda to get a deal was so firm. But whether Pompeo ordered Biegun's enthusiasm, allowed it, or was ignorant of it was beside the point; the dangerous consequences were the same.

Since State's negotiators seemed to be spinning out of control, overcome by zeal for the deal, and intoxicated by the publicity, I considered what to do with Trump personally to prevent mistakes in Hanoi. I concluded that Trump's pre-Hanoi briefings needed to be significantly different from those before Singapore, which had had little impact. The first Hanoi prep session was on February 12 in the Sit Room, starting at four forty-five and lasting forty-five minutes. We showed a film, opening with news clips of Carter, Clinton, Bush, and Obama all saying they had achieved great deals with North Korea, then turning to North Korea's actual conduct since Singapore and how they were still deceiving us. The film ended with clips of Reagan describing his 1986 Reykjavik Summit with Gorbachev. Reagan's point was that when you held firm, you got better deals than when you gave in. There was a smooth flow of discussion, Trump asked good questions, and the session was remarkably focused. When we finished, Trump himself said the key points he carried away were: "I've got the leverage," "I don't need to be rushed," and "I could walk away." The briefing allowed Trump to conclude that Hanoi was not make-or-break; if no real progress emerged, he could simply proceed as before. I couldn't have scripted it better.

Our economic pressure on North Korea was greater than before, but it was a matter of degree. The sanctions nonetheless gave us a near-term advantage. Kim Jong Un was the one more desperate for the deal because the squeeze, while far from perfect, continued to frustrate his efforts to deliver economic improvement inside his country. Over the long term, time always benefited the proliferator, but my definition of "long term" was now two weeks: getting past the Hanoi Summit without making catastrophic concessions and compromises. If we stalled any rush to make a deal just to say we had, which was the State Department's every inclination, I would be satisfied. I foresaw the pressure on us to deal declining once we were past the second Trump-Kim summit. We could instead refocus on the very grave threat the North still represented, whether or not they were actively testing nuclear weapons and ballistic missiles. I felt enormously relieved the briefing hadn't been a disaster and that we might even have made progress with Trump.

The second briefing, on February 15, just after two o'clock, again lasted about forty-five minutes. We ran an excerpt from a North Korean propaganda film showing them still engaged in robust war games, even if we weren't, pursuant to Trump's orders. He was very interested in the video and asked to have a copy. We focused on the most important point: the meaning of "complete denuclearization." Trump asked for the conclusions on a single sheet of paper, which we had already prepared. After a good discussion, Trump said, "Clean this up and get it back to me," which suggested he might hand it to Kim Jong Un at some point. I stressed the importance of getting a full baseline declaration, not the piecemeal approach that the State Department would accept. I thought this second briefing also went extremely well, accomplishing all we could expect to get Trump into the right frame of mind so as not to give away the store in Hanoi.

Even another phone call with South Korea's Moon Jae-in, persistently pushing South Korea's agenda, on February 19 didn't cause major damage. Trump proclaimed that he was the only person who could make a nuclear deal with Kim Jong Un. He pressed Moon to let the media know that progress was being made, since they typically tried to put a negative spin on whatever he did. He promised to keep South Korea's interests in mind, but stressed that Kim wanted a deal. They all wanted deals. Later that morning, Pompeo, Biegun, the NSC's Allison Hooker, and I yet again had a meeting with Trump, during which he said, "If we walk away, it's okay," the main point made in the briefings. To Biegun, Trump said, "Tell them [the North Koreans] how much I love Chairman Kim, but also tell them what I want."

After further discussions, Pompeo and I went back to my office to talk about Hanoi. I stressed again why a baseline declaration by North Korea was the starting point for any intelligible negotiation. I also underlined why we couldn't give up economic sanctions and why we needed more pressure. Pompeo bristled at my "interference" with his turf, but he didn't disagree on the substance, which he rarely did when we talked alone. At a Principals Committee later that day on North Korea, the clear weakness Biegun displayed disturbed many of those present, especially Shanahan and Dunford, even Pompeo. Was he managing Biegun or wasn't he? Dunford wanted to be sure that any "end-of-war declaration" would not have binding legal effect, which of course raised the question of why we were considering it at all. The North had told us they didn't care about it, seeing it as something Moon wanted. So why were we pursuing it?

The third and final North Korea briefing, on February 21, followed a call with Abe the day before that couldn't have teed it up better. We had prepared a set of "wild cards" that Kim Jong Un might bring to Hanoi to surprise Trump and get him to make unnecessary concessions. Once again lasting about forty-five minutes, the session was a successful conclusion to our briefing efforts. Whether they would suffice to prevent catastrophic concessions to Kim remained to be seen.

I left for Hanoi early on February 24. Flying toward our refueling stop in Anchorage, we received a draft US–North Korea statement. The NSC's Allison Hooker said Biegun had "table-dropped" it at a meeting with the North, without previously clearing it. It read as if drafted by North Korea, enumerating all Trump's prior "concessions" to Kim Yong Chol in the Oval Office without seeking anything in return beyond another vague statement that North Korea would agree to define "denuclearization." It was a complete mystery to me why Pompeo would allow such a text. What if the North Koreans simply accepted it word for word? This was another massive process foul, and a political time bomb. I had Kupperman show the draft to Mulvaney and Stephen Miller in Washington, and Mulvaney agreed it was both a first-magnitude political mistake and a deliberate violation of the established interagency process. They were flying with Trump to Hanoi on Air Force One and explained the problems to him en route. Trump was completely unaware of the draft, so Biegun had no authority from on high. I also called Pence on Air Force Two, as he flew back to Washington from the Lima Group meeting in Bogotá, and he had the same reaction to the Biegun draft that I did.

Having been overwhelmed by Venezuela before leaving for Hanoi, once there and ensconced in the US delegation's hotel, the JW Marriott, I tried to learn what was going on. The record was very confused, but the State Department was working overtime to lock down everything they could on Biegun's draft, excluding NSC and Defense Department representatives, before Trump arrived late that evening. It was all bad news.

The next morning, Wednesday, February 27, Mulvaney told Pompeo and me that Trump was very unhappy about a *Time* magazine story[4] on his intelligence briefings and how little he paid attention or understood them. I hadn't heard of the story, although Pompeo had, saying *Time* was doing a profile of him, which was perhaps where it had come up. He was willing to issue a statement, similar to one he had made months before, that Trump was deeply involved in the briefings. I had not made such a statement before and was looking for exits from the hotel room so I wouldn't have to now. The *Time* article nearly severed an already tense relationship with the intelligence community. Trump called Director of National Intelligence Dan Coats "an idiot" and asked Pompeo and me in the elevator later, "Did we make a mistake with [CIA Director] Gina [Haspel]?"

We then trooped to another room set up to brief Trump for the day's events. Trump was still on fire because of the *Time* article but started by telling Pompeo he didn't like Biegun's comments, which were "too much," referring to the draft statement Kupperman and Mulvaney had shown him on Air Force One. The import was clear to everyone in the room. After a detour on the *Time* article, Trump again criticized Biegun, repeating what he had said just minutes before. (For the record, when he saw Biegun the next morning, he didn't recognize him.) Trump said he saw three possible outcomes: a big deal, a small deal, or "I walk." He immediately rejected the "small deal" because it would mean weakening the sanctions. The "big deal" wasn't going to happen because Kim Jong Un remained unwilling to make a strategic decision to renounce nuclear weapons. The idea of "I walk" came up repeatedly, which meant Trump was at least prepared for it, and might even prefer it (ditch the girl before she ditches you). There would be criticism no matter what he did, Trump said with a shrug, so I mentioned Reagan's walking away at Reykjavik and the important boost that gave to later negotiations (ironically, on the INF Treaty, which we were leaving). Trump mused about what he would say at the concluding press conference ("We still like each other; we'll keep talking") and, looking at me, said, "You should go out and defend it."

Trump seemed consumed by the coming testimony in Washington of Michael Cohen, one of his former lawyers, a rare occasion when I saw his personal problems bleed into national security. I was relieved the earlier briefings were still top of mind and that the option of walking away was live. We spent the rest of the day in meetings with Vietnam's top leadership, up until Trump's dinner with Kim Jong Un. By that time, morning in Washington, the news coverage was all Michael Cohen. The North Koreans excluded me from the dinner, with only Pompeo and Mulvaney attending with Trump, following a one-on-one with the two leaders. I didn't like it but figured it was a cost of doing business.

Mulvaney called me to his room after the dinner ended at nine p.m. to debrief with Pompeo and others. Trump had wanted to avoid substance until the next morning, but as the dinner was ending, Pompeo said Kim had proposed that the North give up its Yongbyon nuclear facilities, in exchange for the lifting of all post-2016 UN Security Council sanctions.[5] This was a typical "action for action" ploy, giving them economic relief they desperately needed but giving us very little, since even without Yongbyon, it was publicly well known that North Korea had many other facilities with which to continue its nuclear program. I asked if Kim Jong Un had something else up his sleeve, but Pompeo didn't think so. I also asked if Trump had raised the Japanese-abductee issue, which he had, meaning he had fulfilled his commitment to Japan.

I thought that was it for the evening, but word soon came that Shanahan and Dunford wanted to talk to Pompeo and me about a ballooning crisis between India and Pakistan. After hours of phone calls, the crisis passed, perhaps because, in substance, there never really had been one. But when two nuclear powers spin up their military capabilities, it is best not to ignore it. No one else cared at the time, but the point was clear to me: this was what happened when people didn't take nuclear proliferation from the likes of Iran and North Korea seriously.

The next morning, February 26, was the big day. Having stayed up well into the night watching Cohen testify, Trump canceled the preparatory briefings. I worried that his every instinct would be to do something to drown out Cohen's hearings in the media, which he could only do with something dramatic and unexpected. Walking out would certainly achieve that objective. So too, however, would making a deal he could characterize as a huge success, even if it was badly flawed. The flaws wouldn't catch up until later. Trump had Mulvaney, Pompeo, and me ride with him to the Metropole hotel in the Beast. He had heard from someone that we should ask the North Koreans to give up their ICBMs, which I thought secondary to dismantling the nuclear warheads. Eliminating just the ICBMs would not reduce the dangers to South Korea, Japan, and our deployed forces, nor protect against shorter-range, submarine-launched missiles fired just off our coasts, which the North was pursuing. Trump was irritable and frustrated, asking whether it was a bigger story if we got a small deal or if we walked away. I thought walking away was a far bigger story, if that was what he was looking for. Trump wondered how to explain taking a walk, and Pompeo offered a line: "The teams had met, we had made progress, there was still no testing, and we would meet again notwithstanding the failure of this summit," which Trump liked. It made me gag, but as long as Trump was comfortable with the explanation and walked away, I was not going to complain. He was moving in the right direction, but a fluttering leaf could have turned him 180 degrees. As we arrived at the Metropole, I had no sense of how the rest of the day would play out.

Trump and Kim had a one-on-one at nine a.m., which broke after about forty minutes. They went to an inner courtyard, where they were joined by Pompeo and Kim Yong Chol for what was intended to be a short, perhaps ten-minute, break. Kim Jong Un did not like the heat and humidity, so they went inside a greenhouse-type structure in the inner courtyard used as a café, undoubtedly air-conditioned. The discussion continued, as we watched it through the greenhouse windows. My take was that Kim did not look particularly happy. His sister stood stoically outside in the heat and humidity, while the Americans, needless to say, went inside nearby where it was air-conditioned. After about an hour, this meeting broke, and Trump came into the main structure of the hotel for what was described as a thirty-minute break.

In the holding rooms allocated to us, Trump immediately switched on Fox News to see how the late-night shows were covering Cohen's testimony, as well as events in Hanoi. Pompeo said the discussion that had just concluded, like the one at dinner, had been all about

North Korea's closing down Yongbyon in exchange for sanctions relief, which wasn't going anywhere. Kim Jong Un, he said, was "very frustrated" and was "getting angry" that Trump wasn't giving him what he wanted. There had been no talk of ballistic missiles; the rest of the North's nuclear, chemical, or biological weapons programs; or anything other than Yongbyon. Trump was visibly tired and irritated. It was clear he too was frustrated no satisfactory deal was at hand. That told me we were still in perilous territory. It was never over with Trump until he announced it at a press conference, and sometimes not even then. He still seemed comfortable walking away; there was no "big deal" in sight, and he could not sustain a "small deal" politically. I believed Trump's "head for the barn" instincts were kicking in; he wanted to get it over with and return home (after, of course, the big press conference).

The larger meeting (Trump, Pompeo, Mulvaney, and I on our side of the table; Kim Jong Un, Kim Yong Chol, and Foreign Minister Ri Yong Ho on their side; plus interpreters) was scheduled for eleven a.m. We arrived first, then the North Koreans, and we all shook hands. I said to Kim Jong Un, "Mr. Chairman, it's very nice to see you again," which I hoped would be true. The press mob came in and out, and Trump asked Kim, "Does the press give you a hard time?" Somewhat stunned, Kim said, "That's an obvious question. I don't have that burden," and laughed. On human rights, Trump said happily we could say we talked about human rights because the press asked Kim a question. Another laugh-fest. Turning serious, Trump asked what Kim had come up with during the break. Kim was unhappy that he had traveled all the way to Hanoi with a proposal he claimed was incomparable to all those put on the table by all of their predecessors, and even so Trump was not satisfied. This went on for some time.

While Kim was talking, Trump asked me for the definition of "denuclearization" we had discussed in the Washington briefings, and also for what we called the "bright future" page, which I gave him. He handed both pages to Kim, and offered to fly him back to North Korea, canceling his evening in Hanoi. Kim laughed and said he couldn't do that, but Trump observed happily that that would be quite a picture.

He asked what North Korea could add to its offer; he knew Kim didn't want him to look bad because he was the only one on Kim's side. Kim readily returned the compliment, since he was the only one on Trump's side. Doubtless without intending the pun, Trump observed that Kim called the shots in North Korea. Kim seemed surprised that Trump saw things that way, but said that even a leader who controlled everything still could not move without providing some justification. Trump said he understood Kim wanted to achieve consensus.

Kim stressed again how significant the Yongbyon[6] "concession" was for North Korea and how much coverage the idea was getting in the US media. Trump asked again if Kim could add something to his offer, such as asking only for a percentage reduction in the sanctions rather than completely removing them.[7]

This was beyond doubt the worst moment of the meeting. If Kim Jong Un had said yes there, they might have had a deal, disastrously for America. Fortunately, he wasn't biting, saying he was getting nothing, omitting any mention of the sanctions being lifted.

Trump tried changing the subject, asking about prospects for reunifying North and South Korea, and what China thought. Kim, growing tired of diversions, asked to get back to the agenda.

Still trying to improve Kim's package, Trump suggested he offer to eliminate his long-range missiles, the ones that could hit the United States. I saw this as an obvious dismissal of what I said earlier about the concerns of Japan and South Korea for the short- and medium-range missiles that could hit them. Then came the unexpected from Trump: "John, what do you think?"

I wasn't going to miss the chance. We needed a full baseline declaration of North Korea's nuclear, chemical, biological, and ballistic-missile programs (echoing the paper Trump had given Kim Jong Un), I said. This was a traditional step in arms-control negotiations, and prior negotiations had failed without one.

Trump responded that what I had just said was a little complicated, but looked to Kim for his reaction.

Kim wasn't buying, urging that if we went step by step, that would ultimately bring us a comprehensive picture. He complained, as he had in Singapore, that North Korea had no legal guarantees to safeguard its security, and Trump asked what kind of guarantees the North wanted. There were no diplomatic relations, seventy years of hostility and eight months of personal relations, Kim answered, obviously unwilling to respond with specifics. What would happen if a US warship entered North Korea territorial waters? he asked, and Trump suggested Kim call him.

After more back-and-forth, Trump acknowledged that they had reached an impasse that it was politically impossible for him to resolve in the current meeting.

Kim now looked visibly frustrated, but I was worried. After sustained efforts to explain to Trump how dangerous North Korea's nuclear threat was, we were reduced to hoping that the politics of avoiding a mass Republican Party revolt was enough to stop a bad deal. Trump turned to Pompeo, asking him to repeat what he had said in the Beast on the way to the Metropole, which Pompeo rendered as, "The takeaway is the progress we have made; we understand each other better; we trust each other more; there was real progress made here. We can hold our heads high." I was glad I didn't have to say it.

We turned to closing statements, which Kim wanted to be one joint document. Trump initially preferred separate statements, then decided he didn't. This went back and forth until Trump said again that he wanted to do a complete deal. Kim said flatly that the most he could do was what he had already proposed, which obviously wasn't going to happen. He asked instead for a "Hanoi Statement" to show that progress was made, perhaps mentioning that we were thinking about Yongbyon. This was now going in the wrong direction again, but I had been shot down earlier by Trump for saying that a joint statement risked showing we hadn't achieved anything. "I don't need risks. I need positives," Trump responded. Pompeo wanted to talk about progress: "We have made progress in the last eight months, and we will build on that." Even Kim wouldn't accept that, saying that we had obviously not reached a good point. Trump interjected emphatically that if we accepted Kim's proposal, the political impact in the United States would be huge, and he could lose the election. Kim reacted quickly, saying he didn't want Trump to do anything that would harm him politically. Oh great. Kim kept pushing for a joint statement, but lamented that he felt a barrier between the two leaders, and felt a sense of despair. Kim was smartly playing on Trump's emotions, and I worried it might work. Trump said Kim shouldn't feel that way, and then, fortunately, we all laughed. Kim again stressed how important the Yongbyon package was. I said North Korea had already repeatedly promised to denuclearize, starting with the 1992 Joint North-South Declaration, so they already knew to a great extent what was required of them. Trump asked what had happened to the Joint Declaration, and I explained that Clinton had shortly thereafter negotiated the 1994 Agreed Framework. Trump lamented that it was Kim's proposal to lift the sanctions that was the deal breaker. Kim agreed that it was a shame, because he had thought the deal would receive a lot of applause.

Instead, inside the room, there was total silence for several seconds, as we all thought the meeting had come to its end. But it hadn't ended, as Kim kept pushing for some reference to Yongbyon that showed he and Trump had made progress beyond what their predecessors had achieved. I jumped in again, and pitched hard for two separate statements. I said if they were looking for a positive ending, we could each be positive in our own way. Kim said he didn't want his own statement, which brought several more seconds of silence. Trump said he wanted Kim to be happy. No words for that. Trump made it clear he wanted a joint statement, assigning it to Kim Yong Chol and Pompeo to draft. With that, the North Koreans trundled out, leaving the US delegation alone in the room.

While we were milling around, Trump asked me how we could be "sanctioning the economy of a country that's seven thousand miles away." I answered, "Because they are building nuclear weapons and missiles that can kill Americans."

"That's a good point," he agreed. We walked over to where Pompeo was standing, and Trump said, "I just asked John why we were sanctioning seven thousand miles away, and he had a very good answer: because they could blow up the world."

"Yes, sir," said Pompeo. Another day at the office. Trump went back to his holding room, and Pompeo told me that this larger meeting had been essentially a replay of the earlier, smaller meeting, with Kim's relentlessly pushing the Yongbyon deal, hoping Trump would fold.

In the holding room, we found Trump tired, but he expressed the correct insight that "walking away" in Hanoi made clear to the world he could do it elsewhere, such as in the China trade negotiations. Beyond that, however, he had no appetite for anything else, even lunch, which was canceled, along with the joint signing ceremony tentatively on the calendar. Trump said he wanted both Pompeo and me on the stage with him at the press conference, but I explained I had to get to the airport to meet my takeoff slot to avoid a lengthy crew-rest stop in Alaska, which he didn't seem entirely enthusiastic about. Pompeo said to me a few minutes later, "Lucky you." I left the Metropole for the airport at about one p.m., learning after takeoff that negotiations with the North on a joint statement had broken down (no surprise). Trump told Sanders just to put out a White House statement. Pompeo and Biegun did their own briefing, trying to make the summit sound like a success so Biegun's negotiations could continue. In fact, he was following the same failed approach of the three prior Administrations, doomed to produce the same failed outcome.

Flying to Washington, I concluded that Hanoi showed the US still didn't know how to deal with North Korea and its ilk. We spent endless hours negotiating with ourselves, whittling away at our own position before our adversaries even got to it, a fine art the State Department had perfected. The North Koreans and others were expert at taking full advantage of those who wanted a deal, any deal, as a sign of success. We were a perfect mark. The real irony here was how similar Trump was to the Foreign Service. Another key mistake was constantly briefing the press on how successful the working-level negotiations were, raising media expectations of agreement and exaggerating the effects of getting no deal. Perhaps most important, through the pre-Hanoi briefing process, we had helped Trump conclude that walking away was no failure, thereby derailing the unhealthy negotiation path Biegun was on. But as with every success in government, this was a momentary triumph, and one I knew would not last long. The bureaucracy's inexorable drive to keep "the process" going would inevitably ignite again, as would Trump's deathless belief that everyone wanted to talk to him, that everyone was "dying for a deal."

After Hanoi, we learned from press sources such as South Korea's *Chosun Ilbo* that Kim Yong Chol had endured forced labor, although he was later rehabilitated; that Kim Hyok Chol, Biegun's counterpart, had been executed, along with several others; that, in penance, Kim Jong Un's sister had receded from public view for a time; and that Shin Hye Yong, Kim's interpreter, was in a political prison camp for making an interpretation mistake. That at least was better than the previous report that she had been executed for failing to stop Trump from interrupting her translation of Kim Jong Un's glowing words.[8] It was hard to verify any of this, but everyone knew the North Korean leader was fully capable of ordering such punishments. A *Washington Post* reporter, in yet another exercise of its responsible journalism, tweeted: "Looks like [Trump]'s erratic diplomacy, including adopting maximalist Bolton positions in Hanoi, got some people killed."[9]

Reactions to the Hanoi Summit almost uniformly reflected surprise if not stunned disbelief. Condi Rice and Steve Hadley both called and expressed support for Trump's walkout, and Rice told me she had recounted to Pence one of my favorite Bush 43 anecdotes. Bush had likened Kim Jong Il to a child in a high chair, constantly pushing his food onto the floor, with the US and others always picking it up and placing it back on the tray. Things hadn't changed much. The Communists wouldn't learn until the food just stayed on the floor, if then. I spoke a few days later with South Korea's Chung Eui-yong, who had an interesting take. He said they were surprised Kim Jong Un had come to Hanoi with only one strategy and no Plan B. Chung also reflected Moon Jae-in's schizophrenic idea that while we were right to reject North Korea's "action for action" formula, Kim's willingness to dismantle Yongbyon (never defined clearly) was a very meaningful first step, showing that the North had entered an irreversible stage of denuclearization. This last contention was nonsense, as was Moon's endorsement of China's "parallel and simultaneous approach," which sounded a lot like "action for action" to me. Chung was the first to predict, based on coverage of the summit in the North's *Rodong Sinmun* (available to "ordinary people," as Chung described it), that "some officials [would] be replaced," which turned out to be an understatement. Making a mistake in North Korean foreign policy could be fatal not only to your career but to yourself.

The surprise many people felt, especially US commentators, stemmed from the State Department's relentless pre-Hanoi efforts to foreshadow that we would indeed accept some version of "action for action." Speeches, quiet interviews with reporters and pundits, and seminars at think tanks all heralded we were about to reach those "broad sunlit uplands" where one concession after another would flow from Washington. This was what State Department negotiators for years had understood to be "the art of the deal." The people who really had no Plan B after Hanoi were America's High-Minded, who wanted nothing more than to return to the Clinton Administration's Agreed Framework, or the Bush Administration's Six-Party Talks, or the Obama Administration's "strategic patience" strategy. It turned out, on the road to Panmunjom, they were more patient than I gave them credit for.

As time passed, however, the North was moving from being surprised to being outraged. On March 15, our favorite North Korean Vice Foreign Minister, Choe Son Hui, blasted Pompeo and me for creating "an atmosphere of hostility and mistrust" in Hanoi through our "uncompromising demands."[10] I should have issued a statement thanking her. By contrast, she said the Trump-Kim relationship "is still good, and the chemistry mysteriously wonderful." Indeed. Then came the threat. Choe said Kim Jong Un would decide shortly whether to resume nuclear and ballistic-missile testing, which induced enormous concern in South Korea's government. I spoke to Chung the same day, and he said Choe's statement had taken them by surprise. Nonetheless, they hoped her remarks were just reiterating what she had said in Hanoi in a late-night press conference after Trump had walked away. We watched Moon continue to press harder for another Moon-Kim summit, focused only on nuclear issues, perhaps because he saw his own inter-Korean policy being impacted.

I sensed Trump beginning to worry he had been too tough in Hanoi, which manifested itself in several ways. He began saying again, "We shouldn't spend ten cents on war games," referring to our exercises with South Korea. On the other hand, he never relented in supporting the economic "maximum pressure" campaign against North Korea. I held a Principals Committee on March 21 to assess whether the campaign was as "maximum" as it could be and to consider how to stiffen it up. The major issue for discussion was whether the United States should do more to inhibit ship-to-ship transfers at sea, coal being exported from North Korea and oil being imported. Through the ship-to-ship transfers, the North obviously hoped to escape surveillance, and I wanted to see if there were steps short of using force that would make it harder for these exchanges to take place. There was no discussion of additional sanctions against North Korea, only how to better enforce those already in place.

The next day, a Friday, we were in Mar-a-Lago for Trump's meeting with the leaders of five Caribbean island states (the Bahamas, Haiti, the Dominican Republic, Jamaica, and Saint Lucia), another encounter I several times urged him to do despite his objections, but which he later touted as his own idea. Trump pulled me and a few others into the "library" (really a bar) off the lobby lounge and said he wanted recent Treasury enforcement actions against two Chinese companies for violating North Korea sanctions rolled back. We had approved these decisions—all of which had been signed off on personally by Pompeo, Mnuchin, and me—which were enforcement measures under existing sanctions, not "new" sanctions broadening or enlarging what was already there. After Singapore, we had expressly reviewed this distinction with Trump. He agreed strict enforcement of existing sanctions would continue, and pursuant to that understanding, we had, in over nine months since Singapore, penalized a significant number of companies and individuals for violations.

Why Trump wanted to roll back these latest enforcement actions was anybody's guess, other than that he was feeling Kim Jong Un's pain. Trump dictated a tweet that could only be read as reversing the Treasury Department's recent announcement. I argued as strenuously as I could not to do so, with which Mulvaney fully agreed. We had no effect. The whole point, said Trump, was that the tweet was "for an audience of one" with whom he was trying to make a deal. "It won't affect anything else," he said, ignoring my obviously futile efforts to explain that lots of other people would also see this tweet and would inevitably interpret it as weakening the sanctions and a public repudiation of his own advisors, especially Mnuchin. Trump simply didn't care. He wanted to send a message to Kim Jong Un, just as he had wanted to send a message to Xi Jinping when he rolled back Ross's ZTE sanctions after they had been publicly announced. Sanders asked what to say about why Trump had tweeted, and he replied, "I like Kim Jong Un, and these sanctions were unnecessary." The tweet went out.

After we concluded with the Caribbean leaders, discussing common regional challenges, and headed for the airport, we saw media reports that Trump's North Korea tweet did not refer to what Treasury had announced on Thursday but to other, unspecified future sanctions that weren't yet public. Pompeo called me from the Middle East a little after six p.m. Eastern time, and I tried to explain what was happening, but it was still confusing. We were, however, both thoroughly disheartened by what Trump's tweet had done. And this day, March 22, marked the first anniversary of Trump's offering me the NSC position. It only seemed like ten years ago.

On Saturday morning at about seven thirty, I called Mulvaney, who had stayed at Mar-a-Lago. Mnuchin had called him Friday afternoon to speak with Trump, to urge that pulling down the new Treasury sanctions would be embarrassing to him. Mulvaney put the call through, and Mnuchin gave Trump the same analysis I had. Trump agreed, hours after disagreeing with precisely the same points, to keep the decisions in place. Hearing this, I asked Mulvaney if I had not been clear about this the day before. "You were very clear about it," said Mulvaney, "but sometimes it takes two or three tries to get it through." As for the "future" sanctions, Mulvaney said this was merely Treasury's "ham-fisted way of explaining things." He and I decided to conference Mnuchin in. Mnuchin said he was trying to protect Trump from embarrassment by saying we wouldn't do additional sanctions, although he agreed that the rest of the world could conclude we were receding from "maximum pressure." We all agreed, however, that correcting the correction (our new synonym for "reversing") would only make things worse.

Although I didn't initially like Mnuchin's cover story, as the day wore on, I couldn't think of anything better. We, or more accurately, Trump, might have appeared confused, but at least we didn't look too weak. I spoke later to Pompeo, and he also agreed we should just let matters lie. In any other Administration, this affair would have been a major story, but for us, it passed almost unnoticed. The release of the Mueller report, which ended the "Russia collusion" issue, dominated news coverage. On Monday, with Pompeo and me in the Oval with Trump, and Mnuchin on the phone, we reaffirmed what we had decided after Singapore, namely that enforcement actions would continue, but that we would not impose additional prohibitions on North Korea without Trump's approval. If Trump had simply listened on Friday, all this drama could have been avoided.

One issue that bedeviled relations with South Korea (and Japan, and to a lesser extent the European allies) was the question of what share of the costs of US military bases the host country should pay. Virtually everywhere we had bases, the host country paid some costs, but the amounts and formulas varied, and there was no real agreement on what the actual costs were. Under the Defense Department's creative accounting techniques, almost any "cost" figure could be justified, high or low. As with other military funding issues, Trump thought our allies weren't paying enough. This fit with his notion, unshakeable after countless discussions, that we were in, say, South Korea, to defend *them*. We were not there for "collective defense" or "mutual security" or any of that complex international stuff. We were defending Germany, or defending Japan, or defending Estonia, whatever, and they should pay for it. Moreover, as any good businessperson would tell you, we should make a profit from defending all these countries, in which the US had no particular interest ("Why are we in all these countries?" Trump would ask), or at least we should get a better bargaining strategy, starting at the outset of negotiations each time the host-country support agreements came up for renewal.

Trump had long had the idea that host countries should pay "cost plus X percent" of US costs, as he said back in April 2018, pressing for Arab forces to replace us in Syria (see chapter 2). In time, he was persuaded that "cost plus 50 percent" sounded too raw, so he called what he was asking for by various other names, such as "fair share" or "full and fair reimbursement of our costs."[11] Make no mistake, however, the actual dollar amount he wanted, or at least wanted to start negotiations with, remained "cost plus 50 percent." In South Korea's case, under our Special Measures Agreement, that amount was $5 billion annually, an enormous increase over the less than $1 billion per year Seoul was paying. The current agreement was nearing expiration on December 31, 2018, causing enormous concern at both the State Department and the Pentagon. They didn't want to charge host countries as if we were mercenaries, and also because they knew it would be hard to obtain such major increases. South Korea happened to be first because of the agreement's expiration date, and Japan was next, but all were ultimately in line to face the question.

Because I feared Trump's ultimate threat—withdrawing our troops from any country not paying what he deemed to be an adequate amount—was real in South Korea's case, I tried to develop a strategy other than just refusing to do what Trump wanted. The latter was Mattis's approach, which had worked right up until Trump exploded and did what he wanted to do anyway. To State and Defense, withdrawing US forces from South Korea was inconceivable, so their sustained opposition to significantly raising host-country payments just increased the risk. Unfortunately, I knew where the edge of the cliff was. In 2018, after inconclusive negotiations at the end of the calendar year, with December 31 bearing down on us, South Korea agreed to an increase in its costs well above current levels, but still less than $1 billion per year. That meant we now had another year to get a resolution both Trump and the South Koreas would accept, hopefully avoiding withdrawing US forces. That's how things stood for several months into 2019.

Obviously still concerned about the collapse at Hanoi, Moon Jae-in came to Washington on April 11. Pompeo and I met first with Moon at Blair House at nine a.m., along with Foreign Minister Kang Kyung-wha and Chung Eui-yong. After the usual pleasantries, we learned the South had had no substantive contacts since the Hanoi Summit with North Korea; the North needed more time to get over Hanoi. Moon was very worried that Pyongyang's cold shoulder on both the nuclear and inter-Korean issues was bad news for him politically, since his pitch was that "sunshine" would produce tangible results from the North, which it clearly was not doing. I tried to say as little as possible in this meeting, and in the Moon-Trump meeting, precisely because I knew Moon's government was looking for others to scapegoat, and, within the US team, I was the logical person to target as an obstruc-tionist. And why not? Watching the success of Kim Jong Un's analo-gous strategy on Trump, it obviously worked.

Moon arrived at the White House at noon, and after the usual press scrum in the Oval, Pompeo and I stayed with Trump to meet in a smaller setting with Moon, Kang, and Chung. Trump said he was getting a lot of credit for the way Hanoi had turned out, since it was better to walk away than to sign a bad deal. Moon thought that was fine, but he wanted something dramatic to generate momentum for what he thought could be the summit of the century. He urged a dra-matic approach on timing, venue, and form, which could in turn lead to dramatic results, suggesting meeting either at Panmunjom or on a US naval vessel. Trump cut through the monologue, which was for-tunate, because he had seemed to be falling asleep, stressing that he appreciated Moon's ideas, but underlining that his desire was for the next summit to produce an actual agreement. Meeting once without a deal was not a problem, but no one wanted to walk away twice. Moon, however, was still worried about form rather than substance, but what was really uppermost for him was stressing he was available to join Kim and Trump. Trump was not biting, insisting that there had to be a deal to eliminate North Korea's nuclear weapons before there was another summit.

We adjourned to the Cabinet Room for a working lunch, and after reviewing North Korea developments and a little ramble through bilateral trade issues, Trump raised our base costs in South Korea. Trump explained that the bases cost us $5 billion annually,[12] saying the US lost $4 billion a year for the privilege of South Korea selling us televisions. Other countries had offered to pay significantly more, and in the next phase of the negotiations, South Korea should be more forthcoming. Trump conveyed that he felt he was very protective of Moon, and had great respect for him. Moon tried to reply that many South Korean companies invested in the US, and pleaded that, regarding base costs, Trump's expectations were too high. Trump asked if the US leased the land for its bases, or whether it was free, which Moon didn't answer. Instead, he parried by saying South Korea spent 2.4 percent of its GDP on defense, which led Trump to criticize Germany for its inadequate defense expenditures. Then he was back to South Korea, which was freed from having to defend itself, and therefore free to build. By contrast, the US had spent $5 trillion for the privilege of defending the South, because they were the toughest negotiators of all. Trump wanted a formula fair to the US.

After more North Korea discussions, Trump asked how relations were with Japan. We all saw the increasing difficulties between Tokyo and Seoul, which would worsen rapidly in the next few months. Moon was trying to upend a 1965 treaty between the two countries. That treaty aimed, certainly in Japan's view, to put an end to the animosities created by Japan's colonial rule over Korea from 1905 to 1945, especially World War II's hardships and the well-known "comfort women" issue.

Moon said that history should not interfere with the future of relationships, but, from time to time, Japan made it an issue. Of course, it wasn't Japan that was raising the history, but Moon, for his own purposes. My view was that, like other South Korean political leaders, Moon tried to make Japan an issue when times at home were difficult.

Trump asked if South Korea could fight together with Japan as allies despite not wanting to conduct exercises with Japan. Moon answered frankly that Tokyo and Seoul could conduct joint military exercises, but that having Japanese forces in Korea would remind people of history. Trump pressed again, wondering what would happen if we had to fight North Korea, and whether South Korea would accept Japanese participation. Moon clearly didn't want to answer, saying we shouldn't worry about the issue, and that South Korea and Japan would fight as one, so long as there were no Japanese Self-Defense Forces on South Korean soil.

Moon ended by saying that when he returned to Seoul, he would propose to the North a third US–North Korea summit between June 12 and July 27. Trump said that any date was fine, but only if there were a deal beforehand. Moon kept trying, explaining, as we all knew, that on nuclear issues the North's working-level diplomats had no discretion, and that he therefore wanted higher-level discussions. Trump replied simply that Pompeo and I would work on this.

Prime Minister Abe arrived in Washington on April 26, offering very nearly the opposite view from Moon's. Trump told Abe he had received good reviews by leaving the Hanoi Summit, which people respected. Abe agreed that the outcome was very positive, and that Trump was the only person who could walk away. He emphasized repeatedly that it was important to keep up the sanctions (which Kim hated), and make no easy concessions. Abe stressed that time was on our side, and Trump agreed.

Unfortunately, North Korea continued testing missiles, not the ICBMs Kim had promised Trump he would not test, but short- and medium-range missiles that threatened much of South Korea and Japan. Some were launched in salvos, approximating wartime conditions, the first of which I heard about on the evening of Friday, May 3 (Saturday morning Korea time). I immediately called Pompeo and Shanahan after learning of the first launch, to give them a heads-up.

Shortly thereafter, more launches were reported. After speaking with Dunford, I decided to call Trump to tell him what we knew. The missiles were short range, so there was no immediate threat, but you never knew with the North Koreans.

I called Trump a second time a bit later, after still more launches, to say it looked like things were finished for the night. He said, in a somewhat agitated voice, "Keep it calm, play it down, play it down," obviously worried people might think his friend Kim Jong Un was a touch dangerous. By then, based on public statements by the South Korean Ministry of Defense, press stories were appearing in South Korea, which had more to worry about from short-range missiles. Since State would inevitably be drafting something on our reaction, I concluded, just to be sure, that I needed to check with Trump first. I called him for the third and last time that night about an hour later, and as I suspected, he wanted no statement at all. He ended with "Okay, man," one of his usual ways of saying he was relaxed about how we'd concluded a particular issue. Statement or not, these ballistic-missile tests, whatever the ranges, violated the Security Council resolutions forming the basis of the international sanctions against North Korea. Not that I was concerned about some inviolable status for council resolutions, but I worried pragmatically that if we dismissed clear violations as immaterial, other nations would learn the wrong lesson and start characterizing significant sanctions violations as de minimis. This was more than a little risky.

Just to confirm my fears, when I relayed the latest information to Trump the next morning, he said, "Call it artillery," as if labeling it something it wasn't would make it disappear. He had also tweeted, in part, "[Kim Jong Un] knows that I am with him & does not want to break his promise to me. Deal will happen!" Trump obviously thought these tweets helped him with Kim, but I worried they reinforced the perception he was desperate for a deal and that only his destructive advisors (guess who) stood in the way. We had all given up any idea of stopping the tweeting; all we could do was live with it. Interestingly, South Korea's government was also now calling the rockets "projectiles" to minimize the story.[13] All this because of a regime in Pyongyang that was beseeching the world for food for its supposedly starving people but still had enough spare change to engage in missile and nuclear-weapons development.

Others weren't so resigned. Abe called on Monday, May 6, to say Kim was getting ever-more irritated over the sanctions' effects on North Korea, because they were working effectively, and that these new launches were intended to turn the situation in his favor by undermining international unity over the sanctions. Abe said he would completely support Trump's outstanding policy of aiming for a deal and maintaining sanctions and a robust military posture, a posture he still holds publicly. I understood what Abe was trying to do, but I wondered if constantly telling Trump his strategy was brilliant didn't in fact decrease Abe's ability to keep the Trump train on the rails. In fact, Trump suggested Abe put out a statement that Japan and the United States were totally allied so that North Korea would see unambiguously that Japan was with us. He concluded by committing to keep Abe informed, but not to worry, because the launches were short-range and not really missiles. If he said it enough times, perhaps it would become true.

The next day, Moon called Trump to speak about the weekend launches. Moon was, unsurprisingly, eager to play down the significance of the issue, about which Trump had already persuaded himself. As Moon rambled on about Kim Jong Un's dissatisfaction with the joint US–South Korea military exercises, Trump observed that Moon seemed to have lost his relationship with Kim, who was now not traveling to South Korea as once envisaged. Trump didn't see this breakdown as Moon's fault, but obviously something had happened. Moon conceded there still had been few if any substantive discussions with North Korea since Hanoi. Somehow Moon was able to turn that into an argument the US should be giving direct food aid to the North, instead of simply allowing the South to provide it through UNICEF and the World Food Program.[14] Trump answered by saying that he would surprise Moon by giving his complete blessing to releasing the aid through the UN agencies, and asked Moon to let North Korea know that he had suggested it to him. Trump said he was doing this despite hard-liners who opposed it because he had a good relationship with Kim, and the timing was good.

So much for consistency. North Korea could conclude, "We fire missiles and get free food." This was a terrible signal, showing again how eager Trump was for a deal. I stressed to Pottinger and Hooker to make clear to South Korea that we weren't going to be providing any food ourselves. We were simply not objecting to its providing resources, but also insisting that food aid distributed in the North required very careful monitoring. More missile launches followed through the spring and summer, showing Kim's confidence there would be no retaliation.[15] Maybe just more rice. Trump told me on May 9, after the next salvo, "Put heavy sanctions on," later upgrading that to "massive sanctions," but not to say anything publicly. We made a weathervane look like the Rock of Gibraltar.

In late May, Trump traveled to Japan, the first state visitor in the Era of Reiwa (meaning "beautiful harmony"), the name Emperor Naruhito chose for his reign, which began officially on May 1, the day after his father, Emperor Akihito, abdicated. This was an incredible honor for Trump, and Abe was obviously making it clear what Japan's alliance priorities were. I went a few days early for final preparations on the discussions that would take place, meeting with Abe, who explained his objectives with Trump. What I thought would be an uneventful press briefing on Saturday, May 25, however, left me in an awkward position. A reporter asked if North Korea's recent missile launches violated Security Council resolutions, which I knew full well they did, having helped write the first two, Resolutions 1695 and 1718, when I was US Ambassador to the UN. I wasn't about to ignore what I had pressed so hard for at the time. And, as a matter of logic if not perception, it was entirely possible for the launches to violate the resolutions without violating Kim's pledge to Trump, which involved only ICBM launches. It was equally true that Trump looked foolish for not understanding that Kim had, in effect, sold him the Brooklyn Bridge with that pledge, but we were never able to shake Trump's faith he had scored a coup in getting it. Shortly after Air Force One arrived in Japan, Trump tweeted: "North Korea fired off some small weapons, which disturbed some of my people, and others, but not me. I have confidence that Chairman Kim will keep his promise to me, & also smiled when he called Swampman Joe Biden a low IQ individual, & worse. Perhaps that's sending me a signal?" I could tell already this was going to be a fun trip.

On Monday, May 27, the visiting US delegation attended the honor-guard ceremony with the Emperor on the grounds of the Imperial Palace in central Tokyo, which was impressive. Trump reviewed the honor guard, but the Emperor did not, which I suspected was intended to show a break with pre–World War II Japanese history. After a private meeting between Trump, the First Lady, and the imperial couple, we motorcaded to the Akasaka Palace. The palace, a huge building that looked as though it had been transported from Versailles to Tokyo, was built right after World War I to copy the French style of architecture. Several Japanese told us the palace was now unpopular, because who wouldn't dislike a massive French chateau in the middle of Tokyo?

I tried to focus Trump on North Korea's missile tests. While he might have viewed them as insignificant, the Japanese, who lived a lot closer to North Korea, had a different view. He said, "I don't mind having people who disagree with me," which wasn't really my point. Before I could try again, we were ushered into a large, ornate room for the first meeting, with just the two leaders, Yachi and me, and the interpreters. Abe began by thanking Trump for meeting later with the families of Japanese citizens whom North Korea had kidnapped over the years. North Korea repeatedly denied the kidnappings, but the contrary evidence was overwhelming.[16] Abe himself, early in his political career, had made standing up for the hostage families a signature issue, so he personally appreciated Trump's gesture. (Later, the family members, whom I had previously met several times in Washington, didn't mince words with Trump. "North Korea lied to you and tried to cheat you," said one, and another added, "North Korea has been a terrorist nation for three generations." Trump responded warmly, saying to one relative, "Don't ever stop. Don't ever stop," regarding his attempts to free his family member. To the mother of another abductee, he said, "You'll see her again." In their joint remarks to the press after the meeting, which was a big boost for Abe, Trump said, "We'll work on it together to bring the abductees home.")

After further discussions with Abe, largely on China, when we were in the US holding rooms, Trump asked why the US Trade Representative, Bob Lighthizer, hadn't been in the meeting. I explained about the scheduling of the different subjects, which Trump ignored. "Lighthizer should have heard that speech [on China]," Trump said, and then, looking at me, added, "When you write your book, get it right." I laughed and said I would, and even Trump laughed at that point. Request fulfilled.

At three p.m., Abe and Trump had a joint press conference, with Trump saying again he was not worried by North Korea's missile launches and Abe saying publicly, with Trump standing beside him, that he believed they had violated Security Council resolutions. The press just loved the split, but more important, it showed to North Korea that despite the efforts under way all day to show the solidarity of the US-Japan alliance, it was clear Abe and Trump had different views on North Korea.

In June, Trump returned for the Osaka G20 meeting and met with Abe at eight thirty a.m. on Friday the twenty-eighth. In my view, Trump's best personal relationship among world leaders was with Abe (golf buddies as well as colleagues), although when Boris Johnson became UK Prime Minister, it became a tie. Trump loved mentioning that Abe's father had been a World War II kamikaze pilot. Trump used it to show how tough the Japanese were generally, and how tough Abe was in particular. In one version, Trump described Abe's father as disappointed he hadn't been able to carry out his intended mission for the Emperor, never seeming to realize that had the father succeeded as a kamikaze, there would have been no Shinzo Abe (born in 1954). Mere historical details.

Abe once again warmly thanked Trump for meeting with the abductee families during the state visit. Abe said North Korea urgently wanted a deal, which meant different things to the two leaders. To Abe, it meant that North Korea must start concrete actions toward denuclearization, and there was no need to relax sanctions. Trump, though, said that Kim was directly writing him beautiful letters and birthday cards, and that the North wanted to do something because the sanctions on North Korea were hurting badly. Trump asked if Japan had imposed the same sanctions as the US, recounting yet again that the first time he had met with Abe and Moon, he had asked them both if they were also imposing sanctions on North Korea. They had replied they were not because the sanctions were too expensive. (I had asked both South Koreans and Japanese if they heard this conversation, and none had, all of them saying that of course Japan and South Korea were applying all UN sanctions. Trump was so firmly convinced of the story there was no point in asking him about it.) In any case, Trump stressed that sanctions cost money, but if one didn't do them, one paid later. He thought North Korea was sending signals that they might want to close more than one of their nuclear sites, as they had offered in Hanoi, and wanted another meeting. He laughed that they hated Bolton, Pence, and Pompeo, but they loved him. Abe and the Japanese duly laughed, perhaps mostly out of discomfort. Trump said he didn't care because there were no rocket or nuclear tests.

Trump had other bilateral meetings that same day, customary at these affairs, and in a brief discussion with Germany's Merkel touched on North Korea and his post-G20 visit to the South. Trump complained that the US had soldiers everywhere but didn't get anything out of it. He suggested he might meet Kim Jong Un, whose relationship with him was unparalleled, at the DMZ, because Kim wanted to do something but didn't know how to get it started. This, I think, was the first reference to Trump's wanting to meet Kim at the DMZ that anyone in the US delegation heard.

We also heard about it Saturday morning, waiting to brief Trump for the day ahead. Mulvaney showed me a tweet on his cell phone, asking if I knew about it, which I did not:

> After some very important meetings, including my meeting with President Xi of China, I will be leaving Japan for South Korea (with President Moon). While there, if Chairman Kim

> of North Korea sees this, I would meet him at the Border/
> DMZ just to shake his hand and say Hello(?)!

Mulvaney looked just as flabbergasted as I was. I thought the tweet was a throwaway. In the early afternoon, in the midst of the usual flurry of bilaterals, Mulvaney pulled Pompeo and me aside to say the North Koreans had said the tweet didn't constitute a formal invitation, which they wanted, and which he was preparing. Mulvaney was then off to something else. Pompeo said to me alone, "I have no value added on this. This is complete chaos," which was true for both of us. But the next thing I knew, Trump had signed the "formal" letter of invitation that the North Koreans had asked for. Pompeo had succumbed yet again.

He had also been managing Moon's attempts to get into what seemed increasingly likely to be a Kim-Trump meeting. Trump wanted Moon nowhere around, but Moon was determined to be present, making it a trilateral meeting if he could. I entertained the faint hope that this dispute with Moon could tank the whole thing, because it was certain Kim didn't want Moon around.

Because we had different planes, we traveled from Osaka to Seoul separately, meaning I couldn't make it to a dinner Moon hosted. When I reached our hotel in Seoul, I saw that preparations for the DMZ looked more and more like a done deal. As far as I was concerned, any actual Trump-Kim meeting should be limited to a handshake and a photo, although I had no doubt Trump was already thrilling at the expectation of what the morrow would bring. No way would it end quickly. I had not then made any decision on whether to go to the DMZ and travel later to Mongolia on a long-scheduled trip, or just proceed straight to Ulan Bator. I had not originally planned to join the Trump DMZ visit (rescheduled because bad weather had prevented a visit on his first trip to South Korea).

I felt sick that a stray tweet could actually result in a meeting, although I took some solace from believing that what motivated Trump was the press coverage and photo op of this unprecedented DMZ get-together, not anything substantive. Trump had wanted to have one of the earlier summits at the DMZ, but that idea had been short-circuited because it gave Kim Jong Un the home-court advantage (whereas we would fly halfway around the world), and because we still hadn't figured out how to ensure it was just a Trump-Kim bilateral meeting. Now it was going to happen. North Korea had what it wanted from the United States and Trump had what he wanted personally. This showed the asymmetry of Trump's view of foreign affairs. He couldn't tell the difference between his personal interests and the country's interests.

On Saturday, June 30, I awoke to the surprise that Pompeo was listed as attending the DMZ meeting. I e-mailed to ask if he had decided to go, and he replied, "Feel like I need to be there." I didn't think anyone needed to be there, but I concluded that if he went, I would go too. After a breakfast with South Korean and US business leaders at the hotel, we motorcaded over to South Korea's Cheong Wa Dae ("the Blue House") for meetings with Moon and his team. I learned on the way that North Korea didn't want a large bilateral after the photo op, but instead preferred a leader-plus-one meeting for about forty minutes. Shortly thereafter, I was told they planned to have Foreign Minister Ri Yong Ho as their "plus one," meaning Pompeo would be the "plus one" on our side. Thus, since I wouldn't be in the substantive meeting with Kim Jong Un, I veered toward simply leaving for Ulan Bator, to get us there at a reasonable hour. I had no desire to be standing around in the DMZ while Trump and Kim met, and I had no faith any advice I gave Trump beforehand would take. I filled Mulvaney in, and he said it was up to me.

Meanwhile, at the Blue House, at a very restricted bilateral meeting, Moon asked about the plan for the DMZ. Trump said we didn't know what the plan was. Contrary to reality, Trump said Kim had asked to meet him, but suggested he and Moon go to the DMZ and meet together so it would look great for Moon. This, of course, contradicted what Trump had been telling us, so Pompeo interrupted to describe the latest arrangements with North Koreans, including the format for the Trump-Kim meeting. In response to a Trump question, I seconded Pompeo's account. Trump said we would find out shortly, perhaps we would meet, perhaps not. Moon said the paramount issue for Trump was to have the meeting. However, when Kim entered South Korean territory, it wouldn't look right if Moon wasn't present, suggesting that he greet Kim and then hand him over to Trump and depart. Pompeo interjected again that we had presented Moon's view the night before, and the North Koreans rejected it. Trump said he would much rather have Moon present, but he could only pass along what the North's request was (a completely fanciful account). Moon persisted, recalling that there had been several instances of Presidents visiting the DMZ, but this was the first time South Korean and US Presidents would be there together. Trump said he didn't want to miss this big opportunity, because he naturally had some things to say to Kim, and he could only pass along what the Secret Service said, since they were arranging the trip (another fantasy).

Moon changed subjects, saying working-level negotiations with North Korea were always very difficult, but with a patient approach, results were possible. Trump responded, out of nowhere that he might ask that the next US–North Korea summit be after the US elections. At this point, Trump motioned to Tony Ornato, the head of his Secret Service detail, I thought perhaps to ask about the DMZ meeting. Instead, it turned out he asked why Jared and Ivanka were not in the meeting (for which there was a perfectly good reason) and for Ornato to bring them into the room (for which there was no reason at all). Even the South Koreans were embarrassed. Trump sailed on, saying he thought he understood at least a bit how Kim Jong Un thinks, and he knew Kim wanted to see him. Perhaps, Trump suggested, Moon could send him off to the DMZ from Seoul, and then they could meet again at Osan air base during the meet-and-greet with US soldiers. Moon wasn't having any of that, pressing that it was better if he accompanied Trump to OP Ouellette (a DMZ observation post named for a US soldier killed in the Korean War), then they could decide what to do next. Trump said anything Moon wanted to do was fine with him, and they could go to OP Ouellette together. In response to another Trump question, I assured him that that was the plan.

Trump then turned unexpectedly to base costs, recounting that

Pompeo and I had previously raised the issue with Moon. Trump loved South Korea, but the US was losing $20 billion a year on trade with them. Some people wanted to put tariffs on South Korea so that instead of losing $38 billion (these numbers tended to come and go), the US would make $30 billion, but Trump had resisted because of his relationship with Moon. The year before, he had asked me to calculate the amount of the base costs, and work with South Korea for a fair and equitable share, and that amount had been $5 billion a year, or $5.5 billion (more numbers coming and going). Trump then said that, in all other cases, countries had agreed to pay more for base costs (which wasn't true, at least not yet), noting that at the end of 2018, South Korea had agreed to pay just under $1 billion, postponing the reckoning for one year. Now, we had to come up with something fair and equitable for the US, since we were losing $4 billion a year to defend South Korea from North Korea. The North was nuking up, and there would be serious consequences if the US wasn't present on the Peninsula. He asked Moon to assign someone to deal with Pompeo or me so we could make things happen, stressing how hostile the South's next-door neighbor in Pyongyang was. Trump said that people were talking about this issue, and he had gotten elected on it.

Moon, perhaps forgetting Trump had raised the $5 billion figure at the White House in April, said that on economic issues, the trade surplus had decreased since Trump's inauguration, that South Korea was the biggest importer of U.S. LNG, that Korean investment in the US has increased, and that the bilateral balance of trade was now more favorable to the US. Nonetheless, the South would engage in consultations, noting the $1 billion payment Trump had mentioned and the free land and construction for various facilities, as well as weapons purchases, all of which amount to significant contributions to our joint defense. By then, Trump was growing visibly frustrated, gesturing for Moon to speed up and giving exasperated looks to us and the other South Koreans. More embarrassment. Trump said the US shouldn't pay real estate taxes for land to protect the South since we didn't own the land, and perhaps we would leave when things were peaceful. Trump said he had an obligation to do this; we didn't want a profit, just reimbursement from a very wealthy nation for protecting it from its northern neighbor.

Trump was now waving his hands, shrugging and sighing, tired of listening, obviously eager to move on, but Moon obviously was not. South Korea paid 2.4 percent of GDP for its defense budget, the highest level of all US allies, he urged. Trump agreed, saying Germany and Japan were in the same boat as South Korea, and they were not under threat. Trump wanted $5 billion, and told me to lead the negotiations. The US had been the South's military for seventy years, and now he was going to see Kim Jong Un so we could save the South. Moon resisted, while acknowledging the vast amounts of US assistance, arguing that it wasn't true that Seoul had only been a recipient of aid. South Korea had sent troops to Vietnam and Afghanistan, for example. But Trump was done, telling me to call up someone and start dealing.

During lunch, after the press had exited, Trump repeated that Kim wanted to meet very badly. Trump asked the US side again about the arrangement for Moon, wondering disingenuously in my opinion, why Kim would not want South Korea represented. Moon answered that there had not been meaningful talks between the two Koreas because of North Korea's rigidity, based on the North's perception that because the South was taking the US side, the North would be at a disadvantage. Trump said that in his bilateral meeting, he would stress the aid that the South was providing, and would tell Moon everything that happened between him and Kim. Trump was happy that the world had been going crazy over the meeting, and that it had taken over the G20 (in his mind). Kim had agreed to cross the border and wanted working-level negotiations right afterward, so Trump wanted to leave the lunch early. All of this was nonsense. There was no doubt who wanted to meet badly, and that was the one doing the talking.

Trump restated that the discussion about base costs was very important, and that he was assigning me to it, asking whom I had dealt with before, and suggesting I find someone else, which couldn't have made Chung very happy. Then he was off riffing on Chinese currency manipulations. Moon tried to get the discussion back to Kim's wanting security guarantees for his regime. Trump agreed that Kim wanted a guarantee only from the US, not from China or Russia. Trump said we guaranteed the safety of South Korea already but got nothing out of it. He thought he would have a short but very successful meeting with Kim, which would be very good for Moon. Moon said the Korean people respected and liked Trump, who preened that he knew he was popular. He explained how Korean women in his clubs came up and hugged him, then lectured on how different things were in Korea since he became President. He thought it was a big sign that Kim had agreed to meet based on a tweet. No one else knew how to get him. Moon confessed that the South had set up a hot line to Chairman Kim, but it was in the Korean Workers Party headquarters, and Kim never went there.[17] Nor did the phone work on weekends.

Although the working lunch started twenty minutes late, Trump said, five minutes before its scheduled ending at 1:00 p.m., that he wanted to leave right then.

By this point, I had decided to go straight to Mongolia rather than the DMZ, although I had informed only NSC staff. I waited near the Beast so I could tell Trump what I was doing. I understood what conclusions might be drawn from my not being at the DMZ, but I was past caring at that point.

I left South Korea for Ulan Bator in the early afternoon, watching reports of the events in the DMZ as we flew. As foreshadowed by his earlier comments and the irresistible photo op presented, Trump walked into North Korea, with Kushner and Ivanka nearby. Kim looked delighted in the pictures, as he should have. What an incredible gift Trump had given him, coming to the DMZ for the personal publicity. The whole thing made me ill. It didn't get better later when the media reported Trump had invited Kim to the White House. The Kim-Trump meeting itself lasted about fifty minutes, and the two leaders agreed working-level talks should resume again quickly. Of course, Biegun did not yet have a new counterpart; his former one was now likely lying somewhere in an unmarked grave, but no matter.

After a day of meetings in Ulan Bator on July 1, I left for Washington, reviewing news coverage on the DMZ meeting. Most of it was what I expected, but one story in the *New York Times* stood out as particularly bad.[18] Our policy had not changed at the DMZ, but the briefing the *Times* reported, discussing a "nuclear freeze," closely resembled exactly the road to trouble Biegun had followed before Hanoi. I thought we had buried that approach when Trump walked out, but here it was again, as bad or worse than before. There were other media stories where I thought I detected Biegun's fingerprints,[19] but this one was beyond the pale, in my view, both substantively and in process terms. I asked Matt Pottinger what could have justified this media offensive, concluding Trump hadn't authorized a "nuclear freeze" after the Kim Jong Un meeting, although he was obviously excited about resuming working-level negotiations. Trump wrote Kim yet another letter, which was essentially fluff, but at least it didn't give anything away or provide any basis for what had been briefed to reporters.[20] Biegun had taken Trump's enthusiasm as a license to shape the next talks with North Korea in ways that had consistently failed for thirty years.

Biegun initially denied to Hooker and Pottinger that he was the source for the *Times* story, although the "denial" was carefully phrased, and was in any event discredited when we received from a friendly reporter a transcript of his briefing. So much for interagency coordination. He was out of line, whether with Pompeo's blessing or not. I thought it important to correct the impression we were on the road back to prior Administrations' failed policies before things got out of hand. I knew it was risky to say anything publicly, but it was time to take risks. Besides, if I had to resign, it wouldn't be the end of the world. After some careful drafting, I tweeted the following just before wheels up in Tokyo, where we refueled:

> I read this NYT story with curiosity. Neither the NSC staff nor I have discussed or heard of any desire to 'settle for a nuclear freeze by NK.' This was a reprehensible attempt by someone to box in the President. There should be consequences.

I never heard word one from Trump about this tweet. And I was happy to see Lindsey Graham retweeted it soon after I sent it out:

> Glad to see National Security Advisor Bolton push back hard against the NY Times narrative stating the Administration would accept a nuclear freeze as an acceptable outcome by North Korea.

On July 3, I spoke with Pompeo on several subjects, and he raised the *Times* story and my tweet, complaining bitterly. "Why didn't you call me?" he asked. "What Biegun said"—so much for Biegun's denials—"is a lot closer to the President than you are." This was chilling, if true. I replied that I could ask the same question about him and Biegun: Why hadn't they called me? My tweet still represented official Administration policy, while Biegun's briefing did not, which Pompeo did not dispute. I said I wasn't aiming at him and that we would both be more effective if we stuck together on substance, which he agreed with. He said, laughing, "Our teams like this stuff, but we'll do our best if we grow up, which I at least am still struggling to do."

It was a good clearing of the air, but I thought Pompeo mostly worried I had criticized him publicly from the right, which Graham's tweet had reinforced. More seriously, Pompeo said he feared Trump was back to leaving the Peninsula entirely, which was what fundamentally concerned me about the whole base costs issue, and which echoed what Trump said randomly about Afghanistan, Iraq, Syria, Africa, and sundry other locations. Nonetheless, Pompeo believed "we didn't let anything out of the bag with Kim," meaning nothing would emerge publicly to compromise our position. On the other hand, Pompeo said he had tried to walk Trump back after the DMZ, urging, "We don't want to do what John Kerry would do." Trump answered, "I don't give a shit, we need a victory on this," although he also repeated he was "in no rush." Despite our conversation, however, within days Pompeo was telling Biegun not to participate in NSC meetings on North Korea, as before, exhibiting the same proprietary behavior over North Korea he had done repeatedly on Afghanistan. I understood the imperatives of turf in government affairs, but I could never understand why Pompeo didn't seek allies on these issues. When his policies went off the rails, not only would it be bad for the country, but Pompeo, along with Trump, would be solely identified with them. But, I figured, ultimately that was Pompeo's problem.

How did Trump see the DMZ party? "Nobody else could do what I did. Obama called eleven times and never got an answer," he said later that day.

In my remaining White House days, I worried about unforced concessions to North Korea. Ironically, however, the North mostly stonewalled, except when it was launching ballistic missiles or attacking Administration officials other than Trump. I also worried about the harmful potential of the basing-costs issue in both South Korea and Japan, and the growing rift between those two countries, which threatened America's overall strategic position in East Asia.

Back in Washington, on July 16, Pompeo and I spoke about yet another Trump demand to stop a joint US–South Korea military exercise that agitated the ever-sensitive Kim Jong Un. This exercise was mostly a "tabletop" affair, which would once have meant a lot of paper shuffling and moving troop markers around in sandboxes. Today, it was almost all done by computer. Despite repeated assurances that there were no Marines hitting the beaches with B-52s flying overhead, Trump wanted them canceled. I pleaded with Trump to let me make my planned visit to Japan and South Korea to talk about base costs before he made a decision, to which he agreed. More logical arguments, like the need for these and more exercises involving field maneuvers in order to ensure that our troops were at full readiness, able to "fight tonight" if need be, had long since lost their appeal to Trump. Pompeo also told me North Korea was projecting no working-level discussions until mid- to late August, a far cry from the mid-July predictions made by Biegun and others right after the DMZ meeting.

A few days later, I was off to Japan and South Korea to work on the base-costs issue. Stopping first in Tokyo, I raised the question even though the current arrangements expired after South Korea's. The Defense Department, like the State Department, could barely contemplate asking for more funding from the host country, and an underling on the Pentagon's civilian side told Lieutenant General Kevin Schneider, commander of US Forces Japan, which occupied the bases, he could not participate in my meetings, hoping to keep the Defense Department's fingernails clean. The reason I wanted both State and Defense personnel with me was precisely to show that, for a change, the US government actually had one position on an issue. After ascertaining just which civilian underling had caused the problem, I called Dunford and told him. The nation's top military officer had not even heard that civilian policy types were giving orders to his uniformed subordinates about what meetings to attend. Dunford didn't need persuasion, saying he had attended similar meetings when he was US commander in Afghanistan. All of this consumed needless time and energy. Your government at work.

I met first with Yachi to explain why Trump wanted $8 billion annually, starting in a year, compared to the roughly $2.5 billion Japan now paid.[21] I didn't expect him to be happy, and he wasn't, but we were at the beginning of a negotiation; they could prepare themselves, which was more advance notice than South Korea received. Ultimately, only Trump knew what payment would satisfy him, so there was no point now trying to guess what the "real" number was. Trump himself didn't know yet. But at least by alerting Japan and South Korea that they had a real issue, I gave them a chance to figure out a response.

The bulk of the Yachi meeting involved the Japanese explaining their position in the accelerating dispute with South Korea.[22] They believed Moon was undermining a critical 1965 treaty between the two countries, a treaty that, in Japan's view, had two purposes. One was to normalize bilateral relations during the Cold War. The second was to provide final compensation for South Korea's claims for forced labor and other abuses (including the World War II comfort women) during Japanese colonial rule. Japan saw this treaty, which had taken fourteen years to negotiate, as entirely closing the record of the past. From America's perspective, normalizing relations between Tokyo and Seoul, two key allies, was crucial to our efforts in East Asia to deter Russian, North Korean, and Chinese belligerence. We had no NATO counterpart in the Pacific, only a series of "hub and spoke" bilateral alliances, so we always worked for greater South Korean–Japanese cooperation, and to expand it with others like Singapore, Australia, and New Zealand. Even in our otherwise indifferent Administration, the "free and open Indo-Pacific" concept was a way to enhance horizontal ties among like-minded countries. Moreover, high on Trump's priority list for a successful North Korea nuclear deal was his insistence that Japan and South Korea pay a big part of the economic costs; Trump wasn't giving the North any "foreign aid," only the prospect of large, profitable private investment. At that point, Japan was ready to write a substantial check, in my view, but only on the assumption that North Korea would sign an analog to the 1965 South Korea–Japan treaty, resolving all outstanding or potential claims.[23] If the 1965 treaty hadn't really turned the page for Seoul, how could Tokyo expect something comparable from Pyongyang?

Japan had invoked the 1965 treaty's arbitration clause, which South Korea refused to accept. The parties were gridlocked, but Abe wasn't sitting still. South Korea's hard-line position had inflamed Japan's public opinion, so Abe, as shrewd and tough as they come, turned to their export-control laws, based on four international agreements designed to prevent the proliferation of nuclear, chemical, and biological weapons and materials, and certain conventional weapons. Seoul was on Tokyo's "white list" for these purposes, making trade permissible in commodities otherwise barred by the four arrangements, because neither considered the other a proliferation threat. The US also participates actively in these arrangements and has scores of trading relationships similar to those with South Korea and Japan. However, because Seoul and Tokyo had not previously formalized their bilateral relations under the conventional-weapons group (the Wassenaar Arrangement), and under accusations that illicit transshipments under the other three groupings were taking place, perhaps even to North Korea, Japan threatened to remove South Korea from the white list. That would, as a result, require individual licenses for many items traded between the two countries, particularly regarding three sensitive items required to manufacture semiconductors, threatening the South's computer and other high-tech industries.

As if all this were not bad enough, in further response, South Korea was threatening to cancel a bilateral Japan agreement called the General Security of Military Information Agreement. Under this deal, the two countries shared vital military intelligence and other sensitive information, thereby allowing greater bilateral military-to-military cooperation. This was not just a bilateral issue between Japan and South Korea, but directly affected US national security interests as well.[24] As Secretary of Defense Mark Esper said later, the agreement was "critical to sharing intelligence, particularly in a timely manner, with regard to any kind of North Korean actions."[25] If Seoul gave notice and the agreement collapsed, there would be a material negative impact on trilateral defense arrangements in the region, at what was hardly a propitious moment. Timing was critical. The agreement was automatically renewable every year, unless one of the parties gave ninety days' notice to cancel it, the date for which in 2019 was the fast-approaching August 24.

Trump had already told Moon he didn't want to get involved in the dispute, so I didn't see much we could do. But this smoldering issue, about to go big, was bad news. In South Korea the next day, July 24, Ambassador Harris hosted breakfast at his residence with General Robert Abrams, commander of US Forces Korea, and me, just the three of us, to discuss base costs candidly. Harris, former commander of the US Pacific Command before he retired from the military, understood how sensitive this issue was for Trump, having sat through the June 30 meetings where Trump belabored Moon with it. I wanted to be sure I left this breakfast with both of them understanding that simply stonewalling the question, especially as the end of the year approached, was a mistake. I also needed to explain Trump's angst over the upcoming tabletop military exercise, so they could help those of us in Washington to resolve the problem, rather than simply fighting it. Neither Abrams nor Harris could believe what they were hearing, which proved how far removed chatter in the Oval Office with Trump was from the dangerous real world these men inhabited.

We eventually motorcaded to the Blue House to meet with Chung and an interagency team to go over the base-costs issue. It was just as much fun as it had been in Japan, maybe even more so, because the December 31 deadline to renew South Korea's bilateral cost-sharing agreement with the United States was bearing down on all of us. After extensive discussions of the base-costs issue, we turned to the unfolding South Korea–Japan dispute. Needless to say, the South Koreans didn't think they were ripping up the 1965 treaty and claimed they had to act as they did because of decisions by South Korea's Supreme Court.[26] South Korea thought Tokyo's threat to remove Seoul from its white list amounted to "breaching the relationship of trust" between the two countries. Japan's foreign ministry had apparently also deleted from its website a reference to South Korea as a "strategic ally," and that didn't sit well either. That's why the military-intelligence-sharing deal was at risk, and, Chung added, Japan should be aware that without South Korean cooperation, Japan cannot achieve its diplomatic goals. Besides, South Korea was rapidly catching up to Japan; whereas just a few years ago, Japan's economy had been five times the size of South Korea's, now it was only 2.7 times larger, and per capita GDP was almost equal.

When I got back to Washington, I debriefed Trump on the base negotiations (Pompeo and Mnuchin were also with me in the Oval on other issues), and he said, as he did more and more frequently, that the way to get the $8 and $5 billion annual payments, respectively, was to threaten to withdraw all US forces. "That puts you in a very strong bargaining position," said Trump. Fortunately, he was mollified enough by my report to agree the joint tabletop military exercises with South Korea could proceed, although he wasn't happy about it. He repeated his view the next day after hearing more about North Korea's most recent missile launches, saying, "This is a good time to be asking for the money," meaning the increased base payments. Trump went on to tell the others in the Oval, "John got it to one billion dollars this year. You'll get the five billion dollars because of the missiles." How encouraging.

Everything pointed to the Japan–South Korea dispute's taking on a life of its own, expanding without much conscious thought on either side. Despite Trump's disinterest, I proposed to Chung the two countries consider a "standstill agreement" for a month, during which neither country would take any steps to make things worse. That might at least buy time for creative thinking to break the cycle we were in. Chung was willing to consider it, and I said I would talk with the Japanese. They were pessimistic but willing to consider anything that might get us out of the hole they and the South Koreans were busy digging. After several days of intense back-and-forth, we made progress on a standstill. North Korea, in the meantime, had continued firing salvos of short-range missiles, including on July 30, launching two short-range ballistic missiles into the Sea of Japan. We still did not respond. I briefed Trump, but he responded, "What the hell are we doing there to begin with?" That didn't augur well for help from the top if Abe or Moon decided to call Trump again. Japan and South Korea made no progress, and Japan's Cabinet formally decided to remove South Korea from the white list. In response to this, South Korea gave notice it was terminating its military intelligence-sharing deal and removed Japan from its own white list. At that point, having crashed into the ocean floor, the Japan–South Korea crisis rested.[27]

During all this, Trump had a surprisingly good meeting with Mongolian President Khaltmaagiin Battulga, who was visiting Washington. Battulga's son was fighting with US forces in Afghanistan, and Trump signed a photo of the young man that his father brought along. Battulga pulled no punches when Trump asked him what he thought Kim Jong Un really wanted. More than anything else, Kim feared a popular uprising because of the danger to Kim's autocratic regime, said Battulga, stressing that the condition of people's lives in North Korea was grave, and much worse after sanctions.

Trump remained focused on Kim Jong Un, despite his repeated missile launches and the feud between our two main East Asia allies. On August 1, Trump tweeted three messages:

> Kim Jong Un and North Korea tested 3 short range missiles over the last number of days. These missiles tests are not a violation of our signed Singapore agreement, nor was there discussion of short range missiles when we shook hands. There may be a United Nations violation, but . . .

> . . . Chairman Kim does not want to disappoint me with a violation of trust, there is far too much for North Korea to gain – the potential as a Country, under Kim Jong Un's leadership, is unlimited. Also, there is far too much to lose. I may be wrong, but I believe that . . .

> . . . Chairman Kim has a great and beautiful vision for his country, and only the United States, with me as President, can make that vision come true. He will do the right thing because he is far too smart not to, and he does not want to disappoint his friend, President Trump!

That was our North Korea policy.

During the 2020 campaign, there is little doubt North Korea will remain a major White House focus. What we cannot predict is how Kim Jong Un will position himself. Taking advantage of US election-year politics, will he try to entice Trump into a bad deal, the kind of approach that led Trump's predecessors into major mistakes? Or will he conclude that no deal with Trump is possible and that he would be better served waiting to see whether a pliant Democrat with even less foreign-policy experience than Trump emerges as President?

Whatever the answer, North Korea's trajectory toward being a fully capable nuclear-weapons state will continue. And for a fourth Administration in a row, spanning nearly three decades, the United States will have failed to stop the world's most serious nuclear proliferation threat.

That means inevitably that some future Administration will have to face a regime in Pyongyang that can cause incalculable damage to our country (absent a completely effective national missile-defense system we still lack the resolve to build). All this could have been avoided had we only steeled ourselves to act earlier. For nearly thirty years, North Korea's progress toward deliverable nuclear weapons has only increased the threat. We can only hope we yet have a chance to stop it before it becomes imminent.

CHAPTER 12

TRUMP LOSES HIS WAY, AND THEN HIS NERVE

Whenever US attention to Iran faded, especially for Trump, I knew Tehran would help us return it to the top of his agenda. So it was no small matter when the Ayatollah Khamenei, Iran's Supreme Leader, offered a helpful explanation of what Iran's well-organized protesters intended when they shouted "Death to America," along with "Death to Israel," their favorites. "Death to America," said Khamenei, meant "death to Trump and John Bolton and Pompeo."[1] These outbursts of inadvertent truth, like who Iran's leaders were targeting for death, reminded us of the continuing need to exert "maximum pressure" on Tehran. It was due to not just Iran's nuclear-weapons and ballistic-missile programs, but its continuing role as the world's central banker for terrorism, and its aggressive conventional military presence across the Middle East.

One very contentious issue was whether to designate the Islamic Revolutionary Guard Corps as a Foreign Terrorist Organization, a statutory term carrying specified consequences for the organization so named. Trump wanted this designation, as did Pompeo and I, because dealing with a group so listed and its agents risked felony charges. Mnuchin worried that this designation for the elite wing of the Iranian military or even for the Quds Force, its expeditionary arm deployed abroad, currently in Iraq, Syria, Lebanon, and Yemen,[2] would have widespread consequences, a concern I didn't understand. I thought the whole point was to inflict as much pain as possible on these terrorists. Other agencies had varying positions, the general thrust of which was, couldn't we just leave well enough alone without making more work for us?

The real opposition came from the government's permanent bureaucracy. Attorneys in the State Department's Legal Advisor's Office simply held the issue for months, not informing the Legal Advisor herself. Attorneys at Homeland Security did essentially the same thing, hoping the issue would just go away. And, during our efforts in March 2019 to move the process along, lawyer time in many key agencies was consumed by disputes over how to fund Trump's Mexico border wall, which had long been the Administration's very own La Brea tar pit. There were legal issues, such as whether the applicable statute permitted designating all or part of a government as a Foreign Terrorist Organization, or whether the statute only applied to "non-state actors" like al-Qaeda. The Justice Department's Office of Legal Counsel split that baby in March 2019, concluding that a government entity, such as the Revolutionary Guard, could receive the designation, but not an entire government. This Solomonic conclusion limited the potential impact of the decision, which I didn't see as a plus, but we were only after the guard to begin with. Further conceptual debate seemed unproductive.

There was a legitimate concern that action against Iran could increase the risk to US forces in Iraq and across the region. But this argument proved too much. As was too often the case, the Defense Department indiscriminately deployed this objection against numerous ideas to increase pressure on Iran. The answer to the Pentagon's worries about pressuring Iran was to increase our force-protection capabilities in Iraq, assuming you believed US forces should stay there. It was not to ignore the larger strategic threat of Iran, the aspiring nuclear power, by inverting US policy priorities, elevating Iran's threat inside Iraq above Iran's worldwide nuclear and terrorist threats. This inversion increased daily as Iran gained greater influence in both the Baghdad government and through its organization of Iraqi Shia militia groups into surrogate arms of the Quds Force.[3] I worried, as the old admonition said, that the generals were still fighting the last war rather than the current threat. Supporting a government in Baghdad, as we did after the Second Gulf War, hoping it would become representative and functional throughout Iraq, was one thing. Propping up a regime that did not control Iraq's Kurdish territories, had minimal support among Sunni Arabs, and took its orders on truly critical issues from Tehran[4] was something else entirely.

Day after day of bureaucratic guerrilla warfare ensued during the second half of March, but by this time, I was confident the outcome was not in doubt, despite destructive leaks by opponents, predicting the direst of consequences from the terrorist designation. Finally, on April 8, Trump made the announcement, adding a powerful new tool to our "maximum pressure" effort.[5] This "pressure" would have been more "maximum" if it had been applied six months or more earlier, but it demonstrated a seriousness of intention now added to the massive economic effects of the sanctions themselves on Iran. The squeeze was growing.

Commentators remarked periodically how often the Administration resorted to sanctions and tariffs as instruments of national power. This may be true compared to earlier Presidents, but there is no evidence these measures were truly effective, systematic, or well executed. The real story was much more complex, primarily because neither Trump nor Treasury Secretary Mnuchin was interested in or willing to pursue a sanctions policy with resolve and consistency.

To the contrary, Mnuchin argued that the constant use of sanctions, and the pressure we put on the international financial system, would result over time in the tool's being weakened, as states impacted by the sanctions sought to evade them. He argued further that using access to the US financial system as one of our main tools would undermine the status of the dollar as the world's reserve currency and encourage others, like Russia and China, to conduct transactions in euros or through countertrade and other techniques. It was a given that countries would try to evade sanctions. The real reason sanctions were not as successful as they could have been was not that they were used too frequently but that they were used ineffectively, in both the

Trump and Obama Administrations. And while concern for losing the dollar as the reserve currency was legitimate abstractly, there was no real alternative in sight for miscreant nations until far into the future. Moreover, both Mnuchin's arguments amounted to saying that the threat of sanctions was more effective than the application of sanctions, which was manifestly incorrect.

The right way to impose sanctions is to do so swiftly and unexpectedly; make them broad and comprehensive, not piecemeal; and enforce them rigorously, using military assets to interdict illicit commerce if necessary. This was the formula the Bush 41 Administration used immediately after Saddam Hussein's August 1990 invasion of Kuwait, with devastating effect. But even there, it was not sufficient. Although badly weakened, Iraq still smuggled out enough oil to survive, thus ultimately necessitating military force to oust it from Kuwait. But for a road map on imposing sanctions swiftly and comprehensively, UN Security Council Resolutions 661, enumerating the sanctions on Iraq, and 665, authorizing the use of military force to carry them out, remain key documents. Instead, especially under Obama, sanctions began to be applied as if they were individual judicial decisions against specific entities and individuals. This approach did exist under certain sanctions authorities in US law, intended for more limited purposes than dealing with massive threats like Iraq in 1990–91, but it was a mistake to expand the practice. Instead, legislation should have been amended where necessary to allow for sweeping sanctions without quasi-prosecutorial investigations and quasi-judicial determinations at the Treasury Department.

Trump and Mnuchin did not reverse these Obama-era policies; ironically, they were expanded and institutionalized. The sanctions decision-making process came to resemble the *Jarndyce v. Jarndyce* litigation in Charles Dickens's *Bleak House*. Moreover, Mnuchin himself was so averse to negative press coverage that he approached every potentially controversial sanctions decision nervously. In the Administration's early days, Mnuchin relished the publicity he received when imposing new sanctions, but when things got stickier and more complex, he became more and more jumpy. Returning to government after a dozen years, I was surprised to see how large a policy role the Treasury Department now played in sanctions decisions. Rather than being simply an operational enforcement mechanism, Treasury now aspired to do foreign policy, which was, to my mind, inappropriate. It also raised the issue of whether, as with other Treasury law-enforcement functions earlier moved to Homeland Security, the sanctions-enforcement process should go somewhere else: Justice, Commerce, or even Defense.

The risk of undermining the US dollar as the global reserve currency was theoretically important, but that risk existed independent of the effects of US sanctions. Other currencies already had major roles in international financial matters, and the advent of the euro created an even more significant competitor. On the other hand, some countries pegged their currencies to the dollar, and economists spoke of national economies' being "dollarized," sometimes by official decision and sometimes just through real-world practice. Trends were hardly all in one direction. In fact, the "threat" to the dollar's status turned into simply one more Mnuchin argument when he was anxious about imposing sanctions and risking media criticism. As Wilbur Ross said in the context of Venezuela, Mnuchin often seemed more protective of US firms that were sleeping with the enemy than of accomplishing the mission we were trying to achieve. It is rare indeed in the hard, chaotic world of international affairs when the threat of action is actually more powerful than the action itself. If America's economic swords had been sharper during the Trump Administration, we would have accomplished much more.

One issue that should have been among the easiest to resolve, but which was actually one of the most exhausting, was how tightly to squeeze Iran's oil industry. The common response to any proposal to tighten oil sanctions against Iran (or Venezuela, for that matter) was invariably that global oil prices would spike dramatically. Most of this noise came from Mnuchin and Treasury, an unexpected source of expertise on global oil markets. National Economic Council Chairman Larry

Kudlow, Energy Department Secretary Rick Perry, and Council of Economic Advisors Chairman Kevin Hassett repeatedly argued that global supply and capacity levels would mitigate the price effects of tighter sanctions. Hassett stressed the interesting statistic that increases in domestic US oil production since Trump's election dwarfed the decreases in Iran's sales implied by eliminating waivers on purchasing Iranian oil granted to some countries, mistakenly in my view, when sanctions took effect in November 2018. Moreover, he pointed out, given America's enhanced role as an oil producer, rising oil prices actually boosted US GDP, even if higher consumer prices had corresponding negative effects. Overall, for us, it was basically a wash economically.

But Mnuchin's arguments carried weight because Trump invariably believed our allies were not doing enough. This was certainly true on Iran. France, Germany, and the UK spent their time trying to save the Iran nuclear deal rather than pressuring the ayatollahs. Neither they nor Americans who supported Obama's deal ever believed unilateral US sanctions could devastate Iran's economy, although that was exactly their effect. They opposed proving the point more graphically by making the sanctions ever stricter. Accordingly, success in tightening sanctions was mixed. Had we hard-liners persuaded Trump to bear down on Mnuchin, we would have seen even more dramatic economic decline in Iran, but that was not to be. Trump could initiate policies, but his lack of consistency, steadfastness, and resolve invariably undercut them. So it was on Iran sanctions.

One important loophole for Iran was the oil waivers granted to eight countries (Taiwan, China, India, Japan, South Korea, Italy, Greece, and Turkey) when renewed sanctions took effect in November 2018, six months after US withdrawal from the nuclear deal, noted above. Taiwan, Greece, and Italy quickly halted purchases of Iranian oil, so not renewing their waivers was a given. State's bureaucrats found endless reasons to extend the other waivers, as "clientitis" took hold. "But India is so important," or "Japan is so important," said officials, arguing the interests of "their" countries rather than the US interests at stake.[6] One of the worst cases involved India, which, like the others, was buying Iranian oil at prices well below the global market because Iran was so desperate to make sales.[7] India complained it would be disadvantaged not only because of having to find new suppliers, but also because the new sources would insist on prevailing market prices! India's making this argument was understandable, but it was incomprehensible that US bureaucrats echoed it sympathetically.

Pompeo was wobbly, caught between conflicting pressures. He also doubted the Arab oil-producing states would really fulfill their promises to boost production to make up for the "loss" of Iranian oil under the waivers. And of course, global oil prices would spike. Trump, while oscillating on any given day on any given issue, had been vibrating increasingly on the "end the waivers" side of the scale. He said expressly in the Oval on March 25, "I'm ready to cut them off," and on April 12 said, "Increase the sanctions. Max them out, do it right away, including on the oil," and on April 18 said, "Go to zero." In a phone call with Pompeo, Trump had not been sympathetic to India's Prime Minister Narendra Modi, saying, "He'll be okay." I recall a similar conversation reflecting Trump's indifference to notifying allies about waiver decisions. Considering one foreign leader's trip to Washington, which also raised the ending of a waiver, Trump had a ready suggestion: "Do it before he gets here, and then I'll say I didn't know anything about it," and "Do it early in the week. I don't want to be anywhere near it."

On April 22, after six months of endless, needless, time-consuming opposition by many within the Administration, but with widespread Republican congressional support for so doing, the White House announced the end of the waivers.[8] Many in the media, who had listened to the bureaucracy's leaks to the contrary, were surprised. US military and civilian personnel in the region were rightly on alert for an appropriate period, and we made it clear we would hold Iran responsible for any retaliation. This was an important step forward, although the waivers should never have been granted to begin with. The original sanctions were announced in May 2018, taking effect six months later. That was more than enough time for all concerned to make alternative arrangements. The real conclusion was that sanctions for any *new* transactions should have taken immediate effect upon the Iran nuclear deal's termination. It may have been appropriate to grandfather existing transactions that had been "innocently" entered into, but six months to wind these deals down was far too generous. Ninety days was plenty. Giving Iran a full six months before either existing or potential transactions were brought under the ax was a gift from Allah Tehran didn't deserve. The next Administration should fix Mnuchin's approach immediately so everyone will be on notice that sanctions are an economic weapon we will use effectively, not something we feel guilty about deploying.

Another set of waivers causing endless controversy was the "nuclear waivers," allowing for Western assistance or cooperation with elements of Iran's purported "civil" nuclear program. Dating back to the re-initiation of sanctions in November 2018, the State Department, over NSC objections, originally issued seven such waivers. Not all the waivers were equally serious in promoting Iran's nuclear work, but the political symbolism was bad. As the May 2019 sunset of the waivers approached, we sought internal Administration agreement to end at least some and reduce the waiver period to ninety days for others. Our efforts were not as productive as I had hoped, largely because the State Department waged trench warfare to save as many waivers as it could. Nonetheless, in early May, we terminated two waivers, bringing us down to five, and all those remaining were limited in both duration and scope. Before I left, the epicenter of resistance to killing the waivers had shifted to Mnuchin and Treasury. They argued that lifting the waivers would hurt significant Chinese and Russian interests, so we should therefore extend them. Mnuchin, Pompeo, and I argued this out in front of Trump in the Oval on July 25, and Mnuchin's concerns for China and Russia prevailed over my effort to increase pressure on Iran; Pompeo was largely silent.

• • •

Trump often complained that people all over the world wanted to talk to him, but somehow they never got through. So not surprisingly, he eventually began musing about opening discussions with Iran. That country's Foreign Minister, Javad Zarif, gave a series of interviews in New York saying Trump wanted to talk, but that Bibi Netanyahu, Saudi Crown Prince Mohammed bin Salman, and I were trying instead to overthrow the ayatollahs' regime.[9] If only. Beyond that, Iranian President Hassan Rouhani wanted to talk, Putin wanted to talk, everyone wanted to talk to Trump, but someone was cutting him out. Of course, neither Putin nor Rouhani had made any effort to contact us, and to the extent Zarif and others spoke to the media, they were playing to Trump's vanities. The latest variation on this theme, perfected by Kim Jong Un, was to criticize Trump's aides, presumably to convince Trump only he could make a difference. Iran, Cuba, and North Korea all tried it again in late April, and there was every reason to believe the tactic would spread. Such an approach was quite astute, because that's exactly what Trump thought. What he couldn't accept was that these adversaries wanted to talk to him to get a better deal than by negotiating with his troublesome advisors. I figured I'd tell Trump that the day I walked out the door, which was getting closer.

In his April White House meeting with Abe, Trump said neither Pompeo nor I had much of a relationship with Iran, and he had no relationship at all with Iran, but Abe did. This is what Trump thought international geopolitics was all about. Maybe that's how it is in the New York real estate business. In retrospect, these remarks were the first indication Trump had a job in mind for Abe, one that could lead to no good end. This discussion did not go far before Trump, still in the stratosphere over the morning's excellent economic news, veered off to sideswiping Federal Reserve Chairman Jerome Powell as "that idiot at the Fed" for pursuing higher interest rates. On April 30, however, in a phone call with France's Macron, Trump raised the idea again, encouraging Macron, who lived for the Iran nuclear deal, to seize this apparent opening in the US position. Trump, almost alone among world leaders, never saw these bids for conversations as weakening our overall position, although others, friend and foe alike, saw them exactly that way. Trump couldn't stop himself: "I'm a talker, I like to talk." Grand strategy in the Trump Administration.

Simultaneously, Iran was gearing up a major campaign against US interests in the Middle East. Iran armed Yemen's Houthi rebels and Iraqi Shia militia groups with more sophisticated missile and drone weaponry. The Quds Force, effectively the creator of Lebanon's Hezbollah, was a critical prop for Assad's regime in Syria, and both Beirut and Damascus benefited from increased military capabilities supplied by Tehran (at least when Israel wasn't destroying Iranian shipments with repeated air strikes in Syria and later Iraq). Iran also expanded assistance to the Taliban, proving yet again it was an equal-opportunity state sponsor of terrorism, Sunni or Shia, as long as it served Iran's national interest.[10] As a defensive response, the Pentagon increased US military assets in the region, including expediting the deployment of the aircraft carrier *Abraham Lincoln* and its strike force. We issued an explanatory public statement on May 5, which went out over my name.[11] This caused tremors in the press, wondering why it hadn't come from the Pentagon. The answer? Dunford called to say, "Hey, Ambassador, I need some help here," trying to get the statement through the White House bureaucracy, which increasingly felt as cumbersome as the rest of the government. Dunford said to me a few days later, "We have a saying: 'In war, sometimes simple things are hard.'" I was happy to help. Mystery solved.

Iran's escalation was no ad hoc step by Quds Force field commanders but a systematic ratcheting up of what Iran called "maximum resistance"[12] to US pressure. This shift in Iran's strategy, and its continued enhancement of terrorist groups and other surrogate forces, underlined the risks of any perceived weakening of US resolve, which would lead Tehran to conclude it had the upper hand. Over the next four months, Trump's erratic behavior made this risk palpable. In the meantime, on May 8, Rouhani announced that sixty days later Iran was prepared to violate four key elements of the nuclear deal, those: (1) limiting its stockpile of low-enriched (reactor-grade) uranium to

300 kg; (2) limiting its heavy-water stockpile to 130 metric tons (with Iran prepared to sell any excess for export); (3) limiting its level of uranium enrichment to 3.67 percent of the U-235 isotope (that is, moving toward higher enrichment levels approaching weapons grade); and (4) prohibiting the Arak heavy-water reactor from becoming a breeder reactor for plutonium, an alternative to enriched uranium for nuclear-weapons fissile material.[13] Rouhani, in a parallel letter to Putin, threatened to withdraw from the Treaty on the Non-Proliferation of Nuclear Weapons, an interesting twist for a country purportedly not seeking nuclear weapons.[14]

The four limits Iran was rejecting were central to the nuclear deal. If its nuclear program was truly only civil in nature, Tehran had no need to breach any of the restrictions. The only rational explanation for Rouhani's threat was to reduce the "breakout time" for Iran to acquire enough highly enriched uranium to begin fabricating weapons. Rouhani's extortionate demands, and the consequent trajectory toward nuclear weapons, got the Europeans' attention. This could have been a moment of truth for Britain, France, and Germany, but it wasn't. They rejected Rouhani's "ultimatum" for its tone but ignored the substance of his statements.[15]

At the Pentagon, Dunford said he wanted clear objectives and clear orders if he had to take the possibility of action against Iran seriously. In part, this reflected Mattis's argument: the National Security Strategy listed China, Russia, North Korea, and Iran as our major threats, meaning, in Mattis's words, that Iran was a "fourth tier" threat, implicitly unworthy of much attention. Although it had been written before I arrived, I always assumed this meant that these four countries, taken together, represented the "first tier" of threats. In that first tier, Iran may have been fourth, but only because we did not yet believe it had nuclear weapons.

I argued that if the policy was to prevent Iran from getting nuclear weapons, we had to be prepared to use military force. For twenty-five years, people had been unwilling to do what was necessary to stop North Korea from becoming a nuclear-weapons state, and that unwillingness had brought us to the point where North Korea had nuclear weapons. I recounted how Bush 43 had said it was "unacceptable" for Iran to have nuclear weapons, and that I used to say, "I think when the President says it is 'unacceptable,' he means it is 'unacceptable.'" I was wrong. That's not what Bush (or his predecessors or his successors) really meant. We *did* accept North Korea's getting nuclear weapons. To avoid that outcome with Iran, we had to keep upping the pressure, economically, politically, and militarily.

Dunford asked if I really thought the Administration's announced policy of "maximum pressure" would change Iran's behavior. I said it was almost impossible to conceive of the present regime's doing so, and that only full-out regime change would ultimately prevent Iran from possessing nuclear weapons. We were likely near our last chance. Dunford said he assessed it the same way. He believed Iran did not think we were serious about using force, either on the nuclear issue or even on defending ourselves against the attacks we now worried about from the Quds Force in the Persian (or Arabian, depending on where you lived) Gulf, the Red Sea, Iraq, and Afghanistan. That is what Dunford meant when he worried Iran would "miscalculate": Tehran thought it could develop nuclear weapons or even attack us in the region without fear of retaliation.[16] Perhaps Dunford and Shanahan were surprised to hear all this, so I said, "It's not like I have been hiding my views on this over the years," which they laughingly acknowledged. This was a very useful discussion. Unlike Mattis, I thought, Dunford wasn't fighting the conclusion; he just wanted to be sure we understood the implications. It was certainly clear to him when we finished that I did. This was at least a part of the "larger discussion" Dunford wanted on Iran.

During these days, I went to the Hill frequently to brief key House and Senate members, including Mitch McConnell later on May 9, so they knew exactly what we faced. As we were wrapping up, McConnell said, "I don't envy you your job," and I said, "I could say the same about yours." McConnell laughed and replied, "Your job is much harder than mine."

The history of our inadequate responses to direct Iran's strikes against US civilian and military targets in the Middle East was fully in the public record, starting with the seizure of our embassy in Tehran in 1979 and the Iranian-instigated 1983 attack on the Marine barracks in Beirut (resulting in American, French, and Italian forces being withdrawn from Lebanon), and continuing to the absence of US retaliation for Iran's attacks via Shia militia groups on Embassy Baghdad and our Basra consulate in September 2018. This long string of passivity, extending to the current day, had convinced Iran it could act with virtual impunity in the region.

As this latest debate about Iran was on inside the Administration, my view was that the Pentagon clearly had a lot of work to do to make up for Mattis's lack of interest in confronting its nuclear-weapons program. It was during this period of internal discussions over Iran that Trump was asked by a reporter, "Are you satisfied with the advice you received from John Bolton?" Trump answered, "Yeah, John is very good. John is a—he has strong views on things, but that's okay. I actually temper John, which is pretty amazing, isn't it? Nobody thought that was going to happen. I'm the one that tempers him. But that's okay. I have different sides. I mean, I have John Bolton, and I have other people that are a little more dovish than him. And ultimately, I make the decision. No, I get—I like John. I get very good advice from John."[17] Can you imagine which words the media quoted? White House Communications Director Mercy Schlapp described Trump's tone as "affectionate," which I told her struck me as optimistic.

On May 9, we converted Trump's regular intelligence briefing into a larger discussion of Iran, with Shanahan, Dunford, and Pompeo also attending, along with the regular crew. As we were sitting down in front of the *Resolute* desk, Trump said, "Congratulations," to Shanahan, producing a look of confusion, until Trump said, "I'm nominating you as Secretary of Defense," which brought general approval and handshakes, although the decision was long overdue. Pompeo briefed Trump on his recent visit to Iraq, which inevitably kick-started Trump into enumerating the Bush 43 Administration's errors: "Worst President we ever had," said Trump. As was often the case when discussing Iran, Trump raised John Kerry. Trump was obsessed with the idea of prosecuting Kerry for violating the Logan Act, a rarely invoked 1799 law prohibiting private citizens from negotiating with foreign governments. Without doubt, Kerry was trying to persuade Iran to stay in the Iran nuclear deal and wait Trump out until 2020, when a Democrat would assuredly win election and revive it. That said, prosecuting him was a nonstarter. The Logan Act violates the First Amendment and, as a criminal statute, is unconstitutionally void for vagueness, but it is still often used to intimidate the unwary. In Trump's mind, Mike Flynn, his first National Security Advisor, had been unfairly threatened with prosecution under it, which was a fair point, and he wanted to wield it against Kerry. In meeting after meeting in the Oval, Trump would ask Attorney General William Barr or anybody listening to launch a prosecution. I am confident no one ever did any such thing. I tried early on explaining to Trump the likelihood the Logan Act would be declared unconstitutional if tested in court, but I failed utterly. As long as Trump is President, and probably thereafter, he will search for a lawyer willing to prosecute Kerry. If I were Kerry, I wouldn't lose any sleep over it.

Back to reality, Dunford stressed that Iran didn't believe we would respond to the attacks they were contemplating. Trump answered immediately, "They don't understand us very well." We talked about the various military and other options, and sure enough, Trump came back to Kerry: "I'm surprised they're not calling. It's because of Kerry [saying,] 'You're going to make me look bad.' We're going to win."

Dunford and others, myself included, were surprised how positive Trump was about striking some of the targets I suggested, with Dunford saying, correctly, "You've got to be prepared for the next step."

"I'm prepared," Trump answered. "Chairman Kim will be watching. You [Shanahan and Dunford] may want to think about building up."

"That's why we're here, Mr. President," Dunford responded, giving specifics on what would be needed.

Trump did not approve carte blanche, but he did say he wanted the Arab allies to pay for it, a familiar theme.

After we discussed North Korea, Venezuela, Israel, Syria, and a few other topics, the meeting broke. I returned to my office, where several of the others had gathered to carry on the conversation. I asked Shanahan and Dunford if they had what they needed from Trump, and it was clear they knew exactly what Trump wanted, which I saw as effectively a reversal of the Mattis approach.

The Sit Room called me early on Sunday, May 12, to report an oil tanker near the Strait of Hormuz had been hit by some kind of munition and was on fire. Perhaps up to four ships had been struck. I told the Sit Room to awaken Kupperman and others if they hadn't already. I took a shower, got dressed, and had my Secret Service detail head for the White House. I called Dunford from the car shortly after 5:00 a.m., finding he had essentially the same information as I. I arrived at the West Wing at about 5:20, immediately calling Dan Coats to make sure he was aware. As I was hanging up with Coats, Dunford called to confirm one tanker was on fire and that none appeared to be American owned or registered. I wondered aloud if Iran was deliberately testing the United States by attacking non-American assets. Dunford said he believed goading us was definitely part of Iran's strategy. It was early, with incomplete information, but a major event was undoubtedly unfolding.

After a few more calls, I went down to the Sit Room, where the round-the-clock staff was gathering all the available data, and where Kupperman had been since his arrival. We now knew the ships under attack had been lying at anchor in the Gulf of Oman, off the United Arab Emirates port of Fujairah. Information was still spotty and sometimes contradictory, such as reports of explosions in Fujairah itself, which the city government promptly denied and which turned out to be untrue. One ship was likely Norwegian, two Saudi, and one Emirati, and the attacks were by either frogmen who had attached limpet mines to the tankers' hulls, or perhaps short-range rockets fired from small naval craft. By the end of Sunday, the frogman option seemed the most viable,[18] and that was confirmed in subsequent days by US special operations personnel.[19]

By about 6:15 a.m., I concluded it was time to call Trump. Although this was the second time in two weeks I would almost certainly be waking him up (the first time being the April 30 uprising in

Venezuela), I decided to go ahead. I briefed him on what we knew, and he asked, "What should we do?" I said we would continue gathering information, be alert for other possible attacks, and start thinking about what a military response could look like. "But why wouldn't we know about this?" he asked, still apparently believing we knew everything. I explained, as I had many times before, that we were not omniscient, and that I would keep him posted. (Later in the day, speaking with Pompeo, Trump would wonder again why we hadn't known of the attack in advance.)

I left messages for Mulvaney, who was at Camp David with House and Senate members on some kind of retreat. I also had the Sit Room contact Embassy Oslo, Embassy Abu Dhabi, and Embassy Riyadh to pulse their host governments and find out what they knew. My tentative thought was that these three governments should call for an emergency Security Council meeting to put the spotlight on Iran. I spoke with Pompeo at about 6:25, and he agreed with this approach. At 7:30, I called Pence and briefed him, having already asked Kupperman to convene a Deputies Committee at 8:00 a.m. to decide how to work on a response, the first of three that day. Several agencies grumbled at being bothered on a Sunday.

By 8:00, information was still fragmentary. The Saudis, for reasons best known to them, at first denied that any attacks had occurred but later reversed themselves. We were closely consulting with all of our affected allies, watching especially carefully the Iranian disinformation campaigns, which were already under way. At 8:20, Norway confirmed publicly that its ship had been hit, saying there were no casualties and the ship remained seaworthy. Starting at 8:40, I spoke to Dunford three times in rapid succession. By then, we had pictures of a hole in the side of one of the ships, taken by the ship's crew, which he said was clearly not caused by a drone. Dunford called again at 8:50 to say allies were confirming much of what we had heard, but Iran's disinformation efforts were picking up, claiming there were seven to ten ships on fire, and that US and French planes had been spotted nearby. Tehran was vying for the chutzpah-of-the-year award, but they knew many around the world were pre-wired to believe them. Dunford and

I talked about what to do if the whole thing was primarily just an Iranian influence operation. It was one reason why, through the day, the US government said nothing officially. We were very sensitive not to do Iran's work for it, saying something that might inadvertently cause or accelerate oil price increases. At 8:57, Dunford called again to say Pentagon officials were recalling an incident a decade ago when Iran tried to lure us into conflict by putting fake mines in front of the *Grace Hopper*, a guided-missile destroyer. Hopper was a pioneering female computer scientist in the Navy, whose work was central to cryptanalysis for breaking enemy codes in World War II, rising to the rank of Rear Admiral. I told Dunford how Yale rewrote history in 2017, renaming my college, Calhoun, for Hopper, one of Yale's first female PhDs in mathematics. I asked for a picture of her eponymous destroyer for the college common room, to see how that suited the leftist faculty and students. At least we had something to laugh about on a potentially grim day.

We worried about further attacks, especially against our embassies and consulates. I called Trump again shortly after noon, just to check in. By then, Trump was moving toward believing there had been no attack at all, so I tried to explain more fully all that we were hearing, although our fact-gathering and research was still ongoing. As time dragged along, new information was scarce. At about 4:45 p.m., Dunford passed on the Pentagon's assessment that damage to the four tankers appeared light and that, at the United Arab Emirates' invitation, we were sending teams to Fujairah the next day to go in the water and assess the damage. I called Trump one last time at 5:15, to update him on what we knew and were watching, as well as our view that we should not say anything publicly until we knew more. "Yes," he said immediately, "low-key it, don't say anything." He wanted the Gulf Arabs to pay the costs of whatever operations we were undertaking, riffing again that we should have taken Iraq's oil after invading in 2003. At the end of the call, he said, "Thanks, John, bye," which indicated he was satisfied with where we were. I left for home around 5:30.

At Trump's regular intel briefing near noon, he asked immediately, "Why aren't they [the Iranians] talking?" He just couldn't believe they didn't want to talk and still harbored the idea that Pompeo and I were blocking their efforts to speak with him. Based on what we knew, however, there was simply no indication Tehran was interested in speaking with us. Trump was even more forceful than before that he wanted the Arab oil-producing countries to bear "the full cost" of whatever we were doing. After discussing the risks to our personnel in Iraq, Trump filibustered on Syria and why we should get out entirely, not to mention Afghanistan, and then Iraq, while we were at it. "Call Pompeo and tell him to remember Benghazi," Trump concluded. On the other hand, Trump was clear, as I explained to Shanahan later, that he wanted a very robust response if Americans were killed, something significantly greater than a "tit-for-tat" retaliation.

One related and potentially important augmentation of Iran's capabilities involved its ballistic-missile program. Testing continued apace in 2018 and 2019, although there were a fair number of test failures, at launch or shortly thereafter. Although we took comfort from the failures, I remembered, growing up in the 1950s and '60s, American scientists' describing Vanguard and Jupiter-C rockets' blowing up on the launchpad as "90% successes." They learned from failures as well as from impressive launches. Almost inevitably, as Iran's launch testing continued and made progress, its threat in the region and ultimately globally would grow. But it was simply not something, despite repeated efforts, I could get Trump to focus on strategically. After a failed Iranian test launch of a Safir missile,[20] however, he did tweet on August 30:

> The United States of America was not involved in the catastrophic accident during final launch preparations for the Safir SLV Launch at Semnan Launch Site One in Iran. I wish Iran best wishes and good luck in determining what happened at Site One.

That set tongues wagging for some time, since he was implying exactly the opposite of what the tweet said. As Trump said later, "I like to fuck with them." More grand strategy.

Early on Tuesday, May 14, we learned Iran had struck again over-night, hitting two pumping stations on Saudi Arabia's East-West pipe-line.[21] Although Yemen's Houthis claimed credit, there were those who believed the attack came from Shia militia groups in Iraq, in ei-ther case launched under Iran's direction and control. This time, the Saudis quickly announced the attacks publicly, so I called Trump at about eight thirty. He reacted calmly but said of Iran, "If they hit us, we will hit them hard, I can tell you that." As he left the White House for Louisiana to dedicate a new liquefied natural-gas export facility (somehow accompanied by Gordon Sondland and some random EU Commissioner Sondland had persuaded Mulvaney to allow onto Air Force One), reporters asked about news reports he was planning to send 120,000 new troops to the Middle East. Trump replied that it was "fake news," adding, "And if we did that, we'd send a hell of a lot more troops than that."[22] By this time, even Democrats were starting to worry that the magnitude and tempo of Iran's threat was growing un-acceptably. Public awareness later that day of the "ordered departure" of over one hundred nonessential personnel from Embassy Baghdad added to the concern.

The next day, Trump chaired an NSC meeting at nine thirty a.m. to get a better sense of his thinking. Dunford and Shanahan, appro-priately, urged Trump several times to look beyond simply the next immediate decision and consider moves farther down the road. Shanahan said they wanted to assess his tolerance for risk, to which Trump responded, "I have an unbelievable capacity for risk. Risk is good," followed by a lecture on his views on Iraq; why he wanted to get out of Syria; why, as he had said elsewhere, such as in the case of Iraq, we should take the oil in Venezuela after ousting Maduro; and why he thought China was "the greatest cheater in the world," as recently proven by their behavior in the trade negotiations, thus precipitating a riff on economic power as the basis of military power. That brought up the subject of aircraft carriers, and another discourse on how the steam systems for lifting planes to and from carrier flight decks were vastly superior to the electronic systems used on the incredibly ex-pensive *Gerald Ford*—$16 billion to date, said Trump (finicky readers can look up the actual cost on their own; I don't want facts slowing down the narrative flow)—despite the seamen themselves saying they could fix the steam systems by hitting them with a hammer but couldn't begin to understand how to fix the electronic systems. That same logic applied to the steam catapults used to help launch planes, which Trump wanted to reinstall on all carriers that had moved to more advanced systems.

Suddenly, the CIA's Haspel, to her credit, broke in and began her portion of the briefing, stopping the Trump train in its tracks. Of course, I can't describe what she had to say, but the rest of us counted our blessings when she started to say it. John Sullivan, in Pompeo's absence, described the drawdown in Embassy Baghdad personnel, which lit Trump off on Afghanistan. "Get the fuck out," said Trump, which I took to mean both Iraq and Afghanistan, although before we could find out Trump was asking, "How long until we get out of Syria except for those four hundred [two hundred in At Tanf and 'a couple hundred' with the projected multilateral observer force]?"

"Just a few months," Dunford replied.

"Iraq doesn't give a shit about us," Trump continued, referring to the Irbil consulate, saying, "Lock the door and leave," then opining, "That aircraft carrier [the *Lincoln*] was a beautiful sight." Perhaps thinking about the Navy reminded Trump of the Army and General Mark Milley, who would succeed Dunford on October 1. Trump asked if we should start inviting Milley to NSC meetings, saying he would leave the decision to Dunford. The notion was thoroughly wrong. Only one of us sat in these chairs at any given point, and there was a time to start and a time to finish. No one, including Milley, with whom I discussed this subject subsequently, thought it was a good idea to have both of them attend until the transition was imminent, if then. Dunford replied evenly, "I'll leave any time you want, Mr. President," which fortunately backed Trump off. (I told Dunford privately, after the meeting, there was no way he was leaving before his term ended, or that Milley would attend NSC meetings until the right time. Dunford remained impassive, but it wouldn't surprise me if he had been an inch away from getting up and walking out of the Sit Room for good.)

After the *Lincoln* reverie, Trump moved to a short-form version of the soliloquy on John Kerry and the Logan Act: "The Iranians aren't talking only because of John Kerry," he mused, but Shanahan, seeing how successful Haspel had been by just ignoring Trump and interrupting, resumed talking about more boring things like risk, cost, and timing regarding the various options we might consider, including the use of force. "I don't think they should start on building nuclear weapons," Trump offered. When Dunford tried to get more specific on what we might do and when in response to an Iranian attack, Trump said the Gulf Arabs could pay. Dunford kept trying to get Trump to focus on specific options along a graduated ladder of possible responses, but, somehow, we veered off to South Africa and what Trump was hearing about the treatment of white farmers, asserting he wanted to grant them asylum and citizenship.[23] The discussion on targets then resumed, much of it to my satisfaction. Unfortunately, the mention of our remaining troop presence in Iraq led Trump to inquire, "Why don't we take them out? In Syria, we got rid of ISIS." What I heard next was shocking, but I distinctly remember hearing him say "I don't care if ISIS comes back into Iraq." On Iran, discussion of possible US actions continued, but we then zoomed to Afghanistan, as Trump complained about how much we were paying soldiers in the Afghan government army, undissuaded when Shanahan said the average was only about $10 a day.

One week after the attack on the four tankers, on May 19, the Sit Room called me in the early afternoon to relay a report of an explosion, perhaps a Katyusha rocket landing in Zawraa Park a kilometer from our embassy in Baghdad.[24] I called Dunford and then Pompeo, neither having heard anything, but we all agreed that a Katyusha launch in Baghdad was hardly news. At about five p.m., Trump tweeted:

> If Iran wants to fight, that will be the official end of Iran. Never threaten the United States again!

The next day, Trump complained at the intelligence briefing about "news" stories that we were asking to speak to Iran's leaders. He tweeted later:

> The Fake News put out a typically false statement, without any knowledge that the United States was trying to set up a negotiation with Iran. This is a false report . . . Iran will call us if and when they are ever ready. In the meantime, their economy continues to collapse—very sad for the Iranian people!

Rouhani himself said publicly, "Today's situation is not suitable for talks."[25]

I thought Iran was doing a better job trolling Trump than he was doing in return. They said publicly they knew Trump wanted to talk but was being frustrated by advisors like me, or that Trump wanted peace but his advisors wanted war.[26] Much like Kim Jong Un's efforts to separate Trump from others and deal with him alone, this was all a head game. It did bother me that the US media credulously reported these foreign assertions as if they were perfectly logical, thus amplifying Pyongyang and Tehran propaganda efforts. Much worse was that Trump also appeared to take the stories seriously. Prior Presidents would have rejected characterizations by foreign adversaries of their own advisors, but Trump seemed to have the opposite reaction. It was difficult to explain this to outsiders but perfectly normal in the Trump White House. The next day for example, he said to me in an accusatory tone, "I don't want people to be asking Iran to talk." I replied, "Well, I sure as hell am not!" Trump acknowledged, "No, you wouldn't be."

While I flew to Japan to help prepare for Trump's state visit with the Emperor, Shanahan and Dunford met with him to discuss increasing the defensive preparations for our forces already in the Gulf, which Pompeo and Kupperman also attended. Before the discussion got too far, however, Trump asked, "When are we going to get out of fucking Afghanistan? Can you use some of them here [meaning the Middle East]?" Dunford explained that the forces in Afghanistan had different skills. "That fucking Mattis," said Trump, and off he went about how he had given Mattis the rules of engagement he wanted in Afghanistan, and we still hadn't won. "When are we going to get out of Syria?" Trump rolled on. "All we did was save Assad." Dunford tried to explain that, in Syria, we were continuing to do what Trump had agreed to months before, which prompted Trump to ask which of two of our Arab friends produced better soldiers. Somewhat startled, Dunford recovered to say which ones he thought were better soldiers, but Trump then asked, "Aren't they all the same size?" Trump asked. Composure now restored, Dunford said there were differences in culture. Somehow, the discussion reverted to the subject at hand, and Trump accepted the Pentagon's deployment recommendations and agreed they should be announced promptly.

Although Trump hadn't told me at the time, he had asked Abe to get involved between Iran and the US, and Abe had taken the request seriously. Given the growing threats to US and allied interests in the Persian Gulf, this was a particularly inopportune time for this latest misdirection, especially since it was clear to me that Trump was pushing Abe into a public role that could only end in failure (which it ultimately did). Abe was thinking of visiting Iran in mid-June, before the Osaka G20 meeting, which made it even more high-profile. When I met with Abe himself while in Japan just before Trump's state visit to meet the Emperor, Abe stressed that he would undertake the trip to Iran only if Trump wanted him to and there was some prospect of being helpful. I obviously couldn't say that I thought the entire initiative was a terrible idea, but I suggested Abe speak to Trump about it privately and form his own judgment on how to proceed.

During Trump's state visit, Abe and Trump got down to business on Monday, May 27, at eleven a.m. in the Akasaka Palace's Asahi-No-Ma room, with just the two leaders, Yachi and myself, and the interpreters. Abe summarized the previous evening's dinner with Trump, reaffirming his visit to Iran on June 12 and 13. By this point, Trump was seriously falling asleep. He never fell out of his chair and didn't seem to miss anything important, but he was, in the immortal words of one of my Fort Polk drill sergeants, "checking his eyelids for pinholes." Zarif had been in Tokyo the week before, and Abe said he had deduced that Iran was suffering, and had a sense of crisis. He said he thought Trump's decision to send the aircraft carrier *Abraham Lincoln* was very effective. He was ready to decide about going to Iran but had recently spoken to some of our Arab friends who were very critical of the idea. Trump interjected that Abe shouldn't be bothered, because the United States was defending them, we were calling our own shots, and that nobody told us what to do. After further exchanges, Trump said inflation was one million percent in Iran, the GDP was minus 10 percent, and the country was hurting badly. Then, somehow, he said that Moon was begging him to come to South Korea on this trip, but he had declined.

Trump thought Iran was dying and had to make a deal. He wanted to meet with them immediately, halfway in between (geographically, I think he meant). Although he didn't want to humiliate Iran, and indeed hoped they would be successful, it was clear they couldn't have nuclear weapons, which were already too prevalent worldwide, a point he repeated twice, urging Abe to call the Iranians and tell them that after he left Japan. Trump especially wanted the Iranians to know they shouldn't listen to John Kerry. He believed he could do the negotiations in one day, not stretched out over nine to twelve months. Of course, Trump was also totally prepared to go to war if he had to, and Iran should understand that; if they didn't, they would never make a deal. Trump had around him large numbers of people who wanted to go to war now, but it would never happen because of him. Vintage Trump, moving from a deal in one day to all-out war in mere seconds. Abe said he would convey Trump's message, concluding by suggesting that, as he prepared for his Iran visit, Yachi and I should finalize our proposal to deliver in Iran. That was the best news all morning. Trump said Abe should proceed as fast as he could. At this point, shortly before noon, the participants in the larger meeting came in, and Abe started off the second meeting by saying he and Trump had had a very productive meeting with their national security advisors, which was one way to look at it.

While traveling onward from Tokyo to London for the UK state visit, I overnighted for refueling and crew rest in Abu Dhabi, where

I had a chance on May 29 to meet with Crown Prince Mohammed bin Zayed of the United Arab Emirates, whom I had known for many years, along with my Emirati counterpart, Sheikh Tahnoon bin Zayed, and others. The Crown Prince repeated several times that he couldn't tell me how important it was that I had come there, and the signal it sent all around the Gulf. He and the Emiratis were very worried about our nonresponse to Iran's recent provocations, and the accelerating buildup of missiles and drones in the hands of the Houthis and the Shia militia in Iraq, and Iran's aid to the Taliban and ISIS in Afghanistan. They also couldn't understand, having heard from Abe,[27] why Trump wanted to talk to Iran; I tried, unsuccessfully, to explain Trump's idea that talking didn't really mean or imply anything other than talking. The Crown Prince and the Gulf Arabs didn't agree with that, and more important, Iran didn't either; they all saw it as weakness. (In fact, after I arrived in London, Saudi national security advisor Musaid bin Mohammed al-Aiban, whom I had not previously met, reached me to say that his Crown Prince, Mohammad bin Salman, wanted me to know how unhappy they were that Abe was going to Iran.[28] I urged that the Crown Prince call Trump directly, thinking he might have better luck than I.) I left for London as discouraged as during the Obama years when one Middle East leader after another would ask why Obama thought the ayatollahs would ever voluntarily give up terrorism or nuclear weapons.

After the UK state visit, the Brits and then the French hosted D-Day seventy-fifth anniversary celebrations, first on June 5 in Portsmouth, from which many of the landing forces had embarked, and then at Normandy itself on June 6. After the Normandy festivities, Macron hosted a lunch for Trump, with Iran the main subject. Macron was fixed on "the July 8 deadline" of Iran's ultimatum to Europe to provide the economic benefits Tehran thought it was owed under the nuclear deal or Iran would begin breaching key limitations in it. In European Union theology, such breaches might well signal the death of the deal. Plus, in my view, Macron wanted in on Abe's action. What would we be willing to give up, Macron wanted to know. Would we be ready to alleviate the sanctions? And what would we want from Iran?

Reducing its military activities in Syria and Yemen? After explaining again the effects on Iran of America's reimposition of sanctions, Trump went after Kerry for violating the Logan Act and convincing Iran not to negotiate. Mnuchin said we could easily turn sanctions off and on regarding Iran, which was flatly incorrect as a matter of sanctions effectiveness and completely unauthorized by anything Trump had said to that point. He may have been moving in that direction, but Mnuchin was pandering, surrendering without even contemplating the signal that would burst worldwide if sanctions were relaxed, or even asking what we would get in return. Macron said expressly that he was worried Iran would flatly reject negotiations, which I thought a near certainty, thereby saving us from ourselves. This entire conversation was a disaster. Abe's visit to Iran was bad enough, but adding the Europeans could only make it worse. They had a completely different agenda, namely saving the nuclear deal at any cost, rather than acting seriously against the underlying problem. Of course, if Iran continued its belligerent actions and struck new US or allied targets, any US military response would stop any Japanese or European diplomacy dead in its tracks. That is what kept my thoughts of resignation in check, for now.

As I was flying back to Andrews, Kupperman called shortly after six p.m. Washington time. Just hours before, a US MQ-9 Reaper drone (a version of the Predator) had been shot down near Hodeida in Yemen, by a surface-to-air missile likely fired by the Houthis (or Iranians from Houthi territory). The Houthis claimed credit, so Kupperman scheduled a Deputies Committee for eight a.m. Friday morning to consider how to respond.[29] As it turned out, we did nothing, in large part because the military, in the person of Joint Chiefs of Staff Vice Chairman Paul Selva, insisted we were uncertain who had actually shot the Reaper down and who had committed the other recent attacks. My assessment could not have been more to the contrary. Selva acted like a prosecutor demanding that we show guilt beyond a reasonable doubt, which we were actually close to here, the emphasis being on "reasonable." Who else would do this besides Iran or its surrogates? But more important, we were not trying criminal cases in court. We were in a messy real world where knowledge was always imperfect. Of course, that real world also includes bureaucrats expert at ensuring they don't do what they don't want to do, which was an especially powerful problem with a President whose views sometimes zigzagged hourly. As if this weren't bad enough, Defense Department civilians were also trying to pressure Israel not to take self-defense measures, which Pompeo told me that he had personally intervened, and rightly so, to overturn. The Mattis spirit lived on.

Yachi called me at eight thirty a.m. on Friday, June 7, to go over Abe's talking points for the Iran visit, which described a proposal that could have come from Macron or Merkel, it was so generous to Iran. Japan was schizophrenic on Iran and North Korea, soft on the former (because of oil) and hard on the latter (because of grim reality), and I strove repeatedly, with mixed success, to make the Japanese see how similar the two threats were. Japan quite rightly understood that "maximum pressure" was the right strategy to apply against North Korea, and if an EU country had proposed for Pyongyang what Abe was proposing for Tehran, he would have emphatically and unhesitatingly rejected it. I wanted to keep as much distance as possible between Japan and the Europeans, because I thought their objectives were so different, inconsistent in fact. Weakening the sanctions against Kim Jong-Un would only have encouraged him to hold out for better terms on the nuclear side, just as easing the strain on Iran would have done the same in Tehran, all of which I explained to Yachi at length. I briefed Yachi on the Iranian threats we faced, just so he knew how serious they were, using the shooting-down of the Reaper drone and the other attacks described above to illustrate the point. I also told Yachi how important Trump thought Abe's trip was, how difficult it was, and how important to get it right. I was hardly going to undercut Abe's mission, but I was just as determined not to give carte blanche, especially with France and Mnuchin stumbling around trying to save the JCPOA.

On Monday, June 10, I spoke to Trump about how Abe's plans were developing. In our discussion, Trump made clear that Abe's idea was acceptable only "if they [Iran] make the deal," meaning not a concession now, but only after Iran had satisfactorily given up nuclear weapons. This was a crucial distinction, but one Trump himself had trouble keeping straight, with respect to both Iran and North Korea. I called Pompeo to tell him the good news, and he said, "I guess that's it then," meaning we were out of danger, at least for now. Nonetheless, he was less optimistic than I about being saved from what could become the Trump Administration's version of the "cash on pallets" delivered to Iran under Obama. Based on his conversations with Japan's Foreign Minister, he worried they were not prepared to accept what Trump had conveyed to me earlier. To both of us, as Iran and North Korea developments converged in June and July, the risks were growing serious. On Iran, Pompeo told me a dozen Foreign Ministers called him once word of Abe's mission began to get around, believing the "maximum pressure" campaign was off and offering to help mediate. It was more proof that only Trump among world leaders believed talking to adversaries was purely content-neutral. As Pompeo put it, if you only want a nuclear deal with Iran, don't care how good it is, and also don't care about ballistic missiles, support for terrorism, or much else, that deal already existed: the Iran nuclear deal! North Korea was just as bad. We were, in Pompeo's words, "in the danger zone" of Trump's completely undercutting his own policies. What the rest of the world made of our disarray and confusion was less certain, because for the moment, courtesy of the *New York Times* and others,[30] the media were focusing on the split between Trump and me on North Korea and Iran. The bigger picture was the split between Trump and Trump.

That evening, Abe called Trump to review his final Iran script, which was about as innocuous as we could make it. Nonetheless, Abe asked about his proposed program, saying he understood that the United States was skeptical about presenting this idea to Iran at this point in time. Trump simply didn't respond to Abe's comment, which signaled to everyone on the call he would be happy if Abe didn't raise it with Iran. I could hardly believe our good fortune. This was not just dodging a bullet but dodging a MIRV'ed ICBM.

On Thursday, June 13, in the middle of the night, the Sit Room called to relay the information that two tankers in the Gulf of Oman had been attacked. The *Front Altair* and the *Kokuka Courageous* (the latter Japanese owned) were reporting fires and potential flooding, and a US naval vessel was en route to render assistance. There was no immediate evidence who had struck, but there was no doubt in my mind. By three hours later, the fires had grown more serious, and nearby commercial vessels, one later determined to be the *Hyundai Dubai*, evacuated both crews. Iranian naval ships approached the *Hyundai Dubai* and demanded the sailors it had rescued be turned over, which they were. (US Central Command later posted these facts on its website, refuting Iran's outrageous claim that its navy rescued one of the crews.)[31] I arrived at the White House at five forty-five a.m., Kupperman having gotten there earlier, and went immediately to the Sit Room. Reuters was already reporting, picked up by Al Jazeera, so the news was spreading rapidly across the Middle East.

I left for the previously scheduled meeting in the Tank. Shanahan and Dunford wanted a strategic discussion on Iran, which I said was fine, but we were now looking at "an attack on the global oil market" we simply couldn't ignore. The Quds Force was continuing up the escalation ladder, and why not? They certainly weren't seeing the United States do anything in response. Nonetheless, we slogged through the usual Pentagon array of charts (called "place mats" because of the size of the paper used). They had lines and columns and arrows, all very artistic. Finally, I said our various policy priorities with Iran (nuclear, terrorism, conventional military aggression) could not be delinked, and we particularly could not separate Iran's nuclear program from all its other malign behavior. This was precisely Obama's mistake on the nuclear deal. Why return to his failed analytical framework? I argued again that, whether or not it was our declared "end state" (a favored bureaucratic term), there would be no "new" Iran deal and no "deterrence" established as long as Iran's current regime remained. You could like it or not, but basing policy on some other reality would not get us to any "end state" we sought. Whether this discussion was productive or not, or whether it would just lead to another set of elaborate place mats, remained to be seen.

Heading back to the White House, I called Trump. I described our meeting in the Tank and also what was happening in the Gulf of Oman, some of which Fox had already broadcast. "Play it down," said Trump, which was yet again the wrong approach, but which reflected his view that if you pretended bad things hadn't happened, perhaps no one else would notice. By the time I reached the West Wing, our information was unambiguous that this was an Iranian attack. We were all amazed to see film of Iranian sailors approach the *Kokuka Courageous* and remove a mine that hadn't detonated from the hull of the ship.[32] How brazen could you get? I briefed Pence, who was in Montana, returning later in the day.

Hearing the results of Abe's meeting with Khamenei later in the day underlined the Tank discussion. Khamenei took notes as Abe spoke but said at the end that he had no response, which was all but insulting. Moreover, Khamenei was far tougher than Rouhani had been the day before. This showed the folly of Macron and others (Trump included) talking to Rouhani rather than the "Supreme Leader." Was there something unclear about that title? Moreover, even before Abe boarded his plane back to Japan, and contrary to his explicit request not to publicize the meeting, Khamenei issued a long string of tweets; the two most critical from our perspective were:

> We have no doubt in @abeshinzo's goodwill and seriousness; but regarding what you mentioned from U.S. president, I don't consider Trump as a person deserving to exchange messages with; I have no response for him & will not answer him.

> We do not believe at all that the U.S. is seeking genuine negotiations with Iran; because genuine negotiations would never come from a person like Trump. Genuineness is very rare among U.S. officials.

The conclusion was plain: Abe's mission had failed. Iran had effectively slapped Abe in the face, attacking civilian ships near Iran, one of which was Japanese owned, even as he was simultaneously meeting with Khamenei. Nonetheless, the Japanese were in denial, perhaps trying to shield Abe from the humiliation Trump had urged him into.

Pompeo and I met with Trump at twelve fifteen, and I showed him Khamenei's tweets. "Nasty," he said, "very nasty," before launching into a long riff on how Kerry was preventing him from negotiating with Iran. Trump wanted to respond to Khamenei's tweets, which eventually emerged as:

> While I very much appreciate P.M. Abe going to Iran to meet with Ayatollah Ali Khamenei, I personally feel that it is too soon to even think about making a deal. They are not ready, and neither are we! It is the assessment of the U.S. government that Iran is responsible for today's attacks in the Gulf of Oman . . ."

On Friday morning, Abe gave Trump a personal readout of his trip, saying that he had seen no willingness from either Rouhani or Khamenei to have a dialogue with the United States as long as the economic sanctions remained in place. At least Abe complained that Iran immediately made the meeting public, but he nonetheless thought Rouhani really did want a dialogue with the US, waxing poetic about how Rouhani had run after him in the hallway after the Khamenei meeting to say that lifting sanctions would be conducive to opening such a dialogue. Worst of all, Abe remained locked into the idea that Iran and North Korea were very different cases, saying we needed a different approach to Iran. They really had blinders on. Trump said Abe should not feel guilty that he had totally and absolutely failed,[33] but he then backed off, perhaps thinking he had been a tad harsh, saying he just wanted to have a little fun. He hadn't expected Abe to succeed, and he was not surprised at all at the result. He turned to what was really on his mind, saying he really appreciated the effort, but that it was really much more important to him personally that Japan buy more U.S. farm products. The US was doing a lot for Japan, defending it and losing a lot of money on trade. Abe acknowledged that he was considering what to do, and Trump said that the sooner he could do it the better, like immediately. Then, back on Iran, Trump said Abe didn't need to bother to negotiate with them anymore, given the very nasty statements Iran had issued after Abe's meetings. Trump would do the negotiating himself, which he tweeted soon after the call.[34]

We had an NSC meeting scheduled to begin right after the Abe call, but it was late getting started. Trump began by summarizing his discussion with Abe, and after a riff on Kerry's violating the Logan Act, Trump looked at Cipollone and Eisenberg, saying, "The lawyers refuse to do it. I can't understand it. It's ridiculous you don't do it." Shanahan and Dunford wanted to get a better sense of Trump's "intent," and in the course of doing that they showed a new set of place mats with some interesting public statistics on oil purchases by various countries from the Middle showing very high imports from the Middle East for China, South Korea, Japan, India, and Indonesia.[35] I knew what was coming: why didn't these importing countries do more, and why didn't they and Middle East oil producers pay more to safeguard their own oil shipments? By the time Shanahan and Dunford got to the fourth or fifth chart, Trump had begun losing interest, saying, "Let's go to the 'what do you want to do?' page." We discussed the various options but came to no conclusions. Then Trump was back to exiting Syria and Afghanistan, and making the Gulf Arab states pay for whatever we decided to do. I explained, as I had before, that the Bush 41 Administration raised substantial support to pay for the 1991 Gulf War. Pompeo assured Trump he would call the appropriate regional countries.

Trump left, although Pence, Pompeo, Dunford, Shanahan, and I continued the conversation. Dunford wanted to be sure Trump understood that if we inflicted casualties on Iran, Iran's "moratorium" on killing Americans would end. I asked, "What moratorium?" given the number of Americans Iran had killed, starting with the Marine barracks in Lebanon in 1983. The casualty issue was much on the minds of everyone in this and other meetings with Trump. Pence said he thought it was clear Trump "want[ed] kinetic options," which is also how I read him. This was one of a long and growing list of discussions where there was no doubt Trump wanted to consider such options—not that he had decided on anything—and that he was getting frustrated at not having more options before him. There was still considerable work before the next meeting on Monday, but I thought at least no one could fault us for not being exhaustive in considering the implications of using military force.

On Monday, June 17, however, we still did not reach a decision. The bureaucracies and key officials took advantage of Trump's impatience and short attention span to delay a response to the attacks on the tankers. That pushed things beyond the point where military action seemed appropriate. The obstructionists didn't have their own plan, but they counted, successfully, on delay to frustrate any alternative. Most important, they continued to miss the point that failing to act not only enabled Iran to advance its hegemonic aspirations in the gulf, but it also taught them the wrong lessons about deterrence. They were not impressed by American "restraint" but were increasingly convinced we were no obstacle at all. We were simply getting in our own way.

Demonstrating the point even before the ten a.m. NSC meeting, a spokesman for the Atomic Energy Organization of Iran announced it was not waiting until July 8 to violate key nuclear deal limits but had already started doing so. Iran would breach the low-enriched uranium storage limit (300 kg) in ten days, and the limit on stored heavy water (130 tons) within two to three months.[36] Enriching to U-235 levels above the deal's 3.67 percent limit could start in a matter of days or hours, since it involved only mechanical changes in the centrifuge cascade systems doing the enrichment. Iran obviously intended to increase pressure on the Europeans, who were desperately trying to save the nuclear deal, but more important, Tehran was also proving that its key objective was the nuclear-weapons program. Asked if Iran would withdraw from the nuclear deal, the spokesman said, "If we continue this way, this will effectively occur."[37]

Shanahan, Dunford, Pompeo, and I met in my office before the NSC meeting to go over the options the Pentagon had prepared. Unfortunately, they had brought basically the same set we had discussed on Friday, as to which Trump said even then, "We should have hit something immediately after the tankers were hit. My military hasn't been giving me options." Pompeo opened the NSC meeting saying he was making progress with the Gulf Arab countries on financing future operations: "I am confident they will write significant checks." "They should," said Trump. "We don't need their oil anymore. I just don't want Iran to have nuclear weapons." By now, he had his own ideas about what targets to hit, and they were well beyond the options the Defense Department proposed. Trump may or may not have realized it, but he was making an important point about how to "reestablish deterrence," a favorite Pentagon phrase. The Joint Chiefs preferred to do so by a "proportionate" response, "tit-for-tat," that no one could criticize them for. But, in my judgment, it was far likelier that a disproportionate response—such as attacking oil refineries or aspects of Iran's nuclear-weapons program—was necessary to reestablish deterrence. The point was to convince Iran it would face costs far higher than it was imposing on us or our friends if it used force. As of now, Iran had paid no costs at all. Even Obama at least threatened attacking Iran, although the seriousness of his statements was open to question.[38] That, unfortunately, was what we were still doing: not pursuing options. We agreed merely to increase personnel making defensive preparations for US forces in the region, and we had trouble even issuing a press release to that effect by day's end. Moreover, that modest news was overwhelmed by Iran's blowing past the nuclear deal limits. Tehran was still on the move toward nuclear weapons, while we watched the grass grow.

The next day, in a *Time* magazine interview, Trump described the initial and most recent attacks as "very minor."[39] I wondered why I bothered coming to the West Wing every morning. This practically invited something more serious. Just as a starter on Wednesday, rockets were fired in Basra, likely by Shia militia groups, aimed at the local headquarters of three foreign oil companies (Exxon, Shell, and Eni), causing several injuries but no fatalities.[40] The response of the Iraqi government was to announce a ban on attacks from its territory against foreign states.[41] It would have been nice if Iraq treated Iranian military forces and Shia surrogates on its territory at least equally to the US, but that was impossible given Iran's dominance in Baghdad. We refused to acknowledge this reality, even as it continued to expand, as it had been doing for several years. And a DC that morning produced no interest in responding to the rocket attacks. The IRGC's new commander, Hossein Salami, and its Quds Force commander, Qassim Soleimani, had to be smiling broadly.

The bigger news that day was that Shanahan withdrew his nomination to be Secretary of Defense. Reports of past family turmoil caused by his former wife had resurfaced, which he did not want sensationalized in his confirmation hearings. It was a great tragedy, but one couldn't begrudge his desire to shield his family from more unhappiness. Trump decided almost immediately to nominate Army Secretary Mark Esper (a West Point classmate of Pompeo's) for the job, calling him immediately from the Oval. Back in my office, I called Esper myself to say congratulations and to get started on his formal nomination. The next day, Esper came to the White House in the late afternoon for pictures with Trump, and we talked beforehand about the current Iran crisis while waiting for the meeting and pictures.

Afterward, Esper and I walked back to my office, where he got a call that a Saudi desalinization plant's power station had been hit by a Houthi missile. Esper departed immediately for the Pentagon, and I called Dunford, who had not yet heard of the attack. I walked to the Oval at 6:20 p.m. to tell Trump, and he asked if we should meet immediately to consider what to do. I was worried this report might be mistaken or overstated, so I said we should wait until Thursday morning to consider what to do.[42] I called Dunford and filled in Pompeo, telling them both that we would caucus the next morning.

While this strike against the Shuqaiq desalinization plant seemed like a big deal at the time, a much bigger deal was the Sit Room's call that night around nine thirty that Iran had shot down another US drone, the second one in less than two weeks, this one an RQ-4A Global Hawk, over the Strait of Hormuz. The weekly breakfast with Shanahan and Pompeo was already scheduled for Thursday morning,

and Esper and Dunford had been added after the attack on the desalinization plant, so we were already ready to confer. We convened the next
morning, June 20, at seven a.m. in the Ward Room. Dunford reported
first that, at the request of the Saudis, Central Command Commander
Frank McKenzie had a team heading to the Shuqaiq plant to assess the
damage and identify what weapons had hit the facility (which, as with
many such Saudi plants, also served as a power-generation station).
We agreed a Central Command officer should give a public briefing as
soon as possible in order to get the word out widely.

Far more important was Dunford's reaction to the downing of the
Global Hawk. He characterized that incident, which resulted in the destruction of a US asset variously estimated in the media to cost between
$120 and $150 million,[43] as "qualitatively different" from the others in
the long list of attacks and provocations over the past several months,
in response to which we had done nothing. Dunford was completely
convinced the remotely piloted surveillance aircraft had always been
in international airspace, although it likely flew through a zone Iran
unilaterally designated as over its waters, which only Iran recognized.
Dunford suggested we hit three sites along Iran's coast. These three
sites, while probably not themselves involved in downing the Global
Hawk, were nonetheless commensurable.[44] One of his key points was
that he thought this response "proportional" and "non-escalatory."
Precisely because I thought we needed a significantly greater response
to reestablish deterrence, I suggested we add other elements from options lists discussed earlier with Trump after the tanker attacks. We
went back and forth for some time, and it was clear all of us thought
we should retaliate for the attack, although Pompeo and I argued for
a stronger response than Dunford and Shanahan. Esper, new to the
issue, was largely silent. Ultimately, we compromised on destroying
the three sites and several other measures. I said I wanted to be sure
we were all in agreement, so I could tell Trump his advisors would
present a unanimous recommendation. This was a good thing for the
President. While he obviously had the final decision, no one could
say he had come down too hard or too soft on Iran if he chose our
package. Nor would there be an opportunity for the media's favorite

pastime of exposing conflict among his advisors. Subsequent press reports, quoting only anonymous sources, asserted that Dunford did not concur with Trump's decision.[45] That is simply not true. Dunford and everyone else at the breakfast agreed.

As we were talking, Trump decided he wanted to meet congressional leaders—there was a meeting with them scheduled for later that afternoon—before making a final decision. I called him immediately upon leaving the breakfast to explain our conversation and said his senior advisors had agreed on a response, and that we thought our unanimity would be helpful to him. Trump instantly agreed, and I had the distinct sense he knew he had to do something in response to the Global Hawk's destruction. This was too much to accept without a military response. His tweet before the NSC meeting was clear: "Iran made a very big mistake!" Mulvaney later said he also thought Trump would act and wanted the Hill briefing to provide political cover for whatever he decided to do.

The NSC meeting actually began on time at eleven a.m., showing even Trump took this seriously. Pence, Esper, Shanahan, Dunford, Pompeo, Haspel, Mulvaney, Cipollone, Eisenberg, and I attended. With so many NSC meetings and other conversations among the key people in the weeks beforehand, the issues were hardly novel or lacking substantial foundations of prior consideration and discussion. I introduced the issues facing us, and then asked Dunford to explain what had happened to the Global Hawk.[46] He said that our unmanned vehicle cost $146 million;[47] it had been flying throughout its mission in international air space, including when it was shot down; and we knew the location of the battery that had launched the missile that destroyed it, based on calculations and experience analogous to airplane crash investigations.[48] Dunford then presented the proposal we had agreed upon at breakfast, namely to hit three other sites and the other measures. The rest of us who attended the breakfast said we agreed with Dunford. Eisenberg said he wanted "to look at it" but expressed no reservation there might be any legal issues. He in no way, shape, or form asked what the level of casualties might be from these strikes. Trump asked if the sites were Russian, and how expensive they were, and Dunford assured him they were Russian made but not as expensive as our drone.[49] We discussed whether there might be Russian casualties, which was doubtful but not impossible. Dunford said the attacks would be in the dead of night, so that the number of people manning the site would be small, although he did not give a precise number. Nor was he asked to by anyone present.

It was clear to me from Trump's manner that he wanted to hit more than what we suggested. When he asked about this possibility in various ways, I said, "We can do it all at once, we can do it in pieces, we can do it as you like," just so Trump understood we couldn't foreclose his looking at other options by presenting an agreed-upon recommendation. Restoring US credibility, and our utterly negligible deterrence against a nuclear-weapons-aspiring, theocratic-militarist rogue state, would have justified a lot more, but I didn't feel I needed to make that argument. I was certain Trump would at least approve the agreed-upon package from breakfast. Dunford opposed anything other than the breakfast idea, although he was very confident of success against that package, as we all were. The discussion went on, although Pompeo sat mostly silent. "Bolton as a moderate," Trump said at one point, because I was supporting the breakfast package, and everyone laughed. Turning to the question of financing, I said, "This will be a profit-making operation," and Pompeo again described his encouraging fund-raising efforts to date, in which he was also seeking actual military participation in joint naval patrols and the like. He was leaving over the weekend for further consultations in the region. "Don't talk about talks," said Trump, "just ask for the money and the patrols."[50]

Trump then set off into the Kerry/Logan Act riff, without which no meeting on Iran was really official. I brought the discussion to a conclusion by summarizing the decision, which was the breakfast package. Trump agreed and wanted to put out a statement, dictating we would "make a minor response to an unforced error by the Iranians." Since the retaliation should have come as a surprise to Iran, no one else agreed, and the idea got lost in the shuffle. Trump asked when the strike would take place, and Dunford said they were estimating nine p.m. Washington time (by which he meant time-on-target). Dunford also said, "Mr. President, we will be back to you if they try to kill Americans in response," and Trump said, "I don't think so. I am worried about our soldiers in Syria. Get them out." Dunford answered, "We want to get to that point," and Trump answered, "Syria is not our friend."

There were three significant aspects about the decision just reached: (1) we were hitting functioning military targets, as explained above, not merely symbolic ones; (2) we were hitting inside Iran, crossing an Iranian red line, and were certainly going to test their repeated assertions that such an attack would be met by a full-scale response; and (3) we were hitting targets likely entailing casualties, which question we had confronted, Trump having heard that the attacks he had ordered meant dead Iranians (and, possibly, dead Russians). After the fact, there were alternative theories about Trump's stunning decision to cancel the strike, but I believe strongly that Trump knew exactly what he was doing when he made the decision.

We had scheduled a congressional briefing, to which Pelosi arrived twenty minutes late. Trump waited with the rest of us in the Cabinet Room, and there was a stilted (to say the least) conversation. Huawei came up, and Chuck Schumer said, "You've got Democrats on your side," regarding being tough on Huawei. Senator Mark Warner, the ranking Democrat on the Senate Select Committee on Intelligence, chimed in to add, "There is no security with a Huawei network. We could lose credibility with our allies if we used it for trade [meaning exacting trade concessions from Beijing in exchange for rescinding the Huawei penalties]." Warner was right on this, but Trump believed everything was open in trade negotiations. When Pelosi finally rolled in, Trump explained the situation. Adam Schiff, the Democratic Chairman of the House Permanent Select Committee on Intelligence, asked what our plans were. Trump ducked by saying, "They [the Iranians] want to talk," but blamed Kerry's violation of the Logan Act for discouraging them. The Democrats worried about the use of military force, but Trump teased the idea of "a hit, but not a hit that's going to be so devastating." Trump said later, "Doing nothing is the biggest risk," prompting Jim Risch to interject, "I agree," and all Republicans concurred. Mike McCaul (R., Tex.) asked whether we could destroy the sites in Iran from which the attack had come. I hope all of us kept straight faces when Trump answered, "I can't comment, but you'll be happy." Mitch McConnell asked, "How is this different from other periodic outbursts over the past number of years?" Trump responded correctly, "It's not this [incident]. It's where they want to go. We can't let them have it [nuclear weapons]." Dunford added, "What's qualitatively different is that it's a direct attack from Iran. It's attributable."

This meeting ended at 4:20, and preparations for the attack accelerated. Expecting I would be in the White House all night, I went home at about 5:30 to get a change of clothes and return. Dunford had confirmed 7:00 p.m. was the go/no go point for the strike against the three Iranian sites, so I figured I had plenty of time before the 9:00 p.m. hit. I called Trump from the Secret Service SUV at about 5:35 and told him everything was on track. "Okay," he said, "let's go." I talked to Shanahan at 5:40 about the kind of statements he and Dunford would make at the Pentagon once the attacks concluded and whether they should take questions or just read written statements. I reached home, changed clothes, and turned around immediately, running into heavy inbound traffic on the George Washington Memorial Parkway. As I was riding in, Shanahan called with what turned out to be an erroneous report that the UK embassy in Iran had been attacked, and that he and Dunford had decided to delay the time-on-target point to 10:00 p.m. The source of this information was a UK liaison officer at the Joint Chiefs of Staff, but Shanahan said Pompeo was checking (and determined that it was a trivial automobile accident). I couldn't believe the Pentagon had changed the time of attack entirely on its own, especially based on the scanty information involved. I called Trump to say we might have to postpone the attack for an hour, although we were still checking things out. Trump also didn't understand why we had to delay things, but he didn't object.

I called Dunford just after hanging up with Trump and was told the two of them were talking. Worried now that perhaps Shanahan and Dunford had gotten cold feet, I called Pompeo (who was at his residence) to compare notes. He thought Shanahan and Dunford were panicking, and were completely out of line; they had argued to him we should wait a couple of days, in light of the "attack" on the British embassy, to see if we could get the Brits to join the retaliation (although in light of subsequent events, this idea never went any further). It got worse. As Pompeo and I were talking, the Sit Room broke in to say Trump wanted to have a conference call with the two of us, Shanahan, and Dunford. Trump came on the line at perhaps 7:20 (I was now slowly crossing the Roosevelt Bridge across the Potomac) to say he had decided to call the strikes off because they were not "proportionate." "A hundred fifty to one," he said, and I thought perhaps he was referring to the number of missiles we might fire compared to the one Iranian missile that had brought down the Global Hawk. Instead, Trump said he had been told by someone unnamed there might be a hundred fifty Iranian casualties. "Too many body bags," said Trump, which he was not willing to risk for an unmanned drone—"Not proportionate," he said again. Pompeo tried to reason with him, but he wasn't having it. Saying we could always strike later, Trump cut the discussion off, repeating he didn't want to have a lot of body bags on television. I tried to change his mind, but I got nowhere. I said I was nearing the White House and would come to the Oval when I arrived.

In my government experience, this was the most irrational thing I ever witnessed any President do. It called to mind Kelly's question to me: what would happen if we ever got into a real crisis with Trump as President? Well, we now had one, and Trump had behaved bizarrely, just as Kelly had feared. As I arrived at the White House entrance on West Executive Avenue, shortly after seven thirty p.m., Kupperman was outside to greet me to say the strike was off. I went by my office to drop off my briefcase and went straight to the Oval, where I found Cipollone, Eisenberg, and a Mulvaney staffer. I had a thoroughly surreal conversation with Trump, during which I learned that Eisenberg, on his own, had gone into the Oval with the "one hundred fifty casualties" number, a figure drawn up somewhere in the Defense Department (on which I learned more the next day), arguing it was illegal to retaliate in such a disproportionate way. This was all utter nonsense,

both the so-called casualty figure, which no senior official had exam-
ined, and the legal argument, which was a grotesque misstatement of
the proportionality principle. (After the event, commentators circulated a quotation from Stephen Schwebel, former US chief judge of
the International Court of Justice, that "in the case of action taken
for the specific purpose of halting and repelling an armed attack, this
does not mean that the action should be more or less commensurate
with the attack.")[51] Trump said he had called Dunford (probably the
point where I tried to reach him) after Eisenberg spoke to him, and
Dunford didn't dispute the decision. Dunford told me the next day
this was incorrect, but the damage was already done. I was at a loss for
words, which must have been apparent to everyone in the Oval. I tried
to explain that the purported "casualty" figures were almost entirely
conjectural, but Trump wasn't listening. He had in mind pictures of a
hundred fifty body bags, and there was no explaining to be done. He
offered no other justification, simply repeating his worry about television pictures of dead Iranians. Trump said finally, "Don't worry, we
can always attack later, and if we do it'll be much tougher," a promise
worth exactly what I paid for it.

I went to my office and called Pompeo at 7:53 p.m. at his residence.
We were both in the same mood. I described the scene in the Oval,
lighting Pompeo off on Eisenberg, who had, when Pompeo was Director of the CIA, once blocked some agency action with the same kind
of irresponsible, half-baked intercession. Pompeo had never forgiven
him. Kupperman, who was in his office right next to mine the entire
time, confirmed that Eisenberg didn't try to speak with him, didn't try
to reach me, and didn't try to find Cipollone or Mulvaney. He simply
rushed into the Oval to tell Trump he was about to kill a hundred fifty
Iranians. This was utterly inaccurate, unfiltered, and unconsidered,
but just the kind of "fact" that inflamed Trump's attention, as it had
here. No process, period. "This is really dangerous," said Pompeo as
we discussed the day's errors, most notably throwing away a decision
based on a consensus analysis and assessment of the relevant data simply because Eisenberg, at the last minute, without consulting anyone,

thought Trump should hear a "fact" that wasn't a fact at all, one that was completely wrong. As Pompeo put it, "There are times when you just want to say, 'You people figure it out.'"

After I got off the phone, Kupperman told me Pence had returned to the White House, still expecting a nine p.m. time-on-target attack, and wanted to know what had happened. I went to the VP's office at about eight o'clock, and we talked for twenty minutes. Pence was as dumbfounded as I was. He agreed to go down the hall to see Trump and find out if there was any way to reverse the decision, but there obviously was not. I left for home about eight forty p.m.

I had thought about resigning several times before, but this for me was a turning point. If this was how we were going to make crisis decisions, and if these were the decisions being made, what was the point? I had been at the White House slightly over fourteen months. I wasn't looking for long-distance records.

On Friday, June 21, with confused media stories rampant,[52] Mulvaney said he had spoken with Cipollone and Eisenberg the night before, and that Eisenberg had conceded he had talked to no one before charging into the Oval, asserting there was no time before the go/no go point. Eisenberg also had no explanation why the Defense Department's "fact" only emerged at the last minute, and, proving how far out of the loop he was, he didn't know the attack had already been set back an hour. There had been ample time for more considered judgment. Mulvaney concluded from Eisenberg's muddled answers and Cipollone's lack of awareness that Eisenberg's behavior was "unacceptable." There had been a number of "unacceptable" process fouls on Thursday, Eisenberg's being the worst.

I spoke with Pompeo afterward, and we rehashed the worst moments of the prior day. On the chimerical idea of the attack on the UK embassy in Tehran, Foreign Minister Jeremy Hunt (whom Pompeo had woken to get the facts) wrote Pompeo an e-mail saying, in Pompeo's paraphrase, "Always glad to talk to you, but why did you wake me in the middle of the night? Some jackass drives a car into the gate at our embassy? Nothing new in our world!" So much for that fantasy. We spoke again later in the morning, and Pompeo said, reflecting again on Thursday's events, "I can't do what he [Trump] wants me to do. It's massively unfair. I can't do it. We put our people at risk. And you know what will happen when I see him today for lunch; he's going to spin me. He's going to say, 'Mike, you know this is the right thing to do,' right?" I asked Pompeo how he planned to handle this spin, which would come not because Trump doubted his decision but because he wanted Pompeo to accept his line. Pompeo responded, "I'll say, 'Sir, that's one view; let me give you my theory. If I were a parent of a child at Asad Air Base, I'd feel more at risk,' to try to make it personal to him. I'd say, 'If we leave this unanswered, the risk of a nuclear Iran goes up.'" That was all true, but neither of us believed it would sway Trump. He never tried to conform me to this line, perhaps because he didn't care anymore, or never had.

Pompeo said he had stayed up until two a.m., so distressed had he been. He felt the Thursday breakfast consensus was firm enough to be the basis for a strike decision. Reversing that decision undercut all our arguments about Iran. He said, "I can give him [Trump] latitude in what he decides he wants, but I can't figure out how to do what he wants. We can keep telling people we are concerned about Iran's missile programs, but who will believe us?" There was more, but Pompeo's comment here actually revealed a significant divergence between us. I was not so prepared to give Trump latitude in what he decided, since so much of it was badly wrong. I urged that we "keep saying what we have been saying." We had just had the crisis Kelly predicted, and Trump had behaved just as irrationally as he feared. We agreed not to resign without calling each other first, which was the first time that subject had come up. I wouldn't at all characterize this as a lengthy exchange on the pros and cons of resigning, which it wasn't, but the subject was obviously hanging in the air.

Trump had a call set with Mohammed bin Salman, and before making it, he asked my opinion about a statement he was thinking of tweeting. I didn't object, thinking to myself, "Why not? Things went so badly wrong the day before, how could a few tweets make it worse?" Here they are:

President Obama made a desperate and terrible deal with Iran – Gave them 150 Billion Dollars plus 1. 8 Billion Dollars in CASH! Iran was in big trouble and he bailed them out. Gave them a free path to Nuclear Weapons, and SOON. Instead of saying thank you, Iran yelled . . .

. . . Death to America. I terminated deal, which was not even ratified by Congress, and imposed strong sanctions. They are a much weakened nation today than at the beginning of my Presidency, when they were causing major problems throughout the Middle East. Now they are Bust! . . .

On Monday they shot down an unmanned drone flying in International Waters. We were cocked & loaded to retaliate last night on 3 different sights when I asked, how many will die. 150 people, sir, was the answer from a General. 10 minutes before the strike I stopped it, not . . .

. . . proportionate to shooting down an unmanned drone. I am in no hurry, our Military is rebuilt, new, and ready to go, by far the best in the world. Sanctions are biting & more added last night. Iran can NEVER have Nuclear Weapons, not against the USA, and not against the WORLD

I suppose I really thought, "If he wants to put something out that foolish, who am I to object?" I believed Trump would own it so totally after those tweets that perhaps people would understand how idiosyncratic the whole thing had been. It was wounding to lay all this out in public, but there was no stopping Trump from revealing himself.

I called Dunford at eight forty-five to get his version of what had happened. He said he had been up until one in the morning trying to chase down the "casualty" point just in case Trump changed his mind again when he woke Friday morning. Dunford was not happy, saying

Trump had basically called him "feckless" during the Sit Room meeting because he thought Dunford's target options were "too small," and then later called off the retaliation entirely because it was too large! Good point. On the casualty issue, Dunford said, well after the Sit Room meeting, Pentagon lawyers asked what the potential Iranian casualties might be. Dunford had said, "We don't know," which is what he had said in the Sit Room. The lawyers then searched for a table of organization that might lay out the manning pattern for the kinds of targets we had selected and somehow concluded it would be fifty people per battery. "This is all lawyers," said Dunford, meaning no one with hands-on combat or command responsibility was involved in this "estimation."[53] As best Dunford knew, as the attack moved toward launch, there was no legal issue. No one had flashed a yellow light. At 7:13 p.m., said Dunford, Trump called to say he had heard there could be one hundred fifty dead Iranians. Dunford said he responded, "No, it's not one hundred fifty." First, said Dunford, we were already down to two sites rather than three because one we had identified had already packed up and moved, and we weren't sure where it was. That meant potential deaths were one hundred at most, even by the lawyers' estimates. As for the two remaining sites, Dunford said they assessed that it would be fifty people per site "max" and tried to explain to Trump why, in the middle of the night Iran time, the numbers at the site were likely to be far smaller. He couldn't break through, as Trump said, "I don't like it. They didn't kill any of our people. I want to stop it. Not a hundred fifty people."

I then explained to Dunford what had happened from my perspective, with Eisenberg's running into the Oval with the lawyers' estimate. I could sense Dunford shaking his head in amazement on the other end of the phone. "I just want the President to own it," he said. "He didn't want to own it last night. There are consequences when that happens . . ." He trailed off. Dunford then said, "And the tweets this morning. He's telling the Iranians, 'Do what you want as long as you don't hurt Americans.' That means they can do everything else they want." That was exactly right.

Trump said later in the morning that his tweets were "perfect" and said, "Tehran is just like here. People are meeting in rooms discussing this"—another example of Trump's mirror-imaging—along with, "The Iranians are dying to talk." And then, we learned later, he deputized Rand Paul to speak to the Iranians. When I passed this news to Pompeo on Saturday, he was simply speechless, having the same reaction as I: it was mind-boggling Trump would entrust anything sensitive to Paul, let alone something that could determine the fate of his presidency.[54] I told Pompeo I was meeting with Netanyahu on Sunday in Jerusalem, and it might well be a landmark performance if I said what I really thought, thereby certainly finishing my tenure as National Security Advisor. Pompeo joked, "It'll be a twofer in that case." After our several Friday conversations, I did think Pompeo was serious about all this. If he was, we would be in uncharted waters if both of us resigned simultaneously. While that was still unlikely, we were a lot closer than we had ever been before. Reporters were asking Trump about me, and he said as he left for Camp David on Saturday: "I disagree very much with John Bolton . . . John Bolton is doing a very good job but he takes a generally tough posture . . . I have other people that don't take that posture, but the only one that matters is me."[55] One had to wonder how much longer I should remain.

In any case, I left for Israel a few hours later, there being no reason not to, since the strike had been called off. In Israel, I reviewed where things stood on Iran. Netanyahu and his team focused on the latest information gleaned from Israel's daring raid on Iran's nuclear archives, and the subsequent International Atomic Energy Agency inspection of the Turquzabad site, which revealed human-processed uranium.[56] It was not enriched uranium, but perhaps yellowcake (uranium oxide in solid form), and certainly evidence contradicting Tehran's repeated assertions it had never had a nuclear-weapons program.[57] Iran had tried to sanitize Turquzabad, as it had tried to sanitize Lavizan in 2004 and the explosive test chambers at Parchin between 2012 and 2015, but it had failed again.[58] This could well be evidence Iran kept alive its "Amad plan" for nuclear weapons well after it was supposedly ended in 2004 and would definitely put Tehran on the defensive internationally.

Back in Washington, the Pentagon, characteristically, was opposing sanctions Trump had finally decided to impose on the Supreme
Leader's office. It was insisting on an NSC meeting before going forward, which was badly timed since both Pompeo and I were out of
the country. Nonetheless, a meeting was convened, which I attended
via a satellite video hookup from the former US consulate building
in Jerusalem, now the "temporary" embassy. Esper and Dunford said
they were worried the proposed sanctions would inhibit our ability to
negotiate with Iran. (Pompeo, unable to participate because of travel,
said he told Esper later that he was "touched" by their concern, but he
thought he could handle it.)

Trump broke in to say, "Even our enemies liked that we didn't
attack." (No kidding!) "We have capital accumulated. It was the most
presidential act in decades. It worked out very well." Mnuchin pressed
for the Executive Order he had drafted, not actually sanctioning
Khamenei but only his office, which I thought was a mistake. Trump
responded, "It would be much more effective if we designated the Supreme Leader," which was unquestionably true. More confused discussion ensued, and Trump said "we really [didn't] know" what the
sanctions' effect would be. "Actually, I think it will help with the talks.
Most would say it helps with the talks. And why aren't we doing [Quds
Force Commander Qasem] Soleimani? Put his name in there." When
someone suggested Soleimani might already be covered by other
sanctions, Trump said, "Put his name in anyway. John, would you put
his name in there?"

"Yes, sir," I said.

"Would you put the Supreme Leader's name in there?"

"Yes, sir," I said again.

"I don't know if it's good or bad, but I want to do it. Put it in. They
have to have a reason to negotiate. Add Zarif," said Trump, further
making my day. "Make them [the sanctions] strong, super strong,"
Trump concluded.[59]

By raising these issues and trying to block the draft Executive
Order, Dunford and Esper had made things worse for their own position. It served them right. I also thought Trump was showing the

others that despite his wretched Thursday evening decision, over my objections, as everyone knew, I was not yet about to be fired. I considered the outcome of the NSC meeting near-total victory. (Secretary of State Paul later persuaded Trump to defer the Zarif sanctions for thirty days. I wonder if he cleared that with Secretary of State Giuliani? By the end of July, however, Trump, reversing course again, was ready to authorize sanctions on Zarif, which we did.) In Washington, Trump tweeted:

> Iran leadership doesn't understand the words "nice" or "compassion," they never have. Sadly, the thing they do understand is Strength and Power, and the USA is by far the most powerful Military Force in the world, with 1.5 Trillion Dollars invested over the last two years alone . . .

> . . . The wonderful Iranian people are suffering, and for no reason at all. Their leadership spends all of its money on Terror, and little on anything else. The U.S. has not forgotten Iran's use of IED's & EFP's (bombs), which killed 2000 Americans, and wounded many more . . .

> . . . Iran's very ignorant and insulting statement, put out today, only shows that they do not understand reality. Any attack by Iran on anything American will be met with great and overwhelming force. In some areas, overwhelming will mean obliteration. No more John Kerry & Obama!

As if the debacle after the Global Hawk downing were not enough, we immediately faced a diplomatic onslaught from Macron. On his own misguided initiative, he had been working Rouhani hard so Iran didn't blow through the nuclear deal's critical limits on its nuclear activities. Macron unquestionably saw easing sanctions against Iran as the key to starting negotiations, or else the European Union's precious nuclear deal would be on the way to the boneyard. Without US concessions, in Macron's view, Iran would never come to the table, which was just fine with me. In preparation for a call with Macron on Monday, July 8, Pompeo and I briefed Trump about what to expect, with Pompeo saying we thought Macron "would propose a steep concession just to begin negotiations," which was "just what Kerry and Obama did, a bad idea." Trump replied, "We can make a deal in a day. There is no real reason to ease sanctions. Once we do that, they're hard to get back on," which was exactly correct. The discussion wandered around for a while, and the subject of Iran's uranium-enrichment activities came up. "We may need to hit it," said Trump, and then he was back to wondering unhelpfully about when Milley would take over from Dunford: "Should we get Milley involved? We may need to do this in two weeks. If you put twenty Tomahawks into a doorway, I don't give a fuck what they say, that's bad." That was correct too, although I had no idea which doorway he had in mind, or from where he had plucked the number "twenty."

What Pompeo and I didn't know (nor did anyone else at State or the NSC), and certainly did not approve, was that Mnuchin had been negotiating quietly with French Finance Minister Bruno Le Maire to do just what Trump said he wouldn't do. I learned this from Mulvaney, who said Mnuchin had called him to report we had a deal with Iran, which Mnuchin essentially repeated to me later. Neither Pompeo nor I knew anything about Mnuchin's discussions with Le Maire (although Mnuchin claimed this was somehow agreed at the Trump-Macron D-Day lunch). Besides, this sounded a lot like Mnuchin's trade negotiations with the Chinese; a deal was always done or just about done. Mnuchin apparently never saw a negotiation where he couldn't make enough concessions to clinch a deal. When Trump spoke with Macron, it struck me maybe even Trump didn't know Mnuchin had been trying to give away the store when Macron raised the Mnuchin–Le Maire negotiations. After a Trump discourse on Kerry and the Logan Act, Macron asked directly what Trump would be willing to give up, thereby precisely demonstrating his mentality to make concessions to Iran without getting anything in return. Although Trump first ducked, they did discuss before the call ended the idea of a significant reduction in the oil and financial sanctions against Iran for a brief period, and Trump seemed to be clearly leaning in that direction. This was exactly what Pompeo and I had been struggling to prevent.

Another disaster. After a customary Oval Office event for new Ambassadors to present their credentials, I stayed behind to ask him to explain his offer to Macron. Trump disparaged Macron but said, he's the kind of guy who could make the deal. It's only some of the oil sanctions for a brief period, he said, which was better than the other proposals he'd discussed with Macron, and which is what I conveyed immediately to my new French counterpart, Emmanuel Bonne. "I don't mind the oil," said Trump, "you can always turn that [the sanctions] back on." This, of course, was exactly the opposite of what he had said to Pompeo and me earlier, prompting Pompeo to say he would call Graham, Cruz, and Tom Cotton to stir up Republican opposition to negotiations. I sent Pompeo the record of the call and spoke to him later in the day. The concession on relieving the oil sanctions was "beyond belief" to him, as it was to me, because it showed that Trump did not understand the damage that would be done to our overall "maximum pressure" effort by dialing sanctions up and down like a rheostat. Once again, Pompeo was ready to resign, and he said it was only a matter of time until we both made that call. He said, "We may put this fire out, but the next one will be worse . . . ," and trailed off. All we could do was hope that Iran would come to our rescue one more time.

I wasn't entirely passive on that score, encouraging Netanyahu to call Trump on July 10 to stiffen his spine.[60] Within two hours, Trump tweeted:

> Iran has long been secretly 'enriching,' in total violation of the terrible 150 Billion Dollar deal made by John Kerry and the Obama Administration. Remember, that deal was to expire in a short number of years. Sanctions will soon be increased, substantially!

We were developing an escort program for commercial vessels in the Gulf, known as Operation Sentinel, with the Saudis and Emiratis participating, as well as Brits and other Europeans, which would at least discourage that form of Iranian interference with global oil markets.[61] Earlier, on July 4, UK Royal Marines, acting at the request of Gibraltar's government, had seized the Iranian-owned *Grace 1* tanker for violating EU sanctions on Syria. In response, on July 10, Iran tried to seize the UK-owned *British Heritage* tanker in the Strait of Hormuz; on July 13 it did capture an Emirati-owned, Panamanian-flagged tanker, the *Riah*; and then on July 19, they finally got what they wanted, seizing the UK-flagged, Swedish-owned *Stena Impero*. Obviously, Iran aimed to swap the *Grace 1* (by now renamed *Adrian Darya 1*) for the *Stena Impero*, although the two seizures were hardly equivalent. Unfortunately, a swap was just what the Brits were looking for.

Clearly, the game was still very much afoot unless and until we had Operation Sentinel in place, which was proving more difficult than anticipated because many countries hesitated to join. Part of the hesitation was doubtless due to the instinct for appeasement, but part of it was due to uncertainty about US resolve and staying power because of Trump's erratic moves. Due both to their devotion to saving the Iran nuclear deal and their desire not to have anything else distract from the existential imperative of achieving Brexit, even Boris Johnson's new government didn't hold firm, releasing the *Grace 1* under a commitment not to offload its oil cargo in Syria, a promise worth exactly what London received in return for it. They simply didn't want to have a struggle. Another bad lesson, doubtless duly noted in Tehran.

The next day, July 11, my new French counterpart Emmanuel Bonne called me from Paris, having just returned from Iran. Khamenei himself, he said, had flatly rejected his efforts. Iran's formula was "maximum resistance to maximum pressure," which was exactly the line Iran began to use publicly.[62] While some sanctions relief could allow negotiations, Iran's ballistic-missile program was off the table entirely, Zarif had made clear. Rouhani had been equally firm: Iran believed it would win in the end, and they were ready to oppose US escalation with any available means. When Bonne said Macron asked for an economic cease-fire, Rouhani said he wanted such a cease-fire, but only the total lifting of US sanctions would bring Iran back into compliance with the nuclear deal, which was ridiculous. Just to be clear, Rouhani had also stressed that the Supreme Leader approved this position.[63] I promised to let Trump know of his report and went to see him about three thirty p.m. Trump responded, "That's it. Withdraw the offer. Sanction the shit out of them. Get ready to hit the [. . .] sites [an ellipsis required here by the pre-publication clearance process]," which we had discussed back and forth. Then Trump was back to getting out of Syria. As I left the Oval, Mnuchin was waiting outside, so I took the opportunity to tell him the good news about the collapse of the French effort with Iran.

Rand Paul, by this time, was working to have Zarif come from New York to Washington to meet with Trump,[64] as North Korea's Kim Yong Chol had done the year before. Just in case, I prepared at home a typed copy of my two-sentence resignation letter, handwritten in June, to bring in at a moment's notice. I was ready.

Despite the rebuff from Iran, Macron's effort to make concessions to keep the nuclear deal alive resumed unabated. This was not improving the nuclear deal but degrading it even further, in desperate and increasingly dangerous ways, simply to keep the shell of the agreement alive. It would have been laughable were Trump not succumbing to the subversion of his own stated policy. Trump had moments where he came back on course, such as when he finally publicly repudiated the Rand Paul gambit on July 19.[65] He said to me the next day, "Rand Paul is not the right person to negotiate this. He's a peacenik. I got out of that yesterday, did you see?" I didn't let the opportunity pass to note that Mark Levin, on his radio show the night before, had said that Paul's foreign policy was essentially the same as that of Ilhan Omar, the radical Democratic House member from Minnesota. On a subsequent Macron call, Trump explained about the defensive action the USS *Boxer*, an amphibious assault vessel, had taken, shooting down an Iranian drone coming unacceptably close to the ship.[66] At least we were still defending ourselves, although the cost of the Iranian drone was trivial compared to that of the downed Global Hawk. Macron had nothing new to offer, and Trump continued to assert he would speak directly with the Iranians. Macron's direction remained unchanged.

Trump seemed to understand this from time to time, as on August 8, when he said to me about Macron, "Everything he touches turns to shit." That had the right tone. Pompeo and I discussed Macron's involvement continuously, and later that day, after meeting with Trump, Pompeo burst into my office and, laughing already, said, "I've solved your problem for you. He has tweeted about Macron by now for sure, look it up," which I quickly did, finding that just minutes earlier, Trump had proclaimed:

> Iran is in serious financial trouble. They want desperately to talk to the U.S., but are given mixed signals from all of those purporting to represent us, including President Macron of France . . . I know Emmanuel means well, as do all others, but nobody speaks for the United States but the United States itself. No one is authorized in any way, shape, or form, to represent us!

Pompeo and I were now rolling in the aisles, believing mistakenly that Macron's effort was effectively dead. It was not.

That was evident as preparations for the Biarritz G7 in late August accelerated. Despite rumors France would invite Rouhani to attend as a guest, Bonne repeatedly denied to me this was true. And it wasn't true—they were inviting Zarif. Trump was wildly unenthusiastic about attending yet another G7 after the fun at Charlevoix in 2018, and several times told me and others he would arrive late and leave early. The French were trying to nibble us to death on "deliverables" from the G7 and being generally unhelpful on logistics and security issues, which was driving the Secret Service and White House advance teams to distraction. Substantively, Bonne and others were clear Iran was Macron's highest priority, which was obviously worrying. Macron was not taking no for an answer, in part because Mnuchin was still encouraging with Le Maire the idea that there was a deal to be done.

Trump was so uninterested in the G7 it was hard for Kudlow and me to schedule a briefing for him, but we finally did on Tuesday, August 20, four days before the summit began. Trump heard a long list of complaints from Kudlow, the Secret Service, and the White House advance people, so he decided to call Macron with us all in the Oval, reaching him at about five p.m. Washington time.[67] Trump had others address the issues and then launched into complaining about how badly Macron had treated him on earlier visits (like the famous insult about nationalism versus patriotism at the November Armistice Day ceremony). Macron broke in to say it was eleven p.m. in France, and that he had asked for a phone call two days earlier. Trump exploded, pausing on the call to turn to me and said, "I wasn't told about that, goddamn it, Bolton, you should have told me. I hear that from everybody. Give me those fucking calls." I said that in fact Macron had not done so, but Trump was not dissuaded. Reportedly, Trump had, early on, accused Michael Flynn of withholding a call to him from Putin.[68] Perhaps Trump thought he was still the victim of an ongoing conspiracy.

I came close to walking out of the Oval at that point, but that would have required resigning, which I was certainly close to doing. I didn't want to do so over this point, however, since he and Macron were both wrong. Bonne had e-mailed me for several days asking when we would arrive in Biarritz, and I had e-mailed back that we were still working on it, looking for a time to hear from Trump what his preference was. The day before, Bonne had asked that Macron brief Trump on his recent meeting with Putin in Moscow. I suggested we schedule it once we had had our G7 planning session with Trump, so the two leaders could discuss both issues. Bonne agreed, which was entirely sensible and efficient for both sides. Of course, I didn't tell Bonne that, in my assessment, Trump had until then paid no attention whatever to the G7.

This conversation with Macron rambled on to six p.m. When it finished, I stayed behind to pin down a decision on whether Trump should travel to Denmark after the summit. Trump had calmed down by then, and began dictating a tweet on why he wasn't going to Denmark but would in the future. With that in hand, as I was leaving the

Oval, I was handed a note from Kupperman saying that another MQ-9 drone had been shot down, this one apparently by the Houthis over Yemen.[69] Although we were still receiving information, the Houthis had already claimed credit in social media, so I went back in to tell Trump. Trump responded immediately, "I want retribution. Bring me some options later," which I said we would do.

Back in my office, I told Kupperman what Trump had said to me in the Macron call, and Kupperman said, "Trump should apologize to you." I said, "That's never going to happen."

The next day, however, after the regular intel briefing, I stayed behind to show Trump the printed-out e-mail exchange between Bonne and myself, showing that a possible Macron-Trump call had been well under control and certainly not withheld from him. I had no expectation Trump would read the e-mails, any more than he read most other things, but I did want him to know I had spoken honestly when I said I had not kept Macron from reaching him. Trump responded, "I shouldn't have yelled at you. I'm sorry, I have too much respect for you. But people don't get through to me." This last sentence was as inaccurate then as it had been the evening before, but it was hardly worth contesting in the abstract.

I left for Biarritz early on Friday, August 23, flying through the day and arriving there in the early evening to make preparations for Trump's arrival midday on Saturday. He reached his hotel at one thirty, and we heard unexpectedly he would have lunch with Macron at two p.m., which was not previously scheduled. I had committed to do other meetings, which I hastily canceled, to get to the Hotel du Palais, where the G7 leaders were staying. When I arrived, Trump and Macron were sitting at a table on the veranda doing a press conference. Others on the French and US delegations were gathered around a separate table nearby. What I did not learn until the next day, Sunday, was that Iran was almost the sole topic between Macron and Trump, specifically whether Trump should meet with Zarif, who was on his way to Biarritz, probably from Paris, where he had been holed up since meeting Macron the day before. Trump later told Abe that the one-on-one lunch with Macron was the best hour and one half he'd ever spent.

On Sunday morning, Trump and Britain's Boris Johnson had breakfast, their first meeting since Johnson had become Prime Minister. Inevitably, the subject of Iraq came up, and Johnson engaged in some friendly teasing by saying, "I agree with the President that 'democracy building' was a mistake. Are we done with the regime change era, John?" I laughed and said, "Well, that's a sensitive subject," but made the point that pursuing "regime change" in certain circumstances was not the same thing as "democracy promotion" or "nation building." Out of nowhere, Trump then said, "John's done a good job. When he walks into a room, Xi Jinping and these others take notice," which caused general merriment, as he turned to me, smiled, and said, "It's true." That was nice. While it lasted.

The G7 meetings proceeded through lunch on Sunday until the bombshell hit, as rumors swept through the Bellevue Conference Center that Zarif was on a plane landing imminently in Biarritz. As we tried to get the facts, I received an e-mail from Pompeo asking that I call him immediately, which I did at about 3:40 P.M. He reported a call he had just had with Netanyahu about an Israeli air strike in Syria the night before, directed against Iranian threats to Israel, a not infrequent occurrence because, unlike the Trump Administration, Israel did not hesitate to squash threats preemptively.[70] We discussed how we should proceed in light of the Israeli strike, and I then told Pompeo what I was hearing about Zarif's showing up in Biarritz, which he didn't know anything about. I explained I was about to head back to the Bellevue and would keep him posted. There, I tracked Mulvaney down, and he said he was unaware of any possible contact with Zarif, although he had heard the same rumors I had. I sent a note into the G7 leaders' meeting for Kelly Ann Shaw, the US sherpa, to pass to Trump, describing what we knew of Zarif's whereabouts. She sent a note back saying Trump had read mine and told her Macron had invited him to meet Zarif today. "POTUS definitely wants to do this," she wrote.

I sat alone in an unused bilateral meeting room to gather my thoughts. I told NSC staff to get in touch with our pilots to create an alternative flight itinerary for later that day or Monday. Instead of going to Kiev and the other stops before Warsaw, I wanted a flight plan back to Joint Base Andrews. I didn't say why, but if Trump met with Zarif, my inclination was to return home and resign. I could see no purpose for continuing the rest of the trip if I knew I would resign when I finally got back to the White House. I decided I might as well do it now and get it over with.

Bizarrely, we then had a Trump bilateral with Australian Prime Minister Scott Morrison, where Iran barely came up, and I rode in Trump's motorcade back to the Hotel du Palais, to talk to him privately about this Zarif meeting. By then I had an e-mail from Pompeo, who had again spoken to Netanyahu. Netanyahu had heard about the possible Zarif meeting and was pressing to call Trump at five thirty p.m. Biarritz time, which was fast approaching. After arriving at the hotel, I spoke again with Pompeo while waiting to meet Trump in his suite. I told him I would do what I could about Netanyahu's call, but I was determined to make one more effort to talk Trump out of meeting with Zarif. Netanyahu and Israel's Ambassador Ron Dermer were also calling me, so I asked Pompeo to tell them I felt like the Light Brigade, outcome TBD. On Trump's floor, I found Mulvaney and Kushner. Kushner was on the phone to David Friedman, US Ambassador to Israel, telling Friedman that he was not going to allow Netanyahu's call to go through. (Now we knew who was stopping all those calls to Trump!) When he hung up, Kushner explained he had stopped this and an earlier effort by Netanyahu because he didn't think it was appropriate for a foreign leader to talk to Trump about whom he should speak to.

I told Mulvaney I needed to brief Trump on Israel's overnight military activity in Syria,[71] as well as Iran. Mulvaney said Trump had told him in the car to the hotel that Macron had used the Saturday lunch with Trump to make the invitation to meet Zarif. Trump had then invited Mnuchin over to their table, to discuss the Zarif issue and to suggest that Mnuchin meet with Zarif in lieu of Trump. Mulvaney said Trump also told him Kushner knew about the possible Zarif meeting. I went into Trump's suite at about 5:25, accompanied by Mulvaney and Kushner. Trump started off by asking why I hadn't wanted to do the Sunday talk shows (!). I explained Mnuchin, Kudlow, and Lighthizer had rightly done them that day because of our effort to refocus the G7 on economic rather than political issues. Trump accepted the explanation, which at least had the small virtue of being true.

I then described to Trump the Israeli military operation. Trump raised Zarif, said he wanted to meet with him, and asked, "Do you think it's a good idea?" "No, sir, I do not," I answered, and then laid out why this was not the moment to meet, let alone to relax the economic sanctions, let alone still further to extend the $5–15 billion credit line France had proposed and Mnuchin had been negotiating with Le Maire.[72] I said that once we took the pressure off Iran, it would be very hard to put it back on (just like with North Korea). Even a little economic relief went a long way to sustaining countries under tough sanctions, but we had no way of knowing how much actual behavioral change we were going to get from Iran. Trump asked Mulvaney and Kushner what they thought. Mulvaney agreed with me, but Kushner said he would have the meeting because there was nothing to lose. These people had an attention span no longer than the deal in front of them. Then, as if a light went off in Trump's head, he said, "They're not getting any line of credit until the whole deal's done. I'm not agreeing to anything just to get them to stop violating the [nuclear deal]." That, of course, was the precise opposite of what Macron was proposing. Although Trump's comment was better than where I feared ending up, I still pressed him not to meet with Zarif. "I still think I'll see him," Trump said, "it would be in private, maybe just a handshake." I again urged him not to do it, and the meeting ended.

Out in the hallway, Mulvaney, Kushner, and I spoke for a few minutes more. I explained that Macron had a screw loose if he thought any reputable financial institution was waiting around to extend a line of credit to Iran. We all at least agreed Macron was a weasel (that was my recollection) and that he would try to take credit for whatever meeting did take place. I came away more convinced that Mulvaney had not known anything about this mess until I spoke with him at the Bellevue center earlier in the afternoon. I called Pompeo a third time at about six fifteen p.m. to fill him in. "So, we have Mnuchin and Jared, two Democrats, running our foreign policy," he said when I finished my report, which struck me as about right. He added, "We have a substance problem here, and a massive process problem," both of which were clear. "It's the President's inclination to have this meeting, and he's canvassing the world until he finds someone who agrees with him" (also correct). I responded that if the meeting took place, I would undoubtedly resign, and that even if it didn't, I might resign anyway. "I'm with you," said Pompeo. I waited into the evening for word Trump's meeting with Zarif had taken place, expecting to be awakened to hear the news at some point, but it never came.

The next day, Monday, August 24, I concluded, amazingly, there had been no meeting. There was certainly no media coverage of a meeting, although French Foreign Minister Jean-Yves Le Drian had met with Zarif for over three hours, joined at one point by Macron.[73] The French told Kelly Ann Shaw that Macron gave Trump a one-on-one readout of those conversations in Trump's hotel room but apparently informed no one else. When I talked to Mulvaney just before Trump's first bilateral that morning, he said he didn't think there had been a meeting with Zarif. I e-mailed this news to Pompeo at about ten thirty a.m., saying I couldn't rule out a phone call, and I also wasn't sure whether Kushner or Mnuchin might have met or spoken with Zarif, to create a future channel of communication. (This latter hypothesis was something that I believed agitated and worried senior Israeli officials, and which of course made Pompeo livid.)

I don't know if I alone talked Trump out of meeting Zarif, but the decision was enough for me to travel on to Kiev rather than return home. Still, how much longer could it be before Trump made a truly bad, irreversible mistake? Yet again, we had only postponed, and maybe not for long, the day of reckoning.

CHAPTER 13

FROM THE AFGHANISTAN COUNTERTERRORISM MISSION TO THE CAMP DAVID NEAR MISS

I knew what I wanted to achieve in Afghanistan, and Trump's other senior advisors shared my two objectives. Tied for first, they were: (1) preventing the potential resurgence of ISIS and al-Qaeda, and their attendant threats of terrorist attacks against America; and (2) remaining vigilant against the nuclear-weapons programs in Iran on the west and Pakistan on the east. This was the counterterrorism platform[1] we wanted to pursue in early 2019.[2] The hard part was getting Trump to agree and then stick with his decision. If these objectives were presented poorly, or timed badly, we risked another outburst in which Trump would demand we withdraw everyone immediately; not presenting them meant withdrawal by default.

Zalmay Khalilzad's ongoing negotiations with the Taliban constituted another layer of complexity. Pompeo believed he was carrying out Trump's mandate to negotiate a deal lowering the US troop presence to zero. I thought this was clearly bad policy. In theory, the US government opposed any such arrangement unless it was "conditions based," meaning we would go to zero only if: (1) there were no terrorist activities in the country; (2) ISIS and al-Qaeda were barred from establishing operating bases; and (3) we had adequate means of verification. I thought this was touchingly naïve, much like the Pentagon's views on arms control: we make a deal with some gang of miscreants, and they adhere to it. How nice.

From the outset, Pompeo insisted it was the Pentagon that wanted a deal with the Taliban, to diminish threats to US personnel as we reduced our presence; without such an agreement, the risks to the shrinking US forces were too great. But again, I thought this was an almost childlike view. I never understood why such a deal gave us any real protection from a group of terrorists we had never trusted. If the Taliban, ISIS, and al-Qaeda concluded from the plain evidence of palpable US troop drawdowns that we were withdrawing, and that raised risks to our diminishing forces, what would those terrorists conclude from a piece of paper that expressly said we were going to zero by October 2020?

"Conditions based," in the Afghan context, was like an opiate. It made some of us (not including me) feel good, but it was merely a temporary, ultimately hollow, experience at best. I doubted there was any deal with the Taliban we *should* find acceptable, given their track record. If "total withdrawal" was the target, violations of the "conditions" would not change that outcome, given Trump's view. Once we were on the nosedive to zero, that's where we would finish. But if continuing negotiations bought us time to prepare and then maintain a sustainable counterterrorism presence, then play on.

Shanahan, Dunford, Pompeo, and I all believed that the sooner we could brief Trump on how such operations would work in practice, the better. A briefing was scheduled for Friday, March 15, and preparations for it began in earnest. Knowing how much was at stake, we had a prep session in the Tank on the Friday before. Curiously, Pompeo had John Sullivan attend in his stead; perhaps he didn't want to reveal what the actual state of play in diplomacy with the Taliban was before the Trump briefing, which would be consistent with his practice of sharing as little about the negotiations as he could. I wasn't bothered by his absence, because I had concluded Afghan diplomacy wouldn't matter much in the long run anyway. My horizon was more limited: how to make the Defense Department's presentation to Trump the following Friday as effective as possible, thereby persuading him we needed to keep substantial counterterrorism resources in country. Typical of its briefings, the Pentagon had prepared charts and slides making everything more complicated than necessary, even when they were conveying "good" news to Trump, such as the substantial reductions in personnel and costs the military would achieve. I urged Shanahan and Dunford to pay close attention to Trump's reactions as they briefed and not simply bull ahead reading the slides and charts. This was the Mattis style, and I had heard the stories, true or not, of Trump tuning out long, exhaustive briefings by McMaster. No need to go through that again. I thought everyone agreed, but the test would come the following week.

On the morning of March 15, Trump called Ethiopian President Abiy Ahmed Ali (who became the 2019 Nobel Peace Prize winner in October) to express condolences for the recent Ethiopian Air crash (leading to the worldwide grounding of all Boeing 737 Max airplanes). While Trump and I were talking, waiting for the call to go through, he raised Afghanistan and said, "We've got to get out of there." It was not an auspicious way to start the day. I called him back after the Abiy call to explain that the briefing would largely consist of the Pentagon's showing how it had redefined the Afghan mission based on his instructions to reduce the US presence. "It won't hurt the negotiations, will it?" he asked, worried that pulling down our numbers would indicate weakness, and I said it would not. He asked that I ride with him in the Beast to the Pentagon, along with Pence, which provided another chance to take his temperature and address any concerns, but the conversation during the ride turned out to be largely about North Korea.

In the Tank, Shanahan said the briefing would explain how to maintain our counterterrorism and other wherewithal now that the Taliban was negotiating. Trump immediately interrupted to ask, "Do we weaken our hand in the negotiations by saying we're dropping our forces?" I had called both Shanahan and Pompeo right after my earlier exchange with Trump, and their answers were well prepared. They said the timing was actually perfect. As is often the case, decimating the opposition often makes the survivors more eager to negotiate. Trump then discoursed on how bad previous commanders had been (unfair, but a frequent complaint), not to mention Mattis's performance, despite Trump's having approved the rules of engagement Mattis requested. "How are the negotiations going?" Trump asked, but cut almost immediately into Pompeo's response, raising the endemic corruption among Afghan officials, especially Afghan President Ghani and his purported riches, although unfortunately confusing Ghani with former President Hamid Karzai, as he did constantly. Hopefully unnoticed, I signaled Dunford to jump in to say that the reduction in violence accomplished by our current strategy meant we could fulfill our ongoing counterterrorism and other missions in practice with reduced resources, even without agreement from the Taliban. "We listened to you," Dunford said to Trump, which was a good line in the post-Mattis era. Dunford also said we could handle any weakening of the Afghan government, if that occurred, and focus on al-Qaeda and ISIS, the real terrorist threats to America. I pointed out that weak central government was Afghanistan's historical default position and would be nothing new for the inhabitants.

Dunford further explained the need to maintain a counterterrorism presence for the broader region. As he launched into his charts and slides to show how our ongoing Afghan operations would be staffed and costed, Trump said, "There are still a lot of people there," but fortunately he went on to say, "Having no one is dangerous, because they [the terrorists] tend to form there and knock down buildings," which was exactly the point. Trump repeated one of his hobbyhorses, namely that it was cheaper to rebuild the World Trade Center than to fight in Afghanistan, inconveniently ignoring the loss of life in the 9/11 attacks, not just the cost of rebuilding. It also ignored the reality that a Trump withdrawal, followed by a terrorist attack, would be devastating politically. Dunford pressed on, saying our military pressure kept the terrorists from reconstituting and was like an insurance policy. He had no precise timetable in mind, but the Pentagon would allow the diplomatic reconciliation process to set the timing. I thought we were approaching dangerous ground here, again opening the question of whether we should be in Afghanistan at all. The discussion meandered around for a while, with Trump asking me why we were fighting in

Iraq and Afghanistan but not Venezuela, which at least showed everyone else in the room what he really wanted to do.

Following more chatter, Shanahan turned to the cost reductions that maintaining the counterterrorism capability would entail, but before he got too far, Trump broke in to complain about Congress's refusal to fund the Mexico border wall. Then he was off: "Why can't we just get out of Syria and Afghanistan? I never should have agreed to the other two hundred [in Syria], and it's really four hundred anyway." Dunford explained that other NATO countries would hopefully contribute to the multilateral observation force in Syria, and Trump responded, "We pay for NATO anyway," which in turn produced another riff about Erdogan and what he was doing in Turkey. Then after literally forty-five seconds back on Afghanistan, Trump asked, "Why are we in Africa?" He soon made it clear he wanted out of Africa altogether, expounding for some time on our $22 trillion national debt, followed by the problems of our balance-of-trade deficits, followed by complaining, again, about how Nigeria received $1.5 billion annually in foreign aid, as he said the President of Nigeria had confirmed to him in an earlier visit, even though they wouldn't buy US farm products. After more Africa discussion, Trump returned to Afghanistan, saying, "Get it [the annual cost] down to ten billion dollars [a figure derived from the resources required by our thinking for the continuing US presence], and get it down fast." That led to the costs of US military bases in South Korea and how much Seoul should contribute to defraying the expenses. Trump said happily we had extracted $500 million more from the South in negotiations at the end of 2018 (it was actually around $75 million, as pretty much everyone else in the Tank knew). He still wanted the South Korea payment to equal US costs plus 50 percent. And whatever our political differences with Iraq, Trump reminded us that, having paid so much to build our bases there, we were not leaving.

After a bit less than an hour, as we were wrapping up, Trump asked Dunford in front of everyone, "How's our Acting Secretary doing?" Dunford, obviously stunned, came back quickly to offer, "Here's where I say what a great job he's doing," and everyone laughed. I just wanted to get out the Tank's door, so Pompeo and I simply stood up and started pulling papers together. Others then rose, and we all walked to the Pentagon's River Entrance, where the motorcade was waiting. Pence and I rode with Trump in the Beast, where the conversation was mostly on the Max 737 grounding. Back in the West Wing, I called Shanahan to congratulate him on the outcome and say he should take the rest of the day off. It wasn't pretty, as I also told Dunford when I called him a few minutes later, but it was definitely a win. Dunford said, "[Trump] now believes we're listening to him, which he didn't believe before," which was emphatically correct. Pompeo, with whom I spoke the next day, also believed the briefing was a win.

The problem still not resolved, however, was the Taliban negotiations. At a breakfast on March 21, Shanahan and Dunford brought a chart showing several ways the State Department had departed from what the Pentagon believed were the agreed negotiating guidelines. Most troubling to me was that the State Department's negotiating objectives were completely detached from what I considered to be our real objectives: being fully capable of preventing a resurgence of terrorism and remaining vigilant against the nuclear dangers of Iran and Pakistan. The resource levels Trump had implicitly approved at the Tank briefing were not near what we would need in a major crisis, but, in my view, at least we would still have several bases in Afghanistan, and the possibility of rapidly scaling up our capabilities. Pompeo and Khalilzad, however, were still negotiating as if we were withdrawing entirely. We may have started there in November, but we had clawed ourselves a long way back, and Shanahan, Dunford, and I feared losing that progress. Within thirty minutes of the breakfast, I called Trump and said it was his decision whether to let Khalilzad and the State Department act with complete independence in the negotiations, but I thought it was dangerous for what Trump said he wanted. "I don't even know who he is," Trump replied of Khalilzad. "Do what you think is best."

That same morning, I met with Khalilzad, someone I had known, as I have said, for nearly thirty years. He said Pompeo had ordered him not to communicate with me because I was undermining

Pompeo with Trump. That happened to be untrue, and I wondered if Pompeo's real motivation was who would get credit for Afghanistan, a common Washington phenomenon. If true, it was misplaced. I didn't think there was any material chance the negotiations would produce an acceptable result, so I was hardly eager to get "credit" for the outcome. Khalilzad agreed to an informal meeting with all the officials involved to work out the misunderstandings before he left Washington to resume talks with the Taliban. I thought this was a good decision. Several days later, however, Pompeo called to complain that senior Pentagon officials and Lisa Curtis, the National Security Council's Senior Director for South Asia, were interfering with Khalilzad and should leave him alone. Normally, such meetings constituted "interagency coordination," but Pompeo saw it as meddling. No wonder we had internal Administration problems on Afghanistan.

In the midst of these difficulties, we received one piece of extraordinarily good news, on April 12, when the International Criminal Court's "pretrial chamber" handed down a thirty-two-page opinion rejecting its prosecutor's request to open an investigation into the conduct of US military and intelligence personnel in Afghanistan. I spoke several times with former Congressman Pete Hoekstra, our Ambassador to the Netherlands, where the court was located, in the Hague, and found him nearly as surprised as I that we had succeeded in stopping this miscarriage of justice. I had long opposed the court,[3] and I had given a speech early in my tenure to the Federalist Society in Washington about why the Administration rejected it as a matter of principle, and the steps we were prepared to take against the court if it presumed to target American citizens.[4] I called Trump at nine fifteen a.m. to tell him about the decision, and he said, "Put out something powerful," which I was delighted to do.

As for the US-Taliban meetings, I was less concerned than before about their substance, and therefore less exercised than the Pentagon, because I thought we had largely won the key battle in Trump's mind. The United States would not be completely withdrawing from Afghanistan but would maintain a persistent troop presence for counterterrorism and other objectives. If it turned out Trump reversed course and one day simply said to leave immediately (which he did in outbursts periodically), even that decision didn't depend on the state of play in the talks. In short, the US military posture was no longer tied to the peace process, if it ever had been. Thus, in my mind, there was no particular pressure for Khalilzad to produce results and no real target date to finish the negotiations.

Yet by July 1, Defense learned that Khalilzad was about to announce a deal with the Taliban without informing anyone in Washington what was in it. Not unreasonably, Esper called Pompeo, his West Point classmate, to suggest bringing the deal back to Washington for review. Kupperman heard from Esper's Chief of Staff that Pompeo "lit up Esper" in no uncertain terms, and his subordinates, for involving themselves in the Afghan negotiations. Pompeo, often screaming, we were told, said Khalilzad was under instructions—he left unstated by whom—to make a deal without outside supervision. Shanahan had tried to be reasonable and failed, and now it was Esper's turn. When I spoke to him the next day, his concerns were actually more tactical, such as his legitimate interest in the safety of withdrawing US forces, rather than aimed at the policy. "Mike got a little animated," Esper put it politely, but as our conversation continued, there was clearly a disjunction between the State Department's objective—zero US forces—and my (and the Pentagon's) desire to preserve counterterrorism and other capabilities. Esper was rightly concerned with how the actual functioning of military operations would be affected if we lost even a foothold in Afghanistan.

I brought this schizophrenia to a head in a discussion with Khalilzad on July 19. My objective was to reach agreement within the US government from among all the various strands of thought, and to resolve the disconnects in our internal deliberations. Specifically, while his instructions from Trump (or Pompeo, whomever) at that time were to get US forces to zero, he also had instructions from Trump to support counterterrorism capabilities consistent with what had been previously briefed to Trump in the Tank, essentially without an end date. The trick was how to get the Taliban and the Afghan government to agree we were going to zero on the existing mission, while

simultaneously creating a modified mission to support counterterrorism capabilities. Khalilzad readily agreed, saying he fully understood
what Trump expected, so I considered this significant progress. My
objective here was ensuring that our government agreed within itself
in the context where we found ourselves at that point. We could have
done this earlier and more easily if Pompeo had let Khalilzad have
these conversations more often and we didn't have to arrange them
like spy encounters. In any case, the Taliban talks continued apace
through the summer.

On Wednesday, August 14, Kupperman first heard from Esper's
Chief of Staff about a Friday meeting on Afghanistan at Trump's Bedminster golf club, where he was staying for about a week. That was
news to us, so at 7:10 a.m. the next morning, I called Mulvaney, who
was also in New Jersey, to see what was up. He said he had heard about
a Friday meeting, and asked Westerhout about it. She said it was with
"the guy from Afghanistan" (meaning Khalilzad) and Pompeo. "You
can come," said Mulvaney, "is [the Defense Department] coming?" I
said I thought so, and the call ended. All this showed yet again how
State was treating the rest of the national security team. I had no doubt
the Taliban were increasingly happy about the terms of the emerging
deal, most of which I believed they had little intention of following. I
suspected Pompeo wanted Trump to sign off with the minimal internal opposition possible but the endless negotiations had produced a
result I and many others believed would have severe negative consequences for America. The National Security Advisor's job is to coordinate between State, Defense, and other NSC members. If I couldn't
perform this role, there was no point in staying. In the meantime, at
least I had "succeeded" in getting invited.

I spoke with Pompeo later that morning, raising the Bedminster
gathering among other issues. He said we were "not done" with the
negotiations, like the nature of the cease-fire, the overall reduction in
violence from the Taliban, and the counterterrorism mission, all of
which were unresolved. I said I was flying up for the meeting, probably
on Air Force Two with Pence, and asked when he was going up. You
could have heard a pin drop. He obviously had not anticipated that

a small army of people would be attending the Bedminster meeting, and certainly not me. It turned out that Haspel, Cipollone, Marc Short (the VP), and Kellogg also attended, along with Mulvaney, Esper, and Dunford.

Lindsey Graham called me, having heard about the Bedminster meeting and stressed to Trump on Wednesday the need for a residual force to counter the terrorist threat and other purposes. Nonetheless, he was very worried about press reports indicating the deal with the Taliban contained no such provisions, and he asked me to speak with Jack Keane, the retired four-star general who was a regular commentator on Fox. I called Keane while waiting to take off from Andrews and urged him to call Trump directly, since he and Trump spoke frequently about such issues. If there was ever a time for Keane to talk to Trump on Afghanistan, this was it. Pence asked me to join him in his cabin for the flight, and I explained the risks in the proposed deal, as best I understood it, as well as the considerable political downside for Trump, noting that Graham and others were already outspoken in their views. We landed at the Morristown, New Jersey, airport and motorcaded to Bedminster.

The meeting began shortly after three p.m., with Pompeo saying, "We are not quite done with the Taliban," but then laying out the broad terms of a deal that sounded almost done. This description contrasted sharply with what Pompeo had said to me on the phone earlier that day. Trump asked questions, especially about one provision for an exchange of prisoners and hostages between the Taliban and the Afghan government, which in numerical terms looked a lot more favorable to the Taliban than to us. Trump didn't like that at all. Then Trump began riffing about Afghan President Ghani and his elaborate house in Dubai, which we knew from actual research Ghani didn't own. But no matter, because Pompeo pointed out the reality that Ghani was now President and controlled the government's armed forces. Completely predictably, Trump asked, "Who pays them?" Esper, new to this movie script, promptly responded, "We do," thereby launching Trump into the riff about how Mattis always said, "These soldiers are fighting bravely for their country," until Trump asked who paid for them, and found out the total cost (including equipment and other supplies) was about $6.5 billion annually. "They are the most highly paid soldiers in the world," Trump concluded. Then he was off on "green-on-blue" attacks, where Afghan government soldiers attacked US forces: "We teach them how to shoot, and then they take the weapons and say, 'Oh, thank you, sir,' and then kill our guys." Then we were off to the Afghan elections and a reprise on why Trump didn't like this or that senior Afghan official. If only Trump could keep it straight that incumbent President Ghani was not former President Karzai, we could have spared ourselves a lot of trouble.

As the discussion proceeded, Trump said at one point, "Making a bad deal is worse than just getting out. I'd rather not make a deal." I thought this comment provided a glimmer of hope. But before we got too far, Trump shifted again to complaining about leaks, including that CNN had earlier reported this very meeting. "These people should be executed, they are scumbags," he said, but then observed it was "not a bad thing that the news [was] out" that we were talking about Afghanistan. This led to one of Trump's favorite legal gambits, namely, that the Justice Department arrest the reporters, force them to serve time in jail, and then demand they disclose their sources. Only then would the leaks stop. Trump told Cipollone to call Barr about it, which Cipollone said he would do. Trump went on: "I like my message. If they come at us, we're going to destroy their whole nation. Not with nuclear weapons though. They hate us too. Taliban wants their land. We went in to take their land, and they've got crooks" in the highest levels of government.

The conversation continued, but I sensed Trump was increasingly distant from it. Something was bothering him, but I couldn't tell what. Suddenly, off to the races again: "I want to get out of everything," he said, criticizing our military programs in Africa, as Esper and Dunford hastened to assure him they were already being reduced. Then it was back to the 2018 NATO summit and how he threatened to withdraw (which was not quite true), and how much we spent in Ukraine. Then he again recounted his first conversation with Angela Merkel, and how even before congratulating him for winning, Merkel had asked what he was going to do about Ukraine. Trump had replied by asking

Merkel what *she* was going to do about Ukraine.[5] Then he asked, "Do we really want Fort Trump [in Poland]?" I said he had agreed to it in several conversations with Polish President Andrzej Duda, that the Poles were paying for its construction, and that he was going to Poland on September 1 to commemorate the eightieth anniversary of the Nazi invasion, which didn't slow him down. He said he didn't remember agreeing to Fort Trump, which reflected on either his memory or his ability to disregard whatever he didn't want to remember.

Esper tried to explain that troops in Poland would be rotational rather than permanent, but Trump was off to his next point, the ongoing war games in South Korea. "You shouldn't have let them go on," he said to me, notwithstanding that he had agreed to them, knowing they were tabletop exercises, not field maneuvers. "I'm trying to make peace with a psycho," he said, which at least acknowledged that Kim Jong Un might be *somewhat* problematic. "The war games are a big mistake. I never should have agreed to the exercises," he finally said. "Get out of there if we don't get the five-billion-dollar deal [for South Korean support of US bases]. We lose $38 billion in trade in Korea. Let's get out." He asked several times when the current exercises ended, which was on August 20, and he said, "End them in two days; don't extend them even for a day."

As if he had already decided to approve the Pompeo-Khalilzad deal, Trump said, "Let's make a big deal about it, like it's a wonderful deal. If they do anything bad [which I understood to mean, if Taliban broke the agreement], we're going to blow their fucking country into a million pieces. [I did not take this to be a well-thought-out military strategy, but simply typical Trump analysis.] And I don't blame the military because you weren't given the tools." This last point would have surprised Mattis, to whom Trump had constantly said he had done just that. Then it was off on the subject of Greenland, but quickly back to Africa: "I want out of Africa and as many other places as you can. I want our soldiers on our soil. Take them out of Germany. I'm going to tell Germany, 'You have to pay immediately.'" Then it was back to Fort Trump, and Esper tried for a second time to explain that US troops there would be rotating in and out, not actually stationed there. "I got elected on getting out of Afghanistan and these war games." Then he said, "We have fifty-two thousand troops in Europe . . . People are so enamored with NATO." Then, switching to Kashmir, "I want to call Modi on Monday," he said. "We have tremendous power [. . .] because of trade."

Pence tried to return the conversation to announcing the Afghan deal, asking if it should be next week. Trump said, "Don't mention 'withdrawal' in the statement, but say we will go to zero in October [2020] right before the election. We could push it past the election. How does it look politically?" Dunford said we could decrease to the proposed resource levels Trump had been briefed on in the Tank (discussed above) and just stop there. Pompeo again pushed for a commitment to zero in the agreement because the Taliban insisted on it. That was the heart of the problem. I said near the meeting's end that I hadn't actually seen the text of the agreement, and Pompeo said, "It's true we've held this very tight, but we will have leaks as soon as we broaden the distribution." That was another problem. Pompeo tried to keep the whole thing between himself, Khalilzad, and Trump (although, as the meeting started, Trump said it had been a long time since he had seen Khalilzad). By keeping it so tight, Pompeo guaranteed he owned it entirely. That was fine with me. If that's what he and Trump wanted, they could have the political blowback to themselves. The meeting ended about 4:50 p.m., without a decision on whether there would be a statement next week or not. In part, that was because significant issues were still unresolved, if they could be resolved at all.

On Monday, I met Khalilzad at his request to follow up the Bedminster meeting. He and Pompeo had clearly taken Friday's outcome to mean they had carte blanche to continue negotiating, which, as I told Khalilzad, I thought overstated their writ. In any case, I had little doubt that Trump reserved the right to reject anything he didn't like, right up to and even after the last minute. Khalilzad first wanted me to read the documents that were mostly agreed, but he couldn't leave copies behind. I said thanks but handed the documents back to him unread, saying there was no way I was going to be rushed on these things. I wanted time to study the documents, and I didn't alter my view even after Khalilzad said Esper, Dunford, and Haspel had all agreed to his proposed approach. He seemed stunned I wouldn't go along, but I was quite clear I wasn't going to consume in ten minutes something he and Pompeo had worked on for ten months. I said I couldn't for the life of me figure out Pompeo's desire to hold all this so tightly, using preventing leaks as an argument never to show it to anyone. Why, I asked, given that we all knew the political risks on this deal were from most Republicans, let alone Democrats, didn't Pompeo want allies? If he wanted all the credit for it, I could understand that, but there would be precious little "credit" when the agreement collapsed, which even Pompeo told me he thought was inevitable. What was the logic? Khalilzad didn't answer, I suspect because he also didn't understand why he operated under so many Pompeo-imposed constraints.

We next discussed what would happen in the negotiations. I explained why a "conditions-based" withdrawal, linked to US forces' going to zero, was inherently unlikely to see the conditions actually met. We could repeat the phrase "conditions based" all we wanted, but in reality, this agreement would be regarded as pulling up stakes and getting out (which Trump probably would have preferred, even though none of the rest of us did), with all the attendant chaos that would likely follow. Khalilzad understood but said this was the best we could do. My strong personal opinion was that I was still prepared to reduce forces to some extent without any deal (albeit unhappily, because while those levels previously briefed to Trump would be the best we could get from him, I remained convinced they were too low). Nonetheless, Khalilzad said he still thought Trump and certainly Pompeo wanted a signed document, period. Always hoping for the best, I asked Khalilzad to stay in touch once he got back to the negotiations.

At a lunch later that day with Esper and me, Pompeo said he read Trump as being "uneasy," which was not far from my own take. Trump didn't want to stop the negotiations, but he was clearly worried he was exposing himself to more political risks than he had anticipated, and perhaps for no good reason. A few days later, on August 27, Pompeo reached me in Kiev to say Khalilzad had everything wrapped up and expected to bring back the final documents. Interestingly, he thought

Trump was leaning toward my option of reducing forces to the counterterrorism-mission level (8,600, which even Trump was now using in public)[6] without signing the deal. Pompeo thought Trump appreciated how devastating it would be to see the "zero" level in writing, especially with all the conditions-based language somewhere out in the weeds, which was certainly my analysis, and what I had argued as strenuously as I could at Bedminster. As to whether the military could live without the "protection" of a deal, Pompeo said he thought the US commander would prefer a deal but could live with it either way. That clinched it for me. Trump also said in a radio interview with Fox's Brian Kilmeade, "We're going to keep a presence there. We're reducing that presence very substantially, and we're always going to have a presence. We're going to have high intelligence . . . But we're bringing it down—if the deal happens. I don't know that it's going to happen . . . You know my attitude on those things, Brian."[7] On August 29, I called Pompeo from my plane on the way to Warsaw, and he said his phone had lit up with NATO foreign ministers and Stoltenberg as Trump made those remarks.

Later that day, because of Hurricane Dorian, Trump canceled his visit to Poland, saying Pence would instead lead our delegation. Therefore, what turned out to be a key meeting on Afghanistan took place on Friday, August 30, with Pence linked up from the outside; Khalilzad connected from Doha, I think; yours truly participating via videoconference from Warsaw; and all the other attendees in the Sit Room, including Kupperman, who later gave me the mood in the room. We were scheduled to cover not just Afghanistan but also Ukraine, so there was a lot riding on this call, which did not actually begin until eight forty-five p.m. Warsaw time. This was a fine irony since the ever-diligent *Washington Post* was about to publish (and did) a story saying I was excluded from key Afghanistan meetings. (These people were a piece of work.) The initial discussion sounded much like the one in Bedminster, with Trump opining, "The Taliban just want their land back," and confusing President Ghani with former President Karzai and their respective net worths.

"Would you sign it, John?" Trump then asked, and I said, "I would not, Mr. President." I explained again my reasons why Trump should just go down to 8,600 service members, plus associated and coalition forces, if that's what he wanted to do, and then wait and await further developments, such as the Afghan elections. There was no way to trust the Taliban and no enforcement mechanism. This was not a New York real estate deal. Khalilzad then explained this was the deal Trump had said he wanted. Esper said he thought I made a lot of good points, but the Defense Department wanted the deal, because after all it was "conditions based." Trump posed what was always his key question: "How bad will this deal make me look? The Democrats would trash a great agreement." Esper suggested bringing in Hill leaders for consultations. Trump asked, "Is this agreement salable?" and I said I didn't think so, largely because, in my view, the Taliban wouldn't adhere to it and everyone knew it.

Then Trump blew the whole meeting away by saying, "I want to speak to the Taliban. Let them come to Washington." I could not have been happier that I was in a secure room deep in Eastern Europe rather than in the Sit Room when I heard that statement. Trump asked Pence what he thought, and Pence replied carefully, "We should reflect before we make that decision. They have abused and oppressed their people. Have they actually changed?" Trump then referred to Billy Graham's grandson, a major who had served in Afghanistan, who said, "We took their land." "Why is he only a major?" Trump asked Dunford. "He's good-looking, right from central casting." We then discussed how Congress would react to a US commitment to withdrawing our troops completely and what we were going to do with the duly-elected Afghan government, whatever Trump's views on Ghani.

Trump said, "I want Ghani here too, as well as the Taliban. Let's do it before it's signed. I want to meet before it's signed. Not a phone call."

"They'd love to come," said Khalilzad.

"Hey, John," Trump said to the screen in the Sit Room, "what do you think?"

My instinct was that this meeting could stop the pending deal dead in its tracks while the Taliban and the Afghan government wrestled with its implications, or at least delay it for a significant-enough period because of the time it would take for the Afghan parties to figure out their positions. That would give us time to find some other way to tank the deal. So, I said, "Okay by me, as long as they have to pass through the world's most powerful magnetometer before they meet with you."

"And chemical," said Trump, correctly.

Only Trump could conceive of a President of the United States meeting with these thugs, but by so doing, he was threatening the very deal Pompeo was pushing. "Maybe they will or they won't come," said Trump.

"We need to think it through," said Pompeo.

Pence asked, "Would you meet with Ghani first?"

"Only if Ghani knows I'm also going to sit down with the Taliban later," said Trump.

Trump's next thought was to start reducing troop levels immediately. No one supported the idea, although only Khalilzad spoke against it. Trump said, "Our attitude is, I'm not looking to get out. I will meet with Ghani first. This could be a home run. The Taliban would like to talk to Donald Trump to talk peace. We should say to the press that the President has agreed to a meeting, and he's looking forward to the meeting." I could sense even through my remote connection (and Kupperman agreed later) that Pompeo and others in the Sit Room were close to meltdown. Pence added, "To meet with Ghani and others in the Afghan government," and Trump agreed, "Yes, and before the meeting with the Taliban."

With that, Trump got up and started to leave. I all but yelled from Warsaw, "What about Ukraine?" and the meeting moved to that subject, which I will describe at length in the next chapter.

I concluded after the call that Trump had suggested meeting the Taliban because he was looking for alternatives to signing the Pompeo-Khalilzad deal. Obviously, he didn't fully agree with me that he shouldn't sign it, but he saw the clear political risks, if nothing else,

if he did sign it. Faced with that unhappy choice, he reached for something to avoid the dilemma and to find an option to put him in the
starring role. What could go wrong? The battle roared on.

Back in Washington, Kupperman heard from Dan Walsh, a Mulvaney deputy, on the Wednesday after Labor Day, that Trump wanted
the Taliban and Ghani meetings at Camp David. I had mistakenly put
the arrangements for this meeting out of mind, assuming the logistics
would be so complicated that delay was inevitable, not to mention the
chance Taliban leaders would smell a trap and reject the invitation
entirely. So, the idea things had progressed to the point where Camp
David was Trump's preference was truly disheartening. I didn't want
the meetings, and I didn't want the deal, and now it seemed we might
get both. The next day, September 5, Mulvaney came to my office just
before eight a.m. to tell me personally this was where things were
headed. He planned to go up to Camp David with Trump on Saturday
and suggested I come up on Sunday with the rest of the gang (Pompeo,
Esper, Dunford, and Khalilzad). Pompeo was handling travel arrangements for the Taliban, and the Qataris were flying in the Taliban thugs.
Also interesting was that Pompeo seemed to be backing away from
the deal, perhaps finally realizing there was political danger for him in
continuing to be the deal's strongest supporter.[8]

Walsh was apoplectic about the physical dangers of this exercise
and the lack of time to plan adequately, but Trump was determined
to proceed. He worried that too-intrusive security measures would
offend the Taliban's dignity. This precipitated chaotic early-morning
meetings among the rest of us to discuss how to protect Trump from
his "dignified" guests. One thing Mulvaney, Kupperman, Walsh, and I
all agreed on was that Pence was not going to Camp David, no matter
what. There is much I cannot describe here, but suffice it to say that,
with one exception, no one in the West Wing was enthusiastic about
this frolic.

Amid these conversations, we heard reports from Afghanistan
about a suicide bombing in Kabul, with ten killed, including one American and one Romanian service member, and several wounded.[9] It was
almost certainly a Taliban attack, although given Iran's recent activity

in Afghanistan, it could have been a joint effort. Mulvaney came into my office a little before nine a.m. to say, "If my Trump-o-meter reading is accurate, I think there's at least a twenty percent chance he will cancel [the Sunday meeting]. He [Trump] said immediately, 'We can't do the meeting,'" which sounded like more than 20 percent to me. I pointed out—not that it probably wasn't too late—that once Trump met with Ghani and the Taliban, he would own this deal beyond any chance of separating himself from it when things went wrong. In fact, commentary was already growing about how bad the underlying deal was, even though no one outside the Administration knew anything about a Taliban meeting, let alone one at Camp David. Thus, there was at least a chance to postpone things further, with the rising attendant possibility of killing the agreement entirely. Moreover, if the meeting proceeded, it would be on September 8, three days before the anniversary of the 9/11 attacks by al-Qaeda, to which the Taliban had given aid and comfort. How could anyone have missed that?

Mulvaney and I agreed to see Trump as early as possible, which turned out to be eleven forty-five, with Pompeo and others, including, for some unknown reason, Mnuchin. Almost before we sat down in the Oval, Trump said, "Don't take the meeting. Put out a statement that says, 'We had a meeting scheduled, but they killed one of our soldiers and nine others, so we canceled it.' There should be a cease-fire, or I don't want to negotiate. We should drop a bomb, hit 'em hard. If they can't do a cease-fire, I don't want an agreement." That pretty well settled that. Pompeo and I spoke after he was back at the State Department to see if his understanding was the same as mine, that not only the Taliban but also the Ghani meeting was canceled, and he agreed that's what he'd heard Trump say. We also concluded, as Mulvaney and I had, that we should make no statement about not meeting the Taliban. Much better to say nothing and hope the possibility never became public. There were media reports in Afghanistan already about Ghani's coming to Washington, but US press stories hadn't picked up the real reason; maybe it would stay that way.[10]

Of course not. On Saturday evening, September 7, with no warning, Trump tweeted:

Unbeknownst to almost everyone, the major Taliban leaders and, separately, the President of Afghanistan, were going to secretly meet with me at Camp David on Sunday. They were coming to the United States tonight. Unfortunately, in order to build false leverage, they admitted to . . .

. . . an attack in Kabul that killed one of our great great soldiers, and 11 other people. I immediately cancelled the meeting and called off peace negotiations. What kind of people would kill so many in order to seemingly strengthen their bargaining position? They didn't, they . . .

. . . only made it worse! If they cannot agree to a ceasefire during these very important peace talks, and would even kill 12 innocent people, then they probably don't have the power to negotiate a meaningful agreement anyway. How many more decades are they willing to fight?

He couldn't restrain himself. The Sunday media were flooded with accounts of the near-disaster of Camp David. The Taliban brashly claimed the US would "be harmed more than anyone" by canceling the meeting, which was totally false, but it also meant Afghanistan's September 28 presidential election would now go forward, which it did. Neither the incumbent, President Ghani, nor Afghanistan's Chief Executive, Abdullah Abdullah, received an absolute majority, necessitating a runoff, likely to be scheduled in 2020. Thus, unfortunately, rather than strengthening the government's hand, the runoff requirement introduced new political uncertainty. Nonetheless, the determination of Afghans who wanted an elected government rather than theocratic rule remained strong, which added at least some muscle to those determined to avoid a sellout to the Taliban.

•   •   •

This was effectively the last of my involvement in Afghanistan. Since I resigned, Trump resumed talks with the Taliban, which were just as detrimental to the United States as before. Combined, however, with the October withdrawal debacle in Syria, a clear unforced error by Trump personally, political opposition to surrendering in Afghanistan grew stronger. Nonetheless, on Saturday, February 29, 2020, the United States and the Taliban signed an agreement that, in my view, looked very much like the agreement that had come unstuck in September. This still being the Twitter presidency, I tweeted my opposition that morning: "Signing this agreement with Taliban is an unacceptable risk to America's civilian population. This is an Obama-style deal. Legitimizing the Taliban sends the wrong signal to ISIS and al Qaeda terrorists, and to America's enemies generally." Trump responded in typical fashion at a press conference a few hours later, saying of me, "He had his chance; he didn't do it."[11] The preceding chapter demonstrates, to the contrary, that this Afghanistan deal is entirely Trump's. Time will prove who is right, and the full effects of the deal may not become apparent until after Trump leaves office. But there should be no mistaking this reality: Trump will be responsible for the consequences, politically and militarily.

CHAPTER 14

THE END OF THE IDYLL

Ukraine seems an unlikely place as a battleground to imperil an American presidency, but that is exactly what happened in 2019, exploding literally just days after I resigned. My timing couldn't have been better. Not only was I a participant in and witness to much of the debacle as it unfolded, but I also seemed poised, for good or ill, to figure in only the fourth serious effort in American history to impeach a President. Throughout my West Wing tenure, Trump wanted to do what he wanted to do, based on what he knew and what he saw as his own best personal interests. And in Ukraine, he seemed finally able to have it all.

Ukraine is under intense Russian political and economic pressure. In 2014, Moscow orchestrated the illegitimate annexation of Crimea after intervening militarily, the first change in European borders due to military force since 1945. Russian troops remained deployed across the Donbas region in eastern Ukraine, supporting and in fact directing separatist forces there. This major Russian-American dispute proves that failing to act earlier to bring Ukraine into NATO left this large, critically important country vulnerable to Putin's effort to reestablish Russian hegemony within the space of the former Soviet Union. At NATO's April 2008 Bucharest Summit, the Bush 43 Administration tried to put Georgia and Ukraine on a path to NATO membership, which the Europeans, especially Germany and France, opposed. The tragic consequences were made plain that August, when Russian troops invaded Georgia, effectively placing two provinces under Moscow's control, which remain so to this day. Ukraine's suffering began later, but the pattern was the same. Western sanctions followed, but

Russia neither withdrew nor modified its belligerent behavior in any substantial way during the Obama Administration, sensing the palpable weakness Obama projected globally.

Trump inherited this debacle, but he paid very little attention to it in his first two years in office, at least officially. In 2017, Tillerson appointed Kurt Volker, a former Foreign Service officer I knew, as Special Representative for Ukraine Negotiations. My first meeting with Volker in this capacity came on May 10, 2018, when he described his role and priorities. He was then advocating a "nonrecognition policy" on Russia's annexation of Crimea and its military presence in the Donbas, along their border. Throughout the remainder of my White House tenure, Volker was a regular visitor, keeping me posted on his efforts. I found him professional and helpful as I engaged with my European counterparts on Ukraine and related issues.

My first major encounter with Ukraine itself in the Trump Administration came in 2018 when I flew to Kiev to celebrate the August 24 anniversary of Ukraine's 1991 declaration of independence from the Soviet Union. Jim Mattis had attended this ceremony in 2017, feeling as I did the importance of demonstrating US resolve in support of Ukraine's continued independence and viability. Given Russia's unilateral annexation of Crimea, plus the obvious Russian assistance to and control over "opposition" forces in eastern Ukraine, this concern was far from hypothetical.

I came from Geneva the night before, after meetings on US-Russian issues with Nikolai Patrushev, my Russian counterpart, where I happily told them I was flying from Switzerland to Ukraine for the celebrations. Smiles all around. Whether by Russian intention or not, Ukraine was one of the last issues on the agenda with Patrushev, and we barely had time for it before we both left the US mission for the Geneva airport. In lieu of a real discussion, but to underscore nonetheless how strongly we felt about Ukraine, I said, "I incorporate herewith everything we have said before, and we still mean it!" Patrushev didn't say much of anything.

On August 24, I had a working breakfast with Prime Minister Volodymyr Groysman on Ukraine's economy and Russia's increasing efforts to interfere in the upcoming 2019 elections. Groysman argued that Ukraine was a line for Putin, and if he could cross it successfully, he would establish impunity for his actions throughout Europe and globally, which posed entirely legitimate concerns for the United States.[1] Marie Yovanovitch, our Ambassador to Ukraine, and several embassy staffers also attended the breakfast and were with me pretty much throughout the entire day. After breakfast, we went to the reviewing stand for the parade on Khreshchatyk Boulevard where the 2013–14 Euromaidan demonstrations had taken place, forcing out the pro-Russian Yanukovych regime. I stood on the platform with President Petro Poroshenko and eight or ten members of his government, next to Prosecutor General Yuriy Lutsenko, ironical in light of future developments. Though reminiscent of May Day pageantry in Moscow's Red Square during the Cold War, the parade was politically the opposite. Poroshenko's speech was viscerally anti-Russian, and his loudest applause line came when he vowed to establish an autocephalous (independent from Moscow) Ukrainian Orthodox church patriarchate.

During the parade, Poroshenko thanked me several times for US-supplied weapons systems and equipment as they passed by, and for the Tennessee National Guard unit that marched with other NATO troops deployed to Ukraine to train its military. Afterward, we rode to the Mariinsky Palace, originally built for Catherine the Great and recently restored by Poroshenko's wife, shortly to be the venue for a large reception Poroshenko was hosting. There, at noon, I met with Poroshenko, Foreign Minister Pavlo Klimkin, National Security Advisor Kostya Yeliseyev, and others. We discussed Ukraine's security posture, particularly vis-à-vis Russia and the various threats it posed, not just militarily, but also Moscow's efforts to subvert Ukraine's 2019 elections. Poroshenko wanted to buy more US weapons, and we elaborated our worries about Ukrainian companies' selling advanced airplane engine designs to China, concerns that only grew more acute over the year before my next visit to Kiev.

After the meeting, Poroshenko took me to another room for a one-on-one, where he asked the US to endorse his reelection campaign. He also asked for a number of things that I addressed, allowing me to slide past the endorsement request without being too rude when I said no. What Poroshenko really wanted was for America to sanction Igor Kolomoisky, a Ukrainian oligarch backing Yulia Tymoshenko, who was, at least at this point, Poroshenko's main competition in the 2019 elections. Although it didn't come up in this conversation, Kolomoisky was also backing Volodymyr Zelensky, then leading the polls but not regarded as serious, because, after all, he was just an actor . . . (For liberal readers, that's a joke. Ronald Reagan, one of America's greatest Presidents, was also an actor.) I told Poroshenko if he had evidence on Kolomoisky, he should send it to the Justice Department. I filled Yovanovitch in on this conversation as we rode to the next event, a press conference with Ukrainian media.

The last meeting was a two forty-five p.m. coffee at Yovanovitch's official residence with various leaders in Parliament, including Tymoshenko, whom I had met in the Bush 43 Administration and later. The State Department didn't want me to meet with Tymoshenko separately because they thought she was too close to Russia, although typical of the department's methods, that's not how they put it. This joint meeting was the closest I could get to a separate meeting, not that it mattered, because Tymoshenko, as the only presidential candidate among the parliamentary leaders, dominated the conversation, not unexpectedly. She reminded me she had read my book *Surrender Is Not an Option*, always a good way to get an author's attention, and mentioned Senator Kyl's advice to keep moving and keep firing, like a big gray battleship. Well prepared. At this point, only Zelensky was doing well in the polls, with all the other candidates aiming to finish among the top two in the first round, thus getting into the expected runoff. After this meeting, we headed for the airport and then back to Andrews.

Not for nearly three months did I again have much involvement in matters Ukrainian, until the early afternoon of Sunday, November 25, when I received word of an incident at sea between Russia and Ukraine. Ukrainian warships and an accompanying tugboat had tried to enter the Sea of Azov through the Kerch Strait, the narrow body of water separating the Crimean Peninsula from Russia proper, and over which Russia had recently built a bridge. Our initial information was that a Russian naval vessel had rammed a Ukrainian ship, but later information indicated that Russians had fired what were perhaps intended as warning shots, one or more of which hit the Ukrainian ships. None of this could be accidental. The Russians seized all three Ukrainian ships and their crews (with some of them reportedly injured), although it was not clear in whose waters the ships were when they were taken. Most of this information came through our Kiev embassy, so we were hearing Ukraine's side of the story, at least initially.

Because escalation was possible, I decided to call Trump. I wanted to be sure he knew that we were monitoring the situation, in case journalists started asking questions. His first response was "What are the Europeans doing about this?" the answer to which, of course, was "Nothing," the same as we were doing. (The European Union did later put out a statement, but it was the usual mush.) Trump's first thought was that Ukraine had been provocative, which was at least possible, given the impending presidential elections. But it was also possible the Russians were looking for a confrontation, perhaps trying in some way to legitimize their "annexation" of Crimea, which very few other countries recognized. Trump wasn't interested in doing anything quickly, even if Russia was entirely in the wrong. By the evening, Poroshenko appeared ready to declare martial law, which seemed a surprising reaction to an incident at sea. The State Department wanted to issue a strong anti-Russia statement, which I blocked because of what Trump had said a few hours earlier. Moreover, there was every prospect of a UN Security Council meeting Monday, ironically called by Russia, during which there would obviously be a US statement, giving us more time to obtain the facts.

Germany's Jan Hecker called me at seven thirty a.m. Monday morning, and the first issue he raised was the Kerch Strait incident. The Germans were cautious, and my impression was that Hecker believed that Poroshenko was not at all unhappy about what happened because of the potential political benefits he foresaw; he would campaign as the strong anti-Russia candidate, Hecker speculated, noting that the

Rada was scheduled to vote in about two and a half hours on a bill proposed by Poroshenko declaring martial law for sixty days. The bill would activate one hundred thousand reservists for training, and also preclude any political activity while in force. Since another Ukrainian law required there be at least ninety days of campaigning immediately prior to a national election, Poroshenko's bill would guarantee the March 31 elections would be pushed back, something surely to his benefit, given his low opinion-poll numbers.[2] Germany opposed postponing the elections, said Hecker; so far, Ukraine and Russia had given competing accounts of the episode, but the facts remained unclear. Merkel was scheduled to speak with Poroshenko imminently, and indeed, as we were speaking, Hecker was called to Merkel's office to listen in, saying he would phone again when it was over.[3]

In the meantime, Pompeo told me he had just spoken with Trump about the briefing he and Mattis were due to give Congress in a few days regarding legislation barring aid to Saudi Arabia related to the Yemen war. During that call, Trump raised the Kerch Strait issue, saying Poroshenko might have provoked something for political purposes. "Let the Europeans own this," said Trump, "I don't want to own it." Pompeo did not raise with Trump State's Sunday request for a White House statement, but he did tell him his staff was trying to water down Nikki Haley's draft Security Council remarks, where she was up in arms against Moscow over the incident. (She was taking advantage of the very few camera appearances left as her time in New York dwindled down.) Pompeo told Trump he and I would make sure Haley followed his instructions. I suggested we treat Haley's prospective statement as the vehicle to convey the definitive US view rather than having several, and he agreed. Pompeo said he would call Haley and tell her to "color within the lines," which sounded right. I then called Trump and told him what Pompeo and I had decided regarding Haley's statement, which he liked, and I also briefed him on Germany's reaction and the Ukrainian martial-law legislation.

While I was waiting for Hecker to call back, I tried to reach Sedwill in London and Étienne in Paris to see how they assessed the situation. Étienne was not in Paris, but Sedwill called back fairly quickly, and we compared notes on what we knew. Sedwill had already heard that Canada, still Chairman of the G7 until the end of 2018, was preparing a draft statement, although neither of us had seen it yet. I told Sedwill what Trump had said over the last twenty-four hours so the Brits could factor it in.[4]

At 11:05, Pompeo called, bouncing off the walls. He said he had called Haley, told her what we had agreed, and that she had also agreed. Then, as he learned subsequently, she immediately called Trump to complain. She read Trump a completely different set of talking points, which Trump accepted. Pompeo wanted a conference call with her and me to get everyone on the same page, but before the call could be arranged, Trump called Pompeo to say Haley's talking points were fine and that he didn't want to be hammered in the press for being too soft. Pompeo and I were perfectly happy to have a stronger statement we could attribute to Trump, but we both knew that Haley was motivated by *her* desire not to get hammered in the press. Shortly thereafter, in the Oval for the regular intelligence briefing, Trump said to me, "You understand the [Haley] statement was a little tougher than I said, but that's okay. You probably wanted it tougher anyway, right?" I said I was fine with the statement, adding that we had called on Russia to release the Ukrainian ships and crews, when Trump interjected, "Don't call for the release of the crews. If they don't do it, it looks like the Iran hostage thing. I don't want that." I said I would tell Haley, but by the time I got out of the Oval, she had already made her remarks. Many other countries said the same thing, so I didn't think we would stand out in a way Trump wouldn't like. In any case, the incident provoked Trump to recount yet again one of his favorite stories, involving his first phone call with Merkel, when she asked what he was going to do about Ukraine, and he had replied by asking her what *she* was going to do about Ukraine.

When Pompeo and I reviewed all this subsequently, it was plain that we were once again seeing how Haley operated when Tillerson was Secretary of State: as a free electron. That would change in a month with her departure, and Pompeo and I saw it exactly the same, that her successor, whoever it turned out to be, would not operate that way. "Light as a feather," as Pompeo described her in a subsequent conversation.

Hecker called at one thirty to finish our conversation and reported that at a just-concluded meeting involving representatives of the Ukraine, Russia, France, and Germany, Russia had said the Ukrainian ships failed to give the required notice for transiting a temporary exclusion zone (permissible under international law for purposes such as military exercises), which seemed ridiculous. In Merkel's conversation with Poroshenko, he said he had modified the martial-law bill pending in the Rada, reducing the period affected from sixty to thirty days, thus permitting the March elections to proceed as scheduled. This was progress, although martial law would help Poroshenko politically, and it would bear watching to see if the thirty-day period was later extended (it was not). Merkel was speaking to Putin in about an hour to urge de-escalation on both sides, specifically asking that Putin engage directly with Poroshenko.[5]

On the morning of November 28, I flew from Andrews to Rio de Janeiro to see newly elected Brazilian President Jair Bolsonaro before the Buenos Aires G20 meeting. I called Trump from the plane at about eight forty-five a.m., to ask if he had any further thoughts on the Putin bilateral scheduled at the G20, since Russia was still holding the Ukrainian ships and crews. Trump said he thought it would be terrible to meet with Putin in these circumstances, and that the press would only talk about the Ukraine issue. He said I should get a message to Putin explaining that he looked forward to meeting, but that Russia needed to release the sailors and ships first, so the meeting could focus on key issues and not Ukraine. I reached Patrushev in Moscow about two hours later to deliver Trump's message, and he said he would convey it immediately to President Putin, who he thought would definitely consider it. Even though he knew I knew the Russian position, he then repeated it to me at some length.

I landed in Brazil, at about eleven p.m. Rio time. Trump called again to say he would do the bilateral if Putin would announce, when it ended, that he was releasing the ships and crews, thus in effect giving Trump credit for springing them. Considering the time differences, I did not call Moscow. Moreover, changing our position at this point would make Trump look desperate for the meeting, which he probably was. The next morning, I spoke with our Moscow Deputy Chief of Mission Anthony Godfrey (Huntsman being away), who said the Russians were charging the crews with trespassing, not a good sign, to say the least. Patrushev reached me as I was in the air to Buenos Aires, saying he had a message he wanted me to convey from Putin to Trump, namely, that because of the "illegal trespassing" of Russia's border, a criminal case, including investigative actions, has been launched. The Russians claimed that, judging by documents they had seized from the ships and the information provided by the crews, it was a military provocation, an operation guided and controlled by the Ukraine security services. Therefore, said Patrushev, in accordance with Russian legal procedures, the formalities were now under way, so releasing the ships and crews was impossible.[6] He said he was convinced we would do the same, analogizing Moscow's actions to Trump's policies along the Mexican border. There followed a lecture on our actions in recent weeks on that subject, and more.

There was little room to mistake Patrushev's message, but I asked how long proceedings against the Ukrainian crews might take. He said he couldn't give me an answer but would find out and let me know. I said I would speak to Trump and see whether there would still be a bilateral meeting. Trump, it turned out, was running late (as usual), so I didn't reach him on Air Force One until 11:20 a.m. Washington time. I described what Patrushev had relayed from Putin, which I took to be "a very hard no." "What would you do?" Trump asked, and I said I would cancel the meeting. Trump immediately agreed, saying, "We can't give anything away." A tweet to that effect went out shortly thereafter, before I could get back to Patrushev, who declined my call to show how irritated they were.

In Buenos Aires, Putin's diplomatic advisor Yuri Ushakov and I met several times to see if there was any way to have a Putin-Trump meeting, which we concluded was not possible, given the two sides' respective public positions on the Kerch Strait incident. Instead, Trump spoke to Putin at the G20 leaders' dinner, with no other Americans around other than the First Lady. They used Putin's interpreter, and the US advance man trailing the President couldn't overhear the conversation. The Russians didn't put anything about the meeting in their press, and Trump related to me the next morning he had essentially told Putin he didn't see how the two of them could meet at any length until the Kerch Strait incident was resolved and the ships and crews returned to Ukraine, which didn't seem likely for some time. In a later Trump-Merkel bilateral, Trump implied that a Ukrainian President sympathetic to Russia could help avoid a third world war. The Russians would have loved that.

Ukraine remained basically quiet as we awaited their first round of presidential elections on March 31, but other matters began coming to the fore. Trump had complained about our Ambassador Yovanovitch, for some time, noting to me on March 21 during a telephone call covering a number of subjects that she was "bad-mouthing us like crazy" and that her only concern was LGBTQ matters. "She is saying bad shit about me and about you," he added, saying he wanted her fired "today." I said I would call Pompeo, who was in the Middle East; I tried several times to reach him but didn't because of meeting schedules and time-zone differences. After Principals Committees later that afternoon, I pulled Deputy Secretary of State John Sullivan aside to convey Trump's direction, so he could inform Pompeo. Sullivan knew Trump wanted Yovanovitch fired, so he understood that this repetition of Trump's instruction was serious.

A few days later, on March 25, Trump called me to the Oval, but I found him in his small dining room with Rudy Giuliani and Jay Sekulow (another of his private attorneys), obviously enjoying discussing the reaction to Mueller's report on his Russia investigation. At this meeting, I learned Giuliani was the source of the stories about Yovanovitch, who he said was being protected by a Deputy Assistant Secretary in State's European bureau, George Kent (I don't think Giuliani knew Kent's job title accurately; Pompeo clarified it for me later). Trump again said Yovanovitch should be fired immediately. I reached Pompeo by phone in the late afternoon to relay this latest news, now with the update that it came from Giuliani. Pompeo said he had spoken with Giuliani before, and there were no facts supporting any of his allegations, although Pompeo didn't doubt that, like 90 percent of the Foreign Service, Yovanovitch probably voted for Clinton. He said she was trying to reduce corruption in Ukraine and may well have been going after some of Giuliani's clients. Pompeo said he would call Giuliani again and then speak to Trump. The next morning, I called Trump about several matters and asked if he and Pompeo had spoken on Yovanovitch. They had not, but he repeated he was "tired of her bad-mouthing us" and her saying he would be impeached and the like. "Really bad," said Trump. I called Pompeo about nine forty-five a.m. to report this conversation. He again protested that Giuliani's allegations simply weren't true and said he would call Trump. I mentioned this to Trump later in the day, just so he knew he wasn't being ignored.

Whether or not Giuliani's importuning was related to Ukraine's impending election, on Sunday, March 31, with the returns fully counted, Zelensky finished first, Poroshenko second, putting them in the April 21 runoff. Shortly thereafter, I discussed with France's Étienne and Germany's Hecker how we would all proceed. Although we had earlier agreed to keep hands off entirely, Hecker said Germany was inviting Poroshenko to Berlin, despite risking a backlash from Ukraine if Zelensky won the runoff. Étienne told me that, even before the runoff, France had invited both Poroshenko and Zelensky to Paris, which was at least more even-handed. None of us knew much about Zelensky's fitness to be President, and there were concerns about how close he was to the oligarch Kolomoisky, which might raise corruption issues. Worrisome allegations were swirling around, and prudence indicated a hands-off approach. The German and French change of heart—their eagerness to engage—struck me as misguided. There was no disagreement Zelensky was headed into the runoff with a big lead in the polls, based largely on his opposition to Ukraine's substantial corruption problem.

Zelensky's support held, and on Easter Sunday, April 21, he defeated Poroshenko with 73 percent of the vote. We had a "call package" ready for Trump if he decided to congratulate Zelensky that day, which he did around four thirty p.m. our time. I briefed Trump in advance of the call that Zelensky might invite him to his inauguration (the date for which had not yet been officially set), and Trump said he would send Pence instead. The call was brief, less than five minutes, but very warm, with Trump opening, "I want to congratulate you on a job well done." Zelensky replied, "Thank you so very much," and said he appreciated the congratulations, adding, "We had you as a great example." Trump said he had many friends who knew Zelensky and liked him, adding, "I have no doubt you will be a fantastic President." Zelensky did invite Trump to his inaugural, and Trump responded he would "look at the date" and said, "We'll get you a great representative for the United States on the great day." Trump also invited Zelensky to the White House, saying, "We're with you all the way." Zelensky pushed for Trump to visit, saying Ukraine was a great country with nice people, good food, and so on. Trump said that, as former owner of the Miss Universe Pageant, he knew that Ukraine was always well represented. Zelensky signed off, saying in English, "I will do big practice in English" (so he could speak it when they met). Trump responded, "I'm very impressed. I couldn't do that in your language."

A couple of days later, April 23, I was called to the Oval to find Trump and Mulvaney on the phone, discussing Yovanovitch again with Giuliani, who was still pressing for her removal. He had spun Trump up with the "news" that she had spoken to President-Elect Zelensky to tell him Trump himself wanted certain investigations by Ukrainian prosecutors stopped. In Giuliani's mind, Yovanovitch was protecting Hillary Clinton, whose campaign was purportedly the subject of Ukrainian criminal investigations, and there was some connection with Joe Biden's son Hunter in there as well. Giuliani was delivering what was all third-or-fourth-degree hearsay; he offered no evidence on the call for his allegations. I said I had spoken with Pompeo on Yovanovitch and would check with him again. Trump couldn't believe Pompeo hadn't fired Yovanovitch yet, and that's what he wanted, no ifs, ands, or buts. Trump said I should find out immediately from Pompeo what was happening, and I should call Zelensky to make it clear Yovanovitch did not speak for the Administration. Of course, since we didn't really know what she had said, it was unclear what I should tell Zelensky to ignore.

I went back to my office and reached Pompeo about four p.m. He said he had already curtailed Yovanovitch from either late November or early December back to June 1, and some time before had so informed Trump, who didn't object. Pompeo wanted to leave it at that. I told him the mood was pretty volcanic because she wasn't gone entirely, which was met with a groan. He again mentioned his previous conversations with Giuliani, who couldn't describe in any detail what had supposedly happened but who had raised it constantly with Trump over the past several months. But Pompeo said also that, in looking at the embassy, the State Department now had a pile of materials they were sending over to Justice that implicated Yovanovitch and her predecessor in some unnamed and undescribed activity that might well be criminal. Pompeo closed by saying that he would order her back to Washington that night. With Yovanovitch ordered home, there was no point in calling Zelensky (which I hadn't wanted to do anyway), so I did not.

I briefed Eisenberg on this latest Yovanovitch development. A bit later, Mulvaney came to my office with Cipollone and Emmet Flood, a White House Counsel's office attorney handling the Mueller investigation. I raised with them something I had asked about before, with either Cipollone or Eisenberg: whether Giuliani had ethical problems under the lawyers' Code of Professional Responsibility for using one attorney-client relationship to advance the interests of another client, a dynamic that I thought might be at work in his dealings on behalf of Trump. I said I thought it was an ethical violation to do so, but I was in the minority; the others did agree it was "slimy." So much for legal ethics.

Earlier that day, I had gone over to Justice to have lunch with Bill Barr, whom I had known since the mid-1980s, before the Bush 41 Administration. Barr had become Attorney General (again) in mid-February, and we had been trying since then to find a convenient date to get together and talk about life in the Trump Administration. In particular,

I wanted to raise my determination to have better coordination when national security interests and prosecutorial equities intersected and might conflict. We needed conscious decisions on US priorities in such events, rather than settling them at random. As someone deeply interested in security issues, Barr was completely amenable to better working relations among the affected departments and agencies.

Specifically, however, I also wanted to brief him on Trump's penchant to, in effect, give personal favors to dictators he liked, such as the criminal cases of Halkbank, ZTE, potentially Huawei, and who knew what else. Barr said he was very worried about the appearances Trump was creating, especially his remarks on Halkbank to Erdogan in Buenos Aires at the G20 meeting, what he said to Xi Jinping on ZTE, and other exchanges. I had had essentially this same conversation with Cipollone and Eisenberg for about an hour on January 22, shortly after Cipollone replaced McGahn on December 10, 2018. At that time, we discussed Halkbank, ZTE, a Turkish agent Israel had arrested (and Trump had gotten released during his July stay at Turnberry in calls with Netanyahu), the question whether to lift US sanctions against Russian oligarch Oleg Deripaska (which was done in early April), Huawei, the implications for China trade negotiations, Trump's personal legal travails, and other issues. I had no doubt of the President's constitutional authority to prioritize among conflicting Executive Branch responsibilities, such as law enforcement and national security. Nonetheless, in the febrile Washington atmosphere caused by the Russia collusion allegations, it wasn't hard to see politically how all this would be characterized. Whether there was anything even more troubling beneath the surface, none of us knew. Cipollone had not had any previous briefing on these issues, and he was plainly stunned at Trump's approach to law enforcement, or lack thereof.

Even earlier, on December 10, prompted by Trump's Christmas party remarks on Huawei and the Uighurs, I spoke to Pompeo on these problems, and also on questions about the settlements of some of Trump's personal legal issues. The pattern looked like obstruction of justice as a way of life, which we couldn't accept. Moreover, leniency for Chinese firms violating US sanctions, cheating our companies, or endangering our telecom infrastructure could only be described as appeasing our adversaries, totally contrary to our interests. Somewhere nearby was resignation territory, I said, which Pompeo agreed with. This didn't yet require drafting a resignation letter, but warning lights were flashing.

Trump called Putin on May 3, because, as he said with no apparent basis, Putin was "dying" to talk to him. In fact, Trump was "dying" to talk, having not had a real conversation with Putin since the Kerch Strait incident forced cancellation of their bilateral at the Buenos Aires G20. Although Trump had announced then that substantive meetings were off until the Ukrainian ships and crews were released, this call to Putin unceremoniously lifted that moratorium, which had lasted since late November, with Russia still holding them. They discussed Ukraine briefly but to no great effect. Putin wondered whether Igor Kolomoisky would get his Ukrainian assets back, given his financial support for Zelensky's successful campaign. Zelensky, said Putin, was quite well-known in Russia because of his television career, and he had lots of contacts there. However, Putin added that he had yet to manifest himself. He said he had not yet spoken with Zelensky because he was not yet the president, and because there was no final result yet. Whether Putin meant the fate of the existing Rada or whether Zelensky would call snap parliamentary elections was unclear.[7]

On May 8, the Ukraine pace began to quicken. At about one forty-five p.m., Trump called me to the Oval, where he was meeting with Giuliani, Mulvaney, Cipollone, and perhaps others. The subject was Ukraine, and Giuliani's desire to meet with President-Elect Zelensky to discuss his country's investigation of either Hillary Clinton's efforts to influence the 2016 campaign or something having to do with Hunter Biden and the 2020 election, or maybe both. In the various commentaries I heard on these subjects, they always seemed intermingled and confused, one reason I did not pay them much heed. Even after they became public, I could barely separate the strands of the multiple conspiracy theories at work. Trump was clear I was to call Zelensky and make sure Giuliani got his meeting in Kiev next week. Giuliani swore he had no clients involved, which I found hard to believe, but I still hoped to avoid getting into this mess. Yovanovitch's firing was already in the press, and a Giuliani visit to Ukraine would certainly find its way there as well. Giuliani also said he was after an official at State, last name of Kent, who Giuliani said was in league with George Soros and very hostile to Trump. I had heard the name before in connection with Yovanovitch but didn't know him from Adam.

I was happy to escape at about 1:55 and return to my office, where I promptly did *not* call Zelensky, hoping the whole thing might disappear. I had barely settled down at my desk before John Sullivan and Marc Short came charging in, saying Trump had dispatched them from the weekly trade meeting in the Roosevelt Room to talk about Kent. (I found these weekly trade meetings so chaotic I largely left them for Kupperman to attend, which punishment he didn't deserve, but life is hard.) Sullivan also barely knew who Kent was, but he described the scene in the Roosevelt Room, Trump talking to him in a loud whisper while Bob Lighthizer went through a series of charts on various trade issues, with Trump obviously not paying attention. After he finished speaking to Sullivan about Kent, Trump turned back to Lighthizer for a few seconds before saying in a loud voice to Sullivan, "Go talk to Bolton about Kent." He then said to Short, "Show him where John's office is." So, there they were. Short departed, and I explained to Sullivan the latest Ukraine conversation I had just had in the Oval, and asked him to talk to Pompeo as soon as he could. Pompeo was arriving back in Washington by nine the next morning, and Sullivan said he would brief him then.

The issue of Giuliani's trip to Ukraine percolated for a few days without a clear decision. Cipollone and Eisenberg came to see me on May 10, with Yovanovitch's firing having received more media coverage (although the mainstream press showed little interest), and with Giuliani on his own generating a fair amount of attention. In a *New York Times* interview published in print that morning,[8] he was quoted as saying, "We're not meddling in an election, we're meddling in an investigation, which we have a right to do . . . There's nothing illegal about it . . . Somebody could say it's improper. And this isn't foreign policy—I'm asking them to do an investigation that they're doing already and that other people are telling them to stop. And I'm going to give them reasons why they shouldn't stop it because that information will be very, very helpful to my client, and may turn out to be helpful to my government." The three of us agreed Giuliani couldn't be allowed to go to Ukraine, but the brouhaha also made it uncertain who from the Trump Administration could attend Zelensky's inauguration, given the adverse publicity it might receive.

Pence's participation therefore looked doubtful, complicated because the inauguration's exact date was still not set. Embassy Kiev was quite surprised on May 16 to hear that Ukraine's Rada had picked May 20, which didn't leave us much time to check schedules and choose the US delegation. By then, Trump had concluded Pence could not go, and Pompeo decided not to for his own reasons. By the end of the day on May 16, it looked like Energy Secretary Rick Perry would be the lead, which was justifiable because of the significant energy issues Ukraine posed, and the importance of Kiev-Washington cooperation in the face of Moscow's exploitation of energy resources throughout Central and Eastern Europe. US Ambassador to the European Union Gordon Sondland worked hard to be added to the US delegation, but because he had no legitimate reason to attend, I repeatedly deleted his name. Yet, in the end, he was on the delegation, because, we learned, Mulvaney had insisted. Why the Rada chose such an early inauguration was unclear, but our observers on the ground believed Poroshenko's party decided it was prepared to risk snap parliamentary elections, believing Zelensky could not possibly meet the expectations growing around him. That turned out to be a miscalculation by Poroshenko's advisors and a huge boost to Zelensky.

In fact, Zelensky's May 20 inauguration brought the further surprise that he was calling Poroshenko's bluff and scheduling early parliamentary elections. No exact date was set, but the voting was expected to be at some point in July. It also became increasingly plain, not only to me but to others as well, including Fiona Hill, the NSC Senior Director for Europe and Russia, that Trump completely accepted Giuliani's line that the "Russia collusion" narrative, invented by domestic US political adversaries, had been run through Ukraine. In other words, Trump was buying the idea that the Ukraine was actually responsible for carrying out Moscow's efforts to hack US elections. That clearly meant we wouldn't be doing anything nice for Ukraine any time soon, no matter how much it might help us forestall further Russian advances there.

On May 22, after addressing the Coast Guard Academy's graduation ceremony in New London, Connecticut, I left Andrews for Japan, for final preparations for Trump's state visit, the first under the new Emperor Naruhito. Two days later, from Tokyo, I spoke with Kupperman, who had attended Trump's debriefing earlier that day (it was still May 23 in Washington when we spoke) from our delegation to Zelensky's inaugural: Perry, Sondland, Volker, and Senator Ron Johnson. It was a classic. "I don't want to have any fucking thing to do with Ukraine," said Trump, per Kupperman. "They fucking attacked me. I can't understand why. Ask Joe diGenova, he knows all about it. They tried to fuck me. They're corrupt. I'm not fucking with them." All this, he said, pertained to the Clinton campaign's efforts, aided by Hunter Biden, to harm Trump in 2016 and 2020.

Volker tried to intervene to say something pertinent about Ukraine, and Trump replied, "I don't give a shit."

Perry said we couldn't allow a failed state, presumably a Ukraine where effective government had broken down, and Trump said, "Talk to Rudy and Joe."

"Give me ninety days," Perry tried again, but Trump interrupted, saying, "Ukraine tried to take me down. I'm not fucking interested in helping them," although he relented to say Zelensky could visit him in the White House, but only if he was told how Trump felt in the matter. "I want the fucking DNC server," said Trump, returning to the fray, adding, "Okay, you can have ninety days. But I have no fucking interest in meeting with him." Afterward, Perry and Kupperman agreed Zelensky should not be invited until after the July Rada elections, to see if he had any chance of governing effectively. (Several nearby leaders, such as Hungary's Viktor Orban, thought Zelensky's prospects were grim, which was not inconsistent with Putin's standoffish views.) There were also rumors Perry was leaving the Administration in the near future, so the "ninety day" figure squared with the notion he wanted the time to achieve something in Ukraine. Senator Johnson told me several weeks later, regarding this Trump meeting, "I was pretty shocked by the President's response." I thought it sounded like just another day at the office.

Nonetheless, in the following weeks, Sondland, who apparently didn't have enough to do dealing with the European Union at its Brussels headquarters, kept pushing for an early Zelensky visit to Washington. Pompeo didn't care much one way or the other. It was clear he had no appetite for reining Sondland in, despite his normal insistence that Ambassadors reported to him (which they did, usually through Assistant Secretaries), and that he didn't want them going around him to the President. This was par for the course in Pompeo's management of the State Department: conflict avoidance. Trump resolved the visit issue just before leaving for the United Kingdom in June by saying not until the fall, the right outcome in my view. Key Europeans also showed caution on Zelensky's prospects. Both German Foreign Minister Heiko Maas and French Foreign Minister Jean-Yves Le Drian visited Zelensky in Kiev in late May but formed no definite conclusions. When Trump met with French President Macron on June 6, Macron seemed to be warming to Zelensky, as was Merkel when Trump met with her at the Osaka G20. However, based on Trump's recent call with Putin, there was no sign Putin was prepared for serious discussions about Crimea or the Donbas, certainly not before the Rada elections.

The next discussion with Trump on Ukraine that I recall was not until June 25. I was in Israel to meet Netanyahu and for a trilateral meeting with Patrushev and Ben-Shabbat, but I attended an NSC meeting via videoconferencing from our former Jerusalem consulate, near the David Citadel Hotel, where I was staying. The meeting, held in Washington in the Sit Room with the usual crew attending, was to discuss other matters, but at one point, Trump riffed on Nord Stream II, complaining about "our great European allies" and Germany's low spending on defense: "Angela [Merkel] saying she'd be there [two percent of GDP] by 2030, remember that, John," he said to the screen in the Sit Room, where I was visible from Israel.[9] "I listen to my advisors despite what people think," Trump laughed (so did I), and then he was off again in full roar: "Everyone screws us on trade. This is going to be the best June in years. The tariffs have a lot of money pouring in." Then it was off to Ukraine and a $250 million assistance program for weapons purchases. "Did you approve it, John?" I said it was a congressional earmark that the Defense Department was proceeding with. "How stupid is this?" Trump asked. "Germany doesn't spend on neighboring countries. Angela says, 'We don't spend because it's a neighboring country.'[10] John, do you agree on Ukraine?" I didn't answer directly, worrying about what had suddenly made Trump pay attention to this particular military assistance. Instead, I suggested that Esper raise all these questions about NATO and Ukraine burden-sharing at the NATO Defense Ministers' meeting scheduled in the coming days. This was likely the first time I heard security assistance to Ukraine called into question, but the real issue was how Trump found out about it, and who came up with the idea to use it as leverage against Zelensky and his new government. I never learned the answers to these questions, but Mulvaney, in his continuing capacity as the Director of the Office of Management and Budget, was certainly one possible source. The key point that I carried away from this conversation was that the Ukraine security assistance was at risk of being swallowed by the Ukraine fantasy conspiracy theories.

On July 10, I met in my office with my Ukrainian counterpart, Oleksandr Danylyuk, the new Secretary of their National Security and Defense Council. Danylyuk was a pro-Western reformer. Formerly Poroshenko's Finance Minister, he had resigned because he didn't believe Poroshenko's government was committed to real reform.[11] Perry, Sondland, and Volker all asked to attend (did Sondland spend any time in Brussels?), and it was clear immediately that the three of them were trying to squeeze me into inviting Zelensky to the White House before the July parliamentary elections. Since I knew, and they should have realized after their May 23 Oval Office meeting with Trump, that he didn't want to have anything to do with Ukrainians of any stripe (influenced, wrongly, by the nonsense Giuliani had been feeding him), I didn't play along. Danylyuk obviously wanted a closer relationship with us, which I strongly supported and which was much easier to talk about. Danylyuk was surprised and uncomfortable that I didn't readily agree to a Zelensky visit, which came from the incessant boosterism of the others in the meeting, but I wasn't about to explain to foreigners that the three of them were driving outside their lanes. The more I resisted, the more Sondland pushed, getting into Giuliani territory I saw as out of bounds.

In the later congressional hearings, Fiona Hill accurately testified that after the meeting and a picture with Danylyuk and the hordes of US officials at the meeting, I told her to get into a meeting Sondland held on his own in the Ward Room with the Ukrainians and others from the meeting in my office. I was stunned at the simplemindedness of pressing for a face-to-face Trump-Zelensky meeting where the "Giuliani issues" could be resolved, an approach it appeared Mulvaney shared from his frequent meetings with Sondland. I told her to take this whole matter to the White House Counsel's office; she quoted me accurately as saying, "I am not part of whatever drug deal Sondland and Mulvaney are cooking up." I thought the whole affair was bad policy, questionable legally, and unacceptable as presidential behavior. Was it a factor in my later resignation? Yes, but as one of many "straws" that contributed to my departure. Earlier, Hill testified, I had called Giuliani "a hand grenade who's going to blow everybody up," which still sounds right today. Perry and Sondland in particular kept pushing, including on Danylyuk to press me at least for a Trump-Zelensky phone call before the Rada elections. I continued to fend them off, fearing the call could backfire.

I was off to Japan and South Korea on Saturday morning, July 20, the day before the parliamentary elections, to discuss the base-cost issues. I called Kupperman from the air, now that it was clear any Trump call would be after the Rada elections, asking him to call Danylyuk and politely tell him to stop listening to Sondland. Kupperman told me shortly thereafter that Danylyuk was very grateful to receive this news, as was Bill Taylor, our Chargé in Kiev, who knew just as we did Sondland was freelancing. Most interesting, Danylyuk said the Trump-Zelensky meeting (or call) was not his idea but Sondland's. The whole thing was a complete goat rope. Zelensky's supporters did very well in the elections, receiving about 43 percent of the vote, enough to give his party and like-minded independent candidates a working majority in the Rada. I hoped this was an important step toward moving things back into proper channels.

I returned from Asia the evening before Trump's now-famous July 25 call to Zelensky. I briefed him quickly ahead of the call at nine a.m., which I expected to be a repeat of the essentially pro forma congratulatory call Trump made on the evening of Zelensky's own victory in the presidential runoff. I explained that Ukraine had just seized a Russian tanker and crew in retaliation for the Russian seizures that touched off the Kerch Strait incident in 2018, which showed real spine on the part of Zelensky and his new team. Sondland, whom I had kept off my briefing call (which would have been the first time in my tenure that any Ambassador would have participated in such a briefing), had, through Mulvaney, spoken with Trump at seven thirty a.m. on God knows what agenda.

The "call record" of the Trump-Zelensky discussion, which I listened to, as is customary, compiled by NSC notetakers, now released publicly, is not a "transcript" like that produced by a court reporter of testimony in trial or in depositions. Soon after arriving at the White House, on May 18, 2018, I met with Eisenberg to discuss the process for creating these call records and how it had evolved. We decided to leave things as they were, to avoid recording as final, under the Presidential Records Act, things that shouldn't be kept for posterity. Until the Ukraine controversy broke, I was not aware we ever deviated from that policy, including "storage" procedures. Nor, at the time, did I think Trump's comments in the call reflected any major change in direction; the linkage of the military assistance with the Giuliani fantasies was already baked in. The call was not the keystone for me, but simply another brick in the wall. These are my recollections of what was important in the conversation, not from the call record.

Trump congratulated Zelensky on the Rada elections, and Zelensky thanked Trump, adding, "I should run more often, so we can talk more often. We are trying to drain the swamp in Ukraine. We brought in new people, not the old politicians."

Trump said, "We do a lot for Ukraine, much more than the European countries, who should do more, like Germany. They just talk. When I talk to Angela Merkel, she talks about Ukraine but doesn't do anything. The US has been very, very good to Ukraine, but it's not reciprocal because of things that have happened [Giuliani's conspiracy theories]."

Zelensky answered, "You are absolutely right, one thousand percent. I did talk and meet with Merkel and Macron, and they're not doing as much as they should do. They are not enforcing sanctions [against Russia]. The EU should be our biggest partner, but the US is, and I'm very grateful to you for that. The US is doing much more on sanctions." He then thanked the US for its defense assistance, saying he wanted to buy more Javelins.

Trump turned to the real issue: "I would like you to do us a favor, because our country has been through a lot, and Ukraine knows a lot about it. Find out about CrowdStrike [a cyber company the DNC used], the server, people say Ukraine has it. I would like our Attorney General to call you and get to the bottom of it. The whole thing ended yesterday with Mueller [his televised House hearing[12]]: impotent, incompetent. I hope you can get to the bottom of it."

Zelensky answered: "This is very important for me as President, and we are ready for future cooperation, and to open a new page in our relations. I just recalled the Ukrainian Ambassador to the United States, and he will be replaced to make sure our two countries are getting closer. I want a personal relationship with you. I will tell you personally one of my assistants just spoke to Giuliani. He will travel to Ukraine, and we will meet. I will surround myself with the best people. We will continue our strategic partnership. The investigation will be done openly and candidly. I promise as the President of Ukraine."

Trump said, "You had a good prosecutor. Mr. Giuliani is a highly respected man. If he could call you along with the Attorney General, and if you could speak to him, it would be great. The former Ambassador from the United States was bad news. The people she was dealing with were bad news. There is lots of talk about Biden's son stopping the prosecution [against those formulating and executing the Russia collusion operation]. He went around bragging that he stopped the prosecution. It sounds horrible."

Zelensky said, "Since we have an absolute majority in parliament, the next Prosecutor General will be one hundred percent my candidate. He will start in September. He will look at the company. The investigation is to restore honesty. If you have any additional information to provide us, please do so. With regard to the US Ambassador to Ukraine, Yovanovitch, I am glad you told me she was bad. I agree one hundred percent. Her attitude toward me was far from the best. She would not accept me as President."

Trump responded, "I will tell Giuliani and Attorney General Barr. I'm sure you will figure it out. Good luck with everything. Ukraine is a great country. I have many Ukrainian friends."

Zelensky said he had lots of Ukrainian-American friends too, and added, "Thank you for your invitation to Washington. I'm very serious about the case. There is a lot of potential for our two countries. We want energy independence."

Trump said, "Feel free to call. We'll work out a date."

Zelensky then invited Trump to Ukraine, noting both would be in Warsaw on September 1 for the eightieth anniversary of Germany's invasion of Poland, launching World War II, suggesting Trump could then come to Kiev, which Trump politely discouraged.

These were, to me, the key remarks in the July 25 call that later raised so much attention, deservedly so, whether impeachable, criminal, or otherwise. When, in 1992, Bush 41 supporters suggested he ask foreign governments to help out in his failing campaign against Bill Clinton, Bush and Jim Baker completely rejected the idea.[13] Trump did the precise opposite.

The next week, the State and Defense Departments pressed to transfer nearly $400 million of security assistance to Ukraine, calling for high-level meetings, as bureaucracies do reflexively. Of course, the bureaucrats didn't know that Pompeo, Esper, and I had been discussing this subject quietly for some time, making efforts with Trump to free

up the money, all of which had failed. (By the time I resigned, we cal-
culated that, individually and in various combinations, we had talked
to Trump between eight and ten times to get the money released.) If
the bureaucrats believed that a Principals Committee would change
Trump's mind, they hadn't been paying much attention for two and a
half years. I told Tim Morrison, Fiona Hill's successor, to have the State
and Defense Departments stop focusing on meetings, but I wanted to
have the funds ready in case Trump did agree to release them. For that
to happen, we needed to prepare the necessary paperwork, to be sure
we could obligate the security assistance before the fiscal year's looming September 30 end. Under long-standing budget rules applicable
to the legislation earmarking these funds, they would disappear if not
obligated by that point. That's why the bureaucracy was beginning to
show signs of agitation. Of course, one might ask why the bureaucracy
didn't start agitating earlier in the fiscal year, rather than waiting until
the end and blaming their potential troubles on someone else. One
might ask, but that's the way bureaucracies operate, painfully slowly,
and then blaming others when things go wrong.

On August 1, I spoke with Barr to brief him on what Trump said
to Zelensky about Giuliani, and Trump's references to Barr himself. I
suggested he have someone rein Giuliani in before he got completely
out of control. We also discussed the status of Halkbank, and the
still-pending question of sanctioning Turkey for purchasing Russian
S-400 air defense systems. Barr said he was waiting to hear back from
Halkbank's counsel on the Justice Department's latest settlement offer.
(On October 15, just after I left the Administration, the Justice Department returned a blistering indictment against Halkbank in New
York, having obviously found the final settlement offer by the bank's
attorneys inadequate.)[14]

Esper, Pompeo, and I continued exchanging thoughts about how
to persuade Trump to release the security assistance before September 30. We could have confronted Trump directly, trying to refute the
Giuliani theories and arguing that it was impermissible to leverage
US government authorities for personal political gain. We could have,
and we almost certainly would have failed, and perhaps have also

created one or more vacancies among Trump's senior advisors. The correct course was to separate the Ukraine security assistance from the Ukraine fantasies, get the military aid approved, and deal with Giuliani and the fantasies later. I thought, in fact, I had already initiated the second, Giuliani-related track, with the White House Counsel's office and subsequently with Bill Barr. There was also no point in encouraging more fruitless grinding at lower levels of the bureaucracy. None of that would have any impact on Trump's decision-making and could only risk press stories that would dig Trump in even more deeply against releasing the aid. That, at least, was my assessment at the time, and one that I believe Esper and Pompeo agreed with.

We fully appreciated the implications of the approaching deadline, but we also knew our maneuvering room was limited, with the usually unstated problem of the 2016 and 2020 election conspiracy theories at the root. We all knew just what Trump's thinking was, which was why we believed it was critical to move the issue for his decision only at the right moment. Timing the approach incorrectly could doom the assistance once and for all. Thus, when Trump raised the issue of Ukraine during the discussion of Afghanistan at Bedminster on Friday, August 16, asking how much we were spending there, I was worried that, in the heat of the contentious Afghan discussion, the Ukraine aid could be lost for good. Esper surprised me with his response, saying that Acting Office of Management and Budget Director Russ Vought had "stopped that," meaning stopped attempts to keep the aid from being released. This implied the decision was made and further discussion foreclosed, which I definitely did not believe. Fortunately, Ukraine passed into and out of Trump's free-flowing monologue without further incident.

The Office of Management and Budget had, of course, by then entered the picture, ostensibly for budgetary reasons, but we suspected more likely because Trump used Mulvaney to put a stop to any efforts by the State or Defense Departments to move funds they respectively supervised. The budget office was also trying to rescind more than $4 billion of foreign economic assistance (which affected only the State Department, not the Pentagon), an annual exercise. As in 2018, the budgeteers ultimately backed down, mostly because there would have been open warfare with Congress had Trump decided to proceed with rescission. Mulvaney and others later argued that the dispute over Ukraine's security assistance was related to rescinding the economic assistance, but this was entirely an ex post facto rationalization.

With time drawing short, I suggested to Pompeo and Esper that I again see how Trump was leaning, and the three of us then coordinate our schedules to talk to Trump together, with which they agreed. The next morning, August 20, I took Trump's temperature on the Ukraine security assistance, and he said he wasn't in favor of sending them anything until all the Russia-investigation materials related to Clinton and Biden had been turned over. That could take years, so it didn't sound like there was much of a prospect that the military aid would proceed. Nonetheless, with time running out, I said that Esper, Pompeo, and I would like to see Trump about the issue later in the week, which he accepted. Because of scheduling difficulties for Pompeo and Esper, and because I left Friday morning for the Biarritz G7 summit, Kupperman sat in for me on August 23 to discuss Ukraine. Unfortunately, it was during a meeting where Trump once again decided to do nothing after an Iranian-Houthi downing of yet another US drone, the third in recent months. The discussion on Ukrainian aid was brief. Trump punted, saying, "Let me think about it for a couple of days. I will talk to others at the G7 about it." Esper, about to attend a NATO defense ministerial meeting, said he would press other members to do more on Ukraine, which could also help. It could have been worse, but time was still slipping away.

At the G7, it seemed France and Germany were more optimistic that Putin might take steps to decrease tensions with Ukraine, such as an exchange of hostages and the ship crews detained in November. Because Biarritz was so fraught with dangerous near misses on Iran, however, Ukraine played a relatively minor role (although most other G7 members strongly opposed inviting Russia to the US-hosted G7 in 2020). After Biarritz, having come close to resigning, I flew to Kiev to meet Zelensky personally, as well as key members of his incoming team. I hoped to ensure that the upcoming Zelensky-Trump meeting in Warsaw, which could not be avoided, would be a success. Flying to Kiev on August 26, I spoke with Volker about Ukrainian Independence Day two days before, which he thought Zelensky had handled well. Volker stressed that Zelensky had no wish to become involved in US domestic politics, although he was happy to have investigated whatever may have happened in 2016, before his time.

In Kiev, I met again with Danylyuk, accompanied by Chargé Bill Taylor and several NSC officials, for an extended discussion on how a Ukrainian National Security Council might function, as well as dealing with the Russians in Crimea and the Donbas. Taylor and I then laid a wreath at a memorial for the approximately thirteen thousand Ukrainians killed in the ongoing war with Russia. The next day, we had breakfast with Ivan Bakanov, then the Acting Chairman of the Ukrainian Security Service, confirmed a few days later to delete the "Acting" from his title. Bakanov was responsible for reforming the security services, a formidable task, but our embassy officials believed he was the right person for the job. Much of our conversation, as with Danylyuk the day before, was about Motor Sich and Antonov, two key aerospace companies that were in danger of slipping under Chinese (or other foreign) control, which would make it almost impossible for the US to cooperate with them. These firms (and many others) were the legacy of Soviet days, put there by those expert Communist economic planners for no particular reason, but left an independent Ukraine with significant assets it didn't want to see slip away. Now here was a strategic interest that should have been a high priority for US decision-makers.

Next was a meeting with Minister of Defense–designate Andriy Zagorodnyuk, who was determined to make significant reforms in Ukraine's military, in the midst of ongoing armed conflict with Russia and its surrogate forces in the Donbas. He favored using the pending US security aid not just to buy weapons from US firms, though he certainly wanted to do that, but also to obtain US help in building the Ukraine military's institutional capabilities. By so doing, he expected to multiply the effects of the assistance into the future. (At the end of the day, I also met with General Ruslan Khomchak, Chief of the Ukraine General Staff, with whom I discussed the Donbas and Crimea at length. Khomchak was also an enthusiastic supporter of US military assistance: He stressed the need to change the culture of Ukraine's military, including through providing English-language training and other reforms to break free from Moscow's influence. He was also very worried about Russian efforts to build up military strength in the region, which would be a direct threat to both Poland and Ukraine. These were serious matters that I found both Zagorodnyuk and Khomchak taking seriously.)

We then rode to the Presidential Administration Building for a meeting with Zelensky's chief of staff, Andriy Bohdan, and one of his deputies, Ruslan Ryaboshapka. Bohdan had been Zelensky's lawyer in private life, and also represented the oligarch Igor Kolomoisky. There was visible tension between Bohdan and Danylyuk, who joined us a bit later, foreshadowing Danylyuk's mid-September resignation as national security advisor to Zelensky.[15] Danylyuk's arrival also brought Ivan Bakanov, Vadym Prystayko (the Foreign Minister–designate), and Aivaras Abramovicius (the head of the state-owned holding company that effectively controlled Ukraine's defense industrial base, including Motor Sich and Antonov) into the meeting. Bohdan stressed that Ukraine was counting on US support for the reform program. Although Zelensky had an absolute majority in the Rada, most of the new parliamentarians, along with Zelensky's own inner circle, had no government experience at all. The Cabinet, accordingly, had been selected on the basis of technical expertise and included people from a number of the other political parties, and some career officials like Prystayko, who was then serving as Ukraine's Ambassador to NATO, pressing its case for admission.

We talked about a wide range of issues, following which I had forty-five minutes alone with Prystayko to talk foreign policy. Interestingly, Ukraine, along almost unimaginably with State's Legal Advisor's office, had concluded that our withdrawal from the INF Treaty meant that the entire treaty had expired.[16] Accordingly, as a successor state to the USSR, and previously therefore theoretically bound by the treaty, Ukraine was now free to develop its own INF-noncompliant missile systems. Given the situation with the Crimea annexed and the Donbas in jeopardy, this was no small matter for Ukraine, Europe, or the United States. Whatever the Western Europeans thought, Ukraine and other Eastern European states had their own ideas about how to respond to Russia's intermediate-range missile capabilities.

As the larger meeting ended, before meeting with Prystayko, I pulled Ryaboshapka aside to speak with him one-on-one. He had not said much during the meeting, which I hoped showed his discretion. Ryaboshapka, as the soon-to-be equivalent to the US Attorney General, was the Zelensky Cabinet official most likely required to deal with Giuliani's conspiracy theories, and also the Ukrainian official Bill Barr would turn to for any legitimate government-to-government legal issues. Here, I had my only conversation in Ukraine on Giuliani's issues, and a very brief one at that. I urged Ryaboshapka to speak directly to Barr and the Justice Department as soon as he took office, figuring this was the best way to prevent fantasy from overwhelming reality. I didn't mention the words "Rudy Giuliani," hoping the omission spoke volumes. Time would tell.

The Zelensky meeting began at twelve thirty p.m. and lasted until about two. On the Ukrainian side were basically all those who had participated in the earlier meetings. Bill Taylor, NSC officials, and several embassy officers comprised the US side. Zelensky was impressive throughout, very much in command of the issues. He started by thanking us for keeping our Crimea sanctions in place and our continued nonrecognition of Russia's purported annexation. I thought: If only he knew how close we were to giving all that away! We discussed Crimea, the Donbas, the failing Normandy Format peace process, and his desire to get the US and the UK more active in resolving the Russia-Ukraine dispute. Domestically, Zelensky said the fight against corruption, the centerpiece of his presidential campaign, was his highest priority. His "Servant of the People Party," named after his TV show, had 254 Rada members, and he said that when the new session opened, they would introduce 254 reform bills, one for each party member to shepherd through. Zelensky emphasized that the time for promises alone was over, and it was now time to implement the promises he had campaigned on.

He said the issue that prompted his first call to Putin was trying to get the Ukrainian sailors released. He was determined to get the Donbas back as soon as possible and end the war within the Minsk agreements. Zelensky had very specific ideas for a cease-fire, starting at one particular town and then expanding it. There would be no diplomatic games from him, he said, but Ukraine needed to see reciprocal steps from Russia: he wanted to resolve the issue, not let it drag out for years. We also discussed the tricky issue of what would happen if the Donbas were resolved but not Crimea. No one, including the US, had a way around this dilemma, but Zelensky stressed that the West as a whole had to keep sanctions tied to the Crimea problem, not just ending the Donbas war. After discussing Belarus and Moldova, and their common problems with Russia and corruption, we concluded. There was no discussion of Hillary Clinton, Joe Biden, or anything in Giuliani land. If this didn't demonstrate what America's real interests were, and what Zelensky should raise with Trump in Warsaw, I didn't know how else to do it.

I left Kiev confident Zelensky understood the magnitude of the task facing him, at home and abroad, as did his incoming team. These were people we could work with, so long as we didn't get lost in the fever swamps, which remained to be seen. Taylor, who had been in all my meetings except my brief Ryaboshapka one-on-one, spoke to me alone before I left for the airport, asking what he should do about the swirling Giuliani issues. I sympathized with his plight, so I urged him to write a "first-person cable" to Pompeo telling him what he knew. "First-person cables" are rare, direct messages from a Chief of Mission straight to the Secretary of State, reserved for extraordinary circumstances, which we obviously had here. Besides, it was past time to get Pompeo more actively into the fray. Taylor's subsequent congressional testimony made him one of the most important witnesses in the House impeachment investigation.[17]

On August 29, I flew from Kiev to Moldova and Belarus, continuing my travels in the former republics of the USSR. I wanted to show Russia we had a sustained focus on its periphery and were not content simply to leave these struggling states to contend with Moscow alone. Had I stayed in the White House longer, I had more substantive plans for US relations with the former Soviet states, but that was not to be. Particularly in Minsk, despite Alexander Lukashenko's less-than-stellar human-rights record, I wanted to prove the US would not simply watch Belarus be reabsorbed by Russia, which Putin seemed to be seriously considering. One aspect of my strategy was a meeting the Poles arranged in Warsaw on Saturday, August 31, among the national security advisors of Poland, Belarus, Ukraine, and the United States. Let the Kremlin think about that one for a while. I obviously had much more in mind than just having additional meetings, but this was one that would signal other former Soviet republics that neither we nor they had to be passive when faced with Russian belligerence or threats to their internal governance. There was plenty we could all do diplomatically as well as militarily. After I resigned, the Administration and others seemed to be moving in a similar direction.[18]

Flying from Minsk to Warsaw, I called Pompeo to brief him on the trip to Ukraine, Moldova, and Belarus. I relayed specifically what Taylor had told me candidly in Kiev: he had left the private sector to rejoin the government temporarily as Chargé in a country where he had been Ambassador (a rare occurrence, if it ever happened before), because of how strongly he supported a close Ukraine-US relationship. If we took an indifferent or hostile approach toward Ukraine, he said, "I'm not your guy here," which Pompeo confirmed Taylor had also said explicitly before taking on the post in the spring, after Yovanovitch was removed. Neither Pompeo nor I had any doubt that Taylor's resignation was nearly certain if the military assistance did not go through.

I asked whether it might be possible to get a decision on the security funds before Trump left for Warsaw. Pompeo thought it was, noting also that he would have another chance on Air Force One, which was leaving Andrews Friday night and arriving in Warsaw Saturday morning. The meeting with Zelensky was scheduled for Sunday morning, so there was also at least some time in Warsaw. Jim Inhofe, Chairman of the Senate Armed Services Committee, was trying to reach me, and Pompeo and I reviewed the several Hill options we had been considering and discussing quietly to get some relief from the September 30 deadline. There might be ways to buy more time, usually impossible at a fiscal year's end but doable here in a variety of ways because of the overwhelming bipartisan support for security assistance to Ukraine.

That night, we learned Trump would not travel to Poland because of Hurricane Dorian's approach to Florida, and that Pence would come instead, not landing until Sunday morning. Both Pompeo and Esper dropped off the trip, and the Warsaw schedule was thrown into disarray because Pence would arrive twenty-four hours later than planned for Trump. In particular, the Zelensky meeting would now have to be after the ceremony for the eightieth anniversary of the Nazi attack on Poland rather than before. All of that could be done, but it obviously meant that a Trump decision on Ukraine military aid had again been pushed to the back burner. Time was now racing away from us.

On Friday evening Warsaw time, August 30, I participated from Warsaw via videoconference in an NSC meeting on Afghanistan with Trump and most others in the Sit Room. As I have described, so consuming was the Afghanistan discussion that Trump was leaving the room before I realized the meeting was breaking up. I all but yelled at the screen, "Wait, what about Ukraine?" and everyone sat back down. Trump said, "I don't give a shit about NATO. I am ready to say, 'If you don't pay, we won't defend them.' I want the three hundred million dollars [he meant two hundred fifty million dollars, one piece of the assistance earmarked for Ukraine] to be paid through NATO." Of course, none of that was physically possible, reflecting Trump's continued lack of understanding of what these funds were and how they came to be earmarked, but there was nothing new there. "Ukraine is a wall between us and Russia," he said, meaning, I think, a barrier to closer Moscow-Washington relations. He then said to Pence, "Call [NATO Secretary General] Stoltenberg and have him have NATO pay. Say 'The President is for you, but the money should come from

NATO,'" which still didn't make any sense. "Wait until the NATO meeting in December," Trump said, implying, at least in my mind, that he was going to announce we were withdrawing.

This was not good news, although Kupperman told me Senator Inhofe spoke with Trump for nearly thirty minutes after the NSC meeting, working on the security assistance question. Trump finally said to him, "Pence will soften my message," whatever that meant. Senator Ron Johnson told me a few days later he had also spoken to Trump, and made the political point that support for Ukraine in Congress was nearly unanimous. He was not sure he had moved Trump, but I knew the number of House and Senate members preparing to call or meet with Trump was growing rapidly. Raw politics might yet do better with Trump than substantive arguments. In any case the meeting ended inconclusively.

Pence called Saturday night while flying to Warsaw to discuss Trump: "I thought I heard him say that he knew it was the end of the fiscal year, and there had been no prior notification [to Ukraine] we would want to cut the money off, but he had real concerns. I think I know the President well enough that he might be saying, 'Let's do this, but get our allies to do more in the future.'" I hoped that was the message he would deliver in Warsaw. Neither of us, however, yet knew. Pence landed in Warsaw on Sunday morning, slightly ahead of schedule, just before ten a.m. To my surprise, Sondland had flown on Air Force Two and also managed to crash the briefing the VP's staff had arranged, notwithstanding the advance team's efforts to keep him out. Sondland later testified that he had been "invited at the very last minute." He invited himself over near-physical efforts by the VP's advance people to keep him out. At the briefing, I told Pence in abbreviated form about my trip to the three eastern European countries, especially my meeting with Zelensky and the other Ukrainians in Kiev. Subsequently, Sondland testified he had said in this same meeting that aid to Ukraine was being tied to the "investigations" Trump and Giuliani wanted, and that his comment had been "duly noted" by Pence. I don't recall Sondland's saying anything at that meeting.

Time was tight before we had to leave for Pilsudski Square, the venue for the ceremony, and where Pope John Paul II had given the famous 1979 mass that many Poles believe marked the beginning of the end of the Cold War. We didn't return to the hotel until two thirty, well behind schedule because of the complex logistics for all the national leaders attending. In another opportunity to brief Pence, without Sondland's being present, I explained I had to leave the Zelensky meeting (which began at three thirty, almost an hour late) no later than three forty-five. Pence and I concentrated on the security assistance issue, and he acknowledged we still didn't have a good answer to give. Once Zelensky arrived, the press mob stumbled in, asking questions on the subject, which Pence ducked as adroitly as possible. The press left, as did I simultaneously so my plane didn't lose its takeoff slot at Warsaw's crowded airport. I didn't hear until later, therefore, when Morrison called, that Zelensky had homed in on the security package as soon as the press departed. Pence danced around it, but the lack of a "yes, it's definitely coming" statement was impossible to hide. Fortunately, Sondland did not raise the Giuliani issues during the meeting with Zelensky, as he had pressed us to do. Afterward, however, said Morrison, Sondland had grabbed one of Zelensky's advisors, Andriy Yermak, who handled "US affairs" and who had previously met with Giuliani. Morrison was not fully aware of what Sondland and Yermak had discussed, but I doubted it had to do with Crimea or the Donbas, let alone the implications of the demise of the INF Treaty. Morrison told me in a subsequent conversation that Sondland had raised the Giuliani issues with Yermak.

After a quiet Labor Day, I spent Tuesday at the White House, catching up. When Haspel and the intelligence briefing team arrived before seeing Trump, she said, "You can't do that again!" "What?" I asked. "Go away for a week," she said, and we all laughed. On September 4, I spoke to Pence, still in Europe at Trump's Doonbeg, Ireland, golf resort, which had become the latest scandal of the day. Pence was impressed with Zelensky, and so informed Trump, concluding, "My recommendation and the consensus recommendation of your advisors is that we move forward with the two hundred fifty million dollars." Pence also pressed Trump to meet Zelensky at the UN General

Assembly and said that "just between us girls," he thought Trump was looking for a news peg to make what we hoped was the right decision. "Zelensky didn't quite close the argument [in their meeting], so I closed it for him," said Pence, which sounded positive. In the meantime, the press was beginning to sniff out the connection between withholding military assistance for Ukraine and Trump's obsession with the 2016 and 2020 elections in the persons of Hillary Clinton and Joe Biden.[19] Bipartisan Hill opposition to withholding the aid continued to rise (which, all else failing, I hoped would produce the right result). It was not until the end of September, however, that the media began to appreciate what had been happening since well before the July 25 call.[20]

Over the weekend, Zelensky's prisoner swap with Russia proceeded, a positive event in its own right, and which Trump had seemingly indicated might be enough to get him to release the security assistance. Pompeo and I discussed this on the morning of September 9, and Esper and I spoke about it by phone later that day, in both cases continuing to press for legislative relief to buy more time. On Wednesday afternoon, Trump decided to release the Ukraine money.[21]

By then, I was a private citizen. At about two fifteen p.m. on Monday, September 9, Trump called me down to the Oval, where we met alone. He complained about press coverage on Afghanistan and the cancellation of the Camp David meeting with the Taliban, not to mention the overwhelmingly negative reaction, certainly among Republicans, both to the deal and the invitation of Taliban to Camp David. Of course, most of the negative reaction he had brought on himself by his ill-advised tweets. Perhaps surprisingly, nothing had leaked before the tweets, but they blew the lid off the story. He was furious he was being portrayed as a fool, not that he put it that way. He said, "A lot of people don't like you. They say you're a leaker and not a team player." I wasn't about to let that go. I said I'd been subject to a campaign of negative leaks against me over the past several months, which I would be happy to describe in detail, and I'd also be happy to tell him who I thought the leaks were coming from. (Mostly, I believed the leaks were being directed by Pompeo and Mulvaney.)

As for the claim I was a leaker, I urged him to look for all the favorable stories about me in the *New York Times*, the *Washington Post*, and elsewhere, which often revealed who was doing the leaking, and he would find none. Trump asked specifically about the meeting with the Taliban, and I reminded him I had said merely the Taliban should go through a powerful magnetometer. What I had said was that I wouldn't have signed the State Department's deal, and Trump pointed his finger at me and said, "I agree." Then he was off again, saying, "You have your own airplane," which I explained briefly I did not. I flew on military aircraft on all official trips, following precisely the same policy that governed my predecessors and many other senior officials involved in national security. I didn't write these rules; I followed them. I knew this specifically was a Mulvaney complaint, the source of a lot of this nonsense. "You've got all your own people back there [on the National Security Council staff]," said Trump, another Mulvaney complaint. Of course, Trump's usual complaint was that the NSC staff included too many members of the "deep state."

At that point, I rose from the chair in front of the *Resolute* desk, saying, "If you want me to leave, I'll leave." Trump said, "Let's talk about it in the morning."

That was my last conversation with Trump. I left the Oval at about two thirty and returned to my office. I told Kupperman and Tinsley about the conversation and said that was it as far as I was concerned. I gave my short resignation letter, written several months before, to Christine Samuelian, my assistant, to put on White House letterhead. I said I was going home to sleep on it overnight, but I was ready to resign the next day. In light of the subsequent controversy, I should note that on Tuesday, Kupperman told me that Dan Walsh, one of Mulvaney's deputies, had called him late Monday, returning with Trump on Air Force One from a North Carolina political rally Trump had departed for right after speaking with me. Trump was still spun up about my use of military aircraft, which Walsh had tried to explain to him unsuccessfully, and said to Walsh, "You tell him he's not getting another plane unless I specifically approve it." This comment from Trump demonstrates that late on Monday he still thought I'd be around making requests for military planes after seeing him on Tuesday.

On Tuesday, September 10, in the morning, I came in at my regular early hour, fulfilled a few remaining obligations, and then left to be at home when the firestorm hit. I asked Christine to take the letter down to the Outer Oval and deliver copies to Pence, Mulvaney, Cipollone, and Grisham at 11:30 a.m. I am confident Trump did not expect it, tweeting at about 11:50 to get his story out first. I should have struck preemptively—there's a lesson in that—but I was content to countertweet with the facts. I know how it actually ended. And with that, I was a free man again.

CHAPTER 15

EPILOGUE

When I resigned as National Security Advisor on September 10, 2019, no one was predicting the subsequent Trump impeachment saga. I was not then aware of the now famous whistleblower's complaint, nor of its handling within the Executive Branch, but that complaint and the publicity it subsequently received transformed the Washington political landscape in completely unforeseen ways. I have no idea who the whistleblower is.

Nonetheless, as the previous chapter demonstrates, I knew more than I wanted to about Trump's handling of Ukraine affairs, and while the nation as a whole concentrated on the unfolding events relating to impeachment, I concentrated on deciding what my personal and constitutional responsibilities were regarding that information. Whether Trump's conduct rose to the level of an impeachable offense, I had found it deeply disturbing, which is why I had reported it to White House Counsel Pat Cipollone and his staff and Attorney General Bill Barr, and why Pompeo, Mnuchin, and I had worried over it in our own conversations. But the importance of maintaining the President's constitutional authority, and what Hamilton called "energy in the Executive" were no small matters either. In the subsequent partisan Armageddon, virtue signalers on both sides of the battle were quick to tell the world how easy the choices were. I didn't see it that way.

Neither I nor my attorneys, an outstanding team led by Chuck Cooper, an old friend and colleague from the Department of Justice during the Reagan Administration, were speaking to the press, for good and sufficient reasons. What little sense of complexity and intellectual rigor political debate in America still retains was quickly lost in the impeachment struggle, and trying to explain my views didn't pass my cost-benefit analysis of time and effort expended, given the predictable results. Many other participants in the impeachment conflict, however, had their own agendas, often more vigorously pursued in the media than in the real world. Inevitably, therefore, press coverage was often badly wrong, reflecting both the not-so-hidden agendas of many other players, and the usual media bias, laziness, lack of education and professionalism, and short attention span. I felt then, and feel now, no obligation to correct reporters' mistakes about me piecemeal; if I did that, I would barely have time for anything else. I believed that I would have my say in due course (one of the few comments I did make to the press, on several occasions), and I was content to bide my time. I believed throughout, as the line in *Hamilton* goes, that "I am not throwing away my shot," especially not to please the howling press, the howling advocates of impeachment, or Trump's howling defenders.

My substantive views on the impeachment process were decidedly mixed. Most important, from the very outset of proceedings in the House of Representatives, advocates for impeaching Trump on the Ukraine issue were committing impeachment malpractice. They seemed governed more by their own political imperatives to move swiftly to vote on articles of impeachment in order to avoid interfering with the Democratic presidential nomination schedule than in completing a comprehensive investigation. Such an approach was not serious constitutionally. If Trump deserved impeachment and conviction, the American public deserved a serious and thorough effort to justify the extraordinary punishment of removing an elected president from office. That did not happen. The Democrats' perceived imperatives posed by the electoral calendar may have raised hard political questions and difficult logistical problems for impeachment advocates, but that was their own fault. Their self-imposed scheduling limitations hardly rose to a constitutional level at all, let alone one equivalent to impeaching a President, one of Congress's gravest Constitutional responsibilities. Neither did scheduling issues justify the subsequent tactical decisions by the impeachment proponents, such as not pursuing subpoena enforcement actions in court, or otherwise building not just an "adequate" evidentiary record, but a compelling one. Indeed, in some senses it was a mirror image of what impeachment advocates were accusing Trump of doing: torquing legitimate governmental powers around an illegitimate nongovernmental objective.

The consequences of this partisan approach by the House were twofold. First, it narrowed the scope of the impeachment inquiry dramatically and provided no opportunity to explore Trump's ham-handed involvement in other matters—criminal and civil, international and domestic—that should not properly be subject to manipulation by a President for personal reasons (political, economic, or any other). This is not to say that I have any doubts about a President's Article II authority over the Department of Justice. But it does mean that a President's Constitutional obligation to "take care that the laws be faithfully executed" means that the laws must be applied evenhandedly. A President may not misuse the national government's legitimate powers by defining his own personal interest as synonymous with the national interest, or by inventing pretexts to mask the pursuit of personal interest under the guise of national interest. Had the House not focused solely on the Ukraine aspects of Trump's confusion of his personal interests (whether political or economic), but on the broader pattern of his behavior—including his pressure campaigns involving Halkbank, ZTE, and Huawei among others—there might have been a greater chance to persuade others that "high crimes and misdemeanors" had been perpetrated. In fact, I am hard-pressed to identify any significant Trump decision during my tenure that wasn't driven by reelection calculations.

Second, rushed proceedings, combined with the hysterical mood of many impeachment advocates, which brooked no dissent from the proposition that Trump had to be removed from office by any means available, meant that developing a truly accurate record—at a minimum, a *full* record—was not an option House Democrats wanted to pursue. In turn, this resulted, quite literally, in driving away House Republicans who might have been inclined at least to consider articles of impeachment involving broader aspects of Trump's conduct. From the very earliest days of the House proceedings, that meant that the entire affair would be bitterly partisan, which is exactly what it turned out to be. This was particularly true of the second article of impeachment ("obstruction of Congress"), which was frivolous on its face. And what was true of the House was equally true in the Senate, meaning that lines were drawn on party grounds, making Trump's acquittal in the Senate a certainty even before the final House votes to impeach. This scenario was not inevitable ab initio, but it was made so by the conscious decisions of the House impeachment advocates.

That is malpractice pure and simple. And that's how I saw it almost from the outset. Of course, it wasn't long before former Deputy National Security Advisor Charlie Kupperman and I received inquiries from the House Permanent Select Committee on Intelligence about whether we would testify. As did the attorneys for other witnesses who testified before the committee. Cooper asked for subpoenas, and one was duly issued for Kupperman. Immediately, the White House informed Kupperman that the President had ordered that he invoke "testimonial immunity," a more stringent instruction than other witnesses subpoenaed by the intelligence committee had theretofore received, and that he not even appear at the noticed deposition. On Kupperman's behalf, Cooper promptly filed a lawsuit seeking judicial guidance on which of the two contradictory commands to follow, exactly what I would have done had I been in Kupperman's place. The various pleadings Cooper filed on Kupperman's behalf made it plain he was not advocating the substantive merits of either the Executive or the Legislative Branches on what his course of conduct should be, but merely seeking the Judiciary's guidance.

Many of the ensuing developments were misreported in more ways than might seem possible, but the statement that I issued on January 6, 2020, still represents the best summary of these events and my thinking:

> "During the present impeachment controversy, I have tried to meet my obligations both as a citizen and as former National Security Advisor. My colleague, Dr. Charles Kupperman, faced with a House committee subpoena on the one hand, and

a Presidential directive not to testify on the other, sought final resolution of this Constitutional conflict from the Federal judiciary. After my counsel informed the House committee that I too would seek judicial resolution of these Constitutional issues, the committee chose not to subpoena me. Nevertheless, I publicly resolved to be guided by the outcome of Dr. Kupperman's case.

"But both the President and the House of Representatives *opposed* his effort on jurisdictional grounds, and each other on the merits. The House committee went so far as to withdraw its subpoena to Dr. Kupperman in a deliberate attempt to moot the case and deprive the court of jurisdiction. Judge Richard Leon, in a carefully reasoned opinion on December 30, held Dr. Kupperman's case to be moot, and therefore did not reach the separation-of-powers issues.

"The House has concluded its Constitutional responsibility by adopting Articles of Impeachment related to the Ukraine matter. It now falls to the Senate to fulfill its Constitutional obligation to try impeachments, and it does not appear possible that a final judicial resolution of the still-unanswered Constitutional questions can be obtained before the Senate acts.

"Accordingly, since my testimony is once again at issue, I have had to resolve the serious competing issues as best I could, based on careful consideration and study. I have concluded that if the Senate issues a subpoena for my testimony, I am prepared to testify."

The Senate, of course, declined to hear any witnesses, and went on to acquit Trump on the two articles of impeachment the House had adopted. Had a Senate majority agreed to call witnesses and had I testified, I am convinced, given the environment then existing because of the House's impeachment malpractice, that it would have made no significant difference in the Senate outcome.

One incident during the Senate proceedings that generated substantial attention was the leak of what purported to be information from the manuscript of this book to the *New York Times*. In response to this disturbing and unwelcome development, Cooper issued a statement on Saturday, January 26, 2020, attaching the transmittal letter (dated December 30, 2019) of the manuscript to the NSC for pre-publication review. That review is intended to ensure that no classified information is publicly released. Although we did not believe we were required to submit the manuscript, we did so out of an abundance of caution, and because it was always my firm intention not to include anything legitimately deemed classifiable. We had, until then, kept even the fact of submitting the manuscript out of the public eye, but the leak clearly required a public response. Cooper's statement said, in part:

> "It is clear, regrettably, from the *New York Times* article published today that the prepublication review process has been corrupted and that information has been disclosed by persons other than those properly involved in reviewing the manuscript. We submitted the manuscript . . . on the assurance that the 'process of reviewing submitted materials is restricted to those career government officials and employees regularly charged with responsibility for such reviews' and that the 'contents of Ambassador Bolton's manuscript will not be reviewed or otherwise disclosed to any persons not regularly involved in that process.'"

Cooper also said to the *Washington Post*, "I can tell you unequivocally that we had nothing to do with the leak of any information concerning John's manuscript."[1] The next day, January 27, we also issued this statement: "Ambassador John Bolton, Simon & Schuster, and Javelin Literary categorically state that there was absolutely no coordination with the *New York Times* or anyone else regarding the appearance of information about his book, THE ROOM WHERE IT HAPPENED, at online booksellers. Any assertion to the contrary is unfounded speculation." Whoever did undertake these leaks, a question that remains unfortunately unanswered, is certainly no friend of mine.

Trump's subsequent acquittal demonstrated yet another consequence of the impeachment malpractice committed by the House of Representatives. Democrats argued that impeachment itself would forever taint the Trump presidency, thus justifying their actions in the House. Inexplicably, they ignored the palpable reality that the inevitable consequence of a failed impeachment effort meant that Trump could claim vindication, and act accordingly, which is precisely what he did. This is the exact opposite of what House impeachment advocates purportedly intended, and yet they marched in lockstep off the cliff, thereby eliminating yet another "guardrail," the term commonly used, limiting Trump's misuse of governmental power. As Yogi Berra once asked about the hapless New York Mets: "Don't nobody here know how to play this game?"

Impeachment, of course, is, for the most part, only a theoretical guardrail constitutionally. The real guardrail is elections, which Trump faces in November 2020. Should he win, the Twenty-Second Amendment precludes (and should continue to preclude) any further electoral constraint on Trump. While liberals and Democrats focus on impeachment, conservatives and Republicans should worry about the removal of the political guardrail of Trump having to face reelection. As this memoir demonstrates, many of Trump's national security decisions hinged more on political than on philosophy, strategy or foreign policy and defense rationales. More widely, faced with the coronavirus crisis, Trump said, "When somebody is the President of the United States, the authority is total, and that's the way it's got to be."[2] He threatened to adjourn Congress, wrongly citing a constitutional provision that has never been used.[3] No conservative who has read the Constitution could be anything but astonished at these assertions.

Of course, politics is ever present in government, but a second-term Trump will be far less constrained by politics than he was in his first term. The irony could well be that Democrats will find themselves far more pleased substantively with a "legacy"-seeking Trump in his second term than conservatives and Republicans. Something to think about.

• • •

As if impeachment were not enough, I also found myself confronting the daunting challenge of fighting against an incumbent President
determined to prevent publication of a book about my White House
experiences. Trump behaved typically, directing the seizure and withholding of my advisors' personal and other unclassified documents,
despite numerous requests for their return; obstructing my Twitter
account; and outright threats of censorship.[4] His reaction thus ranged
from the mean-spirited to the constitutionally impermissible. My
reaction . . . my response? Game on.

One ostensibly "legitimate" avenue of Trump's attack was the US
government's grinding, bureaucratic, pre-publication review process,
which I reluctantly agreed to undergo so this book could be published.
In order to receive access to classified information while serving as
National Security Advisor, and like many other government officials,
I signed numerous nondisclosure agreements before and during my
tenure.[5] Without question, anyone who receives classified information is under a permanent obligation not to disclose it to unauthorized
persons, something I never intended to do in writing the manuscript
of this book. There was plenty to say without needing to reveal such
material.

These nondisclosure agreements are, at best, obscurely worded on
the circumstances under which such a manuscript is subject to the
pre-publication review process, which is intended to ensure that no
classified information is revealed. I did not, for example, submit *Surrender Is Not an Option* for pre-publication review in 2007, nor, as I
recall, did Colin Powell submit his memoir, *My American Journey*,[6] for
review. By contrast, James Baker told me shortly after his book, *The
Politics of Diplomacy*,[7] was published during the Clinton Administration, that he wished he had not submitted it for review. He was rightly
appalled at the number of objections made because his statements
about, say, US policy toward China did not reflect the Clinton Administration's policy. This resulted in significant delays in publication. All
these experiences counseled against the risk of censorship inherent
in the government review process, especially under a presidency like
Trump's.

On the other hand, it was clear from the outset, based on the circumstances of my departure from the Administration, and during the production of the book, that Trump would do everything he could to prevent its publication, at least until after the 2020 presidential election. In light of this unprecedented hostility, and Chuck Cooper's prudent legal advice, I decided to submit to the pre-clearance review, notwithstanding our conviction that we were not required to do so because the manuscript contained no legitimately classifiable material. In the Trump era, normal rules simply did not apply.

The review process itself was conducted professionally, courteously, and meticulously, but certainly not as expeditiously as I would have liked (although concededly the COVID-19 crisis did have some effect on timing). I made numerous changes to the manuscript in order to obtain clearance to publish, the vast bulk of which, in my view, did not change the facts set forth. In some cases, I simply had to add a phrase like "in my view" (see the previous sentence), to make it clear I was expressing my opinion rather than relying on some highly sensitive information. In other cases, I was required to characterize the facts I was discussing at a slightly higher level of abstraction, such as, for example, describing potential military targets in Iran somewhat more generally than in my initial draft. Readers can, therefore, duly imagine for themselves what I and others, including Trump, actually had in mind.

Two categories of changes stand out. First, in almost every recounting of conversations between Trump and foreign leaders, and between me and my foreign counterparts and other senior foreign officials, I was directed to "take out the quotation marks." In many cases, that is literally all I did: delete the quotation marks. In many other cases, some paraphrasing was necessary to reflect that I was no longer using direct quotations, so that personal pronouns and the like had to be modified to allow the substance to be conveyed clearly. In a very small number of cases, I was prevented from conveying information that I thought was not properly classifiable, since it revealed information that can only be described as embarrassing to Trump, or as indicative of possible impermissible behavior. I plan to continue to fight for either the declassification of these passages, or the right to use direct quotations in subsequent editions of this book or other writings.

Readers can be assured that, in this text, I have as faithfully as I could presented the substance of Trump's conversations with foreign leaders, and mine as well. In some cases, just put your own quotation marks around the relevant passages; you won't go far wrong. And interestingly, almost no changes were required in my discussion of conversations between Trump and his subordinates. This seeming anomaly is because the classification review was intended to shield foreign leaders from having to deny what Trump said to them. Instead of denying direct quotations, they will have to deny paraphrases. There may well be an explanation for this disparate treatment, but I don't see it. Trump may actually like it even less than I do.

The second major set of changes involved roughly tripling the number of endnotes in the book. The purpose of this exercise was to prove the negative that I was not relying on classified material for the information conveyed in the text. This endnoting was tedious, to be sure, but every time I provided a cite, I avoided having to delete substantive material, a tradeoff I was invariably happy to make.

Any number of commentators have observed that the government's pre-clearance review process is riddled with constitutional deficiencies; the potential for obstruction, censorship, and abuse; and harmful to timely debate on critical public policy issues. You can add my name to the list of critics, especially when the process is in the hands of a President so averse to criticism that the idea of banning books comes to him naturally and serenely.

There is one other point worth addressing, not related to the clearance process but to the idea of writing a book like this immediately after leaving government service. A number of critics, having of course not read the book, denounced it as a tell-all that was unseemly at best, and, in the words of Trump himself, traitorous. I addressed precisely these issues in 2014, in writing a review of Robert Gates's memoir, *Duty: Memoirs of a Secretary at War*,[8] addressing criticisms of Gates similar to those now directed at me:

"Gates's critics have made two basic points, one political, one ethical. First, they say, it was inappropriate for him to write about an administration still in office, with the Afghanistan war (a major aspect of the book) still under way, and, more amusingly, with former Secretary of State Hillary Clinton ramping up her expected 2016 presidential campaign.

"Second, they argue that Gates betrayed the trust of President Obama and other senior Defense and Administration colleagues by revealing their conversations, positions, and emotions. . . .

"I believe former senior officials have virtually an obligation to explain what they did while in government. . . . It is jarringly apparent to government veterans that those who have never been 'inside' find it difficult, if not impossible, to understand what goes on and why. Press accounts and 'instant histories' are far too often lacking in insight and understanding of the government in operation. Accordingly, memoirs are critical to parting the curtain for the uninitiated, as Gates does.

"As to Gates's timing, I believe the criticisms are unfair and misplaced. There is no better moment for a prospective author to write than while his memory is still fresh, just after leaving government service. If such timing is inconvenient for the incumbent administration or former colleagues, that is their problem, not the author's. Especially for those subject to the kind of withering criticism Gates levels at Obama, no time is convenient. Imagine what those now complaining about Gates's timing would have said had the book emerged in September 2012.

"Indeed, if Gates is subject to criticism on timing, it is precisely that he did not publish before the 2012 election, where exposing Barack Obama's views on Afghanistan and his lack of interest in the global war on terrorism could have been significant. For example, voters could well have benefited from knowing what Gates was thinking during a March 2011

National Security Council meeting in the White House Situation Room, listening to the Commander in Chief: 'The president doesn't trust his commander, can't stand Karzai, doesn't believe in his own strategy, and doesn't consider the war to be his. For him it's all about getting out.'

"The harder, more important question is whether Gates violated the implicit confidences of the president and other senior colleagues. In some respects, this criticism parallels the justification for 'executive privilege,' namely, that the president must be able to receive candid advice from his subordinates, and that such candor is simply impossible if people expect to read about it thereafter. Since the integrity of Executive Branch decision-making is under siege from virtually every direction imaginable, it is no small matter if it is vulnerable from the very people directly advising the president.

"But the executive-privilege analogy is only superficially accurate. All histories pose a threat to executive privilege, and insiders have been leaking internal administration battles since Alexander Hamilton and Thomas Jefferson propagandized against each other through partisan newspapers. Somehow, President Washington muddled through. Moreover, executive privilege's true justification is to defend against an intrusive congress or judiciary, and its rationale is therefore different from the normal human expectation that confidences do not last forever. Except in the case of classified information, not at issue here, adults in US politics today understand that they are always on stage. There is no rule of omertà in politics, except perhaps in Chicago."

I stand by these views still today.

NOTES

CHAPTER 1: THE LONG MARCH TO A
WEST WING CORNER OFFICE

1 John Bolton, *Surrender Is Not an Option: Defending America at the United Nations* (New York: Simon & Schuster, 2007).

2 For those interested, see ibid.

3 See, e.g., Josh Dawsey et al., "Giuliani pulls name from contention for secretary of state," https://www.politico.com/story/2016/12/giuliani-pulls-name-from-contention-for-secretary-of-state-232439.

4 Elise Labott, "Donald Trump Told Nikki Haley She Could Speak her Mind. She's Doing Just That," https://www.cnn.com/interactive/2017/politics/state/nikki-haley-donald-trump-united-nations/.

5 Emily Smith, "Trump spent Thanksgiving asking: Mitt or Rudy?", *New York Post*, November 27, 2016, https://nypost.com/2016/11/26/trump-spent-thanksgiving-asking-mitt-or-rudy/.

6 See Gregg Jaffe and Adam Entous, "As a general, Mattis urged action against Iran. Now, as a defense secretary, he may be a voice of caution," https://www.washingtonpost.com/world/national-security/as-a-general-mattis-urged-action-against-iran-as-a-defense-secretary-he-may-be-a-voice-of-caution/2017/01/08/5a196ade-d391-11e6-a783-cd3fa950f2fd_story.html; Josh Rogin, "Mattis clashing with Trump transition team over Pentagon staffing," https://www.washingtonpost.com/news/josh-rogin/wp/2017/01/06/mattis-clashing-with-trump-transition-team-over-pentagon-staffing/.

7 Kenneth P. Vogel and Josh Dawsey, "CIA freezes out top Flynn aide," https://www.politico.com/story/2017/02/mike-flynn-nsa-aide-trump-234923.

8 See Gardiner Harris, "Where Is Rex Tillerson? Top Envoy Keeps Head Down and Travels Light," https://www.nytimes.com/2017/02/15/world/europe/germany-rex-tillerson.html?searchResultPosition=2.

9 Matt Apuzzo et al., "Trump Told Russians That Firing 'Nut Job' Comey

Eased Pressure From Investigation," https://www.nytimes.com/2017/05/19 /us/politics/trump-russia-comey.html.

10 See "Remarks by President Trump Before a Briefing on the Opioid Crisis," August 8, 2017, https://www.whitehouse.gov/briefings-statements /remarks-president-trump-briefing-opioid-crisis/.

11 See Conor Finnegan, "Tillerson: Americans should 'sleep well at night' amid N. Korea crisis," August 9, 2017, https://abcnews.go.com/International /tillerson-americans-sleep-night-amid-korea-crisis/story?id=49111147.

12 See Peter Baker, "Trump Says Military Is 'Locked and Loaded' and North Korea Will 'Regret' Threats, August 11, 2017, https://www.nytimes .com/2017/08/11/world/asia/trump-north-korea-locked-and-loaded.html.

13 See Ben Kesling, "On North Korea, Mattis, Mattis Stresses Diplomacy, But Advises Army to Be Ready," https://www.wsj.com/articles/on-north-korea -mattis-stresses-diplomacy-but-advises-army-to-be-ready-1507591261.

14 Shinzo Abe, "Solidarity Against the North Korean Threat," https:// www.nytimes.com/2017/09/17/opinion/north-korea-shinzo-abe-japan .html?searchResultPosition=22.

15 See "Interview with John Dickerson of CBS's Face the Nation," September 17, 2017, https://www.state.gov/interview-with-john-dickerson-of-cbss-face -the-nation/.

16 Jackie Northam, "China Cuts Off Bank Business With North Korea As Trump Announces New Sanctions," https://www.npr.org/2017/09/21 /552708231/china-cuts-off-bank-business-with-north-korea-as-trump -announces-new-sanctions.

17 John Bolton, "Trump must withdraw from the Iran nuclear deal—now," https://thehill.com/blogs/pundits-blog/foreign-policy/342237-opinion -trump-must-withdraw-from-iran-nuclear-deal-now.

18 See Peter Baker, "Trump Recertifies Iran Nuclear Deal, but Only Reluctantly," https://www.nytimes.com/2017/07/17/us/politics/trump-iran-nuclear-deal -recertifyhtml?auth=login-email&login=email&searchResultPosition=1.

19 See Stephen F. Hayes and Michael Warren, "Getting to No: How the Trump Administration Decided to Decertify the Iran Nuclear Deal," https://www.washingtonexaminer.com/weekly-standard/getting-to-no -how-the-trump-administration-decided-to-decertify-the-iran-nuclear -deal-2009955; and Peter Baker, note 18 above.

20 See John R. Bolton, "How to Get Out of the Iran Nuclear Deal," https://www .nationalreview.com/2017/08/iran-nuclear-deal-exit-strategy-john-bolton -memo-trump/.

21 Omer Carmi, "How Will Iran Prepare for Potential U.S. Withdrawal from

the JCPOA?", https://www.washingtoninstitute.org/policy-analysis/view /how-will-iran-prepare-for-potential-u.s.-withdrawal-from-the-jcpoa.

22 John Bolton, "Mr. President, don't put America at risk with flawed Iran deal," https://thehill.com/opinion/national-security/354484-john-bolton -mr-president-dont-put-america-at-risk-with-flawed-iran.

23 See Remarks by President Trump on Iran Strategy, October 13, 2017, https://www.whitehouse.gov/briefings-statements/remarks-president -trump-iran-strategy/.

24 See Bolton, *Surrender Is Not an Option*, especially pp. 233-38.

25 See David M. Halbfinger, "U.S. Funding Cut Reignites Debate on Palestinian Refugee Agency," https://www.nytimes.com/2018/01/17/world/middleeast /palestinian-refugee-agency-unrwa.html?searchResultPosition=2.

26 See Stephen Farrell, "Israel admits bombing suspected Syrian nuclear reactor in 2007, warns Iran," https://www.reuters.com/article/us-israel -syria-nuclear/israel-admits-bombing-suspected-syrian-nuclear-reactor -in-2007-warns-iran-idUSKBN1GX09K.

27 Reuters, "South Korea approves record $2.6 million budget for North Korea's Olympic visit," February 13, 2018, https://www.reuters.com/article /us-olympics-2018-northkorea-payment/south-korea-approves-record-2-6 -million-budget-for-north-koreans-olympic-visit-idUSKCN1FY094.

28 See, e.g., Michael Schwirtz, "U.N. Links North Korea to Syria's Chemical Weapons Program," https://www.nytimes.com/2018/02/27/world/asia /north-korea-syria-chemical-weapons-sanctions.html.

29 See Gordon Corera, BBC, "Salisbury poisoning: What did the attack mean for the UK and Russia," March 4, 2020, https://www.bbc.com/news/uk-51722301.

30 See "Press Briefing by Principal Deputy Press Secretary Raj Shah," https:// www.whitehouse.gov/briefings-statements/press-briefing-principal-deputy -press-secretary-raj-shah-03262018/.

31 Nahal Toosi, " Dunford: Military option for North Korea not 'unimag-inable,'" https://www.politico.com/story/2017/07/22/dunford-north-korea -military-option-not-unimaginable-240851.

32 Dean Acheson, *Present at the Creation* (New York, W.W. Norton & Co., 1969), p.88.

CHAPTER 2: CRY "HAVOC!" AND LET SLIP THE DOGS OF WAR

1 See Ben Hubbard, "Dozens Suffocate in Syria as Government Is Accused of Chemical Attack," https://www.nytimes.com/2018/04/08/world/middleeast /syria-chemical-attack-ghouta.html.

2 See Sarah Almukhtar, "Most Chemical Attacks in Syria Get Little Attention. Here Are 34 Confirmed Cases." https://www.nytimes.com/interactive/2018 /04/13/world/middleeast/syria-chemical-attacks-maps-history.html?search ResultPosition=2.

3 See "Statement from Pentagon Spokesman Capt. Jeff Davis on U.S. strike in Syria, April 6, 2017," https://www.defense.gov/Newsroom/Releases /Release/Article/1144598/statement-from-pentagon-spokesman-capt-jeff -davis-on-us-strike-in-syria/.

4 See Karen DeYoung and Missy Ryan, "Strike on Assad for use of chemical agents unlikely to advance wider US goals in Syria," https://www .washingtonpost.com/world/national-security/strike-on-assad-for-use-of -chemical-agents-unlikely-to-advance-wider-us-goals-in-syria/2018/04/10 /0c5fe3f8-3c0a-11e8-974f-aacd97698cef_story.html.

5 The White House statement after this call said Trump and Macron had agreed on a "strong, joint response." Monique El-Faizy, "Will Macron Do in Syria What Obama Wouldn't?" https://www.france24.com/en/20180 413-france-will-macron-do-syria-what-obama-would-not-russia-ghouta -chemical-weapons.

6 Trump raised the possibility of Russian responsibility publicly later in the day: "So if it's Russia, if it's Syria, if it's Iran, if it's all of them together, we'll figure it out and we'll know the answers quite soon." "Remarks by President Trump at Cabinet Meeting," https://www.whitehouse.gov/briefings -statements/remarks-president-trump-cabinet-meeting-7/.

7 These sorts of consultations among allies are commonplace, and often acknowledged publicly, as in this case: "British officials said Monday they are monitoring the situation in coordination with allies." Carol Morello, "U.N. to meet on chemical attack in Syria, though Russia is expected to stick up for Assad government," https://www.washingtonpost.com /world/national-security/un-to-meet-on-chemical-attack-in-syria-though -russia-is-expected-to-stick-up-for-assad-government/2018/04/09/f2e18176 -3bf4-11e8-a7d1-e4efec6389f0_story.html.

8 See Catherine Lucey and Jill Colvin, Associated Press, "In run-up to missile strike, an orderly, chaotic White House," https://www.militarytimes.com /flashpoints/2018/04/15/in-run-up-to-missile-strike-an-orderly-chaotic -white-house/; and Dion Nissenbaum, Michael Gordon, and Stacy Meichtry, "U.S. Presses Allies to Back a Military Strike on Syria," https:// www.wsj.com/articles/watchdog-agency-to-investigate-syria-chemical -strike-site-1523383551?mod=searchresults&page=1&pos=20.

9 Ibid.

10   See Associated Press, "Macron: France persuaded Trump to strike in Syria,"
     https://www.usatoday.com/story/news/world/2018/04/15/macron-france
     -persuaded-trump-strike-syria/518960002/.

11   Iran clearly thought Israel had conducted the attack, and was threatening
     retaliation. See Thomas Erdbrink, "Iran Threatens Israel Over Air Strike in
     Syria," https://www.nytimes.com/2018/04/10/world/middleeast/iran-israel
     -missile-syria.html?searchResultPosition=1.

12   See Peter Baker et al., "Trump Weighs More Robust Military Strike Against
     Syria," https://www.nytimes.com/2018/04/10/us/politics/trump-military
     -strike-syria.html.

13   Indeed, May was vigorously criticized by the Opposition for avoiding a vote
     in the House of Commons, for all the reasons Sedwill explained. See John
     Rentoul, "Theresa May avoided a vote in parliament on Syrian air strikes
     because she knew she would lose," https://www.independent.co.uk/voices
     /theresa-may-trump-syria-strikes-parliament-vote-britain-russia-chemical
     -weapons-latest-a8303146.html. Not surprisingly, May's statement to the
     House of Commons why she did not seek a parliamentary vote defending
     that decision did not directly address this point. She offered other grounds,
     including that "it was a decision which required the evaluation of intelli-
     gence and information much of which was of a nature that could not be
     shared with Parliament." Ibid. See also Alissa J. Rubin and Stephen Castle,
     "With Eye on Issues at Home, May and Macron Back Trump on Syria
     Strikes," https://www.nytimes.com/2018/04/14/world/europe/france-britain
     -syria-strikes.html?searchResultPosition=21.

14   See Gordon Rayner and Ben Riley-Smith, "Theresa May stands behind
     Donald Trump on Syria strikes, as Russia warns against 'illegal' interven-
     tion," https://www.telegraph.co.uk/politics/2018/04/10/theresa-may-joins
     -donald-trump-emmanuel-macron-condemning-syria/.

15   Russia said publicly that Israeli F-15's had fired eight missiles at the base.
     Israeli officials declined public comment, but Israel struck the same base
     on February 10. See Scott Neuman and Camila Domoneske, "Russia, Syria:
     Israeli Jets Strike Air Base After Alleged Poison Gas Attack in Douma,"
     https://www.npr.org/sections/thetwo-way/2018/04/09/600765750/russia
     -syria-israeli-jets-strike-air-base-after-alleged-poison-gas-attack-in-dou.
     The United States denied attacking Tiyas. See "U.S. denies carrying out
     missile strike in Syria, Russia says Israel did it," https://www.cbsnews.com
     /news/syria-missile-strike-attack-t4-air-base-not-us-retaliation-douma-gas
     -attack-israel-russia-says/.

16   Among other public confirmations of the call was one by Vladimir

Shamanov, Chairman of the State Duma Defense Committee, and former commander in chief of Russian airborne troops. See "President Erdogan, U.S. counterpart Trump, discuss developments in Syria," https://www .dailysabah.com/syrian-crisis/2018/04/11/president-erdogan-us-counter part-trump-discuss-developments-in-syria.

17 Earlier, Macron had said publicly he would act unilaterally if Syria again used chemical weapons, an assertion reiterated by his Foreign Minister on April 9: "In reference to a warning by President Emmanuel Macron last month that France would strike unilaterally if Syria used chemical weapons again, Foreign Minister Jean-Yves Le Drian said that the nation would assume its responsibilities." Carol Morello and Jenna Johnson, "Trump tweets condemnation of Syria chemical attack, saying Putin shares the blame." https://www.washingtonpost.com/world/national-security /trump-tweets-condemnation-of-syria-chemical-attack-criticizing -putin-for-sharing-the-blame/2018/04/08/c9c1c0e5-d063-4133-ae4d-e26 496f79fff_story.html.

18 See Seth J. Frantzman, "Ankara seeks middle path between U.S. and Russia on Syria," https://www.jpost.com/Middle-East/Ankara-seeks-middle -path-between-US-and-Russia-on-Syria-549801.

19 See Mehmet Celik, "Ankara exerts diplomatic efforts to end US-Russia row in Syria," https://www.dailysabah.com/diplomacy/2018/04/13/ankara-exerts -diplomatic-efforts-to-end-us-russia-row-in-syria.

20 See Dan Lamothe et al., "US strikes Syrian military airfield in first direct assault on Bashar al-Assad's government," https://web.archive.org/web /20170407024143/https://www.washingtonpost.com/world/national-secu rity/trump-weighing-military-options-following-chemical-weapons-attack -in-syria/2017/04/06/0c59603a-1ae8-11e7-9887-1a5314b56a08_story.html.

21 See "Timeline of Syrian Chemical Weapons Activity," https://www.arms control.org/factsheets/Timeline-of-Syrian-Chemical-Weapons-Activity.

22 Dunford and Mattis made these points publicly in a briefing right after the retaliation was concluded. See "Mattis, Dunford Detail Attacks on Syrian Chemical Arsenal," https://www.defense.gov/Explore/News/Article/Article /1493636/mattis-dunford-detail-attacks-on-syrian-chemical-arsenal/.

23 See "Assad forces emptying airports, bases over possible US strikes, Syrian Observatory says," https://www.dailysabah.com/syrian-crisis/2018/04/11 /assad-forces-emptying-airports-bases-over-possible-us-strikes-syrian -observatory-says.

24 See comments by LTG Kenneth McKenzie on April 14, cited in Gareth Davies, "Syria fired 40 missiles 'at nothing' after allied air strikes destroyed

three Assad chemical sites," https://www.telegraph.co.uk/news/2018/04/14 /russia-claims-ally-syria-shot-71-103-missiles-launched-us-britain/.

25 See "Readout of President Donald J. Trump's Call with President Emmanuel Macron of France, April 14, 2018, https://www.whitehouse.gov/briefings -statements/readout-president-donald-j-trumps-call-president-emmanuel -macron-france-15/.

26 See Michael R. Gordon, "US Intelligence Finds Syrian Government Conducted Chlorine Rocket Attack in May," https://www.wsj.com/articles /u-s-intelligence-finds-syrian-government-conducted-chlorine-rocket -attack-in-may-11569513600 and Lara Jakes, "US Concludes Syria Used Chemical Weapons in May Attack," https://www.nytimes.com/2019/09/26 /world/middleeast/syria-chemical-weapons-us.html.

CHAPTER 3: AMERICA BREAKS FREE

1 Abe had previously argued that "prioritizing diplomacy and emphasizing the importance of dialogue will not work with North Korea" and that "now is the time to exert the utmost pressure on the North." He wrote expressly that "I firmly support the United States position that all options are on the table," using the familiar phrase that includes military force as the unmentioned option. See Shinzo Abe, "Solidarity Against the North Korean Threat," https://www.nytimes.com/2017/09/17/opinion/north-korea-shinzo -abe-japan.html.

2 See "Treasury Designates Russian Oligarch, Officials, and Entities in Response to Worldwide Malign Activity," https://home.treasury.gov/news /press-releases/sm0338.

3 Many policy commentators shared my skepticism. See, e.g., Derek Grossman, "China's Reluctance on Sanctions Enforcement in North Korea," https://www.rand.org/blog/2018/01/chinas-reluctance-on-sanctions-en forcement-in-north.html.

4 "Trump calls Iran deal 'insane' in meeting with France's Macron," https:// www.cnbc.com/video/2018/04/24/trump-calls-iran-deal-insane-in-meet ing-with-frances-macron.html.

5 Macron revealed this to the press on his own a few days later. See https:// www.efe.com/efe/english/world/macron-believes-trump-will-scrap-iran -nuclear-deal/50000262-3596907.

6 See Peter Baker and Julie Hirschfeld Davis, "Trump Signals Openness to a 'New Deal' to Constrain Iran," https://www.nytimes.com/2018/04/24 /world/europe/trump-macron-iran-climate.html?searchResultPosition=22.

7 Macron used this very phrase in the joint press conference following the bilateral meeting. See "Remarks by President Trump and President Macron of France in Joint Press Conference," April 24, 2018, https://www.white house.gov/briefings-statements/remarks-president-trump-president -macron-france-joint-press-conference/.

8 Trump made essentially these same points in the joint press conference followed the closed meeting. See n. 7 above ("But we'll see also, if I do what some people expect, whether or not it will be possible to do a new deal with solid foundations. Because this is a deal with decayed foundations. It's a bad deal. It's a bad structure. It's falling down.").

9 Ibid.

10 See, e.g., Caroline Houck, "Trump Calls Europe "as bad as China" on trade," https://www.vox.com/world/2018/7/1/17522984/europe-china-trade-war -trump, quoting Trump in an interview with Fox News's Maria Bartiromo.

11 See Julie Hirschfeld Davis, "Trump and Merkel Meet One on One, but Don't See Eye to Eye," https://www.nytimes.com/2018/04/27/us/politics/trump -merkel.html?searchResultPosition=6.

12 BBC, "Merkel lobbies Trump on trade and Iran," https://www.bbc.com /news/world-us-canada-43925422.

13 See Judah Ari Gross, "US officials say Israel behind latest Syria strike, preparing for war with Iran," https://www.timesofisrael.com/us-officials -say-israel-behind-latest-syria-strike-preparing-for-war-with-iran/, quoting Courtney Kube, "Israel seems to be preparing for war with Iran, U.S. officials say," May 1, 2018, https://www.nbcnews.com/news/mideast/israel -seems-be-preparing-war-iran-say-u-s-officials-n870051.

14 See, "Readout of President Donald J. Trump's Call with Prime Minister Theresa May of the United Kingdom," May 5, 2018. https://www.white house.gov/briefings-statements/readout-president-donald-j-trumps-call -prime-minister-theresa-may-united-kingdom-7/.

15 See Boris Johnson, "Don't Scuttle the Iran Nuclear Deal," https://www.ny times.com/2018/05/06/opinion/boris-johnson-trump-iran-nuclear-deal.html.

16 See "Press briefing by National Security Advisor John Bolton on Iran," May 8, 2018, https://www.whitehouse.gov/briefings-statements/press -briefing-national-security-advisor-john-bolton-iran/.

17 See, e.g., Michael Gordon et al., "After Trump's Threat, White House Convenes a Policy Meeting," https://www.wsj.com/articles/after-trumps -threat-to-iran-white-house-convenes-a-policy-meeting-1532597520 ?mod=searchresults&page=1&pos=2.

18 See Michael Gordon, "White House Blames Iranian-Backed Militias for

Attacking U.S. Facilities in Iraq," September 11, 2018, https://www.wsj.com/articles/white-house-blames-iranian-backed-militias-for-attacking-u-s-facilities-in-iraq-1536707458, quoting White House press secretary Sarah Sanders.

19 See, e.g., Editorial Board, "A Swift Iran Decision: Iranian banks have to be expelled from the global financing network," https://www.wsj.com/articles/europes-not-so-swift-diplomacy-1539730896.

CHAPTER 4: THE SINGAPORE SLING

1 See Bolton, *Surrender Is Not an Option*, especially chapters four and eleven.

2 Winston Churchill, Speech in Parliament, May 2, 1935, quoted in John H. Maurer, "Churchill and the Outbreak of the Second World War in Europe," *Orbis*, Summer, 2019, p. 313.

3 Gossip to this effect circulated in Seoul after the summit, and I raised the issue with Chung directly, having suspected it myself. Even before traveling to Pyongyang, Chung intimated that US-North Korea talks were part of his mission: "I plan to hold in-depth discussions on various ways to continue talks between not only the South and the North, but also the North and the United States." See, BBC News, "North Korea's Kim Jong-un meets South Korea's envoys," https://www.bbc.com/news/world-asia-43282807.

4 See point five in the "Joint Statement of the Fourth Round of the Six-Party Talks," Beijing, September 19, 2005, https://2009-2017.state.gov/p/eap/regional/c15455.htm: "The Six Parties agreed to take coordinated steps to implement the aforementioned consensus in a phased manner in line with the principle of "commitment for commitment, action for action."

5 The U.S. and Japan subsequently agreed on a one-year dismantlement program. See note 8, below.

6 See David French, "A Trip Down Memory Lane: In 2015, the Obama Administration Said the Iran Deal Wasn't Even a 'Signed Document,'" May 10, 2018, https://www.nationalreview.com/corner/iran-nuclear-deal-not-signed-document-not-binding/.

7 See, e.g., Shinzo Abe, "Solidarity Against the North Korean Threat," September 17, 2017, https://www.nytimes.com/2017/09/17/opinion/north-korea-shinzo-abe-japan.html..

8 See Adam Mount and Ankit Panda, "North Korea Is Not Denuclearizing," https://www.theatlantic.com/international/archive/2018/04/north-korea-kim-jong-un-trump-nuclear-summit-weapons-missiles/558620/; Joby

Warrick, "Suspicious factory underscores challenge of verifying North Korea's nuclear promises," https://www.washingtonpost.com/world /national-security/suspicious-factory-underscores-challenge-of-verify ing-north-koreas-nuclear-promises/2018/04/21/fad9764e-457d-11e8-8569 -26fda6b404c7_story.html.

9 Nicholas Eberstadt, "North Korea's Phony Peace Ploy," https://www.nytimes .com/2018/04/25/opinion/north-korea-south-korea-peace.html.

10 Given this relative success on timing, I adopted the Moon-Kim one-year period as an accepted agreement. See, e.g., Hyonhee Shin, "U.S. has plan to dismantle North Korea nuclear program within a year: Bolton," https:// www.reuters.com/article/us-northkorea-missiles-usa/u-s-has-plan-to-dis mantle-north-korea-nuclear-program-within-a-year-bolton-idUSKBN 1JR1KP.

11 Choe Sang-Hun, "North Korea Envoy Hails Bolton's Ouster and Trump's Talk of a New Approach," https://www.nytimes.com/2019/09/20/world/asia /north-korea-us-nuclear-talks.html?searchResultPosition=1.

12 "Remarks by President Trump and Secretary General Stoltenberg of NATO Before Bilateral Meeting," https://www.whitehouse.gov/briefings-statements /remarks-president-trump-secretary-general-stoltenberg-nato-bilateral -meeting/.

13 See Statement of Ambassador John Bolton, reported in "Security Council Condemns Nuclear Test by Democratic People's Republic of Korea, Unani- mously Adopting Resolution 1718 (2006)," https://www.un.org/press/en /2006/sc8853.doc.htm.

14 Jamie Tarabay, "To experts, North Korea dismantling nuclear site is like destroying evidence," https://www.cnn.com/2018/05/22/asia/north-korea -destroy-nuclear-site-intl/index.html, quoting Cheryl Rofer: "'If I were going I would want to bring some capability of taking samples, and I would also want to bring a geologist with me. I'd want to have a radiation counter, I would want to go into the tunnel to see if parts of it have caved in in the back, and I would want to take radiation measurements.' All those samples and tests could yield information on the kinds of weapons that were being tested, she said. 'Isotope measurements could tell you about the design of the device, it would tell you what kind of bombs they're making, what they're making them out of, how much uranium and plutonium is in the bombs. We might be able to infer what they're planning and the shape of their progress,' she said."

15 Ibid.

16 See Christina Maza, "China Tells Trump to Stay Calm as North Korea

Threatens to Cancel Historic Talks," May 17, 2018, https://www.newsweek
.com/china-tells-trump-stay-calm-north-korea-threatens-cancel-historic
-talks-931275.

17 See Joyce Lee and Heekyong Lee, "North Korea won't hold talks with
'incompetent' South unless differences settled," Reuters, https://www
.reuters.com/article/us-northkorea-missiles-southkorea/north-korea-says
-wont-hold-talks-with-incompetent-south-unless-differences-settled-idUS
KCN1II0B7.

18 On Monday, May 8, 2019, discussing trade issues with Bob Lighthizer, I
told this anecdote about "breaking up with the girl first." Lighthizer was
incredulous, saying "that's exactly what Trump told me on Friday when I
was briefing him on how the negotiations in Beijing had gone!" This was a
rare mark of consistency in Trump policy.

19 See Joshua Berlinger, "North Korea warns of nuclear showdown, calls Pence
'political dummy,'" https://www.cnn.com/2018/05/23/politics/mike-pence
-north-korea-intl/index.html.

20 See Thomas Maresca and Jane Onyanga-Omara, "South Korean president
calls cancellation of Trump-Kim summit 'very regrettable,'" https://www
.usatoday.com/story/news/world/2018/05/24/trump-cancels-summit-kim
/640452002/.

21 Japan's public reaction was restrained and supportive of Trump's cancellation. See Reiji Yoshida and Daisuke Kikuchi, "Tokyo shows united front
on Trump-Kim summit cancellation, calling for cooperation with U.S. and
South Korea," https://www.japantimes.co.jp/news/2018/05/25/national
/politics-diplomacy/tokyo-understands-trumps-cancelation-u-s-north
-korea-summit-officials/#.XmEfbKhKiF4.

22 See "Full address by South Korean President Moon Jae-In on May 26 inter-
Korea summit," May 27, 2018, https://www.straitstimes.com/asia/east-asia
/full-address-by-south-korean-president-moon-jae-in-on-may-26-inter
-korea-summit.

23 See "South Korea's Moon Jae In might join Trump, Kim in Singapore for
3-way summit: Official," https://www.straitstimes.com/asia/east-asia/south
-koreas-moon-jae-in-might-join-trump-kim-in-singapore-for-3-way
-summit-official.

24 See "Italy's Conte wants G8 with Russia, not quick end to sanctions," June
8, 2018, https://www.reuters.com/article/us-g7-summit-italy/italys-conte
-wants-g8-with-russia-not-quick-end-to-sanctions-idUSKCN1J50MV.

25 There was constant public speculation that China was not enforcing
sanctions strictly. See, e.g., Derek Grossman, "China's Reluctance on

Sanctions Enforcement in North Korea," https://www.rand.org/blog/2018
/01/chinas-reluctance-on-sanctions-enforcement-in-north.html; and
"China is quietly relaxing its sanctions against North Korea, complicating
matters for Trump," https://www.latimes.com/business/la-fg-china-north
-korea-sanctions-2018-story.html.

26 See Gardiner Harris and Choe Sang-Hun, "North Korea Criticizes
'Gangster-Like' U.S. Attitude After Talks with Mike Pompeo," July 7, 2018,
https://www.nytimes.com/2018/07/07/world/asia/mike-pompeo-north
-korea-pyongyang.html.

27 See, e.g., Nuclear Threat Initiative, "North Korea," https://www.nti.org/learn
/countries/north-korea/nuclear/.

28 See https://ustr.gov/trade-agreements/free-trade-agreements/korus-fta
/final-text.

29 See "Press Briefing by Press Secretary Sarah Sanders and National Security
Officials," August 2, 2018, https://www.whitehouse.gov/briefings-statements
/press-briefing-press-secretary-sarah-sanders-national-security-officials
-08022018/.

30 Trump also tweeted later that evening that he was looking forward to
seeing Kim. See John Wagner, "Trump says he is looking forward to
meeting again 'soon' with Kim Jong Un," https://www.washingtonpost
.com/politics/trump-says-he-is-looking-forward-to-meeting-again-soon
-with-kim-jong-un/2018/08/02/7084654e-963b-11e8-a679-b09212fb69c2_
story.html.

31 See "Press Briefing by Press Secretary Sarah Sanders and CEA Chairman
Kevin Hassett," https://www.whitehouse.gov/briefings-statements
/press-briefing-press-secretary-sarah-sanders-cea-chairman-kevin
-hassett-091018/.

CHAPTER 5: A TALE OF THREE CITIES— SUMMITS IN BRUSSELS, LONDON, AND HELSINKI

1 My earlier encounters with Putin are described in *Surrender Is Not an
Option*, especially chapter three.

2 See Jeffrey Goldberg, "The Obama Doctrine," https://www.theatlantic.com
/magazine/archive/2016/04/the-obama-doctrine/471525/; Mark Landler,
"Obama Criticizes the 'Free Riders' Among America's Allies," https://www
.nytimes.com/2016/03/10/world/middleeast/obama-criticizes-the-free
-riders-among-americas-allies.html.

3 See Susan B. Glasser, "Trump National Security Team Blindsided by NATO

Speech," https://www.politico.com/magazine/story/2017/06/05/trump-nato
-speech-national-security-team-215227.

4 Nicholas Fiorenza, "Allies agree to reduce US contributions to NATO
common funding," https://www.janes.com/article/92915/allies-agree-to
-reduce-us-contributions-to-nato-common-funding.

5 See Veronica Stracqualursi, "Trump says Putin meeting "may be the
easiest of them all," https://www.cnn.com/2018/07/10/politics/trump-putin
-meeting/index.html.

6 See "Remarks by President Trump and NATO Secretary General Jens
Stoltenberg at Bilateral Breakfast," July 11, 2018, https://www.whitehouse
.gov/briefings-statements/remarks-president-trump-nato-secretary-gene
ral-jens-stoltenberg-bilateral-breakfast/.

7 Merkel was repeating what she had said earlier on entering the NATO headquarters, having obviously heard about the Stoltenberg-Trump breakfast.
See Steve Erlanger and Julie Hirschfeld Davis, "Trump versus Merkel: Blistering Salvo Meets Quiet Rejoinder," https://www.nytimes.com/2018/07/11
/world/europe/germany-merkel-russia-trump-nato.html.

8 These were all remarks Trump had earlier said publicly. See ibid.

9 See "Statement from the Press Secretary on the Expulsion of Russian
Intelligence Officers," March 26, 2018, https://www.whitehouse.gov/brief
ings-statementsstatement-press-secretary-expulsion-russian-intelligence
-officers/.

10 See Mark Mazzetti et al., "12 Russian Agents Indicted in Mueller Investigation," https://www.nytimes.com/2018/07/13/us/politics/mueller-indictment
-russian-intelligence-hacking.html.

11 See "Remarks by President Trump and Prime Minister May of the United
Kingdom in Joint Press Conference," July 13, 2018, https://www.whitehouse
.gov/briefings-statements/remarks-president-trump-prime-minister-may
-united-kingdom-joint-press-conference/.

12 See "Fearing Russian aggression, Finland tells 900K military reservists to
be prepared 'in the event of war,'" https://nationalpost.com/news/world
/fearing-russian-aggression-finland-tells-900k-military-reservists-to-be
-prepared-in-the-event-of-war, which cites a figure of 285,000 army
reservists.

13 All attributed comments to the two Presidents in this and the following
paragraphs are from "Remarks by President Trump and President Putin of
the Russian Federation in Joint Press Conference," July 16, 2018, https://
www.whitehouse.gov/briefings-statements/remarks-president-trump
-president-putin-russian-federation-joint-press-conference/.

CHAPTER 6: THWARTING RUSSIA

1 See "New START: Treaty Text," https://2009-2017.state.gov/t/avc/newstart /c44126.htm.

2 See "Remarks by President Trump Before Marine One Departure," https:// www.whitehouse.gov/briefings-statements/remarks-president-trump -marine-one-departure-18/.

3 See Reuters, "Bolton says we're a long way from deploying U.S. missiles in Europe," October 23, 2018, https://www.reuters.com/article/us-usa -nuclear-bolton-inf/bolton-says-were-a-long-way-from-deploying-u-s -missiles-in-europe-idUSKCN1MX2L9.

4 See Deutsche Welle, "INF: Vladimir Putin Threatens to mirror US deploy- ment of nuclear missiles in Europe," October 24, 2018, https://www.dw.com /en/inf-vladimir-putin-threatens-to-mirror-us-deployment-of-nuclear -missiles-in-europe/a-46031790.

5 See U.S. Department of Defense, "Nuclear Posture Review," 2018, https:// media.defense.gov/2018/Feb/02/2001872886/-1/-1/1/2018-NUCLEAR -POSTURE-REVIEW-FINAL-REPORT.PDF, at pp. 9 and 53.

6 See Bolton, *Surrender Is Not an Option*, pp.87–92, 97.

7 See Aaron Mehta, "US, Russia remain at 'impasse' over Open Skies treaty flights," https://www.defensenews.com/air/2018/09/14/us-russia-remain -at-impasse-over-nuclear-treaty-flights/.

8 Aric Jenkins, "Why Russia Was Allowed to Fly a Surveillance Plane Over the Capitol and the Pentagon," https://time.com/4895574/open-skies-treaty -russia-surveillance-plane/.

9 Julian Borger, "Trump administration determined to exit treaty reducing risk of war," April 5, 2020, https://www.theguardian.com/us-news/2020 /apr/05/trump-administration-treaty-war-russia-withdraw.

10 See Curtis A. Bradley, "Unratified Treaties, Domestic Politics, and the US Constitution," 48 *Harvard International Law Journal* 307 (Number 2, Summer, 2007), https://scholarship.law.duke.edu/cgi/viewcontent.cgi ?article=2517&context=faculty_scholarship.

11 The story of how we unsigned the ICC is told briefly in *Surrender Is Not an Option*, pp. 85–87.

12 See John R. Bolton, "Vladimir Putin looked Trump in the eye and lied to him. We negotiate with Russia at our peril," at https://www.telegraph.co.uk /news/2017/07/10/vladimir-putin-looked-trump-eye-lied-negotiate-russia -peril/.

13 David Filipov et al., "Putin denies election hacking after Trump pressed

him, Tillerson says," https://www.washingtonpost.com/world/heres-whats
-at-stake-whentrump-finally-meets-putin/2017/07/07/a5c577d2-627c-11e7
-80a2-8c226031ac3f_story.html.

14 See "National Cyber Strategy of the United States of America," September,
2018, https://www.whitehouse.gov/wp-content/uploads/2018/09/National
-Cyber-Strategy.pdf, pp.1-2 and throughout.

15 Ibid.

16 Jacqueline Thomsen, "US to prioritize attacks against foreign adversaries
under new cyber strategy," https://thehill.com/policy/cybersecurity
/407670-us-to-launch-offensive-attacks-against-foreign-adversaries
-under-new.

17 Justin Lynch, "Trump's national cyber strategy praised by experts,"
https://www.fifthdomain.com/congress/policy/2018/09/21/
trumps-national-cyber-strategy-praised-by-experts/.

18 See "Executive Order on Imposing Sanctions in the Event of Foreign
Interference in a United States Election," September 12, 2018, https://www
.whitehouse.gov/presidential-actions/executive-order-imposing-certain
-sanctions-event-foreign-interference-united-states-election/.

19 See, e.g., Eric Geller, "Trump silent as top officials warn of Russia threat,"
https://www.politico.com/story/2018/08/02/trump-russian-election
-hacking-720428.

20 See end note 9, chapter 5.

21 See Ivan Gutterman et al., "A Timeline of All Russia-Related Sanctions,"
https://www.rferl.org/a/russia-sanctions-timeline/29477179.html.

22 Ellen Nakashima and Paul Sonne, "Bolton says US is conducting 'offensive
cyber' action to thwart would-be election disrupters," https://www
.washingtonpost.com/world/national-security/bolton-acknowledges-us
-has-taken-action-to-thwart-would-be-election-disrupters/2018/10/31
/0c5dfa64-dd3d-11e8-85df-7a6b4d25cfbb_story.html.

23 Darwin McDaniel, "Nakasone: 2018 Midterm Elections a Success in
Feds' Cyber Efforts," https://www.executivegov.com/2019/01/nakasone
-2018-midterm-elections-a-success-in-feds-cyber-efforts/.

CHAPTER 7: TRUMP HEADS FOR THE DOOR IN SYRIA
AND AFGHANISTAN, AND CAN'T FIND IT

1 See Greg Farrell and Christian Bertelsen, "Turkey's Halkbank Could Suffer
from Ex-Banker's US Conviction," https://www.bloomberg.com/news
/articles/2018-01-04/turkey-s-halkbank-could-suffer-from-ex-banker-s-u

-s-conviction, and Amanda Sloat, "Why Turkey cares about the trial of Reza Zarrab," https://www.brookings.edu/blog/order-from-chaos/2017/11/22/why-turkey-cares-about-the-trial-of-reza-zarrab/.

2 See "A court case in New York rattles Turkey's president, Recep Tayyip Erdogan," https://www.economist.com/europe/2017/12/09./a-court-case-in-new-york-rattles-turkeys-president-recep-tayyip-erdogan.

3 See "Andrew Brunson: US hits Turkey with sanctions over jailed pastor," https://www.bbc.com/news/world-us-canada-45036378.

4 See Zeynep Bilginsoy, "Turkey slaps sanctions on 2 US officials in retaliation," https://www.apnews.com/4d47a56373e64669b80a3a14f87c0be2.

5 "Turkey expects no fine for Halkbank: finance minister," https://www.reuters.com/article/us-turkey-currency-albayrak-usa/turkey-expects-no-fine-for-halkbank-finance-minister-idUSKCN1LJ0L6.

6 See Jack Ewing and Carlotta Gall, "Qatar Comes to Aid of Turkey, Offering $15 Billion Lifeline," https://www.nytimes.com/2018/08/15/world/europe/turkey-andrew-brunson-tariffs.html.

7 See Carlotta Gall, "Turkey Frees Pastor Andrew Brunson, Easing Tensions With US," https://www.nytimes.com/2018/10/12/world/europe/turkey-us-pastor-andrew-brunson.html.

8 See, e.g., Atlantic Council, "The sticky situation of the final Idlib offensive," August 15, 2018, https://www.atlanticcouncil.org/blogs/syriasource/the-sticky-situation-of-the-final-idlib-offensive/.

9 See, e.g., "Israel says it launched 200 strikes in Syria since 2017," September 5, 2018, https://www.aljazeera.com/news/2018/09/israel-launched-200-strikes-syria-2017-180905063755959.html.

10 See Barbara Starr et al., "Syria accidentally shot down a Russian military plane," https://www.cnn.com/2018/09/17/politics/syrian-regime-shoots-down-russian-plane/index.html.

11 See Jonathan Marcus, "Is Russia taking control of Syria's air defenses?", https://www.bbc.com/news/world-middle-east-45625388.

12 See, e.g., Michael Knights, Washington Institute, "Responding to Iranian Harassment of U.S. Facilities in Iraq," https://www.washingtoninstitute.org/policy-analysis/view/responding-to-iranian-harassment-of-u.s.-facilities-in-iraq; Al Jaazeera, "Rockets hit Iranian Kurdish opposition office's in Iraq's Koya," September 8, 2018, https://www.aljazeera.com/news/2018/09/rockets-hit-iranian-kurdish-opposition-offices-iraq-koya-180908090605503.html; and Edward Wong, "Blaming Iran, U.S.

Evacuates Consulate in Southern Iraq," https://www.nytimes.com/2018
/09/28/world/middleeast/iraq-iran-consulate-basra-closed.html.

13 See Edward Wong, note 12, above.

14 See Glenn Harlan Reynolds, "Turkey's new sultan," July 20, 2016,
    https://www.usatoday.com/story/opinion/2016/07/20/turkey-coup
    -islam-erdogan-sharia-sultan-caliphate-crackdown-democracy
    -column/87344676/.

15 The December 14 call is noted at p. 138 in https://www.govtinfo.gov
    /content/pkg/DCPD-2018DIGEST/pdf/DCPD-2018DIGEST.pdf.
    See also Barbara Starr et al., "Trump orders rapid withdrawal from
    Syria in apparent reversal," https://www.cnn.com/2018/12/19/politics
    /us-syria-withdrawal/index.html; and Karen DeYoung, "Trump Adminis-
    tration tries to head off Turkish assault on Kurds in Syria," December 14,
    2018, https://www.washingtonpost.com/world/national-security/trump
    -administration-tries-to-head-off-turkish-assault-on-kurds-in-syria/2018
    /12/14/6d614120-ffe5-11e8-ad40-cdfd0e0dd65a_story.html.

16 See Mark Landler et al., "Trump to Withdraw US Forces From Syria,
    Declaring 'We Have Won Against ISIS,'" https://www.nytimes.com/2018/12
    /19/us/politics/trump-syria-turkey-troop-wthdrawal.html.

17 See p. 140 at https://www.govinfo.gov/content/pkg/DPCD-2018DIGEST
    /pdf/DPCD-2018DIGEST.pdf.

18 See "Remarks by President Trump to Troops at Al Asad Air Base, Al Anbar
    Province, Iraq," December 26, 2018, https://www.whitehouse.gov/briefings
    -statements/remarks-president-trump-troops-al-asad-air-base-al-anbar
    -province-iraq/.

19 See Zeke Miller and Lolita C. Baldor, "US pushes NATO allies to join observer
    force in Syria," https://apnews.com/1fa36d41b686410e84bfc986c9f56337.

20 See Bolton, *Surrender Is Not an Option*, throughout, on this subject.

21 See David A. Sanger, "Bolton Puts Conditions on Syria Withdrawal,
    Suggesting a Delay of Months or Years," https://www.nytimes.com/2019/01
    /06/world/middleeast/bolton-syria-pullout.html.

22 See "Remarks by President Trump Before Marine One Departure" January
    6, 2019, https://www.whitehouse.gov/briefings-statements/remarks-presi
    dent-trump-marine-one-departure-29/.

23 See note 21 above.

24 See Associated Press, "Turkey slams Pompeo comments on 'slaughtering'
    Kurds," January 4, 2019, https://apnews.com/27fa54d76e8d4fa79453430f
    9e2b57ae.

25   Missy Ryan and Karen DeYoung, "'No different from my original state-
     ments': Trump denies changes to Syria exit plan," https://www.washing
     onpost.com/world/national-security/no-different-from-my-original
     -statements-trump-denies-changes-to-syria-exit-plan/2019/01/07/d939
     22f2-128f-11e9-90a8-136fa44b80ba_story.html.

26   Karen DeYoung and Karoun Demirjian, "Contradicting Trump, Bolton says
     no withdrawal from Syria until ISIS destroyed, Kurds' safety guaranteed,"
     https://www.washingtonpost.com/world/national-security/no-different
     -from-my-original-statements-trump-denies-changes-to-syria-exit-plan
     /2019/01/07/d93922f2-128f-11e9-90a8-136fa44b80ba_story.html.

27   See Australian Broadcasting Corporation, "Turkish president Recep
     Tayyip Erdogan says 'no concession' for Syrian Kurds, snubbing US plea,"
     January 8, 2019, https://www.abc.net.au/news/2019-01-09/turkey-rejects-us
     -request-to-protect-us-kurdish-allies-in-syria/10700680.

28   See Radio Free Europe/Radio Liberty, "White House Now Says 400 'Peace-
     keepers' To Remain In Syria, Up From 200," February 23, 2019, https://
     www.rferl.org/a/us-keeping-peacekeepers-syria-pullout-kurds-russia
     -iran-turkey/29786293.html.

29   See Zachary Cohen, "Inside the dramatic US military raid that killed ISIS
     leader Baghdadi," https://www.cnn.com/2019/10/27/politics/bagdhadi
     -inside-the-raid-timeline/index.html.

30   See Eliza Relman, "Defense Secretary Mattis reportedly wasn't consulted
     before the military dropped the 'mother of all bombs,'" https://www.busi
     nessinsider.com/mattis-mother-of-all-bombs-2017-5.

31   See Julie Turkewitz, "Brent Taylor, Utah Major Killed in Afghanistan,
     Was on 4th Deployment," November 4, 2018, https://www.nytimes
     .com/2018/11/04/us/utah-mayor-killed-afghanistan-brent-taylor.html.

32   The concept of a "counter-terrorism platform" in Afghanistan, to be sure
     going through many variations, had long been under discussion. See, e.g.,
     Andrew deGrandpre, "Before there's another surge in Afghanistan, Mattis
     and his general need to meet," https://www.militarytimes.com/news
     /your-military/2017/02/11/before-there-s-another-surge-in-afghanistan
     -mattis-and-his-general-need-to-meet/.

33   See Mujib Mashal, "U.S. and Taliban Agree in Principle to Peace Frame-
     work, Envoy Says," January 28, 2019, https://www.nytimes.com/2019/01/28
     /world/asia/taliban-peace-deal-afghanistan.html.

34   See "President Donald J. Trump's State of the Union Address," February 5,
     2019, https://www.whitehouse.gov/briefings-statements/president-donald
     -j-trumps-state-union-address-2/.

CHAPTER 8: CHAOS AS A WAY OF LIFE

1 John H. Sununu, *The Quiet Man: The Indispensable Presidency of George H.W. Bush* (New York: Broadside Books, 2015).

2 See Jeane J. Kirkpatrick, "Dictatorships and Double Standards," https://www .commentarymagazine.com/articles/dictatorships-double-standards/.

3 See Helene Cooper, "Fraying Ties With Trump Put Jim Mattis's Fate in Doubt," posted at https://www.nytimes.com/2018/09/15/us/politics/jim -mattis-trump-defense-relationship.html.

4 See Ashley Parker and Phillip Rucker, "'A rising star': Haley poses a potential threat to Trump even if she doesn't run in 2020," https://www .washingtonpost.com/politics/a-rising-star-haley-poses-a-potential -threat-to-trump-even-if-she-doesnt-run-in-2020/2018/10/09/bca850d8 -cbd9-11e8-920f-dd52e1ae4570_story.html.

5 See Christina Zhao, "Nikki Haley Denies 'False Rumors' of a Possible Trump/Haley 2020 Ticket: Pence 'Has My Complete Support,'" https://www .newsweek.com/nikki-haley-denies-false-rumors-possible-trump-haley -2020-ticket-pence-has-my-complete-1455584.

6 See, e.g., BBC, "France's Macron pushes for 'true European army.'" November 6, 2018, https://www.bbc.com/news/world-europe-46108633.

7 See Scott McDonald, "John Kelly's 'Yes Man' Comments on Trump Ripped Through Social Media," https://www.newsweek.com/john-kellys-yes-man -comments-trump-ripped-through-social-media-1467986.

8 See Caroline Kelly et al., "White House: John Kelly 'was totally unequipped to handle the genius of our great President,'" https://www.cnn.com/2019/10 /26/politics/john-kelly-trump-yes-man/index.html.

9 See Rachel Frazin, "Grisham: John Kelly ill-equipped to work with 'the genius of our great president,'" https://thehill.com/homenews /administration/467602-grisham-john-kelly-ill-equipped-to-work-with -the-genius-of-the.

CHAPTER 9: VENEZUELA LIBRE

1 See, e.g., the interview with Elliott Abrams, the State Department's point person on Venezuela, in David Luhnow and José de Córdoba, "Venezuela's Government Held Talks With Government on Ousting Maduro," May 1, 2019, https://www.wsj.com/articles/venezuelas-opposi tion-held-talks-with-government-on-ousting-maduro-11556767656.

2 See *New York Times*, "Trump Alarms Venezuela With Talk of a 'Military

Option,'" August 12, 2017, https://www.nytimes.com/2017/08/12/world
/americas/trump-venezuela-military.html and Christopher Woody,
"Trump: 'I'm not going to rule out a military option' for Venezuela, August
11, 2017, https://www.businessinsider.com/trump-im-not-going-to-rule
-out-a-military-option-for-venezuela-2017-8.

3 See Siobhán O'Grady, "As Maduro clashes with opposition, Washington
engages in 'careful little dance' with Venezuela," January 12, 2019, https://
www.washingtonpost.com/world/2019/01/12/maduro-clashes-with
-opposition-washington-engages-careful-little-dance-with-venezuela/.

4 State Department spokesman Robert Palladino said, "It is time to begin
the orderly transition to a new government. We support the National
Assembly's call for all Venezuelans to work together, peacefully, to restore
constitutional government and build a better future." Ibid.

5 See Ana Vanessa Herrero, "Venezuela Opposition Leader Is Arrested
After Proposing to Take Power," January 13, 2019, https://www.nytimes
.com/2019/01/13/world/americas/venezeula-juan-guaido-arrest.html.

6 Indeed, confusion within Maduro's regime, see ibid., was one indication
that outside forces might have been at work. The Cuban presence in
Venezuela, and particularly the key role they play in keeping the Maduro
regime in place, is amply documented. Predictably, Cuba denies everything.
See, e.g., Ethan Bronner, Alex Vasquez, and David Wainer, "How Has
Maduro Survived? With Lots of Help from Cuban Operatives," April 1,
2019, https://www.bloomberg.com/news/articles/2019-04-01/how-has
-maduro-survived-with-lots-of-help-from-cuban-operatives; Jorge C.
Carrasco, "Venezuelan Democracy Was Strangled by Cuba," May 14, 2019,
https://foreignpolicy.com/2019/05/14/venezuelan-democracy-was-stran
gled-by-cuba/; "https://www.geopoliticalmonitor.com/author/josemi
guel/" Jose Miguel Alonso-Trabanco, "Cuba's intelligence Masterstroke in
Venezuela," August 9, 2018, https://www.geopoliticalmonitor.com/cubas
-intelligence-masterstroke-in-venezuela/; and Adam Taylor, "How many
Cuban troops are there in Venezuela? The U.S. says over 20,000. Cuba says
zero." May 2, 2019, https://www.washingtonpost.com/world/2019/05/02
/how-many-cuban-troops-are-there-venezuela-us-says-over-cuba-says-zero/.

7 See Jennifer Hansler, Flora Charner and Zachary Cohen, "US orders
non-emergency personnel out of Venezuela," January 25, 2019, https://www
.cnn.com/2019/01/24/politics/pompeo-bolton-venezuela-maduro/index.html.

8 See Associated Press, "The Latest: Venezuela opposition leader backs US
sanctions," January 29, 2019, https://apnews.com/aea46490266049c6a20a6a
ba29efc2ca.

9   See Nick Paton Walsh, Natalie Gallón, and Diana Castrillon, "Corruption
    in Venezuela has created a cocaine superhighway to the US," April 17, 2019,
    https://www.cnn.com/2019/04/17/americas/venezuela-drug-cocaine
    -trafficking-intl/index.html.

10 See "Remarks by President Trump and President Duqué of Colombia
    Before Bilateral Meeting," September 25, 2018, https://www.whitehouse
    .gov/briefings-statements/remarks-president-trump-president-duque
    -republic-colombia-bilateral-meetings/.

11 This was exactly what we were saying publicly throughout the crisis, at
    Trump's behest. See, e.g., John Allen, "Bolton: All options are on the table
    for Trump in Venezuela," January 28, 2019, https://www.nbcnews.com
    /politics/white-house/bolton-all-options-are-table-trump-venezuela
    -n963681; and Ellen Mitchell, "Bolton says 'all options are on the table'
    in Venezuela as protests intensify," April 30, 2019, https://thehill.com
    /homenews/administration/441426-bolton-says-all-options-are-on-the
    -table-in-venezuela-as-protests

12 See Mary Beth Sheridan, "Maduro's muscle: Politically backed motorcycle
    gangs known as 'colectivos' are the enforcers for Venezuela's authoritarian
    leader," March 14, 2019, https://www.washingtonpost.com/world/the
    _americas/maduros-muscle-politically-backed-motorcycle-gangs
    -known-as-colectivos-are-the-enforcers-for-venezuelas-authoritarian
    -leader/2019/03/13/2242068c-4452-11e9-94ab-d2dda3c0df52_story.html.

13 Reuters reported that "Private military contractors who do secret missions
    for Russia flew into Venezuela in the past few days to beef up security
    for President Nicolas Maduro in the face of US-backed opposition
    protests, according to two people close to them." See Maria Tsvetkova
    and Anton Zverev, Reuters, "Exclusive: Kremlin-linked contractors help
    guard Venezuela's Maduro—Sources," January 25, 2019, https://www
    .reuters.com/article/us-venezuela-politics-russia-exclusive/exclusive
    -kremlin-linked-contractors-help-guard-venezuelas-maduro-sources
    -idUSKCN1PJ22M.

14 See Jessica Donati, Ian Talley and Andrew Scurria, "Venezuela's Opposition
    Leader Guaidó to Name New Citgo Board, Rubio Says," February 6, 2019,
    https://www.wsj.com/articles/venezuelas-opposition-leader-guaido-to
    -name-new-citgo-board-sen-rubio-says-11549501327.

15 See Keith Johnson, "Kerry Makes It Official: 'Era of Monroe Doctrine Is
    Over,'" November 18, 2013, https://blogs.wsj.com/washwire/2013/11/18
    /kerry-makes-it-official-era-of-monroe-doctrine-is-over/.

16 See "Statement from President Donald J. Trump Recognizing Venezuelan

National Assembly President Juan Gaidó as the Interim President of Venezuela," January 23, 2019, https://www.whitehouse.gov/briefings-statements/statement-president-donald-j-trump-recognizing-venezuelan-national-assembly-president-juan-guaido-interim-president-venezuela/.

17 See Deutsche Welle, "Venezuelan opposition leader Juan Guaidó declares himself acting president," January 23, 2019, https://www.dw.com/en/venezuelan-opposition-leader-juan-guaido-declares-himself-acting-president/a-47201512.

18 See BBC News, April 1, 2019, "Venezuela crisis: Opposition's Guaidó awaits army support," https://www.bbc.com/news/world-latin-america-47769121.

19 See, e.g., Patricia Laya, Ethan Bronner, and Tim Ross, January 25, 2019, "Maduro Stymied in Bid to Pull $1.2 Billion of Gold From U.K.," https://www.bloomberg.com/news/articles/2019-01-25/u-k-said-to-deny-maduro-s-bid-to-pull-1-2-billion-of-gold.

20 See Hollie McKay, "As Venezuela crisis deepens, US embassy faces security challenges," January 26, 2019, https://www.foxnews.com/world/venezuela-political-aggression-puts-us-diplomats-at-risk.

21 See, e.g., Reuters, "Venezuela's Guaidó considering request for funds from IMF: sources," January 25, 2019, https://www.reuters.com/article/us-venezuela-politics-guaido/venezuelas-guaido-considering-request-for-funds-from-imf-sources-idUSKCN1PJ21Q, and Lesley Wroughton. Reuters, "Latam lender replaces Venezuela's Maduro representative with Guaidó economist," March 15, 2019, https://www.reuters.com/article/us-venezuela-politics/iadb-ousts-venezuelas-maduro-representative-replaces-with-guaido-economist-idUSKCN1QW29J.

22 See Kirk Semple, "With Spies and Other Operatives, a Nation Looms Over Venezuela's Crisis: Cuba," January 26, 2019, Editorial Board of the Wall Street Journal, "Cuba out of Venezuela," January 24, 2019, https://www.wsj.com/articles/cuba-out-of-venezuela-11548376414.

23 See Daniel Chang, "'End this nightmare,' Pompeo urges U.N. member nations on Venezuela's political crisis," https://www.miamiherald.com/news/nation-world/world/americas/venezuela/article225107520.html.

24 See Adry Torres, "Venezuelan President Maduro's right-hand man evacuates his two youngest children to China under fake names," February 25, 2019, https://www.dailymail.co.uk/news/article-6743013/Venezuelas-second-command-flies-two-children-China-using-wifes-surname.html.

25 A subsequent press statement from Sanders and Trump tweets essentially

repeated the highlights of this call. See, Rebecca Morin, "Trump congratu-
lates Venezuelan opposition leader in call," January 30, 2019, https://www
.politico.com/story/2019/01/30/trump-juan-guaido-call
-1136918.

26 See Reuters, "Trading arm of Russia's Lukoil stops swap operations in
Venezuela," February 14, 2019, https://www.reuters.com/article/us
-venezuela-politics-russia-lukoil/trading-arm-of-russias-lukoil-stops
-swap-operations-in-venezuela-idUSKCN1Q3225.

27 See "PetroChina Drops Venezuela's State oil Company," February 1, 2019,
https://financialtribune.com/articles/energy/96482/petrochina-drops
-venezuela-s-state-oil-company.

28 See Tatiana Voronova, "Russia's Gazprombank freezes accounts of Venezuela's PDVSA: Source," February 17, 2019, https://www.reuters.com/article
/us-venezuela-politics-gazprombank/russias-gazprombank-freezes
-accounts-of-venezuelas-pdvsa-source-idUSKCN1Q60BK.

29 See Christine Armario and Fabiola Sanchez, "Venezuela opposition leader
to police: Leave my family alone," January 31, 2019, https://apnews.com
/c6916be2bce147e486e8e7915272077c.

30 See Dylan Baddour and Anthony Faiola, "As U.S. amasses aid on
Venezuelan border, Colombian town braces for showdown," February 17,
2019, https://www.washingtonpost.com/world/the_americas/as-us-amasses
-aid-on-venezuelan-border-colombian-city-braces-for-showdown/2019/02
/17/7bcf57b0-3140-11e9-8781-763619f12cb4_story.html.

31 See "'John Bolton tried to assassinate me': Interview with Venezuelan
president Nicolas Maduro," https://thegrayzone.com/2019/08/06/interview
-venezuelan-president-nicolas-maduro/.

32 See Roberta Rampton, "Move Over Ayatollahs: Bolton Turns Tweets and
Talons on Maduro," February 27, 2019, https://www.usnews.com/news
/world/articles/2019-02-27/move-over-ayatollahs-bolton-turns-tweets
-and-talons-on-maduro.

33 See Alex Daugherty, "Rubio says sanctioned Maduro loyalists can receive
amnesty, but only if they act soon," February 11, 2019, https://www.miami
herald.com/news/nation-world/world/americas/venezuela/article226085
225.html.

34 Press reporting from these remote border areas was scanty, but clearly
showed clashes with regime authorities. See Antonio Maria Delgado, "Two
dead, fourteen injured after Venezuela soldiers fire at civilians near border
with Brazil," February 22, 2019, https://www.miamiherald.com/news
/nation-world/world/americas/venezuela/article226624859.html.

35 See, e.g., AFP, "Guaidó arrives at border concert, dealing blow to Maduro," February 23, 2019, https://www.france24.com/en/20190223-venezuela -guaido-border-concert-humanitarian-aid-maduro.

36 See, e.g., Beatrice Christofaro, "567 Venezuelan soldiers defected to Colombia, and it could be a sign that Maduro's once rock-solid power base is starting to crumble," March 2, 2019, https://www.businessinsider.com /venezuela-soldiers-defect-to-colombia-threaten-maduro-power-2019-3.

37 See Maria Ramirez, "Soldiers held hostage, villagers killed: the untold story of Venezuelan aid violence," May 21, 2019, https://www.reuters.com /article/us-venezuela-politics-pemon-insight/soldiers-held-hostage -villagers-killed-the-untold-story-of-venezuelan-aid-violence-idUSKCN 1SR1L0.

38 See note 36 above.

39 See Jeff Mason, Reuters, "U.S. considers sanctions to restrict Visa, Master-card in Venezuela: official," March 14. 2019, https://www.reuters.com /article/us-usa-venezuela-sanctions/u-s-considers-sanctions-to-restrict -visa-mastercard-in-venezuela-official-idUSKCN1QV2VS.

40 See Reuters, "More than 40 dead, 850 detained in Venezuela violence, U.N. says," January 29, 2019, https://www.reuters.com/article/us-venezuela -politics-un/more-than-40-dead-850-detained-in-venezuela-violence-u -n-says-idUSKCN1PN16Y.

41 See Larry Neumeister, Associated Press, "Ex-Venezuelan vice president accused of aiding drug dealers," March 8, 2019, https://apnews.com/ff89b f5c8f5445fab11e6fdf6d91640f.

42 See note 19, above.

43 See, e.g., Ryan C. Berg, "Russia Is Gearing Up for a Conflict with the United States in the Caribbean," October 9, 2019, https://foreignpolicy .com/2019/10/09/russias-putin-venezuela-evade-oil-sanctions-prepar ing-conflict-united-states/; and Joshua Goodman, Associated Press, "Oil tankers 'go dark' off Venezuela to evade US sanctions," November 14, 2019, https://apnews.com/84cabe36652c4194ae2db852e8bab2c4.

44 See Reuters, "Trump threatens 'full' embargo on Cuba over Venezuela secu-rity support," April 30, https://www.reuters.com/article/us-venezuela -politics-trump-tweet/trump-threatens-full-embargo-on-cuba-over -venezuela-security-support-idUSKCN1S62PD

45 See Nicholas Casey, "'It Is Unspeakable': How Maduro Used Cuban Doctors to Coerce Venezuela Voters," https://www.nytimes.com/2019/03/17/world /americas/venezuela-cuban-doctors.html?auth=login-email&login=email.

46 See "US-sanctioned Venezuelan defects to Colombia, Slams Maduro,"

https://www.reuters.com/article/us-venezuela-politics-general/u-s-sanc
tioned-venezuelan-defects-to-colombia-slams-maduro-idUSKCN1QZ1YB.

47 See David Luhnow, "Maduro Loses Grip on Venezuela's Poor, a Vital
Source of His power," https://www.wsj.com/articles/maduro-loses-grip-on
-venezuelas-poor-a-vital-source-of-his-power-11553014207.

48 See Nathan Hodge and Anna-Maja Rappard, CNN, "Russia confirms
its military personnel are in Venezuela," March 29, 2019, https://www.cnn
.com/2019/03/28/europe/russia-venezuela-military-personnel-intl/index.html

49 See "Remarks by President Trump and First Lady Fabiana Rosales of the
Bolivarian Republic of Venezuela before Bilateral Meeting," March 27, 2019,
https://www.whitehouse.gov/briefings-statements/remarks-president
-trump-first-lady-fabiana-rosales-bolivarian-republic-venezuela-bilateral
-meeting/.

50 These remarks were very similar to what she had said in the presence of the
press. Ibid.

51 See "Venezuelan minister tells US' Bolton 'right thing' is respecting the
people's will," March 30, 2019, https://www.dailysabah.com/americas/2019
/03/30/venezuelan-minister-tells-us-bolton-right-thing-is-respecting-the
-peoples-will.

52 As documented in previous footnotes, many details of what happened in
Venezuela in March and April in particular, described in the following
pages, have found their way into the public record. We learned them in
real time from the opposition, although as in any domestic conflict like
this, there are often disagreements on many issues. In addition to what has
already been cited above, see, e.g., Nicole Gaouellette, "Bolton says senior
Venezuelan officials committed to backing Guaidó," April 30, 2019, https://
www.cnn.com/2019/04/30/politics/venezuela-us-clashes-bolton/index
.html. The C-SPAN tape of my April 30 interview is found at https://www
.c-span.org/video/?460292-1/national-security-adviser-bolton-calls
-peaceful-transfer-power-venezuela. See also the interview with Elliott
Abrams in "US: Venezuelan officials who were negotiating Maduro exit
have gone dark," May 1, 2019," "https://www.efe.com/efe/english/world
/us-venezuelan-officials-who-were-negotiating-maduro-exit-have-gone
-dark/50000262-3965957" https://www .efe.com/efe/english/world/us
-venezuelan-officials-who-were-negotiating-maduro-exit-have-gone
-dark/50000262-3965957#; and Uri Freedman, "How an Elaborate Plan to
Topple Venezuela's President Went Wrong," May 1, 2019, https://www
.theatlantic.com/politics/archive/2019/05/white-house-venezuela-maduro
-failed/588454/.

53 See John Otis, NPR, "Venezuelan Officers Who Fled to Colombia Are 'Adrift' As Maduro Holds On to Power," July 22, 2019, https://www.npr .org/2019/07/16/742275893/venezuelan-officers-who-fled-to-colombia-are -adrift-as-maduro-holds-onto-power.

54 See MacKenzie Sigalos, "China and Russia loaned billions to Venezuela— and then the presidency went up for grabs," February 7, 2019, https://www .cnbc.com/2019/02/07/venezuela-china-and-russia-owed-debts-as -presidential-fight-rages.html.

55 After his defection, Cristopher Figuera became a major public source of information about the Maduro regime, and specifically about the Cuban presence. See, e.g., Anthony Faiolo, "Maduro's ex-spy chief lands in U.S. armed with allegations against Venezuelan government," June 24, 2019, https://www.washingtonpost.com/world/the_americas/maduros -ex-spy-chief-lands-in-us-armed-with-allegations-against-venezuelan -government/2019/06/24/b20ad508-9477-11e9-956a-88c291ab5c38_story .html. Excerpts from the *Washington Post* interview with Cristopher Figuera are found at https://www.youtube.com/watch?v=__Pk9WS06-g. See also Martin Arostegui, "Exiled Venezuelan Spy Chief Speaks Out About Corruption, Cuban Ties," https://voanews.com/americas /exiled-venezuelan-spy-chiefs-speak-out-about-corruption-cuban-ties.

56 See Abrams interview, notes 1 and 52 above, and Freedman, note 52 above.

57 Ibid.

58 Cristopher Figuera described the dialogue: "On April 29, Figuera said, he learned that Maduro's feared colectivos were preparing a large-scale assault on a May Day protest that could result in a 'bloodbath.' He told Padrino of the new timetable himself. 'Are you crazy?' Padrino responded, in Figuera's telling. 'What about the [TSJ] ruling? How are you going to do it?' 'It's happening,' Figuera said he responded. 'If not, May 1 will be bloody. . . . We have to move fast.' Figuera and other plotters said they received confirmation that Moreno was prepared to issue his ruling on April 30. But after hearing Padrino's skepticism, Figuera said, he began calling other military figures." See Faiola, note 55 above.

59 See Associated Press, "Venezuela's Maduro Calls for Military Unity After Clashes," May 2, 2019, https://www.usnews.com/news/world/articles /2019-05-01/venezuela-awaits-more-protests-after-a-day-of-turmoil.

60 See note 44 above.

61 Juan Forero, José de Córdoba and Kejal Vyas, "Venezuela's Opposition Came Close to Ousting the President—but the Plan Fell Apart," May 3,

2019, https://www.wsj.com/articles/how-plan-to-oust-venezuelan-leader
-fell-apart-115569266837?mod+searchresults&page=3&pos+8.
62 See, e.g., Antonella Davalos, "Why Is Cuba Propping Up the Maduro
Regime? A Look at the History of this Special Relationship," February 23,
2019, https://www.democracyspeaks.org/blog/why-cuba-propping-maduro
-regime-look-history-special-relationship.
63 On the afternoon of April 30, I tweeted, "@vladimirpadrino, @ivanr_
HD, @MaikelMorenoTSJ: You know well the role you played in planning
today's move for democracy in Venezuela. You must now stand and do
what is right for Venezuela. We, and the world, will hold you accountable
for those Venezuelans who are injured today." And the next day, in a lengthy
radio interview with Hugh Hewitt, I elaborated on the complex dealings
between key regime figures and the opposition before the uprising. See
transcript, https://www.hughhewitt.com/ambassador-john-bolton-on
-uprising-in-venezuela.

CHAPTER 10: THUNDER OUT OF CHINA

1 See, e.g., "Whither China: From Membership to Responsibility?" Speech by
Robert B. Zoellick, Deputy Secretary of State, found at https://2001-2009
.state.gov/s/d/former/zoellick/rem/53682.htm.
2 See Remarks by Assistant Secretary Christopher A. Ford, "Huawei and Its
Siblings, the Chinese Tech Giants: National Security and Foreign Policy
Implications," September 11, 2019, https://www.state.gov/huawei-and-its
-siblings-the-chinese-tech-giants-national-security-and-foreign-policy
-implications/.
3 See, e.g., Kate O'Keefe et al., "China Taps Its Private Sector to Boost Its Military, Raising Alarms," https://www.wsj.com/articles/china-taps-its-private
-sector-to-boost-its-military-raising-alarms-11569403806.
4 See, e.g., Rachel Botsman, "Big data meets Big Brother as China moves to
rate its citizens," https://www.wired.co.uk/article/chinese-government
-social-credit-score-privacy-invasion.
5 And see "National Security Strategy of the United States of America,"
December 2017, https://www.whitehouse.gov/wp-content/uploads/2017
/12/NSS-Final-12-18-2017-0905.pdf.
6 See "A Free and Open Indo-Pacific: Advancing a Shared Vision," November
3, 2019, https://www.state.gov/a-free-and-open-indo-pacific-advancing
-a-shared-vision/.

7 See Department of Justice, "ZTE Corporation Agrees to Plead Guilty and Pay Over $430.4 Million for Violating U.S. Sanctions by Sending U.S.-Origin Items to Iran," March 7, 2017, https://www.justice.gov/opa/pr/zte-corporation-agrees-plead-guilty-and-pay-over-4304-million-violating-us-sanctions-sending.

8 See David J. Lynch, "U.S. companies banned from selling to China's ZTE telecom maker," April 16, 2018, https://www.washingtonpost.com/news/business/wp/2018/04/16/u-s-companies-banned-from-selling-tochinas-zte-telecom-maker/.

9 Hassett later stated publicly that "the actions we've taken against China have had a big negative effect on their markets and their economy but very little effect . . . here in the U.S." See Emily McCormick, "White House economist: Tariffs are hurting China much more than the US," September 20, 2018, https://www.finance.yahoo.com/news/white-house-economist-kevin-hassett-need-fair-reciprocal-trade-155519844.html .

10 See Karen Freifeld, "Exclusive: U.S. may soon claim up to $1.7 billion penalty from China's ZTE - sources," June 1, 2018, https://www.reuters.com/article/us-usa-trade-china-zte-exclusive/exclusive-u-s-may-soon-claim-up-to-1-7-billion-penalty-from-chinas-zte-sources-idUSKCN1IX5T2.

11 Under the existing judicial rulings orders, the court-appointed monitor will be in place observing ZTE until 2022. See Dan Strumpf, "U.S. Judge Orders China's ZTE to Two More years of Monitoring," October 4, 2018, https://www.wsj.com/articles/u-s-judge-orders-chinas-zte-to-two-more-years-of-monitoring-1538634469.

12 See "Remarks by President Trump at the United Nations Security Council Briefing on Counterproliferation," September 26, 2018, https://www.whitehouse.gov/briefings-statements/remarks-president-trump-united-nations-security-council-briefing-counterproliferation-new-york-ny/.

13 See "Remarks by Vice President Pence on the Administration's Policy Toward China," October 4, 2018, https://www.whitehouse.gov/briefings-statements/remarks-vice-president-pence-administrations-policy-toward-china/.

14 This phrase is well-known from the thesis and eponymous title of Michael Pillsbury's book, The Hundred-Year Marathon: China's Secret Strategy to Replace America as the Global Superpower, Griffin, reprint edition 2016.

15 See Ana Swanson and Alan Rappeport, "Trump Delays a Tariff Deadline, Citing Progress in China Trade Talks," February 4, 2019, https://www.nytimes.com/2019/02/24/us/politics/us-china-trade-truce.html.

16 See "Remarks by President Trump and President Xi of the People's Republic of China Before Bilateral Meeting, Osaka, Japan," June 19, 2019, https://

www.whitehouse.gov/briefings-statements/remarks-president-trump
-president-xi-peoples-republic-china-bilateral-meeting-osaka-japan/.

17 See note 2 above.

18 For a classic statement of this utterly misguided thinking, see George
    Gilder, "Huawei Is an Asset, Not a Threat," posted at https://www.wsj.com
    /articles/huawei-is-an-asset-not-a-threat-11558390913.

19 The United Kingdom ultimately rejected the U.S. position. See, Adam
    Satariano, "Britain Defies Trump Plea to Ban Huawei from 5G Network,"
    January 29, 2020, https://www.nytimes.com/2020/01/28/technology
    /britain-huawei-5G.html.

20 See Simon Denyer, "Japan effectively bans Huawei and ZTE from
    government contracts, joining U.S.," December 10, 2018, https://www
    .washingtonpost.com/world/asia_pacific/japan-effectively-bans-chinas
    -huawei-zte-from-government-contracts-joining-us/2018/12/10/748fe98a
    -fc69-11e8-ba87-8c7facdf6739_story.html; and "Huawei Loses key 5G
    Contract in Japan to Nokia and Ericsson," May 31, 2019, https://www
    .straitstimes.com/asia/east-asia/huawei-loses-key-5g-contract-in-japan-to
    -nokia-and-ericsson.

21 Ibid.

22 See Anna Fifeld and Jeanne Whalen, "Canadians detained in China after
    Huawei arrest have now spent a year in custody," December 10, 2019,
    https://www.washingtonpost.com/world/canadians-detained-in-china
    -after-huawei-arrest-have-now-spent-a-year-in-custody/2019/12/10
    /3a55cd4c-1af0-11ea-977a-15a6710ed6da_story.html.

23 See Robert Fife and Steven Chase, "Chrétien proposes cancelling Meng's
    extradition case to unfreeze relations with China," October 2, 2019,
    https://www.theglobeandmail.com/politics/article-chretien-suggests
    -huawei-executives-extradition-case-should-end/.

24 The Administration has imposed other penalties on ZTE and Huawei since
    I resigned, but the overall policy direction remains unclear. See, e.g., Ryan
    Tracy et al., "FCC Targets China's Huawei and ZTE," https://www.wsj.com
    /articles/fcc-moves-to-cut-off-huawei-zte-from-subsidies-11572289868.

25 See Echo Xie, "Chinese state media warns 'end is coming for those
    attempting to disrupt Hong Kong," September 1, 2019, https://www.scmp
    .com/news/hong-kong/politics/article/3025284/chinese-state-media-warns
    -end-coming-those-attempting.

26 Although the House of Representatives has passed a bill authorizing
    sanctions on China relating to the Uighurs, there is no change in Trump's
    opposition to such sanctions. See, Alan Rappeport and Edward Wong, "In

Push for Trade Deal, Trump Administration Shelves Sanctions Over China's Crackdown on Uighurs," May 4, 2019, https://www.nytimes.com /2019/05/04/world/asia/trump-china-uighurs-trade-deal.html.

27 See John Pomfret, "Trump abandoned the Kurds in Syria. Could Taiwan be next?" https://www.washingtonpost.com/opinions/2019/10/18/trump -abandoned-kurds-syria-could-taiwan-be-next/.

28 See, e.g., Josephine Ma, "Coronavirus: China's first confirmed Covid-19 case traced back to November 17," March 13, 2020, https://www.scmp.com /news/china/society/article/3074991/coronavirus-chinas-first-confirmed -covid-19-case-traced-back.

29 See, e.g., Javier C. Hernández, "Chinese Tycoon Who Criticized Xi's Response to Coronavirus Has Vanished," March 15, 2020, https://www .nytimes.com/2020/03/14/world/asia/china-ren-zhiqiang.html?searchResult Position=2.

30 See Guy Taylor, "Surge of coronavirus lies by adversaries seeking to blame the U.S. floods web," March 16, 2020, https://www.washingtontimes.com /news/2020/mar/15/coronavirus-lies-pushed-china-blame-virus-us-biowe/; and, Fred Lucas, "Coronavirus Coverup? Trump's National Security Advisor Puts China On Notice," March 15, 2020, https://nationalinterest.org/blog /buzz/coronavirus-coverup-trumps-national-security-advisor-puts-china -notice-132497.

31 See Ivana Kottasová and Paul P. Murphy, March 13, 2020, "Satellite images show Iran building burial pits for coronavirus victims," https://www.cnn .com/2020/03/13/middleeast/iran-coronavirus-mass-graves-intl/index.html.

32 See Fred Imbert, "Larry Kudlow says US has contained the coronavirus and the economy is holding up nicely," February 26, 2010, https://www.cnbc .com/2020/02/25/larry-kudlow-says-us-has-contained-the-coronavirus -and-the-economy-is-holding-up-nicely.html?__source=twitter%7Cmain.

33 See Aram Roston, Marisa Taylor, Reuters, March 11, 2020, "Exclusive: White House told federal health agency to classify coronavirus deliberations– sources," https://www.reuters.com/article/us-health-coronavirus-secrecy -exclusive/exclusive-white-house-told-federal-health-agency-to-classify -coronavirus-deliberations-sources-idUSKBN20Y2LM.

34 See Tim Morrison, "No, the White House didn't 'dissolve' its pandemic response office," March 16, 2020, https://www.washingtonpost.com/opinions /2020/03/16/no-white-house-didnt-dissolve-its-pandemic-response-office/. Daniel Lippman and Meredith McGraw, "Inside the National Security Council, a rising sense of dread," April 2, 2020, https://www.politico.com /news/2020/04/02/nsc-coronavirus-white-house-162530; and Andrew

Kaczynski and Em Steck, "Top administration officials said last year threat of pandemic kept them up at night," April 3, 2020, https://www.cnn .com/2020/04/03/politics/kfile-officials-worried-over-pandemic-last-year /index.html.

35 A number of commentators agreed with the reorganization. See, e.g., Tom Rogan, "No, the Trump Administration didn't weaken US biode-fenses," March 15, 2020, https://www.washingtonexaminer.com/opinion /no-the-trump-administration-didnt-weaken-us-biodefenses; and Alexander Muse, March 14, 2020, "Fact check: Did Trump disband the US pandemic response team?" https://partisan.space/pandemic-team/. Fact checkers agreed that the dispute over the reorganization was a matter of opinion, not verifiable fact: Glenn Kessler and Meg Kelly, "Was the White House office for global pandemics eliminated?" https://www.washington post.com/politics/2020/03/20/was-white-house-office-global-pandemics -eliminated/, and Lori Robertson, "Dems Misconstrue Trump Budget Remarks," https://www.factcheck.org/2020/03/dems-misconstrue-trump -budget-remarks/.

36 See Alex M. Azar II, Robert R. Redfield, and Anthony S. Fauci, "On the Front lines of the Trump Administration's Ebola Response," November 4, 2019, https://foreignpolicy.com/2019/11/04/trump-administration-ebola -response-azar-redfield-fauci-congo/.

37 See "National Biodefense Strategy," www.whitehouse.gov/wp-content /uploads/2018/09/National-Biodefense-Strategy.pdf.

38 See "Presidential memorandum on the Support for National Biodefense," September 18, 2018, https://www.whitehouse.gov/presidential-actions /presidential-memorandum-support-national-biodefense/.

39 See "Executive Order on Modernizing Influence Vaccines in the United States to promote National Security and public health," September 19, 2019, https://www.whitehouse.gov/presidential-actions/executive-order -modernizing-influenza-vaccines-united-states-promote-national -security-public-health/.

40 See Eric Lipton, David A. Sanger, Maggie Haberman, Michael D. Shear, Mark Mazzetti, and Julian E. Barnes, "Despite Timely Alerts, Trump Was Slow to Act," April 12, 2020, https://www.nytimes.com/2020/04/11/us /politics/coronavirus-trump-response.html.

41 The NSC structure is now analogous to the U.S. Army Medical Research Institute for Infectious Diseases. See, usamriid.army.mil.

CHAPTER 11: CHECKING INTO THE HANOI HILTON, THEN CHECKING OUT, AND THE PANMUNJOM PLAYTIME

1 See Choe Sang-Hun, "Kim Jong-un Praises Trump's 'Unusual Determination' to Hold Second Summit," January 23, 2019, https://www.nytimes .com/2019/01/23/world/asia/trump-kim-jong-un-summit-korea.html? searchResultPosition=1.

2 See Gus Taylor, "Team Trump quietly filling 'pot of gold' encouraging Kim Jong Un to denuclearize," posted at https://www.washingtontimes .com /news/2019/jan/28/stephen-biegun-preps-north-korea-economic -package-/.

3 See Stephen Biegun, "Remarks on DPRK at Stanford University," https:// www.state.gov/remarks-on-dprk-at-stanford-university/.

4 See John Walcott, " 'Willful Ignorance.' Inside President Trump's Troubled Intelligence Briefings," https://time.com/5518947/donald-trump -intelligence-briefings-national-security/.

5 All of this was subsequently amply reported in numerous press sources. See, e.g., Adam Taylor, "Nukes and sanctions: What actually went wrong for Trump and Kim Jong Un," March 1, 2019, https://www.washingtonpost .com/world/2019/03/01/nukes-sanctions-what-actually-went-wrong-trump -kim-jong-un/.

6 Trump himself expressly mentioned Yongbyon in subsequent press discussions. See, e.g., Reuters, "Trump says he and North Korea's Kim discussed dismantling of Yongbyon nuclear plant," February 28, 2019, https:// www.reuters.com/article/us-northkorea-usa-trump-yongbyon/trump -says-he-and-north-koreas-kim-discussed-dismantling-of-yongbyon -nuclear-plant-idUSKCN1QH0WN.

7 North Korea itself fully confirmed their version of the offer at a press conference late in the evening after the Summit ended. See, e.g., https:// www.scmp.com/author/lee-jeong-ho" Lee Jeong-ho and https://www.scmp .com/author/bhavan-jaipragas" Bhavan Jaipragas, "Trump-Kim Summit 2019: North Korea stages late-night press conference to deny US president's claims about why summit ended, February 28, 2019, https://www.scmp .com/week-asia/geopolitics/article/2188052/trump-kim-summit-2019 -ends-disarray-talks-break-down.

8 See Hyonhee Shin and Joyce Lee, Reuters, "North Korea executes envoy to failed U.S. summit – media; White House monitoring," May 30, 2019, https:// www.reuters.com/article/us-northkorea-usa-purge/north-korea-executes-envoy -to-failed-u-s-summit-media-white-house-monitoring-idUSKCN1T02PD.

9 "Jackson Diehl@JacksonDiehl, "Looks like @realDonaldTrump's erratic

diplomacy, including adopting maximalist Bolton position in Hanoi, got some people killed."

10 See Choe Sang-Hun, "North Korea Threatens to Scuttle Talks with the U.S. and Resume Tests," March 15, 2019, https://www.nytimes.com/2019/03/15 /world/asia/north-korea-kim-jong-un-nuclear.html.

11 See, e.g., Hiroyuki Akita, "Trump demands Japan and South Korea Pay for nuclear umbrella," February 4, 2020, https://asia.nikkei.com/Spotlight/Com ment/Trump-demands-Japan-and-South-Korea-pay-for-nuclear-umbrella.

12 See, e.g., Joyce Lee, Sangmi Cha, and Hyonhee Shin, Reuters, "US breaks off defense cost talks, as South Korea balks at $5 billion demand," November 18, 2019, https://www.reuters.com/article/us-southkorea-usa-talks /us-breaks-off-defense-cost-talks-as-south-korea-balks-at-5-billion -demand-idUSKBN1XT0EN.

13 See Simon Denyer and Moon Joo Kim, "Kim personally supervised 'guided weapons' test, North Korea says," May 4, 2019, https://www.washingtonpost .com/world/north-korea-fires-several-short-range-projectiles-south -korean-military-says/2019/05/03/511efe92-6e0f-11e9-be3a-33217240a539 _story.html.

14 See Dagyum Ji, "South Korea to push ahead with delivery of $8 million in aid to North: MOU," May 17, 2019, https://www.nknews.org/2019/05/south -korea-to-push-ahead-with-delivery-of-8-million-in-aid-to-north-mou/.

15 See David E. Sanger, William J. Broad, Choe Sang-Hun, and Eileen Sullivan, "New North Korea Concerns Flare, as Trump's Signature Diplomacy Wilts," May 9, 2019, https://www.nytimes.com/2019/05/09/world/asia/north-korea -missile.html.

16 See Steven Borowiec, Asia Society, "The Sad but True Story of North Korea's Abduction Project," https://asiasociety.org/korea/sad-true-story-north -koreas-abduction-project.

17 See, e.g., Chad O'Carroll, "Hotline between the two Koreas: why hasn't it been used yet?" May 10, 2019, https://www.nknews.org/2019/05 /hotline-between-the-two-koreas-why-hasnt-it-been-used-yet/.

18 Michael Crowley and David E. Sanger, "In New Talks, US May Settle for a Nuclear Freeze by North Korea," https://www.nytimes.com/2019/06/30 /world/asia/trump-kim-north-korea-negotiations.html.

19 See, e.g., Rebecca Balhaus et al., "Trump's Twitter Invitation to Kim Set Off 24-Hour Scramble." https://www.wsj.com/articles/trumps-twitter -invitation-to-kim-set-off-24-hour-scramble-11561943026.

20 See Straits Times, "North Korea's Kim Jong-Un receives personal letter from Trump, KCNA says," June 24, 2019, https://www.straitstimes.com

/asia/east-asia/north-koreas-kim-jong-un-receives-excellent-letter-from
-trump-state-media.

21 See Lara Seligman and Robbie Gramer, "Trump Asks Tokyo to Quadruple
Payments for U.S. Troops in Japan," November 15, 2019, https://foreign
policy.com/2019/11/15/trump-asks-tokyo-quadruple-payments-us-troops
-japan/.

22 There has been considerable press attention and commentary on this
ongoing dispute. See e.g., Kim Tong-hyung, "South Korea Will Keep Its
Military Intelligence Pact with Japan - For Now," November 23, 2019,
https://thediplomat.com/2019/11/south-korea-will-keeps-its-military
-intelligence-pact-with-japan-for-now/; Simon Denyer and Min Joo Kim,
"South Korea axes pact on sharing military intelligence with Japan,"
August 22, 2019, https://www.washingtonpost.com/world/asia_pacific
/south-korea-axes-pact-to-share-military-intelligence-with-japan/2019
/08/22/fe57061c-c4be-11e9-8bf7-cde2d9e09055_story.html; and Victor
Cha, "The Meaning of GSOMIA Termination; Escalation of the Japan
-Korea Dispute," August 22, 2019, https://www.csis.org/analysis/meaning
-gsomia-termination-escalation-japan-korea-dispute.

23 See Treaty between Japan and Republic of Korea, dated June 22, 1965,
Number 8473, https://treaties.un.org/doc/Publication/UNTS/Volume%
20583/volume-583-I-8473-English.pdf.

24 See "Sharing military intel with Japan 'difficult,' Moon tells visiting
U.S. defense chief," November 15, 2019, https://www.japantimes.co.jp
/news/2019/11/15/national/sharing-military-intel-japan-difficult-moon
-tells-visiting-u-s-defense-chief/#.XmOlqKhKiF4.

25 Ibid.

26 See, e.g., Brian Kim, "Korea and Japan Clash Over History and law," August
16, 2019, https://www.lawfareblog.com/korea-and-japan-clash-over-history
-and-law; Yosuke Onchi and Jada Nagumo, "Five things to know about
South Korea's wartime labor ruling," October 30, 2018, https://asia.nikkei
.com/Politics/International-relations/Five-things-to-know-about-South
-Korea-s-wartime-labor-ruling; and Choe Sang-Hun and Rick Gladstone,
"How a World War II-Era Reparations Case Is Roiling Asia," October
30, 2018, https://www.nytimes.com/2018/10/30/world/asia/south-korea
-japan-compensation-world-war-two.html.

27 On November 22, South Korea suspended its withdrawal from GSOMIA.
Whether bilateral relations would thereupon improve, or simply remain as
they were, was unclear. See, e.g., "Japan-South Korea friction flares again

after GSOMIA intel pact rescue," https://www.japantimes.co.jp/news/2019
/11/25/national/politics-diplomacy/japan-south-korea-bickering-gsomia/#
.Xez2X-hKiF4.

CHAPTER 12: TRUMP LOSES HIS WAY, AND THEN HIS NERVE

1   See Thomas Erdbrink, " 'Death to America' Means 'Death to Trump,' Iran's
    Supreme Leader Says," https://www.nytimes.com/2019/02/08/world/middle
    east/iran-trump-death-to-america.html.
2   See Alma Keshavarz, "A Review of Iran's Revolutionary Guards and Qods
    Force: Growing Global Presence, Links to Cartels, and Mounting Sophisti-
    cations," https://smallwarsjournal.com/jrnl/art/a-review-of-iran%E2%80%
    99s-revolutionary-guards-and-qods-force-growing-global-presence-links
    -to-car.
3   See, e.g., Tim Arango, "Iran Dominates in Iraq After U.S. 'Handed the
    Country Over,'" July 15, 2019, https://www.nytimes.com/2017/07/15
    /world/middleeast/iran-iraq-iranian-power.html; James Risen, Tim Arango,
    Farnaz Fassihi, Murtaza Hussain, Ronen Bergman, "A Spy Complex
    revealed," November 18, 2019, https://theintercept.com/2019/11/18
    /iran-iraq-spy-cables/; and NPR, "Iran's Powerful influence in Iraq,"
    January 4, 2020, https://www.npr.org/2020/01/04/793662756/iran
    -s-powerful-influence-in-iraq.
4   Ibid.; and John Davison and Daphne Psaledakis, "Washington blacklists
    Iran-backed Iraqi militia leaders over protests," December 6, 2019, https://
    www.reuters.com/article/us-iran-usa-iraq-sanctions/washington-blacklists
    -iran-backed-iraqi-militia-leaders-over-protests-idUSKBN1YA206.
5   See "Statement from the President on the Designation Of the Islamic Revo-
    lutionary Guards Corp as a Foreign Terrorist Organization," April 8, 2019,
    https://www.whitehouse.gov/briefings-statements/statement-president
    -designation-islamic-revolutionary-guard-corps-foreign-terrorist
    -organization/.
6   "Clientitis" and other institutional problems of State's bureaucracy are
    discussed in Boston, *Surrender Is Not an Option*, on pp. 447–455.
7   See, e.g., Florence Tan, Reuters, "Iran keeps oil prices in Asia at wide
    discounts against Saudi oil in January," December 10, 2019, https://www
    .reuters.com/article/us-oil-iran-prices/iran-keeps-crude-prices-in-asia-at
    -wide-discounts-against-saudi-oil-in-january-idUSKBN1OA056 and Irina
    Slav, "Iran is desperately trying to save its oil share ahead of US sanctions,"

August 15, 2018, https://www.businessinsider.com/iran-us-oil-sanctions -drive-barrel-discounts-before-november-2018-8.

8 See Lesley Wroughton et al., "US to end all waivers on imports of Iranian oil, crude price jumps," https://www.reuters.com/article/us-usa-iran-oil /us-to-end-all-waivers-on-imports-of-iranian-oil-crude-price-jumps -idUSKCN1RX0R1.

9 See "Zarif: B-Team targeting Iranian people with economic terrorism," https://en.mehrnews.com/news/144632/Zarif-B-Team-targeting-Iranian -people-with-economic-terrorism.

10 See, e.g., Ariane Tabatabai, "Iran's cooperation with the Taliban could affect talks on U.S. withdrawal from Afghanistan," August 9, 2019, https://www .washingtonpost.com/politics/2019/08/09/irans-cooperation-with-taliban -could-affect-talks-us-withdrawal-afghanistan/; and Reuters, "In new claim, Pompeo says Iran has been working with Taliban to undermine Afghan peace effort," January 7, 2020, https://nationalpost.com/news/world /in-new-claim-pompeo-says-iran-has-been-working-with-the-taliban -to-undermine-afghan-peace-efforts.

11 See "Statement from the National Security Advisor John Bolton," May 5, 2019, https://www.whitehouse.gov/briefings-statements/statement-national -security-advisor-ambassador-john-bolton-2/.

12 See *Tehran Times*, "'Maximum pressure' has produced 'maximum resistance,' says Iran's Araqchi," September 23, 2019, https://www.tehran times.com/news/440423/Maximum-pressure-has-produced-maximum -resistance-says-Iran-s.

13 See Tamer El-Ghobashy, Michael Birnbaum and Carol Morello, "Iran announces it will stop complying with parts of landmark nuclear deal," May 8, 2019, https://www.washingtonpost.com/world/iran-to-take -steps-to-reduce-its-commitment-to-landmark-nuclear-deal/2019/05 /07/90cc3b1c-70fe-11e9-9331-30bc5836f48e_story.html.

14 Ibid., and "Kremlin: Russia warned Iran against withdrawing from nuclear non-proliferation treaty," May 30, 2019, https://uawire.org /kremlin-russia-warns-iran-not-to-withdraw-from-nuclear-non -proliferation-treaty.

15 See Michael Peel and Najmeh Bozorgmehr, "European power reject Iran 'ultimatums,'" https://www.ft.com/content/247236ba-7234-11e9-bf5c -6eeb837566c5.

16 For public remarks by Dunford along these lines, see Adam Twardowski, "At Brookings, Gen. Joseph Dunford comments on threats from China, Russia, North Korea and beyond," June 4, 2019, https://www.brookings.edu

/blog/order-from-chaos/2019/06/04/at-brookings-gen-joseph-dunford
-comments-on-threats-from-russia-china-north-korea-and-beyond/.

17 See "Remarks by President Trump on Ending Surprise Medical Billing,"
    May 9, 2019, https://www.whitehouse.gov/briefings-statements/remarks
    -president-trump-ending-surprise-medical-billing/.

18 See, e.g., RFE/RL, "Saudi Arabia, U.A.E., Norway at U.N. Blame 'State Actor'
    for May 12 Tanker Attacks," June 9, 2019, https://www.rferl.org/a/saudi
    -arabia-uae-norway-blame-state-actor-tanker-attack/29985842.html.

19 Ibid.

20 See David A. Sanger and William J. Broad, "In a Tweet Taunting Iran,
    Trump Releases an Image Thought to Be Classified," August 30, 2019,
    https://www.nytimes.com/2019/08/30/world/middleeast/trump-iran
    -missile-explosion-satellite-image.html.

21 See Stephen Kalin and Rania El Gamal, Reuters, "Saudi oil facilities
    attacked, US sees threat in Iraq from Iran-backed forces," May 14, 2019,
    https://www.reuters.com/article/us-saudi-oil-usa-iran/saudi-oil-facilities
    -attacked-us-sees-threat-in-iraq-from-iran-backed-forces-idUSKCN1SK0YM.

22 See "Remarks by President Trump Before Marine One Departure," May 14,
    2019, https://www.whitehouse.gov/briefings-statements/remarks-president
    -trump-marine-one-departure-42/.

23 This was a long-standing refrain. See Kimon de Greef and Palko Karasz,
    "Trump Cites False Claims of Widespread Attacks Against White Farmers
    in South Africa," August 23, 2018, https://www.nytimes.com/2018/08/23
    /world/africa/trump-south-africa-white-farmers.html.

24 See Alissa J. Rubin and Falih Hassan, "Rocket Hits Green Zone in Baghdad
    as Tensions Flare Between U.S. and Iran," May 19, 2019, https://www.ny
    times.com/2019/05/19/world/middleeast/rocket-baghdad-greenzone.html.

25 See Reuters, "Iran's Rouhani: Today's situation isn't suitable for talks; resis-
    tance is our only choice – IRNA," May 21, 2019, https://uk.reuters.com
    /article/usa-iran-rouhni/irans-rouhani-todays-situation-isnt-suitable-for
    -talks-resistance-is-our-only-choice-irna-idUKL5N22X01X.

26 See Michelle Nichols, Lesley Wroughton, and Phil Stewart, "Exclusive: Iran's
    Zarif belies Trump does not want war, but could be lured into conflict,"
    April 24, 2019, https://www.reuters.com/article/us-iran-usa-exclusive
    /exclusive-irans-zarif-believes-trump-does-not-want-war-but-could
    -be-lured-into-conflict-idUSKCN1S02VK.

27 See Michael MacArthur Bosack, "Success or failure for Abe in Tehran?"
    June 18, 2019, https://www.japantimes.co.jp/opinion/2019/06/18/commen
    tary/japan-commentary/success-failure-abe-tehran/#.Xn97SIhKiF4.

28 Ibid.

29 See Reuters, "US blames Iran for helping Houthi rebels shoot down drone in Yemen," June 16, 2019, https://www.reuters.com/article/us-mid east-attacks-usa-drone/us-blames-iran-for-helping-houthi-rebels-shoot -down-drone-in-yemen-idUSKCN1TH0LA.

30 See, e.g., Peter Baker et al., "Trump Undercuts Bolton on North Korea and Iran," https://www.nytimes.com/2019/05/28/us/politics/trump-john -bolton-north-korea-iran.html?searchResultPosition=3.

31 See "U.S. Central Command Statement on June 13 Limpet Mine Attack in the Gulf of Oman," June 13, 2019, https://www.centcom.mil/MEDIA /STATEMENTS/Statements-View/Article/1875666/us-central-command -statement-on-june-13-limpet-mine-attack-in-the-gulf-of-oman/.

32 See ibid., which contains a link to the film.

33 Trump's view was widely shared. See e.g., Ishaan Tharoor, "Shinzo Abe's mission to Iran ends in flames," June 14, 2019, https://www.washington post.com/world/2019/06/14/shinzo-abes-mission-iran-ends-flames/.

34 See Conor Finnegan, "Iran's Ayatollah Khameini said he rejects Trump's offer to talk," June 13, 2019, https://abcnews.go.com/Politics/irans -ayatollah-khamenei-rejects-trumps-offer-talk/story?id=63687413.

35 Publicly available statistics make the same point, although varying depending on what time period is used to measure the imports. See, e.g., Reuters, "Factbox: Asia region is most dependent on Middle East crude oil, LNG supplies," January 8, 2020, https://in.reuters.com/article/asia-mideast -oil-factbox/factbox-asia-region-is-most-dependent-on-middle-east-crude -oil-lng-supplies-idINKBN1Z71VW.

36 See Laurence Norman and Gordon Lubold, "Iran to Breach Limits of Nuclear Pact, as US to Send More Troops to Mideast," https://www.wsj.com /articles/iran-to-breach-limits-of-nuclear-pact-putting-bid-to-save-deal-in -doubt-11560765015.

37 Ibid.

38 See Mark Landler, "Obama Says Iran Strike Is an Option, but Warns Israel," March 3, 2012, https://www.nytimes.com/2012/03/03/world/middleeast /obama-says-military-option-on-iran-not-a-bluff.html.

39 See Tessa Berenson, "Exclusive: President Trump Calls Alleged Iranian Attack on Oil Tankers 'Very Minor,'" https://time.com/5608787/iran-oil -tanker-attack-very-minor/.

40 See Alissa J. Rubin, "2 Rockets Strike Oil Fields in Southern Iraq," June 19, 2019, https://www.nytimes.com/2019/06/19/world/middleeast/iraq

-rocket-attacks-basra.html. https://www.nytimes.com/2019/06/19/world
/middleeast/iraq-rocket-attacks-basra.html.

41 See Bethan McKernan, "Iraq rocket attack: oil firms begin evacuating staff
from Basra site," June 19, 2019, https://www.theguardian.com/world/2019
/jun/19/iraq-rocket-attack-basra-injured-foreign-oil-companies.

42 Sarah Sanders issued a short statement that Trump had been briefed on the
attack that evening. See Saudi Desalination Plant Struck by Missile from
Yemen, U.S. Drone Shot Down–Reports," June 20, 2019, http://sustg.com
/saudi-desalination-plant-struck-by-missile-from-yemen-u-s-drone-shot
-down-reports/.

43 See, e.g., Henry Fernandez, Fox News, "US navy drone shot down by
Iranian missile cost $130M," June 20, 2019, https://www.foxbusiness.com
/politics/us-navy-drone-shot-down-iranian-missile-cost.

44 See, e.g., Michael D. Shear, Eric Schmitt, Michael Crowley, and Maggie
Haberman, "Strikes on Iran Approved by Trump, Then Abruptly Called
Back," June 20, 2019, https://www.nytimes.com/2019/06/20/world
/middleeast/iran-us-drone.html?smid=nytcore-ios-share and James LaPorta
and Tom O'Connor, "Donald Trump Decided to Strike Iranian Missile
System, Then Changed His Mind," June 21, 2019, https://www.newsweek
.com/us-military-strikes-iran-drone-1445116.

45 See, e.g., Peter Baker et al., "Urged to Launch an Attack, Trump Listened to
the Skeptics Who Said It Would Be a Costly Mistake," posted at https://www
.nytimes.com/2019/06/21/us/politics/trump-iran-strike.html.

46 CENTCOM also issued public statements. See, https://www.centcom.mil
/MEDIA/STATEMENTS/Statements-View/Article/1881682/us-central
-command-statement-iranians-shoot-down-us-drone/; and https://www
.centcom.mil/MEDIA/STATEMENTS/Statements-View/Article/1882519
/us-air-forces-central-command-statement-on-the-shoot-down-of-a-us
-rq-4/.

47 As previously noted, estimates varied depending in part on what
equipment each drone carried. Dunford's cost citation here was within
the range previously cited. Other public estimates were as high as $220
million. See,Lily Hay Newman, "The Drone Iran Shot Down Was a $220M
Surveillance Monster," June 20, 2019, https://www.wired.com/story/iran
-global-hawk-drone-surveillance/.

48 CENTCOM released a map showing the location from which where it
believed the Iranian SAM missiles had been fired. See Amy McCullough,
Jennifer-Leigh Oprihory, and Jennifer Hlad, "CENTCOM: Iranian SAM

Shoots Down US Drone Over Strait of Hormuz," June 20, 2019, https://www.airforcemag.com/centcom-iranian-sam-shoots-down-us-drone-over-strait-of-hormuz/.

49 Russia has an extensive military-sales-and-cooperation relationship with Iran, frequently involving train-and-assist elements. See, e.g., Michael Eisenstadt, "Russian Arms and technology Transfers to Iran: Policy Challenges for the United States," https://www.armscontrol.org/act/2001-03/iran-nuclear-briefs/russian-arms technology-transfers-iranpolicy-challenges-united; and Maxim A. Suchkov, "Intel: How Russia is deepening military ties with Iran to counter the US," June 30, 2019, https://www.al-monitor.com/pulse/originals/2019/07/intel-russia-deepening-military-ties-iran-counter-us.html.

50 CENTCOM issued a statement shortly after the attack on its development of "Operation Sentinel," which was intended to employ naval patrols in and around the Gulf through a multilateral cooperative effort. See "U.S. Central Command Statement on Operation Sentinel," July 19, 2019, https://www.centcom.mil/MEDIA/STATEMENTS/Statements-View/Article/1911282/us-central-command-statement-on-operation-sentinel/.

51 See Schwebel, Judge Stephen, Nicaragua vs. U.S., 1986 I.C.J. 14, 259 (June 27), quoted in "Draft Articles on State Responsibility–Comments of the Government of the United States of America", U.S. State Department, http://www.state.gov/documents/organization/28993.pdf, March 1, 2001.

52 See, e.g., Michael D. Shear et al., "Strikes on Iran Approved by Trump, Then Abruptly Pulled Back," https://www.nytimes.com/2019/06/20/world/middleeast/iran-us-drone.html ; and Michael D. Shear, et al., "Trump Says He Was 'Cocked and Loaded' to Strike Iran, but Pulled Back," June 21, 2019, https://www.nyt.com/2019/06/21/us/politics/trump-iran-attack.html.

53 See Peter Baker, Eric Schmitt, and Michael Crowley, "An Abrupt Move That Stunned Aides: Inside Trump's Aborted Attack on Iran," September 21, 2019, https://www.nytimes.com/2019/09/21/us/politics/trump-iran-decision.html.

54 See Maya King, "Trump: Rand Paul to help with Iran negotiations," July 19, 2019, https://www.politico.com/story/2019/07/19/rand-paul-iran-trump-1423779.

55 See "Remarks by President Trump Before Marine One Departure," June 22, 2019, https://www.whitehouse.gov/briefings-statements/remarks-president-trump-marine-one-departure-49/.

56 See David E. Sanger and Ronen Bergman, "How Israel, in Dark of

Night, Torched Its Way to Iran's Nuclear Secrets," July 15, 2018, https://www.nytimes.com/2018/07/15/us/politics/iran-israel-mossad-nuclear.html.

57 See Reuters, "Chronology on Iran's Nuclear Program," August 8, 2019, https://www.nytimes.com/2005/08/08/international/chronology-of-irans-nuclear-program.html; AFP, "'Uranium particles' detected at undeclared site in Iran: IAEA," November 11, 2019, https://www.france24.com/en/20191111-uranium-particles-detected-at-undeclared-site-in-iran-iaea-1; and Alexander Ma, "Investigators found uranium particles at a secret facility in Iran, suggesting a further rejection of the nuclear deal," November 12, 2019, https://www.businessinsider.com/iran-nuclear-watchdog-uranium-secret-facility-bbc-2019-11. Like any product of mining, uranium is processed mechanically and chemically in advance of actually being put to use, in uranium's case, before it can be enriched. Milling separates uranium from the associated ore by chemical leeching, and subsequent refinement produces U_3O_8, or yellowcake, a solid, which is how uranium is typically stored and shipped prior to actually being put to use within the nuclear fuel cycle. Before uranium can be enriched, it is converted chemically from a solid to a gas, usually UF_6, before it can be injected into centrifuges. Of course, Israel knows for certain what form the uranium is in since it has the stolen documents, as does the IAEA, which has collected samples, but the likelihood is that the uranium at Turquzabad was yellowcake, rather than something further along in the nuclear fuel cycle.

58 See RFE/RL, "Israel Accuses Iran Of Having 'Secret Atomic Warehouse' Near Tehran," September 28, 2018, https://www.rferl.org/a/israeli-prime-minister-netanyahu-accuses-iran-having-secret-atomic-warehouse-outside-tehran/29514107.html.

59 See U.S. Department of the Treasury, Treasury Designates Iran's Foreign Minister Javad Zarif for Acting for the Supreme Leader of Iran, July 31, 2019, https://home.treasury.gov/news/press-releases/sm749.

60 See p. 64 in https://www.govinfo.gov/content/pkg/DCPD-2019DIGEST/pdf/DCPD-2019DIGEST.pdf.

61 See note 50 above; and Simon Newton, "Operation Sentinel: The Naval Task-force Protecting Gulf Shipping," November 15, 2019, https://www.forces.net/news/operation-sentinel-naval-taskforce-protecting-gulf-shipping

62 See, e.g., "'Maximum pressure' has produced 'maximum resistance,' says Iran's Araqchi," September 23, 2019, https://www.tehrantimes.com

/news/440423/Maximum-pressure-has-produced-maximum-resistance
-says-Iran-s

63 See Reuters, "Macron says he warned Iran's Rouhani about breaking nuclear commitments," June 27, 2019, https://www.reuters.com/article/us-iran -nuclear-france/macron-says-he-warned-irans-rouhani-about-breaking -nuclear-commitments-idUSKCN1TS0YU.

64 See note 54 above.

65 See "Remarks of President Trump Before Boarding Marine One," July 19, 2019, https://www.whitehouse.gov/briefings-statements/remarks-president -trump-marine-one-departure-53/

66 See Mosheh Gaines et al., "U.S. Marines jam an Iranian drone in the Gulf, destroying it," July 18, 2019, https://www.nbcnews.com/politics/national -security/trump-says-u-s-navy-ship-shot-down-iranian-drone-n1031451.

67 See p. 75 in https://www.govinfo.gov/content/pkg/DCPD-2019DIGEST /pdf/DCPD-2019DIGEST.pdf.

68 Peter Bergen, *Trump and His Generals*, Penguin Press, New York, 2019, pp. 69–70.

69 See Helene Cooper, "American Military Drone Shot Down Over Yemen," August 21, 2019, https://www.nytimes.com/2019/08/21/us/politics /american-drone-yemen.html

70 See David Halbfinger, "Israel Says It Struck Iranian 'Killer Drones' in Syria," August 24, 2019, https://www.nytimes.com/2019/08/24/world/middleeast /israel-says-it-struck-iranian-killer-drones-in-syria.html.

71 Ibid.

72 See John Irish and "Parisa Hafezi, "France Pushes for $15 billion credit line plan for Iran, if US allows it," September 3, 2019, https://www.reuters.com /article/us-iran-usa-france/france-pushes-15-billion-credit-line-plan-for -iran-if-us-allows-it-idUSKCN1VO1AF.

73 See, e.g., Peter Baker, "Iranian Official Makes Surprise Appearance on Side-lines of G7 Summit," https://www.nytimes.com/2019/08/25/world/europe /g7-iran-trump-biarritz.html.

CHAPTER 13: FROM THE AFGHANISTAN COUNTERTERRORISM MISSION TO THE CAMP DAVID NEAR MISS

1 The notion of a continuing Afghanistan counterterrorism platform was basic at the outset of the Trump Administration, and had been for many years. See Brian Dodwell and Don Rassler, "A View from the CT Foxhole: General John W. Nicholson, Commander, Resolute Support and U.S.

Forces-Afghanistan," February, 2017, https://ctc.usma.edu/a-view-from-the
-ct-foxhole-general-john-w-nicholson-commander-resolute-support-and
-u-s-forces-afghanistan/.

2 The prepublication review process has insisted that I insert the following
note: "In February/March 2020, the United States signed an agreement with
the Taliban, but what follows in this chapter is the policy debate while I was
National Security Advisor in 2019."

3 See Bolton, *Surrender Is Not an Option*, pp. 85–87.

4 See Ken Bredemeier, "US: No Cooperation with ICC Probe of Alleged
Afghan War Crimes," https://www.voanews.com/usa/us-no-cooperation
-icc-probe-alleged-afghan-war-crimes.

5 This exchange with Merkel, somewhat embellished from time to time, was a
staple in Trump's repertoire of exchanges with foreign leaders. It would arise
again in the Ukraine context, as the next chapter indicates.

6 See Rebecca Kheel, "Trump: US to keep 8,600 troops in Afghanistan after
Taliban deal," August 29, 2019, https://thehill.com/policy/defense/459281
-trump-us-to-drawdown-to-8600-troops-in-afghanistan.

7 Ibid. A recording of the full interview is found at https://radio.foxnews
.com/2019/08/29/president-trump-talks-china-trade-afghanistan-and-fox
-news-with-brian-kilmeade-on-fox-news-radio/.

8 See Kimberly Dozier, "Exclusive: Secretary of State Pompeo Declines to
Sign Risky Afghan Peace Deal," https://time.com/5668034/pompeo
-afghanistan-peace-deal/.

9 See Phil Stewart and Jason Lange, Reuters, "Trump say he cancelled peace
talks with Taliban over attack," September 7, 2019, https://ru.reuters.com
/article/idUSKCN1VS0MX.

10 See Pamela Constable, and Siobhán O'Grady, "Afghanistan's Ghani to
visit Washington as peace deal limps and violence surges," September 6,
2019, https://www.washingtonpost.com/world/asia_pacific/afghanistans
-ghani-to-travel-to-washington-as-peace-deal-limps-ahead-and-violence
-surges/2019/09/06/215e1c5e-d07c-11e9-a620-0a91656d7db6_story.html.

11 See "Remarks by President Trump, Vice President Pence, and Members
of the Coronavirus Task Force in Press Conference," February 29, 2020,
https://www.whitehouse.gov/briefings-statements/remarks-president
-trump-vice-president-pence-members-coronavirus-task-force-press
-conference-2/.

CHAPTER 14: THE END OF THE IDYLL

1 Groysman had made similar comments previously, for example in October,
   2017, remarks to committees of Canada's House of Commons in Ottawa:
   "The international community must continue to enforce sanctions and
   the stiffest penalties possible in order to dissuade Russian President Vladimir Putin from any further aggression—and from repeating Russia's 2014
   annexation of Crimea in other Eastern European states.'This should be
   unbearable for them,' he urged." See Amanda Connolly, "Ukrainian PM
   urges 'unbearable' consequences for Russian aggression," https://ipoli
   tics.ca/2017/10/31/ukrainian-pm-urges-unbearable-consequences-for
   -russian-aggression/. See also the June 26, 2018, op-ed by Danish Prime
   Minister Lars Lokke Rasmussen and Groysman, entitled "A new Ukraine
   rising," https://euobserver.com/opinion/142167: "It is our hope, that the
   rising of a reformed new Ukraine will demonstrate to Russia that 19th
   century aggression will not be tolerated nor prove itself worthwhile in
   our 21st century Europe." See also "National Security Advisor, Ambassador John Bolton's Press Conference at Ukrainian Crisis Media Center
   (UCMC)," https://ua.usembassy.gov/national-security-advisor-ambassa
   dor-john-boltons-press-conference-at-ukrainian-crisis-media-center-
   ucmc/.

2 This proposed legislation was already the subject of public debate in
   Ukraine. See Andrew E. Kramer, "Ukraine, After Naval Clash with Russia,
   Considers Martial Law," https://www.nytimes.com/2018/11/25/world
   /europe/ukraine-russia-kerch-strait.html.

3 See Reuters, "Merkel expressed concern about situation in Ukraine
   in call with Poroshenko: spokesman," November 28, 2018, https://
   www.reuters.com/article/us-ukraine-crisis-russia-germany/merkel
   -expressed-concern-about situation-in-ukraine-in-call-with-poroshenko
   -spokesman-idUSKCN1NV22U.

4 See, "Canada led joint G7 statement condemning Russian aggression in
   Ukraine, says Freeland," November 30, 2018, https://www.thestar.com/news
   /canada/2018/11/30/canada-led-joint-g7-statement-condemning-russian
   -aggression-in-ukraine-says-freeland.html.

5 See, Andrew Osborn and Anton Zverev, "European politicians call for
   new sanctions on Russia over Ukraine," November 27, 2018, https://www
   .reuters.com/article/us-ukraine-crisis-russia-germany/european-politicians
   -call-for-new-sanctions-on-russia-over-ukraine-idUSKCN1NW0WW.

6 When the Russian criminal case was filed shortly thereafter, all the elements

of the Russian theory, described in the text, went on the public record. See Patrick Reevell. "Russia brings captured Ukrainian sailors to court," https://abcnews.go.com/International/russia-bringing-captured-ukrainian -sailors-court/story?id=59440311; Patrick Reevell, "Russia extends deten- tion of captured Ukrainian sailors," https://abcnews.go.com/International /russia-brings-captured-ukrainian-sailors-court/story?id=60398214, and Radio Free Europe/Radio Liberty, "Russian Court Jails Captured Ukrainian Sailors for Two Months," https://www.rferl.org/a/west-rallies-behind -ukraine-calls-on-russia-release-detained-sailors-kerch-azov/29623124.html.

7 See "Telephone conversation with US President Donald Trump," http:// en.kremlin.ru/events/president/news/60469. A subsequent press report referred to Russians' knowledge of Zelensky: "members of [Zelensky's] foreign policy team want to move the battlefield of ideas away from Ukraine right into Russia, taking advantage of Mr. Zelensky's long experi- ence appealing to Russians with his mostly lowbrow, sometimes raunchy, comedy shows and movies. His comedic work was widely seen in Russia." Andrew E. Kramer, "In Ukraine, a Rival to Putin Rises," https://www.ny times.com/2019/08/04/world/europe/ukraine-president-putin-russia .html?searchResultPosition=1.

8 See Kenneth P. Vogel, "Rudy Giuliani Plans Ukraine Trip for Inquiries That Could Help Trump," https://www.nytimes.com/2019/05/09/us/politics /giuliani-ukraine-trump.html.

9 Trump frequently referred to this Merkel statement that Germany would not reach the 2014 NATO agreement that its members' defense spending would reach 2 percent of GDP by 2024 until 2030. At the June 2018 NATO Summit in Brussels, for example, Trump complained publicly about the German position: "Germany's plan to increase its defence expenditure to the Nato target of 2% of GDP by 2030 was not good enough, Trump said. 'They could do it tomorrow,' he added." Ewen MacAskill, "Angele Merkel hits back at Donald Trump at Nato summit," https://www.theguardian.com /us-news/2018/jul/11/nato-summit-donald-trump-says-germany-is -captive-of-russians. Chacellor Merkel has herself publicly mentioned the 2030 date for Germany, rather than NATO's 2024 target. See Guy Chazan, "Merkel warns Europe can't defend itself without Nato," https://www.ft.com /content/4a208660-10f8-11ea-a225-db2f231cfeae.

10 Trump made essentially this same point in the July 25, 2019, telephone call with Zelensky. See below.

11 See Matthias Williams, "Ukraine's sacked finance minister says no will in cabinet for gas price hike," June 8,2018, https://www.reuters.com/article

/us-ukraine-danylyuk/ukraines-sacked-finance-minister-says-no-will-in
-cabinet-for-gas-price-hike-idUSKCN1J4288.

12 See Julie Hirschfeld Davis and Mark Mazzetti, "Highlights of Mueller's
    Testimony to Congress," https://www.nytimes.com/2019/07/24/us/politics
    /mueller-testimony.html.

13 See Peter Baker, "'We Absolutely Could Not Do That': When Seeking
    Foreign Help Was Out of the Question," https://www.nytimes.com/2019/10
    /06/us/politics/trump-foreign-influence.html?searchResultPosition=3.

14 See the DoJ press release announcing the indictment, https://www.justice
    .gov/opa/pr/turkish-bank-charged-manhattan-federal-court-its-participa
    tion-multibillion-dollar-iranian.

15 See "Senior Ukrainian Security Official Quits," https://www.rferl.org/a
    /senior-ukrainian-security-official-quits/30187540.html.

16 See, Polino Sinovets and Oleksii Izhak, "Ukraine's Position on the INF
    Treaty Suspension," May, 2019, https://www.researchgate.net/publiation
    /337161190_Ukraine's_Position_on_the_INF_Treaty_Suspension.

17 See https://www.nytimes.com/interactive/2019/10/22/us/politics/william
    -taylor-ukraine-testimony.html for Taylor's written testimony; for a news
    report, see Michael D. Shear et al., "Ukraine Envoy Testifies Trump Linked
    Military Aid to Investigations," https://www.nytimes.com/2019/10/22
    /us/trump-impeachment-ukraine.html?action=click&module=Top%20
    Stories&pgtype=Homepage.

18 See Yaroslav Trofimov, "A Russian Ally's Solo Course Alters Western
    Calculations," https://www.wsj.com/articles/a-russian-allys-solo-course
    -alters-western-calculations-11572958804?mod=searchresults&page=
    1&pos=1.

19 See, e.g., Editorial Board, "Trump tries to force Ukraine to meddle in the
    2020 election," https://www.washingtonpost.com/opinions/global-opinions
    /is-trump-strong-arming-ukraines-new-president-for-political-gain/2019
    /09/05/4eb239b0-cffa-11e9-8c1c-7c8ee785b855_story.html.

20 See, e.g., Greg Miller et al., "Giuliani pursued shadow Ukraine agenda as
    key foreign policy officials were sidelined," found at https://www.washing
    tonpost.com/national-security/giuliani-pursued-shadow-ukraine-agenda
    -as-key-foreign-policy-officials-were-sidelined/2019/09/24/ee18aaec-deec-11
    e9-be96-6adb81821e90_story.html.

21 See, e.g., Patricia Zengerle, Reuters, https://www.reuters.com/article/us-usa
    -ukraine/trump-administration-reinstates-military-aid-for-ukraine-idUSK
    CN1VX213.

CHAPTER 15: EPILOGUE

1 See Karen DeYoung and Josh Dawsey, "Bolton book roils Washington as onetime allies turn on Trump's former national security adviser," https:// www.washingtonpost.com/national-security/bolton-book-roils-wash ington-as-onetime-allies-turn-on-trumps-former-national-security-ad viser/2020/01/27/f8ab83d8-4145-11ea-b503-2b077c436617_story.html.

2 "Remarks by President Trump, Vice President Pence, and Members of the Coronavirus Task Force in Press Briefing," April 13, 2020, whitehouse.gov /briefings-statements/remarks-president-trump-vice-president-pence -members-coronavirus-task-force-press-briefing-25/.

3 "Remarks by President Trump, Vice President Pence, and Members of the Coronavirus Task Force in Press Briefing, April 15, 2020, www.whitehouse .gov/briefings-statements/remarks-president-trump-vice-president-pence -members-coronavirus-task-force-press-briefing-26/.

4 "We're going to try and block the publication of the book," Trump reportedly said at luncheon of network television anchors on February 4, 2020. See Josh Dawsey, Tom Hamburger, and Carol D. Leonnig, "Trump wants to block Bolton's book, claiming most conversations are classified," https:// www.washingtonpost.com/politics/trump-wants-to-block-boltons-book -claiming-all-conversations-are-classified/2020/02/21/6a4f4b34-54d1-11 ea-9e47-59804be1dcfb_story.html.

5 The basic document is the "Classified Information Nondisclosure Agreement," Standard Form 312 (Rev. 7-2013), which I signed on April 5, 2019, and the "Sensitive Compartmented Information Nondisclosure Agreement," Form 4414 (Rev. 12-2013), the first of which I also signed on April 5, 2019. There was never any claim that any material in my manuscript implicated information governed by this second agreement.

6 Colin Powell, with Joseph E. Persico, *My American Journey*, Random House, New York, 1995.

7 James A. Baker, III, with Thomas M. DeFrank, *The Politics of Diplomacy: Revolution, War and Peace 1989–1992*, G.P. Putnam's Sons, New York, 1995.

8 Book Review of *Duty: Memoirs of a Secretary at War, by Robert Gates, American Review* (Australia), May, 2014, Number 16, Page 54, reprinted at https://www.algemeiner.com/2014/04/24/robert-gates-memoir-is-a-jaw -dropping-read-review/.

INDEX